The Feeling of Risk

The Feeling of Risk

New Perspectives on Risk Perception

Paul Slovic

earthscan
from Routledge

First published by Earthscan in the UK and USA in 2010

Earthscan
2 Park Square, Milton Park, Abingdon, Oxon OX14 4RN
Simultaneously published in the USA and Canada by Earthscan
711 Third Avenue, New York, NY 10017

Earthscan is an imprint of the Taylor & Francis Group, an informa business

British Library Cataloguing-in-Publication Data
A catalogue record for this book is available from the British Library.

Library of Congress Cataloging-in-Publication Data
Slovic, Paul, 1938-
  The feeling of risk : new perspectives on risk perception / Paul Slovic.
    p. cm.
  Includes bibliographical references and index.
  ISBN 978-1-84971-149-4 (hardback) -- ISBN 978-1-84971-148-7 (pbk.) 1. Risk perception. 2.
  Risk assessment. 3. Decision making. 4. Risk--Social aspects. I. Title.
  BF637.R57S55 2010
  153.7'5--dc22
                                                                          2010001827

ISBN 13: 978-1-84971-149-4 (hbk)
ISBN 13: 978-1-84971-148-7 (pbk)

Typeset by MapSet Ltd,Gateshead,UK
Cover design by Benjamin Youd

Earthscan publishes in association with the International Institute for Environment
and Development

Contents

I Risk as Feelings

II Culture, Cognition and Risk

III Psychometric Studies

IV Risk Knowledge and Risk Communication

List of Figures and Tables

Figures

Tables

Acronyms and Abbreviations

ANOVA	analysis of variance
ATSDR	Agency for Toxic Substances and Disease Registry
CA	completely avoidant
FDA	Food and Drug Administration
FTP	future time perspective
GMO	genetically modified organism
IRSA	Industrial Relations and Social Affairs
LULU	locally unwanted land-use
MANOVA	multivariate analysis of variance
NCA	not completely avoidant
NIMBY	not in my back yard
NIMTOF	not in my term of office
NRC	National Research Council
ppm	parts per million
RT	response time
SARF	social amplification of risk framework
SWL	subjective well-being
SUNY	State University of New York
UEA	University of East Anglia
USDHHS	US Department of Health and Human Services
USEPA	US Environmental Protection Agency

Acknowledgements

My profound thanks go to the co-authors of the chapters in this book, who have played such an important role in extending risk-perception research into this new century. What a pleasure it has been to work with you.

As the introductory chapter indicates, the inspiration and support for the present work began in the middle of the last century with the research and guidance of Clyde Coombs and Ward Edwards, and the work of their students and colleagues in the fields of judgment, decision making, and risk analysis. Among the many, Paul J. Hoffman, Lew Goldberg, Sarah Lichtenstein, Baruch Fischhoff, Amos Tversky, Danny Kahneman, and Howard Kunreuther were particularly inspirational to my early efforts in this field.

I wish also to acknowledge the numerous public and private sources who funded the research reported in this book. Special thanks go to the Decision, Risk and Management Science Program at the National Science Foundation, the primary sponsor for research on risk and decision making. Other important sponsors of this research have been the Annenberg Foundation, through its support of the Annenberg Public Policy Center of the University of Pennsylvania, and Paul Brest of the Hewlett Foundation.

I thank Ragnar Löfstedt, editor of the Earthscan Risk, Society and Policy Series, for encouraging me to undertake this book and for his valuable editorial guidance during the course of its development. Alison Kuznets, as well, provided excellent editorial guidance and support.

Close to home, very special thanks go to Leisha Wharfield, who did her usual outstanding job of keeping track of the innumerable vital details that accompany the making of a book and coordinating the assembly of the contents. This book would not have been accomplished without her skilled efforts. She was ably assisted by Valerie Dayhuff, Jennifer Kristiansen, Jozee Adamson, Cecelia Hagen, and Janet Macha. The support and encouragement of my other fine colleagues at Decision Research is also greatly appreciated. Thanks!

Once again, I dedicate this book to Roz Slovic, a remarkable woman who has been at my side since 1959, and to our children, Scott, Steven, Lauren, and Daniel. Scott and Lauren have even written papers with me, one of which appears in this volume.

Paul Slovic
Eugene, Oregon
June, 2010

Introduction and Overview

My earlier book, *Perception of Risk* (Slovic, 2000a), presented a selection of articles describing a 25-year programme of research that took place during the latter part of the 20th century. The present book, *The Feeling of Risk*, picks up where the last one left off, and describes the extension of risk-perception research into the first decade of the new century.

Risk as feelings

Although the present book follows in the same tradition as the first book, centred around the 'psychometric paradigm,' there are clear new paths with both theoretical and practical implications. The last chapter of Slovic (2000a) by Finucane et al introduced the *affect heuristic*, a cognitive process in which people look to their positive and negative feelings as a guide to their evaluation of an activity's risks and benefits. According to this view, information must convey emotion or feeling to be meaningful. This general notion, 'risk as feelings,' has continued to play an important role in research and has been highlighted in the title of the present volume and in the first section of the book.

Before launching into the specific contents of *The Feeling of Risk*, I would like to reminisce a bit about the long journey that led to my interest in this topic.

I was enticed to begin my study of risk in 1959. My first mentor, Clyde Coombs, gave me a draft of his paper using choices among gambles as a way to test the theory that people choose the gamble with the highest expected value (the sum over outcomes of the probability times the value of the outcome; Coombs and Pruitt, 1960). I was captivated by the idea that psychologists could do research with gambles and my first study was designed to replicate and extend Coombs' experiment. Close to 50 years later, I find myself still doing research on simple gambles (see Chapter 1).

In 1959, there was little consideration of the possibility that feelings might play a role in people's judgements and decisions about risk. An important paper by my second mentor, Ward Edwards, introduced psychologists to the 'theory of decision making' (Edwards, 1954). The focus was on an ideal decision maker, 'economic man,' who was completely informed, infinitely sensitive, and rational in the sense of making choices that maximized expected value (what Coombs was testing) or a subjective version of value, expected utility. Edwards, like Coombs, questioned these assumptions as accurate descriptions of how people actually behave and he encouraged psychologists to conduct empirical research to test the economic theories. To be sure, Edwards pointed out that the concept of utility, as originally conceived by Jeremy Bentham (1789/1823), centred around the pleasure or pain-giving properties of an object. Edwards also noted the similarity of the notion of utility to the notion of valence espoused by social psychologist Kurt Lewin (1946). Thus, said Edwards (1954), 'psychologists might consider the experimental study of utilities to be the experimental study of valences' (p389).

Researchers inspired by Edwards began to study utility as an expression of value that could be measured by observing choices, with little regard for the underlying psychological processes. The theories of this era described conscious, deliberate and rather mechanical processing of probabilities and payoffs.

A major change in direction occurred around 1970, when pioneering studies by Amos Tversky and Danny Kahneman began to shed light on fascinating mental strategies called 'heuristics' that could explain people's judgements of probability and their risk-taking decisions (Kahneman et al, 1982). For example, in some situations people seemed to be judging the probability of an event by the ease with which past instances of the event could be recalled or the ease with which the event could be imagined, a process named the *availability heuristic*. Further studies uncovered situations in which people judged probability by the extent to which an event was similar to its parent population, a process named the *representativeness heuristic*. Studies of choice uncovered other mental strategies; elimination by aspects, choosing according to the most important attribute, and so on.

I recall, in the midst of this growing collection of heuristic strategies, wondering how people decided when it was safe to cross a busy street. Certainly they were not calculating probabilities and utilities or their summed products, and the known judgement heuristics did not seem to offer any insight.

Some years later, I think I know the answer. The information available to us conveys positive and negative feelings that we rely upon when deciding when to cross the street or, indeed, when making any decisions involving risk. My first glimmer of this occurred one day when my car ran out of gas on a busy freeway. I had to cross the freeway on foot to get to the gas station. I surveyed the traffic coming toward me at high speed, trying to assess a safe distance to begin the crossing. Several times I took a few steps into the road only to jump back to the curb when the distance to the nearest car closed so fast as to send a chilling fear through my body. Only when my emotions remained calm as I began and continued the crossing did I proceed the whole way. No numerical calculations aided me; only my feelings.

Although this experience may have primed me to be receptive to the idea of risk as feelings at some later date, it did little to change my research, which continued to examine rather deliberate, mechanistic strategies for processing information.

The change in my thinking came gradually. My colleagues and I were asked by officials of the State of Nevada to advise them about the potential for adverse economic impacts to occur in southern Nevada if the government decided to locate a repository for storing high-level nuclear waste 90 miles from Las Vegas. We knew we could ask people whether such a facility would deter them from coming to Nevada for recreation, or to retire or start a business. We also knew that the answers might not be trustworthy. A previous survey had found that people insisted they would stop swimming at a popular beach if a nuclear power plant were located nearby. The plant was built. No decline was observed in attendance at the beach.

Clearly survey questions are limited in their ability to forecast actual behaviours, especially with regard to a unique facility with which no one has had any experience, and in response to events that will take place far into the future. For several decades marketers had been assessing imagery and associations to consumer products to figure out how to make their products maximally appealing. Following the marketing approach and borrowing a method for studying imagery developed by Szalay and Deese (1978), we first tested whether we could predict people's preferences for visiting cities and states by eliciting images and associations to those places along with the feelings attached to those responses: for example, What word or phrase comes to mind when you hear the word 'Colorado'? It worked: we could predict a person's location preferences by the rated favourability or unfavourability of the images and associations linked to those places. We also found that a nuclear waste repository evokes many strongly negative images, consistent with perceptions of extreme risk and stigmatization. We advised the state that there was a real possibility that, to the extent that adverse events and publicity linked Nevada with nuclear waste (highly negative imagery), visitation to the state would probably be reduced.

We also began appreciating the link between risk and feelings that was being demonstrated in other studies. Our earliest perception studies had found that perceived risk and acceptable risk were most closely associated with the feelings of dread evoked by a hazard (Fischhoff et al, 1978). Another important early finding was that perceived risk and perceived benefit were inversely correlated across diverse hazards. The relevance of this inverse relationship for risk as feelings became clear to us only some 15 years later when my student, Ali Alhakami, decided to investigate it for his doctoral thesis. He found that the extent of this inverse relationship was related to the degree to which people judged an activity as good or bad (Alhakami and Slovic, 1994). This insight, supported further by controlled laboratory experiments (Finucane et al, 2000a), became the basis for the affect heuristic (Slovic et al, 2002), a model asserting that feelings serve as an important cue for risk/benefit judgements and decisions. If we like an activity, we tend to judge its benefits as high and its risks as low; if we dislike it, we judge it the opposite – low benefits and high risk. These inversely structured judgements may not correspond at all to the environment where risks and benefits tend to be positively correlated across activities.

Another important step in the development of risk as feeling came from a dissertation by Alida Benthin (Benthin et al, 1993), who used imagery and associations to study adolescents' perceptions of risk and benefit associated with a variety of behaviours known to be dangerous to youth, such as smoking, drinking, marijuana and sexual intercourse, or health-enhancing (exercise and seat belts). Positive and negative image scores were found to be highly predictive of engagement in the target behaviours. Images and associations produced by frequent participants in an activity were much more favourable than associations produced by non-participants.

These ideas and findings were the scaffolding upon which the notion of risk as feelings was constructed. We soon began seeing links to many other findings in the risk and decision-making literature, such as the discovery by Chris Hsee and colleagues that information had to be evaluable (in the sense of conveying feelings) in order to be useful for judgements and decisions (Hsee, 1996b). An earlier finding by Slovic et al (2000b), regarding the different response to risk expressed as a frequency such as 1 in 10 vs. a risk expressed as a percentage such as 10 per cent, could be linked to images and feelings created by the frequency format: 'Who is the 1 in the 1 of 10? Is she doing something bad?'

Important influences also came from connecting the work of many other theorists during the past half century. Charles Osgood (Osgood et al, 1957) demonstrated the importance of positive and negative affect for understanding the meaning of words. Affect was shown to be an important factor for explaining animal learning studies (Mowrer, 1960a, b), for motivating and guiding all rational human behaviour (Damasio, 1994), and for helping to explain the very nature of human thinking (Berkowitz, 2000). At about the same time that my colleagues and I were integrating much of this work into our review paper 'The Affect Heuristic' (Slovic et al, 2002), George Loewenstein and colleagues crafted a similar story and gave us the rubric 'Risk as Feelings' in their excellent review article (Loewenstein et al, 2001).

So, in this way, over many years, stimulated by personal experiences and by the findings from diverse studies, I have come to appreciate the important role that feelings play in guiding human behaviour in general and risk perceptions and risk decisions in particular.

With this as background, let's examine Part I of the present book, illustrating the variety of risk judgements and decisions that have been investigated recently through the lens of the affect heuristic and risk as feelings. The first chapter, by Bateman et al, shows that 50 years after beginning to study people's judgements of gambles, my colleagues and I found that there is still something that can be learned from this experimental paradigm. We focus on a very simple prospect, offering a 7/36 chance to win $9, otherwise win nothing. We find, consistent with Hsee's notion of evaluability, that even a very familiar outcome such as winning $9 is not very evaluable. We lack a firm feeling of how good or bad $9 is in this context. As a result, it carries little weight in the judgement of the gamble. But we can inject positive feeling into the $9 by changing the other outcome in the gamble to lose 5¢. The $9 win now 'comes alive with feeling,' looking very good in comparison to the small loss. It is evaluable (good) and carries weight in the judgement, thus making the gamble with a small loss more attractive than the gamble with no loss.

The second chapter demonstrates that feelings are important in determining our reactions to risks from a broad range of personal or societal threats. Building on the distinction between experiential and analytic thinking about risk, Slovic et al demonstrate ways that emotional reactions (risk as feelings) are associated with vividness of imagery, proximity in time, and other variables that play a minimal role in analytic evaluations. The difference between analytic and experiential reactions poses a dilemma for policy makers who are urged to follow deliberative approaches (e.g. cost–benefit analysis) that act as a check against unwarranted fears (e.g. Sunstein, 2005) but are also advised to respect the public's sensitivity to important value-laden considerations that are often ignored in expert deliberations (e.g. National Research Council [NRC], 1996). This dilemma is explored in depth in Chapter 12 by Kahan et al.

An important chapter in Slovic (2000a) by Fetherstonhaugh et al (1997) documented a form of insensitivity to the value of human life that parallels the insensitivity observed in early psychophysical studies of sensory perceptions. Just as a fixed increase in light energy leads to a greater increase in perceived brightness when the original intensity is small than when it is large, saving a fixed number of lives seems more valuable when fewer lives are at risk to begin with – a form of 'psychophysical numbing.' Subsequent research has linked this numbing to a limitation in our ability to 'feel the meaning' in large numbers. Chapters 3, 4, 5 and 6 describe studies attempting to better understand the importance of feelings in motivating decisions to help people in need.

The study by Dickert and Slovic (Chapter 3) demonstrates the role that attention plays in the generation of feelings toward people who are at risk. One experiment shows that sympathy toward a child in need is reduced when that child's image is presented in the context of distracting images. A second study finds that sympathy judgements made when the child's image is in view are greater than those made from a memory of the child's image.

The research described by Small, Loewenstein and Slovic in Chapter 4 shows that donations to a starving child in Africa were greatly reduced when potential donors were informed that this child was one of millions in need. Other research demonstrates that people help others, in part, to make themselves feel good (e.g. Andreoni, 1990). The data in Chapter 4 suggest that making donors aware of needy persons 'out of reach' may trigger negative feelings that counter the good feelings that come from giving aid. This is non-rational. We should not be deterred from helping those we can help by knowledge that there are others we cannot help.

Chapter 5 argues that our attitudes and behaviours towards saving lives are guided more by the feelings associated with our moral intuitions than by the reasoned actions that would result from a more deliberative form of thinking, moral judgement. Because moral intuition tends to be insensitive to large losses of life, moral judgement must be invoked to create laws and institutions dedicated to preventing and halting mass abuses of human beings, even when our feelings convey no sense of alarm.

Chapter 6 further explores the problem of insensitivity to mass tragedies. Paul Slovic describes the difficulties that people have in understanding the meaning of large-scale human and environmental catastrophes represented numerically by dry statistics, '... human beings with the tears dried off.' Scott Slovic, a writer and eco-critic, provides a brief introduction to ways that writers attempt to overcome this insensitivity and create feelings and meanings through stories. Stories have the power to help us understand larger, complex problems – including threats to the environment – that we cannot apprehend through quantitative information alone.

Chapter 7 argues that the initiation of cigarette smoking is based on experiential thinking (feelings) rather than an analytic evaluation of risk. It describes important ways in which young smokers fail to understand the risks they are taking. Chapter 8 applies the affect perspective to explaining the impact of the South Asia tsunami (in which 600 Swedes were killed) on the lives of the Swedish population. The study suggests that the negative affect elicited by thinking about a recent major natural disaster leads to a more pessimistic view of the future. The implications of this infusion of affect in everyday judgement are vast, perhaps influencing decisions about consumption, health, social interactions and finance.

Culture, cognition and risk

Part II highlights another important perspective on risk, documenting the interplay between cultural factors and cognition. The first three chapters (9, 10 and 11) take the 'white male effect' as a starting point for deeper analysis of race, gender and cognition. The original study of this effect by Flynn et al (1994) found that 30 per cent of the white male population in the United States had extremely low perception of risk across a diverse array of hazards. In Chapter 9, Finucane and colleagues replicate and extend the original study, finding sizeable differences between white males and other respondents on a variety of sociopolitical attitudes. Finucane et al speculate that the world seems safer and hazardous activities seem more beneficial to white males than to others. Using the same National Survey data, Satterfield et al (Chapter 10) show that feelings of vulnerability, linked to experience with discrimination and injustice, are important drivers of the effect such that even white males have relatively high perceptions of risk if they, too, have had these experiences. Chapter 11, by Kahan and colleagues, proposes a new explanation for why white men fear risks less than women and minorities. According to this view, individuals selectively acknowledge or dismiss associated dangers in a manner supportive of their cultural identities. Thus the white-male effect can be seen as a reflection of the scepticism that hierarchist and individualistic white males display when activities integral to their cultural identities are challenged as harmful.

Much of the early research on risk perception documented striking differences of opinion between experts and the public that were quite resistant to change (Slovic, 2000a). In 2005, Cass Sunstein published a careful and comprehensive analysis of this literature and its implications for a normative account of how the law should respond to public risk perceptions (Sunstein, 2005).

Concerned that numerous social and cognitive mechanisms drive members of the public to exaggerate risks, Sunstein proposed a number of important institutional mechanisms designed to shield 'deliberative democracy' from the influence of risk panics. Chapter 12 by Kahan et al, written as a review of Sunstein's work, critiques his arguments from the perspective of cultural cognition. A model is proposed whereby individuals behave neither as rational nor irrational judges but rather as cultural evaluators of risk.

Chapter 13 by Satterfield et al examines culture in a different way, documenting the despair and life-disruption that took place when a close-knit African-American community in Georgia was told by the Environmental Protection Agency that their neighbourhood was severely contaminated by chemical releases from a nearby pesticide manufacturing factory. One of the well-documented effects on technologies, products and places that have become associated with an abnormal degree of risk is stigmatization (Gregory et al, 1995). Satterfield et al convey what it feels like to be forced to live in a risk-stigmatized community.

New psychometric studies

Much of the research presented in Slovic (2000a) and the present volume grew out of what was called the 'psychometric paradigm.' This paradigm encompasses a theoretical framework that assumes risk is subjectively defined by individuals who may be influenced by a wide array of psychological, social, institutional and cultural factors. The paradigm assumes that, with appropriate design of survey instruments, many of these factors and their interrelationships can be quantified and modelled in order to illuminate the responses of individuals and their societies to the hazards that confront them.

Part III of the present volume presents a short selection of recent studies that have applied the psychometric paradigm to specific, and sometimes new, hazard domains.

Finucane, Slovic and Mertz (Chapter 14) examined American attitudes toward blood transfusion. At the time of data collection, 1997, it was clear that transfusion was a stigmatized activity, with a substantial proportion of people believing that the US blood supply was unsafe. The authors conclude that perceptions of risk from blood transfusion need to be monitored and the study methodology provides a guideline for doing this.

Savadori et al (Chapter 15) compared experts and a public sample on perceptions of risk associated with medical and food applications of biotechnology. Compared to the public, experts perceived less risk for every biotech application, but both groups judged the risk from food-related applications as higher than the risk from medical applications.

During the period 1987–1991, national surveys in Sweden and Canada examined public attitudes and perceptions regarding the risks and benefits of prescription drugs. Chapter 16 by Slovic et al describes similar results from a national study in the United States, more than a decade later. Prescription medicines were perceived to be high in benefit and low in risk and were sharply differentiated from other chemicals.

Burns and Slovic (Chapter 17) demonstrate how basic psychometric surveys can provide insights vital to modelling the consequences of a terrorist attack in an urban area. Not surprisingly, a terrorist act is much more alarming than non-terrorist events (e.g. accidents, diseases) that cause equivalent direct harm. But not all terrorism is equivalent. Disease agents (e.g. anthrax) are more scary than bombs and the motives of the terrorists matter to risk perception. But, consistent with the findings described in Chapters 4, 5 and 6, the number of victims (ranging from 0 to 495) did not seem to matter. The study, while exploratory, provides a model for research that can inform policy decisions in this important risk domain.

Kahan et al (Chapter 18), working within the framework of 'cultural cognition,' find that members of the public who hold relatively egalitarian and communitarian worldviews perceive the risks from nanotechnology to be greater and its benefits smaller than do persons who hold hierarchist and individualistic worldviews.

Risk knowledge and risk communication

Part IV examines the role of risk perception within a broader context of knowledge and communication.

One of the most important theoretical frameworks to emerge out of the study of risk perception is that of the 'social amplification of risk.' This framework attempts to integrate findings from media and communication research, from the psychometric and cultural schools of risk-perception research, and from studies of organizational responses to risk. In Chapter 19, Kasperson et al review research on the framework that took place during the 15 years subsequent to its introduction in 1988. Among various applications, social amplification appears to have been particularly useful for studying risk-induced stigma and its policy implications.

Much information about risk comes to us in the form of statistics and probabilities. In Chapter 20, Peters et al introduce the important concept of numeracy, showing that individuals who differ in their ability to understand numbers often fail to comprehend risk information adequately. Those who design health risk communications need to consider what can be done to help less-numerate people make better health care decisions.

But even more basic than understanding risk numbers is understanding the consequences being quantified by the numbers. Risk perception has been shown to be a layered process starting with superficial knowledge (e.g. smoking is harmful) and progressing (sometimes) to deeper levels of understanding (e.g. what forms of harm are caused by smoking and how does it feel to experience them?). In Chapter 21, Weinstein et al demonstrate that, although people may recognize that smoking can lead to adverse health effects, they do not have even a basic understanding of the nature and severity of these harmful consequences. Graphic images of smoking-induced disease have been assumed to boost knowledge and produce negative affective reactions that may counter the positive images conveyed by billions of dollars in tobacco advertising. In support of this assumption, Chapter 22 by Peters et al shows, by means of controlled experiments, that putting graphic images on cigarette packages may help to reduce smoking initiation and increase quit attempts.

Where do we go from here?

It is exciting to view the profound improvement in our understanding of judgement and decision making under risk that has occurred during the past 50 years. If anything, new technological advances involving computers, Internet testing, high-fidelity simulations, and neuroimaging, coupled with the ability to easily communicate and collaborate with others around the world, have speeded up innovation and discovery.

In particular, I hope that 50 years from now we will have found ways to overcome insensitivity to large-scale tragedies. Perhaps new methods of education, starting in the early years of school, will teach us how to understand the reality underlying large numbers, so we can act effectively to prevent and halt mass destruction of people and nature. I also hope that a vastly improved understanding of the feeling of risk will enable us to integrate feelings with technical analysis so that we can communicate about risk more effectively and make wiser decisions, even when dealing with people of different worldviews and cultures. Certainly sophisticated methods of neuroimaging will add valuable new insights into risk perception. But will the study of simple gambles still be part of our methodological toolkit a half-century from now? I wouldn't bet against it.

Paul Slovic
Eugene, Oregon

Part I

Risk as Feelings

Chapter 1

The Affect Heuristic and the Attractiveness of Simple Gambles

*Ian Bateman, Sam Dent, Ellen Peters, Paul Slovic
and Chris Starmer**

Introduction

The gamble has been to decision research what the fruit fly has been to biology – a vehicle for examining fundamental processes with presumably important implications outside the laboratory. Judgement and decision researchers have been studying people's preferences among gambles for more than 50 years. This chapter will describe a series of experiments with gambles that add to the growing literature on preference construction (Lichtenstein and Slovic, 2006) and provide what we hope are useful insights about the interplay of affect, reason, risk and rationality in life's most important gambles.

In recent years there has been much interest in using the concept of affect to understand a wide range of decision behaviours (Loewenstein et al, 2001; Slovic et al, 2002; Peters et al, 2006a). In this chapter, experimental studies with simple gambles are used to examine the roles of affect and the related concept of evaluability in determining judgements and decisions. We begin by providing some theoretical background on the key concepts. We next describe experiments demonstrating an anomalous finding: introducing a small loss as a component of a gamble increases its attractiveness. We then hypothesize an explanation for this anomaly based upon affect and describe several experiments that test and confirm this hypothesis. Finally, we discuss evidence that the subtle, context-dependent valuations we have observed with gambles in simple laboratory experiments appear to occur as well in many types of important decisions outside the laboratory.

* Reprinted from Bateman, I., Dent, S., Peters, E., Slovic, P. and Starmer, C. (2007) 'The affect heuristic and the attractiveness of simple gambles', *Journal of Behavioral Decision Making*, vol 20, no 4, pp365–380.

Background and theory: The importance of affect

In this chapter, following Slovic et al (2002), we use the term affect to refer to experienced feeling states associated with positive or negative qualities of a stimulus. Slovic et al (2002) present a wide range of evidence supporting the notion that images, marked by positive and negative affective feelings, guide judgement and decision making. In light of this evidence, they propose that people use an affect heuristic to make judgements. That is, in the process of making a judgement or decision, people consult or refer to the positive and negative feelings consciously or unconsciously associated with the mental representations of the task. Then, just as imaginability, memorability and similarity serve as cues for probability judgements (e.g. the availability and representativeness heuristics), affect may also serve as a cue for many important judgements and decisions (Kahneman, 2003). Affective responses tend to occur rapidly and automatically. As such, using an overall, readily available affective impression can be quicker and easier – and thus sometimes more efficient – than weighing the pros and cons or retrieving relevant examples from memory, especially when the required judgement or decision is complex or cognitive resources are limited.

The concept of evaluability has been proposed as a mechanism mediating the role of affect in decision processes. Affective impressions vary not only in their valence, positive or negative, but in the precision with which they are held. There is growing evidence that the precision of an affective impression substantially impacts judgements. In particular, Hsee (1996a, b, 1998) has proposed the notion of evaluability to describe the interplay between the precision of an affective impression and its meaning or importance for judgement and decision making. Evaluability is illustrated by an experiment in which Hsee (1996b) asked people to assume they were looking for a used music dictionary. In a joint-evaluation condition, participants were shown two dictionaries, A (with 10,000 entries in 'like new' condition) and B (with 20,000 entries and a torn cover), and were asked how much they would be willing to pay for each. Willingness-to-pay was far higher for Dictionary B, presumably because of its greater number of entries. However, when one group of participants evaluated only A and another group evaluated only B, the mean willingness to pay was much higher for Dictionary A. Hsee explains this reversal by means of the evaluability principle. He argues that, in separate evaluation, without a direct comparison, the number of entries is hard to evaluate, because the evaluator does not have a precise notion of how good 10,000 (or 20,000) entries is. However, the defects attribute is evaluable in the sense that it translates easily into a precise good/bad response and thus it carries more weight in the independent evaluation. Most people find a defective dictionary unattractive and a 'like-new' dictionary attractive. Under joint evaluation, the buyer can see that B is far superior on the more important attribute, number of entries. Thus the number of entries becomes evaluable through the comparison process.

According to the evaluability principle, the weight of a stimulus attribute in an evaluative judgement or choice is proportional to the ease or precision with which the value of that attribute (or a comparison on the attribute across alternatives) can be mapped into an affective impression. In other words, affect bestows meaning on information (cf. Osgood et al, 1957; Mowrer, 1960a, b) and the precision of the affective meaning influences our ability to use information in judgement and decision making. Evaluability can thus be seen as an extension of the general relationship between the variance of an impression and its weight in an impression-formation task (Mellers et al, 1992).

Hsee's work on evaluability is noteworthy because it shows that even very important attributes may not be used by a judge or decision maker unless they can be translated precisely into an affective frame of reference. The implications of these findings may be quite wide-ranging: Hsee (1998) demonstrates evaluability effects even with familiar attributes such as the amount of ice cream in a cup. Slovic et al (2002) demonstrate similar effects with decisions about options saving different numbers of human lives.

Evaluability and the attractiveness of gambles

In this section we propose evaluability as an explanation for some early findings in the judgement and decision literature pertaining to gambles. In subsequent sections we shall discuss a series of newer studies, also conducted with gambles, which test this explanation.

A number of studies have found that attractiveness ratings of simple gambles are influenced more by probabilities than by payoffs. Evidence for this claim can be found in Slovic and Lichtenstein (1968a), Goldstein and Einhorn (1987), Schkade and Johnson (1989) and, more recently, in data from a pilot study conducted by the present authors at the University of Oregon. In this pilot study, the relative importance of probabilities and payoffs was evaluated with 16 gambles, created by crossing four levels of winning probability (7/36, 14/36, 21/36 and 28/36) with four levels of payoff ($3, $6, $9, $12). University of Oregon students ($N = 297$) were randomly assigned to one of the 16 gambles and were asked to rate its attractiveness on a 0 (not at all attractive) to 20 (extremely attractive) scale. The mean ratings, shown in Table 1.1, indicated that attractiveness increased monotonically as probability increased, with the largest (and statistically significant differences) occurring when the two highest probabilities (21/36 and 28/36) were compared with the two lowest (7/36 and 14/36). Mean attractiveness varied little across a fourfold increase in payoffs (no column mean differences were significant statistically). A subsequent study using the same probabilities but increasing the payoffs to $30, $60, $90, and $120 showed essentially the same weak influence of payoff.[1]

The concept of evaluability provides one possible interpretation of these results. Following Hsee's reasoning one may argue that, because probabilities are represented on a fixed scale from 0 to 1, they can be more readily mapped into a relatively precise affective response: a probability close to zero can readily be interpreted as a 'poor' chance to win. By contrast, payoff outcomes such as those in Table 1.1 have less obvious affective connotations, at least in the absence of

Table 1.1 *Mean attractiveness ratings in the pilot study*

Probability	$3	$6	Payoff $9	$12	Mean
7/36	5.3	5.3	8.9	6.2	6.4
14/36	6.5	7.8	8.4	9.0	7.9
21/36	12.8	13.8	11.9	12.2	12.7
28/36	13.2	13.3	15.0	14.5	14.0
Mean	9.5	10.1	11.2	10.8	

Note: Each respondent saw one probability/payoff combination (e.g. 14 chances out of 36 to win $6) and was asked to rate the attractiveness of playing this gamble on a 0 (not at all attractive) to 20 (extremely attractive) scale.

further context. To illustrate the point, ask yourself the question 'how good is $9'? This $9 question, we contend, has no clear answer without further context. For instance, while it may be difficult to evaluate the goodness of an abstract and context-free $9, when further context is provided, the same amount of money may then 'come alive with feeling' (Slovic et al, 2002). For instance, although a $9 tip on a $30 restaurant bill may immediately be judged good by a waiter, a $9 increase on a monthly salary of $2000 may be judged quite negatively by an employee. If it is accepted that, in the context of these studies, probabilities are more evaluable than monetary outcomes, evaluability implies that attractiveness ratings will be relatively more sensitive to probabilities than to payoffs.[2]

In what follows, we seek to construct a test of the hypothesis that context may influence the evaluability of a stimulus and hence the affect and importance of that stimulus to judgements and decisions about simple gambles.

Testing the evaluability principle: The base task

Consider the decision task described in Figure 1.1. In this task, an individual is required to rate the attractiveness of a bet offering a probability of 7/36 to win $9 (otherwise win nothing). We shall refer to this as the USbase task (when data are collected in the US). The bet is described in terms of winning numbers on a roulette wheel and subjects respond on an attractiveness scale having 20 intervals ranging from 0 ('not at all an attractive bet') to 20 ('extremely attractive bet'). Applying the reasoning of the previous section, we should expect the winning probability (7/36) to produce a fairly precise affective impression. It is an unattractive chance; one is much more likely to not win than to win. In contrast, the affective impression of $9 may be diffuse, reflecting the difficulty of evaluating this sum of money without any particular context in which to place it apart from this novel gamble. Thus, the impression formed by the gamble offering $9 to win with no losing payoff is expected to be dominated by the relatively precise and unattractive impression produced by the 7/36 probability of winning.

Now consider a variant of this task, modified so that the stated gamble below the first sentence in Figure 1.1 reads instead:

Evaluating the Attractiveness of a Bet

We would like you to rate how attractive the prospect of playing the following bet is to you.

7/36 to win **$9.00**

This means that there are 7 chances out of 36 that you will win the bet and receive **$9.00** and 29 chances out of 36 that you will win nothing.

Visualize a roulette wheel on the left with 36 numbers along the

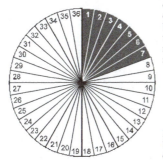 circumference. If a ball lands on any of the 7 numbers between 1 and 7 inclusive, you win **$9.00**. If it lands on numbers 8–36, you win nothing.

Indicate your opinion of this bet's attractiveness by **circling** one number on the rating scale below:

There is no right or wrong answer, we are interested only in your opinion about the **attractiveness** of playing this bet.

0	1	2	3	4	5	6	7	8	9	10	11	12	13	14	15	16	17	18	19	20

Not at all an   Moderately   Extremely
attractive bet   attractive bet   attractive bet

Figure 1.1 *Instructions for the attractiveness rating task*

7/36 to win $9
29/36 to lose 5¢

The text alongside the gamble is changed from 'you win nothing' to 'you lose 5¢.' We shall refer to this task as US−5. Notice that this new task is identical to the baseline task except that the zero outcome associated with the 29/36 probability has been replaced by a very small loss of 5¢. Consequently, the modified gamble is dominated by the base gamble and so any preference theory embodying the principle of monotonicity would imply that the modified gamble is strictly worse.

The evaluability principle, however, suggests a contrary implication because adding a very small loss to the payoff dimension provides new context for evaluating the $9. For instance, notice that the combination of a possible $9 gain and a 5¢ loss is a very attractive win/loss ratio. Hence introducing the small loss provides new perspectives from which the gamble can be evaluated. Whereas the imprecise mapping of the $9 carries little weight in the averaging process, the more precise and now favourable impression of ($9; −5¢) potentially carries more weight. Hence following the logic of evaluability, the modified gamble could, in principle, receive a higher rating.

Over a period of years, we have conducted numerous studies in the US and the UK exploring behaviour in relation to this and related tasks. We now bring these results together here for the first time.[3]

Table 1.2 *Baseline studies of the attractiveness of three gambles on a 0–20 rating scale*

Group	Gamble	Mean rating
USbase	(7/36, +$9.00; 29/36, win nothing)	9.4
US–5	(7/36, +$9,00; 29/36, –$0.05)	14.9
US–25	(7/36, +$9.00; 29/36, –$0.25	11.7

The original studies were conducted with three groups of subjects at the University of Oregon. Each group evaluated only one gamble, either USbase (7/36 win $9; otherwise win nothing), US–5 (7/36 win $9; otherwise lose 5¢), or US–25 (7/36 win $9; otherwise lose 25¢). The gambles were rated on the 0–20 scale of attractiveness shown at the bottom of Figure 1.1. The results are shown in Table 1.2. The gamble US–5 was rated more attractive than the gamble with no loss ($p < .001$) as was gamble US–25 ($p < .05$). Gamble US–25 was rated less attractive than gamble US–5, but the difference was not statistically significant.

These findings have more recently been replicated in the UK with 105 students (three groups of approximately 35) from the University of East Anglia (UEA). One group faced a task (UKbase) identical to USbase task but with a payoff of £9 (UK pounds) instead of $9. As in the Oregon experiments, the UEA experiments included a second task (UK–5) which replaced the otherwise win nothing outcome in the base task with a small loss (5 pence) and a third task (UK–25) which involved a larger (but still small) loss of 25 pence.

The mean attractiveness ratings for the three tasks are shown in Table 1.3. The overall pattern of results is almost identical to the results obtained earlier in the United States. Application of t-tests and Mann-Whitney tests (these always agreed) showed that bets UKbase and UK–5 differed at $p < .01$, UKbase and UK–25 differed at $p < .05$ and UK–5 and UK–25 did not differ significantly (though the lesser attractiveness of the gamble with the 25p loss replicated the result found in the original US study).

Joint evaluation

Perhaps the enhanced attractiveness of the gamble with the small loss is due, not to increased appreciation of the $9 or £9 payoff but rather to the attractiveness of taking a small risk? An additional study in the UK speaks to this explanation. 44 subjects from the UEA saw both gambles, UKbase and UK–5 together. They rated each gamble on the 0–20 scale of attractiveness. The results were almost the

Table 1.3 *Mean attractiveness ratings for three tasks*

Group	Gamble	Mean rating
UKbase	7/36 +£9; 29/36 win nothing	9.28
UK–5	7/36 +£9; 29/36 –£0.05	13.24
UK–25	7/36 +£9; 29/36 –£0.25	12.61

mirror-image of the between-groups findings described above. Under joint evaluation, the base gamble was judged far more attractive (mean rating 13.09) than the gamble with the small loss (mean rating 9.82). The difference was statistically significant ($t = 2.50$; $p < .02$). Much as Hsee (1996b) has demonstrated preference reversals in going from joint to separate evaluations, the same occurred here with these gambles. The results do not support the hypothesis that our subjects are attracted by the risk of a small loss. They also show that there are several ways to create a context to evaluate these gambles: by adding a small loss or by adding another gamble for comparison (see also Parducci, 1995) and Birnbaum, 1999) for further examples of these sorts of contextual effects).

Other variations

A subsequent study was conducted at the State University of New York (SUNY) at Plattsburgh with five separate groups each comprising 50 subjects. Each subject was presented with just a single gamble to rate (Bateman et al, 2006). The gambles studied were analogues of USbase and US–5 (designated NYbase and NY–5) plus two new gambles: 'NY+5' replaced the small loss outcome with a small gain; 'NYbase*10' is the base problem but with the winning outcome increased by a factor of 10. Participants in each group rated only one gamble. The results are shown in Table 1.4.

Comparing NYbase and NY–5 we see the now familiar effect of between-groups studies with these gambles: introducing a small loss increases the mean attractiveness rating ($t = 3.31$, $p < .001$). Interestingly, the mean for NY+5, offering the possibility of either $9 or a 5¢ gain, was 11.40. Although this is still significantly higher than NYbase ($t = 2.81$, $p < .01$), it is slightly lower than the mean for NY–5 with the 5¢ loss. The difference between the mean rating of NY+5 and NY–5 is not statistically significant ($t = 0.75$), but their relative ordering appears to stem from a small percentage of high ratings for NY+5 (only 24 per cent of subjects gave it a score of 16 or above) relative to those for NY–5 (which had 42 per cent of ratings at 16 or above). We can speculate that, relative to the positive affect of the NY–5 bet, the prospect of winning just 5¢ rather than $9 causes the NY+5 bet to be viewed somewhat negatively; i.e. while NY–5 offers a 'good loss' relative to the possible payout, the $0.05 outcome of NY+5 might be perceived as a 'bad gain.' However, as NY+5 has no possibility of loss, it also received fewer low ratings than NY–5 such that, the variance of the distribution of ratings for NY–5 is greater (33.0) than the variance for NY+5 (23.4),

Table 1.4 *Mean attractiveness ratings for SUNY Plattsburgh tasks*

Group	Gamble	Mean rating
NYbase	7/36 + $9; otherwise win nothing	8.66
NY–5	7/36 +$9; 29/36 −$0.05	12.20
NY+5	7/36 +$9; 29/36 +$0.05	11.40
NYbase*10	7/36 +$90; 29/36 +$0.05	10.48

though the difference is not statistically significant (Levene's test statistic is 1.89, $p = .17$).

The mean rating for NYbase*10 was only 10.48. This is not significantly higher than the rating for the base problem and it is lower than the ratings for NY−5 and NY+5 which feature a prize one-tenth as large. This result provides further evidence that the rating response scale is not particularly sensitive to variation of payoffs.

Taken together, these results show that very small changes (in terms of expected value) in the patterning of gamble payoffs can have very large effects in gamble evaluations, while large changes (in expected value) can have negligible effects. We also suggest that these effects have a natural interpretation as consequences of affective responses. The basis for this claim is that the hypothesis based on affect provides a way of making sense of what would otherwise appear perverse effects. In particular, why would the introduction of a small loss increase its attractiveness? The joint evaluability study in the UK did not support an explanation based on an attraction to the risk of a small loss. We suggest, instead, that affect and evaluability provide a credible explanation for this anomalous effect.

Later in this chapter we provide specific evidence supporting this interpretation based on affect. Before doing so, however, we turn to two additional studies, which address a possible criticism of our results so far.

Response mode robustness

One limitation of the results we have provided so far is that they are all generated from rating tasks using a similar response mode. A natural question to ask, therefore, is whether our results are peculiar to that type of task? It seems at least possible that this could be so. For instance, recall that our response scale was bounded on the attractiveness interval 0–20 with its midpoint at 10. Notice that probabilities also have bounds and a midpoint at 0.5. Note also the jump in mean attractiveness going from 14/36 to 21/36 (crossing the midpoint) in Table 1.1. Maybe it is simply easier to map 7/36 onto this bounded, linear attractiveness scale (below the midpoint) than to map $9 onto it, without the aid of a small loss? If so, it could be that the effect we are observing is a feature of this particular response scale and not a more general result of affective reactions to the gamble stimuli.

We provide a first test of this conjecture by replicating the study with a response mode that is unbounded and without a midpoint. Specifically, 201 students at the University of Oregon were asked to indicate the attractiveness of a gamble (either USbase, or US−5), by drawing a circle. According to the instructions, the more attractive the gamble, the larger the circle that should be drawn.[4] USbase was evaluated by 98 persons, and 103 judged the gamble US−5. A scoring template made up of different sized circles was constructed and placed over the responses in order to assign a number to each circle drawn. The median responses, presented in Figure 1.2, showed a strong and statistically significant difference in attractiveness favouring US−5 ($p < .01$; median test). Thus, the 5¢ loss effect does not depend upon the 0–20 scale of attractiveness.

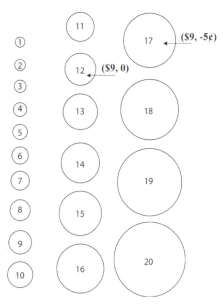

Figure 1.2 *Size of median circles indicating the attractiveness of two gambles*

While this replication is reassuring, the 'circles' response mode still has a generic similarity with the initial response modes: both are rating tasks requiring the responder to indicate the attractiveness of a single gamble. In view of this, a second robustness check was performed by testing for our original effect in a choice task rather than a rating task. Two studies, one in the US and one in the UK, used choice as the mode of response.

The choice experiments compare the attractiveness of the base gamble (USbase or UKbase) and the small-loss gamble (either US–5 or UK–5) against a sure gain. Of course, if the sure gain is large, many may choose it, thus obscuring any differential attractiveness of the two gambles. We therefore used two different values for the sure gain, one half the size of the other.

The US study asked 96 University of Oregon students to choose between playing a gamble and receiving a sure gain of $4. For 45 (51) students, the gamble was USbase (US–5). Whereas only 29.9 per cent chose USbase over the $4, 35.5 per cent chose US–5. This difference, however, was not statistically significant ($\chi^2 = 1.83$; $p < .20$). The same subjects made a second choice with $2 as the sure gain. This again favoured the gamble with the small loss (US–5) which was chosen over the $2 gain by 61.0 per cent participants, compared to 33.3 per cent who selected USbase over the sure gain. The difference was statistically significant ($\chi^2 = 7.22$; $p < .01$).

The UK study tested 120 adults in Aberdeen, Scotland, with essentially the same design, except for the payoffs being in pounds and pence. The results were quite similar to those in the US study. Against the sure gain of £4, UK–5 was selected by 36.7 per cent of the respondents compared with 33.3 per cent for UKbase. This difference was not statistically significant. However, as in the US study, the gamble with the 5p loss (UK–5) was selected far more often against the sure gain of £2 (63.3 per cent) than the gamble without the loss (41.7 per cent; $p < .02$).

Together, the studies employing circle responses and choices suggest that the increased attractiveness of the gamble with the small loss generalizes across response modes.

Direct tests of the affect account

Rating affect

The affect explanation of the 5¢ loss effect proposes that $9 within the payoff combination ($9, win nothing) is not evaluable, and that adding the 5¢ loss makes $9 'come alive with feeling' and causes it to become weighted in the judgement of attractiveness. In order to challenge this interpretation, more direct tests of the affect account were designed and conducted.

In these tests, subjects were asked to rate the affective valence of the stated probability and payoff as well as rating the overall attractiveness of the gamble. In the first of two experiments, 33 University of Oregon students rated the attractiveness of USbase and 34 rated US–5. The now familiar result was obtained: the gamble with the loss was rated more attractive ($t = 1.82$; $p < .05$, one-tailed test). In addition to rating attractiveness, subjects were asked to judge the affective valence of the 7/36 probability and the valence of the payoff combination (either $9, win nothing or $9, –5¢) by indicating how many people out of 100 would like or dislike these attributes to varying degrees (see instructions in Figure 1.3). The seven response categories were coded –3 (dislike very much) to +3 (like very much) for the analysis. Means and correlations are shown in Table 1.5.

The results in Table 1.5 support the affect account of the 5¢ loss effect. First, the mean affect for the 7/36 probability was slightly negative for both gambles, and did not differ significantly between the gambles. However, the liking for the $9, –5¢ payoff combination was much greater than liking for the $9, win nothing combination ($t = 2.71$; $p < .01$). The correlations, across subjects, between attractiveness ratings and the valences are also revealing. Attractiveness was correlated primarily with liking for probability in the no-loss gamble and primarily with liking for payoff in the –5¢ loss condition. Thus, the –5¢ loss did seem to enhance the meaning and importance of the gamble payoffs.

In the second direct test, 285 University of Oregon students rated the attractiveness of one of three gambles: either USbase or US–5 or a new gamble US+5 (i.e. 7/36 win $9; 29/36 win 5¢).

After making their rating, they were asked to indicate how they felt about the $9 outcome on a nine-point scale going from very bad (–4) through neutral (0) to very good (+4). They were then asked to rate the other outcome of the gamble, either win nothing, lose 5¢ or win 5¢, depending upon which gamble they had seen. The results, presented in Table 1.6, again support the affect explanation. As

Now imagine 100 people like those who are participating in this experiment. Suppose these 100 people were looking at the bet you just rated:

7/36 to win $9.00

29/36 to lose 5¢

Think first about the 7/36 chance of winning. Of these 100 people, how many of them do you believe would dislike this probability, how many would feel neutral about it, how many would like it, etc.? Indicate your answers by putting numbers in the blank spaces below the 7/36. **These numbers should add to 100.**

Next, do the same for the bet's possible payoffs: win $9 or lose 5¢. How many of 100 would dislike these two payoffs, how many would feel neutral about them, how many would like them? Again, put the number of people in each blank space below the payoff.

Category Code	7/36	Number of people	$9 or −5¢	Number of people
-3	dislike very much	_____	dislike very much	_____
-2	dislike moderately	_____	dislike moderately	_____
-1	dislike slightly	_____	dislike slightly	_____
0	neutral	_____	neutral	_____
1	like slightly	_____	like slightly	_____
2	like moderately	_____	like moderately	_____
3	like very much	_____	like very much	_____
	Total	_____	Total	_____
		(should =100)		(should =100)

Figure 1.3 *Instructions and coding for the first valence rating experiment*

before, the 5¢ loss enhanced attractiveness relative to the ($9, win nothing) gamble ($t = 5.73; p < .001$). Note that the gamble with the 5¢ gain was less attractive than the gamble with the loss. Although this difference was not statistically significant, it replicates prior findings. Table 1.6 also shows that the affect valence for $9 was substantially more positive for US−5 compared with the other two conditions. When $9 was paired with win nothing, 40 per cent of its affect ratings were neutral compared with 21 per cent when it was paired with −5¢. Similarly, the percentage of +3 and +4 (*very good*) ratings was only 9 per cent for USbase compared to 44 per cent for US−5. These results provide clear support for the hypothesis that that $9 did indeed 'come alive with feeling' when paired with a small loss.[5]

Turning to the 'other outcome,' the valence was much more positive for the 5¢ loss than for the win nothing outcome ($t = 7.3; p < .001$). The 5¢ loss was even rated slightly more favourably than the 5¢ gain, though this difference was not statistically significant.

Affect ratings were correlated, across subjects, with attractiveness ratings. Affect for $9 correlated positively with attractiveness in each condition, but the

Table 1.5 *Results of the first affect rating experiment*

	USbase (7/36 $9; otherwise win nothing)	US−5 (7/36 $9; −5¢)
Liking for probability (7/36)[a]	−0.07	−0.16
Liking for payoff outcomes[a]	0.16	0.92
($9; win nothing) or ($9; −5¢)		
Correlations with 0–20 ratings of attractiveness		
Liking for probability	0.52	0.10
Liking for payoff outcomes	0.21	0.60

Note: [a] Mean values: The 7-category affect ratings scale ran between *dislike very much* (coded −3) and *like very much* (coded +3).

highest correlation ($r = 0.73$) occurred when $9 was combined with the 5¢ loss. Affect toward the other outcome correlated most highly with attractiveness when that outcome was the 5¢ loss. Interestingly, that correlation was positive ($r = 0.36$; $p < .05$). The more attractive the 5¢ loss, the more attractive the gamble, consistent with our speculation that the 5¢ loss is a 'good' loss.

These results confirm that the combination of $9 and −5¢ conferred a special affective quality on that gamble, enhancing the attractiveness and the importance of both the $9 payoff and the 5¢ loss.

One hallmark of affect is the degree to which subtle features of a stimulus representation can manipulate feelings and thus influence judgements and decisions, especially when other attributes of the stimulus are low in evaluability. An example of this is the importance of the book's condition ('like new' vs. 'torn cover') in Hsee's dictionary example described earlier. We attempted a 'torn cover' type manipulation by varying the representation of the win nothing outcome for the $9 gamble. Two rating conditions, each with 50 subjects, were run in Plattsburgh, comparing:

US-NoWin 7/36 win $9; 29/36 you win nothing

and US-NoLoss 7/36 win $9; 29/36 you lose nothing

Table 1.6 *Results from the second affect rating study*

	Condition		
	USbase ($9; win nothing)	US−5 ($9, −5¢)	US+5 ($9; +5¢)
Attractiveness (0–20)	7.2	12.8	11.8
Affect for $9	0.4	1.8	1.0
Affect for other outcomes			
(0, −5¢, or +5¢)	−1.5	0.4	0.3
N	72	72	141

Note: The rating scale for affect ranged from −4 (*very bad*) to +4 (*very good*).

We predicted that the more positive tone of 'you lose nothing' would cause US-NoLoss to be rated more attractive than US-NoWin where 'you win nothing.' This prediction was confirmed. The US-NoWin gamble received a mean rating of 9.0; but the US-NoLoss gamble, where the 0 outcome was reframed as 'you lose nothing,' received a much higher mean rating of 13.2 ($t = 3.8$; $p < .001$). Interestingly, the 'lose nothing' bet rating of 13.2 is significantly greater ($t = 2.51$; $p < .02$) than that for the bet with a potential $90 payoff. This was the NYbase*10 bet (7/36 + $90; 29/36 win nothing), for which the mean rating was 10.48.

Discussion

What have we learned from inflicting these few simple gambles on hundreds of individuals, on both sides of the Atlantic? At one level, we have learned that the rated attractiveness of the gamble in the base task (7/36 to win 9 ($ or £); 29/36 to win nothing) is reliably enhanced when the second outcome is changed to a small loss. This effect occurred with attractiveness expressed as the size of a freely drawn circle as well as with a numerical rating scale. The effect also occurred with choices between a gamble and a sure gain. Though some may be tempted to dismiss the basic effect as merely making a gamble more interesting or exciting by adding the chance of loss, this explanation fails because side-by-side comparison showed a clear attractiveness advantage for the gamble without a loss.[6]

Although these findings are certainly a narrow starting point for general theory, the plot thickened when affect was invoked as an explanatory factor and an affect account was supported by experiments in which the gambles' component attributes were rated on valence (i.e. their goodness, badness or likeability). The $9 outcome was found to evoke rather neutral feelings in the context of its alternative, 'win nothing.' The mediocre attractiveness of the no-loss gamble is driven by the somewhat negative feelings associated with its 7/36 probability of winning. But $9 is seen in a favourable light and becomes an important factor contributing to the gamble's attractiveness, when it is paired with a 5¢ loss. This result is congruent with the concept of evaluability that has been shown to influence a wide range of judgements and decisions (Hsee, 1996a). The essence of evaluability is that affect conveys meaning upon information. Without affect, information lacks meaning and will not be given weight in decision making.

Taking a broader perspective, our studies of these few simple gambles demonstrate the importance of context in the 'construction' of utility and preference. One might expect that a lifetime of learning would imbue us with a clear sense of the value of such a familiar quantity as $9 or £9. Instead, we find that this value depends greatly on context. In this light, we see a link between the 5¢ loss effect and the many diverse observations that led Kahneman and Tversky (1979) to propose a value function for Prospect Theory that was defined on gains and losses ('goods' and 'bads') rather than on total wealth (likely to be less evaluable). Indeed the present findings contribute to a broader conception in which important preferences may not exist within us, waiting to be elicited but, instead, are constructed during the very process of elicitation or decision (Slovic, 1995; Lichtenstein and Slovic, 2006). In an interesting twist to this general story Peters et al (2006b) hypothesized and found that the effect of the small loss is driven by individuals higher in 'numeracy' (skill with numbers) presumably because they draw more meaning from the numerical comparison of the $9 and 5¢ loss, compared to those low in numeracy.

Generalization to decisions with real consequences

Although the experiments described in this chapter were all conducted with hypothetical payoffs, there is evidence that the affect-driven context dependency we observed would be as strong for gambles with real payoffs. Indeed, Bateman et al (2006) have conducted a study in which both the UKbase gamble and the UK−5 gamble were embedded in a set of 13 diverse items (e.g. you receive an envelope containing £5; you receive a box of 11 handmade Belgian chocolates; you receive a free, medium-sized box of Cornflakes; etc.). Each item was rated on the same 0–20 scale of attractiveness. At the outset, participants were told that, after they had rated each item, 2 of the 11 would be selected at random and they would receive the item they had rated more attractive. Thus, if the most attractive item in a pair was one of the gambles, they actually played the gamble and received either £9 or the other outcome (0 or −5p). The first-time ratings of the two real gambles were virtually identical to the ratings of the hypothetical gambles described in this chapter. The gamble with the 5p loss was rated far more attractive.

One referee of this chapter questioned whether the results would generalize to gambles involving losses. Perhaps losing $9 would produce a more precise affective impression than winning $9. We did not test this hypothesis. However, there is ample evidence that numerical representations of large losses of life, as occur in mass murder or genocide, often convey little or no affect (Slovic, 2007). But some large numbers do appear to carry special affective 'prominence' or meaning (Albers, 2001), as when the outcome reaches $1000 or $1 million or, in the case of the lottery, hundreds of millions of dollars (see e.g. Associated Press, 2001).

One might also ask whether the present results could generalize to gambles evaluated in terms of buying and selling prices. Because prices have been shown to be constructed by means of an anchoring and adjustment process and because the likely anchor ($9) was the same for both loss and no-loss gambles, we would expect little or no price advantage for the loss bet.

Another referee questioned the seriousness of the mistakes made by participants in our studies who found the 5¢ loss gambles attractive. What is the boundary of this effect? How large will the loss have to be before the attractiveness of the gamble with the negative outcome becomes equal in attractiveness to the gamble with the zero outcome? We found that boosting the loss to 25¢ or 25p decreased the attractiveness only slightly, compared to US−5 or UK−5 (see Table 1.2), leaving the loss gamble still significantly more attractive than the base gamble. We did not examine gambles with losses any larger than 25¢ (25p).

On reflection, this is too narrow a perspective on the importance of the affect-induced contextual effects documented here. A broader perspective would take account of the fact that affective processes similar to those underlying the 5¢ loss effect can be seen as contributing to the construction of preferences in many areas of economic, social and political life. Consider, for example, the well-known asymmetric dominance effect observed in choice experiments. First studied by Huber et al (1982), an asymmetrically dominated alternative is dominated by one item in the choice set but not by another. Huber et al observed that adding such an alternative to a choice set can increase the probability of choosing the item that dominates it. This violates a fundamental assumption of most choice theories – namely that the addition of a new alternative cannot increase the probability of choosing a member of the original set (see also Bateman et al, 2005). Asymmetric dominance bears a resemblance to the 5¢ loss effect described in this chapter. If alternative X is paired with alternative Y in the original choice set, adding a new alternative, Z, that is dominated by X but not by Y, makes X 'look good,' thus enhancing its attractiveness in competition with Y. Note the similarity with the effect that the 5¢ loss has in making $9 look good. Doyle et al (1999) demonstrated the asymmetric dominance effect with real purchases in a grocery store. They concluded that the effect is robust, sizeable and of practical significance.

Other judgement and decision-making contexts in which affective processes have been shown to be important include destination preferences for vacations, jobs and retirement (Slovic et al, 1991c), risk perception (Loewenstein et al, 2001; Slovic et al, 2004), consumer product scares (Mitchell, 1989; Powell, 2001), marketing and advertising (Packard, 1957; Clark, 1988), insurance purchases (Hsee and Kunreuther, 2000), punitive damage awards by juries (Kahneman et al, 1998), environmental protection (Slovic and Slovic, 2004/2005) and response (or non-response) to life-saving opportunities (Fetherstonhaugh et al, 1997; Slovic et al, 2002; Slovic, 2007).

Affect and rationality

Contemplating the workings of the affect heuristic may help us to appreciate neuroscientist Antonio Damasio's (1994) contention that rationality is not only a product of the analytical mind, but of the experiential mind as well:

> *The strategies of human reason probably did not develop, in either evolu-tion or any single individual, without the guiding force of the mechanisms of biological regulation, of which emotion and feeling are notable expres-sions. Moreover, even after reasoning strategies become established ... their effective deployment probably depends, to a considerable extent, on a continued ability to experience feelings.* (pxii)

Consistent with this view, Damasio documents the difficulties that individuals have in making good decisions when brain damage has impaired their ability to attach feelings to the anticipated outcomes of their actions. However, affective feelings are not always beneficial. Strong feelings can desensitize us to differences among probabilities and outcomes (Loewenstein et al, 2001; Rottenstreich and Hsee, 2001; Sunstein, 2003; Hsee and Rottenstreich, 2004).

In addition, affect can sometimes deceive us through its strong dependency upon context and experience (Slovic, 2001; Slovic et al, 2002). As we have seen in this chapter, affect appears to have led the objectively inferior gamble to appear more attractive under certain circumstances. A challenge for future research is to better identify when affect facilitates good judgements and decisions and when it leads us astray.

Acknowledgements

Support for this chapter has come from the following grants from the National Science Foundation to Decision Research: SES-9876587, SES-0241313 and SES-0339204. Chris Starmer is grateful to The Leverhulme Trust (award F/00204/K) for financial support. The Programme on Environmental Decision Making is supported by the UK Economic and Social Research Council. The authors are grateful to staff and students at State University of New York, Plattsburgh and University of East Anglia for assistance in running various of the data collection exercises described in this chapter. The authors also thank three anonymous reviewers for their thoughtful and constructive comments on the manuscript.

Notes

1   There are also some circumstances in which payoffs are given more weight than probabilities. This occurs when people use a pricing response to evaluate a gamble (e.g. Lichtenstein and Slovic, 1971; Goldstein and Einhorn, 1987; Schkade and Johnson, 1989) and also when the gamble offers massive, highly exciting gains, as with a lottery (Loewenstein et al, 2001). Preferences within certain pairs of gambles can be predicted by a 'priority heuristic' which looks at a gamble's minimum gain as a first reason for choice (Brandstätter et al, 2006). The priority heuristic, however, would not predict the type of anomalous preferences that are the focus of the present study.

2   This interpretation is consistent with the link between evaluability, affect and monetary worth put forth by Hsee et al (1999). They observed that:
   ... an attribute can be difficult to evaluate even if its values are precisely given ... For example, everybody knows what money is ... but the monetary attribute of an option can be difficult to evaluate if the decision maker does not know the evaluability for that attribute in the given context ... To say that an attribute is difficult to evaluate ... means that the decision maker has difficulty determining the desirability of its value in the given decision context. (p580, emphasis in the original)

3   The motivation for the earlier studies predates our interest in affect and evaluability. Rather, notions of compatibility (Slovic et al, 1990a) stimulated the original design. However, recent research has led us to interpret these studies and design new ones within the framework of the affect heuristic.

4   Specifically, instead of responding to the gamble on the 0–20 scale of attractiveness, respondents were instructed to: 'Indicate your feeling about the attractiveness of playing this bet by drawing a circle on the back of this page. If the bet appears rather unattractive, draw a small circle. If it appears very attractive, draw a large circle. If it is somewhere in between, drawn an in-between size circle.'

5   The greater attractiveness of $9 in the loss condition perhaps may answer a puzzling question raised by the choice study reported above: Why did gambles US–5 and UK–5 fare only slightly better against the $4 (£4) sure gain than did their no-loss counterparts? Perhaps the relatively greater attractiveness of $9 in the loss bet also enhanced the attractiveness of the $4 alternative via an anchoring process. The $2 (£2) sure gain, being smaller, may not have been as influenced by the $9 anchor. This speculative answer could be tested using the methods described earlier for directly assessing affect.

6   A referee of this chapter asks why the zero outcome does not provide as good a level of comparison as either the 5¢ loss or the 5¢ gain: 'Is it because people take the ratio of outcomes and don't know how to divide by zero?' Our sense is that the description of the gambles called attention to the small loss and small gain, which were placed right under the 7/36 win $9. The win nothing outcome appeared only in text in two places not immediately below the gamble (see Figure 1.1). This may have reduced any tendency to compare $9 with 0. Also, the effect of the zero outcome is probably quite sensitive to subtle aspects of its description. As we saw in the Plattsburgh replication, placing 29/36 win nothing in the description of the gamble did not enhance its attractiveness and, in fact, produced a much lower rating than did 29/36 lose nothing.

Chapter 2

Risk as Analysis and Risk as Feelings: Some Thoughts about Affect, Reason, Risk and Rationality

Paul Slovic, Melissa L. Finucane, Ellen Peters and Donald G. MacGregor[*]

Introduction

Risk in the modern world is confronted and dealt with in three fundamental ways. Risk as feelings refers to our fast, instinctive and intuitive reactions to danger. Risk as analysis brings logic, reason and scientific deliberation to bear on hazard management. When our ancient instincts and our modern scientific analyses clash, we become painfully aware of a third reality – risk as politics. Members of the Society for Risk Analysis are certainly familiar with the scientific approach to risk, and Slovic (1999) has elaborated the political aspect. In this chapter we will examine what recent research in psychology and cognitive neuroscience tells us about the first dimension, 'risk as feelings,' an important vestige of our evolutionary journey.

That intuitive feelings are still the predominant method by which human beings evaluate risk is cleverly illustrated in a cartoon by Garry Trudeau (Figure 2.1). Trudeau's two characters decide whether to greet one another on a city street by employing a systematic analysis of the risks and risk-mitigating factors. We instantly recognize that no one in such a situation would ever be this analytical, even if his or her life was at stake. Most risk analysis is handled quickly and automatically by what we shall describe later as the 'experiential' mode of thinking.

[*]   Reprinted from Slovic, P., Finucane, M. L., Peters, E. and MacGregor, D. G. (2004) 'Risk as analysis and risk as feelings: Some thoughts about affect, reason, risk, and rationality', *Risk Analysis*, vol 24, pp311–322.

Figure 2.1 *Street calculus*

Background and theory: The importance of affect

Although the visceral emotion of fear certainly plays a role in risk as feelings, we shall focus here on a 'faint whisper of emotion' called affect. As used here, 'affect' means the specific quality of 'goodness' or 'badness' (1) experienced as a feeling state (with or without consciousness) and (2) demarcating a positive or negative quality of a stimulus. Affective responses occur rapidly and automatically – note how quickly you sense the feelings associated with the stimulus word 'treasure' or the word 'hate.' We argue that reliance on such feelings can be characterized as 'the affect heuristic.' In this chapter, we trace the development of the affect heuristic across a variety of research paths followed by us and many others. We also discuss some of the important practical implications resulting from ways that this heuristic impacts the way we perceive and evaluate risk and, more generally, the way it effects all human decision making.

Two modes of thinking

Affect also plays a central role in what have come to be known as dual-process theories of thinking, knowing and information processing (Sloman, 1996; Chaiken and Trope, 1999; Kahneman and Frederick, 2002). As Epstein (1994) observed:

> There is no dearth of evidence in every day life that people apprehend reality in two fundamentally different ways, one variously labeled intuitive, automatic, natural, non-verbal, narrative, and experiential, and the other analytical, deliberative, verbal, and rational. (p710)

Table 2.1, adapted from Epstein, further compares these modes of thought. One of the main characteristics of the experiential system is its affective basis. Although analysis is certainly important in some decision-making circumstances, reliance on affect and emotion is a quicker, easier and more efficient way to navigate in a complex, uncertain and sometimes dangerous world. Many theorists have given affect a direct and primary role in motivating behaviour (Mowrer, 1960a; Tomkins, 1962, 1963; Zajonc, 1980; Clark and Fiske, 1982; Le Doux, 1996; Forgas, 2000; Barrett and Salovey, 2002). Epstein's (1994) view on this is as follows:

> The experiential system is assumed to be intimately associated with the experience of affect ... which refer[s] to subtle feelings of which people are often unaware. When a person responds to an emotionally significant event ... the experiential system automatically searches its memory banks for related events, including their emotional accompaniments ... If the activated feelings are pleasant, they motivate actions and thoughts antici-pated to reproduce the feelings. If the feelings are unpleasant, they motivate actions and thoughts anticipated to avoid the feelings. (p716)

Whereas Epstein labelled the right side of Table 2.1 the 'rational system,' we have renamed it the 'analytic system,' in recognition that there are strong elements of rationality in both systems. It was the experiential system, after all, that enabled human beings to survive during their long period of evolution. Long before there was probability theory, risk assessment and decision analysis, there were intuition, instinct and gut feeling to tell us whether an animal was safe to approach or the water was safe to drink. As life became more complex and humans gained more control over their environment, analytic tools were invented to 'boost' the rational-ity of our experiential thinking. Subsequently, analytic thinking was placed on a pedestal and portrayed as the epitome of rationality. Affect and emotions were seen as interfering with reason.

The importance of affect is being recognized increasingly by decision researchers. A strong early proponent of the importance of affect in decision making was Zajonc (1980), who argued that affective reactions to stimuli are often

Table 2.1 *Two modes of thinking: Comparison of the experiential and analytic systems*

Experiential system	Analytic system
1. Holistic	1. Analytic
2. Affective: pleasure–pain oriented	2. Logical: reason oriented (what is sensible)
3. Associationistic connections	3. Logical connections
4. Behaviour mediated by 'vibes' from past experiences	4. Behaviour mediated by conscious appraisal of events
5. Encodes reality in concrete images, metaphors and narratives	5. Encodes reality in abstract symbols, words and numbers
6. More rapid processing: oriented toward immediate action	6. Slower processing: oriented toward delayed action
7. Self-evidently valid: 'experiencing is believing'	7. Requires justification via logic and evidence

the very first reactions, occurring automatically and subsequently guiding information processing and judgement. If Zajonc is correct, then affective reactions may serve as orienting mechanisms, helping us navigate quickly and efficiently through a complex, uncertain and sometimes dangerous world. Important work on affect and decision making has also been done by Janis and Mann (1977), Johnson and Tversky (1983), Schwarz and Clore (1988), Kahneman and Snell (1990), Isen (1993), Rozin et al (1993), Wilson et al (1993), Loewenstein (1996), Mellers et al (1997), Kahneman et al (1998), Mellers (2000), Loewenstein et al (2001), Rottenstreich and Hsee (2001) and Slovic et al (2002).

Damasio (1994), a neurologist, presented one of the most comprehensive and dramatic theoretical accounts of the role of affect and emotion in decision making. In seeking to determine 'what in the brain allows humans to behave rationally,' Damasio argued that thought is made largely from images, broadly construed to include perceptual and symbolic representations. A lifetime of learning leads these images to become 'marked' by positive and negative feelings linked directly or indirectly to somatic or bodily states. When a negative somatic marker is linked to an image of a future outcome, it sounds an alarm. When a positive marker is associated with the outcome image, it becomes a beacon of incentive. Damasio hypothesized that somatic markers increase the accuracy and efficiency of the decision process and their absence, observed in people with certain types of brain damage, degrades decision performance.

We now recognize that the experiential mode of thinking and the analytic mode of thinking are continually active, interacting in what we have characterized as 'the dance of affect and reason' (Finucane et al, 2003). While we may be able to 'do the right thing' without analysis (e.g. dodge a falling object), it is unlikely that we can employ analytic thinking rationally without guidance from affect somewhere along the line. Affect is essential to rational action. As Damasio (1994) observes:

The strategies of human reason probably did not develop, in either evolution or any single individual, without the guiding force of the mechanisms of biological regulation, of which emotion and feeling are notable expressions. Moreover, even after reasoning strategies become established ... their effective deployment probably depends, to a considerable extent, on a continued ability to experience feelings. (pxii)

The affect heuristic

The feelings that become salient in a judgement or decision-making process depend on characteristics of the individual and the task as well as the interaction between them. Individuals differ in the way they react affectively, and in their tendency to rely upon experiential thinking (Gasper and Clore, 1998; Peters and Slovic, 2000). As will be shown in this chapter, tasks differ regarding the evaluability (relative affective salience) of information. These differences result in the affective qualities of a stimulus image being 'mapped' or interpreted in diverse ways. The salient qualities of real or imagined stimuli then evoke images (perceptual and symbolic interpretations) that may be made up of both affective and instrumental dimensions.

The mapping of affective information determines the contribution stimulus images make to an individual's 'affect pool.' All of the images in people's minds are tagged or marked to varying degrees with affect. The affect pool contains all the positive and negative markers associated (consciously or unconsciously) with the images. The intensity of the markers varies with the images.

People consult or 'sense' the affect pool in the process of making judgements. Just as imaginability, memorability and similarity serve as cues for probability judgements (e.g. the availability and representativeness heuristics, Kahneman et al, 1982), affect may serve as a cue for many important judgements (including probability judgements). Using an overall, readily available affective impression can be easier and more efficient than weighing the pros and cons of various reasons or retrieving relevant examples from memory, especially when the required judgement or decision is complex or mental resources are limited. This characterization of a mental short cut has led us to label the use of affect a 'heuristic' (Finucane et al, 2000a).

Empirical support for the affect heuristic

Support for the affect heuristic comes from a diverse set of empirical studies, only a few of which will be reviewed here.

Early research: Dread and outrage in risk perception

Evidence of risk as feelings was present (though not fully appreciated) in early psychometric studies of risk perception (Fischhoff et al, 1978; Slovic, 1987). Those studies showed that feelings of dread were the major determiner of public perception and acceptance of risk for a wide range of hazards. Sandman, noting that dread was also associated with factors such as voluntariness, controllability, lethality and fairness, incorporated these qualities into his 'outrage model' (Sandman, 1989). Reliance on outrage was, in Sandman's view, the major reason that public evaluations of risk differed from expert evaluations (based on analysis of hazard, e.g. mortality statistics).

Risk and benefit judgements

The earliest studies of risk perception also found that, whereas risk and benefit tend to be positively correlated in the world, they are negatively correlated in people's minds (and judgements, Fischhoff et al, 1978). The significance of this finding for the affect heuristic was not realized until a study by Alhakami and Slovic (1994) found that the inverse relationship between perceived risk and perceived benefit of an activity (e.g. using pesticides) was linked to the strength of positive or negative affect associated with that activity as measured by rating the activity on bipolar scales such as good/bad, nice/awful, dread/not dread and so forth. This result implies that people base their judgements of an activity or a technology not only on what they think about it but also on how they feel about it. If their feelings toward an activity are favourable, they are moved toward judging the risks as low and the benefits as high; if their feelings toward it are unfavourable, they tend to judge the opposite – high risk and low benefit. Under this model, affect comes prior to, and directs, judgements of risk and benefit, much as Zajonc proposed. This process, which we have called 'the affect heuristic' (see Figure 2.2), suggests that, if a general affective view guides perceptions of risk and benefit, providing information about benefit should change perception of risk and vice versa (see Figure 2.3). For example, information stating that benefit is high for a technology such as nuclear power would lead to more positive overall affect that would, in turn, decrease perceived risk (Figure 2.3).

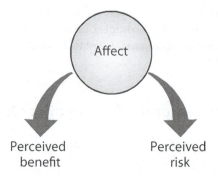

Note: Judgements of risk and benefit are assumed to be derived by reference to an overall affective evaluation of the stimulus item.

Source: Finucane et al (2000a)

Figure 2.2 *A model of the affect heuristic explaining the risk/benefit confounding observed by Alhakami and Slovic (1994)*

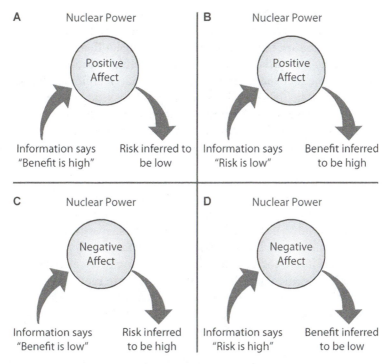

Figure 2.3 *Model showing how information about benefit (A) or information about risk (B) could increase the positive affective evaluation of nuclear power and lead to inferences about risk and benefit that coincides affectively with the information given. Similarly, information could make the overall affective evaluation of nuclear power more negative as in C and D, resulting in inferences about risk and benefit that are consistent with this more negative feeling*

Finucane et al (2000a) conducted this experiment, providing four different kinds of information designed to manipulate affect by increasing or decreasing perceived benefit or by increasing or decreasing perceived risk for each of three technologies. The predictions were confirmed. Because by design there was no apparent logical relationship between the information provided and the non-manipulated variable, these data support the theory that risk and benefit judgements are influenced, at least in part, by the overall affective evaluation (which was influenced by the information provided). Further support for the affect heuristic came from a second experiment by Finucane et al finding that the inverse relationship between perceived risks and benefits increased greatly under time pressure, when opportunity for analytic deliberation was reduced. These two experiments are important because they demonstrate that affect influences judgement directly and is not simply a response to a prior analytic evaluation.

Further support for the model in Figure 2.2 has come from two very different domains – toxicology and finance. Slovic et al (1997b) surveyed members of the British Toxicological Society and found that these experts, too, produced the same inverse relation between their risk and benefit judgements. As expected, the strength of the inverse relation was found to be mediated by the toxicologists, affective reactions toward the hazard items being judged. In a second study, these same toxicologists were asked to make a 'quick intuitive rating' for each of 30 chemical items (e.g. benzene, aspirin, second-hand cigarette smoke, dioxin in food) on an affect scale (bad–good). Next, they were asked to judge the degree of risk associated with a very small exposure to the chemical, defined as an exposure that is less than 1/100th the exposure level that would begin to cause concern for a regulatory agency. Rationally, because exposure was so low, one might expect these risk judgements to be uniformly low and unvarying, resulting in little or no correlation with the ratings of affect. Instead, there was a strong correlation across chemicals between affect and judged risk of a very small exposure. When the affect rating was strongly negative, judged risk of a very small exposure was high; when affect was positive, judged risk was small. Almost every respondent (95 out of 97) showed this negative correlation (the median correlation was −0.50). Importantly, those toxicologists who produced strong inverse relations between risk and benefit judgements in the first study also were more likely to exhibit a high correspondence between their judgements of affect and risk in the second study. In other words, across two different tasks, reliable individual differences emerged in toxicologists, reliance on affective processes in judgements of chemical risks.

In the realm of finance, Ganzach (2001) found support for a model in which analysts base their judgements of risk and return for unfamiliar stocks upon a global attitude. If stocks were perceived as good, they were judged to have high return and low risk, whereas if they were perceived as bad, they were judged to be low in return and high in risk. However, for familiar stocks, perceived risk and return were positively correlated, rather than being driven by a global attitude.

Judgements of probability, relative frequency and risk

The affect heuristic has much in common with the model of 'risk as feelings' proposed by Loewenstein et al (2001) and with dual-process theories put forth by Epstein (1994), Sloman (1996) and others. Recall that Epstein argues that individuals apprehend reality by two interactive, parallel processing systems. The rational system is a deliberative, analytical system that functions by way of established rules of logic and evidence (e.g. probability theory). The experiential system encodes reality in images, metaphors and narratives to which affective feelings have become attached.

To demonstrate the influence of the experiential system, Denes-Raj and Epstein (1994) showed that, when offered a chance to win $1 by drawing a red jelly bean from an urn, individuals often elected to draw from a bowl containing a greater absolute number, but a smaller proportion, of red beans (e.g. 7 in 100) than from a bowl with fewer red beans but a better probability of winning (e.g. 1 in 10). These individuals reported that, although they knew the probabilities were against them, they felt they had a better chance when there were more red beans.

We can characterize Epstein's subjects as following a mental strategy of imaging the 'numerator' (i.e. the number of red beans) and neglecting the denominator (the number of beans in the bowl). Consistent with the affect heuristic, images of winning beans convey positive affect that motivates choice.

Although the jelly bean experiment may seem frivolous, imaging the numerator brings affect to bear on judgements in ways that can be both non-intuitive and consequential. Slovic et al (2000b) demonstrated this in a series of studies in which experienced forensic psychologists and psychiatrists were asked to judge the likelihood that a mental patient would commit an act of violence within six months after being discharged from the hospital. An important finding was that clinicians who were given another expert's assessment of a patient's risk of violence framed in terms of relative frequency (e.g. 'of every 100 patients similar to Mr Jones, ten are estimated to commit an act of violence to others') subsequently labelled Mr Jones as more dangerous than did clinicians who were shown a statistically 'equivalent' risk expressed as a probability (e.g. 'patients similar to Mr Jones are estimated to have a 10 per cent chance of committing an act of violence to others').

Not surprisingly, when clinicians were told that '20 out of every 100 patients similar to Mr Jones are estimated to commit an act of violence,' 41 per cent would refuse to discharge the patient. But when another group of clinicians was given the risk as 'patients similar to Mr Jones are estimated to have a 20 per cent chance of committing an act of violence,' only 21 per cent would refuse to discharge the patient. Similar results have been found by Yamagishi (1997), whose judges rated a disease that kills 1286 people out of every 10,000 as more dangerous than one that kills 24.14 per cent of the population.

Follow-up studies showed that representations of risk in the form of individual probabilities of 10 per cent or 20 per cent led to relatively benign images of one person, unlikely to harm anyone, whereas the 'equivalent' frequentistic representations created frightening images of violent patients (e.g. 'some guy going crazy and killing someone'). These affect-laden images probably induced greater perceptions of risk in response to the relative-frequency frames.

Although frequency formats produce affect-laden imagery, story and narrative formats appear to do even better in that regard. Hendrickx et al (1989) found that warnings were more effective when, rather than being presented in terms of relative frequencies of harm, they were presented in the form of vivid, affect-laden scenarios and anecdotes. Sanfey and Hastie (1998) found that compared with respondents given information in bar graphs or data tables, respondents given narrative information more accurately estimated the performance of a set of marathon runners. Furthermore, Pennington and Hastie (1993) found that jurors construct narrative-like summations of trial evidence to help them process their judgements of guilt or innocence.

Perhaps the biases in probability and frequency judgement that have been attributed to the availability heuristic (Tversky and Kahneman, 1973) may be due, at least in part, to affect. Availability may work not only through ease of recall or imaginability, but because remembered and imagined images come tagged with affect. For example, Lichtenstein et al (1978) invoked availability to explain why judged frequencies of highly publicized causes of death (e.g. accidents, homicides, fires, tornadoes and cancer) were relatively overestimated and under-publicized causes (e.g. diabetes, stroke, asthma and tuberculosis) were underestimated. The highly publicized causes appear to be more affectively charged, that is, more sensational, and this may account both for their prominence in the media and their relatively overestimated frequencies.

Proportion dominance

There appears to be one generic information format that is highly evaluable (e.g. highly affective), leading it to carry great weight in many judgement tasks. This is a representation characterizing an attribute as a proportion or percentage of something, or as a probability.

Proportion or probability dominance was evident in an early study by Slovic and Lichtenstein (1968b) that had people rate the attractiveness of various two-outcome gambles. Ratings of a gamble's attractiveness were determined much more strongly by the probabilities of winning and losing than by the monetary outcomes. This basic finding has been replicated many times (Goldstein and Einhorn, 1987; Ordóñez and Benson, 1997).

Slovic et al (2002) tested the limits of this probability dominance by asking one group of subjects to rate the attractiveness of a simple gamble (7/36, win $9), on a 0–20 scale and asking a second group to rate a similar gamble with a small loss (7/36, win $9; 29/36, lose 5¢) on the same scale. The data were anomalous from the perspective of economic theory, but expected from the perspective of the affect heuristic. The mean response to the first gamble was 9.4. When a loss of 5¢ was added, the mean attractiveness jumped to 14.9 and there was almost no overlap between the distribution of responses around this mean and the responses for the group judging the gamble that had no loss.

Slovic also performed a conjoint analysis where each subject rated one of 16 gambles formed by crossing four levels of probability (7/36, 14/36, 21/36, 28/36) with four levels of payoff ($3, $6, $9, $12 in one study and $30, $60, $90, $120 in another). He found that, although subjects wanted to weight probability and payoff relatively equally in judging attractiveness (and thought they had done so), the actual weighting was 5–16 times greater for probability than for payoff.

We hypothesize that these curious findings can be explained by reference to the notion of affective mapping. According to this view, a probability maps relatively precisely onto the attractiveness scale, because it has an upper and lower bound and people know where a given value falls within that range. In contrast, the mapping of a dollar outcome (e.g. $9) onto the scale is diffuse, reflecting a failure to know whether $9 is good or bad, attractive or unattractive. Thus, the impression formed by the gamble offering $9 to win with no losing payoff is dominated by the rather unattractive impression produced by the 7/36 probability of winning. However, adding a very small loss to the payoff dimension puts the $9 payoff in perspective and thus gives it meaning. The combination of a possible $9 gain and a 5¢ loss is a very attractive win/lose ratio, leading to a relatively precise mapping onto the upper part of the scale. Whereas the imprecise mapping of the $9 carries little weight in the averaging process, the more precise and now favourable impression of ($9–5¢) carries more weight, thus leading to an increase in the overall favourability of the gamble.

Proportion dominance surfaces in a powerful way in a very different context, the life-saving interventions studied by Baron (1997), Fetherstonhaugh et al (1997), Jenni and Loewenstein (1997) and Friedrich et al (1999). These studies found that, unless the number of lives saved is explicitly comparable from one intervention to another, evaluation is dominated by the proportion of lives saved (relative to the population at risk), rather than the actual number of lives saved.

The results of our life-saving study (Fetherstonhaugh et al, 1997) are important because they imply that a specified number of human lives may not carry precise affective meaning, similar to the conclusion we drew about stated payoffs (e.g. $9) in the gambling studies. The gambling studies suggested an analogous experiment with life saving. In the context of a decision pertaining to airport safety, we asked people to evaluate the attractiveness of purchasing new equipment for use in the event of a crash landing of an airliner. In one condition, subjects were told that this equipment affords a chance of saving 150 lives that would be in jeopardy in such an event. A second group of subjects was told that this equipment affords a chance of saving 98 per cent of the 150 lives that would be in jeopardy. We predicted that, because saving 150 lives is diffusely good, hence only weakly evaluable, whereas saving 98 per cent of something is clearly very good, support for purchasing this equipment would be much greater in the 98 per cent condition. We predicted that other high percentages would also lead to greater support, even though the number of lives saved was fewer. The results, reported in Slovic et al (2002), confirmed these predictions (see Figure 2.4).

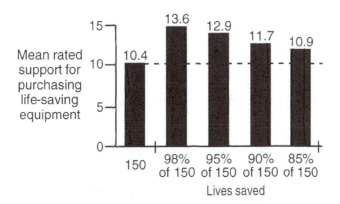

Figure 2.4 *Saving a percentage of 150 lives received higher support than saving 150 lives*

Insensitivity to probability

Outcomes are not always affectively as vague as the quantities of money and lives that were dominated by proportion in the above experiments. When consequences carry sharp and strong affective meaning, as is the case with a lottery jackpot or a cancer, the opposite phenomenon occurs – variation in probability often carries too little weight. As Loewenstein et al (2001) observe, one's images and feelings toward winning the lottery are likely to be similar whether the probability of winning is one in 10 million or one in 10,000. They further note that responses to uncertain situations appear to have an all or none characteristic that is sensitive to the possibility rather than the probability of strong positive or negative consequences, causing very small probabilities to carry great weight. This, they argue, helps explain many paradoxical findings such as the simultaneous prevalence of gambling and the purchasing of insurance. It also explains why societal concerns about hazards such as nuclear power and exposure to extremely small amounts of toxic chemicals fail to recede in response to information about the very small probabilities of the feared consequences from such hazards. Support for these arguments comes from Rottenstreich and Hsee (2001) who show that, if the potential outcome of a gamble is emotionally powerful, its attractiveness or unattractiveness is relatively insensitive to changes in probability as great as from 0.99 to 0.01.

Affect and insurance

Hsee and Kunreuther (2000) demonstrated that affect influences decisions about whether to purchase insurance. In one study, they found that people were willing to pay twice as much to insure a beloved antique clock (that no longer works and cannot be repaired) against loss in shipment to a new city than to insure a similar clock for which 'one does not have any special feeling.' In the event of loss, the insurance paid $100 in both cases. Similarly, Hsee and Menon (1999) found that students were more willing to buy a warranty on a newly purchased used car if it was a beautiful convertible than if it was an ordinary-looking station wagon, even if the expected repair expenses and cost of the warranty were held constant.

Failures of the experiential system

Throughout this chapter, we have portrayed the affect heuristic as the centrepiece of the experiential mode of thinking, the dominant mode of risk assessment and survival during the evolution of the human species. But, like other heuristics that provide efficient and generally adaptive responses but occasionally get us into trouble, reliance on affect can also mislead us. Indeed, if it was always optimal to follow our affective and experiential instincts, there would have been no need for the rational/analytic system of thinking to have evolved and become so prominent in human affairs.

There are two important ways that experiential thinking misguides us. One results from the deliberate manipulation of our affective reactions by those who wish to control our behaviours (advertising and marketing exemplify this manipulation). The other results from the natural limitations of the experiential system and the existence of stimuli in our environment that are simply not amenable to valid affective representation. The latter problem is discussed below.

Judgements and decisions can be faulty not only because their affective components are manipulable, but also because they are subject to inherent biases of the experiential system. For example, the affective system seems designed to sensitize us to small changes in our environment (e.g. the difference between 0 and 1 deaths) at the cost of making us less able to appreciate and respond appropriately to larger changes further away from zero (e.g. the difference between 500 and 600 deaths). Fetherstonhaugh et al (1997) referred to this insensitivity as 'psychophysical numbing.' Albert Szent-Gyorgi put it another way: 'I am deeply moved if I see one man suffering and would risk my life for him. Then I talk impersonally about the possible pulverization of our big cities, with a hundred million dead. I am unable to multiply one man's suffering by a hundred million.'

Similar problems arise when the outcomes that we must evaluate are visceral in nature. Visceral factors include drive states such as hunger, thirst, sexual desire, emotions, pain and drug craving. They have direct, hedonic impacts that have a powerful effect on behaviour. Although they produce strong feelings in the present moment, these feelings are difficult if not impossible to recall or anticipate in a veridical manner, a factor that plays a key role in the phenomenon of addiction (Loewenstein, 1999):

> *Unlike currently experienced visceral factors, which have a disproportionate impact on behavior, delayed visceral factors tend to be ignored or severely under-weighted in decision making. Today's pain, hunger, anger, etc. are palpable, but the same sensations anticipated in the future receive little weight.* (p240)

The decision to smoke cigarettes

Cigarette smoking is a dangerous activity that takes place one cigarette at a time, often over many years and hundreds of thousands of episodes. The questionable rationality of smoking decisions provides a dramatic example of the difficulty that experiential thinking faces in dealing with outcomes that change very slowly over time, are remote in time, and are visceral in nature.

For many years, beginning smokers were portrayed as 'young economists,' rationally weighing the risks of smoking against the benefits when deciding whether to initiate that activity (Viscusi, 1992), analogous to the 'street calculus' being spoofed in Figure 2.1. However, recent research paints a different picture. This new account (Slovic, 2001) shows young smokers acting experientially in the sense of giving little or no conscious thought to risks or to the amount of smoking they will be doing. Instead, they are driven by the affective impulses of the moment, enjoying smoking as something new and exciting, a way to have fun with their friends. Even after becoming 'regulars,' the great majority of smokers expect to stop soon, regardless of how long they have been smoking, how many cigarettes they currently smoke per day, or how many previous unsuccessful attempts they have experienced. Only a fraction actually quit, despite many attempts. The problem is nicotine addiction, a visceral condition that young smokers recognize by name as a consequence of smoking but do not understand experientially until they are caught in its grip.

The failure of the experiential system to protect many young people from the lure of smoking is nowhere more evident than in the responses to a survey question that asked smokers: 'If you had it to do all over again, would you start smoking?' More than 85 per cent of adult smokers and about 80 per cent of young smokers (ages 14–22 years) answered 'no' (Slovic, 2001). Moreover, the more individuals perceive themselves to be addicted, the more often they have tried to quit, the longer they have been smoking, and the more cigarettes they are currently smoking per day, the more likely they are to answer 'no' to this question.

The data indicate that most beginning smokers lack the experience to appreciate how their future selves will perceive the risks from smoking or how they will value the trade-off between health and the need to smoke. This is a strong repudiation of the model of informed rational choice. It fits well with the findings indicating that smokers give little conscious thought to risk when they begin to smoke. They appear to be lured into the behaviour by the prospects of fun and excitement. Most begin to think of risk only after starting to smoke and gaining what to them is new information about health risks.

These findings underscore the distinction that behavioural decision theorists now make between decision utility and experience utility (Kahneman and Snell, 1992; Kahneman, 1994; Loewenstein and Schkade, 1999). Utility predicted or expected at the time of decision often differs greatly from the quality and intensity of the hedonic experience that actually occurs.

Managing emotion, reason and risk

Now that we are beginning to understand the complex interplay between emotion, affect and reason that is wired into the human brain and essential to rational behaviour, the challenge before us is to think creatively about what this means for managing risk. On the one hand, how do we apply reason to temper the strong emotions engendered by some risk events? On the other hand, how do we infuse needed 'doses of feeling' into circumstances where lack of experience may otherwise leave us too 'coldly rational?'

Can risk analysis benefit from experiential thinking?

The answer to this question is almost certainly yes. Even such prototypical analytic exercises as proving a mathematical theorem or selecting a move in chess benefit from experiential guidance. The mathematician senses whether the proof 'looks good' and the chess master gauges whether a contemplated move 'feels right,' based upon stored knowledge of a large number of winning patterns (de Groot, 1978). Analysts attempting to build a model to solve a client's decision-making problem are instructed to rely upon the client's sense of unease about the results of the current model as a signal that further modelling may be needed (Phillips, 1984). A striking example of failure because an analysis was devoid of feeling was perpetrated by Philip Morris. The company commissioned an analysis of the costs to the Czech government of treating diseased smokers. Employing a very narrow conception of costs, the analysis concluded that smokers benefited the government by dying young. The analysis created so much hostility that Philip Morris was forced to issue an apology (*New York Times*, 2001).

Elsewhere we have argued that analysis needs to be sensitive to the 'softer' values underlying such qualities as dread, equity, controllability and so on that drive people's concerns about risk, as well as to degrees of ignorance or scientific uncertainty. A blueprint for doing this is sketched in the Academy report *Understanding Risk: Decision Making in a Democratic Society* (NRC, 1996). Invocation of the 'precautionary principle' (Wiener, 2002) represents yet another approach to overcoming the limitations of what some see as overly narrow technical risk assessments.

Someone once observed that 'Statistics are human beings with the tears dried off.' Our studies of psychophysical numbing demonstrate the potential for neglect of statistical fatalities, thus raising the question: 'How can we put the tears back on?' There are attempts to do this that may be instructive. Organizers of a rally designed to get Congress to do something about 38,000 deaths a year from handguns piled 38,000 pairs of shoes in a mound in front of the Capitol. After 11 September 2001, many newspapers published biographical sketches of the victims, a dozen or so each day until all had been featured. Writers and artists have long recognized the power of the written word to bring meaning to tragedy. *The Diary of Anne Frank* and Elie Wiesel's *Night* certainly bring home the meaning of the Holocaust more powerfully than the statistic, 'six million dead.'

How can an understanding of 'Risk as Feeling' help us cope with threats from terrorism?

Research by Rottenstreich and Hsee (2001) demonstrates that events associated with strong feelings can overwhelm us even though their likelihood is remote. Because risk as feeling tends to overweight frightening consequences, we need to invoke risk as analysis to give us perspective on the likelihood of such consequences. For example, when our feelings of fear move us to consider purchasing a handgun to protect against terrorists, our analytic selves should also heed the evidence showing that a gun fired in the home is 22 times more likely to harm oneself or a friend or family member than to harm an unknown, hostile intruder.

In some circumstances, risk as feeling may outperform risk as analysis. A case in point is a news story dated 27 March 2002 discussing the difficulty of screening 150,000 checked pieces of baggage at Los Angeles International Airport. The best analytic devices, utilizing X-rays, computers and other modern tools, are slow and inaccurate. The solution – rely upon the noses of trained dogs.

Some species of trouble, such as terrorism, greatly strain the capacity of quantitative risk analysis. Our models of the hazard-generating process are too crude to permit precise and accurate predictions of where, when and how the next attacks might unfold. What is the role of risk analysis when the stakes are high, the uncertainties are enormous, and time is precious? Is there a human equivalent of the dog's nose that can be put to good use in such circumstances, relying on instinctual processing of affective cues, using brain mechanisms honed through evolution, to enhance survival? What research is needed to train and test experiential risk analysis skills?

Conclusion

It is sobering to contemplate how elusive meaning is, due to its dependence upon affect. Thus the forms of meaning that we take for granted and upon which we justify immense effort and expense toward gathering and disseminating 'meaningful' information may be illusory. We cannot assume that an intelligent person can understand the meaning of and properly act upon even the simplest of numbers such as amounts of money or numbers of lives at risk, not to mention more esoteric measures or statistics pertaining to risk, unless these numbers are infused with affect.

Contemplating the workings of the affect heuristic helps us appreciate Damasio's contention that rationality is not only a product of the analytical mind, but of the experiential mind as well. The perception and integration of affective feelings, within the experiential system, appears to be the kind of high-level maximization process postulated by economic theories since the days of Jeremy Bentham. These feelings form the neural and psychological substrate of utility. In this sense, the affect heuristic enables us to be rational actors in many important situations. But not in all situations. It works beautifully when our experience enables us to anticipate accurately how we will like the consequences of our decisions. It fails miserably when the consequences turn out to be much different in character than we anticipated.

The scientific study of affective rationality is in its infancy. It is exciting to contemplate what might be accomplished by future research designed to help humans understand the affect heuristic and employ it beneficially in risk analysis and other worthy endeavours.

Acknowledgements

This article received a Best Paper Award at the 2002 Annual Meeting of the Society for Risk Analysis. Research for this article was supported by Grants SES-02413131, SES-0112158 and SES-0111941 from the National Science Foundation.

Chapter 3

Attentional Mechanisms in the Generation of Sympathy

Stephan Dickert and Paul Slovic[*]

Introduction

Witnessing the suffering of others often invokes emotional reactions in the observers. The link between empathic responses and willingness to provide help to others has been the subject of recent research on emotional responses and prosocial behaviour. Feelings such as empathy, sympathy, compassion, distress, pity and even anticipated regret are typically involved in decisions to provide assistance or donate money to those in need (Batson, 1990; Kogut and Ritov, 2005a, b; Batson et al, 2007; Loewenstein and Small, 2007; Small et al, 2007; Dickert, 2008).

Given the prominent role of emotions in prosocial behaviour, research has begun to tackle the important question of what drives the generation of feelings relevant for helping others. Slovic (2007) suggests a model by which mental images and attention are two vital precursors for emotional reactions towards others in distress. Mental images can contain affective tags that serve as a signal for the selection of behavioural alternatives (Damasio, 1994; Peters and Slovic, 2000; Slovic et al, 2002). A direct consequence of this mechanism is that people are more likely to generate sympathetic responses when they are able to mentally imagine the victim. In fact, research on perspective taking (e.g. Davis, 1994; Batson et al, 2007) supports this notion and shows that more empathic concern is generated for victims that are similar to the perceiver (Loewenstein and Small, 2007). Additionally, we seem to 'feel' more for individual victims than for groups of victims because mental images of single, identified victims are more vivid and

[*]   Reprinted from Dickert, S. and Slovic, P. (2009) 'Attentional mechanisms in the generation of sympathy', *Judgment and Decision Making*, vol 4, pp297–306.

concrete (Jenni and Loewenstein, 1997; Kogut and Ritov, 2005a; Slovic, 2007; Västfjäll et al, 2009).

The predisposition to perceive groups of people as less unitary is closely connected to Gestalt theories of perception (Hamilton and Sherman, 1996), an association which highlights that perceptual processes are closely related to other, more complex impression formation processes (Kahneman, 2003; Glöckner and Betsch, 2008). The connection between Gestalt principles of perception and impression formation is of particular interest, as perceptual processes impose limitations on our ability to process large numbers of people in the same way that psychological processes may restrict our ability to feel compassion for large numbers of victims. Additionally, it shows that perceptual and attentional processes can influence affective reactions, as posited by Slovic (2007).

The interaction between emotions and attention

Research on the interplay between emotions and attention has often highlighted the selective effects of emotions on people's attentional focus (e.g. Fox, 2002). Highly relevant affective stimuli are processed faster and hold attention longer than affectively neutral stimuli (Eastwood et al, 2001). The apparent effects of emotional stimuli (such as threatening or fearful stimuli) on behavioural responses (e.g. orienting reaction times) prompted researchers to suggest neural networks that allow for attentional and emotional modulation of visual processes (Vuilleumier and Driver, 2007). Top–down modulation of emotionally significant stimuli on attentional tasks indicates that neural networks exist that allow for rapid communication between attentional and emotional neural systems (Bush et al, 2000). Whereas emotions can direct attention to affectively salient objects (Vuilleumier et al, 2003; Vuilleumier, 2005; Ochsner and Phelps, 2007), attention can influence emotional reactions by inhibiting as well as enhancing and generating emotional reactions to stimuli (Fenske and Raymond, 2006). The ability to shift attention helps in regulating one's own negative emotional state (Gross, 2002; Rueda et al, 2005; Posner and Rothbart, 2007), while focal (spatial) attention facilitates subsequent and more elaborate emotional processing and can have a profound effect on the generation of emotions (Holmes et al, 2003).

The effects of attention on the generation of emotions were demonstrated in a series of insightful experiments that highlight the emotional inhibitory consequences of attending to specific locations in one's visual field (Raymond et al, 2003; Fenske et al, 2004, 2005). These authors consistently show that not attending to distractor stimuli devalues these on affective as well as other dimensions, a phenomenon that they term the attentional inhibition hypothesis (Fenske and Raymond, 2006). For example, smiling and neutral distractor faces were seen as less trustworthy than attended target faces, and abstract Mondrian stimuli were evaluated as less cheerful when unattended.

In this chapter, we expand on the attentional inhibition hypothesis by examining the facilitating effects that attention has on the generation of sympathy. Groups and individuals are processed differently on cognitive (Hamilton and Sherman, 1996; Ariely, 2001) and emotional dimensions; affective reactions towards single identified victims are often more intense compared to groups of victims (Slovic, 2007). A peculiar and inherent property of a group of individuals is that attention to any single individual can be decreased by the presence of the other victims. If attentional focus is indeed facilitating the generation of empathic emotions for individual victims, then other members of a group can assume a distracting role for single individual members. Sympathy for individual victims would then be dependent on the constraints that the distraction places on the ability to attend to each individual.

In two experiments, we used a paradigm that placed participants in a position to react empathically to victims in need of help and manipulated their ability to visually attend to a single target victim. It was expected that distracting attention away from individual targets decreases emotional responses. We hypothesized that visual distractors, in the form of other victims, negatively influence the attention needed to generate sympathy towards a target victim, and that sympathy judgements are higher for a single target victim presented alone vs. with distractor victims. Additionally, we were interested in whether these emotional reactions are different when targets were evaluated online (i.e. while visually focusing on a picture of the target) vs. when these evaluations were made from memory. Hastie and Park (1986) propose that judgements from memory are more effortful than spontaneous online judgements, and that attending to a target is easer when judged online vs. from memory. Affective reactions are thought to be stronger when mental representations are attended to and more vivid (Slovic et al, 2002; Pham, 2007). Judgements based on memory retrieval, on the other hand, can lead to less vivid impression formation (e.g. Reyna and Brainerd, 1995) and subsequently to weaker emotional responses.

Experiment I

Method

Participants
Fifty-eight participants (79 per cent female) with an average age of $M = 21.9$ ($SD = 4.5$) at the University of Oregon completed Experiment 1. All participants had normal or corrected-to-normal vision.

Design and materials
Online vs. memory judgements and presence vs. absence of distractors were manipulated in a fully factorial 2×2 within-subjects design. Participants rated their sympathy for victims identified by a spatial cue that appeared either before or after a target picture. Online judgements were realized by a spatial cue presented before the target picture, while memory judgements featured a cue that appeared after the presentation of the target picture. Thus, in the online judgement condition, participants were able to focus on the specific location where the target picture would appear and make an online sympathy judgement while attending to the picture. In the memory condition, the spatial cue appeared after

the presentation of the target picture, and sympathy judgements were based on a memory representation. Target pictures were either flanked by seven distractor victims or presented alone. The primary dependent variable was sympathy ratings for the target picture. Reaction times for these sympathy ratings were also recorded.

The target and distractor pictures were part of the same set of eight pictures (four female children and four male children, taken from Kogut and Ritov, 2005a, b). Participants saw each picture an equal number of times in the four conditions. In each condition the eight possible pictures served as the target victim twice, resulting in 64 experimental trials.

Apparatus and procedure

Participants were seated 65cm in front of a 17" computer screen (resolution = 1024 × 768) and were informed that they would see pictures of children in need of a financial contribution due to a life-threatening disease. Participants were further told that the child that elicited the highest average sympathy would receive a donation from the experimenters on behalf of the participants. Each trial started with a fixation cross presented for 150ms at the centre of the screen, as shown in Figure 3.1. In the online judgement conditions, a red dot cue (size = 0.5°) appeared at one of eight possible locations (on a horizontal line) at the exact spatial location where the target picture (size = 4.5°) would appear later. Dot cues were shown for 500ms, pictures for 3000ms, and between dots and pictures a 150ms blank screen was interleaved. After seeing the target picture, participants rated how much sympathy they felt on a vertical sliding scale (300 pixels = 8.7° anchored by 0 = No sympathy at all to 300 = Very much sympathy) with a vertically movable cursor corresponding to movements of the mouse. The memory

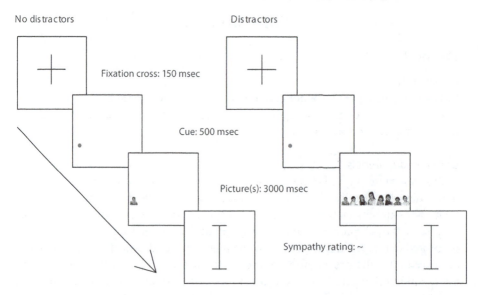

Figure 3.1 *Design schematic (online judgement pair)*

judgement condition was identical to the online judgement condition, except that pictures were presented before the cues, such that participants first saw one (or eight) pictures, but could identify the target only after the pictures disappeared and the spatial cue was presented. The order of pictures presented was determined with a Latin-square to ensure that any effect of picture order on sympathy would be counterbalanced.

Results

Sympathy judgement

Sympathy ratings were averaged across pictures for each condition. The results, depicted in Figure 3.2, suggest that, regardless of whether judgements were made online or from memory, target victims received higher sympathy ratings when they were presented without distractor victims. Sympathy ratings were lowest when the target victim was presented with distractors and judgements were made from memory.

A repeated-measures analysis of variance (ANOVA) with judgement mode and presence of distractors as within-subject factors revealed a significant main effect for judgement mode, such that sympathy ratings were significantly higher when made online ($M = 179.6$, $SD = 70.8$) vs. from memory ($M = 173.7$; $SD = 72.5$), $F(1,57) = 4.8$, $p < .05$, $\eta_p^2 = 0.08$. Participants also gave higher sympathy ratings when target pictures were presented without distractors ($M = 183.4$, $SD = 70.1$) vs. with distractors ($M = 169.5$; $SD = 73.2$), $F(1,57) = 10.7$, $p < .01$, $\eta_p^2 = 0.16$. Furthermore, a significant interaction between judgement mode and presence of distractors emerged from the data, $F(1,57) = 10.8$, $p < .01$, $\eta_p^2 = 0.16$. To further elucidate this interaction, simple contrasts were conducted and revealed that, for memory judgements, targets without distractors ($M = 184.4$; $SD = 70.1$)

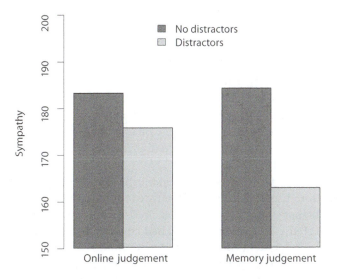

Figure 3.2 *Mean sympathy ratings for Experiment 1*

received significantly higher sympathy ratings compared to targets with distractors ($M = 163.1$; $SD = 75.0$), $t(57) = 3.8$, $p < .01$, Cohen's $d = 0.51$. This difference was still marginally significant for online judgements, with participants expressing higher sympathy for targets without distractors ($M = 183.3$; $SD = 70.2$) vs. with distractors present ($M = 175.8$; $SD = 71.2$), $t(57) = 1.8$, $p < .08$, Cohen's $d = 0.24$.

It is possible that the observed decrease of sympathy judgements in the memory condition with distractors was due to participants not being able to remember which target picture they were rating and making an average judgement instead. If this was indeed the case, we would expect lower variance in sympathy responses especially in the memory judgement condition when distractors were presented. However, we found no evidence for decreased variance in this condition relative to the other conditions. In fact, F-tests revealed that variances were similar in all four conditions, $Fs < 1.1$, $ps > .31$. To further exclude the possibility that participants were making average judgements in the memory condition, we also examined whether significant differences in sympathy judgements existed for the individual pictures. If participants did not recall which picture to judge, we would expect that their responses differ systematically compared to the online condition. A 2 judgement condition (online vs. memory) × 8 picture, repeated-measures ANOVA with sympathy ratings as the dependent variable revealed that some pictures evoked more sympathy than others, $F(7,399) = 56.4$, $p < .001$, $\eta^2 = 0.50$. However these ratings did not interact with the judgement condition, $F(7,399) = 1.7$, $p = .10$, $\eta^2 = 0.03$, showing no evidence that the differences in ratings of the individual pictures were dependent on the judgement condition.

Reaction time analysis

A similar 2×2 repeated-measures ANOVA was conducted on participants' average reaction times for each condition. Results show that memory judgements took longer than online judgements, $F(1,57) = 9.8$, $p < .01$, $\eta_p^2 = 0.15$, and participants' reaction time was slower when distractors were present, $F(1,57) = 23.4$, $p < .001$, $\eta_p^2 = 0.29$. Additionally the interaction between these two factors was also significant, $F(1,57) = 15.7$, $p < .001$, $\eta_p^2 = 0.22$. As can be seen in Figure 3.3, reaction times were longer for memory judgements when distractors were present. In this condition, participants had to first recall which of the previously seen pictures corresponded to the cue before indicating their sympathy rating. Given that the reaction times are similar in the other conditions, it is possible that the difficulty and compound effects of memory retrieval and distractors are responsible for the longer reaction times.

We further investigated whether participants' sympathy judgements correlated with reaction times. Although faster reactions times were generally accompanied by higher sympathy ratings in each of the four conditions (rs ranged from $-.24$ to $-.01$), the correlation approached conventional significance levels only in the online judgement/no-distractor condition, $r(57) = -.24$, $p < .08$. However, across all observations, the correlation between sympathy ratings and reaction times was statistically significant $r(230) = -.13$, $p = .037$.

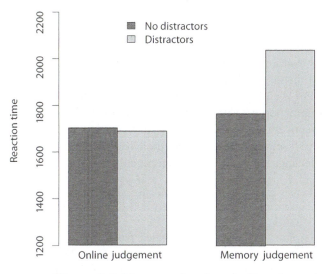

Figure 3.3 *Mean reaction times for Experiment 1*

Discussion

Experiment 1 was designed to investigate the role of attention in the generation of sympathy. Results supported the hypothesis that a single target victim evokes more sympathy when presented alone vs. flanked by distractor victims, which is in line with findings that emotional responses decrease as the number of victims increase (Slovic, 2007). This effect was present when judgements were made online as well as from memory; however, it was especially pronounced when affective judgements were made based on memory. It seems likely that online processing enabled more vivid images and, in turn, stronger empathic responses than memory processing, an explanation that dovetails nicely with research on person perception (Hamilton and Sherman, 1996) and affect (e.g. Loewenstein et al, 2001; Slovic et al, 2002).

A possible alternative explanation of the results in Experiment 1 is that participants gave lower sympathy ratings in the memory judgement/distractor condition simply because they were unable to clearly identify which target they were supposed to rate. However, similar results (albeit less pronounced) were obtained for the online judgement condition, which cannot be explained by an account that focuses solely on unsuccessful retrieval of the target picture. Moreover, if participants were unable to identify the individual pictures in the memory judgement/distractor condition and instead gave average ratings, we would expect little difference in how the individual pictures were rated in this condition. This was not the case, and differences in sympathy ratings for individual pictures did not depend on the judgement condition. Nonetheless, we addressed this concern directly in Experiment 2 to clarify the role that correct identification plays in empathic responses.

Experiment 2

Experiment 2 sought to replicate the general findings in Experiment 1 and rule out the possibility that lower sympathy ratings were mainly a product of unsuccessful retrieval of the target picture. The number of distractors was reduced and the viewing time for the pictures was extended to facilitate better encoding. We also added a manipulation check to verify that participants could indeed identify the target retrospectively. Moreover, we were in a position to replicate the basic findings in a different setting to test whether the effects of attention on the generation of empathic feelings generalize to a different culture.

Method

Participants

Forty-eight participants (53 per cent female) from the University of Bonn, Germany, and community members with an average age of 25.7 ($SD = 7.4$) took part in this study and were paid an average of €12 as compensation for their time in a test battery that included other experiments unrelated to this study.

Design and materials

The design and materials were similar to those used in Experiment 1. Participants saw a total of 64 experimental trials, in which they rated their sympathy for one of eight possible children suffering from an unspecified disease. The two variables of interest (judgement mode and presence of distractors) were manipulated in the same fashion as in Experiment 1. However, unlike Experiment 1, here we reduced the number of distractor pictures to three and used a block-design where trials were blocked by judgement mode. Half of the participants made online judgements for the first 32 trials and memory judgements for the second 32 trials, and this order was reversed for the other half. Within each block, target pictures were presented randomly with and without distractors. The target and distractor pictures could appear in four locations: above, below, right or left at an equal distance from a central fixation cross. As in Experiment 1, the distractor variable was crossed with judgement mode. On half of the trials a spatial cue appeared before the picture(s), and followed the pictures on the other half of the trials. The spatial cue was presented for 500ms and the pictures for 4000ms. At the end of each trial, participants rated their respective sympathy level of the target picture with a sliding scale (500 pixels = 13.8°, anchored by 0 = *No sympathy at all* to 500 = *Very much sympathy*).

After completion of the 64 experimental trials, 24 manipulation check trials were added in which participants had to correctly identify a target picture. The correct identification of the target picture was a concern only for trials in the memory condition with distractors. Thus, the manipulation check trials had a similar structure as the memory judgement condition: in each of these trials, four pictures were presented after the fixation cross, followed by a cue. Participants were then asked to judge whether a test picture corresponded to the target picture identified by the cue. Three types of manipulation check trials were used, each presented a total of eight times: The test picture was (1) identical to the target picture, (2) not identical to the target picture but part of the picture set used in the study, and (3) not identical to the target picture and belonged to a completely different set of pictures not used in the 64 experimental trials.

Results

Manipulation check

Overall, every participant answered more than 87 per cent of the manipulation check trials correctly, and none performed below 75 per cent in any of the three manipulation check trial types. We took this as evidence that participants were quite able to correctly identify the target picture and base their sympathy judgement on the correct mental representation when target pictures were presented with distractors in the memory condition.

Sympathy judgements

A preliminary analysis confirmed that no significant difference existed between the orders in which the blocked online and memory judgements were made, which justified simplifying further analyses to a 2 (online vs. memory judgement) × 2 (distractors vs. no distractors) within-subjects design. An ANOVA with judgement mode and presence of distractors revealed a significant main effect for distractors, $F(1,47) = 4.19, p < .05, \eta_p^2 = 0.08$. Participants gave higher sympathy judgements when pictures were presented without distractors ($M = 230.5, SD = 69.4$) than when distractors were present ($M = 218.8, SD = 90.6$). The main effect for judgement mode was not significant $F(1,47) = 1.01, p = .32, \eta_p^2 = 0.02$, however the mean difference was in the predicted direction such that participants gave higher sympathy judgements when making their judgement online ($M = 227.3, SD = 86.6$) vs. from memory ($M = 222.0, SD = 73.8$). Finally, although the interaction between judgement mode and presence of distractors was not significant, $F(1,47) < 1, p = .72, \eta_p^2 = 0.01$, simple contrasts revealed that participants gave significantly higher sympathy judgements without distractors ($M = 228.5, SD = 71.0$) vs. with distractors ($M = 215.5, SD = 76.5$) only in the memory judgement condition, $t(47) = 4.06, p < .001$, Cohen's $d = 0.59$. This effect was also present but not significant when participants made online judgements ($M = 222.1, SD = 105.3$ and $M = 232.4, SD = 67.8$ for with and without distractors, respectively), $t(47) = 1.13, p = 0.26$, Cohen's $d = 0.16$. See Figure 3.4 for details.

As in Experiment 1, we tested whether the decrease in sympathy judgements in the memory condition with distractors was based on participants' not being able to identify the target picture retrospectively and instead making an average judgement. A 2 judgement condition (online vs. memory) × 8 picture repeated-measures ANOVA indicated that although sympathy ratings differed for the pictures, $F(7,329) = 13.5, p < .001, \eta^2 = 0.22$, this did not depend on whether pictures were seen in the memory or online judgement condition as indicated by a non-significant interaction, $F(7,329) = 0.4, p = .87, \eta^2 = 0.01$.

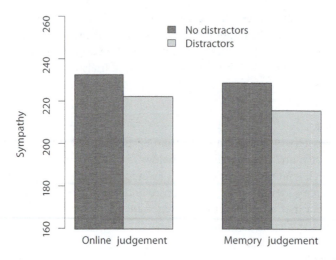

Figure 3.4 *Mean sympathy ratings for Experiment 2*

Reaction time results

A similar 2 × 2 factorial ANOVA for reaction times showed a significant main effect for judgement mode, $F(1,47) = 26.52, p < .001, \eta_p^2 = 0.36$, and presence of distractors, $F(1,47) = 10.75, p = 0.01, \eta_p^2 = 0.19$. As expected, sympathy judgements were faster when made online than when made from memory. Additionally, sympathy judgements were faster when targets were presented without distractors. Apart from the main effects, the interaction between judgement mode and distractors was also significant, $F(1,47) = 11.37, p = 0.01, \eta_p^2 = 0.20$. Figure 3.5 illustrates that judgements were generally slower when distractors were present, but that this effect was particularly present when judgements were made online, $t(47) = 5.5, p < .001$, Cohen's $d = 0.79$. In the memory condition, the effect of distractors on participants' reaction times was minimal, $t(47) = 0.1, p = 0.93$, Cohen's $d = 0.01$. Unlike in Experiment 1, we did not find that reaction times correlated with sympathy ratings, (rs ranged from 0.14 to −0.02), ps > 0.35.

Discussion

Experiment 2 was designed to replicate and extend the finding that presenting distractors reduces emotional responses to individual targets while controlling whether participants could successfully recall the target picture in the memory condition. As predicted, participants gave lower sympathy ratings towards individual victims when distractor victims were presented simultaneously. Additionally, in Experiment 2 sympathy judgements from memory were lower than online judgements, as was expected, albeit not significantly so.[1] It is of note that reducing the number of distractors from seven to three across experiments did not eliminate the effect of distractors on sympathy judgements. However, compared to Experiment 1, participants in Experiment 2 gave lower sympathy ratings in general.

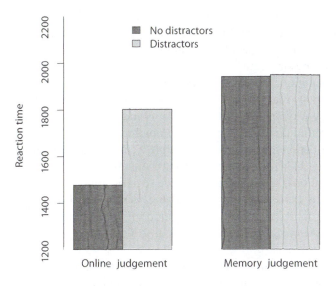

Figure 3.5 *Mean reaction times for Experiment 2*

Reaction times in Experiment 2 were slightly different compared to Experiment 1. Memory judgements took longer than online judgements in both Experiments, but the effect of distractors was most prominent in the memory condition in Experiment 1, whereas in Experiment 2 the effects of distractors was most visible in the online condition. It would be expected that seven distractors are more attention diverting than three, resulting in slower judgements in the memory condition in Experiment 1 compared to Experiment 2. However, it is unclear why participants were faster in the online judgement/no-distractor condition compared to the distractor condition in Experiment 2 and could be due to the change in distance between distractors and target. Additionally, it is possible that having fewer distractors leads to a slower, more comparative process underlying the sympathy judgement of the target. Hyde and Spelke (2009) show that a fundamental difference exists in how small and large numbers are processed, and that adults treat small numbers (i.e. 1–3) as separate objects that are individually compared.

General discussion

Two experiments were conducted to test the hypothesis that distractors and judgement mode influence the generation of emotions. Specifically, these studies were designed to test whether attention is a precursor for empathic feelings, as proposed by Slovic (2007). Across both experiments, sympathy for others was lower when distractor victims were present. Additionally, we found evidence that sympathy judgements were higher when made online vs. from memory. Both of these results indicate that attention to a target can intensify an emotional response. Reaction time results further show that judgements from memory take longer, which is indicative of a more difficult retrieval process compared to online judgements. We found partial evidence that longer reaction times coincide with lower sympathy ratings indicating that sympathy judgements may be sensitive to the timing of the emotional response. Greater temporal distance between encountering and emotionally reacting to a victim might be related to and contribute to other determinants of sympathy, such as vividness and newness (Loewenstein and Small, 2007). Our findings also suggest that empathic concern for others and the often observed reduction in empathy for multiple victims is, at least partly, a result of divided attention. This result contributes to recent advances made in the exploration of how attentional mechanisms influence social-emotional evaluations, and extends research by Fenske and colleagues (e.g. Fenske and Raymond, 2006), who examined the inhibitory effects of attention on judgements of trustworthiness of faces (Fenske et al, 2005; Raymond et al, 2005) and cheerfulness (Fenske et al, 2004).

Our results are best viewed from the perspective that the effects of attention are not unilateral, and can inhibit as well as facilitate emotional reactions. Thus, we suggest that sympathy is not generated to a similar degree when target victims are flanked by distractor victims due to attentional constraints of the perceptual system (e.g. Posner and Raichle, 1994). Furthermore, our results also shed new light on the identified-victim and singularity effects reported in research on prosocial behaviour (e.g. Kogut and Ritov, 2005a, b; Small et al, 2007) by suggesting that a precursor to affective reactions is attentional focus.

In our studies we used pictures of other victims as distractors to target victims. It is possible that the observed attention effects on sympathy ratings are not limited to the use of other victims as distractors and could be visible with other classes of stimuli. However, evidence exists that human faces tend to be processed differently and are more attention grabbing than other, non-face stimuli (Ro et al, 2001; Lavie et al, 2003; Downing et al, 2006; Theeuwes and Van der Stigchel, 2006). In fact, Ro et al demonstrate that faces are preferentially attended to in comparison to other common objects, and Theeuwes and Van der Stigchel argue that the discrimination of human faces from other objects is based on pre-attentive and unconscious processing, which automatically draws focal attention to the faces.

Alternative accounts and limitations

Alternative accounts for how perceptual experience translates into affective evaluations (such as the mere exposure effect and perceptual fluency) could potentially explain our results. However, the fact that participants saw each victim an equal amount of times makes explanations based on theories that capitalize on the mere exposure effect less likely (Zajonc, 1968; Murphy and Zajonc, 1993). The result that individual victims received higher sympathy ratings when presented alone seems to be better explained by the influence that distractors have on participants' attention to the individual target when other victims were present. Research on perceptual fluency (e.g. Winkielman et al, 2003) posits that easier cognitive processing elicits differential emotional reactions. Recall that sympathy judgements were lowest in the distractor/memory condition, which is also cognitively most demanding. However, the effect of distractors was also present in the cognitively less demanding online judgement condition. Furthermore, the perceptual fluency account suggests that ease of processing results in distinctly positive affect. However, empathic concern is usually classified as an arousal state with distinctly negative valence that motivates prosocial behaviour in order to reduce this negative feeling (Batson, 1990).

A possible limitation in our design was that we did not collect sympathy judgements for distractors, which would have allowed us to directly compare whether attended targets receive more sympathy than unattended distractors. Additionally, because we were interested in the connection between perceptual systems and emotions we specifically investigated the role of focal visual attention, which does not allow definite conclusions for other forms of attention (Posner and Rothbart, 2007).

Implications and future research

Our results point to exciting relationships between attentional and affective systems, which are of importance in understanding the generation of feelings and its consequences for behaviour. Presenting a group of people in need of help can increase the difficulty of attending to any single individual, leading to lower sympathy. Consequently, in order to elicit more empathic concern and possibly a higher willingness to help others, it might be better to use presentation formats that take advantage of attentional processes (e.g. single presentation). While we have used a research task specified to prosocial behaviour, the attentional mechanisms discussed in this chapter are important for other tasks that capitalize on the relationship between emotions and decision making (such as the endowment effect). Future research should address the extent to which attention is a precursor to affective reactions related to the construction of preferences and valuations.

Acknowledgements

We kindly thank Tehila Kogut and Deborah Small for sharing their picture stimuli, and Michael Posner, Ellen Peters and Andreas Glöckner for their valuable comments on earlier drafts. Support for this research was provided by the National Science Foundation under Grant SES-0649509 and by the William and Flora Hewlett Foundation.

Note

1   In order to increase power, we reanalysed our sympathy data combining both experiments. The results showed that participants gave higher sympathy ratings when target pictures were shown without distractors ($M = 205$, $SD = 73.1$) compared to when they were presented with distractors ($M = 191.8$, $SD = 85.5$), $F(1,105) = 14.0$, $p < .001$, $\eta^2 = 0.12$. Sympathy ratings were also higher when participants made their judgements online ($M = 201.2$, $SD = 82.4$) vs. from memory ($M = 195.6$, $SD = 77.0$), $F(1,105) = 4.1$, $p < .05$, $\eta^2 = 0.04$. The interaction between presence of distractors and judgement mode was also significant, $F(1,105) = 4.6$, $p < .001$, $\eta^2 = 0.04$. Of note is that sympathy judgements were higher for targets shown without distractors in both the online and memory condition, $t(105) = 1.86$, $p = 0.065$ and $t(105) = 5.2$, $p < .01$, respectively.

Chapter 4

Sympathy and Callousness: The Impact of Deliberative Thought on Donations to Identifiable and Statistical Victims

*Deborah A. Small, George Loewenstein and Paul Slovic**

If I look at the mass, I will never act. If I look at the one, I will.
                                                            Mother Teresa

Charities struggle to raise money to feed the thousands of starving children in third world countries and advocates struggle to raise public support for highway safety measures that would reduce future accident fatalities. Yet, people often become entranced by specific, identifiable, victims. In 1987, one child, 'Baby Jessica,' received over $700,000 in donations from the public, when she fell in a well near her home in Texas. Similarly, the plight of a wounded Iraqi boy, Ali Abbas, captivated the news media in Europe during the Iraq conflict and £275,000 was quickly raised for his medical care. More than $48,000 was contributed to save a dog stranded on a ship adrift on the Pacific Ocean near Hawaii (Song, 2002).

These cases demonstrate that when an identifiable victim is made into a cause, people appear to be quite compassionate and generous. However, at other times, people appear rather self-interested and callous – giving nothing despite the enormity of need. In this chapter, we examine the consequences of attempting to debias the effect by educating people about it – by teaching them about the inconsistent sympathy evoked by statistical and identifiable victims.

---

* Reprinted from Small, D. A., Loewenstein, G. and Slovic, P. (2007) 'Sympathy and callousness: Affect and deliberations in donation decisions', *Organizational Behavior and Human Decision Processes*, vol 102, pp143–153.

Debiasing the discrepancy in giving is important because concentrating large sums of money on a single victim is inefficient. In many cases, society would be better off if resources were spread among victims such that each additional dollar is spent where it will do the most good. Yet, when making a decision to donate money toward a cause, most people probably do not calculate the expected benefit of their donation. Rather, choices are made intuitively, based on spontaneous affective reactions (see Schwarz and Clore, 1983a; Slovic et al, 2002). To the extent that an identifiable victim is more likely to evoke sympathy and move people to give, excessive resources are likely to be allocated toward identifiable as compared to statistical victims (Small and Loewenstein, 2003).

Can individuals be taught to value life consistently? From a utilitarian perspective, it is straightforwardly normative to value lives equivalently. However, there is no 'correct' value of a life or answer to the question of how much one should give to help someone in need. Therefore, it cannot be argued that the 'identifiable victim effect' is a bias to give too much to identifiable victims or to give too little to statistical victims. The bias is simply that people care inconsistently. Therefore, an interesting and practical second question concerns the direction of correction for the effect. To the extent that debiasing the identifiable victim effect does lead to a more consistent treatment of statistical and identifiable victims, will it tend to increase generosity toward statistical victims or to decrease generosity toward identifiable victims?

The identifiable victim effect

Prior research delineates two contributing factors behind the identifiable victim effect. First, when valuing life and other commodities with non-transparent market values, people show greater sensitivity to proportions than to absolute numbers of lives (Baron, 1997; Fetherstonhaugh et al, 1997; Jenni and Loewenstein, 1997; Friedrich et al, 1999). For example, an event or calamity that causes ten deaths within a very small community of 200 evokes a great amount of concern. Ten deaths out of 200 is a fairly large proportion. However, people exhibit much less concern if that same event or calamity causes ten deaths throughout a large population of many million people. Ten deaths out of many million is merely a 'drop in the bucket.'

This 'proportion of the reference group effect' results, because it is difficult to evaluate the goodness of saving a stated number of lives, since an absolute number of lives does not map easily onto an implicit scale (Slovic et al, 2002). Proportions of lives are, however, at least superficially easy to interpret, since the scale ranges from 0 to 100 per cent. A high proportion elicits, for example, stronger support for life-saving interventions, even when the absolute number of lives saved is small. In contrast, interventions that save larger numbers of absolute lives but smaller numbers of relative lives are likely to evoke weaker support.

For a proportion to dominate evaluation, a particular reference group (denominator) must be salient. Intuitively, the reference group for an identifiable victim is itself; there was only one 'Baby Jessica' to be saved. Therefore, an identifiable victim represents the highest possible proportion of a reference group (1 of 1, or 100 per cent). Extraordinarily generous behaviour toward identifiable victims, then, could simply result from the tendency for altruistic behaviour to increase with the proportion of the reference group.

In addition to the proportion effect, there is also a qualitative distinction between identifiable and statistical victims. Small and Loewenstein (2003) and Kogut and Ritov (2005a) both found that the individuals gave more to help an identifiable victim than a statistical victim, even when controlling for the reference group. In one study, Small and Loewenstein (2003) modified the dictator game to produce a situation in which fortunate participants who retained their endowment could contribute a portion of it to 'victims' who had lost theirs. The identity of victims (based solely on a number) either had already been determined (identifiable) or was about to be, but had not yet been, determined (unidentifiable). Gifts to determined victims were significantly greater than gifts to undetermined victims. A field experiment examining donations to Habitat for Humanity to build a house for a needy family replicated this result. Identifiability was manipulated by informing respondents that the family either 'has been selected' or 'will be selected.' In neither condition were respondents told which family had been or would be selected; the only difference between conditions was in whether the decision had already been made. Contributions to the charity were significantly greater, when the family had already been determined. Kogut and Ritov (2005a) likewise found that a single, identified victim (identified by a name and face) elicited greater emotional distress and more donations than a group of identified victims and more than both a single and group of unidentified victims. Moreover, emotional distress partially accounted for differences in contributions.

This finding parallels our conjecture that identifiable targets stimulate a more powerful emotional response than do statistical targets. Recent dual-process models in social cognition identify two distinct modes of thought: one deliberate and calculative and the other affective (e.g. Epstein, 1994; Sloman, 1996; Chaiken and Trope, 1999; Kahneman and Frederick, 2002). The affective mode may dominate depending on a variety of factors, including when the target of thought is specific, personal and vivid (Epstein, 1994; Sherman et al, 1999). The deliberative mode, in contrast, is more likely to be evoked by abstract and impersonal targets. The identifiable victim effect, it seems, may result from divergent modes of thought, with greater felt sympathy for identifiable victims because they invoke the affective system.

Indeed, there is some evidence that identification intensifies feelings. In a study that compared punitive actions taken against statistical and identified perpetrators (a target that evokes negative rather than positive feelings), Small and Loewenstein (2005) found greater anger toward identifiable perpetrators, and also found that affective reactions mediated the effects of identifiability on punitiveness. Thus, it makes sense that the discrepancy in giving toward identifiable and statistical victims is similarly mediated by affect (sympathy).

Two hypotheses

Several theorists, beginning with Zajonc (1980), have proposed that the affective system is a faster, more automatic system, whose output occurs before the output of the deliberate system, which involves slower, more effortful processing (see also Epstein, 1994; Wilson and Brekke, 1994; Shiv and Fedorikhin, 1999; Wilson et al, 2000; Strack and Deutsch, 2004). Offshoots of this research have also shown that it is possible to 'overshadow' or suppress these initial affective reactions by inducing people to think in a deliberative fashion (Wilson and Brekke, 1994; Wilson et al, 2000). As a body, this research suggests that inducing people to weigh the scope of predicaments and to deliberate about alternative uses for money might diminish the impact of an affective response toward identifiable victims. Yet, the primacy of the affective system also implies that when an affective reaction is initially weak, as is true of sympathy toward statistical victims, then supplementing this reaction with more deliberation should not result in much of a difference, since this latter processing is similarly unfeeling. This logic implies that reasoning about identifiability is likely to have an asymmetric effect on generosity toward identifiable and statistical victims, decreasing giving directed toward identified victims but not increasing it toward statistical victims. Such an asymmetry lends itself to two predictions regarding the effects of debiasing identifiability:

> *Hypothesis 1.* Thinking analytically about the value of lives should reduce giving to an identifiable victim.

> *Hypothesis 2.* Thinking analytically about the value of lives should have no effect on giving to statistical victims.

These are the two central predictions that we test in the four studies reported below.

Overview of studies

Each of the four studies attempted to manipulate the level of analytic thought when people made decisions involving statistical and identifiable victims. Study 1 examines the impact on generosity toward statistical and identifiable victims of explicitly informing people about the identifiable victim effect. Study 2 rules out a potential artefactual explanation for the findings from Study 1. Study 3 attempts to teach the same lesson in an implicit, rather than explicit manner. By providing victim statistics alongside of a request for donations to an identifiable victim, we confront individuals with both targets, but do not directly inform them of any bias. Finally, Study 4 examines how priming a calculating mode of thought versus a feeling mode of thought influences donation decisions to both presentations of targets (identifiable and statistical).

Study I

This study examined generosity toward an identifiable victim or statistical victims following an intervention that taught donors about the tendency for individuals to give more to identifiable victims than to statistical victims. We tested the effects of the intervention on giving behaviour toward both presentations of victims.

Method

The experiment consisted of a 2 × 2 between-subjects design. The first factor was identifiability, each participant received a description of either an identifiable or a statistical victim. The second factor was the intervention, half of the participants received a brief lesson about research demonstrating a discrepancy in giving toward identifiable and statistical victims, the other half received no such intervention.

Participants

An experimenter approached individuals (N = 121), who were seated alone, in the student centre at a university in Pennsylvania and asked them if they would complete a short survey in exchange for $5.00. The experimenters knew that there were different versions of the charity request, but did not know which version each participant received and was not informed about the specific research hypotheses.

Procedures

Participants completed a survey about their use of various technological products. The survey was wholly unrelated to the present research and contained no experimental manipulations. After completing the survey, each participant received five one-dollar bills, a receipt, a blank envelope and a charity request letter. The experimenter instructed the participant to read the letter carefully before signing the receipt and then to return both the letter and receipt sealed in the envelope.

The letter informed the participant of the opportunity to donate any of their just-earned five dollars to the organization Save the Children. All participants were told that 'any money donated will go toward relieving the severe food crisis in Southern Africa and Ethiopia.' The donations in fact went directly to Save the Children.

Intervention

Half of the participants (randomly assigned) first read a brief lesson about the research on identifiability. The lesson consisted of the following text:

> *We'd like to tell you about some research conducted by social scientists. This research shows that people typically react more strongly to specific people who have problems than to statistics about people with problems.*

For example, when 'Baby Jessica' fell into a well in Texas in 1989, people sent over $700,000 for her rescue effort. Statistics – e.g. the thousands of children who will almost surely die in automobile accidents this coming year – seldom evoke such strong reactions.

Identifiability

In the statistical victim condition, the charity request letter described factual information taken from the Save the Children website (www.savethechildren.org) about the problems of starvation in Africa. In the identifiable victim condition, participants saw a picture of a little girl and read a brief description about her. Again, the picture and description were taken directly from the website. The stimuli are reproduced in the appendix.

Finally, the letter instructed all participants:

Now that you have had the opportunity to learn about how any money you donate will be used, please fill out the following page and include it with any money you donate in the envelope you have been given. Even if you do not choose to donate, please fill out the form and return it to us in the envelope.

The following page asked participants to indicate the amount of their donation, $0, $1, $2, $3, $4 or $5. Then, participants were asked several questions about their affective and moral reactions to the situation described on a five-point Likert scale ranging from 1 (Not at all) to 5 (Extremely). The questions included: (1) How upsetting is this situation to you? (2) How sympathetic did you feel while reading the description of the cause? (3) How much do you feel it is your moral responsibility to help out with this cause? (4) How touched were you by the situation described? and (5) To what extent do you feel that it is appropriate to give money to aid this cause? These five items produced a reliable scale ($\alpha = 0.87$), which we heretofore will refer to as feelings.

The experimenter gave the participant space and a few minutes to read the letter, and to donate privately the amount that they chose without any social pressure from the experimenter to give.

Results and discussion

Figure 4.1 presents means for each of the four treatments. To assess the effects of the manipulations on giving behaviour, we subjected participants' donations to a 2(identifiability) × 2(intervention) analysis of variance (ANOVA). Both factors, identifiability and the intervention, resulted in main effects. Participants who faced an identifiable victim gave more ($M = 2.12, $SD = 2.13) than those who faced a statistical victim ($M = 1.21, $SD = 1.67$), $F(1,115) = 6.75$, $p < .05$, $\eta_p^2 = 0.06$; The intervention reduced donations ($M = 1.31, $SD = 1.82) relative to no intervention ($M = 2.00, $SD = 2.03), $F(1,115) = 4.15$, $p < .05$, $\eta_p^2 = 0.04$. However, as revealed by a significant interaction between the treatments

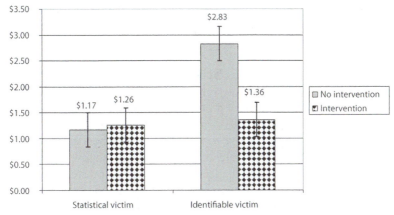

Figure 4.1 *Effects of teaching about identifiability on donations in Study 1*

$(F(1,115) = 5.32, p < .05, \eta_p^2 = 0.04)$, the intervention had an asymmetric impact on generosity in the two identifiable conditions; learning about identifiability decreased giving only toward identifiable victims. Post-hoc contrast tests reveal a significant difference between the identifiable/no intervention cell ($M = \$2.83$, $SD = \$2.10$) and the other three ($M = \$1.26$, $SD = \$1.74$), $t(117) = -4.06$, $p < .001$.

Given the large number of zeros in the dependent variable and the non-normal distribution, we also analysed the data with an ordered probit regression (Kennedy, 1998). The results were consistent with those obtained using simple ANOVA, there was a significant effect of identifiability $\chi^2(1) = 10.06$, $p < .01$, no effect of the intervention $\chi^2(1) = .01$, $p = 0.92$, and a significant interaction between identifiability and the intervention $\chi^2(1) = 4.72$, $p < .03$. In all subsequent studies, we also replicated the main analyses with ordered probit and obtained qualitatively similar results, but report only the ANOVA results.

A two-way ANOVA with feelings as the dependent variable revealed no significant main effects for either the identifiability factor [$F(1,114) = 1.80$, $p = 0.18$] or the intervention [$F(1,114) = 0.24$, $p = 0.63$], and the interaction term was insignificant as well, $F(1,114) = 2.00$, $p = 0.16$. The same pattern held, when the feelings factor score was replaced by each of the five items that made up the feelings scale. However, correlations between feelings and donations reveal an interesting pattern. In the three cells for which donations were relatively low (statistical/no intervention, statistical/intervention, and identifiable/intervention), the Pearson correlation between the factor score of the five feelings items and donations are all relatively small (0.39, 0.33 and 0.34, respectively). However, in the identifiable/no intervention condition, the correlation between feelings and giving is relatively strong, $r = 0.55$, $p < .01$. This is at least suggestive that affect and behaviour are particularly linked when people face an identifiable victim.

These results are consistent with our prediction that forcing people to think more analytically about the choice to give has an asymmetric effect. Reactions to the affective target, the identifiable victim, were negatively affected by the teaching intervention, but reactions to the non-affective target, statistical victims, were not affected significantly.

Study 2

A limitation of the first study is a potential demand effect that we were made aware of after running it. Participants may have attempted to correct for their gut intentions about how much to give to please the researchers after learning about the bias. If this were true, one would expect participants to give more to statistical victims in addition to giving less to identifiable victims. However, it is possible that participants inferred that the bias was specifically located on donations to identifiable victims. The intervention stated that people give 'more' to identifiable victims than to statistical victims, and 'more' could potentially be interpreted as 'too much.' If this is true, then the results of Study 1 may simply be due to experimental demand rather than to learning about identifiability per se.

If the intervention in Study 1 had stated 'People give less to statistical victims' rather than stating the equivalent but alternatively framed 'People give more to identifiable victims,' would the results have been the reverse? Indeed, a large body of research demonstrates the powerful influence of cognitive frames on judgement. In the current study, we test whether alternative frames used to describe the bias in the intervention would affect the level of donations.

Method

Study 2 employed a 2×2 factorial design manipulating (a) identifiability and (b) frame of the intervention. Half of participants were exposed to an identifiable victim and the other half to statistical victims. Since the purpose was to test differences among frames in the intervention rather than comparing the presence versus the absence of an intervention, as in Study 1, all individuals received a teaching intervention. For half of the participants, the discrepancy in giving described in the intervention was framed as 'more to identifiable victims.' For the other half, the discrepancy was framed as 'less to statistical victims.'

Participants

As in Study 1, a hypothesis-blind experimenter approached individuals in public places around a university in Pennsylvania and asked them to complete a short survey in exchange for $5. The sample consisted of 99 individuals who consented to fill out the survey.

Procedures

The basic procedures followed those in Study 1. After participants completed their surveys, the experimenter paid them $5 in one-dollar bills and gave them a receipt, an envelope and a charity request letter. The experimenter instructed them to read the letter and to return it with the receipt sealed in the envelope.

Framing the intervention

To test for the possibility that the response to the intervention revealed in Study 1 was due to the frame of the intervention, we manipulated the frame between subjects. Half of the participants read an intervention with the frame more to identifiable victims:

> ... *research shows that people typically react more strongly to specific people who have problems than to statistics about people with problems. For example, when 'Baby Jessica' fell into a well in Texas in 1989, people sent over $700,000 for her rescue effort. Statistics – e.g. the 10,000 children who will almost surely die in automobile accidents this coming year – seldom evoke such strong reactions.*

The other half read the alternative less to statistical victims frame:

> ... *research shows that people typically react less strongly to statistics about people with problems than to specific people who have problems. For example, statistics – e.g. the 10,000 children who will almost surely die in automobile accidents this coming year – seldom evoke strong reactions. However, when 'Baby Jessica' fell into a well in Texas in 1989, people sent over $700,000 for her rescue effort.*

All other information described about the cause was identical to Study 1.

Results

Figure 4.2 presents the basic pattern of results. We performed a 2(identifiability) × 2(frame) ANOVA on donations. Although there appears to be a main effect of identifiability on donations in the graph, statistical analysis revealed no significant main effects for either factor [$F(1,95) = 0.073, p = 0.79$ and $F(1,95) = 1.00, p = 0.32$, respectively], nor a statistical interaction [$F(1,95) = 0.01, p = 0.94$]. Most importantly, there is no observable trend in the data toward giving more to identifiable victims (either relatively or absolutely) under the 'more' than under the 'less' frame. We further tested for simple effects of identifiability within each frame. The frame did not significantly affect donations to statistical victims [$F(1,95) = 0.073, p = 0.79$] nor did it affect donations to identifiable victims [$F(1,95) = 1.009, p = 0.32$].

The lack of any effect of framing in this study indicates that the results of the intervention in Study 1 cannot be attributed to the frame of the intervention or experimental demand. Although framing is clearly important in many contexts, framing a discrepancy as more to X versus less to Y does not appear to matter. If the intervention had stated that individuals typically give too much to identifiable victims, then experimental demand would be expected. However the terms 'more' and 'less' convey little about the correct level of giving so subjects cannot gain insight about the desired effect of the researchers.

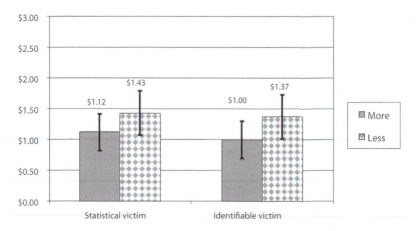

Figure 4.2 *Null effects of framing on donations in Study 2*

Study 3

In Study 3, we attempt to debias identifiability in a more implicit manner. Rather than explicitly teaching participants about the discrepancy, we preceded a request for money for an identifiable victim with the simultaneous presentation of both victim statistics and a description of the identifiable victim.

Kogut and Ritov (2005b) gave some individuals an opportunity to give any amount or nothing to either or both a single, identified victim or a group of identified victims, while others only had the option of giving to one of the two targets (single or group). Although, they gave more to a single identified victim than to a group of identified victims when evaluated separately, they gave similar amounts to each when evaluated jointly. Moreover, more people donated and the mean donation was higher in separate evaluation than in joint evaluation. This result suggests that comparative evaluation blunts caring, possibly because it requires analytic, deliberative thought.

In the present study, we jointly present an identified victim with victim statistics. It is possible that this double presentation could have an additive effect, such that participants would give the most when faced with greatest information. However, we hypothesized that this presentation would reduce caring, since the provision of victim statistics would remind potential donors of the many other victims who would not receive help. This joint presentation should force people to compare the relative importance of helping one victim to the importance of helping the multitudes.

Method

This study consisted of three conditions: (1) identifiable victim, (2) statistical victims and (3) identifiable victim with statistical information. The third condition served as the 'implicit' intervention.

Participants

A hypothesis-blind experimenter approached individuals, who were seated alone, in the university centre and courtyard at a university in Pennsylvania, and asked if they would complete a short survey in exchange for $5.00. A total of 159 individuals agreed to participate.

Procedures

As in Studies 1 and 2, participants completed a survey about their use of various technological products. Again after completing the survey, each participant received five one-dollar bills, a receipt, a blank envelope and a charity request letter, informing the participant of the opportunity to donate to Save the Children.

The stimuli for the identifiable victim and the statistical victims were identical to those used in Studies 1 and 2. In the identifiable victim with statistical information condition, the request was identical to the identifiable victim condition, with the addition of the statistical information provided in the statistical victim condition. In other words, participants faced a choice of whether to help an identifiable victim, but were confronted by victim statistics before making a choice. Once again, the letter instructed all participants to indicate on paper the amount they chose to donate, and to include it with any money they donated in an envelope.

Results and discussion

The main hypothesis in this study is that showing statistical information in conjunction with an identifiable victim will reduce giving relative to just showing an identifiable victim. The means for the three conditions, reported in Figure 4.3, are consistent with this pattern. We conducted a one-way ANOVA on donations, which revealed a significant effect of identifiability $F(2) = 5.67, p < .01. \eta_p^2 = 0.07$. We then performed Bonferroni-adjusted pairwise comparisons, which revealed that individuals who faced an identifiable victim donated more than those who faced victim statistics, $p < .01$, and also donated more than those who faced an identifiable victim in conjunction with statistics, $p < .05$. Thus, the main hypothesis was supported. There was no difference between individuals, who faced statistics only and those who faced an identifiable victim in conjunction with victim statistics, $p = 1.0$.

Apparently, statistical information dampens the inclination to give to an identifiable victim. This result is consistent with the tendency to give less to an identifiable victim after learning about the discrepancy in giving. When jointly evaluating statistics and an individual victim, the cause evidently becomes less compelling. This could occur in part because statistics diminish the reliance on one's affective reaction to the identifiable victim when making a decision.

We have argued that asymmetric effects of the intervention in this and the previous two studies result from processing differences inherent in reactions to the two victim presentations. However, an alternative explanation is possible.

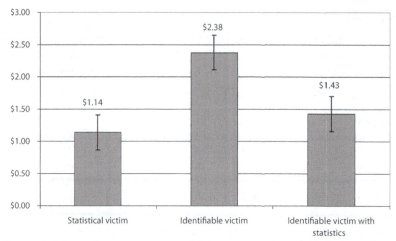

Figure 4.3 *Donations to separate and joint presentation of victim types in Study 3*

Perhaps people do not contribute to the statistical victims, because they feel that any contribution would not make an appreciable contribution to the problem. Such an account would be consistent with the literature, reviewed earlier, showing that people are sensitive not only to the absolute number of victims but to the size of the reference group (Baron, 1997; Fetherstonhaugh et al, 1997; Jenni and Loewenstein, 1997). In fact, such a 'drop in the bucket' effect may also have contributed to the discrepancy in treatment of the statistical versus identifiable victims in the first two studies, though it is difficult to explain the effect of the teaching intervention in such terms. In the next study, we avoid this possible confound by directly manipulating modes of processing information (e.g. feeling based vs. calculation based).

Study 4

Unlike the previous studies in this chapter, Study 4 does not incorporate an attempt to teach individuals about the identifiability effect, either explicitly or implicitly. Instead, we use an intervention designed to induce either a calculation-based or a feeling-based mode of thought. By doing so, we test whether it is possible to reverse the dominant reaction to each victim presentation. Importantly, this approach avoids the confound just discussed between modes of processing and the drop in the bucket effect. We would not expect the latter to be affected by an intervention targeted only at mode of processing.

Altering mode of thought could lead to several different patterns. First, it could have no effect on giving, if the initial response to a presentation of a cause is powerful and uncompromising. If instead, processing modes are flexible and only loosely dependent on the target, then inducing feeling-based processing could lead to greater caring and giving, whereas inducing calculation-based processing could lead to reduced caring and giving.

We contend, in accordance with the primacy of affect, that it should be more feasible to reverse reactions based on feeling than to add feelings where they do not automatically arise. If this reasoning is correct, then inducing a calculating mode should lessen caring toward identifiable victims, since the impact of the initial affective reaction to them can be mitigated by deliberate thinking. Caring about statistical victims, in contrast, should be less amenable to induced feeling.

Methods

This study employed a priming task developed by Hsee and Rottenstreich (2004) to manipulate a calculating mode versus a feeling mode of processing. This priming task was crossed with a manipulation of identifiability, such that the design was a 2(identifiability) × 2(priming) between-subjects design.

Participants

Students and other people on campus at a university in Pennsylvania ($N = 165$) were recruited to complete a few short questionnaires. Each received a packet of questionnaires and received $5 in one-dollar bills for participating.

Procedures

The questionnaire packet consisted first of the survey on the use of technology as in Studies 1, 2 and 3. Second, in the packet was a short questionnaire which served as the priming manipulation. In the calculation-priming condition, the questionnaire was entitled 'Calculations Questionnaire.' It instructed participants to work 'carefully and deliberatively to calculate the answers to the questions posed below': Five questions followed, which were all similar to the first one: 'If an object travels at five feet per minute, then by your calculations how many feet will it travel in 360 seconds? _____ feet.'

In the feeling-priming condition, the questionnaire was entitled 'Impression Questionnaire' and instructed participants to 'base your answers to the following questions on the feelings you experience': Representative of these questions was: 'When you hear the word "baby" what do you feel? Please use one word to describe your predominant feeling: _____.'

After completing the packet, including the prime, participants received $5 in one dollar bills, an envelope, a receipt and a charity request of the same nature as the previous studies, which they were instructed to read before leaving, as in previous studies. The procedure for donating their earnings by sealing it in the envelope anonymously was identical to the previous studies.

Results and discussion

As is evident from Figure 4.4, which presents means for the four conditions, the results support our hypotheses that calculative thought lessens the appeal of an identifiable victim, but feeling-based thought does not improve the appeal of statistical victims. A two-way ANOVA revealed that the priming manipulation had

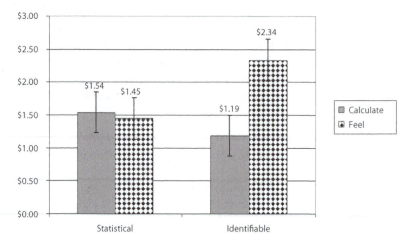

Figure 4.4 *Donations following processing primes in Study 4*

a marginal effect on generosity, $F(1,160) = 3.49$, $p = 0.063$, $\eta_p^2 = 0.02$, and no main effect of victim type, $F(1,160) = 0.87$, $p = 0.35$, $\eta_p^2 = 0.01$. However, the primes interacted with victim type, $F(1,160) = 4.67$, $p < .04$, $\eta_p^2 = 0.03$. When primed to calculate, participants donated significantly less to the identifiable victim than when primed to feel, $F(1,160) = 3.49$, $p < .01$, $\eta_p^2 = 0.05$. However, priming had no effect on donations to statistical victims, $F(1,160) = 0.87$, $p = 0.35$, $\eta_p^2 = 0.01$.

These results strongly support the notion that modes of processing, and specifically the distinction between affect and deliberation, play an important role in the identifiable victim effect and in the impact of explicit and implicit education about the effect. Priming analytic thinking reduced donations to an identifiable victim relative to a feeling-based thinking prime. Yet, the primes had no distinct effect on donations to statistical victims, which is symptomatic of the difficulty in generating feelings for these victims.

General discussion

Certain victims trigger a disproportionate level of sympathy. In this chapter, we find that debiasing, through deliberative thinking, reduces the discrepancy in giving to statistical and identifiable victims. We contend that deliberative thinking reduces the reliance on sympathy when evaluating an identifiable victim.

Our findings resonate with the 'affect heuristic' (Slovic et al, 2002) and the 'feelings as information' (Schwarz and Clore, 1983a) frameworks. Consistent with the affect heuristic (Slovic et al, 2002), stimuli that generate sympathetic affect induce individuals to place a high value on the identifiable victim.

A key aspect of the 'feelings as information' framework (Schwarz and Clore, 1983a) is that the impact of feelings on evaluative judgements depends on the perceived informational value of the feelings. The finding from our studies that generosity is reduced when additional information is given, either in the form of an intervention (Study 1) or additional statistics (Study 3), could be interpreted in such terms. Perhaps these interventions led people to believe that their feelings were less relevant to the decision of how much to give than was true in the absence of the interventions.

The finding that sympathetic reactions are undermined by deliberative thinking further supports the two-systems approach, in which an affective response can be blunted or controlled through thoughtful deliberation (see Epstein, 1994; Shiv and Fedorikhin, 1999; Wilson et al, 2000; Strack and Deutsch, 2004). Although donations to identifiable victims decreased following the intervention, it is possible that the feelings persevered. In a study on prejudice, Wilson et al (2000) demonstrated that initial negative information that was later deemed to be false had a lasting impression at an implicit level but not an explicit level. Essentially, people could override the discredited initial affective attitude when they had capacity and motivation, but the affective attitude persevered in implicit attitude measures. Thus, the reduction in donations to an identifiable victim following intervention in our studies may represent a change only in the explicit attitudes of participants.

An unresolved question is how people manage their sympathy and prevent it from contaminating their judgements and decisions. Wilson et al (1998) outline five strategies which people believe they can adopt to avoid contamination: exposure control, preparation, resistance, remediation and behaviour control. Any of these might be involved in our interventions. Participants could have skipped over the charity request after reading the intervention as a means to control exposure to the sympathetic plea; they could prepare themselves by strengthening their mental defences against their feelings and resist their feelings once exposed; finally, they could attempt to undo the effects of their sympathy and/or attempt to prevent their feelings from influencing their behaviour. Future research could tease apart the mix of mental strategies involved in correcting for unwanted sympathy when trying to make efficient and fair decisions.

Our findings also dovetail with research on proportional reasoning, which shows that people value lives less as the denominator of the proportion increases (Baron, 1997; Fetherstonhaugh et al, 1997; Jenni and Loewenstein, 1997; Friedrich et al, 1999). For example, Study 3 in this chapter demonstrates that providing statistics reduced generosity toward an identifiable victim. One possible mechanism through which this effect may have occurred is by effectively priming a large denominator. However, our other studies show that other methods (explicit teaching and inducing an analytic mindset) that are unlikely to prime large denominators have a similar effect. Thus, while the proportion effect undoubtedly contributes to the disproportionate weight placed on identifiable victims, it is unlikely that it, alone, accounts for the identifiable victim effect.

Implications for social welfare

The results from these studies might appear to be somewhat discouraging. On the one hand, teaching about identifiability led individuals to donate similar amounts regardless of whether victims were identifiable or not. Hence, it at least increased people's consistency toward the two types of victims. Yet, the intervention had a pernicious effect on overall caring, since people gave less after each of our interventions in the identifiable condition, but gave no more to statistical victims. Insight, in this situation, seems to breed callousness.

In some ways, this conclusion seems well founded. Faced with almost any disaster of any magnitude, it is almost always possible to think of worse things that have happened or even that are currently happening in the world. The deaths of 11 September 2001, for example, compared with the slaughter in Rwanda, seem almost inconsequential. But the slaughter in Rwanda, in turn, is dwarfed by the problem of AIDS in Africa. Thinking about problems analytically can easily suppress sympathy for smaller-scale disasters without, our research suggests, producing much of an increase in caring for larger-scale disasters.

However, we believe that this simple interpretation is probably somewhat off the mark. A more precise account of what is going on is that, in certain situations, affective responses to victims diverge from more deliberative responses. It is possible that deliberate thinking could sometimes lead to more charity. For example, contrary to the difference between statistical and identifiable victims, we often experience little visceral sympathy for needy victims who are from other countries or of a different race or socio-economic status, but thinking about their plight may lead us to recognize their deservingness. In such instances, we conjecture, interventions that encourage deliberate thinking like those presented in the four studies just presented might lead to greater generosity rather than less.

Some support for this is evident in a study by Skitka et al (2002). In this study, participants read about a number of individuals with AIDS who differed in how they contracted the disease. For each case, participants judged whether the individual was to blame for their situation and how deserving he/she was of subsidies for drug treatment. Half of the participants performed this task while under cognitive load, thereby reducing the ability for deliberate thinking. Under cognitive load, both self-described liberals and conservatives were less likely to provide subsidies to blameworthy than to non-blameworthy individuals. Conservatives followed the pattern without load, yet, liberals provided just as much assistance to blameworthy individuals as to non-blameworthy individuals. Thus, deliberative thinking increased generosity, at least for liberals.

Other evidence that deliberation can generate affect comes from Drolet and Luce (2004). They find that cognitive load mitigates the affective turmoil of emotion-laden trade-off decisions. This suggests that affect does not always have primacy. Rather, in certain cases cognitive resources are necessary to generate affect. Future research would benefit from delineating when affect is automatic and when requires deliberation.

A second best optimum

Improvements to social welfare could certainly be made, if dollars of aid were shifted from identifiable victims like Baby Jessica and Ali Abbas to other more desperate victims. However, it is possible that the failure to equate marginal benefits per aid dollar is still consistent with a 'second best' optimum (Loewenstein et al, 2006). Although the money spent on Baby Jessica and Ali Abbas could save more lives in theory if not concentrated as such, the absence of identifiability effects might reduce the impetus to give at all. Thus, although victim identification may distort aid allocation somewhat, its impact generates more aid than any other pitch. Charities certainly recognize this, at least implicitly, when they employ a poster child to raise money for a general cause.

Conclusion

In sum, our results demonstrate that sympathy for identifiable victims diminishes with deliberative thought, but remains consistently low for statistical victims. This pattern holds with various manipulations of deliberative thought, including explicit debiasing interventions, providing statistics and priming an analytic mindset.

These findings support the more general notion that certain stimuli naturally evoke more affect than others and that cognitive deliberation can undermine outcomes that typically arise when choices are made affectively. In this case, encouraging people to think about their choices had an unfavourable effect on social welfare. Future research is likely to reveal conditions in which deliberation increases generosity and yields social benefits.

Acknowledgements

This research was supported by the Russell Sage Foundation and the Center for Integrated Study of the Human Dimensions of Global Change, a joint creation of the National Science Foundation (SBR-9521914) and Carnegie Mellon University. We thank Linda Babcock, Margaret Clark and Jennifer Lerner for helpful comments and Jennifer Cerully and Nadia Tuma for research assistance.

Appendix A: Statistical victim

Food shortages in Malawi are affecting more than three million children.

In Zambia, severe rainfall deficits have resulted in a 42 per cent drop in maize production from 2000. As a result, an estimated three million Zambians face hunger.

Four million Angolans – one third of the population – have been forced to flee their homes. More than 11 million people in Ethiopia need immediate food assistance.

Appendix B: Identifiable victim

Any money that you donate will go to Rokia, a seven-year-old girl from Mali, Africa. Rokia is desperately poor, and faces a threat of severe hunger or even starvation. Her life will be changed for the better as a result of your financial gift. With your support, and the support of other caring sponsors, Save the Children will work with Rokia's family and other members of the community to help feed her, provide her with education, as well as basic medical care and hygiene education.

Chapter 5

The More Who Die,
the Less We Care

*Paul Slovic**

A defining element of catastrophes is the magnitude of their harmful consequences. To help society prevent or mitigate damage from catastrophes, immense
effort and technological sophistication is often employed to assess and communicate the size and scope of potential or actual losses. This effort assumes that
people can understand the resulting numbers and act on them appropriately.

However, recent behavioural research casts doubt on this fundamental
assumption. Many people do not understand large numbers. Indeed, large
numbers have been found to lack meaning and to be underweighted in decisions
unless they convey affect (feeling). As a result, there is a paradox that rational
models of decision making fail to represent. On the one hand, we respond
strongly to aid a single individual in need. On the other hand, we often fail to
prevent mass tragedies such as genocide or take appropriate measures to reduce
potential losses from natural disasters. This might seem irrational but I think this
is, in part, because as numbers get larger and larger, we become insensitive; the
numbers fail to trigger the emotion or feeling necessary to motivate action
(Slovic, 2007).

I shall address this problem of insensitivity to mass tragedy by identifying
certain circumstances in which it compromises the rationality of our actions and
by pointing briefly toward strategies that might lessen or overcome this problem.

---

* Reprinted from Slovic, P. (2010) 'The more who die, the less we care', in E. Michel-
Kerjan and P. Slovic (eds) *The Irrational Economist: Making Decisions in a Dangerous
World*, PublicAffairs, New York. Portions of this chapter appeared in the 2007 paper
'If I look at the mass I shall never act: Psychic numbing and genocide', *Judgment and
Decision Making*, vol 2, pp79–95.

Background and theory: The importance of affect

Risk management in the modern world relies upon two forms of thinking. Risk as feelings refers to our instinctive and intuitive reactions to danger. Risk as analysis brings logic, reason, quantification and deliberation to bear on hazard management (see Chapter 2 of this volume). Compared to analysis, reliance on feelings tends to be a quicker, easier and more efficient way to navigate in a complex, uncertain and dangerous world. Hence, it is essential to rational behaviour. Yet it sometimes misleads us. In such circumstances we need to ensure that reason and analysis also are employed.

Although the visceral emotion of fear certainly plays a role in risk as feelings, I shall focus here on a 'faint whisper of emotion' called affect. As used here, 'affect' refers to specific feelings of 'goodness' or 'badness' experienced with or without conscious awareness. Positive and negative feelings occur rapidly and automatically – note how quickly you sense the feelings associated with the word 'joy' or the word 'hate.' A large research literature in psychology documents the importance of affect in conveying meaning upon information and motivating behaviour. Without affect, information lacks meaning and will not be used in judgement and decision making.

Facing catastrophic loss of life

Despite the rationality of risk as feelings, which employs imagery and affect in remarkably accurate and efficient ways, this way of responding to risk has a darker, non-rational side. Affect may misguide us in important ways. Particularly problematic is the difficulty of comprehending the meaning of catastrophic losses of life when relying on feelings. Research reviewed below shows that disaster statistics, no matter how large the numbers, lack emotion or feeling. As a result, they fail to convey the true meaning of such calamities and they fail to motivate proper action to prevent them.

The psychological factors underlying insensitivity to large-scale losses of human lives apply to catastrophic harm resulting from human malevolence, natural disasters or technological accidents. In particular, the psychological account described here can explain, in part, our failure to respond to the diffuse and seemingly distant threat posed by global warming as well as the threat posed by the presence of nuclear weaponry. Similar insensitivity may also underlie our failure to respond adequately to problems of famine, poverty and disease afflicting millions of people around the world and sometimes even some in our own backyard. I next examine this problem in the context of genocide, focusing on the situation in Darfur.

The Darfur genocide

Since February 2003, hundreds of thousands of people in the Darfur region of western Sudan, Africa have been murdered by government-supported militias, and millions have been forced to flee their burned-out villages for the dubious safety of refugee camps. This has been well documented. And yet the world looks away. The events in Darfur are the latest in a long line of mass murders since World War II that powerful nations and their citizens have responded to with indifference. In her Pulitzer Prize winning book *A Problem from Hell: America and the Age of Genocide*, Samantha Power documents in meticulous detail many of the numerous genocides that occurred during the past century. In every instance, American response was inadequate. She concludes 'No U.S. president has ever made genocide prevention a priority, and no U.S. president has ever suffered politically for his indifference to its occurrence. It is thus no coincidence that genocide rages on' (Power, 2003, pxxi).

The UN general assembly adopted the Convention on the Prevention and Punishment of the Crime of Genocide in 1948 in the hope that 'never again' would there be such odious crimes against humanity as occurred during the Holocaust of World War II. Eventually some 140 states would ratify the Genocide Convention, yet it has never been invoked to prevent a potential attack or halt an ongoing massacre. Darfur has shone a particularly harsh light on the failures to intervene in genocide. As Richard Just (2008) has observed,

> ... *we are awash in information about Darfur ... no genocide has ever been so thoroughly documented while it was taking place ... but the genocide continues. We document what we do not stop. The truth does not set anybody free* (p36) ... *how could we have known so much and done so little?* (p38)

Affect, analysis, and the value of human lives

This brings us to a crucial question: how should we value the saving of human lives? An analytic answer would look to basic principles or fundamental values for guidance. For example, Article 1 of the United Nations Universal Declaration of Human Rights asserts that 'All human beings are born free and equal in dignity and rights.' We might infer from this the conclusion that every human life is of equal value. If so – applying a rational calculation – the value of saving N lives is N times the value of saving one life, as represented by the linear function in Figure 5.1.

An argument can also be made for judging large losses of life to be disproportionately more serious because they threaten the social fabric and viability of a group or community (see Figure 5.2). Debate can be had at the margins over whether one should assign greater value to younger people versus the elderly, or whether governments have a duty to give more weight to the lives of their own

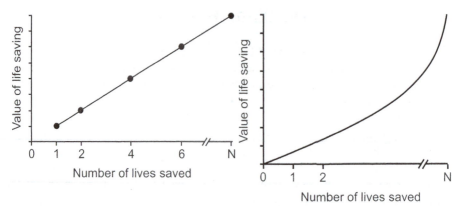

Figure 5.1 *A normative model for valuing the saving of human lives: Every human life is of equal value*

Source: Slovic (2007)

Figure 5.2 *Another normative model: Large losses threaten the viability of the group or society*

Source: Slovic (2007)

people and so on, but a perspective approximating the equality of human lives is rather uncontroversial.

How do we actually value human lives? Research provides evidence in support of two descriptive models linked to affect and intuitive thinking that reflect values for life saving profoundly different from the normative (rational) models shown in Figures 5.1 and 5.2. Both of these descriptive models demonstrate responses that are insensitive to large losses of human life, consistent with apathy toward genocide.

The psychophysical model

There is considerable evidence that our affective responses and the resulting value we place on saving human lives follow the same sort of 'psychophysical function' that characterizes our diminished sensitivity to changes in a wide range of perceptual and cognitive entities – brightness, loudness, heaviness and wealth – as their underlying magnitudes increase.

As psychophysical research indicates, constant increases in the magnitude of a stimulus typically evoke smaller and smaller changes in response. Applying this principle to the valuing of human life suggests that a form of psychophysical numbing may result from our inability to appreciate losses of life as they become larger (see Figure 5.3). The function in Figure 5.3 represents a value structure in which the importance of saving one life is great when it is the first, or only, life saved but diminishes as the total number of lives at risk increases. Thus, psychologically, the importance of saving one life pales against the background of a larger threat – we may not 'feel' much difference, nor value the difference, between saving 87 lives and saving 88.

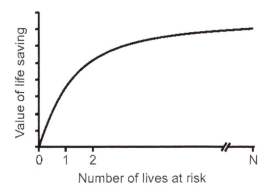

Figure 5.3 *A psychophysical model describing how the saving of human lives may actually be valued*

Source: Slovic (2007)

My colleagues, David Fetherstonhaugh, Steven Johnson, James Friedrich, and I (1997) demonstrated this potential for psychophysical numbing in the context of evaluating people's willingness to fund various life-saving interventions. In a study involving a hypothetical grant funding agency, respondents were asked to indicate the number of lives a medical research institute would have to save to merit receipt of a $10 million grant. Nearly two-thirds of the respondents raised their minimum benefit requirements to warrant funding when there was a larger at-risk population, with a median value of 9000 lives needing to be saved when 15,000 were at risk (implicitly valuing each life saved at $1111), compared to a median of 100,000 lives needing to be saved out of 290,000 at risk (implicitly valuing each life saved at $100). Thus respondents saw saving 9000 lives in the smaller population as more valuable than saving more than ten times as many lives in the larger population. The same study also found that people were less willing to send aid that would save 4500 lives in Rwandan refugee camps as the size of the camps' at-risk population increased.

In recent years, vivid images of natural disasters in South Asia and the American Gulf Coast, and stories of individual victims there, brought to us through relentless, courageous and intimate news coverage, unleashed an outpouring of compassion and humanitarian aid from all over the world. Perhaps there is hope here that vivid, personalized media coverage featuring victims could also motivate intervention to halt the killing.

Perhaps. Research demonstrates that people are much more willing to aid identified individuals than unidentified or statistical victims. But a cautionary note comes from a study where my colleagues and I gave people who had just partici- pated in a paid psychological experiment the opportunity to contribute up to $5 of their earnings to the charity, Save the Children (Small et al, 2007). In one condition, respondents were asked to donate money to feed an identified victim, a seven-year-old African girl named Rokia of whom they were showed a picture.

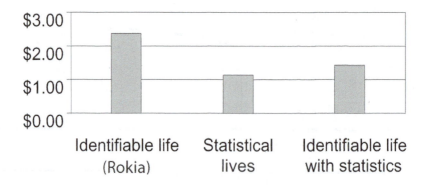

Figure 5.4 *Mean donations*

Source: Reprinted from Small, D. A., Loewenstein, G. and Slovic, P. (2007) 'Sympathy and Callousness: The Impact of Deliberative Thought on Donations to Identifiable and Statistical Victims', *Organizational Behavior and Human Decision Processes*, vol 102, pp143–153. Copyright © 2007, with permission from Elsevier.

They contributed more than twice the amount given by a second group, asked to donate to the same organization working to save millions of Africans (statistical lives) from hunger. A third group was asked to donate to Rokia, but was also shown the larger statistical problem (millions in need) shown to the second group. Unfortunately, coupling the large-scale statistical realities with Rokia's story significantly reduced the contributions to Rokia (see Figure 5.4).

Why did this occur? Perhaps the presence of statistics reduced the attention to Rokia essential for establishing the emotional connection necessary to motivate donations. Alternatively, recognition of the millions who would not be helped by one's small donation may have produced negative feelings that inhibited donations. Note the similarity here at the individual level to the failure to help 4500 people in the larger refugee camp. The rationality of these responses can be questioned. We should not be deterred from helping one person, or 4500, just because there are many others we cannot save!

In sum, research on psychophysical numbing is important because it demonstrates that feelings necessary for motivating life-saving actions are not congruent with the normative/rational models in Figures 5.1 and 5.2. The non-linearity displayed in Figure 5.3 is consistent with the devaluing of incremental loss of life against a background of a large tragedy. It can thus explain why we don't feel any different upon learning that the death toll in Darfur is closer to 400,000 than to 200,000. However, it does not fully explain apathy toward genocide because it implies that the response to initial loss of life will be strong and maintained, albeit with diminished sensitivity, as the losses increase. Evidence for a second descriptive model, better suited to explain apathy toward large of losses of lives, follows.

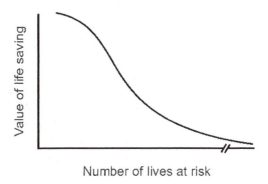

Figure 5.5 *A model depicting psychic numbing – the collapse of compassion – when valuing the saving of lives*

Source: Slovic (2007)

The collapse of compassion

American writer Annie Dillard reads in her newspaper the headline 'Head spinning numbers cause mind to go slack.'[1] She writes of 'compassion fatigue' and asks, 'At what number do other individuals blur for me?' (Dillard, 1999, p131).

An answer to Dillard's question is beginning to emerge from behavioural research. Studies by social psychologists find that a single individual, unlike a group, is viewed as a psychologically coherent unit. This leads to more extensive processing of information and stronger impressions about individuals than about groups. Consistent with this, a study in Israel found that people tend to feel more distress and compassion and provide more aid when considering a single victim than when considering a group of eight victims (Kogut and Ritov, 2005a, b). A follow-up study in Sweden found that people felt less compassion and donated less aid toward a pair of victims than to either individual alone (Västfjäll et al, 2009). Perhaps the blurring that Annie Dillard asks about begins for groups as small as two people.

The insensitivity to life saving portrayed by the psychophysical model is unsettling. But the studies just described suggest an even more disturbing psychological tendency. Our capacity to feel is limited. To the extent that valuation of life saving depends on feelings driven by attention or imagery, it might follow the function shown in Figure 5.5, where the emotion or affective feeling is greatest at $N = 1$ but begins to decline at $N = 2$ and collapses at some higher value of N that becomes simply 'a statistic.' Whereas Robert J. Lifton coined the term 'psychic numbing' to describe the 'turning off' of feeling that enabled rescue workers to function during the horrific aftermath of the Hiroshima bombing (Lifton, 1967), Figure 5.5 depicts a form of psychic numbing that is not beneficial. Rather, it leads to apathy and inaction, consistent with what is seen repeatedly in response to mass murder and genocide.

The failure of moral intuition

Thoughtful deliberation takes effort. Fortunately evolution has equipped us with sophisticated cognitive and perceptual mechanisms that can guide us through our daily lives efficiently, with minimal need for 'deep thinking.'

Consider how we typically deal with risk. Long before we had invented probability theory, risk assessment and decision analysis, there was intuition, instinct and gut feeling, honed by experience, to tell us whether an animal was safe to approach or the water was safe to drink. As life became more complex and humans gained more control over their environment, analytic ways of thinking evolved to boost the rationality of our experiential reactions. We now can look to toxicology and analytic chemistry to tell us whether the water is safe to drink – not only to how it looks or tastes. But we can still use our feelings as well, an easier path.

As with risk, the natural and easy way to deal with moral issues is to rely on our intuitions: 'How bad is it?' Well, how bad does it feel? We can also apply reason and logical analysis to determine right and wrong, as our legal system attempts to do. But, as Jonathan Haidt, a psychologist at the University of Virginia, has demonstrated, moral intuition comes first and usually dominates moral judgement unless we make an effort to critique and, if necessary, override our intuitive feelings (Haidt, 2001, 2007).

Unfortunately, moral intuition fails us in the face of genocide and other disasters that threaten human lives and the environment on a large scale. We cannot trust it. It depends upon attention and feelings that may be hard to arouse and sustain over time for large numbers of victims, not to speak of numbers as small as two. Left to its own devices, moral intuition will probably favour individual victims and sensational stories that are close to home and easy to imagine. Our sizeable capacity to care for others may be demotivated by negative feelings resulting from thinking about those we cannot help. Or it may be overridden by pressing personal and local interests. Compassion for others has been characterized by social psychologist Daniel Batson as 'a fragile flower, easily crushed by self concern' (Batson, 1990, pp344–345). Faced with genocide and other mass tragedies , we cannot rely on our intuitions alone to guide us to act properly.

What to do?

Behavioural research, supported by common observation and the record of repeated failures to arouse citizens and leaders to halt the scourge of genocide and to prevent thousands from perishing in natural disasters, sends a strong and important message. Our moral intuitions often fail us. They seduce us into calmly turning away from massive losses of human lives, when we should be driven by outrage to act. This is no small weakness in our moral compass.

Fortunately, we have evolved a second mechanism, moral judgement, to address such problems, based on reason and argument. In the case of genocides and other mass crimes against humanity, we must focus now on engaging this mechanism by strengthening international legal and political structures that pre-commit states to respond to these tragedies rather than being silent witnesses. The United Nations is the institution that was created in part to deal with such issues, but structural problems built into its very charter have made it ineffective. Appreciation of the failures of moral intuition makes development of new institutional arrangements even more urgent and critical. For it may only be laws and institutions that can keep us on course, forcing us to doggedly pursue the hard measures needed to combat genocide when our attention strays and our feelings lull us into complacency.

Elsewhere, I have proposed that international and domestic law should require officials to publicly deliberate and proffer reasons to justify action or inaction in response to genocide (Slovic, 2009). If enforced, a requirement for public justification would probably heighten pressure to act to save lives rather than allowing people to die.

The stakes are high. Failure to understand how our minds become insensitive to catastrophic losses of human life and failure to act on this knowledge may condemn us to passively witness another century of genocide and mass abuses of innocent people as in the previous century. It may also increase the likelihood that we may fail to take appropriate action to reduce the damages from other catastrophic events.

Acknowledgements

I wish to thank the William and Flora Hewlett Foundation and its President, Paul Brest, for support and encouragement in the research that has gone into this chapter. Additional support has been provided by the National Science Foundation through Grant SES-0649509.

Many individuals have provided constructive criticisms and helpful suggestions on this work as well as other intellectual and logistical support. Among the many, Ellen Peters and Daniel Västfjäll deserve special thanks. Finally, this chapter has benefited greatly from the advice and comments of Dan Ariely, Cass Sunstein, Ryan Goodman, Derek Jinks and Andrew Woods. David Zionts' ideas about legal and policy implications of psychic numbing are especially appreciated.

Note

1   She struggles to think straight about the great losses that the world ignores: 'More than two million children die a year from diarrhea and eight hundred thousand from measles. Do we blink? Stalin starved seven million Ukrainians in one year, Pol Pot killed two million Cambodians ...' (Dillard, 1999, p130)

Chapter 6

Numbers and Nerves: Toward an Affective Apprehension of Environmental Risk

Scott Slovic and Paul Slovic*

There are 1,198,500,000 people alive now in China. To get a feel for what this means, simply take yourself – in all your singularity, impor-tance, complexity, and love – and multiply by 1,198,500,000. See? Nothing to it.

Annie Dillard, *For the Time Being* (1999, p87)

Who among us can perform the act of multiplication described in the epigraph by Annie Dillard? 'Nothing to it,' jokes Dillard. Simply do the maths. It would be difficult to state more graphically that we struggle to understand information described by numbers, whether these numbers describe quantities of things (such as people) or vast processes – either sudden cataclysms or slow, barely perceptible systemic changes – that occur in the natural world. Environmental risks – both the risks we expose ourselves to when we live in the world and the risks of human impacts on the natural world – are often described in language poorly suited to overcome the numbing, desensitizing effects of abstract, quantitative discourse.

In the past decade, cognitive science has increasingly come to support the claim that we, as a species, think best when we allow numbers and narratives, abstract information and experiential discourse, to interact, to work together. Psychologist Seymour Epstein, in the article 'Integration of the cognitive and psychodynamic unconscious' (1994), argues that humans apprehend reality, including risk and benefit, by employing two interactive, parallel systems of

*   Reprinted from Slovic, S. and Slovic, P. (2004/2005) 'Numbers and nerves: Toward an affective apprehension of environmental risk', *Whole Terrain*, vol 13, pp14–18.

processing information: the deliberative, logical, evidence-based 'rational system' and the 'experiential system,' which encodes reality in images, metaphors, and narratives associated with feelings, with affect. In other words: we need numbers and we need nerves.

In recent years, many writers have corroborated the findings of cognitive science, expressing their frustration at the numbing effects of numerical discourse. In an essay called 'The blood root of art,' published in his 1996 volume *The Book of Yaak*, Montana author Rick Bass gets right to the heart of the discussion, stating:

> The numbers are important, and yet they are not everything. For whatever reasons, images often strike us more powerfully, more deeply than numbers. We seem unable to hold the emotions aroused by numbers for nearly as long as those of images. We quickly grow numb to the facts and the math. (p87)

Yet Bass also frets in this essay about the possible inadequacy of art, of language, for the communication of solid information that might have the power to sway government and corporate officials away from the excessive harvesting of natural resources, the destruction of wild places and nearby communities. He states: 'I had ... meant for this whole essay to be numbers, a landslide of numbers, like brittle talus. But I cannot tolerate them at present. There is a space in me this short winter day, that cries out for words' (p93). There is a space in all people, even in the scientists and economists whose daily currency is the worldview we call 'quantification,' that 'cries out for words,' and for images and stories, for the discourse of emotion. What is the function of language – chiefly, 'narrative language' – in helping us, scientists and laypeople alike, to appreciate the meaning of our environmental quandaries?

Over the years, we have discussed the emphasis that both social science and environmental literature have placed on emotion and the language of story in the apprehension and communication of risk. We have repeatedly observed this shared understanding in environmental writing and in the empirical research of contemporary psychologists. Our conversations as a psychologist and a literary critic inspired us to embark upon a father-and-son collaboration, where we joined forces to examine the place where our professional interests coincide. In this essay, we would like to briefly explore our converging disciplines and offer Bill McKibben's book, *Maybe One: A Personal and Environmental Argument for Single-Child Families* (1998), as an example of a narrative that uses emotion to successfully convey the ecological risks posed by human overpopulation.

Psychologists often highlight the importance of emotion or affect in human understanding of environmental risk. Affect is a specific quality of 'goodness' or 'badness,' and affective responses occur rapidly and automatically. Note how quickly you sense the feelings associated with the word 'treasure' or the word 'hate.' In his 1994 book, *Descartes' Error: Emotion, Reason and the Human Brain*, Antonio Damasio presents an account of the role affect plays in human decision making. In seeking to determine how the human brain enables rational behaviour, Damasio argues that thought is made largely from images, broadly construed to include perceptual and symbolic representations. A lifetime of learning marks these images with positive and negative feelings linked directly or indirectly to somatic or bodily states. A negative feeling sounds an alarm when linked to a future outcome. A positive feeling associated with the outcome image becomes a beacon of incentive.

Researchers currently studying the role of affect in risk perception and decision making claim that: (1) affect conveys meaning upon information; (2) without affect, information lacks meaning and will not be used in judgement and decision making; and (3) affect is a key ingredient of rational behaviour (Slovic et al, 2002). These ideas are directly relevant to the perception of risk in a variety of contexts. George Loewenstein and his colleagues, in a paper entitled 'Risk as feelings' (2001), find that emotions such as worry, fear, dread or anxiety sometimes have a more pronounced effect on risk-taking behaviour than logical cognitive evaluations of risks and benefits. Evolution, they argue, has not prepared people to react with appropriate fear to objectively dangerous stimuli such as guns, hamburgers, automobiles, smoking and unsafe sex, while humans react viscerally to such stimuli as spiders, snakes and heights.

Evolution has also shaped our minds to be sensitive to small changes in our environment (e.g. the difference between 0 and 1 deaths) at the cost of making us less able to appreciate and respond appropriately to larger impacts. Robert Jay Lifton and Greg Mitchell refer to this as 'psychic numbing,' a term that David Fetherstonhaugh and his colleagues recast as 'psychophysical numbing' where it refers to numeric insensitivity (Lifton, 1967; Lifton and Mitchell, 1995; Fetherstonhaugh et al, 1997). Annie Dillard's 1,198,500,000 Chinese is precisely the kind of 'dry statistic' that can numb the human mind. A newspaper headline, decrying our inattention to the daily deaths of 35,000 children from poverty and starvation, opens with a variation on this theme:

> *The death of one child can be big news, but the deaths of a million children are rarely news at all.* (Cohen and Solomon, 1994)

> *The concept of 'psychophysical numbing' has powerful implications in the realm of environmental risk. It is why many people care more about the loss of a single tree than about the devastation of vast forests, more about the fate of one bird than about the extinction of entire species. It is why the suffering of a single child may be more poignant for most people than the threat of an uninhabitable planet.*

If, as people sometimes say, 'statistics are human beings with tears dried off,' how can we put the tears back and thus impart the feelings that are needed for rational action? The risks of global climate change, deforestation and biodiversity loss cannot be conveyed without presenting quantitative data – and yet these contemporary environmental phenomena can have little visceral, emotional meaning for the public unless they are also presented by way of stories and images. It is difficult to tell a gripping, intimate story about one's encounters with global climate change, although Mitchell Thomashow shows how this might be done in his book, *Bringing the Biosphere Home: Learning to Perceive Global Environmental Change* (2002).

A good example of a contemporary environmental writer who walks the tightrope between analysis and story, information and image, is journalist Bill McKibben, whose work explores such topics as climate change (1989), the personal and cultural implications of television (1992), and human genetic engineering (2003). McKibben's 1998 book, *Maybe One: A Personal and Environmental Argument for Single-Child Families*, offers a compelling narrative of the author's own engagement with the issues of overpopulation and reproductive responsibility – a crucial environmental topic, and one that seems to require largely quantitative data about the ecological impact of human population growth.

McKibben's approach is a process of telescoping, of moving inward toward intimate, personal aspects of human reproduction and then moving outward to broader, more abstract facets of the issue. This shift from the individual to the global by way of narrative prose makes the topic accessible and meaningful without compromising scientific information the author considers essential for his readers to make informed decisions about reproduction in their own lives. *Maybe One* differs from more conventional examples of population literature, not only because of the author's use of personal narratives of reproductive decision-making, but because of his interest in the emotional and developmental experience of growing up as a single child. As he explains, 'I did it because of Sophie, my four-year-old daughter. I wanted to make sure that growing up without brothers and sisters would not damage her spirit or her mind.' Likewise, the book's final chapter examines what it means to be parents raising 'much smaller families than tradition dictates, or to raise no families at all.' By focusing on the emotional well-being of children and parents and not just on their material existence, McKibben hopes 'to make what has usually been an abstract question very personal and immediate' (p11).

The opening chapter of *Maybe One* begins with a paragraph about the author's fears that his approach to parenting will 'screw up' his daughter Sophie, and the final chapter concludes with a description of a delightful (and implicitly routine) afternoon and evening with his daughter as they play and learn together. In between these frames, McKibben offers clusters of chapters devoted to Family, Species, Nation and Self, presenting research on topics such as child psychology, population biology, resource economics, pollution and contraception, mixed with personal stories and narratives of his research practices, including stories of working in the basement of the library at the State University of New York in Albany, and meeting scholars such as psychologist Toni Falbo for an interview in Washington, DC.

Perhaps the best way, in brief, to explain the ecological discourse of *Maybe One* is to refer to the opening of chapter 8, which begins the section of the book devoted to 'Self.' The chapter starts with a narrative of McKibben's own experience having a vasectomy performed at an Ottawa clinic. The whole story occupies only three pages, but it makes the entire subject of vasectomies profoundly personal and accessible. This is clearly an author who has lived the subject he is discussing. After telling the story of the medical procedure, McKibben backtracks and explores the emotional, philosophical and even religious dimensions of reproduction, asking why it is that humans seem biologically programmed to reproduce ourselves, and how we might come to act in a way that goes against this programming. The discussion is reasonable and respectful, even sympathetic. McKibben seems to appreciate both the dogmatic and personal reasons for having children, pointing out that in his own 'circle of friends and acquaintances, the single most common route to maturity has been through raising children, often lots of children.' But he then walks the reader through his own decision-making process, his choice not to have additional children, as a result of exploring the fact that 'now we live in an era ... when parenting a bunch of kids clashes with the good of the planet' (p196). After reading McKibben's *Maybe One*, the meaning of Dillard's '1,198,500,000 people' finally begins to take shape.

One could argue that there's a limited audience for any work of literature, and perhaps an even narrower audience for literature or literary journalism that explicitly addresses issues of ideology, politics and biology. However, the process of dispersing to the general public new perspectives on ecologically crucial issues, such as human reproduction, requires the development of new modes of discourse – new ways of describing experience, new strategies for translating statistics into stories, new ways of articulating the meaning of both numbers and nerves. We need entire forests as much as individual trees, entire species as much as individual birds. Stories have the power to help us understand large, complex problems – including environmental risks – that we cannot apprehend through quantitative information alone. This convergence of psychology and story invites collaboration among social and natural scientists, humanities scholars and artists, and is one that we continue to pursue.

Chapter 7

Cigarette Smokers:
Rational Actors or Rational Fools?

Paul Slovic[*]

I don't smoke and don't care to be around smoke, but I believe smokers should have the right to smoke if they choose. What I cannot comprehend, however, is why smokers are being allowed to sue tobacco companies for millions of dollars because of choices they made on their own.

No one forces anyone to smoke. We have been warned ever since I can remember about the dangers of smoking. If I choose to smoke, then I also must pay the consequences of whatever that choice leads to, whether it's lung cancer or a home that burns because I fell asleep in bed with a cigarette in my hand.

This whole thing is totally unfair to the tobacco industry. But maybe I can learn something from it. Maybe I'll start smoking so I can die rich some day and leave all my millions to my kids and grandkids.[1]

In numerous legal battles across the United States, lawyers for the cigarette industry have been relying heavily on the argument that smokers know the health risks of smoking and are making rational decisions to smoke because the benefits to them outweigh the risks. Such 'informed consumers,' the lawyers claim, have no cause for complaint if they become ill.

Do individuals really know and understand the risks entailed by their smoking decisions? This question is particularly important in the case of young persons, because most smokers start during childhood and adolescence. After many years of intense publicity about the hazards of smoking cigarettes, it is generally believed that every teenager and adult in the United States knows that smoking is

---

[*] Reprinted from Slovic, P. (2001) 'Cigarette smokers: Rational actors or rational fools?', in P. Slovic (ed) *Smoking: Risk, Perception and Policy*, Sage, Thousand Oaks, CA.

Figure 7.1 *Things everybody knows*

hazardous to one's health. Apart from writers of letters to newspaper editors and editorial cartoonists (see Figure 7.1), the most enthusiastic empirical demonstration of this 'fact' comes from research on perceptions of risk from smoking reported by Viscusi (1992; see also Viscusi, 1990, 1991).

Analysing survey data, Viscusi concluded that young smokers are not only informed about the risks of smoking, they are over-informed in the sense that they overestimate those risks. He also concluded that, despite this overestimation, young people operate rationally on the information they have. In this chapter, I present a counter view based upon work in cognitive psychology that demonstrates the powerful influence of experiential thinking and affect on judgement and decision making. I describe some of this work in the next section. In the final section of the chapter, I examine data from the Annenberg Survey 2 that demonstrate how experiential thinking misleads smokers and, contrary to Viscusi's view, causes them to underestimate the risks of smoking.

Experiential thinking and the affect heuristic

This section introduces a theoretical framework that describes the importance of affect in guiding judgements and decisions. As used here, affect means the specific quality of 'goodness' or 'badness' (a) experienced as a feeling state (with or without conscious awareness) and (b) demarcating a positive or negative quality of a stimulus. Affective responses occur rapidly and automatically – note how quickly you sense the feelings associated with the word 'treasure' or the word 'hate'. Following Finucane et al (2000a), I shall argue that reliance on such feelings can be characterized as the 'affect heuristic.' Below, I briefly trace the development of the affect heuristic across a variety of research paths. A more extensive review can be found in Slovic et al (2002).

Background

A strong early proponent of the importance of affect in decision making was Zajonc (1980), who argued that affective reactions to stimuli are often the very first reactions, occurring automatically and subsequently guiding information processing and judgement. According to Zajonc, all perceptions contain some affect. 'We do not just see "a house": We see a handsome house, an ugly house, or a pretentious house' (p154). He later adds: 'We sometimes delude ourselves that we proceed in a rational manner and weigh all the pros and cons of the various alternatives. But this is probably seldom the actual case. Quite often, "I decided in favor of X" is no more than "I liked X"... We buy the cars we 'like', choose the jobs and houses we find 'attractive', and then justify these choices by various reasons' (p155).

Affect also plays a central role in what have come to be known as 'dual-process theories' of thinking, knowing and information processing. As Epstein (1994) observes, 'There is no dearth of evidence in everyday life that people apprehend reality in two fundamentally different ways, one variously labeled intuitive, automatic, natural, non-verbal, narrative, and experiential, and the other analytical, deliberative, verbal, and rational' (p710). Table 7.1 further compares these two systems. One of the characteristics of the experiential system is its affective basis. Although analysis is certainly important in many decision-making circumstances, reliance on affect and emotion is a quicker, easier and more efficient way to navigate in a complex, uncertain and sometimes dangerous world. Many theorists have given affect a direct and primary role in motivating behaviour. Epstein's view on this is as follows:

> The experiential system is assumed to be intimately associated with the experience of affect ... which refer[s] to subtle feelings of which people are often unaware. When a person responds to an emotionally significant event ... the experiential system automatically searches its memory banks for related events, including their emotional accompaniments ... If the activated feelings are pleasant, they motivate actions and thoughts anticipated to reproduce the feelings. If the feelings are unpleasant, they motivate actions and thoughts anticipated to avoid the feelings. (p716)

Also emphasizing the motivational role of affect, Mowrer (1960a) conceptualized conditioned emotional responses to images as prospective gains and losses that directly 'guide and control performance in a generally sensible adaptive manner' (p30; see also Mowrer, 1960b). Mowrer criticized theorists who postulate purely cognitive variables such as expectancies (probabilities) intervening between stimulus and response, cautioning that we must be careful not to leave the organ-

Table 7.1 *Two modes of thinking: Comparison of the experiential and rational systems*

Experiential system	Rational system
1. Holistic	1. Analytic
2. Affective: pleasure/pain oriented	2. Logical: reason oriented (what is sensible)
3. Associationistic connections	3. Logical connections
4. Behaviour mediated by 'vibes' from past experiences	4. Behaviour mediated by conscious appraisal of events
5. Encodes reality in concrete images, metaphors and narratives	5. Encodes reality in abstract symbols, words and numbers
6. More rapid processing: oriented toward immediate action	6. Slower processing: oriented toward delayed action
7. Self-evidently valid: 'experiencing is believing'	7. Requires justification via logic and evidence

Source: Adapted from Epstein (1994)

ism at the choice point 'lost in thought.' Mowrer's solution was to view expectancies more dynamically (as conditioned emotions such as hopes and fears) serving as motivating states leading to action.

One of the most comprehensive and dramatic theoretical accounts of the role of affect in decision making is presented by the neurologist Antonio Damasio in his book *Descartes' Error: Emotion, Reason, and the Human Brain* (1994). Damasio's theory is derived from observations of patients with damage to the ventromedial frontal cortices of the brain that has left their basic intelligence, memory and capacity for logical thought intact but has impaired their ability to 'feel' – that is, to associate affective feelings and emotions with the anticipated consequences of their actions. Close observation of these patients combined with a number of experimental studies led Damasio to argue that this type of brain damage induces a form of sociopathy (Damasio et al, 1990) that destroys the individual's ability to make rational decisions – that is, decisions that are in his or her best interest. Persons suffering such damage became socially dysfunctional even though they remain intellectually capable of analytic reasoning. Commenting on one particularly significant case, Damasio (1994) observes:

> *The instruments usually considered necessary and sufficient for rational behavior were intact in him. He had the requisite knowledge, attention, and memory; his language was flawless; he could perform calculations; he could tackle the logic of an abstract problem. There was only one significant accompaniment to his decision-making failure: a marked alteration of the ability to experience feelings. Flawed reason and impaired feelings stood out together as the consequences of a specific brain lesion, and this correlation suggested to me that feeling was an integral component of the machinery of reason.* (pxii)

In seeking to determine 'what in the brain allows humans to behave rationally,' Damasio argues that thought is made largely from images, broadly construed to include sounds, smells, real or imagined visual impressions, ideas and words. A lifetime of learning leads these images to become 'marked' by positive and negative feelings linked directly or indirectly to somatic or bodily states (Mowrer and other learning theorists would call this conditioning): 'In short, somatic markers are ... feelings generated from secondary emotions. These emotions and feelings have been connected, by learning, to predicted future outcomes of certain scenarios' (Damasio, 1994, p174). When a negative somatic marker is linked to an image of a future outcome, it sounds an alarm. When a positive marker is associated with the outcome image, it becomes a beacon of incentive. Damasio concludes that somatic markers increase the accuracy and efficiency of the decision process, and their absence degrades performance by 'compromising the rationality that makes us distinctly human and allows us to decide in consonance with a sense of personal future, social convention, and moral principle' (pxii).

Based on ideas about affect-marking images (e.g. Damasio, 1994), which in turn motivates behaviour (e.g. Mowrer, 1960a, b; Epstein, 1994), affect can be portrayed as an essential component in many forms of judgement and decision making. Specifically, Finucane et al (2000a) propose that people use an affect heuristic to make judgements. That is, representations of objects and events in people's minds are tagged to varying degrees with affect. In the process of making a judgement or decision, an individual consults or refers to an 'affect pool' containing all the positive and negative tags consciously or unconsciously associated with the representations. Just as imaginability, memorability and similarity serve as cues for probability judgements (e.g. the availability and representativeness heuristics first described by Tversky and Kahneman, 1974), affect may serve as a cue for many important judgements. Relying on an affective impression can be far easier – more efficient – than weighing the pros and cons or retrieving from memory many relevant examples, especially when the required judgement or decision is complex or mental resources are limited. This characterization of a mental short cut leads to the labelling of the use of affect as a heuristic.

Empirical evidence

This subsection presents and integrates the findings of a series of diverse studies demonstrating the operation of the affect heuristic.

Manipulating preferences through controlled exposures

The fundamental nature and importance of affect have been demonstrated repeatedly in a remarkable series of studies by Robert Zajonc and his colleagues (see e.g. Zajonc, 1968). The concept of stimulus exposure is central to all of these studies. The central finding is that, when objects are presented to an individual repeatedly, the 'mere exposure' is capable of creating a positive attitude or preference for these objects.

In a typical study, stimuli such as nonsense phrases, faces or Chinese ideograms are presented to an individual with varying frequency. In a later session, the individual judges these stimuli on liking, familiarity or both. The more frequent the exposure to a stimulus, the more positive the response. A meta-analysis by Bornstein (1989) of mere exposure research published between 1968 and 1987 included more than 200 experiments examining the exposure–affect relationship. Unreinforced exposures were found reliably to enhance affect toward visual, auditory, gustatory, abstract and social stimuli.

Winkielman et al (1997) have demonstrated the speed with which affect can influence judgements in studies employing a subliminal priming paradigm. A participant was 'primed' through exposure to a smiling face, a frowning face or a neutral polygon presented for 1/250 of a second, an interval so brief that there is no recognition or recall of the stimulus. Immediately following this exposure, an ideogram was presented for two seconds, following which the participant rated the ideogram on a scale of liking. Mean liking ratings were significantly higher for ideograms preceded by smiling faces. This effect was lasting. In a second session, ideograms were primed by the 'other face,' the one not associated with the stimulus in the first session. This second priming was ineffective because the effect of the first priming remained.

Sherman et al (1998) tested the perseverance of induced preferences by asking participants to study Chinese characters and their English meanings. Half of the meanings were positive (e.g. beauty) and half were negative (e.g. disease). Participants were then given a test of these meanings followed by a task in which they were given pairs of characters and were asked to choose the one they preferred. Participants preferred characters with positive meaning 70 per cent of the time. Next, the characters were presented with neutral meanings (desk, linen) and subjects were told that these were the 'true' meanings. The testing procedure was repeated and, despite the participants having learned the new meanings, preferences remained the same. Characters that had been initially paired with positive meanings still tended to be preferred.

These and many other related studies demonstrate that affect is a strong conditioner of preference, whether or not the cause of that affect is consciously perceived. They also demonstrate that affect is independent of cognition, indicating that there may be conditions of affective or emotional arousal that do not necessarily require cognitive appraisal. This affective mode of response, unburdened by cognition and hence much faster, has considerable adaptive value in many situations.

Image, affect and decision making

Consistent with the literature just reviewed, a number of non-laboratory studies have also demonstrated strong relationships among imagery, affect and decision making. Many of these studies have used a word-association technique to discover the affective connections that individuals have learned through life experiences. Researchers using this method present each subject with a target stimulus, usually a word or very brief phrase, and ask him or her to provide the first thought or image that comes to mind. The process is then repeated a number of times, say three to six, or until no further associations are generated. Following the elicitation

Table 7.2 *Images, ratings and summation scores for one respondent*

Stimulus	Image number	Image	Image rating
San Diego	1	Very nice	2
San Diego	2	Good beaches	2
San Diego	3	Zoo	2
San Diego	4	Busy freeway	1
San Diego	5	Easy to find way	1
San Diego	6	Pretty town	2
Total			10
Denver	1	High	2
Denver	2	Crowded	0
Denver	3	Cool	2
Denver	4	Pretty	1
Denver	5	Busy airport	−2
Denver	6	Busy streets	−2
Total			1

Note: Based on these summation scores, this person's predicted preference for a vacation site would be San Diego.

Source: Slovic et al (1991c)

of images, the subject is asked to rate each image he or she has given on a scale ranging from very positive (e.g. +2) to very negative (e.g. −2), with a neutral point in the centre. Scoring consists of summing or averaging the ratings to obtain an overall index.

This method has been used successfully to measure the affective meanings that influence people's preferences for different cities and states (Slovic et al, 1991c) as well as their support for or opposition to technologies such as nuclear power (Peters and Slovic, 1996). Table 7.2 illustrates the method in a task where one respondent was asked to give associations for each of two cities and, later, to rate each image affectively. The cities in this example show the clear affective superiority of San Diego over Denver for this subject. Slovic et al (1991c) showed that summed image scores such as these were highly predictive of expressed preferences for living in or visiting cities. In one study, we found that the image score predicted the location of actual vacations during the next 18 months.

Subsequent studies have found affect-laden imagery elicited by word associations to be predictive of preferences for investing in new companies on the stock market (MacGregor et al, 2000) and of adolescents' decisions to take part in health-threatening and health-enhancing behaviours such as smoking and exercise (Benthin et al, 1995).

The affect heuristic in judgements of risk and benefit

The research that, in conjunction with the sorts of findings reported above, led to recognition of the affect heuristic, had its origins in the early study of risk perception reported by Fischhoff et al (1978). One of the findings in that study and subsequent replications of it was that perception of risk and society's responses to risk were strongly linked to the degree to which a hazard evoked feelings of dread (see also Slovic, 1987). Thus activities associated with cancer (e.g. activities exposing people to radiation or toxic chemicals) are seen as riskier and more in need of regulation than activities associated with less dreaded forms of illness, injury and death (e.g. accidents).

A second finding in the study by Fischhoff et al (1978) has been even more instrumental in the study of the affect heuristic. This is the finding that judgements of risk and benefit are negatively correlated. For many hazards, the greater the perceived benefit the lower the perceived risk, and vice versa. Smoking, use of alcoholic beverages and consumption of food additives, for example, tend to be seen as very high in risk and relatively low in benefit, whereas the use of vaccines, antibiotics and X-rays tend to be seen as high in benefit and relatively low in risk. This negative relationship is noteworthy because it occurs even when the nature of the gains or benefits from an activity is distinct and qualitatively different from the nature of the risks. That the inverse relationship is generated in people's minds is suggested by the fact that risk and benefits generally tend to be positively (if at all) correlated in the world. Activities that bring great benefits may be high or low in risk, but activities that are low in benefit are unlikely to be high in risk (if they were, they would be proscribed).[2]

A study by Alhakami and Slovic (1994) found that the inverse relationship between the perceived risk and perceived benefit of an activity (e.g. using pesticides) was linked to the strength of positive or negative affect associated with that activity. This result implies that people base their judgements of an activity or a technology not only on what they think about it but also on what they feel about it. If they like an activity, they are moved to judge the risks as low and the benefits as high; if they dislike it, they tend to judge the opposite – high risk and low benefit.

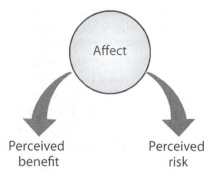

Figure 7.2 *A model of the affect heuristic explaining the risk/benefit confounding observed by Alhakami and Slovic (1994)*

Note: Judgements of risk and benefit are assumed to be derived by reference to an overall affective evaluation of the stimulus item.
Source: Finucane et al (2000a)

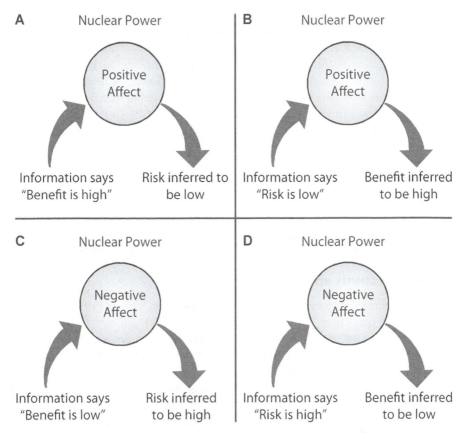

Figure 7.3 *Model showing how information about benefit (A) or information about risk (B) could increase the overall affective evaluation of nuclear power and lead to inferences about risk and benefit that coincide affectively with the information given. Similarly, information could decrease the overall affective evaluation of nuclear power as in C and D, resulting in inferences that are opposite those in A and B*

Source: Finucane et al (2000a)

These findings suggest that use of the affect heuristic guides perceptions of risk and benefit as depicted in Figure 7.2. If so, providing information about risk should change the perception of benefit and vice versa (see Figure 7.3). For example, information stating that benefit is high for some technology should lead to more positive overall affect, which would, in turn, decrease perceived risk. Indeed, Finucane et al (2000a) conducted this experiment, providing four different kinds of information designed to manipulate affect by increasing or decreasing perceived risk and increasing or decreasing perceived benefit. In each case there was no apparent logical relation between the information provided (e.g. information about risks) and the non-manipulated variable (e.g. benefits). The predictions were confirmed. When the information that was provided changed either the perceived risk or the perceived benefit, an affectively congruent but inverse effect was observed on the non-manipulated attribute, as depicted in Figure 7.3. These findings support the theory that risk and benefit judgements are causally determined, at least in part, by the overall affective evaluation.

The affect heuristic also predicts that using time pressure to reduce the opportunity for analytic deliberation (and thereby allowing affective considerations freer rein) should enhance the inverse relationship between perceived benefits and risks. In a second study, Finucane et al (2000a) showed that the inverse relationship between perceived risks and benefits increased under time pressure, as predicted. These two experiments with judgements of benefits and risks are important because they support Zajonc's (1980) contention that affect influences judgement directly and is not simply a response to a prior analytic evaluation.

Is the decision to smoke informed and rational?

Viscusi's account and its shortcomings

In his book entitled *Smoking: Making the Risky Decision*, Viscusi (1992) addresses the following question: 'At the time when individuals initiate their smoking activity, do they understand the consequences of their actions and make rational decisions?' (p11). He goes on to define the appropriate test of rationality in terms of 'whether individuals are incorporating the available information about smoking risks and are making sound decisions, given their own preferences' (p12). Viscusi even questions whether an individual's future self may have different preferences, although he never offers information on any test of this possibility: 'Does the 20-year-old smoker fully recognize how his or her future self will value health as compared with smoking?' (p119).

The primary data upon which Viscusi (1992) relies come from a national survey of more than 3000 persons ages 16 and older in which respondents were asked, 'Among 100 cigarette smokers, how many do you think will get lung cancer because they smoke?' Analysing responses to this question, Viscusi found that people greatly overestimated the risks of a smoker getting lung cancer.[3] They also overestimated overall mortality rates from smoking and loss of life expectancy from smoking. Moreover, young people (ages 16–21) overestimated these risks to an even greater extent than did older people. Viscusi also found that perceptions of risk from smoking were predictive of whether and how much people smoked, for young and old alike.

Viscusi (1992) argues that these data support a rational learning model in which consumers respond appropriately to information and make reasonable trade-offs between the risks and benefits of smoking. With respect to youth, he concludes that his findings 'strongly contradict the models of individuals being lured into smoking at an early age without any cognizance of the risks' (p143). Viscusi further concludes that young people are so well-informed that there is no justification for informational campaigns designed to boost their awareness. Finally, he observes that social policies that allow smoking at age 18 'run little risk of exposing uninformed decision makers to the potential hazards of smoking' (p149). Viscusi's data and conclusions thus appear to lend support to the defence used by cigarette companies to fend off lawsuits brought by diseased smokers: these people knew the risks and made informed, rational choices to smoke.[4]

Viscusi's arguments would seem, at first glance, to have merit from the standpoint of experiential thinking as well as from his analytic perspective. On experiential grounds, the well-known association of cigarettes with cancer, a dread disease, should create enough negative affect to stimulate a powerful drive to avoid this harmful behaviour. Consistent with this view, many people do decide not to smoke or to quit smoking. The minority who initiate smoking or maintain the habit may also be doing so on the basis of informed experiential or analytic thinking that has led them to conclude that the benefits outweigh the risks.

On the other hand, there appear to be a number of ways in which reliance on experiential thinking might lead smokers to fail to appreciate risks and to act in ways that are not in their best interests. In particular, the exposure to information that Viscusi believes causes overestimation of risk cuts both ways. The major exposure comes from massive advertising campaigns designed to associate positive imagery and positive affect with cigarette smoking. A recent ad for Kool Natural Lights, for example, featured a picture of a beautiful waterfall on the cigarette package. In addition, the word natural appeared 13 times in the ad.

More subtle than the content of cigarette ads is the possibility that the 'mere exposure effect' that results from viewing them repeatedly (Zajonc, 1968; Bornstein, 1989) also contributes to positive affect for smoking in general and for specific brands of cigarettes in particular. Through the workings of the affect heuristic, this positive affect would be expected not only to enhance individuals' attraction to smoking but to depress the perception of risk (Finucane et al, 2000a).

Within the experiential mode of thinking, 'seeing is believing,' and young people in particular are likely to see little or no visible harm from the smoking done by their friends or themselves. In this sense, smoking risks are not 'available' (Tversky and Kahneman, 1973).

Viscusi's arguments are also lacking in a number of other respects, as I have indicated in several previous studies (Slovic, 1998a, 2000b, c). Here I shall focus on two failings, both of which relate to experiential thinking. The first reflects the repetitive nature of cigarette smoking and the accumulation of risk over a long period of time. The second reflects young people's failure to appreciate the risks of becoming addicted to smoking.

Cigarette smoking is a behaviour that takes place one cigarette at a time. A person smoking one pack of cigarettes every day for 40 years 'lights up' about 300,000 times. Although most smokers acknowledge a high degree of risk associated with many years of smoking, many believe they can get away with some lesser amount of smoking before the risk takes hold. Many young smokers, in particular, believe that smoking for only a few years poses negligible risk. They are more prone to believe in the safety of short-term smoking than are young nonsmokers (Slovic, 1998a, 2000c).

Belief in the near-term safety of smoking combines in an insidious way with a tendency for young smokers to be uninformed about, or to underestimate, the difficulty of stopping smoking. Recent research indicates that adolescents begin to show evidence of nicotine dependence within days to weeks of the onset of occasional use of tobacco (DiFranza et al, 2000). Many young people regret their decision to start smoking and attempt unsuccessfully to stop. The 1989 Teenage Attitudes and Practices Survey found that 74 per cent of adolescent smokers reported they had seriously thought about quitting, and 49 per cent had tried to quit in the previous six months (Allen et al, 1993). A longitudinal survey conducted as part of the University of Michigan's Monitoring the Future study found that 85 per cent of high school seniors who smoked occasionally predicted that they probably or definitely would not be smoking in five years, as did 32 per cent of those who smoked one pack of cigarettes per day. However, in a follow-up study conducted five to six years later, of those who had smoked at least one pack per day as seniors, only 13 per cent had quit and 69 per cent still smoked one pack or more per day. Of those who smoked one to five cigarettes per day as seniors, only 30 per cent had quit (60 per cent had expected to do so) and 44 per cent had actually increased their cigarette consumption (Johnston et al, 1993; Centers for Disease Control and Prevention, 1994).

The belief pattern that emerges from these and various other studies is one in which many young smokers perceive themselves to be at little or no risk from each cigarette smoked because they expect to stop smoking before any damage to their health occurs. In reality, a high percentage of young smokers continue to smoke over a long period of time and are certainly placed at risk by their habit.

New data: The dominance of experiential thinking

Viscusi's arguments about perceptions of risk and the informed choices made by smokers assume the pre-eminence of the analytic mode of thinking. Viscusi (1992) portrays the beginning smoker as a young economist, weighing the benefits against the risks before making the fateful decision to light up: 'One might expect some individuals to rationally choose to smoke if the weight they placed on the benefits derived from smoking exceeds their assessment of the expected losses stemming from risks' (p135). But the evidence for smokers' short-term perspectives and underestimation of the grip of addiction suggests that experiential and affective forces are leading many young people to make smoking decisions that they later regard as mistakes.

Evidence for this view comes from data collected in a national telephone survey of more than 3500 individuals conducted on behalf of the Annenberg Public Policy Center of the University of Pennsylvania in the fall of 1999 and winter of 1999–2000. Households were selected through random-digit dialling, and within each household a resident aged 14 or older was selected randomly for the interview. Young people were oversampled. Completed interviews were obtained for 2002 members of a 'youth sample' ages 14 to 22 and 1504 members of an adult sample ranging in age from 23 to 95. Within the youth sample there were 478

Table 7.3 *Perceptions and expectations of the beginning smoker (in percentages)*

Questions/Responses	Adult smokers (N = 310)	Young smokers (N = 478)
Q19a. When you first started to smoke, how much did you think about how smoking might affect your health?		
A lot	5.8	13.8
A little	15.5	38.9
Not at all	78.4	46.9
Don't know/Refused	0.3	0.4
Q19c. How much do you think about the health effects of smoking now?		
A lot	53.9	54.6
A little	32.9	36.0
Not at all	12.3	8.6
Don't know/Refused	1.0	0.8
Q19d. Since you started smoking, have you heard of any health risks of smoking that you didn't know about when you started?		
Yes	54.8	33.5
No	43.9	66.3
Don't know/Refused	1.3	0.2
Q19e. When you first started smoking, did you think more about how smoking would affect your future health or about how you were trying something new and exciting?		
Thought about future health	4.5	21.1
Thought about trying something new and exciting	67.4	58.0
Other	18.1	11.5
Don't know/Refused	10.0	9.4
Q19f. When you first started smoking, how long did you think you would continue to smoke?		
A few days	3.9	9.4
A few months	4.5	6.5
Less than a year	3.2	7.7
1–5 years	4.8	10.2
More than 5 years	7.4	4.8
Didn't think about it	75.8	61.3
Don't know/Refused	0.3	0.0

smokers and 1524 nonsmokers; among the adults there were 310 smokers and 1194 nonsmokers.[5]

Recall that the experiential mode is automatic, based on feelings, and not always accessible to conscious awareness. People acting experientially may not sense that they are consciously deliberating. Experiential thinking is evident throughout responses to the survey questions (see Table 7.3). Almost 80 per cent

Table 7.4 *Responses to question 'About how many times, if any, have you tried to quit smoking?' (in percentages)*

Number of times	Adult smokers (N = 310)	Young smokers (N = 478)
0	21.3	38.1
I	16.8	21.8
2–4	38.4	30.1
5–9	11.6	4.0
10+	9.4	4.8
Don't know/Refused	2.6	1.3

of the adult smokers surveyed answered 'not at all' when asked how much they thought about how smoking might affect their health when they first began to smoke (Question 19a). Young smokers appeared more likely to have thought about health when they began to smoke, but their most frequent answer was still 'not at all.' However, now that they smoke, most of these individuals said that they do think about the health effects (Question 19c). A substantial proportion of smokers also said that, since they started smoking, they have heard of health risks they did not know about when they started (Question 19d).

Most telling are the answers to Questions 19e and 19f. Far more beginning smokers were thinking about 'trying something new and exciting' than were thinking about health (19e). When asked how long they thought they would continue to smoke when they first started, the majority of young and older smokers said that they did not think about it (19f).

Table 7.5 *Perspectives on quitting smoking (in percentages)*

Questions/Responses	Adult smokers (N = 310)	Young smokers (N = 478)
Q29. Do you plan to quit smoking?		
Yes	65.5	83.7
No	30.6	13.2
Don't know/Refused	3.9	3.1
Q29a. When are you planning to quit?		
Next 6 months	49.3	57.0
6 months to a year	24.1	19.5
More than a year from now	15.8	18.2
Don't know/Refused	10.8	5.2
Q29b. If we called you again in a year, would you guess you would have successfully quit smoking?		
Yes	77.8	83.3
No	11.4	9.8
Don't know/Refused	10.7	6.9

Table 7.6 *Plans to quit smoking by number of past attempts to quit (in percentages)*

| | Number of attempts to quit | | | | | | | |
| | 0 | | 1–4 | | 5–9 | | 10+ | |
Questions/Responses	AS	YS	AS	YS	AS	YS	AS	YS
Q29. Do you plan to quit smoking?								
Yes	39.4	74.7	67.8	89.5	88.9	100.0	79.3	91.3
No	54.6	22.0	28.1	7.7	11.1	0.0	20.7	8.7
Don't know	6.1	3.3	4.1	2.8	0.0	0.0	0.0	0.0
Q29a. When are you planning to quit?								
Next 6 months	38.5	56.6	46.6	55.0	62.5	57.9	52.2	76.2
6 months to a year	26.9	15.4	27.6	23.0	18.8	21.0	17.4	9.5
More than a year from now	15.4	23.5	17.2	16.3	15.6	15.8	8.7	9.5
Don't know	19.2	4.4	8.6	5.9	3.1	5.3	21.7	4.8
Q29b. If called in a year, would you have quit?								
Yes	88.2	86.7	81.4	85.0	69.2	66.7	56.2	61.1
No	0.0	7.1	9.3	9.2	19.2	26.7	25.0	16.7
Don't know	11.8	6.1	9.3	5.8	11.5	6.7	18.8	22.2

Note: AS = adult smokers; YS = young smokers.

Data from the Annenberg survey indicate that most smokers neither want to continue smoking nor expect to do so. The majority of smokers had made more than one attempt to quit (Table 7.4), and about 65 per cent of the adults and 84 per cent of the young people said that they planned to quit (Table 7.5, Question 29). Of those who planned to quit, about 78 per cent of the adults and 72 per cent of the youth planned to do so within the next year (Table 7.5, Question 29a). When asked whether the researchers would find that they had successfully quit smoking if they were called again in a year (Table 7.5, Question 29b), 78 per cent of the adults and 83 per cent of the young people said yes.

Tables 7.6 and 7.7 present the responses to these same three questions about quitting, conditioned by the number of past attempts to quit (Table 7.6) and by the length of time the individual had been smoking (Table 7.7). In Table 7.6 we see that, except for adults who had never tried to quit, a substantial majority of smokers planned to quit (Question 29) and planned to do so within the next year (Questions 29a and 29b), even though they had unsuccessfully attempted to quit a number of times before. Thus we see that, among youth who had attempted to quit ten or more times, 91.3 per cent still planned to quit, and 85.7 per cent of those expected to do so in the first year (Question 29a). This estimated one-year time line was lower (61.1 per cent) when elicited in Question 29b, but it was still far greater than the 'no' response (16.7 per cent).

Similar optimism about quitting was evident among long-time smokers (Table 7.7). Even among those who had been smoking for more than five years, 64 per cent of adults and 80 per cent of young people planned to quit, and most of these individuals planned to do so within the next year. The median age of the

Table 7.7 *Plans to quit smoking by length of time smoking (in percentages)*

| | Length of time smoking | | | | | | | |
| | 1 month or less | | About 1 year | | 1–5 years | | > 5 years | |
Questions/Responses	AS	YS	AS	YS	AS	YS	AS	YS
Q29. Do you plan to quit smoking?								
Yes	—	81.4	—	82.5	74.2	87.3	63.7	80.2
No	—	15.2	—	14.3	25.8	11.0	32.2	15.9
Don't know	—	3.4	—	3.2	0.0	1.8	4.1	4.0
Q29a. When are you planning to quit?								
Next 6 months	—	85.4	—	55.8	39.1	15.8	50.0	54.5
6 months to a year	—	6.2	—	28.8	17.4	21.6	25.6	16.8
More than a year from now	—	2.1	—	7.7	17.4	22.1	15.7	23.8
Don't know	—	6.2	—	7.7	26.1	4.5	8.7	5.0
Q29b. If called in a year, would you have quit?								
Yes	—	90.9	—	86.4	92.3	81.5	75.4	80.6
No	—	6.8	—	6.8	7.7	10.3	12.3	12.5
Don't know	—	2.3	—	6.8	0.0	8.2	12.3	6.9

Note: AS = adult smokers; YS = young smokers.

adults who had been smoking for more than five years was 41, which makes it likely that they had actually been smoking for more than 20 years (more than five years was the longest time in the response options presented by the interviewers). It is noteworthy that these older smokers were as optimistic as young smokers about quitting within the next year.

Although we have seen above that most smokers were not thinking about health risks when they first began to smoke, some of those who were may have been reassured by the thought that there is little or no harm to smoking in the short run. I had earlier observed this in a survey of a sample of high-school-age smokers (Slovic, 2000c), and the present findings replicate this result. When asked to 'imagine someone who starts to smoke a pack of cigarettes a day at age 16,' 29.7 per cent of adult smokers and 26.4 per cent of young smokers agreed with the statement 'There is usually no risk to the person at all for the first few years.' Agreement was lower among nonsmokers (18.8 per cent for adults and 20.6 per cent for youth). When asked, 'How long, if ever, do you think it takes for smoking to seriously harm the health of a new smoker?' 44.8 per cent of adult smokers and 32.0 per cent of young smokers answered five years or more.

Addiction

Loewenstein (1999) has proposed a theoretical perspective that portrays addiction as an extreme form of a class of behaviours that are controlled by 'visceral factors.' Visceral factors include drive states such as hunger, thirst, sexual desire, moods and emotions, physical pain and, for addiction, intense craving for a drug

Table 7.8 *Responses to the question: 'Do you consider yourself addicted to cigarettes?'*
(in percentages)

Questions/Responses	Adult smokers			Young smokers		
	Yes	No	Don't know	Yes	No	Don't know
Q30. About how many times, if any, have you tried to quit smoking?						
0	59.1	37.9	3.0	41.2	57.7	1.1
1	76.9	23.1	0.0	56.7	43.3	0.0
2–4	78.2	21.0	0.8	75.7	24.3	0.0
5–9	91.7	8.3	0.0	73.7	26.3	0.0
10+	93.1	6.9	0.0	91.3	8.7	0.0
Q31. How long have you smoked?						
Few months or less	—	—	—	3.4	96.6	0.0
About a year	—	—	—	33.3	65.1	1.6
1–5 years	64.5	35.5	0.0	64.5	35.5	0.0
More than 5 years	79.6	19.6	0.7	88.1	11.1	0.8
All respondents	76.4	22.6	1.0	58.8	40.4	0.8

or cigarette. From the experiential perspective, it is very difficult, if not impossible, to appreciate one's own susceptibility to visceral influences. As Loewenstein observes: 'Unlike currently experienced visceral factors, which have a disproportionate impact on behavior, delayed visceral factors tend to be ignored or severely underweighted in decision making. Today's pain, hunger, anger, etc. are palpable, but the same sensations anticipated in the future receive little weight' (p240).

The Annenberg survey data provide abundant evidence regarding the difficulties of stopping smoking. First, as shown earlier in Table 7.4, the majority of the adult and young smokers had attempted to quit, usually more than once. Second, despite their lack of success in quitting, most of these individuals planned to stop smoking in the near future (Tables 7.5–7.7). Another indication of the short-term perspective of smokers and their misperception of the ease of quitting comes from the finding that only 7.4 per cent of the adult smokers and 4.8 per cent of the young people expected to smoke for more than five years when they began (Table 7.3, Question 19f), yet 87.1 per cent of these adults and 26.4 per cent of these youth reported that they had been smoking for more than five years.

When asked whether they considered themselves addicted to cigarettes, 76.4 per cent of the adult smokers and 58.8 per cent of the young people said yes (bottom row of Table 7.8). The proportions of adults and young people who considered themselves addicted increased sharply with the number of attempts to quit and length of time smoking (Table 7.8, Questions 30 and 31).

Viscusi's quantitative risk estimates are unreliable

Viscusi (1992) places great weight on the validity of his quantitative questions about smoking risk perceptions. However, there are a number of reasons to be suspicious about the reliability of answers to his questions about the relative frequency of lung cancer among 100 smokers. First, he asked respondents to estimate the risks to 100 smokers, not to themselves. Answers for themselves would probably be lower, as a result of optimism bias (Weinstein, 1998). Second, Tversky and Koehler (1994) have developed and tested a theoretical model, support theory, that shows that respondents asked to judge the likelihood for one focal event (e.g. lung cancer) produce higher probabilities than do respondents asked for judgements of the same event in the context of other alternative events. Third, we would expect that young smokers, as experiential rather than analytic thinkers who do not expect to be smoking much longer, would not be paying careful attention to tracking lung cancer rates among smokers. Hence they would not have firm quantitative estimates in their heads.

The Annenberg survey tested these suspicions by first replicating Viscusi's line of questioning and then adding a variation in the question format along the lines suggested by Tversky and Koehler's theory. Early in the survey, respondents were asked to 'imagine 100 cigarette smokers, both men and women, who smoked cigarettes their entire adult lives. How many of these 100 people do you think will die from lung cancer?' This was immediately followed by a similar question asking about the number of lung cancer deaths among 100 nonsmokers. Next, a third question asked for respondents' estimates of the number of deaths among the same 100 smokers from (a) automobile accidents, (b) heart disease, (c) stroke, (d) lung cancer and (e) all other causes combined (the order of a, b and c was randomized).

Table 7.9 presents the means and standard deviations of the estimates for lung cancer among the 100 smokers enquired about in the first and third questions. The answers to the first question, about lung cancer alone, were in the range obtained in Viscusi's surveys, with estimates by the youth sample being larger than estimates by the adults (60.4 versus 48.5). However, the estimates for lung cancer decreased by more than 50 per cent when made in the context of the other causes (Question 3). The proportions of respondents who reduced their first estimates when given a small number of alternative causes of death in Question 3 were 72.6 per cent (adults) and 80.9 per cent (youth). Furthermore, the correlation between

Table 7.9 *Judged deaths from lung cancer among 100 smokers*

	Adult sample (N = 1416)		Youth sample (N = 2002)	
	Mean	SD	Mean	SD
Question 1	48.5	27.4	60.4	25.1
	r_{13} = 0.33		r_{13} = 0.19	
Question 3	23.5	17.5	28.3	19.4
Percentage Q3<Q1	72.6		80.9	

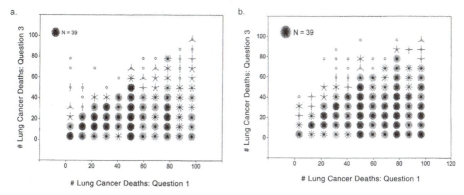

Figure 7.4 *Sunflower plot showing the relationship between (a) adult respondents'*
and (b) young respondents' estimates of lung cancer deaths among 100 smokers

Note: Question 1 asked only about lung cancer. Question 3 asked about lung cancer and other causes of death.
Open circles represent one respondent. Multiple cases at a point are represented by the number of petals on
the sunflower.

the two estimates, a form of reliability, was very low, only 0.33 for the adults and
0.19 for the younger respondents (see the scatterplots in Figures 7.4 and 7.5).
These results thus replicate and extend findings obtained earlier with a sample of
university students (Slovic, 2000b). They demonstrate that one can get a wide
range of estimates for lung cancer (or other smoking-induced causes of death)
simply by varying the number of other causes respondents are also asked to judge.

Quantitative judgements of lung cancer risk were also elicited in other ways in
the survey, but these judgements, too, were unreliable. Question 6 in the survey,
also given in two forms, asked: 'If you smoked a pack of cigarettes a day, how
much do you think it would increase your chances of getting lung cancer?'[6] Possible responses were as follows:

Question 6, Format A	*Question 6, Format B*
No more likely	No more likely
Twice as likely	Twice as likely
5 times as likely	3 times as likely
10 to 20 times as likely	5 times as likely
50 times as likely	10 or more times as likely

The results from Question 6 are displayed in Table 7.10. Note that, in both versions, the estimated rates of increase in lung cancer were higher for the young
smokers than for the adults. More salient is the fact that the proportion of adult
smokers estimating the increase at ten times or greater was 41.1 per cent under
Format A but only 14.6 per cent under Format B. For young smokers, the corresponding figures were 57.1 per cent (A) and 30.9 per cent (B). We thus see that
size of the estimated effect of smoking on lung cancer was strongly dependent on
response format, much as was found with Questions 1 and 3.

Table 7.10 *Response distributions for Question 6:*
Increases in lung cancer (in percentages)

Format A	Adult smokers (N = 153)	Young smokers (N = 245)	Format B	Adult smokers (N = 157)	Young smokers (N = 233)
No more likely	9.2	2.9	No more likely	14.6	4.3
Twice as likely	28.1	24.5	Twice as likely	36.9	13.7
5 times as likely	16.3	15.5	3 times as likely	10.8	17.6
10 to 20 times as likely	25.5	35.1	5 times as likely	19.1	31.3
50 times as likely	15.6	22.0	10 or more times as likely	14.6	30.9
Don't know/Refused	5.2	0.0	Don't know/Refused	3.8	2.2

Another quantitative risk response upon which Viscusi (1992) relies was elicited by this question: 'The average life expectancy for a 21-year-old male (female) is 53 (59) years. What do you believe the life expectancy is for the average male (female) smoker?' Here, too, Viscusi's respondents seemed to appreciate or even overestimate the risks. Their mean loss of life expectancy was 11.5 years.

The Annenberg survey included two versions of a question asking about the extent to which smoking a pack of cigarettes a day 'would shorten your life.' Possible responses were as follows:

Question 7, Format A	Question 7, Format B
Not at all	Not at all
1 year	A few months
5 to 10 years	1 year
15 years	2 to 3 years
20 years or more	5 to 10 years

We see in Table 7.11 that, in both versions, young smokers estimated somewhat greater loss of life expectancy than did adults. More important, however, is the strong influence of response scale format. For adults, 77.0 per cent of the sample estimated a life shortening of five years or more under Format A, compared with only 48.1 per cent under Format B. Corresponding figures for young smokers were 82.7 per cent (A) and 52 per cent (B).

The data from nonsmokers (not shown here) reveal a pattern of format effects quite similar to those of smokers in Tables 7.10 and 7.11. Taken together, these results and those in Table 7.9 indicate that the survey respondents, young and old alike, did not have reliable quantitative knowledge about smoking risks. The judgements they provided depended on how the response options were framed. This conclusion is consistent with other theoretical and empirical research demonstrating the dependence of quantitative judgements such as these on the form of the question and (e.g. Slovic et al, 2000b; Tversky and Koehler, 1994). It is also consistent with the view that smokers do not think analytically about the risks they are taking.

Table 7.11 *Response distributions for Question 7: Shortening of life (in percentages)*

Scale Format A	Adult smokers (N = 152)	Young smokers (N = 230)	Scale Format B	Adult smokers (N = 158)	Young smokers (N = 248)
Not at all	6.6	1.7	Not at all	9.5	3.2
I year	9.9	13.0	A few months	6.3	10.1
5 to 10 years	53.3	50.9	I year	5.7	5.2
15 years	11.2	18.3	2 to 3 years	20.3	26.6
20 years or more	12.5	13.5	5 to 10 years	48.1	52.0
Don't know/Refused	6.6	2.6	Don't know/Refused	10.1	2.8

The failure of rationality

Viscusi (1992) argues that smokers make informed, rational decisions to smoke. Viscusi has also asserted that the key question pertaining to the failure of the rational model is one in which an individual, asked to go back in time to the moment of decision and repeat the choice, would not make the same choice again. I asked that question in a small survey of smokers at the University of Oregon and in a poll of Oregon residents (Slovic, 2000b). The Annenberg telephone survey asked it as well of all smokers: 'If you had it to do over again, would you start smoking?' The results, shown in Table 7.12, are clear. More than 85 per cent of adult smokers and about 80 per cent of young smokers answered no. Moreover, the pattern of responses shown in the table was similar for both young and adult smokers. The more they felt addicted to cigarettes, the more often they had tried to quit, the longer they had been smoking, and the more cigarettes they were smoking per day, the more likely they were to say no.[7]

Recall Viscusi's central question: 'At the time when individuals initiate their smoking activity, do they understand the consequences of their actions and make rational decisions?' The data presented here indicate that the answer to this question is no. Most beginning smokers do not appreciate how their future selves will perceive the risks from smoking and value the trade-off between health and the need to smoke.

This is a strong repudiation of the model of informed rational choice. It fits well with findings that indicate that smokers give little conscious thought to risk when they begin to smoke. They appear to be lured into the behaviour by the prospects of fun and excitement. Most begin to think of risk only after they have started to smoke and have gained what to them is new information about health risks. The increased likelihood of smokers' repudiating their earlier decision exhibited by those who have been smoking for the longest time, those who are currently smoking the most cigarettes, those who perceive themselves at high risk from smoking, those who have tried most often to quit, and those who acknowledge their addiction, paints a sad portrait of individuals who are unable to control a behaviour that they have come to recognize as harmful.

Table 7.12 *Smoking: Would you start again? (in percentages)*

Questions/Responses	Adult smokers (N = 310)		Young smokers (N = 478)	
	Yes	No	Yes	No
Overall	11.9	85.5	17.0	80.1
Q32. Do you consider yourself addicted to cigarettes?				
Yes	11.4	86.9	13.9	84.3
No	14.3	81.4	21.8	74.6
More than average	7.7	90.4	7.1	92.9
Same as average	11.1	85.6	15.3	80.9
Less than average	16.2	83.8	20.4	77.0
Q30. Number of times tried to quit?				
0	27.3	66.7	22.5	73.1
1–4	9.4	88.3	14.5	83.9
5–9	8.3	91.7	10.5	84.2
10+	0.0	100.0	4.4	95.6
Q31. How long have you smoked?				
Few months or less	—	—	22.0	74.6
About 1 year	—	—	20.6	76.2
1–5 years	19.4	80.7	16.7	79.4
More than 5 years	11.1	86.3	13.5	86.5
Q26. Cigarettes smoked per day last 30 days?				
Less than 1	16.1	83.9	25.3	69.5
1–5	10.5	89.5	18.9	77.5
6–10	10.0	88.0	19.4	79.6
11–14	11.1	86.1	13.4	83.6
15–19	15.4	82.0	5.9	91.2
20	10.4	85.1	7.0	93.0
More than 20	11.4	86.4	12.1	87.9

These disturbing findings underscore the distinction that behavioural decision theorists now make between decision utility and experience utility (Kahneman and Snell, 1992; Kahneman, 1997; Loewenstein and Schkade, 1999). This distinction arises from numerous studies of persons who have experienced very good outcomes, such as winning the lottery, or very bad ones, such as becoming paraplegic or testing positive for HIV. Winning the lottery leaves people much less happy than they had expected, and people adjust to being paraplegic or HIV-positive much better than they had expected (Brickman et al, 1978). In the case of smoking, the discrepancy between decision utility and experience utility underscores the veracity of Loewenstein's visceral account of addiction.

Cigarette smokers: Rational actors or rational fools?

Rationality is a product not only of the analytic mind but of the experiential mind. As Damasio (1994) observes:

> *The strategies of human reason probably did not develop, in either evolution or any single individual, without the guiding force of the mechanisms of biological regulation, of which emotion and feeling are notable expressions. Moreover, even after reasoning strategies become established ... their effective deployment probably depends, to a considerable extent, on a continued ability to experience feelings.* (pxii)

Ironically, the perception and integration of affective feelings, within the experiential system, is exactly the kind of high-level maximization process postulated by economic theorists since the days of Jeremy Bentham. In this sense, the affect heuristic enables us to be rational actors in many important situations – but not in all situations. It works beautifully when our experience enables us to anticipate accurately how much we will like the consequences of our decisions. It fails miserably when the consequences turn out to be much different in character from what we had anticipated. In such situations, exemplified well by the smoking of cigarettes, the rational actor becomes the rational fool.[8]

Notes

1   This quote comes from a letter to the editor that was published in the *Register-Guard* in Eugene, Oregon, 12 April 2000 (p10a).
2   This inverse relationship is found as well when the correlation is computed across individuals judging the same activity. Thus one person may judge nuclear power to be high in risk and low in benefit, whereas another might judge it low in risk and high in benefit.
3   The mean estimate was 43 of 100, compared with an actuarial value that Viscusi (1992) claims was only 10–15 of 100. Similar overestimation was found in subsequent studies that asked about lung cancer mortality rather than incidence (Viscusi, 1998a).
4   Viscusi (1992) interprets his findings as follows: 'There is substantial evidence that individuals make tradeoffs with respect to smoking risks and other valued attributes. This behavior is consistent with ... models of rational behavior ... it is unlikely that smoking rates greatly exceed what would prevail in a fully informed market context' (p144). Other scholars, quoted on the dust jacket of Viscusi's book, appear to buy Viscusi's argument. A blurb from Alan Schwartz of the Yale Law School notes:

> *This book combines two disciplines, cognitive psychology and the economics of risk, to make an important contribution to the smoking debate. Viscusi shows that persons in all age groups overestimate smoking risks, as theory predicts, and that persons behave rationally respecting the smoking decision given their perception of the facts. After these findings, the smoking decision can justifiably be regulated only in consequence of third party effects, not because consumers make poor health choices.*

And Robert D. Tollison of George Mason University asserts:

> *Viscusi's book will provide the intellectual basis and framework for a long overdue reassessment of the role of government in protecting consumers and workers from certain types of risky behavior. It should come as no surprise that the government has once again been overzealous in their protection of consumers and workers from the dangers of smoking by mandating hazard warnings on packages, restricting television advertising and imposing restrictions on where smoking is permitted. Viscusi analyzes the government's actions and offers us some interesting routes out of the swamp of overprotection.*

5   A smoker was defined as someone who said he or she had smoked at least one cigarette within the past 30 days.

6   This was not a question used by Viscusi; rather, it was selected as another way to elicit quantitative estimates of the lung cancer risk associated with smoking.

7   The perception that smoking is risky to one's health was also correlated strongly with the 'no' response for both young and adult smokers.

8   I have borrowed the notion of the rational fool from Amartya Sen's (1977) penetrating critique of the behavioural foundations of economic theory.

Chapter 8

Affect, Risk Perception and Future Optimism After the Tsunami Disaster

Daniel Västfjäll, Ellen Peters, and Paul Slovic[*]

Introduction

Major societal events such as natural disasters and terrorist attacks influence our thoughts and feelings. In the face of a major environmental event, many people tend to react with emotion and emotion-laden decisions (Lerner et al, 2003). The 2004 East Asian tsunami disaster had a profound psychological impact on many countries, not only those that were directly hit by the tsunami waves. Sweden (population 9 million) had an unusually high number of tourists visiting the area at the time of the disaster, resulting in over 600 Swedes being killed or missing. The tsunami disaster was therefore considered a major national tragedy in Sweden (Grandien et al, 2005). A consequence of this tragedy, and the media attention it received (Mann, 2007), was that many Swedes felt deeply involved and saddened (Grandien et al, 2005).

The feelings elicited by such an event may also have an impact on everyday decisions. Previous research in judgement and decision making has shown that preferences are constructed on the basis of various contextual factors (such as incidental affect or mood; Johnson and Tversky, 1983; Lichtenstein and Slovic, 2006; Peters, 2006) and people tend to rely on their affective reactions when making decisions (Slovic et al, 2002; see also Pfister and Böhm, 2008).

Affect is defined here as the specific quality of goodness or badness experienced as a feeling state (with or without awareness) and demarcating a positive or negative quality of a stimulus.[1] Reliance on such feelings in judgement and

[*]   Reprinted from Västfjäll, D., Peters, E. and Slovic, P. (2008) 'Affect, risk perception and future optimism after the tsunami disaster', *Judgment and Decision Making*, vol 3, no 1, pp64–72.

decision making has earlier been described as an affect heuristic (Finucane et al, 2000a; Slovic et al, 2002). Most previous research on affect and decision making has focused on integral affect (affect attached to mental representations of objects; Slovic et al, 2002). However, in many judgements other sources of affect are also present. A large number of studies shows that affective states that are unrelated to the judgemental target influence judgements and decisions nonetheless (Schwarz and Clore, 1983b; Isen, 1997). In a famous example, Johnson and Tversky (1983) found that incidental affect (i.e. a mood state) induced by reading a newspaper article influenced subsequent risk judgements.

However, the effect of incidental affect on judgements is not a stable, unchangeable or unavoidable fact; it should rather be seen as a constructive process where the individual tries to determine if their affective reactions to a target are a reliable and relevant source of information (Clore and Huntsinger, 2007). At the core of this argument lies the notion that when asked to make an evaluative judgement, individuals seek information to determine how they should make this judgement. People tend to use whatever information is available to them at the time of making a decision (Schwarz, 2004; Clore and Huntsinger, 2007). In the absence of other relevant or more salient information, people use their affective reactions to the target to evaluate the object (Pham, 1998; see also de Vries et al, 2008). People in positive moods tend to evaluate objects more favourably than participants in a negative mood (mood-congruence; Schwarz and Clore, 1983b; but see Andrade, 2005 for a discussion about mood-incongruent effects). One important point here is that people incorrectly attribute their incidental moods as a reaction to the target. This misattribution can be corrected or changed by introducing information that questions the diagnostic value of the affective reaction for the judgement. For instance, in Schwarz and Clore's (1983b) study participants were given a simple reminder about the cause (sunny vs. cloudy weather) of their moods which resulted in mood no longer influencing judgements of well-being. Importantly though, it was the diagnostic value of the affective reaction for the judgement task, not the affective reaction itself, that was affected by this manipulation (Schwarz, 2004).

Incidental mood is only one of many sources of experiential information that can be used in judgements. The meta-cognitive experience of the ease or fluency of information processing has been shown to be an important experiential factor informing judgements and decisions (Schwarz and Clore, 2007). In a study on the effect of fluency on decision making, participants were more likely to defer choice when they generated more reasons for making the choice (thus decreasing fluency; Novemsky et al, 2007). Studies on perceptual fluency (the subjective ease of perceptual processing) have found that if the colour in which a statement is printed makes it easy to read, this can impact the perceived truthfulness of the statement (with an easier-to-read font leading to a higher probability of endorsing a statement as true; Reber and Schwarz, 1999). Thus, as Schwarz (2004, p341) notes, it seems that 'the subjective experiences that accompany our thought processes are informative in their own right.' Consequently, meta-cognitive feelings may further modulate the impact of affect on judgements. Supporting this, a study by Lerner and Gonzalez (2005) showed that fluency manipulations influenced the effect of specific emotions on risk perception.

The conceptual model guiding this research can be described in the following way:

1   We expect that major environmental events such as a natural disaster may influence experienced affect even among individuals not directly affected by the disaster.
2   The experienced affect will, in turn, impact various affective and cognitive judgements.
3   The effects of affect incidental to the judgement task can be diminished by introducing information (such as fluency manipulations) that questions the diagnostic value of experienced feelings for judgements.

Specifically, we tested the prediction that affect elicited by thinking about a recent major natural disaster would influence judgements of well-being (Schwarz and Clore, 1983b) and future pessimistic/optimistic thinking (Wright and Bower, 1992) in a mood-congruent manner (Schwarz and Clore, 2007). Previous research has documented the effects of laboratory-induced mood using standardized mood induction procedures (autobiographical recall or affect-inducing scenarios). We extended this research by inducing affect through a procedure in which participants were asked to think about a recent and relevant major environmental disaster.

Our research strategy compared ratings of affect and ratings of future personal and societal events in two groups of participants, one reminded about the tsunami and a control group. We hypothesized that reminding participants about the tsunami would elicit negative affect associated with the event. We further anticipated that this affect would spill over to judgements of well-being as well as optimistic/pessimistic thinking.

In Study 1, participants in both conditions completed a measure of future pessimism (future time perspective (FTP) scale, Lang and Carstensen, 2002) and rated their well-being (Pavot and Diener, 1993). The FTP scale was originally developed as an individual difference measure of the perceived time remaining in life (Carstensen, 2006). In Study 1, we used the FTP scale as a dependent variable and we expected to find that individuals reminded about the tsunami perceived life as more finite and limited than participants in a control condition. In Study 2, half of the participants in the tsunami-remind condition were given an additional experimental manipulation (ease-of-thought-generation; Schwarz, 2004). Participants then made risk estimates of various future positive and negative events (Lerner and Gonzalez, 2005). We expected that this manipulation of the ease with which examples of other disasters comes to mind would influence the diagnostic value of feelings for judgements of future risk, but it does not change the feelings themselves.

Study 1.
Future time perspective

As people grow older they experience time as more limited, closed, and finite (Carstensen, 2006). However, chronological age is not the only determinant of how the future is perceived. For instance, Fung and Carstensen (2006) showed that younger adults prioritized emotional goals, a behaviour indicative of a limited time perspective, when facing a major environmental event (i.e. the SARS epidemic). Building on these findings, we hypothesized that participants reminded about the tsunami would experience a more limited future time perspective than participants in a control condition. In addition, we expected that participants reminded about the tsunami would experience stronger negative affect and lessened well-being compared to the control group and that this differ-ence would account for the hypothesized difference between conditions.

Method and measures

28 men and 77 women with a mean age of 25.3 ($SD = 4.1$) participated. Data were collected in Sweden during the Spring of 2005, roughly 3–5 months after the tsunami disaster. The tsunami was still very actively covered by the media in Sweden during this time (Mann, 2007).

To manipulate access to feelings, we used an experimental approach resem-bling the techniques developed by Lerner et al (2003) and studies on affective imagery and decision making (Slovic, 1995). In a between-groups design, half of the participants were asked to write down the first three images that came to mind when hearing the word 'tsunami'. The other half of the participants (the control condition) were asked to produce images to a neutral word ('round'). Pretesting showed that this priming manipulation made affect[2] associated with the tsunami disaster salient (Siemer and Reisenzein, 1998) and provided us with the opportu-nity to study the relative impact of affect in the two conditions.

After the experimental manipulation, participants responded to a series of questions. To measure future time perspective, a version of the FTP scale (Lang and Carstensen, 2002) was used. The measure contains eight items:

1   Many opportunities await me in the future.
2   My future is filled with possibilities.
3   Most of my life lies ahead of me.
4   My future seems infinite to me.
5   There is plenty of time left in my life to make new plans.
6   I have the sense that time is running out.
7   There are only limited possibilities in my future.
8   As I get older, I begin to experience time as more limited.

Participants responded to the question 'How well does each question describe you' by circling a number between 1 (not at all) and 7 (very well). The measure was reverse-scored where appropriate and averaged across the eight items (Cronbach's alpha = 0.77) into a single index; higher values indicated a more closed or limited future time perspective. In addition, the Pavot and Diener (1993) subjective well-being scale as well as mood and specific-emotion scales (Västfjäll et al, 2002) were administered. The mood scale consisted of six adjective pairs found in previous research (Västfjäll et al, 2002) to tap valence and activation, respectively. Sleepy–awake, dull–peppy and passive–active were used to define the activation scale, displeased–pleased, sad–glad and depressed–happy were used to define the valence scale. Participants were asked to circle a number (range = −4 to 0 to +4) that best corresponded with their current feeling. The three adjectives tapping each dimension were averaged into two index variables corresponding to valence and activation, respectively.

The specific emotion scale consisted of the adjectives sad, depressed, anxious, worried, afraid and angry. Participants were asked to rate how intensely they felt each emotion by circling a number on a unipolar scale anchored by 0 (not at all) to 6 (very much).

Results and discussion

To show that affect indeed was more negative in the tsunami-remind condition than in the control condition, the mood and emotion ratings were submitted to a series of independent t-tests. Negative affect ratings were significantly higher in the experimental condition suggesting that the manipulation was successful (see Table 8.1).

In order to test the primary research hypotheses, that well-being should be lower and FTP more limited in the tsunami-remind condition than in the control condition, two contrasts were performed. As expected, participants reminded about the tsunami rated their overall well-being as lower (M = 3.81) than participants in the control condition (M = 4.50), t(103) = 9.09, p < .001. Similarly, FTP was more limited (M = 4.80) in the tsunami-remind condition than in the control condition (M =3.22), $t(103)$ = 2.92, p < .001.

Table 8.1 *Means and inferential statistics (df = 102) for mood and specific emotion ratings obtained in the experimental and control conditions*

Measure	Tsunami-remind	Control	t	p <
Mood scales				
Valence	−1.11	0.67	13.20	0.01
Activation	1.33	0.20	9.16	0.01
Emotion scales				
Sad	2.71	0.99	14.42	0.001
Depressed	2.14	1.08	8.11	0.001
Anxious	2.34	1.02	6.92	0.01
Afraid	1.99	0.53	9.40	0.001
Worried	2.25	0.87	10.65	0.001
Angry	2.04	0.46	15.19	0.001

The finding that the experimental manipulation increased negative affect which, in turn, decreased overall subjective well-being is a replication of Schwarz and Clore's (1983b) findings. The result that future time perspective changed with experienced affect is, however, a novel demonstration. To further show that affect influenced FTP judgements, we conducted a mediation analysis. Because both affect and well-being ratings were more negative in the experimental condition, we decided to test whether well-being (as an overall proxy of affect) mediated the effect of condition on FTP. The choice of well-being ratings as an overall measure of affect was motivated by literature on happiness that suggested that current feelings are integrated into more global assessments of affective well-being (Schwarz and Clore, 1983b; Schwarz and Strack, 1999). The subjective well-being measure, however, includes aspects other than experienced feelings (e.g. life circumstances; Diener, 1984; Pavot and Diener, 1993) and when used as a variable in a mediation analysis it may be more conservative than ratings of current affect.[3] To test mediation, a series of regression models were estimated (Baron and Kenny, 1986). To examine the degree of mediation, we first regressed subjective well-being on the condition variable, then regressed FTP on the condition variable, and finally regressed FTP on both the condition variable and subjective well-being. The degree to which the influence of condition on FTP is reduced when accounting for the influence of subjective well-being expresses the degree of mediation.

The results of these regression analyses are depicted in Figure 8.1. Subjective well-being (SWL) mediated the influence of condition on FTP. Specifically: (a) condition predicted SWL ($F(1,103) = 8.59$, regression weight = 0.27, $p < .05$); (b) condition predicted FTP ($F(1,103) = 82.69$, regression weight = 0.67, $p < .01$); (c) SWL predicted FTP ($F(1,103) = 25.91$, regression weight = 0.45, $p < .01$); and (d) the condition variable dropped significantly when controlling for SWL ($F(2,102) = 6.37$, regression weight = -0.08, ns.).

Taken together, these findings suggest that thinking about a major environmental event such as the tsunami disaster elicits negative feelings (as indexed by specific emotion/mood ratings as well as well-being ratings). These feelings in turn influence how people think about and view their future possibilities. Negative feelings lead individuals to be more pessimistic, viewing time as more limited and holding fewer possibilities. Although the FTP scale was originally developed as an individual difference measure (Lang and Carstensen, 2002), the findings here suggest that it also can be used as a dependent variable measuring group differences. In contrast to the present findings, previous research has shown that the FTP measure is relatively uncorrelated with current mood (Lang and Carstensen, 2002). However, these studies have not experimentally manipulated moods which may be why mood effects were not obtained. The FTP scale is used here as a measure of pessimism and the link between mood and optimism–pessimism is well documented in the mood literature (Wright and Bower, 1992; Isen, 1997). Although the finding that participants in the experimental condition experienced a more limited FTP may be predicted from previous research without involving experienced affect as an explanatory

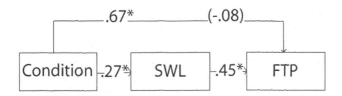

Figure 8.1 *Mediation analysis of condition and subjective well-being (SWL) on future time perspective (FTP)*

variable (Fung and Carstensen, 2006), we extend this research by showing that well-being mediates the effect.

A limited future time perspective may have many detrimental consequences for different individual behaviours such as preference for immediate consumption of food and money at the cost of long-term health behaviour and well-being (Shiv et al, 2005). In Study 2, we study risk perception in different domains of one's future life and also test potential measures to counteract the negative impact of feelings on judgements.

Study 2.
Future life expectations and ease-of-thought

In Study 2, future pessimism was assessed by obtaining risk estimates of future events across different decision domains. As in Study 1, a between-groups comparison was used (remind about the tsunami vs. a control group). In addition, we assessed whether the ease with which thoughts about other natural disasters comes to mind may modulate the impact of feelings on risk perception. Previous research has demonstrated that the ease or fluency of thoughts and feelings determines the impact of those thoughts and feelings on judgement (Schwarz, 2004). For example, participants asked to generate eight examples of behaviours that increased the risk of heart disease (a relatively difficult task) were more likely to report that they were invulnerable to heart-disease problems than participants asked to generate three examples (an easy task; Rothman and Schwarz, 1998). The explanation for this result is that the participants in the generate-eight condition noticed how difficult it was to think of examples and, on the basis of that difficulty, thought that they must be relatively invulnerable to heart disease.

Building on this logic, we asked participants to list a more difficult six (versus an easier two) examples of major natural disasters during the last one hundred years. We expected that participants in the difficult condition should notice that such events are very rare and thus experience less confidence in their feelings about the tsunami disaster as a basis for risk judgements. In other words, the difficult ease-of-thought generation should render incidental affect from the tsunami disaster relatively less diagnostic for judgements (Pham, 1998).

The design of Study 2 closely resembles Lerner and Gonzalez's (2005) Study 1, but with one important difference: Rather than studying the effects of specific emotions we focus on the effects of generalized moods on risk perception. We predict (in line with Lerner and Gonzalez's findings for specific emotions) that an ease-of-thought manipulation will interact with the effects of incidental affect on judgements, effectively debiasing risk estimates in the hard (list many) condition but not in the easy (list few). However, since the affect induced by thinking about the tsunami does not directly rely on the ease with which one can list six vs. two other major disasters, it may be predicted that well-being ratings will be relatively untouched by this manipulation. Thus, we expect that one experimental manipulation (tsunami-remind vs. control) will influence both well-being and risk perception, whereas the second experimental manipulation (ease-of-thought) will only influence risk perception.

Method and measures

50 men and 75 women with a mean age of 27.1 ($SD = 6.2$) participated. The study was run in Sweden 3–4 months after the tsunami disaster.

In addition to the tsunami-reminder manipulation used in Study 1, half of the participants in the remind condition were given an 'ease-of-thought-generation' manipulation (Schwarz, 2004) in which they were asked to list either six (hard) or two (easy) other major natural disasters that occurred anywhere in the world during the last 100 years.[4] After the experimental manipulation, participants responded to a series of questions. To measure risk perception, we used a modified version of the scale developed by Lerner and Gonzalez (2005). Participants indicated from 1 (extremely unlikely) to 7 (extremely likely) the likelihood that each of 15 events would happen to them at any point in their future life. This measure is thus similar to the FTP scale in that it taps future pessimism. However, rather than asking specific questions about the remaining time in life and the possibility of changing one's circumstances, the risk perception scale asks participants to judge the likelihood of various positive and negative events in different life domains (social, health, financial, recreational). The 15 items were:

1   I enjoyed my job.
2   I had a heart attack before age 50.
3   My achievements were written up in a newspaper.
4   I chose the wrong career.
5   I married someone wealthy.
6   I received recognition in my profession.
7   I could not find a job for 6 months.
8   My income doubled within 10 years after my first job
9   I developed gum problems in my mouth.
10 I did something in a job interview that made me embarrassed.
11 I said something idiotic in front of my class mates.
12 I got lost at night for more than 15 minutes.

13 I was on an airplane that encountered severe turbulence.
14 I received favourable medical tests at age 60.
15 I encountered a dangerous snake while on vacation.

The measure was averaged (with reverse scoring for the appropriate items) across the 15 items into an overall pessimistic future risk index (Cronbach's alpha = 0.89). In addition, the Pavot and Diener (1993) subjective well-being scale used in Study 1 was administered.[5]

Overall, we expected that participants in the tsunami-remind condition who were asked to list few natural disasters (easy condition) would give more pessimistic risk estimates than participants in the control and tsunami-remind difficult (list many natural disasters) condition. Furthermore, we expected that participants in the tsunami-remind conditions would report an overall lower well-being than participants in the control condition, independent of the ease-of-thought manipulation.

Results and discussion

To test the hypotheses, three contrasts were performed for both the subjective well-being ratings and the risk estimates. As expected, participants in the control condition reported significantly higher well-being ($M = 4.86$) than participants in the tsunami-remind difficult ($M = 3.95$, $t(74) = 3:30$, $p < .05$) and the tsunami-remind easy ($M = 3.82$, $t(82) = 3.79$, $p < .05$) conditions. The difficult and easy conditions did not differ ($t(88) = 0.43$, ns).

For the risk estimates, participants in the control condition reported less pessimistic estimates ($M = -0.19$) than participants in the tsunami-remind easy condition ($M = -0.96$, $t(74) = 5.18$, $p < .01$), but similar estimates to the participants in the tsunami-remind difficult ($M = -0.22$, $t(73) = -0.13$, ns). Further, risk estimates in the easy condition were significantly higher than those in the difficult condition ($t(87) = 4.75$, $p < .01$).

Taken together, these findings suggest that thinking about the tsunami decreased perceived well-being and systematically biased risk estimates. In addition, the effect on risk estimates was modulated by the ease with which participants could list few versus many natural disasters. Combining the logic of research on fluency (Schwarz, 2004) and mood effects (Schwarz and Clore, 2007), generating many disasters (hard condition) likely produced the experience of difficulty/low fluency, which then caused the participants in the hard condition to question the diagnostic value of their feelings for estimating risk. In the easy condition, the subjective ease-of-thought/fluency should explain why these participants were less likely to question the validity of their feelings for the judgement task. These findings are consistent with previous research on fluency and decision making (Lerner and Gonzalez, 2005; Novemsky et al, 2007). In addition to this replication, we found that the ease-of-thought manipulation did not substantially influence ratings of well-being. Schwarz (2004) suggested that the subjective experience of fluency is a form of meta-cognitive experience that helps inform judgements. While the validity and relevance of feelings as a proxy of risk estimates may have been called into question by the fluency manipulation, there is little reason why the validity of the feelings per se should be questioned by this manipulation. However, previous research has noted that the experience of fluency may generate positive affect which potentially could influence the obtained difference between the easy and hard conditions (Reber et al, 2004). Several suggestions regarding why fluency is marked with positive affect have been offered, ranging from perceptual harmony to the adaptive value of process-ing information with ease (Schwarz and Clore, 2007). While we cannot completely refute the possibility that the fluency manipulation induced positive affect in the present research, the finding that well-being ratings were comparable in the hard vs. easy conditions suggests that this effect was minor. Most impor-tantly, even if participants in the easy condition had more positive affect than participants in the hard condition, this feeling did not impact the judgement task. If the positive affect associated with fluency had spilled over to the risk estimates, we would expect that participants in the easy condition would have rated the risk of future negative outcomes lower than participants in the hard condition. However, the reverse pattern was found, suggesting that the positive affect associ-ated with fluency experiences neither changed the negative affect elicited by the experimental manipulation, nor did it influence the judgement task.

General discussion

The results of these studies suggest that the negative affect elicited by thinking about a recent major natural disaster leads to a more pessimistic view of the future. Participants reminded about the recent tsunami disaster felt that their life had fewer possibilities and that time was limited (Study 1) and that the risk of future self-relevant negative events was high and the likelihood of positive events was low (Study 2). This finding is consistent with other research documenting the effects of emotions elicited by major events on judgement and decision making (Lerner et al, 2003). The implication of this infusion of affect in everyday judge-ment is vast. Not only may judgements be affected when the affect is considered relevant, such as the perceived risk of travelling to areas affected by the disaster, but also perhaps affected are everyday decisions concerning consumption, health, social and financial domains.

Emotions and moods are usually determined in a highly idiosyncratic manner (Morris, 1999) suggesting that the overall effect of feelings on individual everyday decisions will vary considerably across individuals. Therefore, the net effect on a societal level will vary depending on the mean mood of the population (Hirschliefer and Shumway, 2003). However, in the case of affect elicited by an event that is important or relevant for a whole society or country, the impact of affect on individual decisions as well as societal decisions may be much more homogeneous and far-reaching. The current research does not speak directly to this issue since we did not directly assess this type of national mood change in a whole population. Instead, we studied a sample of people who recently experienced the aftermath of natural disaster. Although it is difficult to conclude with certainty that the experimental approach used here is representative of the effects on a whole population, a comparison with other data suggests that the reactions of our participants resembled that of the larger population. In other studies conducted in Sweden using nationally representative samples immediately following the tsunami, and six months later, we have found effects on judgement tasks similar to those found in the present study, suggesting that the experimental manipulation used here is a reasonably valid approach to investigate the effects of feelings associated with the tsunami disaster (Västfjäll et al, 2007).

Does this suggest that affect elicited by a major natural disaster, and its effect on judgements, is different from other type of mood effects? Previous research studying the emotional impact of natural disasters/major events has found that generalized anxiety and depression (Lau et al, 2006), negative well-being (Grandien et al, 2005) and negative specific emotions (Lerner et al, 2003) tend to increase compared to normal times. The results from the manipulation check in Study 1 seem consistent with this increased negative response in that the experimental manipulation resulted in a general increase in specific negative emotions and negatively valenced mood. Again, this finding is in line with the results of the nationally representative sample; immediately after the tsunami, a generalized negative response was found. When the same negative emotions were measured six months later, all ratings significantly decreased (Västfjäll et al, 2007). Other studies using nationally representative Swedish samples have found similar effects (Grandien et al, 2005). As pointed out earlier, it seems that the main difference between a normal mood change and a change brought about by a natural disaster lies in the fact that national moods are large-scale reactions that may be quite homogeneous across individuals. Further, this type of affect is continually bolstered by new information (from media, other people, etc.; Mann, 2007) that is associated with uncertainty (How many people were killed? Did I know someone who went on vacation in Thailand?), and may therefore not dissipate as quickly as a normal change in mood (Russell, 2003). This type of change in affective tone or affective background may therefore be more similar to chronic impairments of the mood system (Morris, 1999). However, research has demonstrated that chronic affect influences risk perceptions and judgements in similar ways to normal incidental mood (Gasper and Clore, 1998). For that reason, we expect that the present results will be informative for any type of study on affect and its impact on judgements.

Another major finding was that the potentially large impact of affect on behaviour was mitigated by very subtle manipulations of the ease with which examples of other disasters came to mind. The result that participants who were asked to list many (in contrast to few) other natural disasters corrected for the effect of their feelings on risk estimates is consistent with the notion that metacognitive processes have important biasing/debiasing effects on judgements (Schwarz et al, 2007). The extent of correction on judgements may depend on the naive theory used by the participant (Schwarz, 2004). In the present case, it seems likely that participants realized that natural disasters are relatively rare phenomena and tried to correct for this by minimizing reliance on their affective reactions. However, it may be argued that this assumes that participants were aware of their reactions, what caused them, and had a naive theory about how feelings may spill over to judgements. The present results cannot be used to infer the exact psychological mechanisms involved in these correction effects and future research is needed to resolve this issue. However, the mere fact that correction processes could be relatively easily elicited using simple manipulations has important implications for everyday judgements. Many of the negative effects of the feelings associated with a major environmental event such as risk aversion concerning travel after a disaster (Grandien et al, 2005) and over-insurance when affective images of terrorism are made salient (Hsee and Kunreuther, 2000), as well as the impact of those feelings on everyday decisions, could be mitigated by simple reminders of the low probability of the event. However, rather than simply stating that the event is of low probability (experience by description; Hertwig et al, 2004), fluency manipulations allow individuals to experience (through meta-cognitive feelings) that the event is unlikely. Such manipulations may prove to be more effective than traditional means of providing debiasing information (Schwarz et al, 2007). Although beyond the scope of this chapter, future research could further address this issue by contrasting debiasing techniques that rely on description against techniques relying on experiential information. However, the finding that experienced feelings were relatively unaffected by the fluency manipulations suggests that the potential impact of affect may persist over time. The implication of this finding is that debiasing strategies would need to be used repeatedly for each new judgement for the duration of the mood.

Another force counteracting the effects of fluency is motivated information processing. Rothman and Schwarz (1998) found that fluency effects could be reversed when participants were motivated to think about an issue carefully. It is thus possible that strategies relying on low fluency to debias affect-laden risk perception could backfire and individuals still would exhibit biased judgements similar to that of individuals not using these strategies.

Overall, this research suggests that major environmental events may send psychological ripples globally, with the consequence that individuals and societies remote from the actual disaster may change their everyday decision behaviour. The findings reported here may be used to better understand public risk perception and decision behaviour in the aftermath of natural disasters. Further, the present research is a first step towards developing means to counteract the sometimes negative impact of feelings on judgements.

Acknowledgements

The research reported in this chapter was supported by the National Science Foundation; contract/grant numbers: SES-0517770; SES-0526020; SES-0339204; SES-0241313. We thank Gisela Böhm, Wibecke Brun, Jon Baron, Rolf

Reber and three anonymous reviewers for helpful comments on an earlier version of this manuscript.

Notes

1   Affective responses can occur rapidly and automatically, and may be elicited by stimulus properties, physical stimulation, perception of one's immediate environment, thoughts and memories, or proprioceptive cues (Schwarz and Clore, 2007). Mood, one form of affect, is a relatively stable and mild affective state that does not have a specific focal object (Morris, 1999), whereas emotions, another form of affect, are more intense and are of shorter duration. Incidental affect is an affective state, such as a mood state, brought about by environmental or intrinsic stimulation. Integral affect, on the other hand, is elicited by perceiving the target or a mental representation of the target.

2   Pretesting showed that this procedure in general heightened negative feelings such as sadness, depression and anxiety, and no specific emotion was more salient.

3   Analyses with either the valence mood index or the composite specific emotion index as mediating variables yielded comparable results to the well-being ratings. Subjective well-being had strong correlates with these two indices ($r = 0.71$ and 0.68, respectively, $p < .01$).

4   The ease-of-thought manipulation was only used in the tsunami-remind conditions since our hypothesis pertains to the debiasing effect of this manipulation in this experimental condition.

5   Mood and discrete emotion scales were, however, not included in this study. We chose to only include well-being as a measure of affect since both pre-studies and Study 1 consistently showed that negative affect ratings discriminated between the two conditions and, further, that these ratings co-varied with well-being ratings (see note 3).

Part II

Culture, Cognition and Risk

Chapter 9

Gender, Race and Perceived Risk:
The 'White-Male' Effect

Melissa L. Finucane, Paul Slovic, C. K. Mertz,
*James Flynn and Terre Satterfield**

Introduction

Risks tend to be judged as lower by men than by women (see, for example, Brody, 1984; Steger and Witt, 1989; Gwartney-Gibbs and Lach, 1991; Gutteling and Wiegman, 1993; Stern et al, 1993; Flynn et al, 1994). However, progress has been slow in explaining gender differences in perceived risk, and few studies have examined how differences are related to other characteristics of individuals, such as race. Flynn et al (1994) suggest that the role of gender or race in perceived risk may relate to sociopolitical factors. The main aim of this chapter is to examine how gender and race are related to a range of sociopolitical factors thought to influence risk perceptions. The study reported here was designed to oversample minority populations and address a range of sociopolitical issues. Data suggest that general attitudes toward the world and its social organization (which we shall refer to as worldviews and trust) and stigma are different for white males compared with other groups and that this effect is more complex than previously indicated by Flynn et al. We also note that gender and race are politically sensitive issues, and raising them in public discussions about risks (where there is often much at stake) can be emotionally intense and difficult. Therefore, a second aim of this chapter is to provide data about how people of different genders and races perceive risks.

Traditionally, one explanation for differences in risk perceptions is based on an assumption of differences in rationality and education. According to the

---
*   Reprinted from Finucane, M. L., Slovic, P., Mertz, C. K., Flynn, J. and Satterfield,
     T. A. (2000b) 'Gender, race, and perceived risk: The "white male" effect', *Health,
     Risk, & Society*, vol 2, no 2, pp159–172.

'irrationality' perspective, risk perceptions that deviate from estimates of fatality rates or other 'objective' indices are thought to arise from a lack of understanding of complex scientific and technical information (see Cohen, 1983; Cross, 1998). Some risk regulators and health risk communicators seem to believe that arming people with more information should reduce their scientific illiteracy and improve their decision making. That is, risk perceptions would be more accurate if people used more complete information about product or technology attributes (Bettman et al, 1987). Others seem to believe that if people just listened to the facts, they would reach the same conclusions as experts (Wandersman and Hallman, 1993). However, extensive efforts to educate the public about risks and risk assessment, such as advertisement campaigns for nuclear power, have failed to move public opinion to coincide with the experts. When measured by expert views, the public overestimates some risks and underestimates others (Adler and Pittle, 1984; see also Svenson et al, 1985). Furthermore, addressing risk controversies with technical solutions may contribute to conflict (Kunreuther and Slovic, 1996).

Research on gender differences suggests that discrepancies in risk perceptions of men and women may not reflect differences in rationality or education (Gardner and Gould, 1989). For instance, Barke et al (1997) showed risk perception differences between men and women scientists. Thus, men and women with considerable technical understanding of risk and knowledge of risk assessment procedures still differ in their risk perceptions. Similar data were reported by Slovic et al (1997a), who found that among members of the British Toxicology Society, females were far more likely than males to judge societal risks as moderate or high (see also Kraus et al, 1992; Slovic et al, 1995). Furthermore, biased risk judgements have been demonstrated within expert populations, suggesting even the most highly educated are influenced by the specific context of risk estimation questions. For example, McNeil et al (1982) showed that framing outcomes in terms of the probability of survival rather than the probability of death affected physicians' preferences for different lung cancer treatments, despite the survival and death probabilities being objectively equivalent.

Another common explanation for gender differences in risk perceptions is based on biological differences. However, recent research (for example, Flynn et al, 1994; and see also Slovic, 1997) has reduced the salience of a purely biological approach. Flynn, Slovic and colleagues found that: (i) nonwhite males and females are more similar in their perceptions of risk than are white males and females; and (ii) white males are different from everyone else in their perceptions and attitudes toward risk. Biological explanations imply that the differences between men's and women's risk perceptions would transcend racial boundaries.

In the study by Flynn et al (1994), 1512 Americans were asked, for each of 25 hazard items, to indicate whether the hazard posed (1) little or no risk, (2) slight risk, (3) moderate risk, or (4) high risk to society. Results showed that the percentage of high-risk responses was greater for women than men on every item. Similar analyses showed that the percentage of high-risk responses was greater among people of colour than among white respondents for every item studied. The most

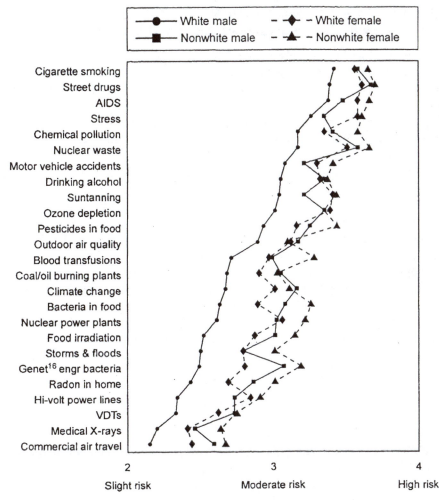

Figure 9.1 *Mean risk-perception ratings by race and gender*

Source: Flynn et al (1994), reprinted with permission

striking result, however, is shown in Figure 9.1, which presents the mean risk ratings separately for white males, white females, nonwhite males and nonwhite females. For all 25 hazards, white males' risk perception ratings were consistently much lower than the means of the other three groups.

This 'white-male' effect seemed to be caused by about 30 per cent of the white male sample that judged risks to be extremely low. When these low-risk white males (LRWM) were compared with the rest of the respondents, they were found to be better educated, had higher household incomes, and were politically more conservative. They also held very different attitudes, characterized by trust in institutions and authorities and by anti-egalitarianism, including disinclination toward giving decision-making power to citizens in areas of risk management.

The role of sociopolitical factors:
People vary in their worldviews, trust and control

The results described above led to the hypothesis that differences in worldviews, trust, control and other sociopolitical factors could be key determiners of gender and race differences in risk judgements and that risk perceptions may reflect deep-seated values about technology and its impact on society (Barke et al, 1997). White males may perceive less risk than others because they are more involved in creating, managing, controlling and benefiting from technology. Women and nonwhite men may perceive greater risk because they tend to be more vulnerable, have less control, and benefit less. Indeed, some research suggests that risk perceptions are related to individuals' levels of decision power (for example, whether they have high or low ability to influence decisions about the use of hazards such as liquefied petroleum gas) and their interest in a hazard (for example, direct, indirect or adversarial) (see, for example, Kuyper and Vlek, 1984; Baird, 1986; Bord and O'Connor, 1997).

Understanding how sociopolitical factors differ by gender and race is important because it would help explain why attempts to impose the elite view of the world have often failed to improve public acceptance of risks. In the present research we expected to find that white males differ from others in that they have lower risk perceptions across a range of hazards and tend to endorse hierarchical and anti-egalitarian views.

Method

This chapter reports data collected as part of a national telephone survey designed to test hypotheses about risk perceptions over a range of hazards. The survey contained questions about worldviews, trust and a range of demographic variables. Also included were questions designed to assess the respondent's recognition of potential adverse effects from risk-induced stigmatization of places and products associated with transport of chemical and radioactive wastes (see, for example, Gregory et al, 1995).

Procedure

A stratified random sample of household members over 18 years of age in the United States was surveyed by telephone from 27 September 1997 through to 3 February 1998. A total of 1204 completed interviews were obtained with an overall response rate of 46.8 per cent. Interviewing was conducted within a sample of US households and three racial/ethnic groups (African-American, Hispanic and Asian) were oversampled to permit reliable analyses of differences among these minorities. Race and ethnicity were combined in one question for the survey: 'What is your race or ethnic background? Do you consider yourself White, Hispanic, Black, Asian, American Indian, multiracial or multiethnic, or other?' This procedure relies on self-definition, which as Cooper (1994) points

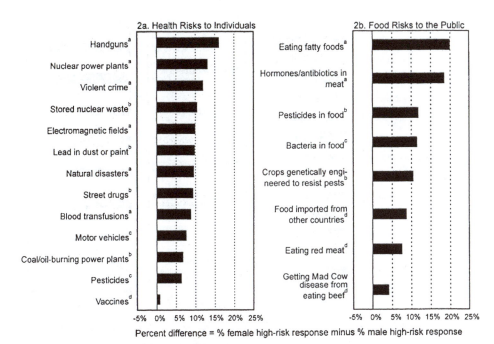

Figure 9.2 *Percentage difference in high-risk responses of males and females for (a) perceived health risks to individuals (you and your family) and (b) perceived food risks to the American public*

ª Significant at *p* < .001 by chi-square tests. ᵇ Significant at *p* < .05 by chi-square tests.
c Significant at *p* < .01 by chi-square tests. ᵈ Not significant by chi-square tests.
Source: 1997 National Risk Survey, N = 859, data weighted for race and gender

out is the 'only legal basis for racial classification' in the United States. The final survey database contains responses for 672 white Caucasians, 217 African-Americans, 180 Hispanics, 101 Asians and 34 respondents of Native American, multiracial/ethnic, or other origin. Interviews were conducted in English and Spanish. The mean age was 43.5 years and 45 per cent were males and 55 per cent were females. The average interview length was approximately 35 minutes. Data displays that include both race and gender characteristics are unweighted. All other uses of the data are weighted to the US census estimates of the 1997 US population in terms of race and gender, resulting in a weighted sample size of 859 respondents. The data are weighted so that individual ethnic/racial groups within the nonwhite group will be representative of the US nonwhite population.

Survey design

The survey contained questions on a wide variety of environmental and health hazards. Only the items relevant to this chapter are described here.

All respondents were asked to consider health and safety risks 'to you and your family' and to indicate whether there is almost no risk, slight risk, moderate

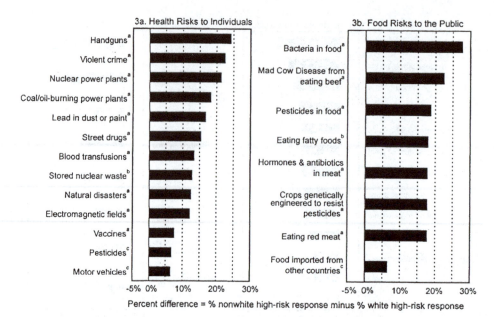

Figure 9.3 *Percentage difference in high-risk responses of whites and nonwhites for (a) perceived health risks to individuals (you and your family) and (b) perceived food risks to the American public*

[a] Significant at $p < .001$ by chi-square tests. [b] Significant at $p < .01$ by chi-square tests.
[c] Not significant by chi-square tests.
Source: 1997 National Risk Survey, $N = 859$, data weighted for race and gender

risk or high risk from each of 13 hazardous activities and technologies (for example, blood transfusions, motor vehicles, nuclear power plants, vaccines). We shall refer to these data as perceived risk to individuals, in contrast to the next series of questions in which all respondents were asked to indicate (on the same four-category scale) the level of health and safety risks from 19 hazards for 'the American public as a whole' (including most of the 13 hazards for which perceptions of risk to individuals and their families were elicited). A general risk perception index was calculated for each respondent by averaging ratings of risk to the public across the 19 hazards.

An additional eight items specifically about food hazards (for example, bacteria in food, hormones and antibiotics in meat, eating fatty foods) were rated for their risks to the public on the four-category scale described above.

Finally, all respondents were asked a series of questions regarding the effects of stigma, worldviews, trust and demographics (including gender and race).

Results

Risk perceptions

Gender differences
We found differences in the high-risk responses of males and females (see Figure 9.2a) with the percentage of high-risk responses greater for females on every item. A similar pattern was found for ratings of health risks to the American public, and ratings of the public risks of food hazards (see Figure 9.2b).

Racial differences
Likewise, examining the differences between the percentages of whites and nonwhites who rate a hazard as a 'high risk' to individuals, the percentage of high-risk responses was greater for nonwhites on every item (see Figure 9.3a). A similar pattern was found for ratings of health risks to the American public, and ratings of the public risks of food hazards (see Figure 9.3b).

The white-male effect
Examining the differences between the percentages of white males and the rest of the sample who rated hazards as a 'high risk' to individuals and to the public, we

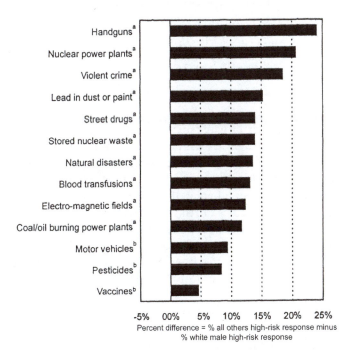

Figure 9.4 *Percentage difference in high-risk responses of white males and others: Perceived health risks to individuals (you and your family)*

[a] Significant at $p < .001$ by chi-square tests. [b] Significant at $p < .01$ by chi-square tests.
Source: 1997 National Risk Survey, N = 859, data weighted for race and gender

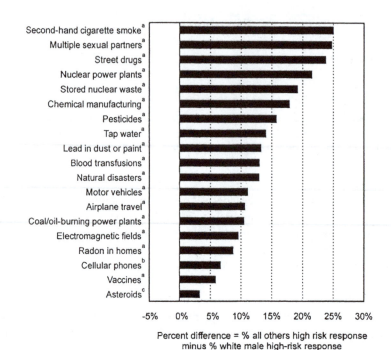

Figure 9.5 *Percentage difference in high-risk responses of white males and others: perceived health risks to American public*

ª Significant at $p < .001$ by chi-square tests. ᵇ Significant at $p < .01$ by chi-square tests.
ᶜ Significant at $p < .05$ by chi-square tests.
Source: 1997 National Risk Survey, $N = 859$, data weighted for race and gender

found high-risk responses were lower for white males on every item (see Figures 9.4 and 9.5). That is, white males were always less likely to rate a hazard as posing a 'high risk.' This was particularly true for handguns, nuclear power plants, second-hand cigarette smoke, multiple sexual partners and street drugs.

Similarly, white males differed from others in their ratings of perceived risks to individuals and the public. Mean ratings of risks to individuals were lower for white males than for white females, nonwhite males and nonwhite females (see Figure 9.6a). A similar pattern was found when ratings of risks to individuals were considered separately for males and females in each racial group (see Figure 9.6b), although the Asian males scored lower (2.68) than white males (2.80) in rating the risks of motor vehicles.

The mean ratings of risks to the American public showed that white males differed from white females, nonwhite males and nonwhite females (see Figure 9.7a). Nonwhite females show the highest risk estimates for several hazards (for example, lead in dust or paint, blood transfusions). When perceived public risk ratings are considered separately for males and females in each racial group (see Figure 9.7b), Asian males show similar or lower perceptions of public risks than white males for several hazards (for example, motor vehicles, tap water, vaccines,

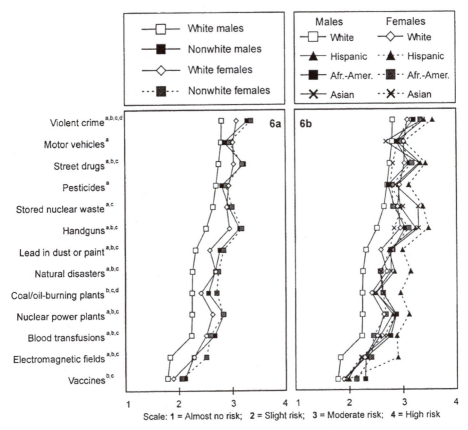

Figure 9.6 *Mean ratings of perceived risks to individuals and their families for*
(a) white and nonwhite males and females, and
(b) white, Hispanic, African-American and Asian males and females

For 6a, Turkey post-hoc paired comparisons showed significant differences between: [a] White males and White females; [b] White males and Non-white females; [c] White males and Non-white males; [d] White females and Non-white females. The results of comparisons for 6b can be obtained upon request.

Note: Data in (a) are weighted for race and gender (N = 859); data in (b) are not weighted (N = 1170)

Source: 1997 National Risk Survey

cellular phones). Some hazards (for example, pesticides) display greater variance in risk ratings across the groups than others (for example, motor vehicles).

Perceptions of risk to the American public from food hazards showed that, compared with white females and nonwhite males and females, white males had lower mean ratings for all items (see Figure 9.8a). Nonwhite females again show the highest risk estimates for several items (for example, bacteria and pesticides in food). When ratings from males and females were considered separately for each racial group, the 'white-male' effect was less apparent. Asian males gave less risky ratings than white males did for several food hazards, such as imported food, eating red meat and hormones/antibiotics in meat (see Figure 9.8b).

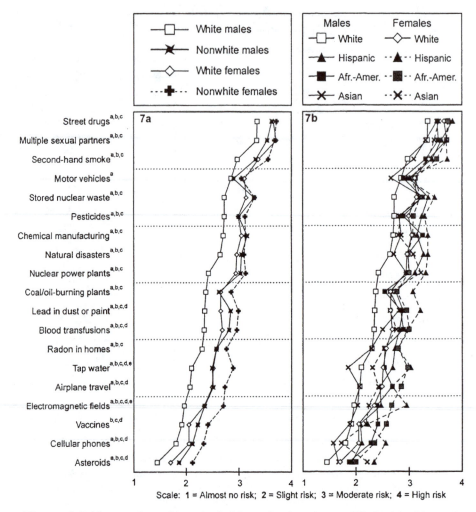

Figure 9.7 *Mean ratings of perceived risks to the American public for (a) white and nonwhite males and females, and (b) white, Hispanic, African-American and Asian males and females*

For 7a, Turkey post-hoc paired comparisons showed significant differences between:
[a] White males and White females; [b] White males and Non-white males; [c] White males and Non-white females; [d] White females and Non-white females; [e] Non-white males and Non-white females. The results of comparisons for 7b can be obtained upon request.

Note: Data in (a) are weighted for race and gender (N = 859); data in (b) are not weighted (N = 1170)

Source: 1997 National Risk Survey

Behavioural intentions

Gender and racial differences were also evident on items measuring behavioural intentions about risky activities and technologies (administered to only half of the sample; weighted $N = 426$). For example, responses to the statement 'If I were hospitalized and my physician recommended a blood transfusion, I would accept

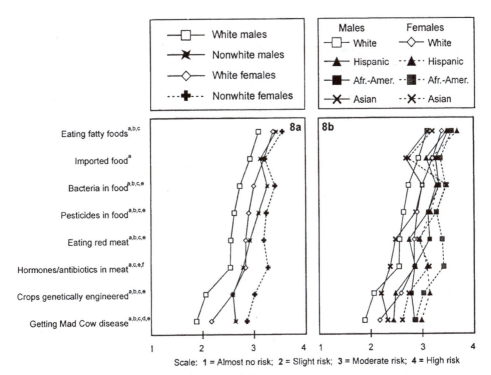

Figure 9.8 *Mean ratings of perceived risks to the American public for (a) white and nonwhite males and females, and (b) white, Hispanic, African-American and Asian males and females*

For 8a, Turkey post-hoc paired comparisons showed significant differences between:
[a] White males and White females; [b] White males and Non-white males; [c] White males and Non-white females; [d] White females and Non-white males; [e] White females and Non-white females; [f] Non-white males and Non-white females. The results of comparisons for 8b can be obtained upon request.

Note: Data in (a) are weighted for race and gender (*N* = 859); data in (b) are not weighted (*N* = 1170)

Source: 1997 National Risk Survey

blood from a blood bank' showed that a higher proportion of females than males disagreed or strongly disagreed that they would accept blood (44.3 per cent vs. 23.6 per cent, data weighted for race and gender, N = 426). Hispanic people disagreed or strongly disagreed more than whites (44.7 per cent for Hispanics vs. 30.5 per cent for whites); likewise African-American people disagreed or strongly disagreed more than whites (43.6 per cent for African-Americans vs. 30.5 per cent for whites; in these comparisons the data were weighted for gender only, N = 611). White males were less likely to disagree or strongly disagree than Asian females (23.0 per cent for white males vs. 42.9 per cent for Asian females) but more likely to disagree or strongly disagree than Asian males (17.6 per cent) (data unweighted). All differences were significant at $p < .05$ by chi-square tests, except for Asian males versus white males.

Sociopolitical factors

What differentiates white males from the rest of the sample? Turning to attitudes, we found that white males seemed to demonstrate different views from others on a range of questions about worldviews, trust, and potential for chemical and radioactive waste hazards to stigmatize places and products. (For the items below, all analyses used data weighted for race and gender to match the US population as a whole, $N = 859$. All differences are significant by chi-square tests at $p < .05$, with the exception of item (c) where $p = 0.05$.)

Worldviews

White males displayed more hierarchical and individualistic views and less fatalistic and egalitarian views. Fatalism is reflected in statement (a) below; hierarchical views by statements (b) and (c); egalitarianism by (d) and (e); individualistic views by (f) and (g). Specifically, when compared to all other respondents, white males were more likely to:

(a) disagree that 'I have very little control over risks to my health' (83.4 per cent vs. 76.3 per cent);

(b) disagree that 'I often feel discriminated against' (81.3 per cent vs. 67.6 per cent);

(c) agree that when a risk is very small, it is OK for society to impose that risk on individuals without their consent (20.8 per cent vs. 15.6 per cent);

(d) disagree that the world needs more equal distribution of wealth (40.1 per cent vs. 23.3 per cent);

(e) agree that we have gone too far in pushing equal rights (49.8 per cent vs. 37.5 per cent);

(f) agree that people with more ability should earn more (88.9 per cent vs. 81.6 per cent);

(g) disagree that the government should make rules about people's personal risk-taking activities (86.8 per cent vs. 74.6 per cent).

Trust

White males seemed more trusting of technological hazards and less trusting of government, possibly because they prefer to be in control of policy and decision making. They were more likely than the others to:

- disagree that people living near a nuclear power plant should be able to vote and to close the plant if they think it is not being run safely (34.3 per cent vs. 12.9 per cent); and

- disagree that the federal government can be trusted to properly manage the risks from technology (74.7 per cent vs. 67.8 per cent).

Stigma

White males were far less worried about adverse public responses from risk exposure to chemical and radioactive waste hazards. They were more likely than the others to:

- disagree that the selection of an existing highway for future transportation of nuclear and chemical waste would lower the value of nearby homes (40.5 per cent vs. 16.4 per cent); and
- disagree that farm products are less acceptable to the public when radioactive waste is transported past farms (59.9 per cent vs. 32.0 per cent).

Other social and demographic variables

Since gender and race are correlated with other variables such as age, income, education and political orientation, we conducted regression analyses to see if gender and race were still significant predictors of overall risk perceptions after these other variables were controlled statistically. The analyses showed that gender, race and 'white male' remained highly significant predictors of the hazard index, even when the other variables were controlled statistically.

Discussion

As expected, our survey revealed that men rate a wide range of hazards as lower in risk than do women. This result is consistent with gender differences found previously in many studies (for example, Brody, 1984; Steger and Witt, 1989; Gwartney-Gibbs and Lach, 1991; Gutteling and Wiegman, 1993; Stern et al, 1993; Flynn et al, 1994). Our survey also revealed that whites rate risks lower than do nonwhites. Nonwhite females often gave the highest risk ratings. The group with the consistently lowest risk perceptions across a range of hazards was white males, a result replicating the earlier research by Flynn et al (1994). A few exceptions were found: compared with white males, Asian males gave lower risk ratings to six items (motor vehicles, tap water, cellular phones, imported food, eating red meat and hormones/antibiotics in meat). Furthermore, we found sizeable differences between white males and other groups in sociopolitical attitudes. Compared with the rest of the sample, white males were more sympathetic with hierarchical, individualistic and anti-egalitarian views, more trusting of technology managers, less trusting of government and less sensitive to potential stigmatization of communities from hazards. These positions suggest greater confidence in experts and less confidence in public-dominated social processes.

Our data support the view that differences cannot be explained entirely from a biological perspective. Explanations based on biological factors would require men and women to show discrepancies in their risk perceptions regardless of race. Clearly, this is not the case, at least for the environmental and health hazards studied here. Sociopolitical explanations are made more salient by our finding that compared with others, white males seem to promote individual achievement, initiative and self-regulation, trust in experts and risk proponents, and intolerance of community-based decision and regulation processes. As a consequence, we speculate that the world seems safer and hazardous activities seem more beneficial to white males than to other groups. For people who place less weight on the importance of individual achievement and more weight on distributing wealth equitably and endorsing community-based regulation, many hazardous technologies and activities are viewed as posing great risks. Compared with white males, many females and nonwhite males tend to be in positions of less power and control, benefit less from many technologies and institutions, are more vulnerable to discrimination, and therefore see the world as more dangerous. Further investigation of the role of a broad array of sociopolitical factors in risk judgements is recommended to clarify gender and racial differences. It may be that the low-risk white males see different things at risk than do other citizens.

Although our data showed that white males stood apart from others, the data also revealed substantial heterogeneity in risk perceptions among the race and gender groups that comprised the 'other' category. That is, risk perceptions varied considerably across African-American, Asian and Hispanic males and females. The heterogeneity implies that risk perceptions depend importantly on the characteristics of the individuals facing the risk. Researchers should examine more closely the variation across individuals within these groups. Although resources did not permit finer analyses in the present study, Flynn et al (1994) found that about 30 per cent of their white males had extremely low risk perceptions. Their results suggest that race/gender groupings may be decomposed further into subgroups with particularly high or low risk perceptions.

Furthermore, while there is a tendency for gender and racial groups to align along social and political attitudes, it does not rule out the idea that sociopolitical attitudes also vary within groups. That is, perhaps some individuals are more prone than others to endorsing individualism or egalitarianism, regardless of gender or race. Some white males may be closer to typical Hispanic women in their views on the value of community-based regulation and equitable distribution of wealth. Some African-American women may be closer to typical white males in their endorsement of individual achievement and reward. Clearly, aligning particular socio-demographic groups with certain perspectives may overlook the possibility that there is variation across individuals regarding their sociopolitical attitudes and associated risk perceptions.

Viewing risk as a social construct dependent on characteristics of individuals raises important questions. What might be found in societies not dominated by white males? Are women bigger risk takers in matrilineal societies and are there some Asian or African countries where nonwhites perceive lower risk than do whites? Furthermore, even within societies seemingly dominated by the white male perspective, there seem to be some hazardous activities for which women are willing to take the greatest risks (such as smoking).

Can differences in worldviews, feelings of trust, and sensitivity to potential product and community stigmatization explain risk perception differences across cultures and sub-cultures?

Furthermore, given that we found risk perceptions varied more for some hazards (for example, tap water, genetically engineered crops) than for other hazards (for example, stored nuclear waste, eating fatty foods), the type of hazard typically examined in risk perception research should be considered. Our findings of lower risk ratings by Asian males than by white males on several items suggested an interaction between characteristics of the hazard being rated and of the individual doing the rating. It seems possible that we may have found white women to have the lowest risk perceptions if household rather than technical risks were studied, for instance.

Research on the heterogeneity of risk perceptions across various socio-cultural groups has important practical implications. Despite knowing very little about the risk perceptions and sociopolitical attitudes of minority groups, they are perhaps precisely the people who might be at greatest risk (and who might receive most benefit) from some activities or technologies. Without understanding the complex factors influencing perceptions, risk communicators and regulators cannot tailor their messages or policies appropriately to the target populations.

Overall, efforts to explain risk perception differences among people of different genders and races would be best addressed by incorporation of what we can learn about social roles, status differentiation, political values and concepts of fairness. Attempts to realign risk perceptions according to the white male view of the world are likely to be unsuccessful. We expect that risk controversies can be better avoided and/or resolved when discussions and negotiations include the full spectrum of interested and affected parties. Some may fear such an approach may be more expensive because of the transaction costs. However, the current stale-mates in managing numerous hazardous conditions from nuclear power to chemical contamination clean-ups show that social conflict has extremely high costs, economic and otherwise. Whether decision-sharing approaches that depend upon compromise and negotiation work as well or better than the current approaches is a question that can be answered with empirical research. Investigators should be careful, however, to pay close attention to the inevitability that just as risk perceptions are based on a wide range of value-laden judgements, views on how to define the economic and health benefits and costs will be disparate. Acknowledging the complexity of perspectives within an already diverse sample of US residents is the first step towards increasing the efficiency and effectiveness of social decision making in general, and risk management and communication in particular.

Acknowledgements

This research was supported by a grant from the Annenberg Public Policy Center and the Annenberg School for Communication of the University of Pennsylvania and by the National Science Foundation under Grant No. SBR-9631635. Our thanks to Kathleen Hall Jamieson of the Annenberg School for her support of this survey work, to Stephen Johnson and Professor Patricia Gwartney of the Oregon Survey Research Laboratory for assistance in design and administration of the survey reported here, and to Janet Douglas for her help with manuscript preparation.

Chapter 10

Discrimination, Vulnerability and Justice in the Face of Risk

*Terre Satterfield, C. K. Mertz and Paul Slovic**

Introduction

This chapter examines the American public's ideas about discrimination, vulnerability and (in)justice as they pertain to African-American, Hispanic, Asian and Anglo-American perspectives on health and environmental risks. It is rooted in studies of perceived health and environmental risks (Flynn et al, 1994; Slovic, 1987, 1999), but extends that work by recognizing the possible influence on perceptions of risk of (1) beliefs closely affiliated with the environmental justice thesis and (2) the subjective experience of discrimination, and economic and physical vulnerability.

Considerable attention has been granted of late to the relationship between gender, race, environmental values and environmental risks. Gender differences regarding the values, beliefs and attitudes affiliated with pro-environmental positions have been found in multiple studies (Stern et al, 1993; Davidson and Freudenburg, 1996; Bord and O'Connor, 1997). Kalof et al (2002) recently found significant differences in pro-environmental beliefs between whites (less pro) and Hispanics (more pro), and white males (less pro) and white females (more pro).

Studies of the effects of gender on perceived health and environmental risks have found that women are more risk-averse than men (Gutteling and Wiegman, 1993; Davidson and Freudenburg, 1996). A study by Flynn and colleagues (Flynn et al, 1994) found a 'white-male effect' wherein nonwhite Americans tended to report higher risk perceptions than did whites. The authors further

*   Reprinted from Satterfield, T. A., Mertz, C. K. and Slovic, P. (2004) 'Discrimination, vulnerability, and justice in the face of risk,' *Risk Analysis*, vol 24, no 1, pp115–129.

discovered that it is a subset of white males that tends to be different from every-one else in terms of its perceptions of risk. Across a set of 25 environmental health-risk items, white males consistently saw less risk than nonwhites (males and females) and white females. The perceptions of risk held by white females were very similar to those of nonwhites. Survey evidence from the Detroit metro-politan area reported by Mohai and Bryant (1998) also indicated that African-Americans were more concerned than whites about environmental risks, particularly in reference to the health and safety effects of pollution, and the environmental conditions of one's community. Jones (1998) similarly found greater concern, among African-Americans, for risks attributed to nuclear power and toxins. These demographic differences have been upheld in examinations of specific risk domains. For example, a recent study of outdoor air pollution found that differences in perceived risks were greatest for white men and nonwhite women and that differences between men and women were less frequent than between whites and nonwhites (Johnson, 2002).

Race and gender differences in reference to perceived risk have been attrib-uted to the reduced social and formal decision-making power held by women and minorities as compared with white men (Gutteling and Wiegman, 1993); to women's greater role as caregivers (Bord and O'Connor, 1997); to the greater likelihood of exposure to environmental harm facing members of minority groups (Mohai and Bryant, 1998); and to income, education and political orientation (Flynn et al, 1994). Interestingly, however, little work has been done on the relationship between support for the environmental justice thesis and risk percep-tion or the relationship between perceived vulnerability and perceived risk.

The environmental (in)justice thesis is that minority populations are dispro-portionately burdened by the health- and community-compromising by-products of industrialization. Early studies by the National Association for the Advancement of Colored People (NAACP) and Bullard (1990) found that technological hazards are more apt to be located in and less likely to be properly remediated in minority communities. Subsequently, the thesis has been exten-sively tested and refined as concerns the distribution of different contaminants (Beck, 1992, 1999), hazardous wastes, and the siting of noxious facilities, demon-strating the specific circumstances under which inequitable distribution, treatment and compensatory actions are evident (Sexton and Anderson, 1993; Zimmerman, 1993; Greenberg and Schneider, 1995; Graham et al, 1999). It is reasonable to assume that significant support for the environmental justice thesis will be found across survey respondents, given the burgeoning of the environ-mental justice movement and the accompanying (and trenchant) mobilizing claims that assert that law and regulation need to address widespread inequities in the distribution of environmental health risks (Greenberg, 1993; Szasz, 1994; Taylor, 2000; Lester et al, 2001). Further, belief statements that support or reject these justice propositions are easily tested and can, in turn, be examined in refer-ence to perceived risk.

Vulnerability to risk has been studied by geographers who are principally concerned with the political economy within which a community is nested and hence its vulnerability to famine, hunger or natural hazards and/or that community's ability to recover from such shocks, crises or stressors (Watts and Bohle, 1993). But only very few risk articles have posited substantive links between perceived vulnerability and perceived risk. In a review of the literature on gender and risk, Bord and O'Connor (1997) reference several studies that find that 'women consistently exhibit much stronger perceptions of vulnerability to illness and physical debilitation' (p832). The authors interpret white women's high-risk perceptions as an artefact of perceived vulnerability. A study by Kraus et al (1992) of toxicological knowledge and risk perceptions designated perceptions of vulnerability 'as a key factor mediating [toxicologists'] attitudes toward public fear of [chemicals]' (p226). Toxicologists who believe that humans are less vulnerable (than are animals) to the adverse effects of chemicals and who also disagree with the reliability of animal studies (i.e. see them as poor indicators of human response), believe that people are unnecessarily alarmed by small amounts of pesticides.

Vulnerability is covertly defined in these above studies as a generalized feeling of enhanced susceptibility to harm. The idea is akin to early social-psychological studies of discrimination that emphasized the action-paralysing effects of discrimination (Jones, 1998). It is thus plausible to consider discrimination as a dimension of vulnerability, but a fuller definition of vulnerability should recognize that vulnerability can be expressed across multiple dimensions. The operational definition of vulnerability developed herein thus includes ideas about perceived personal fragility, perceived economic insecurity and/or physical vulnerability (e.g. such as that affiliated with poor health or health care).

Research questions

Concern with demographic as well as justice- and vulnerability-driven responses to risk raises four core research questions to which this chapter turns. First, and fundamental, is the 'concern gap' posited by Mohai and Bryant (1998) and Jones (1998) or the 'white-male effect' found by Flynn et al (1994) upheld by a representative national sample and by oversampling in minority communities to ensure a robust representation of African-American and Hispanic populations?

Specifically, are white males less concerned about health and environmental safety problems, particularly those attributed to toxins, nuclear hazards and coal and oil facilities, as compared with all other groups (nonwhite men, white and nonwhite women)? Second, to what extent does an experience of discrimination, and vulnerability more broadly, drive that concern/effect? Third, to what extent do beliefs about environmental justice and/or a stated sociopolitical awareness of environmental injustices also explain the perception of risk? Fourth, are white and nonwhite differences in perceived risk erased or significantly reduced when expressions of vulnerability and injustice are accounted for? And, are these new variables more important than education or income?

Methods

The data presented herein were collected as part of a national telephone survey designed to examine topics ranging from perceived risks, worldviews, trust, environmental values, discrimination, vulnerability and justice. These question sets are detailed more fully in the appropriate results sections. The survey design included an oversampling of nonwhite groups to provide a more reliable and robust data set from which to allow further examination of the relationship between risk, race and gender. Only those portions of the survey data relevant to this chapter are discussed.

Administration of the survey

A stratified random sample of household members over 18 years of age in the United States was surveyed by telephone from 27 September 1997 through to 3 February 1998. The objective was to obtain a general population sample plus three oversamples of Hispanic, African-American and Asian census tracts. Random digit dialling was used. All American households with telephones had an equal chance of being selected. For the oversamples, numbers were randomly generated using telephone exchanges in census tracts with incidences of over 75 per cent for the Asian population and over 80 per cent for the Hispanic and black populations. This oversample covered 12.7 per cent of the Hispanic population, 12.6 per cent of the black population, and 14.0 per cent of the Asian population of the United States. For the Asian group, additional pieces of sample were added from Genesys Sampling System, Inc. The Genesys sample was randomly generated by last name from all American telephone exchanges and had a purported incidence of 90 per cent.

A total of 1204 completed interviews were obtained, for an overall response rate of 46.8 per cent. The response rates ranged from 32.6 per cent for the Asian oversample to 54.4 per cent for the Hispanic oversample. The mean age was 43.5, with 45.0 per cent males and 55.5 per cent females. The average interview length was approximately 35 minutes. Interviewing resulted in a sample of 672 white Caucasians, 180 Hispanics, 217 African-Americans, 101 Asians, 22 American-Indian and multiracial persons, and 12 who defined themselves as 'other.' As the demographic characteristics of the 12 others were unknown, they were omitted from our analyses, resulting in a sample of 1192. When necessary for the analysis, the African-American, Hispanic, Asian, American-Indian and multiracial groups were collapsed as an aggregate 'nonwhite' male or female group. This resulted in 289 white males, 383 white females, 245 nonwhite males and 275 nonwhite females. However, when generalizing to the US population as a whole, weighting is necessary due to the oversampling of nonwhites. The general and oversamples were weighted to the 1997 US population as a whole in terms of race and gender, resulting in a weighted sample of 861 respondents.

Results

Risk ratings – demographically defined

Studies of perceived risk have shown that the qualities of a hazard or risk object strongly influence the perception of risk. In particular, it has been established that risks the public views as dreaded, likely to be fatal, involuntarily or unfairly imposed, beyond any one individual's control, or generated by mistrusted institutions tend to evoke strong risk-averse responses (Slovic, 1987, 1992; Slovic et al, 1979).

In this study, respondents rated 19 different sources of risk. Most of the risk items are the product of technological hazards (e.g. pesticides, coal- and oil-burning plants, stored nuclear waste, lead in paint or dust); a few items are affiliated with health-risky behaviours (multiple sex partners, street drugs); others are the product of natural phenomena (asteroids, natural disasters); a few final risk items are specific to consumer goods (motor vehicles, cellular phones). Respondents were asked to rate each risk object as posing almost no risk, a slight risk, a moderate risk, or a high risk to the American public.[1] These response categories were coded 1 to 4, respectively. An overall risk-perception index was created by computing an average score across the 19 individual risk items for each respondent. The Cronbach alpha for this index is 0.90, which indicates high reliability.

Mean risk ratings by race, ethnicity (for Hispanic respondents) and gender are represented in Figure 10.1.[2] The highest mean risk scores were assigned by respondents to 'street drugs' and 'multiple sexual partners.' The lowest risk scores were assigned to vaccines, cellular phones and asteroids.

In Figure 10.1, all male and female respondents identifying themselves as African-American, Hispanic, Asian, Native-American or multiracial are represented, respectively, as nonwhite males and nonwhite females. The figure shows that white males offer uniformly lower risk ratings as compared with the ratings offered by nonwhite females, nonwhite males and white females. This pattern is consistent across 18 of the 19 possible hazards. There existed two deviations from this general pattern. First, for 'motor vehicles,' nonwhite and white males offer similar and slightly lower risk ratings as compared with those offered by white and nonwhite females. Second, nonwhite females offer higher risk ratings than do most other groups. Using a Tukey post hoc significance test, the risk ratings of nonwhite females are higher than (and significantly different from) those offered by white males on all 19 items; they differ significantly from white females on 11 risk items and from nonwhite males on 10 items.[3] In this sense, 'white males' are not the only 'atypical' group, as to a lesser degree nonwhite females exhibit an atypical pattern.

It is admittedly reductionist to categorize African-American, Hispanic, Asian, Native-American and multiracial men and women as, simply, nonwhite (males and females). However, for our purposes here, a fuller accounting of race- and gender-specific responses indicates no consistent pattern of between-group

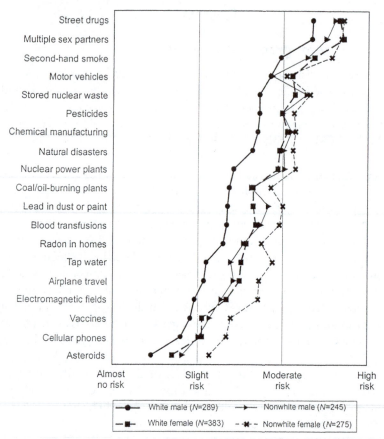

Figure 10.1 *Perceived risks to American public: Means by race and gender – white vs. nonwhite*

Note: 'Nonwhite' includes Hispanic, African-American, Asian, Native-American and multiracial groups

Source: 1997 National Risk Survey

differences that are race or race-and-gender specific. No single (male or female) or combined (male and female) group of African-American, Hispanic or Asian respondents emerges as consistently and comparatively risk-averse or risk-tolerant. When comparing, however, within-group differences between men and women (African-American men as compared with African-American women, etc.), women in the respective nonwhite groups are somewhat more likely to provide higher risk ratings. African-American and Hispanic females' mean risk ratings are higher than those offered by corresponding males on 13 of 19 rated hazards. An exception is the group of Asian women who provided higher ratings on only 5 of the 19 posed risks.

These findings confirm earlier results summarized as the 'white-male effect' that found that white men have substantially lower mean responses to hazards than do any other male or female group (Flynn et al, 1994; Finucane et al,

2000b). As with these earlier studies (Flynn et al, 1994; Finucane et al, 2000b), we too found that a subset of white males offered the lowest risk ratings. They tended, in turn, to drive down the overall risk ratings for white men. This subset of white males was arrived at by starting with the lowest-scoring white male on the risk perception index and moving up the distribution, adding white males until the mean score on the index for the remaining white males matched the mean score for all other persons (all females and all nonwhite males) in the sample. This resulted in 48 per cent of the white males in the sample remaining in the low risk-perception white male subgroup. This subset of white men was found to perceive the benefits from science, technology and industry as outweighing the risks and to be disinclined toward citizen-driven decision making (i.e. they were more author-itarian than egalitarian in outlook). They were also more likely to have accessed higher levels of education, to be politically conservative, and/or to have higher average incomes than did other respondents.[4] Using the same data set recorded here, Finucane et al (2000b) found equally that white males were more likely to be individualistic and fatalistic (vs. egalitarian) in their worldview and were less likely than all others to be bothered by the stigmatizing effects of risk events (e.g. the stigmatizing of properties or businesses because of their proximity to transporta-tion routes used for the shipping of nuclear wastes to storage sites).[5]

The 'white-male effect,' confirmed herein with a broader sampling and oversampling of minority populations, thus counters the common misperception that minority groups, in particular African-Americans, are unconcerned about the environment (Jones et al, 1984). Specifically, this white-male effect is most clearly upheld when considering cross-group perceptions of health and environmental hazards, particularly toxins and nuclear hazards, as was predicted by Mohai and Bryant (1998) and Jones (1998).

Risk as a sociopolitical expression

Discrimination and vulnerability

If we begin with the knowledge that (1) the perceptions of health and environ-mental risks held by African-Americans are similar to most other nonwhite male and all female groups, and (2) that a substantial percentage of white males see the world as much less risky than does everyone else, then some effort must be taken to explain these differences. Flynn et al (1994) found that when they controlled for such demographic variables as age, education and income as well as variables such as perceived importance of technology, gender and race remained highly significant predictors of the risk. This led them to conclude that sociopolitical (not demographic) variables probably explained the influence of gender and race on risk perceptions. White males, they surmised, may see less risk in the world because they in fact create, manage, control and benefit from the major technolo-gies and activities affiliated with many of the above environmental risks. Women and nonwhite men might see the world as more dangerous because in many cases they have less power and control over what happens in their communities and their lives. As noted earlier, Bord and O'Connor (1997) interpret white women's high risk perceptions as an artefact of perceived vulnerability.

To examine in greater detail the vulnerability and sociopolitical underpinnings of this race and gender effect on perceived risk, we first looked at the relationship between respondents' risk ratings and their subjective expressions of discrimination and vulnerability. Self-reports of discrimination as well as multiple expressions of vulnerability were operationalized using a six-item question set.[6] These survey items are as follows:

1   I often feel discriminated against.
2   My whole world feels like it's falling apart.
3   People like me aren't benefiting from the growth of the economy.
4   I have very little control over risks to my health.
5   Would you rate your personal health as excellent, good, fair or poor?
6   How would you rate the quality of medical care that is available to you?

Together these items identify respondents who, regardless of race, 'feel discriminated against.' More broadly, the question set identifies those who feel they have poor control over their lives and feel they do not benefit from economic opportunities or medical services available to other persons. The response-frequency distributions for the six vulnerability questions are represented in Table 10.1.

We expected and did find that white respondents, male and female, differed considerably from nonwhite respondents in their agreement with the discrimination/vulnerability items. A comparison across respondent groups reveals that the vast majority of white males (81.3 per cent) and females (78.3 per cent) do not 'feel discriminated against' whereas about one-half of nonwhite men (49.4 per cent) and women (50.6 per cent) report frequent ('often') feelings of discrimination. A small majority of nonwhite females (54.6 per cent) report that 'people like me aren't benefiting from the economy' whereas only a small minority of white males (29.4 per cent) agree with the same statement. White females and nonwhite males fall somewhere in between at 41.3 per cent and 43.7 per cent disagreement, respectively. The majority of respondents disagree with or rate as good/excellent the other index items (about the world falling apart and health status), although the percentage disagreement is higher for white men than for all other respondent groups on the health status question.

A social vulnerability score for each respondent was created by calculating the mean score across the six items. Items were scored so that a high score on this index indicated high social vulnerability. Individual item responses were coded 1 (*strongly disagree/excellent*) to 4 (*strongly agree/poor*). The scale reliability was examined by calculating the Cronbach alpha for the six items, which was 0.65. Although the coefficient alpha is lower than desirable, factor analysis found all six items loaded on one factor, thus we felt the index adequate to proceed with analyses (DeVellis, 1991). Comparison of the aggregate mean scores for the vulnerability index as a whole is instructive. At the low end, white males' mean vulnerability score is 1.96; at the high end, nonwhite females' score is 2.30. The difference between white males and all other groups is significant as is the differ-

Table 10.1 *Distributions for items comprising the vulnerability index*

Items	White males (%)	White females (%)	Nonwhite males (%)	Nonwhite females (%)
I often feel discriminated against.[*]				
Strongly agree/agree	18.0	20.9	49.4	50.6
Strongly disagree/disagree	81.3	78.3	49.8	48.0
My whole world feels like it is falling apart.[*]				
Strongly agree/agree	7.3	12.3	23.3	21.8
Strongly disagree/disagree	92.4	87.5	75.5	77.8
People like me aren't benefiting from the growth of the economy.[*]				
Strongly agree/agree	29.4	41.3	43.7	54.6
Strongly disagree/disagree	69.2	56.7	53.9	43.3
I have very little control over risks to my health.[*]				
Strongly agree/agree	16.3	19.1	31.4	29.5
Strongly disagree/disagree	83.4	80.7	67.4	69.5
Would you rate your personal health as excellent, good, fair, or poor?[**]				
Excellent/good	82.7	84.6	76.7	76.0
Fair/poor	17.0	15.4	23.3	24.0
How would you rate the quality of medical care that is available to you and your family?[*]				
Excellent/good	81.3	78.6	66.9	66.2
Fair/poor	18.7	20.6	32.7	33.8
Social vulnerability index mean[***]	1.96	2.05	2.24	2.30
N	289	383	245	275

Note: Percentages might not add to 100 as DK and NA are not shown *Significant at $p < .0001$ by chi-square test.
** Significant at $p < .01$ by chi-square test.
*** Social vulnerability index significance differences: white males with all other groups, white females with all other groups (Tukey, $p < .05$).
Source: 1997 National Risk Survey

ence between white females and all other groups. (The implications of these indices for risk scores are elaborated on pp153–155.)

Discrimination and risk

One item – 'I often feel discriminated against' – is particularly instructive. The pattern of response is representative of the other vulnerability items. Mean scores for the 19 risk items were compared with those for the respondents who agreed vs. disagreed with this 'discrimination' statement. Figure 10.2 indicates that those who agree with the statement 'I often feel discriminated against' rate the risks posed by all 19 hazards as higher than do those who disagreed. Moreover, the largest differentiations in risk scores were specific to environmental health

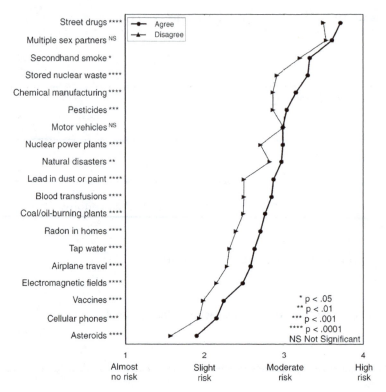

Figure 10.2 *Risk perception means by response to 'I often feel discriminated against'*

Source: 1997 National Risk Survey

hazards: stored nuclear waste, chemical manufacturing, lead in paint and dust, coal/oil-burning plants, radon in homes, and electromagnetic fields. Stored nuclear waste is the technological hazard most dreaded in many risk studies (Slovic, 1987). The presence of lead has been linked to developmental disabilities in children (Bellinger et al, 1987; Agency for Toxic Substances and Disease Registry (ATSDR), 2007; Needleman et al, 1990). Lead in dust and plumbing infrastructure is also prevalent in the physically decaying urban neighbourhoods, some of which house a disproportionately large number of poor and minority populations. Differences in perceived risk were not, however, pronounced for acts of God (natural disasters with the exception of asteroids). Differences were also minimal for risk items that are extremely familiar (motor vehicles) and for those risks over which individuals have personal control (multiple sexual partners, secondhand smoke).

Environmental justice and risk

Vulnerability and discrimination are characterized by the above index items as (largely) subjective expressions.[7] This is logical to the extent that people living in contaminated African-American communities have linked the experience of toxic exposure to the experience of discrimination (Satterfield et al, 2001). But it is also the case that judgements about risk develop with substantial reference to one's social, and not solely subjective, context. Increasingly, in minority communities attentive to environmental concerns, that social context is characterized by the framing of hazards and toxins as risks that are unjustly imposed on minority communities. That is, many risk problems are framed by minorities as questions of justice and fairness and not as technical, scientific or economic problems per se (Vaughan, 1995, p172). Further, several authors have aptly identified the environmental justice movement as a master ideological frame whereby activists are compellingly mobilized to make 'causal attributions or develop vocabularies of motive' that interpret toxic exposure as a persistent expression of societal racism (Capek, 1993; Taylor, 2000, pp514–515).

For these reasons, the language of environmental justice offered a viable source for developing survey questions that captured socially oriented explanations or judgements about the equity of risk distributions in public life. We therefore developed a question set that sought to identify respondents who support the environmental justice hypothesis and believe that hazardous facilities ought not be sited in minority communities. These environmental justice items are as follows:

- I think hazardous facilities are more common in minority communities.
- For economic reasons, minority communities are forced to accept more industrial pollution than non-minority communities.
- Minority communities lack the political clout to stop hazardous facilities from being located near them.
- The government should restrict the placing of hazardous facilities in minority communities.

Table 10.2 discloses the frequency distributions for the question items across the four race- and gender-specified respondent groups. Once again there is considerable variation between the judgements offered by white males as compared with nonwhite male and female respondents. On the first three questions, the opinion of white men is relatively close to that of white women; the point spread between these two groups does not exceed five percentage points on any of these three items. On the fourth question, slightly more white women (71.8 per cent) than white men (63.7 per cent) agree that 'the government should restrict the placing of hazardous facilities in minority communities.' Conversely, the response variation for white males as compared with nonwhite females is substantial. Approximately 19 per cent to 20 per cent more nonwhite females and nonwhite males agree that 'minority communities lack the political clout to stop hazardous facilities from being located near them,' as compared with white males and females. Similarly, as many as 27.2 per cent more nonwhite women and 17 per cent more nonwhite men agree that 'the government should restrict the siting of hazardous facilities in minority communities' as compared with white males. Also noteworthy is the finding that nonwhite males and nonwhite females do not hold

Table 10.2 *Distributions for items comprising the environmental justice index*

Items	White males (%)	White females (%)	Nonwhite males (%)	Nonwhite females (%)
I think hazardous facilities are more common in minority communities.[*]				
Strongly agree/agree	50.5	47.0	66.5	71.6
Strongly disagree/disagree	43.6	46.0	29.8	24.7
For economic reasons, minority communities are forced to accept more industrial pollution than non-minority communities.[*]				
Strongly agree/agree	54.0	57.2	76.3	76.4
Strongly disagree/disagree	41.2	37.9	21.6	20.0
Minority communities lack the political clout to stop hazardous facilities from being located near them.[*]				
Strongly agree/agree	56.4	56.1	76.3	75.3
Strongly disagree/disagree	42.2	39.7	22.0	21.8
The government should restrict the placing of hazardous facilities in minority communities.[*]				
Strongly agree/agree	63.7	71.8	80.8	90.9
Strongly disagree/disagree	30.5	21.2	17.6	8.0
Environmental justice index mean[**] 2.58		2.64	2.88	2.96
N	289	383	245	275

Note: Percentages might not add to 100 as DK and NA are not shown.

* Significant at $p < .0001$ by chi-square test.

** Environmental justice index significance differences: white males with nonwhite males and nonwhite females, white females with nonwhite males and nonwhite females (Tukey, $p < .05$).

Source: 1997 National Risk Survey

divergent views about environmental justice. The mean index scores (based on a four-point agree/disagree scale) are also listed at the bottom of Table 10.2.

An environmental justice score for each respondent was created by computing the mean score across the four items. The items are scored so that a higher score indicates greater perceived environmental injustice. The index is internally consistent, as indicated by the Cronbach alpha for the four items, which was 0.79. The scores in Table 10.2 indicate that only 0.08 points separate nonwhite men and women; conversely, a 0.30 point difference in mean scores separates the opinion of white and nonwhite men and 0.38 points between white men and nonwhite women.

As with the discrimination statement in the vulnerability index, one item in the environmental justice index emerges as particularly instructive with regard to risk ratings. Figure 10.3 shows that those who disagreed with the statement, 'The government should restrict the placing of hazardous facilities in minority communities,' have consistently lower risk ratings than do those who agree with the statement. Figure 10.3 indicates that differences in mean risk scores are greatest

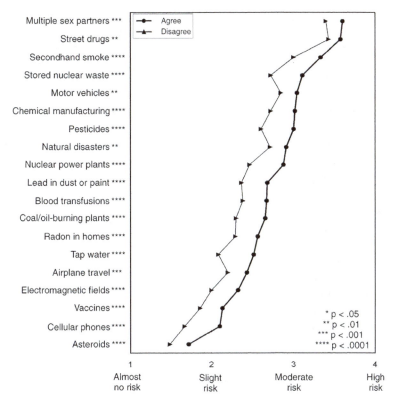

Figure 10.3 *Risk perception means by response to 'The government should restrict the placing of hazardous facilities in minority communities'*

Source: 1997 National Risk Survey: US population as a whole

for stored nuclear waste, pesticides, nuclear power plants, tap water and, for reasons that are not clear, cellular phones.

Justice and vulnerability as it applies to risk

The implications for perceived risk of the combined findings on the vulnerability and environmental justice indices can be examined by comparing 'high' and 'low' responses on both indices to respondents' risk ratings. This comparison was accomplished by separating the distributions for each of the two indices into approximately equal size high, medium and low groups. Those identified as 'high' on the vulnerability index had a mean score of at least 2.3 points, whereas the mean score for low respondents in the vulnerability group did not exceed 1.8 points. Respondents in the high environmental justice group scored 3.0 points or higher, whereas respondents in the low group scored a maximum of 2.5 points. Respondents who were 'high' on both indices were combined to create a 'high justice/high vulnerability subgroup' (weighted, $n = 129$). Similarly, respondents who were low on both indices were combined to create a 'low vulnerability/low

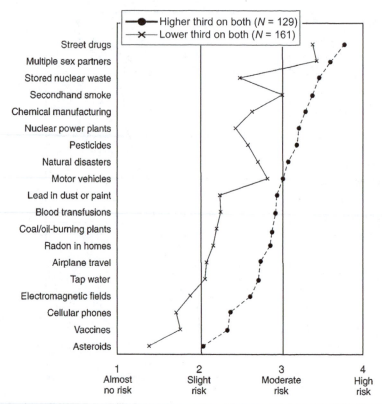

Figure 10.4 *Risk perception means by respondents in the highest third and lowest third of scores on the vulnerability and environmental justice indices*

Source: 1997 National Risk Survey: US population as a whole

justice' subgroup (weighted, $n = 161$). These graphed results are displayed in Figure 10.4.

The consistently lower risk ratings offered by respondents in the low as compared with high justice/vulnerability group suggests that, combined, justice and vulnerability are powerful predictors of risk. For no hazard item do respondents in the respective vulnerability-justice groups offer similar risk ratings. Rather, the difference across groups is substantial for all but two risk items – risks posed by motor vehicles and the risk of multiple sexual partners, both of which are voluntary risks and whose consequences are relatively familiar. The mean differences between the two groups for all other hazard items exceed 0.37 and are statistically significant. More importantly, the difference on 13 of 19 items is 0.60 or greater, with differentiation greatest (0.69 and higher) for the items on stored nuclear waste, nuclear power plants, chemical manufacturing, coal/oil-burning plants, lead in dust or paint and radon in homes.[8]

Table 10.3 *Vulnerability and justice mean index scores:*
Low-risk white males vs. others[a]

Variables/Scale	Low-risk white male (n = 157)	Non-low-risk white male (n = 169)	All others (n = 533)	Tukey significant differences[b]
Vulnerability	1.84	2.08	2.13	a b
Environmental justice	2.43	2.72	2.75	a b

Note: [a] See Note 8. [b] Significant differences identified by Tukey test (*p* < .05). a: low-risk white male vs. non-low-risk white male. b: low-risk white male vs. all others.

Source: 1997 National Risk Survey (weighted data)

Justice, vulnerability and the white-male effect

Re-examining 'the white-male effect'

Given the strength of the above indices as they apply to risk, it is appropriate to re-examine the stability of the 'white-male effect' when that effect is further quali-fied by judgements of vulnerability and justice. That is, what happens to the 'white-male effect' when high environmental justice and vulnerability scores are accounted for? In the comparative risk ratings first reported in Figure 10.1, the risk responses recorded for white males were consistently and significantly lower than were responses by all of the female and male nonwhite respondents. When plotted, this produced the discrete 'white male' line on the graph's left-hand side. This effect is, however, substantially altered when risk ratings are examined for only those respondents recorded as having combined high vulnerability and environmental injustice scores. The sample sizes for this combined high vulnera-bility/injustice group are relatively small, thus the results can only be regarded as suggestive (white male, *n* = 34; white female, *n* = 40; nonwhite male, *n* = 53; nonwhite female, *n* = 95).[9] Further, there are considerably more nonwhite females in this group. A full one-third (34.5 per cent) of nonwhite female respon-dents fall in the high vulnerability/high justice group as compared with 11.8 per cent of white males. Figure 10.5 plots the risk ratings for these high vulnerability/injustice subsamples.

The results recorded in Figure 10.5 indicate that white males who scored high on both the vulnerability and environmental injustice indices are no longer a group with risk perceptions markedly different from all other females and all nonwhite males. This is evidenced by the intermingling of the line representing the plotted white male ratings with the lines representing all other groups. That is, much of the race and gender effect previously documented in Figure 10.1 is eroded when social vulnerability and environmental justice are accounted for in this way.

Regression analysis of the white-male effect

Further testing to determine whether the 'white-male effect' is a vulnerability and justice effect or a demographic effect (i.e. driven primarily by race or gender) can

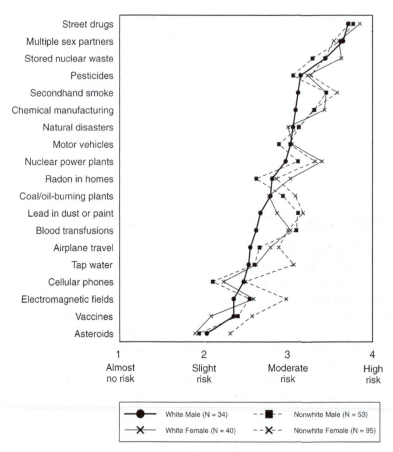

Figure 10.5 *Risk perception means by vulnerability and environmental justice by race and gender: High on both*

Source: 1997 National Risk Survey

be accomplished by using a regression model to predict risk responses based on race and gender only (Model 1), and thereafter, by expanding the model to see whether our measures of social vulnerability and environmental justice can account for the race–gender effect. The results of this two-step analysis are recorded in Table 10.4.

Model 1, which attends only to race and gender, was highly significant ($F(2, 1189) = 87.03, p < .0001$) as can be seen in Table 10.4. The standardized coefficients for both gender and race (0.28 and −0.22, respectively) were significant as well with women and nonwhites exhibiting higher perceptions of risk. This effect was, however, somewhat diminished when controlling for vulnerability and environmental justice as demonstrated by the results from the Model 2 analysis. Race and gender were still significant predictors of risk perception, but the standardized coefficient for race was lower (−0.10) in Model 2. The coefficient for gender (0.24) was slightly diminished after controlling for these new factors.

Table 10.4 *Two regression models predicting risk perception index*

Independent variables	Standardized coefficients	R^2	Increment in R^2
Model I			
Gender	0.28****		
Race	−0.22****		
F value	87.03		
$p > F$	0.0001		
R^2	0.1277		
Model 2			
First 2 variables forced in first			
Vulnerability	0.27****		
Environmental justice	0.18****	0.1668	
Gender	0.24****	0.2249	0.0581
Race	−0.10***	0.2346	0.0097
F value (full model)	90.33		
$p > F$	0.0001		

Note: Coding – Gender: 0 = men, 1 = women; Race: 0 = nonwhite, 1 = white
*** $p < .001$; **** $p < .0001$.

Source: 1997 National Risk Survey

When combined, vulnerability and environmental justice explained 16.68 per cent of the variance in risk perception. When race and gender are added to the model, 23.46 per cent of the variance is explained, an increase of 6.8 per cent. To test whether race and gender still contributed independently to the prediction of risk perception, an R^2 test of the change in proportion of variance explained was performed. The results found that the explanatory power of gender and race remain significant though somewhat diminished. Gender provided a 5.81 per cent increase in R^2, the largest effect over and above the variables of environmental justice and vulnerability, as compared to race, which garnered an R^2 increase of just below 1 per cent. The respective F values for the change in R^2 were $F(3, 1180) = 88.49$, $p < .0001$ and $F(1, 1179) = 14.85$, $p < .001$. Thus, while vulnerability and beliefs about environmental injustice are important predictors of risk perception, they do not completely explain or account for the effect of race and gender. Gender, in particular, remains robust in its own right. Race retains a smaller, but still significant, influence on perceptions of health risks.

In sum, all four variables are important independent predictors of risk perception, with social vulnerability and gender being the strongest predictors followed by environmental injustice and then race.

Additional regression analyses were conducted to determine whether the white-male effect could be accounted for by factors such as age, education, income, political orientation (liberal vs. conservative) and religious commitment (church attendance). It could not. The coefficient for vulnerability (0.20) was somewhat lower after controlling for these other variables. However, education

Table 10.5 *Regression model predicting risk perception index from other socio-demographic variables*

Independent variables	Standardized coefficients	R^2	Increment in R^2
Model 3			
First 2 variables forced in first			
Vulnerability	0.20****		
Environmental justice	0.19****	0.1615	
Gender	0.22****	0.2199	0.0584
Education	−0.18****	0.2464	0.0265
Race	−0.09**	0.2547	0.0083
Church attendance	0.08**	0.2604	0.0057
Political orientation	−0.05	0.2622	0.0018
Age	0.02	0.2627	0.0005
Income	−0.01	0.2627	0.0001
F value (full model)	41.54		
$p > F$	0.0001		

Note: Coding – Gender: 0 = men, 1 = women; Race: 0 = nonwhite, 1 = white; Political orientation: 1 = very liberal, 5 = very conservative; Church attendance: 1 = never, 5 = more than once a week; Education: 1 = 8th grade or less, 8 = Doctorate.
* $p < .05$; ** $p < .01$; *** $p < .001$; **** $p < .0001$.

Source: 1997 National Risk Survey

emerges as a significant predictor of risk, a finding already noted by others (e.g. Finucane et al, 2000b). Gender and race remained strong predictors of risk perception, even after all of the above variables were entered into the regression equation (see Table 10.5).

Discussion

Four important results have emerged from this study. First, these results replicate the 'white-male effect,' which found that across the American population, white males rate the risks that hazards pose as lower than most other demographic groups.[10] In addition, nonwhite females provide higher risk ratings than all others; thus white males cannot be characterized accurately as 'the only atypical group.' These results also uphold the supposition of Mohai and Bryant (1998) and Jones (1998) that African-Americans in the United States are more rather than less concerned about environmental risks, particularly when those risks concern the health and safety effects of pollution. Second, strong (affirmative) feelings of discrimination and vulnerability and evaluative judgements of justice, as well as strong support for environmental injustice claims, are closely linked to high perceptions of environmental health risks. This suggests in turn that both subjective experiences of vulnerability and evaluative judgements of (in)justice are central to the perception of risk. Third, white males with high perceptions of vulnerability and environmental justice tend to rate risks in a manner that is similar to all other groups (white females, and nonwhite males and females). Fourth, vulnerability, gender, environmental justice and race (in order of strength) are significant predictors of health and environmental risk perceptions. Gender remains a robust predictor of risk as does – to a lesser extent – race, but the influence of these two demographic variables (particularly race) is explained in part by our measures of vulnerability and environmental injustice.

It should be emphasized that these are preliminary results to the extent that (1) the subsamples from all groups whose high vulnerability/high injustice perspective diminished the original white-male effect were relatively small, and (2) the indices we developed for measuring vulnerability and environmental injustice represent first attempts and as such may have insufficiently characterized these constructs. Regression analysis confirms that our measures are only partially, at best, responsible for the race and gender effect on perceived risk. Gender, as a particularly robust predictor of risk, is still relatively unexplained. Thus, expanding both indices to better accommodate explanations for the gender effect might well be productive.

Upon reviewing the literature on gender and risk, Davidson and Freudenburg (1996) have argued that the best explanation for differences in risk perception between white men and women is the hypothesis that the risks posed by health and safety problems are more salient to women due to their socially prescribed roles as nurturers and care providers. This provides a viable starting point, particularly as concerns the vulnerability index. But the nurturer hypothesis does not explain the perceptions of nonwhite men, perceptions that were found herein to be somewhat similar to those held by white and nonwhite women. It is possible that while some insights have been achieved here and elsewhere as to the subjective and sociopolitical perspectives of risk perceivers, we do not as yet fully understand precisely what different risks mean to different perceivers. Gustafson has convincingly argued that: 'what appears ... in a questionnaire to be one and the same risk may not always mean the same thing to women and men' (Gustafson, 1998, p807). His analogous case is that men and women alike fear or see violent crime as risky. Yet, investigations of meaning reveal that men read physical violence into the term 'violent crime,' whereas women primarily fear rape and other forms of sexual assault and thus read this latter meaning into the term 'violent crime.'

Improved indices aside, our findings have implications for risk communication and risk remediation practices. That is, procedures employed by regulatory agents to both communicate about risk and physically manage the hazards that demand remediation attention (e.g. many Superfund sites) could benefit from greater sensitivity to cross-group perspectives on the perceived relationship between risk, vulnerability and justice. If, for instance, high risk ratings are a product of subjective states of vulnerability, such states could reasonably be expected to influence the uptake and response to risk messages. Such messages may be met with resistance, denial, anxiety or misinterpretation due to one's heightened perception of susceptibility to possible consequences. In a different vein, and in reference to justice, Vaughan (1995) has noted that risk experts communicating behavioural precautions to those living in minority communities may regard their information as, say, technical discussions of chronic risk exposure, whereas those receiving risk information may be thinking more fully in terms of distributive justice or the relationship between risk exposure and racial equality. Risk communicators might, alternatively and wisely, reframe their messages with reference to justice by explaining, for example, how their actions in site A (a minority community) are similar to those taken in site B (a non-minority community), or how considerations of justice and risk exposure have been addressed in the site in question versus related contexts.

Similarly, Satterfield et al (2001) have argued that in risk remediation contexts, clean-up workers who enter minority neighbourhoods fully clothed in protective suits or machinery may inadvertently become signals that evoke, among residents, justice- and vulnerability-relevant conclusions. In one contaminated African-American community it was found that: 'Visually compelling recollections of heavy machinery and workers in prophylactic suits seemed to say that the residents [there] ought to have been safeguarded these many years ... or, more cynically, that the residents were a socially disposable population, unworthy of protection in the first place' (p76). The tragic irony in remediation contexts is that remedies for protecting exposed communities may exacerbate the very concerns they ought ideally to alleviate.

In the end, fuller recognition of the fact that subjective and sociopolitical factors (vulnerability and justice included) shape the perception of risk may move us toward policy that is both responsive to and genuinely reflects diverse meanings of risk and diverse experiences of risk management.

Acknowledgement

This study was supported by a grant to Decision Research from the National Science Foundation (Grant No. SES-9876581).

Notes

1   Respondents were also asked to rate a subset of these items in terms of health and safety 'risks to you and your family.' The pattern of results was similar to those found for the American public.
2   We recognize that 'race' is (and should be) a contested term in the social sciences as efforts to distinguish biophysical features of racial groups have largely failed. The construct 'race' is nonetheless widely meaningful in public life and remains an important social basis through which humans define themselves and are defined by others.
3   When a Bonferroni test was performed, significant differences were found between nonwhite females and white females on 8 (not 11) items. The Bonferroni test also reduced the number of significant differences between nonwhite males and nonwhite females to two from ten under the Tukey post hoc test.

4   The specific demographic and attitudinal variables that distinguish the subset of
    white males with lower risk perceptions (vs. non-low-risk white males, white females,
    and nonwhite males and females; Finucane, 2000b) are listed below. The comparisons
    reported are statistically significant at $p < .05$. There were no differences in age distri-
    butions across respondent groups. However, white males were more likely to hold
    college or postgraduate degrees (46.0 per cent college or postgraduate degree, vs.
    26.7 per cent for all other groups), have higher household incomes (58.3 per cent
    above $45,000 vs. 33.2 per cent), and be politically conservative (45.3 per cent vs.
    34.3 per cent). They were also more likely to:

    •   agree that the economic benefits from industries located in their community are
        greater than the risks (69.1 per cent vs. 55.9 per cent);
    •   agree that the benefits from science and technology outweigh the risks they create
        (69.1 per cent vs. 54.4 per cent);
    •   agree that in a fair system, people with more ability should earn more (89.9 per
        cent vs. 83.2 per cent);
    •   disagree that people in positions of authority tend to abuse their power (30.2 per
        cent vs. 18.4 per cent);
    •   disagree that what this world needs is a more equal distribution of wealth (54.0
        per cent vs. 24.3 per cent);
    •   disagree that people living near a nuclear power plant should be able to vote and
        to close the plant if they think it is not being run safely (46.8 per cent vs. 15.3 per
        cent);
    •   disagree that there are serious environmental health problems where they live
        (80.6 per cent vs. 62.3 per cent).

5   Interestingly, Finucane et al (2000b) did find that, although white males believed that
    it was acceptable to impose small risks on society without their knowledge, white
    males' trust of the institutions that manage risks was qualified, indicating that they
    preferred (more than others) to control or manage risks themselves.

6   Some of the items in this set were inspired, in part, by Srole's (1965) early 'political
    alienation' question set.

7   We do not mean to imply that discrimination should be causally explained as feelings
    of vulnerability and discrimination. We assume, rather, that injustice is structurally
    rooted but that it may manifest, personally, in these and other feelings.

8   A comparison of vulnerability and justice index scores for the low-risk white male
    group (as defined in the 'Results' section) versus the non-low-risk white male group is
    also instructive. The vulnerability and justice mean index scores for low-risk white
    males are significantly lower than are the mean scores for all other white males as well
    as all other nonwhite groups. These data are recorded in Table 10.3.

9   The sample sizes here total 222 and are unweighted because we are looking at race
    and gender effects. The earlier sample size of $n = 129$ reflects weighting to adjust
    oversampled groups back to their respective proportions within the US population as
    a whole.

10 Interestingly, Greenberg and Schneider (1995) argue that no demonstrable gender
    differences in risk perceptions are found 'among males and females who actually live
    in stressed neighborhoods with multiple hazards' (p503). Men, they argue, are as
    likely as women to be personally threatened by hazards that are figuratively and
    sometimes literally 'in their face' (p509). They regard their findings as consistent with
    the 'white-male effect' in that the difference in their data between men and women in
    non-stressed neighbourhoods may well be an artefact of extremely low levels of

concern expressed by a subset of white males. This does not negate the fact, however, that the experience of actually living in a stressed neighbourhood may substantively alter one's perception of risk.

Chapter 11

Culture and Identity-Protective Cognition: Explaining the White-Male Effect in Risk Perception

Dan M. Kahan, Donald Braman, John Gastil,
*Paul Slovic and C. K. Mertz**

Fear discriminates. Numerous studies show that risk perceptions are skewed across gender and race: women worry more than men, and minorities more than whites, about myriad dangers – from environmental pollution to handguns, from blood transfusions to red meat (Brody, 1984; Steger and Witt, 1989; Gutteling and Wiegman, 1993; Stern et al, 1993; Flynn et al, 1994; Davidson and Freudenburg, 1996; Bord and O'Connor, 1997; Jones, 1998; Mohai and Bryant, 1998; Kalof et al, 2002; Satterfield et al, 2004).

To date, no compelling account has been offered of why risk perceptions vary in this way. It is not convincing to suggest that women and minorities have less access to, or understanding of, scientific information about risk. Gender and race differences persist even after controlling for education. Indeed, gender variance exists even among scientists who specialize in risk assessment (Kraus et al, 1992; Barke et al, 1997; Slovic, 1999).

Also unsatisfying is the suggestion that women are more sensitive to risk because of their role as caregivers. This argument not only fails to explain variance across race, but also cannot account for the relative uniformity of risk assessments among women and African-American men, who presumably are no more socially or biologically disposed to be caring than are white men (Flynn et al, 1994).

Women and African-Americans feel less politically empowered than white men and have less confidence in government authorities. These perceptions might

*   Abridged from Kahan, D. M., Braman, D., Gastil, J., Slovic, P. and Mertz, C. K. (2007) 'Culture and identity-protective cognition: Explaining the white-male effect in risk perception', *Journal of Empirical Legal Studies*, vol 4, pp465–505

incline them to feel more vulnerable to dangers generally. Research shows that such attitudes do play a role, but that both gender and race continue to predict risk perceptions even after these factors are taken into account (Satterfield et al, 2004).

In this chapter, we consider a new explanation. Previous studies have found that race and gender differences in risk perception can be attributed to a discrete class of highly risk-sceptical white men (Flynn et al, 1994). The distorting influence of this seemingly fearless group of men on the distribution of risk perceptions has been referred to as the 'white-male effect' (Finucane et al, 2000b). Research also has shown that these men are more likely to hold certain anti-egalitarian and individualistic attitudes than members of the general population (Finucane et al, 2000b; Palmer, 2003). This finding suggests that the white-male effect might derive from a congeniality between hierarchical and individualistic worldviews, on the one hand, and a posture of extreme risk scepticism, on the other.

We designed a study to test this hypothesis. Our findings strongly support the conclusion that the white-male effect is an artefact of variance in cultural worldviews. Across various types of hazards, gender and race per se did not influence risk perception among the members of our large and broadly representative sample. Rather, these characteristics influenced risk perception only in conjunction with distinctive worldviews that themselves feature either gender or race differentiation or both in social roles involving putatively dangerous activities.

Indeed, the results of this study complicate the conventional account of who is best described as fearful and who fearless in this setting. We find that individuals are disposed selectively to accept or dismiss risk claims in a manner that expresses their cultural values. It is natural for individuals to adopt a posture of extreme scepticism, in particular when charges of societal danger are levelled at activities integral to social roles constructed by their cultural commitments. The insensitivity to risk reflected in the white-male effect can thus be seen as a defensive response to a form of cultural identity threat that afflicts hierarchical and individualistic white males.

But white individualistic and hierarchical males are by no means uniquely vulnerable to this condition. Other groups, including women and African-Americans as well as white men holding egalitarian and communitarian worldviews, also face cultural-identity threats that generate distinctive patterns of risk perception. Indeed, the impact of risk regulation on competing understandings of culture and identity helps explain why the highly technical problems this body of law addresses tend to provoke such impassioned and divisive political conflict (Slovic, 1999).

Our study makes it possible to chart the impact of culturally grounded identity threats on a variety of risk perceptions. We begin with a discussion of the theory that informs the study. We then present a description of the study design, and a detailed description of its results. Finally, after briefly summarizing the principal findings, we discuss their implications for the study of risk perception and the regulation of risk.

Theoretical background: Culture, risk and identity threat

We propose that variance in risk perceptions – across persons generally, and across race and gender in particular – reflects a form of motivated cognition through which people seek to deflect threats to identities they hold, and roles they occupy, by virtue of contested cultural norms. This proposition derives from the convergence of two sets of theories, one relating to the impact of culture on risk perception and the other on the influence of group membership on cognition.

The cultural theory of risk

The *cultural theory of risk perception* (Douglas and Wildavsky, 1982; Rayner, 1992) asserts that individuals' perceptions of risk reflect and reinforce their commitments to visions of how society should be organized. Individuals, according to the theory, selectively credit and dismiss claims of societal danger based on whether the putatively hazardous activity is one that defies or instead conforms to their cultural norms. Debates that on the surface feature instrumental, and often highly technical, claims of risk and benefit are in essence 'the product of an ongoing debate about the ideal society? (Douglas and Wildavsky, 1982, p36).

The competing positions at stake in this debate are reflected in Mary Douglas's (1970) 'group-grid' typology, which classifies competing sets of norms, or 'worldviews,' along two cross-cutting dimensions (Figure 11.1). The 'group' dimension represents the degree to which 'the individual's life is absorbed in and sustained by group membership' (Douglas, 1982, p202). Those with a low group or *individualistic* orientation expect individuals to 'fend for themselves and there-

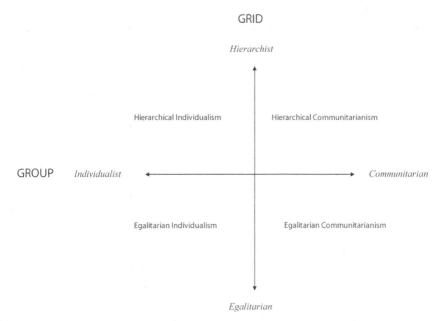

Figure 11.1 *'Group-grid' worldview typology*

fore tend to be competitive'; those with a high group or communitarian worldview assume that individuals will 'interact frequently ... in a wide range of activities' in which they must 'depend on one another,' a condition that 'promotes values of solidarity' (Rayner, 1992, p86). The 'grid' dimension measures the pervasiveness and significance of social differentiation within a worldview. Persons who have a high grid or hierarchical orientation expect resources, opportunities, respect and the like to be 'distributed on the basis of explicit public social classifications, such as sex, color, ... holding a bureaucratic office, [or] descent in a senior clan or lineage' (Gross and Rayner, 1985, p6). Low grid orientations value 'an egalitarian state of affairs in which no one is prevented from participating in any social role because he or she is the wrong sex, or is too old, or does not have the right family connections' and so forth (Rayner, 1992, p86). Groups of like-minded persons, moreover, typically form within the interior of the quadrants demarcated by the intersection of group and grid, thereby becoming committed to social arrange-ments that combine elements of either 'hierarchy' or 'egalitarianism,' on the one hand, and with either 'individualism' or 'communitarianism,' on the other (Douglas, 1982; Thompson et al, 1990).

These preferences, cultural theory posits, explain political conflict over risk regulation. Persons who are relatively egalitarian and communitarian are naturally sensitive to environmental and technological risks, the reduction of which justifies regulating commercial activities that produce social inequality and legitimize unconstrained self-interest. Those who are more individualistic predictably dismiss claims of environmental risk as specious, in line with their commitment to the autonomy of markets and other private orderings. So do relatively hierarchical persons, who perceive assertions of environmental catastrophe as threatening the competence of social and governmental elites (Douglas and Wildavsky, 1982; Wildavsky and Dake, 1990). Building on Douglas's and Wildavsky's work, numerous empirical studies have shown that perceptions (lay and expert) of various types of environmental and technological hazards do vary in patterns that conform to these categories (Wildavsky and Dake, 1990; Dake, 1991; Jenkins-Smith and Smith, 1994; Peters and Slovic, 1996; Ellis and Thompson, 1997; Marris et al, 1998; Gyawali, 1999; Steg and Sievers, 2000; Jenkins-Smith, 2001; Poortinga et al, 2002).

Identity-protective cognition

Group membership, it has been shown, 'can affect how people process informa-tion about nearly all categories of stimuli in the social world' (Baumeister and Leary, 1995, p504). Individuals tend to adopt the beliefs common to members of salient 'in-groups.' They also resist revision of those beliefs in the face of contrary factual information, particularly when that information originates from 'out-group' sources, who are likely to be perceived as less knowledgeable and less trustworthy than 'in-group' ones (Clark and Maass, 1988; MacKie et al, 1992; MacKie and Quellar, 2000).

Identity-protective cognition is one proposed mechanism for this set of dynam-ics. Individual well-being, this account recognizes, is intricately bound up with group membership, which supplies individuals not only with material benefits but a range of critical non-material ones, including opportunities to acquire status and self-esteem. Challenges to commonly held group beliefs can undermine a person's well-being either by threatening to drive a wedge between that person and other group members, by interfering with important practices within the group, or by impugning the social competence (and thus the esteem-conferring capacity) of a group generally. Accordingly, as a means of identity self-defence, individuals appraise information in a manner that buttresses beliefs associated with belonging to particular groups (Cohen et al, 2000, 2007; Cohen, 2003).

The existence of identity-protective cognition is most convincingly supported by studies that investigate how group membership interacts with diverse forms of reasoning. Even someone whose sense of worth was not invested in any profound way in group membership might treat the views of those he or she associates with and trusts as a rough indicator of the accuracy of a commonly held belief. However, experimental studies show the impact of group membership on belief formation is not confined to this heuristic; the perceived predominance of a belief within a group influences information processing even when a member of that group uses systematic reasoning, which is characterized by a relatively high degree of deliberate, critical analysis (Cohen, 2003). In effect, an unselfconscious desire to affirm group beliefs motivates both heuristic and systematic reasoning, determining which form a person will employ and to what end. The motivational effect of group membership on information processing is most easily explained by the inference that individuals do have a profound emotional and psychic invest-ment in seeing their group's beliefs confirmed (Giner-Sorolla and Chaiken, 1997; Chen et al, 1999).

Synthesis: Cultural-identity-protective risk perception

At least as a matter of theory, a marriage of the cultural theory of risk and identity-protective cognition would seem to confer benefits on both. The latter supplies the former with something it notoriously lacks: a straightforward account of why individuals form the beliefs associated with the group-grid culture types. Douglas (1986) and other cultural theorists (Thompson et al, 1990) have suggested functionalist explanations that assume individuals adopt beliefs congenial to the groups to which they belong precisely because their holding such beliefs promotes their groups' interests. By supplying a psychological mechanism rooted in individuals' perceptions of their own interests, identity-protective cogni-tion extricates cultural theory from the well-known difficulties that plague functionalist accounts (Balkin, 1998, pp176–180; Boudon, 1998).

The cultural theory of risk, in turn, supplies a vivid and realistic picture of the types of groups and associated beliefs likely to generate identity-protective forms of cognition. In the laboratory, in-group effects on cognition can be elicited on the basis of seemingly peripheral or even wholly contrived groups, and with respect to wholly inconsequential issues. But in the real world, we associate with myriad diverse groups: we are disciples of religions and members of health clubs; practi-tioners of professions and devotees of professional sports teams; citizens of nation-states and residents of neighbourhoods. It is not merely implausible but logically impossible for persons to react with identity-protective cognition with respect to all the beliefs that might predominate among all such groups, whose (often shifting) majorities are bound to disagree with one another on particular issues.

'Group-grid' furnishes a parsimonious typology of highly salient commitments that are likely to shape individuals' identities, and to determine their group-based affinities, in a manner that transcends the scores of associations they might happen to form with like- and unlike-minded persons. The established empirical correlation between membership in cultural groups of these types and beliefs about societal risks constitutes a fertile testing ground for hypotheses about the contribution identity-motivated cognition is making to real-world conflict on issues of tremendous consequence.

Among such hypotheses are ones that relate to gender and racial variance in perceptions of risk. It is possible that these characteristics predict some level of agreement about societal dangers because they tend to correlate with the identity-generative outlooks represented in the group-grid scheme. In that case, we should expect to see demographic variation in risk perception largely dissipate once individuals' cultural worldviews are taken into account.

But even once worldviews are controlled for, we might still see race or gender differences of a distinctively cultural nature. Particular sets of cultural norms are likely to feature greater degrees of gender and race differentiation in social roles than are others. For example, because hierarchical norms explicitly tie obligations and entitlements, goods and offices, to conspicuous and largely immutable characteristics such as 'kinship, race, gender, age, and so forth' (Rayner, 1992, p86), those norms are more likely than egalitarian ones to distinguish the sorts of activities that are esteem conferring and otherwise appropriate for men and women, minorities and whites. Where such role differentiation exists, the occasion for identity-protective forms of risk scepticism or risk receptivity will vary across gender and race within culturally defined groups, depending on whose cultural identity – men's or women's, whites' or minorities' – is being enabled or interfered with by some putatively dangerous activity. If sufficiently pronounced, this type of cultural-identity-protective cognition would resolve the mystery of the 'white-male effect' in risk perception.

Study design

Overview

To test these conjectures about the relationship between cultural worldviews, identity-protective cognition, and demographic variance in risk perception, we conducted a large-scale opinion survey. The sample consisted of 1844 US residents, 18 years of age or older, contacted by random-digit dialling to participate in a telephone interview. To ensure a sample large enough to facilitate meaningful assessment of the relative effects of cultural worldviews across persons of diverse races, the study included an oversample of 242 African-Americans, the group whose risk perceptions we expected to diverge most from those of whites.[1] As described in more detail below, information was collected on our subjects' perceptions of various types of societal risks, their cultural worldviews and various other individual characteristics.

The basic premise of the study was that the distribution of risk perceptions across persons can yield insight about the formation of those perceptions. One prominent position asserts that individuals (in aggregate, and over time) process information in a manner consistent with expected utility (Viscusi, 1983). An opposing view holds that individuals systematically mis-process risk information as a result of cognitive limits and biases (Sunstein, 2005). These theories generate different predictions about the influences that determine risk perception, but neither predicts that cultural worldviews will be one of them: there is no reason to think that hierarchs and individualists have more or less access to information about risk than do egalitarians and communitarians, or that one or the other of these types is more bounded in its rationality. If it turns out, then, that perceptions of risk do in fact strongly correlate with individuals' worldviews even after other pertinent individual characteristics are taken into account, that result would supply strong evidence that culture is motivating identity-protective cognition in the way we surmise.

Hypotheses

Stated generally, our hypothesis is that cultural-identity-protective cognition will generate two sorts of variance in risk perception. First, individuals holding differing worldviews should disagree with one another when their respective norms clash on the value of a putatively dangerous activity. And second, individuals sharing a cultural worldview should diverge along gender or race lines when their shared norms feature gender or race differentiation with respect to social roles involving such an activity. We selected for study three types of risks – environmental, gun-related and abortion-related – in which this basic hypothesis generated more specific, testable predictions.

Environmental risks
Perceptions of environmental danger are the central phenomena of enquiry for the cultural theory of risk and are well known to reflect race and gender variance. We hypothesized, consistent with Douglas and Wildavsky (1982), that relatively hierarchal and individualistic worldviews would diminish concern with environmental risks, whereas relatively egalitarian and communitarian worldviews would accentuate it. We predicted the influence of cultural worldviews would be strong relative to other individual characteristics that might influence risk perception, including other potential group bases of identity-protective cognition such as political and religious affiliations.

We also hypothesized that the 'white-male effect' for environmental risks would derive from variance along the grid or egalitarianism-hierarchy dimension of cultural outlook. Within a hierarchical worldview, women are primarily assigned to domestic roles, men to public ones within civil society and within the government. Accordingly, to the extent that assertions of environmental risk are perceived as symbolizing a challenge to the prerogatives and competence of social and governmental elites (Douglas and Wildavsky, 1982), it is *hierarchical men* – and particularly *white* ones, insofar as minorities are more likely to be disproportionately egalitarian in their outlooks – whose identities are the most threatened, and who are thus most likely to form an extremely dismissive posture toward asserted risks.

For persons of an individualist orientation, market roles are likely to be seen as esteem conferring for both men and women, and for both whites and minorities. Accordingly, the disposition toward an individualist worldview should generate relatively uniform scepticism across gender and race about assertions of danger directed at commercial activities. Likewise, egalitarianism and communitarianism should generate relatively uniform concern about environmental and technological risks.

Gun risks

The gun-control debate can be framed as one between competing risk claims. Control proponents argue that too little control increases the risk of gun violence and accidents (e.g. Cook and Ludwig, 2000), whereas control opponents argue that too much control risks depriving innocent persons of the ability to defend themselves from violent criminals (e.g. Lott, 2000).

We hypothesized that which of these risks individuals find more important would turn on their cultural orientation. Persons of hierarchical and individualistic orientations should be expected to worry more about being rendered defenceless because of the association of guns with hierarchical social roles (hunter, protector, father) and with hierarchical and individualistic virtues (courage, honour, chivalry, self-reliance, prowess). Relatively egalitarian and communitarian respondents should worry more about gun violence because of the association of guns with patriarchy and racism and with distrust of and indifference to the well-being of strangers (Kahan and Braman, 2003). Again, we predicted that these influences would be large relative to those of other individual characteristics, including affiliations that might generate identity-protective cognition.

It is well documented that men and whites view guns more favourably than do women and African-Americans (e.g. Smith, 2000). We hypothesized that this 'white-male effect,' too, would derive from differences in cultural orientation. The social roles that guns enable and the virtues they symbolize are stereotypically male roles and virtues (Buckner, 1994). Moreover, 'in the historic system of the South, having a gun was a white prerogative,' making gun ownership an enduring 'symbol of white male status' in particular (Hofstadter, 1970, p84). Accordingly, it is individualistic and hierarchical white males whose identities are threatened most by regulation of guns and who should therefore form the most sceptical attitude about asserted gun risks. Hierarchical and individualistic worldviews should, we hypothesized, produce relatively *less* scepticism among women and minorities because they have less of an identity investment in guns being freely available. Because egalitarianism and communitarianism do not tie antipathy to guns to race and gender roles, those worldviews should uniformly incline whites and minorities, men and women, toward gun-risk sensitivity.

Abortion risks

Hierarchical and individualistic white men are not the only cultural subgroups facing threats to their status. Hierarchical women are experiencing a similar challenge as norms conferring status on women who successfully occupy professional roles have come to compete with and perhaps overtake traditional patriarchal norms that assign status to women for occupying domestic roles. This, according to Luker (1984), is the status conflict that informs political dispute over abortion, the free availability of which is thought to symbolize the ascent of egalitarian and individualist norms over hierarchical ones that celebrate motherhood as the most virtuous social role for women.

We predicted that these culturally grounded disagreements would generate identity-protective cognition on the health risks of abortion, an issue that has emerged as central to the rationale for a new generation of abortion regulations (Siegel, 2007).[2] Conforming their factual beliefs to their cultural commitments, relatively hierarchical individuals, we hypothesized, would see abortion as more risky than persons who are relatively egalitarian and individualistic. Moreover, because they are the ones whose identities are most threatened by abortion's symbolic denigration of motherhood, hierarchical women, we anticipated, would be the most receptive of all to the claim that abortion is dangerous; all else equal, commitment to hierarchical norms, we predicted, would have a less dramatic impact in accentuating the abortion-risk concerns of men. In addition, because egalitarian and individualistic norms confer status to women as well as men who master professional roles, the disposition toward those worldviews, we surmised, should uniformly incline women and men to the view that abortion is in fact safe. We also anticipated that any race effect on abortion-risk perceptions would originate in either the correlation of race with cultural outlooks or an interaction between race and cultural worldviews.

Measures

Cultural worldviews

The survey contained 32 worldview items (see Appendix), consisting of statements to which respondents indicated their level of agreement or disagreement on a four-point scale. Item development consisted of the adaptation of items used in previous studies based on the cultural theory of risk (including Dake, 1991; Peters and Slovic, 1996; Ellis and Thompson, 1997), as well as the creation of new items based on focus-group discussions and survey pretesting.

The statements were intended to form (and did form) two reliable scales: Communitarianism–Individualism ($\alpha = 0.77$), which is patterned on the group dimension of the Douglas typology; and Egalitarianism–Hierarchy ($\alpha = 0.81$), which is patterned on the grid dimension. The Communitarianism–Individualism scale measured concern for individual versus collective interests (e.g. 'The government should do more to advance society's goals, even if that means limiting the freedom and choices of individuals'), as well as how responsibility for meeting individual needs should be allocated between individuals and the community (e.g. 'Too many people today expect society to do things for them that they should be doing for themselves?'). The Egalitarianism–Hierarchy scale measured attitudes toward group stratification (e.g. 'We have gone too far in pushing equal rights in this country') and toward deviance from dominant norms and roles (e.g. 'It's old-fashioned and wrong to think that one culture's set of values is better than any other culture's way of seeing the world'). We computed continuous worldview scores ('Individualism' and 'Hierarchy') by averaging the items for each scale, with high scores indicating a more individualistic and a more hierarchical orientation, respectively.

To facilitate analysis, we also assigned individual respondents to cultural groups. We thus designated respondents as either 'Hierarchs' or 'Egalitarians,' and as either 'Individualists' or 'Communitarians,' depending on the relationship of their scores and the median score on each scale. Consistent with the expectation that coherent groups tend to form in the quadrants delineated by the group-grid framework (Douglas, 1982; Thompson et al, 1990), we classified respondents as either 'Hierarchical Individualists,' 'Hierarchical Communitarians,' 'Egalitarian Individualists,' or 'Egalitarian Communitarians' depending on where their scores fell in relation to the median scores of both scales.

Other individual characteristics

In addition to soliciting respondents' gender, race and age, the survey collected data on other individual characteristics that have been found to correlate with risk perceptions. These include demographic characteristics such as education level, household income and the type of community in which respondents reside. They also include a general predilection for risk-taking, which we measured with a two-item 'sensation-seeking' scale (Sensation-Seeking) that has been shown to be a strong and reliable predictor of individuals' propensity to engage in personally hazardous behaviour (Stephenson et al, 2003).

We also collected information on other group affiliations that might be viewed as supplying alternative bases of identity-protective cognition. Respondents were thus asked to report their religious affiliations. They were also asked to characterize their political views on a conventional seven-point ideology scale (Conservative) ranging from extremely liberal to extremely conservative. Finally, they identified their party affiliation, if any, and rated its intensity on a five-point scale (Democrat) ranging from strong Republican to strong Democrat.

Risk perception

Environmental-risk perceptions The survey solicited evaluations of three putative environmental risks: nuclear power generation, global warming and environmental pollution generally (see item wording in Appendix). Participants rated their perception of these risks on a four-point scale based on how strongly they agreed or disagreed that the risk in question was serious. Responses were averaged to form a single environmental-risk perception scale ($\alpha = 0.72$), with higher scores indicating greater concern about environmental risks.

Gun-risk perceptions Those involved in the gun debate disagree about the relative magnitude of the risks associated with insufficient and excessive regulation of guns. Accordingly, to test their perceptions of these competing risks, respondents indicated their level of agreement or disagreement with opposing statements about the impact of guns in either promoting or undermining personal and societal safety. Because risk evaluations are also frequently qualitative and not just quantitative in nature (Slovic et al, 1979), respondents were also asked to react to opposing 'dreadedness' items: one asked them to relate how disturbing they found the prospect that they or a loved one might be injured or killed as a result of insufficiently strict gun-control laws; the other asked them to relate how disturbing they found the prospect that overly strict gun-control laws might interfere with their use of firearms to defend themselves or loved ones from attack (see Appendix). The items were combined into a scale ($\alpha = 0.83$), with higher scores indicating greater concern that gun ownership on balance reduces public safety.

Abortion-risk perceptions We measured respondents perceptions of the risk of obtaining an abortion by asking them to state the strength of their agreement or disagreement with the proposition: 'Women who get abortions are putting their health in danger.'

Results

We present the results of the study in two general steps. First, we report raw means for risk perceptions based on demographic characteristics, worldviews, and combinations of the two. Second, to enable testing of study hypotheses, we report a set of multivariate regression analyses that enable us to assess the relative and interactive effect of culture and other individual characteristics for each type of risk perception.

Preliminary analysis: Comparison of mean risk perceptions

Our sample displayed the conventional 'white-male effect' (Figure 11.2). White males were significantly less concerned about each risk evaluated in the study. The relative concerns of white females and male and female nonwhites varied across risks.

There was also a clear cultural effect (Figure 11.3). As expected, persons who held relative hierarchical and individualistic outlooks – and particularly both simultaneously – were the least concerned about environmental risks and gun risks, while persons who held relatively egalitarian and communitarian views were most concerned. With regard to abortion risks, in contrast, persons who were both relatively hierarchical and communitarian in their views were most concerned;

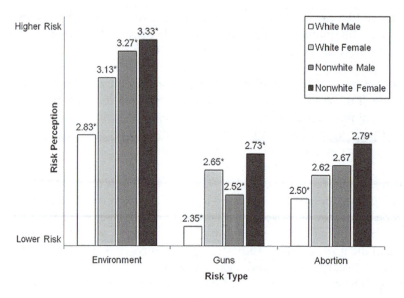

Figure 11.2 *'White-male effect' on risk perceptions*

individuals who had an egalitarian outlook, particularly those who qualified as Egalitarian Individualists, were least worried about the risk of abortion for women's health. This pattern, too, conformed to the anticipated influence of group-grid cultural dispositions.

When risk perceptions were examined for groups defined by combinations of demographic characteristics and cultural worldviews, the 'white-male effect'

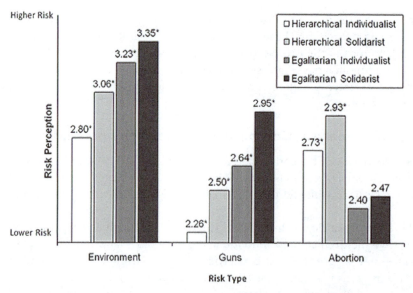

Figure 11.3 *Cultural worldview effect on risk perceptions*

Table 11.1 *Mean risk perceptions of white males and everyone else within cultural groups (N = 1602, oversample excluded)*

	Environmental risks		Gun risks		Abortion risks	
	White males	Everyone else	White males	Everyone else	White males	Everyone else
Hierarch	**2.66**	3.02*†	**2.13**	2.47*†	**2.61**	2.92*†
Egalitarian	**3.18**	3.33*†	**2.80**	2.81†	**2.27**	2.41†
Individualist	**2.73**	3.10*†	**2.19**	2.53*†	**2.49**	2.66*
Communitarian	**3.05**	3.29*†	**2.72**	2.80†	**2.52**	2.64

Note: Risk perception is coded on a four-point scale. Bold font indicates that the white-male cultural group differs significantly ($p \leq 0.01$) from the opposing white-male cultural group. For 'everyone else,' * denotes a significant difference ($p \leq 0.05$) with white males of the same cultural group; † denotes a significant difference ($p \leq 0.05$) with 'everyone else' of the opposed cultural group.

turned out to be highly culture specific (Table 11.1; Figure 11.4).[3] The difference between the mean risk perceptions of white men and those of white females and minorities was pronounced among persons subscribing to hierarchical world-views and individualistic worldviews for every one of the risks examined. Differences between the perceptions of white males and others were relatively muted among persons holding egalitarian and communitarian worldviews and were non-significant with respect to gun risks and abortion risks.

These patterns are suggestive of the hypothesized interaction of the white-male effect with culture-specific forms of identity-protective cognition. But for definitive testing, it is necessary to disentangle the influences of demographic characteristics and cultural outlooks through multivariate regression analyses.

Discussion

Summary of key findings

Our study was designed to see if the 'white-male effect' could be explained as a form of motivated cognition aimed at protecting identities individuals form through their commitment to cultural norms. The results strongly suggest that it can.

Each type of risk perception had the hypothesized relationship with cultural worldviews. Egalitarian and communitarian worldviews predicted risk sensitivity, hierarchical and individualistic worldviews risk scepticism, toward environmental risks. Abortion-risk sensitivity, in contrast, grew in proportion to respondents' commitment to a hierarchical worldview but receded in proportion to their commitment to an individualistic as well as an egalitarian one. Which type of gun risks alarmed respondents most also depended on cultural orientation: the more egalitarian and communitarian respondents became, the more concerned they were that insufficient regulation would lead to gun accidents and crime, whereas

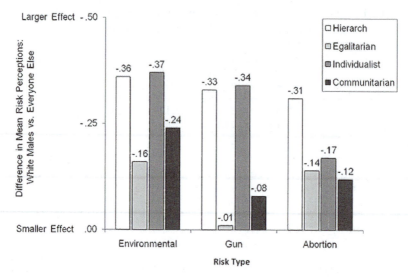

Figure 11.4 *Size of 'white-male effect' on risk perception across cultural groups*

the more hierarchal and individualistic they became, the more worried they were that excessive regulation would undermine the ability of law-abiding persons to defend themselves from violent lawbreakers. These effects were all large, moreover, relative to that of other individual characteristics that might be thought to bear on risk perception, including other group affiliations (such as political party affiliation and religion) that might be expected to produce identity-protective cognition.

Demographic variance in risk perceptions, we found, grew out of cultural variance. Gender affects risk perception only in conjunction with particular worldviews. The influence of gender on both environmental- and abortion-risk concerns is conditional on holding a relatively hierarchical outlook. Similarly, being male predicts less fear of gun risks conditional on holding either a hierarchical or an individualistic worldview. Racial disparities were also highly dependent on culture. When cultural orientations were controlled for, being African-American no longer led to greater apprehension about either environmental risks or gun risks.

The impact of cultural worldviews is consistent with the hypothesized relationship between risk perception and cultural-identity-protective cognition. In keeping with the association of gun ownership with hierarchical and individualistic norms, for example, respondents who held hierarchical and individualistic worldviews were predictably disposed to reject the assertion – levelled by their egalitarian and communitarian rivals – that guns are dangerous. The respondents inclined to see guns as safest of all were hierarchical and individualistic white men. Their stance of fearlessness is convincingly attributable to identity-protective cognition insofar as they are the persons who need guns the most in order to occupy social roles and display individual virtues within their cultural communities.

Identity-protective cognition also plausibly explains the white-male effect for environmental-risk perception. All the gender and race variance with respect to this attitude, we found, was attributable to hierarchical white men. Their extreme risk scepticism makes sense under the cultural theory of risk perception, since their identity is threatened by the indictment of societal and governmental elites implicit in the claim that commerce is hazardous (Douglas and Wildavsky, 1982). Hierarchical women are less threatened, and thus less risk sceptical, because their identity is tied to domestic roles. Assertions of environmental risk should pose an identity challenge to relatively individualistic persons, who equate success in the market with personal virtue. But, as we hypothesized, because individualistic norms treat commercial and professional roles as status enhancing for both men and women, an individualistic orientation disposed respondents to risk scepticism without regard to gender. Our data also demonstrated that male and female African-Americans were uniformly receptive to environmental-risk claims – and no more so than whites once cultural orientation was controlled for.

White hierarchical and individualistic males are by no means the only persons for whom identity threats generate distinctive risk perceptions. Hierarchy more powerfully disposed white women to perceive danger in abortion. We hypothesized that hierarchical women would be more risk sensitive insofar as abortion rights are perceived to denigrate hierarchical norms that confer status on women for occupying domestic rather than professional roles.

Some practical implications

Our findings have important practical implications. The connection between risk perceptions and cultural worldviews should influence both the regulation and the communication of risk.[4]

Risk regulation

Normally, risk regulators use risk–benefit or related forms of analysis to evaluate hazardous activities and proposed measures for abating them (e.g. Revesz, 1999). When employing this approach, analysts often take as given public assessments of the benefits associated with putatively dangerous activities, as revealed in market transactions and other forms of private behaviour (Viscusi, 1983). However, many analysts propose discounting public evaluations of the risks associated with such activities on the ground that those judgements are likely to be distorted by cognitive biases or errors to which experienced risk experts are less likely to succumb (e.g. Breyer, 1993; Margolis, 1996; Sunstein, 2005).

Our study complicates this strategy for risk regulation. To start, the relationship between cultural worldviews and risk perceptions blurs the line between public assessments of the 'risks' and 'benefits' of putatively dangerous activities. The cultural theory of risk perception suggests that individuals conform their view of how dangerous an activity is to their moral assessment of it. Accordingly, when expert risk regulators dismiss public estimations of various risks as uninformed, they can just as easily be understood to be discounting the benefits that individuals attach to activities by virtue of their cultural worldviews.

At the same time, our findings cast doubt on the usual assumption that regulators should always credit the value members of the public attach to hazardous activities. The law takes public estimations of the benefits of dangerous activities as given on the liberal democratic ground that no person's valuation of safety relative to other goals is entitled to more or less weight than anyone else's. But once the connection between risk perception and cultural worldviews is exposed, it becomes clear that individual tolerance of danger does not reflect a 'safety' preference in any straightforward sense. In selecting some risks for attention and dismissing others as unimportant, individuals are, effectively, advancing one culturally partisan vision of the ideal society over others (Kahan, 2007). It is unclear that risk-regulation policy should be responsive to such demands. One might argue, for example, that the law should repudiate the low environmental-risk evaluations reflected in the 'white-male effect' not simply because those evaluations are erroneous, but because they express inappropriate hierarchical and individualistic norms. Alternatively, one might oppose, say, the demand for stricter forms of gun control on the ground that it derives not from an acceptable desire for personal safety but from an illiberal desire to erect an egalitarian or communitarian orthodoxy in law. We take no position on these issues here; we merely draw attention to the normative complexities that a cultural theory of risk perception reveals.

Risk communication

The implications of our study for risk communication are more straightforward. The influence of cultural worldviews on risk perception demonstrates that it would be a profound mistake to assume that the simple ascertainment and dissemination of empirical truth will lead to public enlightenment on various societal and personal risks. Where the activities associated with those risks are conspicuously emblematic of one cultural worldview or another, identity-protective cognition will induce individuals to credit or dismiss scientific information, depending on its congeniality to their cultural norms.

This conclusion does not necessarily mean, however, that it is impossible to educate the public about the risks of such activities. What it does imply is that information must be transmitted in a form that makes individuals' acceptance of it compatible with their core cultural commitments. It is not enough that the information be true; it must be framed in a manner that bears an acceptable social meaning.

In this respect, experimental work on identity-affirmation and cognition is particularly apt. Researchers have shown that individuals who are either personally affirmed or exposed to group-affirming stimuli thereafter display less bias when processing information that is contrary to beliefs dominantly held by their peers (Cohen et al, 2000, 2007; Sherman and Cohen, 2002). Identifying conditions of information dissemination that would exploit this effect in the context of real-world policy debates would enable citizens of diverse cultural persuasions to converge on facts that bear on their common welfare (Kahan et al, 2006).

Evidence of the sort we have presented in this chapter will be highly useful to risk communicators intent on employing this type of strategy. By identifying the cultural worldviews of those most disposed to process risk information in an identity-protective fashion, our study would furnish the risk communicator with information relevant to crafting an appeal that affirms rather than denigrates recipients' values.

Conclusion

Our aim in this study was to investigate the origins of variance in risk perception, particularly racial and gender variance. The source of it, we hypothesized and our data support, is a form of motivated cognition aimed at protecting persons' cultural identities. As surmised by Douglas and Wildavsky (1982), individuals tend to conform their view of the risks of putatively dangerous activities – commerce and technology, guns, abortion – to their cultural evaluations of them. Because individuals' identities are threatened when they encounter information that challenges beliefs commonly held within their group (Cohen et al, 2007), the result is political conflict over risk regulation among groups committed to opposing hierarchical and egalitarian, individualistic and communitarian worldviews.

Similar dynamics explain gender and race disparities in risk perception. Different ways of life feature distinctive forms of gender and racial differentiation in social roles involving putatively dangerous activities. Accordingly, men and women, whites and minorities, form distinct attitudes toward risk in a manner that protects from interference the activities on which their identities depend.

The data we have presented have important practical implications. Normatively, our data raise difficult questions about whether and how identity-protective attitudes toward risk should be factored into the social-welfare calculus that guides risk regulators. Prescriptively, our data suggest the need for expressively sophisticated modes of risk communication, ones that avoid identity-protective resistance to public acceptance of empirically sound risk information.

Fear does discriminate. But it does so in a more even-handed way than had been previously realized. Women and minorities are more fearful of various risks, but the reason they are is that men, particularly individualistic and hierarchical white ones, tend to be more fearful of the threat to their identities that would occur were the law to accept that activities essential to these individuals' identities are dangerous and worthy of regulation. White hierarchical and individualistic men are not the only ones, moreover, impelled toward extreme stances toward risk by identity-protective cognition. The phenomenon is ubiquitous.

These findings solve many long-standing theoretical puzzles about the nature and significance of variance in risk perception. However, they also expose a host of new practical and moral challenges for reconciling the rational regulation of risk with democratic decision making.

Appendix: Survey items

All the items shown below used a four-point response scale: 1 = *strongly agree*, 2 = *agree*, 3 = *disagree* and 4 = *strongly disagree*.

Cultural worldview Items

Egalitarianism–Hierarchy scale
Items beginning with 'E' are reversed.

HCHEATS	It seems like the criminals and welfare cheats get all the breaks, while the average citizen picks up the tab.
HEQUAL	We have gone too far in pushing equal rights in this country.
HFEMININ	Society as a whole has become too soft and feminine.
HREVDIS1	Nowadays it seems like there is just as much discrimination against whites as there is against blacks.
HREVDIS2	It seems like blacks, women, homosexuals and other groups don't want equal rights, they want special rights just for them.
HTRADFAM	A lot of problems in our society today come from the decline in the traditional family, where the man works and the woman stays home.
HWMNRTS	The women's rights movement has gone too far.
EDISCRIM	Discrimination against minorities is still a very serious problem in our society.
EDIVERS	It's old-fashioned and wrong to think that one culture's set of values is better than any other culture's way of seeing the world.
EGAYMAR	A gay or lesbian couple should have just as much right to marry as any other couple.
ERADEQ	We need to dramatically reduce inequalities between the rich and the poor, whites and people of colour, and men and women.
EROUGH	Parents should encourage young boys to be more sensitive and less 'rough and tough'.
EWEALTH	Our society would be better off if the distribution of wealth was more equal.
EXSEXIST	We live in a sexist society that is fundamentally set up to discriminate against women.

Communitarianism–Individualism scale
Items beginning with 'S' are reversed.

IENJOY	People who are successful in business have a right to enjoy their wealth as they see fit.
IFIX	If the government spent less time trying to fix everyone's problems, we'd all be a lot better off.
IGOVWAST	Government regulations are almost always a waste of everyone's time and money.

IINTRFER	The government interferes far too much in our everyday lives.
IMKT	Free markets – not government programmes – are the best way to supply people with the things they need.
INEEDS	Too many people today expect society to do things for them that they should be doing for themselves.
INEEDY	It's a mistake to ask society to help every person in need.
IPRIVACY	The government should stop telling people how to live their lives.
IPROFIT	Private profit is the main motive for hard work.
IPROTECT	It's not the government's business to try to protect people from themselves.
IRESPON	Society works best when it lets individuals take responsibility for their own lives without telling them what to do.
ITRIES	Our government tries to do too many things for too many people. We should just let people take care of themselves.
SHARM	Sometimes government needs to make laws that keep people from hurting themselves.
SLIMCHOI	Government should put limits on the choices individuals can make so they don't get in the way of what's good for society.
SNEEDS	It's society's responsibility to make sure everyone's basic needs are met.
SPROTECT	The government should do more to advance society's goals, even if that means limiting the freedom and choices of individuals.
SRELY	People should be able to rely on the government for help when they need it.

Risk perception items

Environmental risks

ENVIRON	Environmental pollution is a serious risk to public health in our country.
GLOBWARM	Global warming poses a serious danger for the future of our planet.
NUKES	It is dangerous to live near a nuclear power plant.

Gun risks

HOMEACC	When people keep a gun in their home, there is a serious risk that someone will be accidentally shot.
HOMEDEF	Keeping a gun in the home is an effective way for those who live there to defend themselves from an intruder. (Reversed)
SOCSAFE	The more guns there are in our society, the less safe our society becomes.
HANDCRIM	Fewer people commit violent crimes when private citizens are allowed to carry concealed handguns. (Reversed)
DREAD1	I am very disturbed by the thought that I or my loved ones might be injured or killed because gun-control laws aren't strict enough.

DREAD2   I am very disturbed by the thought that gun-control laws might
              interfere with my ability to defend myself or my loved ones.
              (Reversed)

Abortion risks
ABORTION   Women who get abortions are putting their health in danger.

Acknowledgements

Research for this chapter was funded by National Science Foundation Grant
SES-0242106. We are grateful to Paul von Hippel for advice on data imputation;
to Geoffrey Cohen for comments on an earlier draft; and to John Darley, Don
Green, Paul Sniderman and Christopher Winship for their invaluable guidance as
members of our study advisory panel. Most of all, we are indebted to the late
Mary Douglas for inspiration and for supportive, albeit often painfully direct,
counsel on our research methods.

Notes

1   Relatively few studies have examined the risk perceptions of distinct minority groups
     relative to one another. However, one study has found that Taiwanese-American
     males, like white American males, rate health and technology risks to be low relative to
     white females, Taiwanese-American females, and African-Americans and Mexican-
     Americans generally (Palmer, 2003). Finucane et al (2000b) also found that Asian
     males are more akin to white American males in their perception of certain risks.
2   The US Supreme Court in fact recently cited the government's legitimate interest in
     protecting women from '[s]evere depression and loss of esteem' as a ground for
     upholding the federal partial-birth abortion law (Gonzales v. Carhart, 127 S. Ct.
     1610, 1634 (2007)).
3   The African-American oversample was excluded from this analysis to avoid
     overweighting the perceptions of African-Americans relative to white women and
     other minorities in computing the means for individuals in the 'everyone else'
     category.
4   For more systematic discussions of the normative and prescriptive significance of the
     influence of cultural worldviews on perceptions of risk, see Kahan et al (2006) and
     Kahan and Braman (2006a).

Chapter 12

Fear of Democracy: A Cultural Evaluation of Sunstein on Risk

A review of *Laws of Fear: Beyond the Precautionary Principle* (2005) by Cass R. Sunstein

Dan M. Kahan, Paul Slovic, Donald Braman and John Gastil*

To secure the public good ... and at the same time to preserve the spirit and the form of popular government, is then the great object to which our inquiries are directed.

James Madison (1787)

The only thing we have to fear is fear itself.

Franklin D. Roosevelt (1933)

The effective regulation of risk poses a singular challenge to democracy. The public welfare of democratic societies depends on their capacity to abate all manner of natural and man-made hazards – from environmental catastrophe and economic collapse to domestic terrorism and the outbreak of disease. But the need to form rational responses to these and other dangers also challenges democratic societies in a more fundamental way: by threatening their commitment to genuinely deliberative policy making. Effective risk regulation depends on

* Reprinted from Kahan, D. M., Slovic, P., Braman, D. and Gastil, J. (2006) 'Fear of democracy: A cultural critique of Sunstein on risk,' *Harvard Law Review*, vol 119, pp1071–1109

highly technical forms of scientific information – epidemiological, toxicological, economic and the like. Most citizens don't even have access to such information, much less the inclination and capacity to make sense of it. Why, then, should regulatory law afford any weight to the uneducated opinions of ordinary citizens as opposed to the reasoned judgements of politically insulated risk experts?

It is the urgency of this question that makes the study of risk perception a policy science of the first order. Employing a diverse array of methods from the social sciences, the field of risk perception seeks to comprehend the diverse processes by which individuals form beliefs about the seriousness of various hazards and the efficacy of measures designed to mitigate them. Risk perception scholars are not of one mind about the prospects for making public opinion conform to the best available scientific information on risk. But no one who aspires to devise procedures that make democratic policy making responsive to such information can hope to succeed without availing herself of the insights this field has to offer.

Cass Sunstein's *Laws of Fear: Beyond the Precautionary Principle* (2005) is a major contribution to the field of risk perception written in precisely this spirit. In Sunstein's view, the major thing proponents of democratically grounded risk regulation have to fear, in essence, is fear itself. Adroitly synthesizing a vast body of empirical literature, Sunstein catalogues the numerous social and cognitive mechanisms that drive members of the public to form wildly overstated estimates of various societal dangers. He also proposes a number of important institutional devices designed to shield 'deliberative democracy' from the pernicious influence of these 'risk panics' (p1). They include, principally, a form of expert cost–benefit analysis that would separate out considered public values from irrational public fears and a set of administrative procedures that would make law responsive to the former and impervious to the latter. Few recent works in the field of risk perception rival Sunstein's in breadth, intelligence and relevance.

But as masterful as Sunstein's account is, its persuasiveness is undercut by his inattention to one of the most important recent advances in the science of risk perception. A growing body of work suggests that *cultural worldviews* permeate all of the mechanisms through which individuals apprehend risk, including their emotional appraisals of putatively dangerous activities, their comprehension and retention of empirical information, and their disposition to trust competing sources of risk information. As a result, individuals effectively conform their beliefs about risk to their visions of an ideal society. This phenomenon – which we propose to call 'cultural cognition' – not only helps explain why members of the public so often disagree with experts about matters as diverse as global warming, gun control, the spread of HIV through casual contact, and the health consequences of obtaining an abortion; it also explains why experts themselves so often disagree about these matters and why political conflict over them is so intense.

The phenomenon of cultural cognition underwrites a strong critique of the analysis that Sunstein presents in *Laws of Fear*. Once the influence of culture is taken into account, what Sunstein sees as public hysteria is often revealed to be a complex form of status competition between the adherents of competing cultural visions. This reformulation of public risk sensibilities, in turn, undermines much of Sunstein's normative account of how the law should respond to public risk perceptions. Because citizens' fears express their cultural visions of how society should be organized, the line between 'considered values' and 'irrational fears' often proves illusory. Reliance on expert cost–benefit analysis, in these circumstances, becomes less a strategy for rationally implementing public values than a device for strategically avoiding political disputes over individual virtue and collective justice.

Unfortunately, though, it's not clear that incorporating cultural cognition into the science of risk perception reduces the complexity of reconciling rational risk regulation with democratic decision making. A theory of risk perception that incorporates cultural cognition is teeming with insights on how to structure risk communication; by linking risk perception to cultural values, it identifies myriad new strategies for managing public impressions of what risks are real and what risk-mitigation strategies are effective. But at the same time that such a theory makes the prescriptive dimension of risk regulation more tractable, it makes the normative dimension considerably harder to assess. If risk disputes are really disputes over the good life, then the challenge that risk regulation poses for democracy is less how to reconcile public sensibilities with science than how to accommodate diverse visions of the good within a popular system of regulation. Fear itself may indeed be what democratic societies, or at least pluralistic ones, most have to fear – not because governmental responses to risk are likely to be irrational, but because risk regulation is inherently fraught with the potential for illiberality.

We develop this response to Sunstein's *Laws of Fear* in four steps. First, we explicate Sunstein's account. Sunstein's theory is best understood within the context of a debate over two competing models of risk perception – one that sees individuals as rational weighers of risk and another that sees them as irrational weighers.

Second, we examine the dynamic that Sunstein's account overlooks: cultural cognition. We show how cultural cognition supports a distinct model of risk perception – one in which individuals behave neither as rational nor irrational weighers but rather as cultural evaluators of risk. Third, we use this model to challenge the central positive, normative and prescriptive components of Sunstein's account.

Finally, we examine what the cultural-evaluator model of risk perception reveals about the tension between risk regulation and liberalism. Surprisingly, one response to this tension might be to base policy making on an irrational-weigher theory such as Sunstein's, precisely because that model overlooks the cultural underpinnings of public risk perceptions.

Sunstein and the 'irrational-weigher' model

Advances in the field of risk perception have been fuelled by an energetic debate between the proponents of two opposing theories. These theories, which we will call the 'rational-weigher' and 'irrational-weigher' models, posit competing accounts of the nature of individual judgements of risk and how the law should respond to them. Sunstein's account is most readily understood within the context of this debate. Thus, we begin with a general overview of the points of contention between the rational-weigher and irrational-weigher models and then turn to the particulars of Sunstein's sophisticated articulation of the latter.

Two conceptions of individual risk perception: Rational versus irrational weighing

Grounded in the assumptions and methods of neoclassical economics, the rational-weigher model asserts that individuals, in aggregate and over time, form judgements toward risk that maximize expected utility. Decisions to take a hazardous job (say, as a construction worker; Viscusi, 1983, p37), to purchase a potentially dangerous consumer good (perhaps a chainsaw; Schwartz, 1988, p358), or even to engage in manifestly unhealthy forms of personal recreation (smoking cigarettes, see Viscusi, 1992; or unsafe sex, Philipson and Posner, 1993, pp57–83) – all ultimately embody a considered balancing of costs and benefits.

To be sure, people suffer from imperfect information, make mistakes, and even lack the capacity to follow through on what they correctly perceive to be in their best interests. But as a result of chance variation and market-based forms of social selection, whatever departures from utility maximization these impairments might induce in particular individuals can be expected to cancel each other out across individuals. Accordingly, even if no individual approaches risk in a perfectly rational fashion, people behave as if they were doing so in aggregate (Viscusi, 1983, p4; Schwartz, 1988, pp374–384).

The rational-weigher model counsels a restrained role for governmental risk regulation. If people left to their own devices generally make choices that maximize their well-being, then devising legal regimes and institutions to regulate risk-taking is largely unnecessary and indeed ultimately destructive of societal wealth and individual freedom (Viscusi, 1983, p4; Schwartz, 1988, p383). The only circumstance in which regulatory intervention is clearly warranted is when utility-maximizing individuals are likely to expose others to risks the expected costs of which are not fully borne by those creating them. But when imposing regulation to combat externalities of this sort, regulators should not, according to proponents of the rational-weigher model, be guided by their own personal judgements of what types of risk-taking are socially desirable. Rather they should try to base regulatory standards on the preferences implicit in the behaviour of persons who do fully internalize both the costs and benefits of putatively dangerous activities. In effect, regulatory responses to risk should mimic the individual responses revealed in markets and related forms of collective behaviour (Viscusi, 1983, pp114–135).

The irrational-weigher model, in contrast, posits that people, considered individually or collectively, approach matters of risk in a manner that systematically fails to maximize their utility. Drawing on social psychology and behavioural economics, the proponents of this position have catalogued a vast array of cognitive limitations and defects that distort popular perceptions of risk (Noll and Krier, 1990; Slovic, 2000a, pp1–50). Thus, individuals are disposed to wildly overestimate the magnitude of highly evocative risks (say, of a nuclear power accident) and to ignore less evocative ones (say, of developing cancer from peanut butter; Kasperson et al, 1988, p178; Noll and Krier, 1990, pp754–755; Slovic, 2000a, pp37–38). Far from cancelling each other out, the types of risk-estimation errors that people make on an individual level tend to become even more exaggerated as individuals interact with one another. Various mechanisms of social influence cause popular risk perceptions to reinforce and feed on themselves, generating waves of mass incomprehension (Kasperson et al, 1988, pp179–186).

The irrational-weigher model counsels a much more aggressive programme of governmental regulation. The cognitive defects and social forces that tend to distort risk perceptions have the largest impact on members of the lay public; scientifically trained experts are less vulnerable to these influences because they routinely access and comprehend accurate sources of information, form more balanced mental inventories of the harms and benefits associated with various putatively dangerous behaviors, and converge on consensus judgements through rigorous exchanges with other, similarly well-informed observers (Margolis, 1996, pp71–97). It thus makes sense to entrust matters of environmental regulation, consumer protection, workplace safety and the like to such experts, who should be insulated as much as possible from politics to avoid the distorting influence of the public's misapprehension of risk (Slovic, 2000a, pp137–153, 285–315).[1]

We have sketched out the rational-weigher and irrational-weigher models in their purest forms. It's possible, of course, to formulate intermediate positions that include elements of both.[2] Even more important, it's possible to qualify either model based on considerations external to both. Some exponents of the irrational-weigher model, for example, are careful to distinguish divergences between lay and expert risk assessments that reflect the bounded rationality of the public from those that reflect 'rival rationalities': one, on the part of experts, that reduces all issues of risk to a unitary expected-utility metric; and another, on the part of the public, that includes qualitative elements of appraisal that defy such a metric (Slovic, 2000a, pp137–53, 285–315).[3] But the pure forms of the rational-weigher and irrational-weigher models are well represented in the study of risk perception and furnish useful reference points for making sense of any particular scholar's position.

Sunstein on risk

Sunstein's position, as reflected in *Laws of Fear*, embodies the premises of the irrational-weigher model in an essentially unqualified form. Indeed, based on his systematic description of the dynamics that drive public risk perceptions and his detailed prescriptions for shielding risk regulation from the distorting influence of these forces, Sunstein's theory can be viewed as the most instructive account to date of what the irrational-weigher model entails for law.

Descriptive

Sunstein's conception of the irrational-weigher model of risk perception contains two components. The first comprises the psychological mechanisms that dispose individuals to systematically misestimate risk. The second highlights the social forces that magnify popular assessments of risk as individuals interact with one another.

Among the former is the 'availability heuristic.' This dynamic refers to the tendency of individuals to 'assess the magnitude of risks' based on how 'easily [they can] think of … examples' of the misfortunes to which these risks give rise (p36; Slovic, 2000a, pp37–38). Thus, nuclear power triggers alarm because of the notoriety of the accidents at Three Mile Island and Chernobyl; the hazards of toxic waste disposal assume massive proportions because of the publicity that surrounded the Love Canal affair; arsenic levels in drinking water generate apprehension because 'arsenic is [a] well known … poison,' in part due to the 'classic movie about poisoning, *Arsenic and Old Lace*' (pp37–38). The influence of the availability heuristic can easily distort public judgement, insofar as calamitous misfortunes, however isolated, are much more likely to grab media attention and stick in the public memory than are the myriad instances in which risky technologies, processes or chemicals generate benefits for society (compare Margolis, 1996, pp94–97).

Another mechanism that distorts public risk perceptions is 'probability neglect.' This is Sunstein's term for characterizing an asserted disposition of persons 'to focus on the worst case, even if it is highly improbable' (p35). To maximize expected utility, individuals ought to discount the gain or loss associated with a course of action by the probability that such an outcome will occur (Sklansky, 1999, pp9–11). Experimental research shows, however, that individuals are less likely to discount in this fashion when they are evaluating outcomes that provoke strongly negative emotions such as fear; the cost individuals are willing to incur to avoid such outcomes is relatively insensitive to the diminishing probability that such outcomes will occur (Rottenstreich and Hsee, 2001). For Sunstein, this finding implies that ordinary citizens are likely to support expensive preventative measures, however remote the risks and however cost-ineffective the abatement procedures. Examples, he argues, include massive investments in toxic waste clean-up and cumbersome procedures for screening mail for anthrax (pp83–85).

Additional related mechanisms converge to make individuals unduly insensitive to the benefits of risky technologies. One of these mechanisms is 'loss aversion.' Typically, 'a loss from the status quo is seen as more undesirable than a gain is seen as desirable' (p41).[4] Another is the 'endowment effect.' Individuals value goods more once they have them than they did before they acquired them (Kahneman et al 1991, p193); as a result, they are likely to resist courses of action that require them to risk goods they have to achieve outcomes they would value even more (p42). Individuals also display a form of 'status quo bias' (Kahneman et al 1991, p193): in appraising a potentially beneficial but also risky course of action, they fall back on the maxim '[b]etter safe than sorry' to justify inaction (p47).[5] In tandem, these dispositions generate a species of conservatism that causes individuals to seize on the potential 'losses produced by any newly introduced risk, or by any aggravation of existing risks,' to block new technologies without 'concern for the benefits that are forgone as a result' (p42, emphasis omitted). This is the explanation, according to Sunstein, of why persons are 'so concerned about the risks of nuclear power' even though 'experts tend to believe that the risks are ... lower, in fact, than the risks from competing energy sources, such as coal-fired power plants' (p47).

Another distorting mechanism is affect. The emotional responses that putatively dangerous activities trigger in persons have been shown to be one of the most robust predictors of how risky they perceive such activities to be (Finucane et al, 2000a; Loewenstein et al, 2001; Slovic et al, 2004). Indeed, Sunstein plausibly depicts the impact of affect as foundational to nearly all other mechanisms of risk perception. The availability of risks is regulated by how emotionally gripping the images of misfortune they provoke are (pp38–39). It is 'when intense emotions are engaged [that] people tend to focus on the adverse outcome, not on its likelihood' (p64). Persons react conservatively and display status quo bias or loss aversion because 'when [they] anticipate a loss of what [they] now have, [they] can become genuinely afraid, in a way that greatly exceeds [their] feelings of pleasurable anticipation when [they] look forward to some supplement to what [they] now have' (p41).

The distorting influence that these psychological mechanisms exert on individual risk perceptions is magnified, according to Sunstein, by two social forces. Sunstein calls the first of these forces 'availability cascades.' For the same reason that 'fear-inducing accounts' of misfortune with 'high emotional valence' are likely to be noticed and recalled, they are also likely 'to be repeated, leading to cascade effects, as the event becomes available to increasingly large numbers of people' (p96). 'A process of this sort,' Sunstein maintains, 'played a large role in the [reaction to the] Washington area sniper attacks, the Love Canal scare, [and] the debate over mad cow disease' (p94). Availability cascades also help explain 'moral panics' in which large segments of society suddenly perceive 'religious dissidents, foreigners, immigrants, homosexuals, teenage gangs, and drug users' as sources of danger (p98).

'Group polarization,' the second social force Sunstein discusses, magnifies the impact of individual biases when individuals engage in deliberations over risks and how to abate them (Lord et al, 1979). Individuals don't moderate their views when they engage in such discussions, Sunstein argues; on the contrary, 'they typically end up accepting a more extreme version of the views with which they began' (p98). If one view is even slightly predominant within a group when it starts deliberation, arguments in favour of that position will predominate in discussions, fortifying the confidence of those who hold that position and making a bigger impact on the undecided. This effect will be reinforced by the subconscious desire of persons to conform their view to the apparent majority and by the reluctance of those who perceive themselves to be in the minority to take a public stance that might expose them to ridicule.

Despite his emphasis on 'risk panics,' Sunstein recognizes that the same dynamics that make persons 'fearful when they ought not to be' can also make them 'fearless when they should be frightened' (p1). Indeed, one state almost entails the other. This is the case partly because so many risks are offsetting. A society that pays inordinate attention to the risks of nuclear power necessarily pays too little to the risks associated with fossil fuels (for example, global warming and acid rain; pp27–28). Many societies that fear the carcinogenic effects of the pesticide DDT are insufficiently mindful of the increased incidence of malaria associated with using less effective substitutes (p32).

Excessive fear and insufficient fear also tend to mirror each other, according to Sunstein, because of the largely hidden – and hence emotionally tepid – financial impact of risk-reducing regulation. Sunstein cites studies suggesting that every \$7 million to \$15 million in costs incurred to comply with governmental regulation is itself associated with the expected loss of one human life given the adverse effect of such expenditures on the economy (pp32–33; the author cites Keeney, 1990; Hahn et al, 2000). Accordingly, many costly programmes that only slightly reduce the magnitude of risks (such as the amount of arsenic in drinking water) actually end up costing more lives than they save (pp28–29).

It thus becomes impossible (practically and maybe even conceptually) to say which – excessive fear or excessive fearlessness – dominates in public risk perceptions. But one conclusion that can be drawn from Sunstein's account is that the public, impelled by emotion and waves of hysteria to fixate on some risks and wholly disregard others, can never be expected to get it right. The greatest risk to the public's health may be its own risk assessments.

Normative and prescriptive

Sunstein has just as much to say about what the law should do to respond to distorted public perceptions of risk as he does about the forces responsible for distorting them. Not surprisingly, he unequivocally rejects 'populist systems' (p1) of regulation that take public risk evaluations at face value. Indeed, one of the major objectives of *Laws of Fear* is to critique the so-called 'precautionary principle' as unduly responsive to public sentiments. That principle, which enjoys worldwide support among environmentalists and regulatory authorities (pp15–18), asserts, essentially, that 'when there is scientific uncertainty as to the nature of [the] damage or the likelihood of the risk' posed by some activity, 'then decisions should be made so as to prevent such activity ... unless and until scientific evidence shows that the damage will not occur' (p19).[6] When enforced by democratically responsive institutions, this approach, Sunstein maintains, yokes regulatory law to the various mechanisms – availability, probability neglect, status quo bias and various forms of social influence – that make the public irrationally fearful of 'low-probability risks' (p26). At the same time, because fixation on particular risks is always accompanied by inattention to offsetting risks and the adverse societal impact of regulatory expenditures, the precautionary principle inevitably forces society to forgo 'technologies and strategies that make human lives easier, more convenient, healthier, and longer' (p25).

Unfortunately, Sunstein concludes, public irrationality of this sort cannot be dispelled by education. The same mechanisms that cause members of the public to form exaggerated perceptions of risk will also prevent them from processing scientifically sound information in a rational way. Because 'people neglect probability,' for example, even accurate disclosure of risks may induce them to 'fix, or fixate, on the bad outcome,' thereby 'greatly alarm[ing] people … without giving them any useful information at all' (p123). Rather than emphasize how small a risk is, a better way to dispel irrational fear, Sunstein argues, is to 'change the subject' – 'discuss something else and … let time do the rest' (p125).

Ultimately, though, even this strategy of distraction is unlikely to calm public anxieties, because scientists and enlightened regulators aren't the only ones speaking (or not) to the public. 'Terrorists, … environmentalists, and corporate executives,' among others, can all be expected to strategically 'exploit probability neglect' and related dynamics (p65). Propelled by 'economic self-interest,' the news media, too, will intensify risk hysteria by reporting 'gripping instances' of misfortune, 'whether or not representative' of the activities that give rise to them (p103).

For Sunstein, there is only one credible treatment for the pathologies that afflict public risk assessments: the delegation of regulatory authority to independent expert agencies. 'If the public demand for regulation is likely to be distorted by unjustified fear, a major role should be given to more insulated officials who are in a better position to judge whether risks are real' (p126).

Such experts, Sunstein maintains, are relatively immune from the influences that inevitably distort public risk estimations. Drawing on social psychology's 'dual-processing' model of cognition, Sunstein contrasts two forms of information processing: 'System I,' which is 'rapid, intuitive, and error prone' because pervaded by 'heuristic-based thinking' of the sort responsible for exaggerated estimations of risk; and 'System II,' which is 'more deliberative, calculative, slower, and more likely to be error free' (p68).[7] By virtue of their training, the time they have to reflect, and their reliance on one another rather than misguided popular sources of information, scientific experts can be expected to use System II reasoning when appraising risks (pp85–87).

Investing politically independent experts with substantial authority, Sunstein insists, would not make risk assessment fundamentally undemocratic. 'Well-functioning governments,' he observes, 'aspire to be deliberative democracies' (p1). They take account of the public's anxieties, but their 'responsiveness is complemented by a commitment to deliberation, in the form of reflection and reason giving' (p1). Accordingly, 'if highly representative institutions, responding to public fear, are susceptible to error, then it is entirely appropriate to create institutions that will have a degree of insulation. Democratic governments should respond to people's values, not to their blunders' (p126).

The principal device that expert regulators should use to distinguish public values from public misperceptions is cost–benefit analysis. Using this technique, regulators would assess the efficiency of risk-abatement measures by comparing their own calculations of the magnitude and probability of harm associated with risky technologies and substances to the value individuals (as revealed largely through market behaviour) attach to life and limb (p131).[8]

Although he acknowledges that this methodology is far from perfect, Sunstein holds that cost–benefit analysis furnishes an indispensable tool for the rational regulation of risk in a democracy. Because it cleanses risk assessment of the contaminating influences of availability, probability neglect, affect and the like, 'it is an important way of disciplining public fear – of creating a kind of System II corrective against System I heuristics and biases' (p130).

Sunstein allows that cost–benefit analysis 'provides [only] a place to start' and 'should not be taken as decisive' for the law (p174). On reflection, popularly accountable lawmakers might well conclude that other values, including the welfare of poor people, the protection of endangered species or the preservation of pristine areas, are worth the cost of enduring economically inefficient regulation (p129).

There is one particular type of popular veto, however, that Sunstein's conception of 'deliberative democracy' can rarely if ever abide: second-guessing of the magnitude that experts assign to various risks.

Here, as elsewhere, Sunstein (2002, pp1122–1137, reviewing Slovic, 2000a) reacts with deep scepticism toward the 'rival rationality' hypothesis, which depicts many disagreements between expert and lay perceptions of risk as grounded in differences of value, not knowledge. 'Often experts are aware of the facts and ordinary people are not' (p86). 'Hence a form of irrationality, not a different set of values, often helps explain the different risk judgements of experts and ordinary people' (p86). It is precisely to root out public irrationality in perceptions of the 'cost' of risky technologies, in particular, that cost–benefit analysis by independent agencies is essential.

The cultural-evaluator model

Sunstein's account rests on an admirably comprehensive synthesis of the empirical literature on risk perception. This literature, however, features an important dynamic to which Sunstein is strikingly inattentive: the impact of *cultural worldviews*. To set up our assessment of how this omission detracts from Sunstein's account, we begin with a summary of the recent work in this area, which, we argue, supports an alternative to both the rational-weigher and irrational-weigher models of risk perception.

Cultural cognition: Theory and evidence

The claim behind cultural cognition is that culture is prior to facts in societal disputes over risk. Normatively, culture might be prior to facts in the sense that cultural values determine what significance individuals attach to the consequences of environmental regulation, gun control, drug criminalization and the like. But more importantly, culture is cognitively prior to facts in the sense that cultural values shape what individuals believe the consequences of such policies to be. Individuals selectively credit and dismiss factual claims in a manner that supports their preferred vision of the good society.

The priority of culture to fact is the organizing premise of the 'cultural theory of risk.'[9] Associated most famously with the work of anthropologist Mary Douglas and political scientist Aaron Wildavsky (1982), the cultural theory of risk links disputes over environmental and technological risks to clusters of values that form competing cultural worldviews – egalitarian, individualistic and hierarchical. Egalitarians, on this account, are naturally sensitive to environmental hazards, the abatement of which justifies regulating commercial activities that produce social inequality. Individualists, in contrast, predictably dismiss claims of environmental risk as specious, in line with their commitment to the autonomy of markets and other private orderings. Hierarchists are similarly sceptical because they perceive warnings of imminent environmental catastrophe as threatening the competence of social and governmental elites.

Although one can imagine alternative explanations for cultural variation in risk perceptions,[10] cultural cognition offers a distinctively psychometric one.[11] On this view, the impact of cultural worldviews is not an alternative to, but rather a vital component of, the various psychological and social mechanisms that determine perceptions of risk. These mechanisms, cultural cognition asserts, are endogenous to culture. That is, the direction in which they point risk perceptions depends on individuals' cultural values.

Consider the affect heuristic. Emotional responses to putatively dangerous activities strongly determine risk perceptions (Slovic et al, 2004), but what determines whether those responses are positive or negative? The answer, according to cultural cognition, is culture: persons' worldviews infuse various activities – firearm possession (Cultural Cognition Project, undated-a), nuclear power generation (Peters et al, 2004), red-meat consumption (Allen and Ng, 2003) – with despised or valued social meanings, which in turn determine whether individuals react with anxiety or calmness, dread or admiration, toward those activities. This account recognizes, in line with the best psychological accounts, that emotions are not thoughtless surges of affect, but rather value-laden judgements shaped by social norms.[12]

A similar account can be given of probability neglect. Individuals display less sensitivity to the improbability of a bad outcome when that outcome is attended by intensely negative affect. But insofar as the valence and strength of individuals' affective responses are influenced by their cultural appraisals of putatively dangerous activities (guns, nuclear power plants, drug use, casual sex, etc.), probability neglect will again be culture dependent.

Availability, too, is likely to be endogenous to culture. The magnitude of a perceived risk depends on how readily an individual can recall instances of misfortune associated with that risk. But how likely someone is to take note of such misfortunes and to recall them almost certainly depends on her values: to avoid cognitive dissonance, individuals are likely to attend selectively to information in a way that reinforces rather than undermines their commitment to the view that certain activities (say, gun possession, or economic commerce) are either noble or base.[13]

Culture will also condition the impact of social influences on risk perceptions. Most individuals are not in a position to determine for themselves whether childhood vaccines induce autism, silicone breast implants cause immune system dysfunction, private firearm possession reduces or increases crime, and so on. Accordingly, they must trust others to tell them which risk claims, supported by which forms of highly technical empirical evidence, to believe. And the people they trust, not surprisingly, are the ones who share their cultural worldviews – and who are likely to be disposed to particular positions by virtue of affect, probability neglect, availability and similar mechanisms. Risk perceptions are thus likely to be uniform within cultural groups and diverse across them. Accordingly, group polarization and cascades are endogenous to culture, too.

A considerable body of recent empirical research supports this account. Using a variety of methods, researchers have demonstrated the influence of cultural worldviews on perceptions of environmental risks, particularly those associated with nuclear power (Dake, 1991; Peters and Slovic, 1996, pp1445–1451; Jenkins-Smith, 2001, pp107–111).

We have conducted our own National Risk and Culture Survey, designed to establish the influence of cultural cognition on a broad scale.[14] The study utilized Douglas's well-known typology, which categorizes cultural ways of life along two cross-cutting dimensions, 'group' and 'grid' (Douglas, 1970, pviii). Within 'high group' ways of life, individuals 'interact frequently and in a wide range of activities' in which they must 'depend on each other,' a condition that 'promotes values of solidarity'; in 'low group' ways of life, in contrast, individuals are expected to 'fend for themselves and therefore tend to be competitive' (Rayner, 1992, pp87–88). Persons who participate in a 'high grid' way of life expect resources, opportunities, respect and the like to be 'distributed on the basis of explicit public social classifications, such as sex, color, ... holding a bureaucratic office, [or] descent in a senior clan or lineage' (Gross and Rayner, 1985). Those who adhere to a 'low grid' way of life favour a 'state of affairs in which no one is prevented from participating in any social role because he or she is the wrong sex, or is too old, or does not have the right family connections,' and so forth (Rayner, 1992, p87). After conducting an extensive review of ethnographic materials, conducting our own focus group discussions, and pretesting a wide variety of survey items, we developed two highly reliable attitude scales, 'Individualism–Solidarism' and 'Hierarchy–Egalitarianism,' that capture the key value conflicts among persons located in different quadrants of the group/grid typology (Kahan et al, 2005, pp38–40).

In a random national survey of 1800 persons, we used these scales to measure the impact of cultural worldviews on a diverse array of risk perceptions. Our results confirmed Douglas and Wildavsky's (and other researchers') conclusions on the relationship between cultural worldviews and perceptions of environmental risks. The more egalitarian and solidaristic persons are, the more concern they have about global warming, nuclear power and pollution generally, whereas the more hierarchical and individualistic persons are, the less concern they have (Kahan et al, 2005, p15).

We found a similar relationship between cultural worldviews and perceptions of gun-related risks. Relatively egalitarian and solidaristic persons believe that widespread private ownership of guns undermines public safety by increasing the incidence of crime and gun accidents; relatively hierarchical and individualistic persons, in contrast, believe that widespread restrictions on private gun ownership undermine public safety by rendering law-abiding persons unable to defend themselves from violent predation (Kahan et al, 2005, pp18–21). These opposing perceptions of gun risks cohere with the negative and positive social meanings that guns bear, respectively, for persons of these cultural orientations (Kahan and Braman, 2003, pp1299–1302).

Whereas individualists and hierarchists square off against solidarists and egalitarians on environmental and gun risks, on other issues individualists and hierarchists part ways. Hierarchists worry, for example, about the societal dangers of drug distribution and promiscuous sex, and the individual dangers of marijuana smoking; individualists do not (Cultural Cognition Project, 2006a). Likewise, egalitarians and individualists don't worry much about the personal risks of obtaining an abortion or contracting AIDS from surgery; hierarchists worry a great deal about these risks (Cultural Cognition Project, 2006b). These patterns also conform to the logic of the worldviews in question: hierarchists morally disapprove of behaviour that defies conventional norms, and thus naturally believe that deviant behaviour is dangerous; egalitarians morally disapprove of norms that rigidly stratify people, and individualists disapprove of norms that constrain individual choice generally, so these types naturally believe that deviant behaviour is benign.

Cultural evaluation versus rational and irrational weighing

The empirical evidence supporting the phenomenon of cultural cognition generates a distinct model of risk perception. We call it the 'cultural-evaluator' model to emphasize the role that cultural values play in determining not only which outcomes individuals are willing to take risks to obtain, but also which empirical claims about risk they are likely to believe.

This label also underscores our view that individual risk perceptions do not typically embody any sort of expected-utility weighing, rational or irrational. Indeed, for most persons, such weighing is completely unnecessary: studies show that individuals' perceptions of the benefits and risks of various putatively dangerous activities (from nuclear power to commercial aviation to handgun ownership) are inversely correlated.[15] Guided by judgement-infused emotions and motivated by their need to preserve their fundamental ties to others, individuals naturally conform their perceptions of both the costs and benefits of such activities to the positive or negative social meanings with which those activities are imbued by cultural norms.

In sum, individuals adopt stances toward risks that express their commitment to particular ways of life. Their risk perceptions might or might not be accurate when evaluated from an actuarial standpoint; policies based on them might or might not be in the interest of society measured according to any welfarist metric. Nevertheless, which activities individuals view as dangerous and which policies they view as effective embody coherent visions of social justice and individual virtue.

Culturally evaluating Sunstein

We've suggested that Sunstein's conception of the irrational-weigher model is inattentive to the phenomenon of cultural cognition. We now consider how this inattention detracts from Sunstein's diagnosis of the pathologies that afflict risk perceptions and from his recommended institutional cures.

Descriptive deficiencies

Sunstein's descriptive account of risk perception draws a sharp distinction between public risk assessments and expert ones. The former are distorted by various cognitive and social dynamics that impel lay persons to fixate obsessively on risks of high emotional salience but often minimal consequence, and to disregard more serious threats to societal well-being. The latter, in contrast, are characterized by the balance and accuracy associated with the calmer and more analytic modes of System II reasoning.

The cultural-evaluator model suggests a richer and more nuanced picture that accounts for certain phenomena that Sunstein's irrational-weigher model does not satisfactorily explain. These include systematic differences in risk perceptions among lay persons, the clustering of public risk perceptions across seemingly discrete issues, systematic differences of opinion among risk experts, and the intensity of political conflict surrounding risk regulation.

Individual differences

Lay persons disagree not only with experts but also with *one another* about the magnitude of various risks. These disagreements, moreover, are far from random. They highly correlate with characteristics such as gender, race, political orientation and religion, and they persist even after controlling for education and other information-related influences.[16]

These systematic individual differences pose an obvious challenge to the rational-weigher model of risk perception. The idea that individuals respond to risk in a manner that maximizes their expected utility certainly allows for heterogeneity in the benefits individuals attach to risky activities. But if individuals, in aggregate and over time, are rationally processing information about risk, differences in their estimations of the magnitude of various risks should essentially just be noise – products of random variation that display no intelligible patterns across persons.

The irrational-weigher model also fails to explain such differences. It's implausible to think that men are more or less vulnerable than women, whites more or less vulnerable than minorities, Republicans more or less vulnerable than Democrats, or Catholics more or less vulnerable than Protestants or Jews to the distorting influence of availability, probability neglect, status quo bias, affect and the like.[17]

To his credit, Sunstein's particular emphasis on social influences does suggest a reason why risk perceptions might vary cross-culturally. Even initially 'small or random' differences in the distribution of perceptions across space will predictably grow in intensity and ultimately become sharply pronounced as a result of 'availability cascades' and 'group polarization':

> *Because different social influences can be found in different communities, local variations are inevitable, with different examples becoming salient in each. Hence such variations – between, say, New York and Ohio, or England and the United States, or between Germany and France – might involve coincidence ... Indeed the different reactions to nuclear power in France and the United States can be explained in large part in this way. And when some groups concentrate on cases in which guns increased violence, and others on cases in which guns decreased violence, availability cascades are a large part of the reason. 'Many Germans believe that drinking water after eating cherries is deadly; they also believe that putting ice in soft drinks is unhealthy. The English, however, rather enjoy a cold drink of water after some cherries; and Americans love icy refreshments.'* (p96; the author quotes Henrich et al, 2001, p353)

But as Sunstein's own description suggests, this type of 'cultural' account predicts that group differences should be largely geographic in nature. If salient or gripping examples of misfortune (as well as overrepresented opinions or arguments) spread from one person to another within geographic communities – in much the same way that an infectious disease does – there would be little reason to expect Jews, African-Americans and women in New York to be more like Jews, African-Americans and women in Ohio than they are like Protestants, whites and men in New York. But in fact religious, racial and gender effects persist even when controlling for region.

Of course, random variations within other, non-geographic communities – professional or occupational ones, for example, or perhaps Internet discussion groups comprising persons with common vocational or political interests – might also blossom into systematic differences in risk perceptions as individuals within those communities interact. But it's necessary to resort to fairly complex and largely ad hoc conjectures to link differences of these sorts to the well-defined forms of variation actually seen across social groups.

The cultural-evaluator model, in contrast, suggests a coherent and parsimonious explanation for such variation. That model explicitly posits that risk perceptions will vary across persons in patterns that reflect and reinforce their cultural worldviews. Gender, ethnicity, religion, political orientation and like characteristics correlate with such outlooks (Kahan et al, 2005, pp6–7).[18] It follows that cultural variation in risk perceptions will manifest itself in systematic differences in risk perception across different social groups.

The results of our National Risk and Culture Survey confirm this conclusion. Consistent with previous research, we found that factors such as income, education, community type (rural or urban), political ideology and personality type do predict various risk perceptions. But we also found that cultural worldviews exert significantly and substantially more predictive power than these characteristics. Seemingly significant gender and race variances in risk perceptions also turn out to be artefacts of culture-specific differences in risk perceptions related to gender and race differences in social roles within hierarchical and (to a lesser extent) individualistic ways of life (Kahan et al, 2005, pp16–18).

Indeed, even the sorts of geographic variations that Sunstein focuses on are best understood as reflecting variance in cultural commitments over space. The difference between French and US attitudes toward nuclear power, and the resulting differences in the regulations of the two nations, are hardly a matter of 'coincidence' or chance. In contrast to members of the public in the United States, those in France are much more likely to hold a hierarchical worldview (Slovic et al, 2000a, pp55, 93–94). This difference not only disposes the French to be more accepting of nuclear power risks, but also to be more confident in the ability of technical and governmental elites to manage any such risks (Slovic et al, 2000a, pp87–90, 93–94, 98).

In other words, membership in various social groups (including sometimes entire nations) predicts risk perceptions only because those groups are proxies for culture. Moreover, because they are only proxies, their unique influence fades to insignificance in a model that directly accounts for cultural worldviews.

Belief clustering

Risk perceptions not only vary systematically across social groups; they also cohere across seemingly discrete issues. How likely one is to perceive global warming to be a threat, for example, predicts how much one worries about gun accidents, which in turn tells us whether one regards abortion as a dangerous medical procedure and marijuana as a dangerous drug (Kahan et al, 2005, pp24–28).

This feature of public risk perceptions also defies the conventional models. Because as an empirical matter nothing about the size of any one of these risks entails anything about the size of any other, we wouldn't expect persons behaving like rational weighers to divide into opposing groups on these matters. Nor is it at all clear why persons behaving like irrational weighers would form these particular packages of risk perceptions. Nothing in the relative salience, familiarity or evocative imagery of any one of these risks connects in any logical or practical way to those features of the others. There's also nothing intrinsic to Sunstein's irrational-weigher model that should lead us to expect those who do or don't take seriously one of these risks (say, of global warming or of marijuana use) to be any more likely to exchange information with others who do or don't take seriously some other risk (say, of gun accidents or of health complications from abortion).

The cultural-evaluator model, however, readily explains belief clustering. The meanings of these diverse risks – the values expressed by the activities that give rise to the risks, and by governmental regulation of the same – cohere in intelligible ways. The idea that guns are dangerous and worthy of regulation, for example, threatens hierarchical roles and denigrates individualistic virtues; the threat of global warming impugns the competence of hierarchical elites and invites interference with markets and other forms of private orderings that individualists prize. It is therefore perfectly sensible to expect hierarchists and individualists to believe both that guns are not dangerous and global warming is not a serious threat, and for egalitarians and solidarists to believe otherwise. Our data found this very pattern, and others that reflect the expressive coherence of these opposing worldviews.

Expert variation

Sunstein's account seeks to identify the mechanisms that impel members of the public to wildly overestimate the importance of risks that experts view with much less concern. But experts themselves are hardly of one mind about societal risks. Nearly every public belief cited by Sunstein as a product of some public 'risk panic' – that nuclear power is dangerous (Kaku and Trainer, 1982), that arsenic in drinking water poses a health threat,[19] that mad cow disease is a serious concern[20] – is shared by some scientists and rejected by others.

Expert disagreement per se does not necessarily defy Sunstein's account. The empirical evidence surrounding many important societal risks is often conflicting and in some instances scant. Employing the methodical and dispassionate forms of analysis associated with System II reasoning, experts could well come to different conclusions in these circumstances.

The problem, however, is that the nature of expert disagreement belies this account of its causes. As is true of disagreements among members of the public generally, disagreements among risk experts are distributed in patterns that cannot plausibly be linked either to access to information or capacity to understand it. Gender, for example, predicts systematic differences in risk perceptions among experts (Barke et al, 1997, pp172–175), as do political ideology and institutional affiliation (academic or industrial; Slovic, 2000a, pp286, 311–312). Because these sorts of characteristics are all plausible proxies for cultural orientation, variance along these lines suggests that cultural cognition is figuring in expert judgements of risk, too. Research that one of us has conducted (independent of the National Risk and Culture Survey) supports exactly this conclusion.[21]

There are at least two possible ways in which cultural cognition could exert this impact on expert risk assessments. One is that cultural worldviews might induce experts, like members of the public generally, to engage in heuristic-driven System I forms of reasoning pervaded by biases such as availability and probability neglect.

But a second and even more plausible explanation is that cultural worldviews are biasing the more reflective System II forms of reasoning associated with expert judgement. Sunstein maintains that System II reasoning is 'more likely to be error free' because it is 'more deliberative [and] calculative' (p68). But a wealth of research on dual-process reasoning suggests that the truth is much more complicated. System II reasoning often furnishes less reliable guidance than System I.[22] Among the reasons this is so is the vulnerability of even System II reasoning to various biasing influences (Chaiken and Maheswaran, 1994; Chen et al, 1999).

One such influence is known as 'defense motivation' (Giner-Sorolla and Chaiken, 1997, p85). Information that challenges beliefs essential to one's group identity poses a threat to one's perception of one's status. To repel that threat, individuals (subconsciously) screen arguments and evidence to protect their existing beliefs. Such screening operates whether individuals are engaged in either heuristic reasoning or more reflective reasoning.[23] In effect, defence motivation biases individuals' use of System II reasoning, causing them to use deliberate, calculating and methodical analysis to support beliefs dominant within their group and to debunk challenges to those beliefs (Chen et al, 1999, p45).

This is most likely the dynamic that generates group-based disagreement among risk experts. Like members of the general public, experts are inclined to form attitudes toward risk that best express their cultural vision. The only difference, if any, is that experts are more likely to use System II reasoning to do so.

Political conflict

Highly charged disputes about risk occupy a conspicuous position in American political life. How (if at all) to respond to global warming, whether to enact or repeal gun control laws, what sorts of policies to adopt to combat domestic terrorism, and like issues generate intense public conflict. The power to explain the prevalence of intense conflict over risk regulation is another advantage of the cultural-evaluator model over Sunstein's irrational-weigher model.

To be sure, the centrality of risk regulation in democratic politics is perfectly compatible with Sunstein's position. Many risk regulation issues are of obvious consequence to the well-being of society. Moreover, because such issues usually involve highly gripping and evocative instances of harm, they predictably trigger a self-reinforcing wave of public anxiety to which democratically accountable institutions inevitably react (indeed, overreact).

What confounds Sunstein's account, however, is the highly conflictual nature of risk regulation politics. If public attention were being driven solely by mechanisms like availability, probability neglect, cascades and group polarization, we would expect members of the public and democratically accountable government officials to be uniformly impelled toward increasingly restrictive forms of regulation of the sort counselled by the precautionary principle. This is the story that Stephen Breyer, Sunstein's irrational-weigher comrade in arms, tells about the regulatory process (Breyer, 1993, pp33–51). But the truth is that risk regulation politics are not nearly so one-sided. Public demand for regulatory responses to global warming, gun accidents, terrorism and similar sources of risk generates equally intense public opposition to the same.

This is exactly the state of affairs one would predict under the cultural-evaluator model. As a result of cultural cognition, individuals of diverse cultural persuasions are endowed with competing affective responses toward putatively dangerous activities, and are thus impelled toward opposing stances on risk issues.

The cultural-evaluator model not only explains why risk regulation politics are conflictual, but also why those on both sides advance their positions with such intensity. Sociologist Joseph Gusfield (1968, 1986) describes as symbolic 'status conflicts' political disputes in which the adherents of opposing cultural styles compete for esteem. In such struggles, opposing cultural groups mobilize to enact legislation that 'glorifies the values of one group and demeans those of another,' thereby 'enhanc[ing] the social status of ... the affirmed culture' at the expense of the one 'condemned as deviant' (Gusfield, 1968, pp57–58). Because individuals care as much about their status as they do about their material welfare, 'the struggle to control the symbolic actions of government is often as bitter and as fateful as the struggle to control its tangible effects' (Gusfield, 1986, p167). Important historical examples include battles over temperance and civil rights (Gusfield, 1986, pp22–24); contemporary examples include the battles over capital punishment (Stolz, 1983), gay rights (Eskridge, 2005, pp1289–1292), and hate crime laws (Kahan, 1999, pp463–467).

Disputes over risk regulation fit this pattern. Because they evocatively symbolize the worldviews of hierarchists and egalitarians, individualists and solidarists, regulations of drugs, guns, sexual promiscuity and other putatively dangerous activities inevitably come to signify whose stock is up and whose down in the incessant competition for social esteem. What seem like highly technical and often highly uncertain empirical disputes among experts galvanize the public because these controversies are in truth 'the product of an ongoing political debate about the ideal society' (Douglas and Wildavsky, 1982, p36).

Normative and prescriptive deficiencies

Although Sunstein purports to be reconciling risk regulation with 'deliberative democracy,' his proposed regulatory reforms are neither particularly deliberative nor particularly democratic. Sunstein's central prescription is to redirect risk regulation from 'highly representative institutions' to 'more insulated' experts (p126). Rather than try to inject scientifically sound information into public discourse, government officials should endeavour to 'change the subject' – 'to discuss something else' in order to divert public attention away from 'facts that will predictably cause high levels of alarm' (pp123–125). The cultural-evaluator model, in contrast, supports an approach to risk regulation that is much more consistent with participatory and deliberative visions of democracy.

Information and cultural-identity affirmation

To start, Sunstein is probably far too pessimistic about the possibility of public education. Sunstein's preference for distracting rather than educating the public reflects his assumption that ordinary citizens lack the time and capacity to process information through reflective System II forms of reasoning as opposed to heuristic-driven System I ones. As we have emphasized, Sunstein overstates the accuracy of System II reasoning relative to System I. But even more important, because he fails to perceive the endogeneity of risk perception mechanisms to culture, Sunstein overlooks the possibility of risk communication techniques that make System I reasoning itself responsive to scientifically sound information.

The best work in dual-process reasoning supports the conclusion that individuals are motivated by a form of status anxiety to resist information that portends regulatory action that would denigrate their cultural values (Kahan et al, 2005, p49). It follows that individuals can be made more receptive to such information when it is communicated to them in forms that affirm their status. Research by social psychologists Geoffrey Cohen, Joshua Aronson and Claude Steele, for example, shows that individuals are much more willing to change their minds on charged issues like the death penalty and abortion immediately after exposure to self-affirming information, such as their high performance on a test or their possession of some desirable personal attribute (Cohen et al, 2000). Self-affirmation of this sort buffers the threat to self that otherwise motivates individuals to resist acceptance of information at odds with beliefs dominant within their identity-defining group (Cohen et al, 2000).[24]

There is a political analogue of this self-affirmation effect. It involves affirming the selves of those who might resist information about a societal danger by tying that information to a proposed policy solution that itself affirms the resisters' cultural commitments.

For a plausible historical example, consider the softening of conservative opposition to air pollution regulation in the late 1980s and early 1990s. Individualists tend to resist the idea that commerce threatens the environment, because that conclusion implies that society ought to constrain market behaviour and like forms of private ordering. Yet when the idea of tradable emissions permits – a market solution to the problem of air pollution – was devised during the highly individualistic first Bush Administration, pro-market forces in the Republican Party stopped resisting (Project 88, 1988; Stavins, 1998). Shown a solution that affirmed their cultural values, it became easier, cognitively, for individualists to accept the idea that there was a problem to be dealt with after all. Hierarchists, who tend to resist claims of environmental danger as implicit criticisms of social elites, also probably felt affirmed by a policy that promised to improve air quality by empowering rather than constraining commercial firms.[25]

For a contemporary example, consider the global warming controversy. The assertion of this risk is also seen by individualists as threatening the autonomy of markets and by hierarchists as impugning the competence of social and governmental elites. Consequently, both downplay the threat posed by global warming (or deny its very existence). But recently, groups with varying ideologies have started to tout renewed investment in nuclear power as a way to reduce the fossil fuel emissions primarily responsible for global warming (see Gilbert, 2001, p16A; Kristof, 2005, pA19). The self-affirmation effect described by Cohen and his collaborators suggests why this strategy might work. Individualists and hierarchists both support nuclear power, which is emblematic of the very cultural values that are threatened by society's recognition of the global warming risk. Shown a solution that affirms their identities, individualists and hierarchists can be expected to display less resistance – not just politically, but cognitively – to the proposition that global warming is a problem after all.

Indeed, when egalitarians and solidarists are exposed to the message that nuclear power can reduce global warming, they are likely to perceive nuclear power to be less dangerous. The affirmation of their identity associated with recognition of the global warming threat reduces a cognitive impediment to accepting information that they have long resisted about nuclear safety.

In these examples, we have assumed scientific consensus both that air pollution and global warming are serious environmental threats and that nuclear power is reasonably safe. But in conditions of scientific uncertainty, the same strategy of cultural-identity affirmation could be used to make a culturally diverse public receptive to whatever empirical information might eventually emerge in support of policies that advance society's shared interests. Comparative law scholar Mary Ann Glendon (1987), for example, discusses an abortion law in France that simultaneously affirmed the identity of hierarchists, by permitting abortion not on demand but only in circumstances of 'personal emergency,' and the identity of egalitarians and individualists, by treating an individual woman's declaration of personal emergency as effectively unreviewable by government officials. According to Glendon, this legislation dissipated cultural conflict and created a climate in which both sides came to accept previously disputed factual information about the efficacy of certain social welfare policies in reducing demand for abortion (Glendon, 1987, pp15–20).

We can imagine a similar strategy to promote receptivity to sound information on gun risks. Egalitarians and solidarists focus on the risk that too little gun control will lead to more gun accidents and crimes, hierarchists and individualists on the risk that too much will leave persons helpless when facing criminal predation (Kahan et al, 2005, pp18–21). We will assume that existing empirical evidence – which is voluminous and conflicting – does not now support a confident conclusion either way.[26] Nevertheless, a policy those on both sides might accept is a 'bounty,' in the form of a tax rebate or other monetary reward, for individuals who register handguns.

A registration bounty would affirm the cultural identities of both control supporters and control opponents simultaneously because both could see it as an effective and fair solution to a collective action problem, albeit a different one for each group. For control supporters, the relevant public good is the reduction of gun crime; registration contributes to that good by making it easier to trace the ownership of weapons used to commit crimes. Consistent with egalitarian and solidaristic sensibilities, control supporters can thus envision the bounty as equitably compensating individuals for being made to bear a burden that benefits society at large. For control opponents, in contrast, the relevant public good is the reduction of violent crime in a community in which a relatively high proportion of individuals own guns. Because they do not believe individuals should be expected to endure disproportionate burdens to benefit society at large, individualists will think it is perfectly appropriate to compensate individual gun owners for the contribution they are making to public safety generally. So will hierarchists, who can see the bounty as a fitting public acknowledgement of the virtuous willingness of gun owners to promote the common good.[27]

Agreement of any sort might be viewed as a step forward in the American gun policy stalemate. But the real payoff is opening the public's mind to facts. Any policy that simultaneously affirms the identities of culturally diverse citizens makes all of them more receptive to information that they might otherwise have found lacking in credibility. The lesson for risk communicators isn't that they have to 'change the subject' so much as change the discourse to make new empirical findings compatible with a plurality of worldviews.

Cultural cognition and deliberative debiasing

In Sunstein's view, any attempt to undertake public discussions would lead inexorably to mass polarization, with pre-existing biases amplifying themselves in the echo chamber of mass media or even in the confines of a face-to-face discussion. Such a result might occur, but to say it is inevitable underestimates persons' discursive capacities and the potential those capacities have to counteract the biasing effects of cultural cognition.

Research on the polarizing effect of deliberation on political decision making is actually quite mixed. Indeed, a formidable body of empirical research shows that deliberation at least sometimes generates convergence and moderation of opinion (Kerr et al, 1996; Gerber and Green, 1999; Sia et al, 2002; Gastil et al, 2008). Group-communication researchers have catalogued various procedures that help ameliorate polarization.[28] In many political decision-making contexts, such procedures have been used to promote successful deliberative solutions on many issues that are culturally fraught (Pearce and Littlejohn, 1997; Dale, 1999, p923; Forester, 1999, p463; Winship, 2006).

These procedures work, in part, because they help dissipate the potential of cultural cognition to generate conflict. First, carefully structured deliberation does sometimes appear to enable individuals to engage in a culturally debiased form of System II reasoning (Gastil and Dillard, 1999, pp19–21). Political scientist James Fishkin has developed deliberative processes, such as the Deliberative Poll, that use expert moderators whose intervention appears at least sometimes to induce citizens to change their minds on contested issues of fact (Fishkin, 1991; Ackerman and Fishkin, 2004, pp44–59; Fishkin and Farrar, 2005, pp72–75). The Twenty-First Century Town Meeting, a deliberative format designed by Carolyn Lukensmeyer, uses similar techniques and has generated similar results (Lukensmeyer et al, 2005, pp157–160).

Deliberation can also improve public information-processing by forging a shared civic identity alternative to individuals' cultural affiliations (Burkhalter et al, 2002, pp415–416). Individuals tend to find the members of any in-group more credible than the members of any out-group (Clark and Maass, 1988, pp388–392; Mackie et al, 1990, pp820–821). The evidence we have collected on culture and risk suggests that cultural affinity is the dominant in-group when individuals appraise risk. But as they engage one another in earnest face-to-face deliberation, individuals committed to resolving an important common problem typically form strong emotional bonds (Pearce and Littlejohn, 1997, pp151–167; Fishkin and Farrar, 2005, pp68–70; Melville et al, 2005, pp37–39, 45–51). It's plausible to imagine that these connections generate a group identity that, for the period of deliberation at least, displaces cultural affiliations as individuals' dominant reference point. If so, individuals, while they are deliberating together, might experience relief from the sense of threat to self that makes them resist information at odds with their culturally grounded prior beliefs. This effect could explain the consensus that some researchers and practitioners report among deliberation participants.[29]

Finally, deliberation can alter individuals' understandings of the relationship between their cultural affiliations and particular beliefs. On this view, what individuals learn in the course of deliberation isn't so much new information about the facts being debated but rather new information about the identities of those who hold particular factual beliefs. If participants come to see either that a particular belief is less dominant among their cultural peers than they had imagined or that cultural peers who deviate from the dominant belief are not censured as severely as they had anticipated, participants are likely to revise their view about the social cost – or more accurately the social meaning (Cohen, 2003) – of changing their mind.

This conjecture is supported by a number of other recognized psychological processes. One is the 'false consensus effect,' which refers to the tendency of individuals to form an exaggerated sense of the degree to which members of their referent group hold a particular position (Quattrone and Jones, 1980, pp149–151). This bias is likely to generate a self-sustaining condition of 'pluralistic ignorance' to the extent that individuals are motivated to represent their adherence of this belief to others, who will in turn feel constrained to represent that they hold the belief, notwithstanding widespread reservations (Prentice and Miller, 1993, p244). Deliberation might conceivably break this cycle of shared misunderstanding if, contrary to expectations, individuals discover that others who share their group identity do not in fact uniformly hold the belief in question.[30] As they revise downward their estimation of the prevalence of the view within their group, individuals will feel less threatened by, and thus become more receptive to, information at odds with their culturally grounded prior beliefs (Cohen, 2003).

Although it is admittedly speculative, this account of how deliberation can ameliorate the distorting influence of cultural cognition is nonetheless supported by one real-world approach to risk management. Social psychologist Robin Gregory has devised deliberative procedures aimed at generating 'science-based, community-supported' environmental risk policies (Gregory and Wellman, 2001, p38). In what he calls 'structured, value-focused' decision making, interested parties from the affected community first deliberate on ends in a manner that exposes rather than suppresses their underlying values. Expert risk analysts and trained facilitators then join the discussion to help the stakeholders identify courses of action that reconcile various values and evaluate the costs (fiscal and environmental) of those options (Gregory et al, 2001a, pp255–262; Gregory et al, 2001b, pp419–426; Gregory, 2002, pp472–484; Gregory and Failing, 2002, pp493–496; Gregory and McDaniels, 2005, pp187–191). Gregory presents empirical evidence showing that this approach generates outcomes that are more consensual and more defensible from a scientific standpoint than either unguided bottom–up approaches to regulation or highly centralized and insulated top–down ones.[31]

Structured, value-focused deliberation of this sort is likely to engage all of the cultural cognition 'debiasing' mechanisms we have identified. Having been candidly exposed to the values of their fellow citizens, participating individuals are likely to form a more realistic and less antagonistic picture of how positions are distributed among their neighbours. Armed with expert information and assisted by mediators, they are likely to engage in more sophisticated appraisals of the costs and benefits of the regulatory options available. And because the matter is being resolved not by remote agencies or administrators, but by them in a context in which experts engage them face-to-face, participants are likely to form trust-inducing emotional bonds that free them from the need to rely entirely on cultural affinities in assessing the credibility of information sources.

Indeed, the generation of culture-independent forms of trust, particularly between lay persons and risk experts, may be the most valuable feature of genuinely democratic policy making. The design and implementation of policies for managing toxic waste disposal, nuclear power generation, and other societal risks inevitably demand substantial reliance on remote expert regulators. Because members of the public know that their fate is in the experts' hands, risk experts can count on enduring political support for their decisions only if members of the public trust them. And one of the most important conditions of such trust, research shows, is the perception that officials have consulted and are responsive to affected members of the public (Slovic, 2000a, pp316–319, 322).

The relationship between trust and deliberation ought to make even those who share Sunstein's confidence in experts wary of granting them the political insulation he and other irrational-weigher theorists advocate. Just as consultation breeds trust in expert risk regulators, the perception that such officials are remote and unaccountable erodes it (Slovic, 2000a, pp322–323, 409–410). Ironically, then, the greater the degree of political insulation the law affords to expert regulators, the less likely popularly responsive institutions of government are to invest those regulators with power to begin with or to respect their decisions as final.

Culture and expert cost–benefit analysis

We have suggested that Sunstein overstates the intractability of error in public risk perceptions. But even if we are wrong, the cultural-evaluator model strongly critiques the anti-democratic nature of Sunstein's programme. Bringing the role of cultural cognition into view severely undermines the foundation for Sunstein's refusal to afford normative significance to public risk evaluations generally.[32]

As we have noted, Sunstein advocates delegating a sizeable amount of discretion to politically insulated risk specialists. The basis for this prescription is his assumption that the differences between lay assessments of risk and expert ones are the product not of 'rival rationalities' but of simple errors on the part of the public, generated by myriad social psychological pathologies (p86). Accordingly, even in a democracy, or at least in the best 'deliberative' conception of one, such public sensibilities are entitled to no respect: 'Democratic governments should respond to people's values, not to their blunders' (p126). Sunstein advocates expert cost–benefit analysis as the principal device for making the law responsive to the former (as reflected primarily in markets and other forms of private behaviour) and not the latter.

The cultural-evaluator model suggests that this strategy borders on incoherence. In the public consciousness, there is no genuine distinction between the 'costs' and 'benefits' of putatively dangerous activities. Adopting the stance that best expresses their cultural values, citizens invariably conclude that activities that affirm their preferred way of life are both beneficial and safe, and those that denigrate it are both worthless and dangerous.[33] Moreover, unlike attitudes that reflect overgeneralization, disregard for small probabilities, inattention to base rates, and similar manifestations of bounded rationality (Slovic, 2000a, pp21–22, 35–39), risk perceptions originating in cultural evaluation are not ones individuals are likely to disown once their errors are revealed to them. Even if individuals could be made to see that their cultural commitments had biased their review of factual information about the dangers of, say, nuclear power, guns or abortion, they would probably view those same commitments as justifying their policy preferences regardless of the facts.

As a result, the idea that expert cost–benefit analysis respects citizens' 'values' but not their 'blunders' is fundamentally misleading. When expert regulators reject as irrational public assessments of the risks associated with putatively dangerous activities – whether nuclear power or handguns, drug use or toxic waste dumping – they are in fact overriding public values. For just as citizens' perceptions of the benefits of these activities express their worldviews, so too do their perceptions of the risks they pose.

As Douglas and Wildavsky argue, public risk disputes, however much they are dominated by technical analyses of empirical data, are in essence 'the product of an ongoing political debate about the ideal society' (Douglas and Wildavsky, 1982, p36). Experts might have a more accurate sense of the magnitude of various risks (although their conclusions, too, are hardly immune from cultural partisanship, but they have no special competence to identify what vision of society – hierarchical or egalitarian, individualistic or solidaristic – the law should endorse. That should be a matter of public deliberation.

Or at least that is the conclusion likely to be reached by anyone who genuinely favours democratic deliberation. Sunstein doesn't. His is not a programme for those who want to reconcile democracy with a rational response to public fears; it is a programme for those who fear democracy and seek to exclude the regulation of risk from its ambit.

Culture, fear and liberalism

But the hard question for anyone who accepts the cultural-evaluator model as a descriptive matter is whether Sunstein's fear of democracy might indeed be warranted. The cultural-evaluator model, precisely because it exposes the clash of cultural visions that inevitably animates public risk disputes, reveals the potentially deep tension between democratically responsive risk regulation and liberalism.

The rational-weigher and irrational-weigher models disagree about the competence of lay persons to assess the costs and benefits of various risks. But both accept that the optimal balance is one that maximizes satisfaction of individual preferences – or at least (in the case of the irrational-weigher model) the preferences individuals would have were they accurately to perceive the costs and benefits of putatively dangerous activities. This position flows naturally from the assumption that the purpose of risk regulation is to induce an efficient level of safety. It also, conveniently, implements a form of liberal neutrality by treating all persons' valuation of safety relative to other goals as entitled to equal weight.

But once the connection between risk perceptions and cultural worldviews is exposed, the justification for this ecumenical stance becomes less obvious. In selecting some risks for attention and dismissing others as unimportant, individuals are, in effect, advancing their culturally partisan visions of the ideal society. At least for anyone who accepts the liberal injunction that the law steer clear of endorsing a moral or cultural orthodoxy,[34] it is questionable whether risk regulation policy should be responsive to such demands.

As a practical example, consider whether hospitals should have an obligation under the informed consent doctrine to inform patients of the HIV-positive status of medical personnel. The answer might be 'of course' if we understand informed consent doctrine as enabling individual patients to secure treatment consistent with their own medical welfare preferences (McIntosh, 1996). But the cultural-evaluator model suggests that the demand for such information probably is not linked to 'medical welfare' preferences in any straightforward sense. Our own study suggests that hierarchists, but not egalitarians, individualists or solidarists, rate the risk of infection from an HIV-positive surgeon as a serious one (Cultural Cognition Project, 2006b). If what makes hierarchists attend to this risk – while shrugging off many more serious ones – is their preference to see the law reflect their contested worldview, why should the law credit that preference at the expense of those who hold competing worldviews that would be denigrated by such a position, not to mention medical personnel and other patients who would be adversely affected by it?

But risk regulation sensibilities animated by the hierarchical worldview are hardly the only ones susceptible to these sorts of concerns. For example, one might oppose the demand for stricter forms of gun control on the ground that it derives not from an acceptable desire for personal safety, but from an illiberal desire to erect an egalitarian or solidaristic orthodoxy in law.[35] At the same time that it extinguishes one ground for interfering with market and political evaluations of risk – that lay sensibilities are irrational – the cultural-evaluator model arguably creates another: that those sensibilities sometimes reflect an unjust desire to use the expressive capital of the law to advance culturally imperialist ends.

Ironically, if one were convinced that illiberal cultural conflicts of this sort were intractable, one solution might be Sunstein's version of the irrational-weigher theory. Normative legal theories do more than justify particular doctrines and institutional arrangements. They also furnish vocabularies that determine how citizens and legal decision makers talk to each other about what the law should be. Those vocabularies, by accentuating or obfuscating conflicts of value, can themselves influence how likely such actors are to reach agreement and how easily they'll be able to get along with each other if they don't (Kahan, 1999, p419).

In this respect, the irrational-weigher theory's analytic deficiencies can be seen as conflict-abating discourse virtues: precisely because it ignores the decisive role that cultural values play in shaping competing perceptions of risk, that theory mutes the function that risk regulation plays in adjudicating between competing worldviews. So defended, the irrational-weigher theory implements in the risk regulation field Sunstein's preference for 'incompletely theorized agreements' – his distinctive strategy for conforming the law to the liberal injunction to avoid endorsement of partisan visions of the good (Sunstein, 1996, pp35–61).

Still, this is a defence of Sunstein's programme that demurs to, rather than acquits it of, the charge that it is fundamentally antidemocratic. A genuinely democratic response to the liberal dilemma implicit in risk regulation might be possible, too. Deliberation with a form of expressively pluralistic politics might enable citizens of diverse worldviews to agree on risk without having to assent to law that denigrates anyone's cultural identity.[36]

The prospects for such a programme, particularly on a national level, are admittedly uncertain. But we are certain that if there is a democratic solution to the liberal dilemma inherent in risk regulation, it can be formulated only on the basis of the knowledge that the cultural-evaluator model furnishes.

Conclusion

Laws of Fear is a masterful work. No book so comprehensively and imaginatively synthesizes and extends existing empirical works on risk perception. None more systematically develops these insights into a programme for guiding risk regulation.

Nevertheless, *Laws of Fear*'s inattention to the impact of cultural worldviews constrains both the descriptive and normative power of Sunstein's irrational-weigher model of risk perception. A growing body of research demonstrates that conflicts in perceptions of risk – not only between lay persons and experts but also among the members of both groups – reflect individuals' adherence to competing visions of how society should be organized. The cultural-evaluator model of risk perceptions supported by this research furnishes a much more complete account of why risk regulation is a matter of such deep and intense conflict. It also undermines both the defence Sunstein offers for delegating significant risk-regulatory responsibilities to politically insulated experts and his claim that such a regime is 'deliberatively democratic.'

Ironically, though, the inattention of Sunstein's account to culture might itself be viewed by some as a strength. The cultural-evaluator model of risk perception ruthlessly exposes the inescapable role that risk regulation plays in adjudicating disputes between competing cultural groups over whose worldview the law will proclaim orthodox. Sunstein's irrational-weigher account strategically obscures this function and thus offers one possible technique for countering the inherently illiberal tendency of regulatory law.

The challenge that risk regulation poses to democracy is more profound than it appears not only upon first inspection but upon second inspection as well. The material well-being of a democratic society depends on its ability to rationally manage a nearly limitless variety of often competing risks. The integrity of such a society's commitment to self-governance depends on its ability to fashion procedures that are genuinely deliberative, open and democratic. And its obligation to reconcile popular rule with respect for individual dignity and freedom requires it to find a mode of regulation and a strategy of regulatory discourse that deflect the ambitions of competing cultural groups to claim the law as theirs and theirs alone.

No account that unqualifiedly celebrates the culturally expressive nature of risk perceptions and risk regulation can hope to achieve all of these critical ends. But none that ignores the impact of culture on risk perceptions can hope to achieve them either.

Acknowledgements

Research for this review was supported by National Science Foundation Grant Numbers 0112158 and 0242106. We are grateful to David Driesen, Douglas Kysar and Jeffrey Rachlinski for comments on an earlier draft, to Jennifer Peresie and Adam Dressner for research assistance, and to Gene Coakley for masterful library assistance.

Notes

1   For an influential statement of this view, see Breyer (1993).
2   One might characterize Kip Viscusi's more recent work, which treats market and other private behaviour toward risk-taking as rational and political responses as irrational, in this way.
3   For an innovative attempt to build qualitative evaluations of risk into a framework of cost–benefit analysis that minimizes the distorting influence of various cognitive biases, see Revesz (1999).
4   This is an application of Daniel Kahneman and Amos Tversky's (1979) famous 'prospect theory.'

5   The author here quotes Margolis (1996, p5). Internal quotation marks have been omitted. See also pp74, 165–189.

6   The author quotes US Senate (2002, statement of Brent Blackwelder, President, Friends of the Earth). An internal quotation mark has been omitted.

7   For the classic statement of the 'dual-processing' position, see Chaiken (1980). The 'System I/System II' terminology comes from Kahneman and Frederick (2002).

8   Here Sunstein advocates an approach that is largely consistent with that favoured by rational-weigher theorists (see e.g. Viscusi, 1998b, pp126–128). The difference, presumably, is that Sunstein would favour regulation in many contexts in which rational-weigher theorists are content to rely on markets. See Viscusi (1998b, pp126–128), arguing that markets, when they internalize relevant costs, better neutralize various forms of individual irrationality than do government agencies, which often magnify them.

9   See generally Rayner (1992), describing the theory and identifying its key theoretical underpinnings.

10 Douglas and Wildavsky, for example, suggest functionalist accounts in which individuals form beliefs congenial to their ways of life precisely *because* such beliefs promote those ways of life (Douglas, 1986, pp31–43; Thompson et al, 1990, pp104–107).

11 See generally Balkin (1998, pp9–10, 173–174), suggesting the need for an account of cultural influences that rests on psychological mechanisms operating at the individual level.

12 See Nussbaum (2001); see also Kahan and Nussbaum (1996), examining the influence of the cognitive conception of emotion in criminal law.

13 See Kahan and Braman (2003, pp1313–1315); see also Douglas (1966, pp34–40), suggesting that cognitive dissonance might cause persons to ignore harms by believing others are mistaken.

14 See Cultural Cognition Project (undated-b), explaining methods and general findings of the survey.

15 See Slovic (2000a, pp404–405), noting that many persons associated high-benefit actions with low risks, and vice versa; Cultural Cognition Project (undated-a), noting the inverse correlation between perceptions of gun risks and benefits.

16 See Kahan et al (2005), presenting data showing the influence of various individual characteristics on risk perceptions.

17 Researchers have explicitly ruled out such differences in the case of gender (see e.g. McKelvie, 1997; Trumbo, 2002, p379; Berger et al, 2003, p758).

18 For this reason, these and similar demographic characteristics are commonly used as proxies for distinctive cultural norms. See, for example, Gastil (1975), charting regional correlations with cultural values; Gilligan (1982), using gender as an indicator of commitment to certain moral sensibilities); Nisbett and Cohen (1996, pp1–2), using region of residence as representative of a shared cultural and psychological background; Kleck (1996), using race, class, gender and region as proxies for cultural norms.

19 Compare the National Research Council's 2001 report concluding, based on epidemiological studies, that arsenic exposure within existing regulatory standards might significantly increase cancer risk, with Bates et al (1995, p523), concluding that cities with levels of arsenic in drinking water below existing standards do not significantly differ in the incidence of bladder cancer from those with levels above the standards.

20 Compare Hagstrom (2004), reporting the view of a Nobel Prize-winning scientist

who discovered the mad cow infectious agent that the disease is 'the greatest threat to the safety of the human food supply in modern times' (quoting Stanley Prusiner, Professor, University of California, San Francisco; internal quotation marks omitted), with Cohen et al (2001, p112): '[E]ven if BSE were somehow to arise in the U.S., few additional animals would become infected, little infectivity would be available for potential human exposure, and the disease would be eradicated. In short, the U.S. appears very resistant to a BSE challenge ...'

21 See Slovic (2000a, pp406–409), describing studies in which cultural worldviews explained variance among scientists. Douglas Kysar and James Salzman (2003, pp1111–1116) convincingly attribute expert, as well as public, disagreement over risk to conflicting worldviews.

22 See Slovic et al (2004, p320), noting that expert chess players and mathematicians perform better when relying on tacit or heuristic rather than purely analytic reasoning, and arguing that 'risk as feeling may outperform risk as analysis' in settings such as security screening at airports.

23 See Giner-Sorolla and Chaiken (1997, pp85–86); see also Cohen (2003), finding that experimental subjects using systematic reasoning are still disposed to credit arguments conditional on sharing a group allegiance with the source of the arguments.

24 See also Cohen et al (2007); see generally Sherman and Cohen (2002), summarizing self-affirmation research.

25 Although the policy was initially proposed by environmentalists who broke with the conventional egalitarian and solidaristic fear of using market mechanisms to induce risk abatement, see Ackerman and Stewart (1988, pp178–188). President Bush seized on this approach to deflect Democratic Party attacks on his commitment to the environment without alienating his conservative, pro-business base, see Hahn and Stavins (1991, p28); Hirsch (1999, pp363–364).

26 See NRC (2004, pp120–150), summarizing studies and determining that evidence is inconclusive.

27 For an elaboration of this proposal and others aimed at resolving the cultural impasse over guns in American society, see Kahan and Braman (2006b).

28 See Crosby and Nethercut (2005, pp112–115), Fishkin and Farrar (2005, pp68, 72–75), Hendriks, 2005, pp83–89), Lukensmeyer et al, 2005, pp154, 157–160) and Sokoloff et al (2005, pp187–191). See generally Gastil (2000, pp165–171), proposing techniques for counteracting conformity pressure, low motivation, and information deficits.

29 Consider one real-world experiment: the British Columbia Citizens' Assembly on Electoral Reform. The Assembly was made up of 160 randomly selected citizens, one man and one woman from each electoral district, and two at-large Aboriginal members. Despite its diverse membership, the Assembly voted by an overwhelming 146–7 margin to replace the existing electoral system with a single transferable vote model. The Assembly's plan emerged from months of face-to-face deliberation and hearings, which are accessible online (Citizens' Assembly on Electoral Reform, 2006).

30 Compare Matza (1964, pp52–55), suggesting this process as one of the mechanisms that steers delinquent youths toward law-abiding behaviour over time.

31 See, for example, Gregory and Wellman (2001, pp43–51), describing an experiment using structured, value-focused deliberation for planning the development of a local estuary; Gregory et al (2001a, pp263–271), describing an experiment involving deliberation over risks associated with a hydroelectric power plant.

32 Although we focus here on the challenge cultural cognition presents to cost–benefit analysis, others have suggested additional telling criticisms of such analysis. See, for example, Ackerman and Heinzerling (2004); Mandel and Gathii (2006); McGarity (2002).

33 See Kysar (2003, pp1740–1741), noting the difficulty posed to risk-utility analysis by the inverse relationship between costs and benefits in public risk perceptions.

34 See, for example, West Virginia State Board of Education v. Barnette (1943, p642), 'If there is any fixed star in our constitutional constellation, it is that no official, high or petty, can prescribe what shall be orthodox in politics, nationalism, religion, or other matters of opinion … '; Ackerman (1980, pp8–12), arguing against invocation of a partisan view of the good to justify policy; Rawls (1993, p217).

35 Most citizens who support gun control, in fact, say they would favour it even if private possession of handguns reduced crime. See Cultural Cognition Project (2006c).

36 See Kahan and Braman (2006b), defending an expressively pluralistic approach to resolving the American gun debate; see also, describing the use of deliberation to generate consensus consistent with sound empirical information on risk.

Chapter 13

Risk Lived, Stigma Experienced

Terre Satterfield, Paul Slovic, Robin Gregory, James Flynn and C. K. Mertz[*]

Introduction

Marshall, Georgia is situated in Pecan County in southern Georgia.[1] It hosts an historically black college, a population of 5000, and a very limited stock of inexpensive housing. Railroad tracks and a major thoroughfare separate the Alouette Chemical Works plant and an adjacent African-American neighbourhood from the town's more prosperous residential and commercial centre. The Alouette Company began operating in 1910 as a lime-sulphur plant, later becoming a supplier of arsenic-based pesticides for agricultural, lawn and garden markets (M. Hillsman and M. Krafter, personal communication, 29 July 1996). Locals refer to the plant as 'the dust house,' a designation that invokes the particulate matter that once permeated neighbourhood air and life. A ditch carrying untreated waste from the plant travelled through the adjacent neighbourhood until it was covered in the late 1970s. Adult residents of the neighbourhood recall playing in the ditch as children while their parents were said to have waded across the ditch to avoid the longer walk to the plank bridges at the ends of each block.

For most of its history, the plant was owned and operated by a prominent local white family; it was sold to a corporate chemical manufacturer in 1985. In 1986 the state Department of Environmental Quality requested that the company clean contaminated areas within the commercial facility where arsenic had adhered to the soil on plant property. Nothing was said to the predominantly African-American residents living nearest the plant at that time. In 1990 the site was recommended to the US Environmental Protection Agency (USEPA) for

[*] Portions of this chapter are excerpted from a paper published in *Human Ecology Review*, vol 7, no 1, pp1–11. Copyright 2000 by the Society for Human Ecology. Reprinted with permission.

listing on the National Priority or 'Superfund' list. Three years passed before the USEPA notified affected citizens and issued clean-up orders to the plant. Beginning in 1993, residents of the plant neighbourhood learned that several probable carcinogens, in particular arsenical compounds, had permeated the soil in neighbourhood yards and the dust inside local homes. Testing in 1994 through to 1997 on the plant property and throughout the adjacent neighbourhood indicated dust- and soil-based arsenic levels of 15 to 800 parts per million (ppm) despite the cessation of arsenic production during the mid-1980s. The plant grounds include hot spots of up to 30,000ppm. The background level for arsenic in comparable geographic regimes was judged to be about 7ppm. Chronic arsenic exposure has been associated with skin, lung, liver, bladder, kidney and colon cancers (Agency for Toxic Substances and Disease Registry (ATSDR), 1990); arsenic is also believed to be a cancer 'progressor' as is benzene and asbestos (Steingraber, 1997, p244). A 1996 study conducted in Marshall, Georgia by the ATSDR concluded that significant dangerous exposures had occurred in the past, but that current post-remediation levels of exposure were not dangerous to residents (ASTDR, 1996).

Risk scholars recognize that physical harm results from exposure to chemicals, heavy metals and/or radioactive isotopes, and that the social and psychological experience of that harm is both fully rational and central to the risk experience (Slovic, 1987, 1992; Edelstein, 1987; Kasperson, 1992; Erikson, 1994). A prominent extension of risk work to which this volume is devoted, studies of technological stigma, commonly defines risk consequences in fiscal or market terms. Stigma occurs when certain products, places or technologies are identified by the public as dangerous and subject to avoidance given their affiliation with health risks (Gregory et al, 1995). The primary experimental evidence for technological stigmas is the correlation of negative cognitions about a place, product or technology – word associations, imagery, affective descriptors and perceived risks – with detrimental changes in consumer behaviour (Flynn et al, 1997, 1998). Risks prone to this designation are those the public views as dreaded, potentially fatal, involuntarily imposed, or regarded as beyond individual control (Slovic, 1987). Ultimately the stigmatized object becomes an epicentre from which severe economic impacts emanate. The millions in lost revenues incurred by Johnson and Johnson in the wake of fear about further Tylenol poisonings, the decline in land values near nuclear facilities, and the devaluation of real property alongside electromagnetic fields are classic cases of (respectively) product, place and technological stigma (Mitchell, 1989; MacGregor et al, 1994; Slovic et al, 1990b).

Defining stigma in terms of market impacts is logical to the extent that economic viability and public acceptance are necessary conditions for the commercial development of modern technology, such as nuclear power. Nonetheless, a focus on pecuniary impacts sustains a model of stigma that implicitly narrows the definition of impact to altered purchasing habits or fluctuating market values. If human stigma responses are reduced to those where consumer spending drops to *avoid* Alar-suspect apples or buyers whose worries prompt them to *think negatively* about housing purchases, something of the 'complex interplay of psychological, social and political forces' (Gregory et al, 1995, p222) that produces stigmas is lost.

In contrast, a model that recognizes the full social expression of stigma has the potential to accommodate the important association between the stigmatizing of a technology or place by external society and adverse effects on the people most immediately affected.

The relationship becomes more pertinent in light of recent findings about the disproportionate presence of technological hazards in socially stigmatized (especially minority) communities (United Church of Christ, 1987; Bullard, 1990; Szasz, 1994; Johnston, 1994, 1997; see also Zimmerman, 1993). Those historically subject to social stigmas – defamation due to race, class or economic status – are often those contemporarily subject to technological hazards, and thus in some circumstances, stigma.

This chapter demonstrates the effects of stigma on one community subjected to the experience of contamination. The research in Marshall shows that the experience of living in a contaminated and stigmatized place includes both physical and psychological invasions. Neighbourhoods are structurally altered; domestic routines are profoundly disrupted and long-time residents come to be haunted by the inversion of home as a safe haven, an inversion that insinuates itself into thoughts about health and leads to the nagging fear that one's body has been infected by toxic substances. Residents notably invoke their sociopolitical experiences of racism, of being socially marginalized, to interpret how it is that they are viewed by the outside world, to explain why some citizens are protected from contaminants while others are not, why their concerns go unheard, or how it is that they are blamed for the economic woes of the larger community. This study suggests that these opinions may be tied to the defeating social climate that can accompany the experience of contamination and thus warrant study as symptoms of the link between technological and social stigmas.

Methods

In the spring and summer of 1996, 206 questionnaire-based interviews employing open and closed-ended questions were administered to 66 past and 140 current residents of the contaminated neighbourhood. Interviewees were selected from over 600 past and current residents listed as plaintiffs in litigation pending against the Alouette plant. Plaintiffs included all but a few past and present residents of the plant neighbourhood who were (a) traceable, (b) had lived in the neighbourhood for at least 5 years and (c) were said, by a medical doctor, to have clinical signs of arsenic exposure. Interviewees (all 206) were selected not at random but because they lived or had lived in the houses closest to the plant and/or because their house or yard had already been tested for the presence of arsenic. Only one of the 206 interviewees currently works at the plant and fewer than ten have ever worked at the plant for more than three months. All but three of those interviewed were African-American, although a larger proportion of the 600 litigants (approximately 5 per cent) are white.[2]

26 of the 140 people referred to here as current residents moved or were moved in response to the news about contamination. The other 114 (of 140) still live in the neighbourhood. The second group of people referred to here as past residents (66) include only those people who left the neighbourhood well before (often many years before) the news of contamination broke. Most in this latter subset of interviewees live in comparable though not contaminated communities elsewhere in rural Georgia. They do not otherwise differ from current residents with regard to age, gender or race: The mean age of past residents is 46.3 years; present residents' mean age is 46.9 years.[3] 39 per cent of all present residents are male, 61 per cent are female. 35 per cent of past residents are male, while 64 per cent are female.

Questionnaire items were developed with reference to the literature on social responses to technological hazards, and on the basis of background ethnographic interviews conducted by the first author. Questionnaire items were pretested and when necessary rewritten for simplicity and ease of administration. The instrument included word-association tasks, affective ratings, reported behaviours, and opinions about remediation procedures. The questionnaire was read aloud to each interviewee and answers were recorded by the interviewer. Questionnaires were administered by nine African-American school teachers all of whom were trained as interviewers. Many of the teachers had taught in the neighbourhood but none of them lived there. After the questionnaires had been completed, approximately 15 follow-up interviews were conducted by the first author. This last group of interviews was, again, open-ended.

The stigmatization of place:
Reconfiguring home and environment

Community studies have documented the physical deterioration of contaminated places including the potential for infrastructural, social and psychological upheaval that follows a disclosure of contamination (Edelstein, 1988; Fitchen, 1989; Erikson, 1994). In Marshall, Georgia, multiple houses on each of the blocks closest to the plant were purchased by the company, torn down and/or encircled with chain-link fences. The '*hazardous – keep out*' signs that hang on the fencing inform residents that the fractured landscape they occupy is no longer, and perhaps never has been, safe. The soil on the plant-purchased lots remains too contaminated for habitation (the plant is not obligated to clean its purchased properties) which negates the potential for rebuilding the neighbourhood's residential infrastructure. Neighbourhood gardens, fruit trees and farm animals (e.g. chickens and some goats) were removed from properties registering 30ppm of arsenic or greater. Remaining residents see the fences and signs appearing where neighbours once lived and conclude that perhaps their properties are also unsafe; consequently, they cease to garden or trade locally produced fruits and vegetables. The overall inability for neighbours to maintain the quotidian behaviours that typify a comfortable domestic routine – to garden, permit children to play outside, complete yard work, visit neighbours, and so on – represents a 'collective trauma ... a blow to the basic tissues of social life' that 'impairs [any] prevailing sense of communality' (Erikson, 1994, p233).

Residents also portray their immediate neighbourhood as a 'ghost town' of vacant lots and the aesthetic quality of the neighbourhood as 'concentration-camp like.'[4] Houses are uneasily occupied, devoid of the intrinsic merits of home as a safe haven from the predicaments of public life. Betty Fields thus prefers to stay late at her job rather than face 'going home to my arsenic house [where] I can't breathe.' Her neighbour, Helene Johnson, finds only that her home 'feels like a trap ... like there's something hiding in the shadows waiting to jump.' Many feel there is little they can do to protect themselves, a defencelessness articulated by Leroy Roberts as the feeling of 'living in a place I'm afraid of, like it's [the contamination] coming in the cracks.' Long-term neighbours regard these insults as historically rooted, a continuation of decades of plant encroachment into residential territory given the meteoric rise of the plant's productive capacity after the Second World War.[5]

Individual expressions of 'feeling trapped' or feeling 'unable to breathe' should not be mistaken as idiosyncratic, indicative only of exemplars of severe impact. Word-association tasks, credited for revealing the content and thought pattern of the respondents' minds without the complication or burden of discursive language (Szalay and Deese, 1978), confirmed that both past and current residents define their environs in extremely negative terms. Respondents were

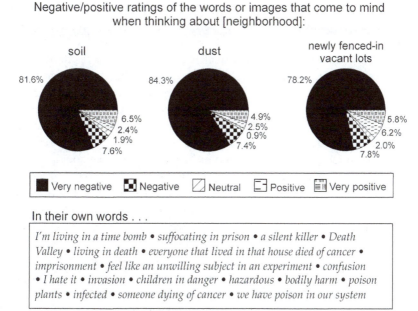

Negative/positive ratings of the words or images that come to mind when thinking about [neighborhood]:

soil	dust	newly fenced-in vacant lots
81.6%	84.3%	78.2%
6.5%	4.9%	5.8%
2.4%	2.5%	6.2%
1.9%	0.9%	2.0%
7.6%	7.4%	7.8%

■ Very negative ▦ Negative ▨ Neutral ⊟ Positive ▤ Very positive

In their own words . . .

I'm living in a time bomb • suffocating in prison • a silent killer • Death Valley • living in death • everyone that lived in that house died of cancer • imprisonment • feel like an unwilling subject in an experiment • confusion • I hate it • invasion • children in danger • hazardous • bodily harm • poison plants • infected • someone dying of cancer • we have poison in our system

Figure 13.1 *Image/word associations and affect ratings (N = 206)*

asked to provide image or word associations for context specific prompts (fences, soil, dust, etc.), and subsequently rated their responses using a five-point affective rating scale: very bad (–2); bad (–1); neutral (0); good (+1); or very good (+2). The rating scores for each stimuli and a sampling of the consistently immoderate image content are displayed in Figure 13.1.

78 per cent of respondents rated their associations with the fenced-in areas in the neighbourhood as highly negative ('very bad' or '–2' on the affect scale), whereas 81.6 per cent and 84.3 per cent of respondents, respectively, rated images associated with 'soil' and 'dust' as highly negative. Across all three stimuli, no single item generated a combined very positive, positive and neutral response in excess of 14.0 per cent. The apparent absence of neutral responses, which usually include synonyms and visual or sensory descriptors (e.g. dimension, colour, sound, etc.), is distinctly revealing in that responses of this kind would be expected in circumstances perceived as benign or generally less threatening. The logical coherence to these affective scores is that the stimuli closest to home and thus closest to one's physical body (dust inside a house and soil immediately outside a house) are rated more negatively than are more distant stimuli (such as fenced-in lots).

Avoidance behaviours

The decayed sense of safety within and around the homes is confirmed, equally, by parallel efforts of residents to avoid activities that normally comprise the acts of everyday life (Edelstein, 1988). Current residents were asked whether they found themselves unable to do some activities given concern about the plant. If the response was affirmative, respondents were then asked if the avoided behaviours were missed a great deal, missed slightly, or not at all missed ('I don't miss it,' 'I miss it slightly' or 'I miss it a great deal'). The majority of residents reported changes in their domestic routines. Responses were nuanced and residents distinguished restrictions that were extremely bothersome from those that were less so. Table 13.1 demonstrates activity avoidance attributed to the plant, and reports frequency distributions for those who missed the avoided activity 'a great deal.'

The response frequencies reflect clear distinctions between restrictions. Residents are much more likely to avoid ordinary activities like opening a window on a breezy day (79.8 per cent) or sitting in the yard on a nice day (74.6 per cent) than less frequent or necessary activities such as going under the house to repair something (44.7 per cent), going up into the attic (47.4 per cent), or allowing children to play in exposed ditches at the edge of the neighbourhood (43.0 per cent). When asked which activities respondents 'miss a great deal,' a similar pattern emerges. Commonplace activities generally associated with a pleasant sense of domestic environment are those most heartily missed. These include opening windows on a breezy day (84.6 per cent), sitting in the yard on a nice day (74.6 per cent), and allowing children to play in the yard (72.6 per cent). Alternatively, activities such as walking near the remaining, though distant, open

Table 13.1 *Activity restrictions: Residents*

Activity	'I do it less often because of the plant'	'I miss it a great deal'	Percentage of total sample[a]
Opening the windows in your house on a breezy day	79.8%	84.6%	67.5%
Sitting in your yard on a nice day	74.6%	84.7%	63.2%
Yard work	66.7%	64.5%	43.0%
Flower gardening	65.8%	70.7%	46.5%
Allowing children in your care to play in your yard	64.0%	72.6%	46.5%
Investing money or time to improve the quality of your house or fix something that is broken	63.2%	66.7%	42.1%
Allowing children in your care to play in a friend's or relative's yard that is near the plant	62.3%	71.8%	44.7%
Walking near the open ditch	54.4%	29.0%	15.8%
Visiting someone whose house or yard is said to have high arsenic levels	50.9%	51.7%	26.3%
Going up in the attic of your house	47.4%	53.7%	25.4%
Going under the house to fix something	44.7%	47.1%	21.1%
Allowing children in your care to play in uncovered ditches	43.0%	34.7%	14.9%

Note: Percentage who do an activity 'less often because of the plant,' who miss the activity 'a great deal,' and the percentage of total respondents who agreed to both (*n* = 114).
[a] Percentage of total sample who do the activity less often because of the plant and reported that they 'miss it a great deal'.

ditches (29.0 per cent), or allowing children to play in those ditches (34.7 per cent) were 'missed a lot' by a minority of respondents.

Embodied stigma

Alterations in household routines signify the inclination of individuals to protect their physical bodies. Worry about bodily harm is often regarded as the defining feature of toxic emergencies: the fear is that contaminants have been absorbed into one's tissues and perhaps the genetic material of survivors (Erikson, 1990, p121; see also Edelstein, 1988; Oliver-Smith, 1996; Kroll-Smith and Floyd, 1997). In Marshall, Georgia residents were forced to interpret these fears while haunted by the image of remediation workers protected from exposure to contaminants, an invading army of clean-up contractors and soil-testing technicians, each of whom benefited from the prophylactic suits used in industrial hygiene. This other-worldly attire seals face, head, body, feet and hands from external contaminants. Workers also were protected and physically distanced from soil and dust through the use of immense backhoes and hep-o-vacs (backhoes assist the removal of contaminated topsoil, while hep-o-vacs function as powerful dust-extracting vacuum cleaners). Such acts of caution are under-standable under the circumstances, yet the symbolic weight of these protected workers lingered in neighbourhood residents' discourse, and helped articulate poignant misgivings. Visually compelling recollections of heavy machinery and 'suited knights' seemed to say that the residents ought to have been safeguarded these many years, that the residents' bodies were already 'poisoned' rendering protection futile, or, more cynically, that the residents were a socially disposable population, unworthy of protection in the first place.

Congruent with this symbolically charged backdrop of protected workers versus vulnerable residents, the interview notes reveal the markings of residents' physical selves. Residents learned to regard the long-familiar patches of atypical skin colour and density on different parts of their bodies as evidence that contaminants were systemically present. Hyperpigmentation, hypopigmentation and hyperkeratoses manifest as epidermal discolorations and lesions, constitute the primary clinical sign of chronic inorganic arsenic exposure (ATSDR, 1990). ATSDR physicians and clinicians examined the health records of 274 current and past residents for signs of exposure. A subset ($n = 75$) of this group showed evidence of simultaneous occurrence of hyperkeratosis, hyperpigmentation and hypopigmentation. Though clinically associated with exposure, these signs are not expertly defined as health risks unless they progress to cancer (ATSDR, 1996, pp3–6). Those diagnosed with skin cancers as well as those merely suspi-cious about the implications of their symptoms treated their skin discolorations as constant reminders that their physical well-being was potentially amiss. During interviews, individuals would draw attention to their 'spots,' point them out, or absentmindedly press upon them as though they were a kind of worry bead, a point of reference that redirected thoughts to the consequences of contamination.

Toxicologists speak of 'body burdens,' the sum total or physical history of exposures through all routes of entry (inhalation, ingestion, skin absorption) and through all sources (food, air, water, office building, etc.; Steingraber, 1997, p236). Denizens of the plant neighbourhood refer instead to the burden of worry: worry about health, childhood exposures, and especially the heightened ex-pectation of pending disease. 88 per cent and 83 per cent of all respondents define themselves, respectively, as 'worrying a lot' about 'birth defects in children' and 'the impact of the plant on my health.' Every child with asthma and every virus is thought to be symptomatic of something larger, more foreboding: 'Am I going to come down with something in my throat and die?' Individual bodies have become physically inscribed (i.e. marked) in the eyes of the owners; atypical pigmentation, perceived risks and socially mediated fears about health have, together, got under the collective skin of neighbourhood residents (Erikson, 1994). Residents thus

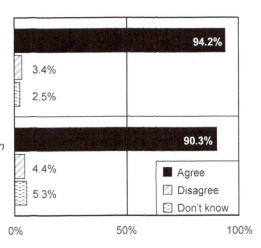

Figure 13.2 *Psychometric dimensions: Fear/dread*

Note: 'Agree' category is 'strongly agree' and 'agree' combined. 'Disagree' category is 'disagree' and 'strongly disagree' combined

come to regard their lives as 'one long lethal injection' or 'feel that they are something that will slowly kill' them.

These observations are corroborated by the vast majority of respondents reporting a deep sense of dread – a quality well documented as central to lay characterizations of toxins (Slovic, 1987) – as well as persistent thoughts about the inhalation and ingestion of contaminants. A full 94.2 per cent of past and current neighbourhood residents agreed that thinking about the contaminants left them with 'a creepy, frightened feeling,' while 90 per cent of current residents agreed with the statement: 'When I'm in my house, I often wonder if I'm breathing in something poisonous.' Figure 13.2 demonstrates these findings graphically.

Older residents carry the additional burden of prior wounds and the unexplained deaths of loved ones. Further, the opportunity to reconsider old griefs in light of recent knowledge about contamination is, for many, unavoidable. Mary Aimes is in her late 60s. Her first child, a daughter, lived only 20 days – the result of a heart defect. Her disabled adult son died of asphyxiation in 1982, the result of a severe allergic reaction to 'something' in the air. Mary's 'bad nerves' began after the release of information about contamination and the concurrent threat that she might be moved from her home.

> You don't worry about it if you don't know, but once you know it makes you remember everything that happened before … All these things I remember. I have nightmares about them now. Like when [as a child and teenager in the late 1940s and 1950s] men from the plant would knock on doors in the middle of the night and tell me and my family to leave the house immediately. There was a leak at the plant. They had giant gas masks, like creatures from outer space. They would tell us we had to run,

Table 13.2 *Stress-related symptoms (N = 206)*

Symptom	Symptom 'bothers me a lot'[a]	Believe plant is the cause[b]	Percentage of total sample[c]
Low energy	85.4%	59.1%	50.5%
Lower back pain	68.4%	41.8%	28.6%
Headaches	68.4%	60.3%	41.3%
Body weakness	65.5%	65.2%	42.7%
Memory trouble	64.1%	50.0%	32.0%
Nervous/shaky feeling	63.6%	62.6%	39.8%
Sore muscles	61.7%	44.9%	27.7%
Trouble getting breath	60.2%	73.4%	44.2%
Tense/keyed up	59.7%	60.2%	35.0%
Heart/chest pains	59.7%	58.5%	35.9%
Heaviness in arms/legs	57.8%	54.6%	31.6%
Depression	53.4%	62.7%	33.5%
Easily annoyed/irritated	52.4%	52.8%	27.7%
Nausea/upset stomach	51.9%	70.1%	36.4%
Trouble concentrating	51.5%	49.1%	25.2%
Heart pounding/racing	51.5%	62.3%	32.0%
Hopelessness	51.0%	74.3%	37.9%
Feeling trapped	49.0%	77.2%	37.9%
Confusion	48.5%	51.0%	24.8%
Faintness/dizziness	48.5%	58.0%	28.2%
Fear	44.2%	64.8%	28.6%
Others do not understand you	43.7%	35.6%	15.5%
Easily hurt feelings	42.7%	38.6%	16.5%
Feeling lonely/alone	41.7%	44.2%	18.4%
Avoidance due to fear	40.8%	67.9%	27.7%
Blaming yourself	37.4%	40.3%	15.0%
Crying easily	33.5%	40.6%	13.6%
Temper outbursts	26.2%	46.3%	12.1%
Critical of others	25.7%	47.2%	12.1%
Poor appetite	22.8%	55.3%	12.6%

Note: [a] Percentage who answered 'yes' to being bothered a lot by the symptom or problem.
[b] Of those who are bothered 'a lot,' percentage who believe the plant is the cause.
[c] Percentage of total sample who are bothered 'a lot' and believe the plant is the cause.

and my mother would try to get all of us up; I was the youngest. When they told me I had to move [due to remediation], I woke up one night in the middle of the night, like as if my mother was trying to get me out of the house. I don't know [Mary stops herself] it's almost more than a body can stand after a certain age.

Mary's psychological and bodily peace is greatly disturbed by this recurrent nightmare and anxious ruminations about the premature deaths of both her children. Her fixation on the 'middle of the night' memory has a particular capacity to crystallize and recreate a pivotal moment of horror for her, and is indicative of the 'intrusive' states that characterize trauma (Herman, 1997, p38).

Extreme distress of this kind is unusual though most residents speak at length about their diseased life histories, and typically enumerate kinship ties and deaths-by-cancers in the same breath ('He was my uncle, he died of bladder cancer, and my sister died last year from breast cancer,' and so on). The reporting of physiological expressions of stress was equally common. A majority of current and past residents reported suffering from 'nausea,' 'feelings of hopelessness,' the 'feeling of being trapped,' 'nervous/shaky feelings,' and the feeling of being 'tense or keyed up.' Over 60 per cent of the subset of respondents who reported being 'bothered a lot' by these symptoms attributed their symptoms to the plant. This did not, however, preclude a credible tendency to attribute other symptoms to non-contaminant causes. Only a minority of respondents reporting symptoms of lower back pain, crying easily or temper outbursts subsequently attributed their sufferings to the plant (Table 13.2, column 2). Similarly, only one symptom, low energy, was reported by a slim majority of all respondents (50.5 per cent) both as 'bothering them a lot' and as 'caused by the plant' (Table 13.2, column 3). Table 13.2 depicts both the distribution of symptoms and the subset of respondents who thereafter attributed their symptoms to the plant.

Sociopolitical stigma

Stigma is a discrediting judgement that in turn evokes a response from those stigmatized (Goffman, 1963; Jones et al, 1984; Gregory et al, 1995). In contaminated communities the complex interplay between technological and social stigmas constructs a tangled mass of attributional actions and reactions. That is, we can speak of those 'constructing' the stigma versus those managing it, we can speak of the racial stigmatization that is probably at play in minority communities versus the technologically derived stigma that residents simultaneously project and suffer because of the plant. Some of this complexity is clarified by acknowledging two basic points. The first is that the occupant of a stigmatized environment can suffer damage simply because of association with that place. This 'suggests that beyond a direct fear of a stigmatizing condition in its own right, there is a concern that any association with the marked setting may serve to mark oneself' (Edelstein, 1987). To this end, residents consciously worry that they are viewed by the outside world as socially contaminated, contagious and therefore unfit as members of the larger human community. Consider by way of example Marvia Lou Smith's characterization of herself as chaffing under media's occasionally ghoulish eye.

> *People come through here now and you see them outside with TV cameras taking pictures and all that. I reckon they said: well what kind of neighborhood is this that has fences and barbed wire. That must be a bad neighborhood. They bad folks that got fences up around here.*

Marvia faults both the physical consequences of remediation (fencing, barbed wire) and the media's amplification of those effects (see Kasperson, 1992) for the negative light they cast upon herself and her community.

Troubling reflections of this kind coexist with a second basic point – that contamination events often involve the stigmatization of the already stigmatized. Exposure to environmental hazards is not random but rather selective of social and economically vulnerable populations. Risks are not distributed equally across social groups, there is a greater-than-average likelihood that the victims of hazardous technologies will be people of colour and/or those occupying the economic margins of society (Bullard, 1990; Johnston, 1997). At the same time, those living in environmentally degraded contexts are often subject to psycho-social debasement and dehumanizing innuendo (lazy, ignorant, backward) that destroys self-esteem and the motivation of individuals to control their destiny (Appell quoted in Johnston, 1994, p10).

In Marshall, this fusion of social stigma and environmental risk engulfs local disputes about the consequences of exposure. To this end all talk about 'the plant' is somehow also talk about race. Arguments about the nature of legitimate evidence for injury, the appropriateness of different compensatory actions, or the logic of soil testing were invariably framed as 'concerns that would have been addressed' or events that 'never would have happened in a white neighbourhood.' In particular, most residents believed the plant and the USEPA ignored pertinent local input that might have ensured a mutually agreeable plan for the testing of soils and thus clean-up. USEPA engineers posited a linear model of contaminant dissemination; properties immediately adjacent to the facility were tested as were those radiating outward from the source. When a safe property was encountered, testing would extend one or two houses further and then cease. It was assumed that all further properties were safe.

Locals opposed this model by insisting that wind patterns, the ditch's history of flooding into some properties and not others, the plant's trucking routes through the neighbourhood, and the historical tendency for employees to carry contaminants into their homes via soiled work clothing had each contributed to an erratic dispersal of contaminants. Widespread discontent of this kind was expressed by survey respondents: 71.8 per cent disagreed with the contention that 'EPA experts considered all the important ways in which chemicals travelled from the plant into the neighbourhood' while 74.8 per cent believed that the EPA did a poor job of 'testing for contaminants in the neighbourhood.' The dismissal of local concerns was eventually tempered by the hiring (on behalf of residents) of outside experts who confirmed a more extensive pattern of contaminant dissemination; the USEPA subsequently verified these findings with further testing by their own technical staff.

Racist motives were also attributed to the USEPA's procrastination regarding the distribution of knowledge about contaminants. The time lag between the 1990 Superfund listing and the 1993 official proclamation of exposure (a fact noted in this chapter's second paragraph) was widely interpreted as an act dismissing Marshall's black community as peripheral and thereby unworthy of urgent attention. Further, black residents cite a late 1980s exodus of white residents from the plant neighbourhood as evidence that knowledge of contamination was divulged well in advance to white residents. The suspicion is that white residents knew about the contamination early on and thus sold damaged residential properties at 'good prices' to unsuspecting Blacks.

Representatives of Marshall's white community deny the persistent accusations of racism, and instead accuse (black) plant-neighbourhood residents of acting against the plant for 'easy' economic gain via the several pending litigation efforts. Residents of the plant neighbourhood are also censured by more affluent locals (white and some black) for denigrating the town's reputation and its commercial prospects through exaggerated and false claims of plant-derived health impacts. Other white residents are not critical per se, but fear the repercussion of voicing support for those in the plant neighbourhood. They fear being socially isolated because of perceived disloyalty toward their white peers (including the plant's founding family) or for being 'too close' to the town's poorest and racially stigmatized residents.

Local African-Americans' pointed critiques of testing procedures and the racist undertones of interactions between local citizens and responsible parties can be read as healthy, proactive signs of resistance to economic and racial stigmatization (Schwab, 1994; Szasz, 1994). Yet the impressions from field observations confirm something different. Neighbourhood residents often appeared to be overwhelmed by a pervasive mood of hopelessness, a few resilient activist voices aside. The neighbourhood's emotional landscape was marred by despair and a resignation not unlike the psychological numbing described in Lifton's (1967) work on radiation poisoning. Similarly, Jones et al (1984) defined the 'essence of the stigmatizing process' as producing 'devastating consequences for emotions, thought and behavior' (p4). The argument is that marked individuals are often unsuccessful at maintaining positive self-regard when the 'evaluations elicited from other people [are] disproportionately negative' (Jones et al, 1984, p111). Other scholars of power and subordination have defined this defeated disposition as a 'quiescence' of political participation despite a relatively open political system (Scott, 1990, p71).

In order to obtain some indication of the injuries of racism as they apply to political will, Srole's (1965) political alienation questions were modified to fit the Georgia context. The responses produced suggestive results. Compare, especially, responses of current residents with those offered by prior residents. These demographically similar groups differ from one another to the extent that current residents have lived through the full range of consequences of exposure – the parade of suited hygiene experts, exacerbated racial tensions, battles for voice in decisions about remediation and, most dramatically, the resonating presence of a

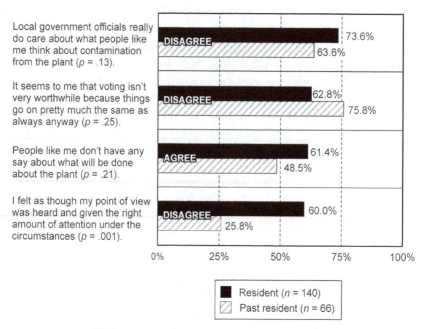

Figure 13.3 *Expressions of political efficacy*

denuded landscape signified as hazardous – while prior residents have faced these events from a more removed and thus arguably protected position.

Both current residents and prior residents demonstrate an impaired sense of political efficacy. This impaired political efficacy is more prominent among current residents than prior residents on each of four questions, though only one of these differences is statistically significant at less than 0.05. Figure 13.3 demonstrates that current residents are more likely (by 10.0 per cent) than prior residents to disagree that 'local officials really do care about what I think'; less likely (by 12.9 per cent) to believe that 'people like me have a say about what will be done about the plant'; and much more likely to disagree with the suggestion that their 'point of view was heard and attended to' (by 34.2 per cent). Both respondent groups disagreed with the contention that voting was no longer 'worthwhile,' though prior residents were more supportive of voting (by a margin of 13 per cent) than were current residents. The combined findings capture something of the flat affect about political efficacy expressed by both groups. The between-group differences suggest, however, that current residents share a greater sense of defeat with regard to political processes than do prior residents. Given that the two groups are demographically similar, save for current residents' greater exposure to plant and clean-up specific events, it is plausible that remediation procedures have had some effect on the loss of democratic control expressed by current residents.

Discussion

This chapter began with the contention that the personal trauma of toxic exposure merits a central position in theorizing about technological, product or geographic stigma. An expanded theory of stigma requires an understanding that extends well beyond the measure of market losses or adverse behaviour by consumers. Accordingly, we considered the ravaging of home, neighbourhood, and individual well-being that characterize Marshall's contamination events. An overwhelming majority of residents adjacent to the chemical plant think only negatively about soil, home and neighbourhood. Individuals change their daily routines, close windows, rest uneasily both inside and outside their homes, and abhor the 'concentration camp' aesthetic that has taken over their lives. Implicit and explicit definitions of home as a place that promises safety for self and family, as an affective anchor in an otherwise chaotic world (Fitchen, 1989), are supplanted by the fear of dust in the attic and the feeling that 'something will slowly kill me.' The fear among Marshall's plant-adjacent residents is a state of mind that 'gathers force slowly and insidiously, creeping around one's defenses rather than smashing through them' (Erikson, 1994, p21). This insidious 'creeping' quality is evident in the psychological recoil that follows the sight of workers in hygiene suits and in individuals' graphic articulations of invasion (e.g. 'My life feels like one long lethal injection').

Both body and place assist the reflective processes fundamental to human thought. The body is the means by which we experience and apprehend the world (Merleau-Ponty, 1962), while place (as in home, neighbourhood, environment, etc.) is a basis for direction and self-reflection, for who one is in the larger social world (Basso, 1996). In Marshall, Georgia, the physical experience of a contaminated neighbourhood and body intersect with disturbing reflections about the self. In this sense, the hazard signs, the emergence of vacant lots, and browning of the neighbourhood can be understood as discrete injuries and as vehicles that repeatedly summon, indeed trap residents, in a vacuum of negative reflections. Dramatic changes in the landscape become insistent reminders of the presence of contaminants, forcing those who live there to cognitively register and re-register the possibility of 'poison in [their] systems.' These reflections interact with larger sociopolitical realities. In the contaminated neighbourhood studied here, worry about one's health or the safety of one's home merged with racial discrimination from some sectors of the town's white community, with anguished musings about denigrating the portrait of one's neighbourhood and its residents on television, with implications about the 'worthiness' of protecting remediation workers but not residents, and with experts' rejection of local complaints about remediation or the testing of soil. This combination of affronts encourages resignation among residents who define themselves as not cared for, listened to, or able to have a say in what will be done about the plant.

Ultimately, the Marshall, Georgia experience can enhance our understanding of the contamination experience and of stigmas. Experienced risk refers here to the contamination experience, that is the physical, psychological and social consequences of exposure. These are direct reactions to hazardous environmental stimuli. Stigmatizing influences consist instead of signals that exacerbate the experience of contamination. The origin of stigmatizing impacts is in part media-fuelled, as suggested by Kasperson et al (1988), and as evidenced by one woman's response to the presence of camera crews in her neighbourhood. More importantly, the Marshall, Georgia context demonstrates unremittingly that public agency (USEPA, ATSDR) efforts to remedy hazards often contribute to the experience of stigmas locally. 'Remedies' for protecting exposed communities (e.g. the stripping of vegetation, the removal of contaminated properties, the invasion of 'suited knights,' and/or the relabelling of pigmentation patterns as exposure symptoms) can foster the very fears they ought ideally to alleviate.

Finally, in this context one must come to some understanding of the combination of racial and technological stigmatization, because persons of colour are often those most immediately impacted by such hazards. We know from Goffman's (1963) early work that visible minorities already need to 'manage' their 'spoiled' identities. In minority communities faced with the ramifications of extant hazards, pre-existing experiences of racial stigmatization can constitute a dominant lens through which the new experience of contamination and technological stigma passes. Technological and social stigmas can thus form an ugly loop, where each follows and so intensifies the impact of the other. A more comprehensive, interactive and socially astute model of technological stigma would acknowledge this interplay and thereby seek to define the links and causal relationships between social stigmas, technological stigmas and the local experience of contamination.

Notes

1   All person, place and company names cited herein have been altered to respect the privacy of those involved.
2   Relying on a litigant sample is admittedly problematic. On the one hand, the legal team did not exclude anyone who fit the above criteria and reported to me that only a very few (less than ten) of all traceable past and present residents declined participation. At the same time, current residents refer to an earlier period (see page 80) where more whites resided on the periphery of the plant neighbourhood. This seems to suggest that more whites should have been included in the litigant list. Nevertheless, the sample for this chapter was drawn from the areas closest to the plant and included those whose properties were regarded by USEPA and litigant experts as appropriate for contaminant testing. These areas represent neighbourhoods that are currently, and were historically, primarily African-American.
3   34 per cent of the resident group are between 18 and 39 years of age, 43.6 per cent are between 40 and 59, and 20.7 per cent are 60 or older (remaining unknown). 33 per cent of non-residents are between 18 and 39 years of age, 39.4 per cent are between 40 and 59, 19.7 per cent are over 60 (remaining unknown).
4   All quoted, unreferenced speech is derived directly from word-association tasks and interview notes.

5   In the United States, the post-1945 production of synthetic organic chemicals
    accelerated exponentially and by 1955 had captured 90 per cent of the agricultural
    pesticide market. By the early 1990s there were 860 active pesticidal ingredients regis-
    tered with the federal government (as compared to 32 ingredients in 1939). They are
    disbursed into more than 20,000 products (Steingraber, 1997, p95).

Part III

Psychometric Studies

Chapter 14

Public Perception of the Risk of Blood Transfusion

Melissa L. Finucane, Paul Slovic and C. K. Mertz [*]

Concern is mounting in Europe and North America about the proportion of people who say they are unwilling to receive a blood transfusion (Compas, Inc, 1995; Industrial Relations and Social Affairs [IRSA], 1995; Lee et al, 1998). In many cases, refusing a transfusion comes with higher risks to health and life than accepting it (US General Accounting Offfice, 1988; Lackritz et al, 1995; Spence, 1995). Health policy makers and regulators would do well to heed warning signals indicating (real or imagined) problems in the blood supply, because they can have devastating health and economic impacts. Fortunately, we may be able to minimize the likelihood of making costly risk management decisions that are too restrictive or, alternatively, not protective enough, by looking at what we know about risk perception and what it implies for acceptability of blood transfusions.

To manage risk best, we need to understand how people think about risk and to recognize that their thoughts, feelings and behaviours are determined by psychological, social, cultural and political forces. Gender, race, worldview, trust and ability to control hazards are human characteristics that have been related systematically to risk perceptions in previous research (Slovic, 1999). Furthermore, sensitivity to stigma has been linked to public opposition to many technologies and consumables (Gregory et al, 1995). Stigmatization occurs when the perception of safety and acceptability of a product is nullified by its association with events that are highly dreaded, have potentially unknown consequences, and receive extensive and dramatic coverage by the news media (Slovic, 1987).

There is limited research to date on the relationship between the perceived risk of blood transfusions and personal characteristics. A better picture of

[*]   Reprinted from Finucane, M. L., Slovic, P. and Mertz, C. K. (2000) 'Public perception of the risk of blood transfusion', *Transfusion*, vol 40, pp1017–1022.

individual differences in response to problems (real or imagined) in the blood supply will help us most effectively tailor risk management strategies to particular groups of people. Thus, this chapter reports data collected as part of a large national telephone survey conducted in the United States to examine how personal characteristics relate to people's perceptions of the risk of blood transfusion. The questions about transfusions were part of a larger assessment of perceptions of the risk of a range of environmental and health hazards (e.g. pesticides, nuclear power, motor vehicles). Only the method and results of the survey that are relevant to perceptions of the risks of transfusions are presented below.

Materials and methods

Survey instrument

Imagery

An imagery exercise was placed at the beginning of the survey. In this exercise, respondents were asked to provide up to three associations to the phrase 'blood transfusions.' This was done by using a version of the method of continued associations (Szalay and Deese, 1978) adapted for use in a telephone survey (Slovic et al, 1991a). This method simply involved the interviewers saying, 'The first question involves word associations. Think about "blood transfusions" for a moment. When you hear the phrase "blood transfusions," what is the first word or brief image that comes to your mind?' Then two more prompts for associations were made. Next, respondents were asked to rate each image they gave on a five-point scale reflecting their feeling from 1 (very positive), 2 (positive), 3 (neutral), 4 (negative), to 5 (very negative). These ratings are called affect ratings.

Only one-third of the sample group ($n = 385$) were asked to give images for blood transfusions. The remaining two-thirds produced images for other activities (eating beef and cloning) that are not relevant to this report. (Respondents were asked to provide associations for only one of the three activities to avoid the confusion in their minds of associations for one stimulus and associations for another stimulus.)

Risk perception

The survey contained three items about the perceptions of the risk of blood transfusions. All respondents were asked to indicate whether blood transfusions carry almost no risk, slight risk, moderate risk or high risk to the health and safety of (1) 'you and your family' and (2) 'the American public as a whole.' Third, respondents were asked if they strongly disagree, disagree, agree or strongly agree with the statement, 'I believe the blood supply in the United States is safe.'

A general risk-perception index was calculated for each respondent by averaging ratings of risk to the public across 18 hazards (e.g. cellular phones, air travel, pesticides), excluding the ratings for the blood transfusion item.

Behaviour

Respondents' behavioural intentions were assessed by asking if they strongly disagree, disagree, agree or strongly agree with the statement, 'If I were hospitalized and my physician recommended a blood transfusion, I would accept blood from a blood bank.' Moreover, respondents were asked if they had ever had a blood transfusion (answers categorized as yes or no).

Other

Finally, all respondents were asked a series of questions regarding stigmatization, worldview, trust and demographics (including gender and race).

To determine significance, values from within each subgroup or for response to each survey item were calculated separately.

Administration of the survey

A stratified random sample of household members over 18 years of age in the United States was surveyed by telephone from 27 September 1997 through to 3 February 1998. A total of 1204 completed interviews were obtained, for an excellent overall response rate of 46.8 per cent. Interviewing was conducted on a sample of the general population and three oversamples of ethnic groups (African-American, Hispanic and Asian). This resulted in a sample of 672 whites, 217 African-Americans, 180 Hispanics, 101 Asians and 34 others. Interviewing was conducted in English or Spanish. Respondents' mean age was 43.5; 45 per cent were men and 55 per cent were women. The general sample and ethnic oversamples were weighted to the 1997 US population as a whole in terms of race and gender, which resulted in a weighted sample of 861 respondents. To minimize the overall interview length, some questionnaire items were administered to only half of the sample (weighted $n = 426$), including the items assessing agreement that the US blood supply is safe, assessing agreement that a transfusion would be accepted if recommended, and determining who had had a transfusion. The average interview lasted approximately 35 minutes.

Results

Imagery and affect ratings

The imagery task yielded 1060 associations to the phrase 'blood transfusions.' A maximum of 1155 images was possible (385 individuals were asked to provide up to three associations each), but fewer images were obtained because some respondents provided only one or two images, and five respondents provided no images.

Associations were assigned to four general categories: health and safety ($n = 529$), functional considerations ($n = 299$), personal considerations ($n = 167$) and other ($n = 65$). All general categories had subcategories, with many containing multiple associations judged to have similar meanings. For example, the general category labelled 'health and safety' contained a subcategory labelled 'Why is

Table 14.1 *Images associated with the phrase 'blood transfusions' by 380 participants*

Image categories	Number of images	Average affect ratings (SD)
Health and safety	529	2.8 (1.2)
Risk of AIDS/HIV	222	3.2 (1.3)
Why is transfusion needed?	174	2.9 (1.0)
Positive consequences of transfusion	57	1.8 (0.6)
Urgency	41	1.8 (0.9)
Questioning safety and risk	35	3.0 (1.2)
Functional considerations	299	2.5 (0.9)
Equipment/places/people	183	2.6 (0.9)
What process is involved?	55	2.3 (0.9)
Physical features of blood	53	2.5 (0.8)
Supply quantity	8	2.8 (1.2)
Personal considerations	167	2.0 (0.8)
Gift giving	89	1.9 (0.6)
Personal relevance	34	1.8 (0.8)
Emotions evoked	33	2.7 (1.2)
Ethics	11	2.0 (0.8)
Other	65	2.9 (1.2)
General	33	2.7 (0.9)
Negative	25	3.4 (1.2)
Positive	7	1.4 (0.5)
Total images	1060	
Overall average		2.6 (0.8)

Note: Ratings coded 1 (very positive); 2 (positive); 3 (neutral); 4 (negative); and 5 (very negative)

transfusion needed?', which included images such as 'sickness,' 'hemophilia,' 'car accidents,' 'childbirth' and 'somebody needing blood' (Table 14.1).

The largest general category, health and safety, contained the largest subcategory, 'risk of AIDS/HIV,' which consisted of images such as 'afraid of contracting AIDS.' The subcategory 'risk of AIDS/HIV' had one of the highest average affect ratings (3.2; $SD = 1.3$), which was in fact around the neutral point (3.0) on the scale.

The average affect rating across all 1060 images for the 380 respondents was slightly positive (2.6; $SD = 0.8$). The majority of the images were positive or very positive (58.5 per cent), but a substantial proportion were negative or very negative (26.0 per cent) or neutral (14.7 per cent).

Risk perception

Nearly half the respondents (46.6 per cent; $n = 401$) gave a moderate or high rating for the perceived risk of blood transfusions to self and family and for the perceived risk of blood transfusions to the American public (52.0 per cent; $n = 447$). Responses to the statement, 'I believe the blood supply in the United States

Table 14.2 *Percentage (and number) of total respondents and in gender, race and education subgroups who disagreed or strongly disagreed with blood safety and acceptance statements*

	Blood supply in the United States is safe	Would accept blood if hospitalized
Total	36.2 (154)	33.3 (132)
Respondent subgroup		
Gender		
Female	44.4* (89)	44.3* (88)
Male	29.1* (66)	23.6* (54)
Race		
African-American	62.7 (32)	43.6† (22)
Hispanic	49.0* (16)	44.7† (15)
White	30.7* (100)	30.5† (100)
Education		
Less than college degree	43.2* (130)	39.0* (117)
College degree	19.2* (24)	19.3* (24)

Note: Significant at $p < .01$ by chi-square test; † Not significant by chi-square test

is safe,' showed that most people (60.9 per cent; $n = 260$) agreed or strongly agreed, although a substantial proportion (36.2 per cent; $n = 154$) disagreed or strongly disagreed with the statement. A higher proportion of disagreement with the statement was found among women than among men, among African-American and Hispanic people than among whites, and among less educated persons than among more educated persons (Table 14.2).

The general risk-perception index was correlated with responses about the safety of the blood supply. As the general perceived risk increased, the blood supply in the United States was perceived as more risky ($r = 0.33$; $p < .001$; $n = 414$).

Behaviour

Responses to the statement, 'If I were hospitalized and my physician recommended a blood transfusion, I would accept blood from a blood bank,' showed that most people (64.7 per cent; $n = 275$) agreed or strongly agreed, but a substantial proportion (33.3 per cent; $n = 132$) disagreed or strongly disagreed. Here too, sex, race and education were related to the extent of disagreement with the statement (Table 14.2).

The general risk-perception index was correlated with responses about behavioural intention. Consistent with expectations, as general perceived risk increased, blood transfusions were perceived as more unacceptable ($r = 0.30$; $p < .001$; $n = 418$).

Responses indicated that 18.8 per cent ($n = 80$) of the sample had had a blood transfusion. The percentage of respondents who have not been transfused

Table 14.3 *Percentage (and number) of respondents who agreed or disagreed with statements about stigma and who rated risks to themselves and their families and to the public from blood transfusions as moderate or high*

| Statements | Percentage (number) judging risk from blood transfusions as moderate or high for | |
	self and family	the public
The selection of an existing highway for future transportation of nuclear and chemical waste would lower the value of nearby homes.		
Agree	50.0 (311)	56.4 (351)
Disagree	36.9 (81)	38.0 (84)
Farm products are less acceptable to the public when radioactive waste is transported past farms.		
Agree	51.5 (227)	59.7 (243)
Disagree	39.3 (144)	42.2 (154)

Note: All percentages were significant at $p < .01$ by chi-square test.

and who rated risk to self and family from transfusions as high was greater than the percentage of those who have been transfused and rated the risk as high (16.2 per cent vs. 7.8 per cent). Similarly, risk to the public was judged as high by a greater proportion of people not transfused than of those transfused (20.6 per cent vs. 11.1 per cent).

Stigma

There was evidence that perceptions of the risk of blood transfusions to individuals and to the public were related to respondents' sensitivity to stigmatization in other risk settings. For example, the more a person thought that transporting nuclear and chemical waste through a region would stigmatize nearby homes and farm products, the higher their perceived risk of blood (Table 14.3).

Trust and control

Risk perceptions of the blood supply were related to respondents' wish to retain control over hazardous activities and to their trust in experts' opinions about risks. For example, a much higher proportion of respondents who agreed that people living near a nuclear power plant should be able to vote to close the plant, if they think it is not being run safely, disagreed with the statement that the US blood supply is safe. Trust in experts' views about pesticide risks was also related to perceived safety of the blood supply (Table 14.4).

There was also other evidence of a relationship between feelings of control of one's immediate environment and risk perceptions. For example, a lower propor-

Table 14.4 *Percentage (and number) of respondents who agreed or disagreed with statements about trust and control, and who disagreed that the US blood supply is safe*

Statements	US blood supply is safe
People living near a nuclear power plant should be able to vote to close the plant if they think it is not being run safely.	
Agree	42.1 (137)
Disagree	17.6 (16)
I trust what experts say about the risk of pesticides.	
Agree	27.7 (60)
Disagree	46.0 (92)
I feel safe from chemical pollutants when inside my home.	
Agree	26.9 (71)
Disagree	51.8 (83)
I often feel discriminated against.	
Agree	51.4 (55)
Disagree	30.9 (97)

Note: All percentages were significant at $p < .01$ by chi-square test.

tion of respondents who agreed with a statement such as 'I feel safe from chemical pollutants when inside my home' disagreed with the statement that the blood supply in the United States is safe. Furthermore, a higher proportion of respondents who agreed with the statement 'I often feel discriminated against' disagreed with the statement that the US blood supply is safe (Table 14.4).

Finally, interesting relationships were found between some individual items about worldviews and ratings of perceived risk (Table 14.5). For example, people who agreed with the statement, 'I have very little control over risks to my health' (which reflects a fatalistic worldview), were more likely to judge transfusions as posing moderate or high risk to self and family. Respondents who agreed with the statement, 'What this world needs is a more equal distribution of wealth' (which reflects an egalitarian worldview), were more likely to judge the risk to self and family from transfusions as moderate or high. Similar patterns were found for judgements of public risk.

Discussion

Many things influence people's risk perceptions, including cognitive and affective factors and personal characteristics. The data presented in this chapter show that people's perceptions of the risk of blood transfusions are no less complicated than their perceptions of other hazards.

What are people thinking and feeling about blood transfusions? A substantial proportion of people do not consider the US blood supply to be safe and say that they would not accept blood if they were hospitalized. Our finding is consistent

Table 14.5 *Percentage (and number) of respondents who agreed or disagreed with statements about fatalistic and egalitarian worldviews and who rated risks to themselves and their families and to the public from blood transfusions as moderate or high*

Statements	Percentage (number) judging risk from blood transfusions as moderate or high for	
	self and family	the public
Fatalistic worldview: I have very little control over risks to my health.		
Agree	54.2* (96)	64.2* (332)
Disagree	44.7* (304)	48.8* (113)
Egalitarian worldview: What this world needs is a more equal distribution of wealth.		
Agree	48.8† (281)	55.4† (318)
Disagree	39.6† (102)	44.2† (113)

Note: Significant at $p < .01$ by chi-square test; † Significant at $p < .05$ by chi-square test.

with previous reports of heightened concern among Europeans and North Americans about real and imagined risks associated with blood transfusions (Compas, Inc, 1995; Industrial Relations and Social Affairs (IRSA), 1995; Lee et al, 1998).

What we learn from the current imagery data is that many people are thinking about the consequences of HIV contamination and AIDS when they think about blood transfusions. Possibly, the prevalence of AIDS/HIV images simply reflects the intense media coverage of the tainted-blood issue in many countries for many years (Picard, 1995). The data here carry both good news and bad news for policy makers and regulators. The good news is that, so far, people's perceptions of the risk of blood transfusions and their related behavioural intentions are not overwhelmingly associated with a negative affect (which would be very hard to undo). The bad news is that the raw materials of stigmatization are already evident, waiting for a precipitating event to heighten their salience. Just as was found with associations to the concept of a nuclear waste repository (Slovic et al, 1991a), images with qualities of dread, revulsion and anger are found in some people's associations to blood transfusions. An event that precipitates a stronger link in people between their images of transfusions and more negative than positive pervasive affect will no doubt escalate the already substantial proportion of people who say they would refuse a blood transfusion.

The imagery in the present study reflects two dimensions that Slovic (1987) found typically to characterize people's risk perceptions. One dimension is dread risk, the extent of perceived catastrophic potential, threat to life, and lack of control. The other dimension is unknown risk, the extent to which the risk associated with the hazard seems unobservable, unknown, new and delayed in its harmful effects. When high dread and unknown risk qualities are associated with a technology, risk perceptions soar and the technology becomes stigmatized and avoided.

There is significant potential for stigmatization of blood and blood components and products. Consider first the dread risk aspects of bad blood. The main cause of concern for the public stems historically from infection of blood in the 1980s with HIV and hepatitis C. Such infection signals catastrophe to people, because the HIV and HCV epidemics have seemed relentless, and they have horrific and potentially fatal consequences. The risk with blood is also involuntary: recipients of blood transfusions would typically face death or severe health consequences if the transfusion were not administered, so they have little choice in the matter. Moreover, unless recipients donate their own blood, the blood used in transfusions is perceived to come from an uncontrollable source. That is, blood is contributed by strangers and is stored in and distributed by a large 'blood bank,' neither of which can be influenced to any great extent by an individual patient.

Bad blood also has elements of unknown risk. Science still does not understand HIV and HCV adequately (there is still no readily available vaccine or cure for either virus), and, despite widespread information campaigns, many people are still somewhat ignorant of how these viruses are spread (Gerbert et al, 1991; Denman et al, 1996). Further, infection of the blood with these viruses, if present, cannot be detected by the transfusion recipient, and their effects are latent. And, of course, the risk is abnormal – blood is supposed to be the elixir of life, not tainted with things like deadly viruses.

Heightened sensitivity to stigmatization is an important component of the perceived risk of blood transfusions. In the present study, sensitivity to stigmatization due to nuclear and chemical waste transport was found to be related to the risk individuals perceived from blood transfusions. Monitoring the potential for stigmatization of technologies or products in a community is important, because, once such stigmatization occurs, it is very hard to reverse. It would be natural to turn to informing and educating people about the risk from blood components to reduce what technical experts may view as 'exaggerated fears.' However, the very nature of a stigma – that it is based in strong feelings – limits the influence of quantitative risk information. Rather, highlighting the qualitative benefits of blood components may reduce negative affect, as there is evidence suggesting that the positive affect associated with benefits can partially offset the negative affect associated with risks (Margolis, 1996; Finucane et al, 2000a).

Other determinants of the perceived risk of blood transfusions

The greatest individual and public risk from blood transfusions is perceived by people who are female, nonwhite and less educated, and who have not previously received a blood transfusion. Lesser feelings of trust and control are related also to greater risk perceptions. This pattern of results is similar to trends found for risk perceptions of many other hazards, from nuclear power to pesticides (Flynn et al, 1994). Flynn et al (1994) postulate that white men may have relatively low perceptions of risk because they create, manage, control and benefit from risky technologies and activities more than anyone else. Women and nonwhite men may have relatively high perceptions of risk, because they are more vulnerable, have less power and control, and benefit less.

The effects of establishing and maintaining trust must not be underestimated. The importance of trust in the blood system has long been recognized by agencies worried that news of tainted blood would result in declining blood donations (Picard, 1995). However, bad blood is of even more significance to people potentially receiving a transfusion, which suggests that building in transfusion recipients legitimate feelings of trust and control regarding the blood supply system should be a priority.

Furthermore, the fact that we found relationships between people's worldviews and their perceived risk of blood transfusions suggests that we need to recognize that people hold different beliefs about what should be considered risky and different goals about how the risk should be managed. People's risk perceptions reflect their deep-seated values about technology and its impact on individuals and society. Consequently, agreeing on particular risk management strategies may be difficult. For instance, Jehovah's Witnesses' refusal of blood components out of their religious conviction presents a special challenge for physicians, whose responsibility it is to preserve life (Vercillo and Duprey, 1988).

Conclusion

Risk perceptions should be monitored to anticipate and deal with problems of public acceptance. It is better to spend resources prophylactically on this issue, because the consequences of not averting potential concerns about (real or imagined) risks, and thus losing public confidence, can be extremely costly. Increasing stigmatization or decreasing trust may be best dealt with via strategies that influence people's perceived control over the blood supply, their focus on potential catastrophic consequences, their familiarity with blood donation, storage and transfusion, and so on. Of course, any strategies adopted should be tailored to the specific characteristics of the people involved, such as gender, race and worldview, which are important determinants of the perceived risk of blood transfusions.

Acknowledgements

The authors thank James Flynn, Howard Kunreuther, Steven Johnson, Patricia Gwartney and numerous other colleagues for their assistance in the design and data collection for the national survey whose results are reported here. They thank Kathleen Hall Jamieson of the Annenberg Center for her financial support of the survey. They give thanks also to Janet Douglas for her help with manuscript preparation.

Chapter 15

Expert and Public Perception of Risk from Biotechnology

*Lucia Savadori, Stefania Savio, Eraldo Nicotra, Rino Rumiati, Melissa L. Finucane and Paul Slovic**

Introduction

The use of genetically modified organisms (GMOs) in food production as well as in medicine and pharmacology has created much public concern, especially in the 15 member states of the European Union (Durant et al, 1998; Gaskell et al, 2000; Gaskell and Allum, 2001; Gaskell and Bauer, 2001). Several risk perception studies have been conducted in the United States and Europe to explore the reasons for public opposition to biotechnology. Some early studies found that the risks of DNA technology were perceived as extremely unknown, with very negative consequences that were delayed in time and not directly observable (Slovic, 1987). In people's minds, DNA technologies were perceived to be very similar to hazards such as nuclear energy, radioactive waste, electromagnetic fields and other technologies that use rays or chemical substances (e.g. food irradiation and food colouring). DNA manipulation (involving both animal and plant genes) has been judged among the most unknown hazards even when compared to hazards in the food domain (such as bacterial food contamination or food colouring; Sparks and Shepherd, 1994; Fife-Schaw and Rowe, 1996).

When the domain of biotechnology and its applications were investigated, other characteristics besides lack of knowledge emerged as important in defining public perceptions. People classified biotech applications by their nature (food-related applications vs. medical-pharmaceutical applications; Zechendorf, 1994;

---

*   Reprinted from Savadori, L., Savio, S., Nicotra, E., Rumiati, R., Finucane, M. and Slovic, P. (2004) 'Expert and public perception of risk from biotechnology', *Risk Analysis*, vol 24, pp1289–1299.

Sparks et al, 1995),[1] and by their specificity (those that involved animal genes vs. those that involved plant genes; Sparks et al, 1995; Frewer et al, 1997). Genetic modification of animals, for example, was more acceptable if it was applied within a medical context than a food-related context (Sparks et al, 1995). Applications involving animal genes were rated riskier than applications involving plant genes (Sparks and Shepherd, 1994; Frewer et al, 1997). Frewer et al (1997) suggested that people's greater concern toward animal genes could be explained by ethical concerns since negative attitudes toward applications involving animal genes were positively correlated with ethical dimensions (immoral, unnatural, unethical). In this chapter we examine the difference between food and medical applications because it allows us to understand how the same organism can be judged to have different risk according to the context in which it is embedded.

In Frewer et al's (1997) study, a factor analysis of ratings on 17 self-generated dimensions of risk revealed two major factors describing people's risk perception of biotech applications. The first, accounting for 88 per cent of the variance, was labelled the 'rejection factor' and covered personal objections, personal worry, negative welfare effects, creation of inequalities, tampering with nature, and whether the application was immoral, unnatural, unethical, harmful, dangerous, risky, not beneficial, not advantageous, not necessary, not progressive and not important. The applications involving animal genes obtained more extreme ratings on the negative pole of this factor. The second factor, accounting for 9 per cent of the variance, was represented only by the dimension of 'long-term effects,' and the most extreme positions on this factor were occupied by medical applications; agricultural applications were perceived to have short-term effects.

Individual differences in risk perceptions

The present study examines expert and lay people's judgements on a set of dimensions (see Appendix), some of which were previously used in studies adopting the psychometric paradigm (Fischhoff et al, 1978) and others that were new, such as harm and benefit. The dimensions related to personal and scientific knowledge were also used because they were found to be important in previous studies of biotechnology risk perceptions (Slovic, 1987; Sparks and Shepherd, 1994; Fife-Schaw and Rowe, 1996).

Reaction to a hazard is not the same in every person. Individual characteristics, such as past experience with the hazard or specific technical knowledge, can affect the importance of some dimensions and result in quite different judgements of risk. For example, when judging risk, the public sometimes relies on aspects such as catastrophic potential or vividness of the effects, while the experts tend to rely more on observed or expected fatalities (Slovic et al, 1979; Flynn et al, 1993a; Kletz, 1996).

Several studies have documented differences between experts and the public in risk perception (Slovic et al, 1980, 1995; Slovic, 1987; Kraus et al, 1992; Flynn et al, 1993a; Savadori et al, 1998), while other studies have not found such differences (Wright et al, 2000). This result probably depends on the type of hazard studied. Compared to experts, the public typically gives higher risk estimates to chemical products (Kraus et al, 1992; Slovic et al, 1995), radioactive waste disposal (Flynn et al, 1993a), nuclear power, police work (Slovic et al, 1980; Slovic, 1987), mountain climbing (Slovic et al, 1980), warfare, inefficiency of health care service, interracial conflicts, shortage of medical equipment (Savadori et al, 1998), hunting and spray cans (Slovic, 1987). In addition, the public typically gives lower risk estimates than experts give to electric power, surgery, swimming, X-rays (Slovic et al, 1980; Slovic, 1987), lawn mowers, downhill skiing (Savadori et al, 1998) and bicycles (Slovic, 1987). Expert and public estimates of the risk derived from oil and gas production tend to be similar (Wright et al, 2000).

A recent analysis of nine empirical studies of expert and lay judgements of risk suggested that too many socio-demographic variables confound the ultimate conclusion that experts and lay people really differ in one quality and nature of their risk judgements (Rowe and Wright, 2001; Sjöberg, 2002). The present study compared a group of experts, which were people with at least a master's degree and specific training in biology such as university professors or PhD students, with a group of non-experts, which were individuals without specific training in biology. The expert and non-expert samples were similar in gender and age.

Trust in information sources

Trust helps us reduce uncertainty to an acceptable level and simplify decisions involving a large amount of information. When we look at consumers' food choices, for example, we discover that they differentiate among brands, retailers or manufacturers based on how much trust they have in them. For this reason, the less we know about an activity, the more we need to rely on others to make decisions and the more our judgements about risk become a matter of trust. Studies have found that risk perception for genetic engineering is negatively correlated with trust while perception of benefits is positively correlated with trust (Siegrist, 1999, 2000; Siegrist and Cvetkovich, 2000; Sjöberg, 2001). Trust was found to be indirectly related to acceptance of gene technology (Siegrist, 1999). Furthermore, the relationship between risk perception and trust strengthened as knowledge of the activity decreased (Siegrist and Cvetkovich, 2000).

The importance of trust in the negotiation process between the public and the government (experts) has often been noted (Slovic et al, 1991a; Flynn et al, 1993a). Trust has been said to be more fundamental to conflict resolution than risk communication (Slovic, 1993). However, trust is fragile. It is created slowly, but can be destroyed instantly. When it comes to winning trust, the playing field is not level: it is tilted toward distrust (Slovic, 1993). Negative (trust destroying) events are more visible or noticeable than positive (trust creating) events. Negative research results were in fact found to be more trusted than positive research results, and this effect was independent of the credibility of the information source (Siegrist, 2000). A similar asymmetry between positive and negative research findings was found also in news media coverage of good and bad events (Lichtenberg and MacLean, 1992).

A survey of the public in 17 European countries showed low trust in national public bodies 'to tell the truth about GM crops grown in fields' (Gaskell et al, 1999). Probably, European governments paid for mishandling information on BSE meat in the United Kingdom and dioxin contamination of dairy and poultry products in Belgium and The Netherlands. Public opinion does not just respond to technology, but it may actively constrain and influence the development of biotechnology (Durant et al, 1998).

Trust may pertain to the overall hazard management process, or it may apply simply to the sources of information. In this case, we talk about 'source credibility' and what we investigate is reliability of information. Previous research has indicated that newspapers and TV are among the most trusted sources of information about food-related hazards, followed by medical sources, the government, friends, industry, magazines and radio, university scientists and consumer organizations. Nevertheless, in the same study, participants were asked to choose the source they would trust the least and newspapers and TV were also more frequently cited as mistrusted sources (Frewer et al, 1996). High credibility of information source, like trust in risk management, was found to be inversely correlated to risk perception (Jungermann et al, 1996).

In the present study, we investigated source credibility in biotech applications to determine how diverse information sources are trusted with regard to different applications. This issue is important to communication with the public. We also tested the relationship between risk perception and source credibility for specific biotech applications. Based on the literature reviewed above, we expected to find that risk perception would be negatively correlated with source credibility.

Method

Sample

A total of 116 persons, 58 experts and 58 non-experts, took part in the research. Experts were professors or PhD students in biology at a northeastern Italian university; 22 were males and 36 females, with a mean age of 30.7 ($SD = 8.74$; ranging from 24 to 72). Non-experts were people with no specific training in biology; 22 were males and 36 females, with a mean age of 29.7 ($SD = 8.57$; ranging from 21 to 54).

We kept the proportion of males and females and age equal in the two samples. Education level was not controlled. The expert group was highly educated (master's degree or more) while the non-expert group was 'mixed' (some were highly educated but not in biology, but most of them were not highly educated). The non-expert sample was intended to represent the general public, including a broad range of education levels. The expert sample was recruited by asking professors and PhD students for unpaid participation in our study. The lay sample was recruited by asking the general population of the same city for unpaid participation.

Material and procedure

Seven biotech applications served as stimuli in our experiment. All the stimuli were written in Italian. Four were food-related applications: to eat vegetables whose DNA was manipulated with plant genes (FOOD/GMO plants), to eat vegetables whose DNA was manipulated with animal genes (FOOD/GMO animals), to introduce into the environment plants whose DNA was manipulated with genes of other plants (PLANTS/GMO plants), and to introduce into the environment plants whose DNA was manipulated with animal genes (PLANTS/GMO animals). Three were medical-pharmaceutical applications: to use medical substances obtained through the cloning of microorganisms (MEDICAL SUBSTANCES/GMO μ-org), to use in transplantation organs created from cloning human cells (MEDICAL TRANSPLANT/GMO human), and to use in transplantation animal organs whose DNA was manipulated in the laboratory (MEDICAL TRANSPLANT/GMO animal). Also included were two filler items representing potential food hazards (food with pesticides and organically grown food). They served to increase heterogeneity of individual judgement across the scale and control for systematic over- or underuse of the scale by the two groups.

Participants were asked for a risk judgement, reporting to what extent each application was risky for an unspecified individual (state to what extent the following applications are risky for the individual). They were instructed to give their rating on a 0–100 scale, where 0 indicated not at all risky and 100 indicated extremely risky. Each application was then rated on 16 dimensions (see Appendix) on a 1–11 scale.

To examine trust in the reliability of an information source, we asked each participant to rate the reliability of information given by a source for each of the applications. Respondents used a 1–11 scale (1 = *absolutely not reliable* and 11 = *extremely reliable*). We enquired about four sources of information:

1 national and European Community political organizations (parliament, government, European Commissions);
2 research institutes (National Research Council, CENSIS, National Nutrition Institute);
3 product producer industries and product commerce industries; and
4 environmental groups.

Thus, for example, the question relative to FOOD/GMO plants and the first source of information was: 'To what extent do you think that information about the risk associated with eating vegetables whose DNA was manipulated with plant genes is reliable when it is provided by national and European Community political organizations (Parliament, Government, European Commissions)?'

Results

Factors predicting biotech risk perception and expert–public differences

For each respondent, the hazards related to food and plants were collapsed into one overall mean judgement labelled 'food applications,' and the hazards related to medical applications were collapsed into another overall mean judgement labelled 'medical applications.' This procedure was done for individuals' judgement of risk and for the judgements on the 16 dimensions. This operation had two aims: we sought to test the prediction that judgement of risk differed for food versus medical biotech applications and we needed to reduce the biotech applications to a fewer number of variables to investigate the factors predicting risk perception both in the expert and public sample. This computation resulted in 17 new variables related to food applications and 17 new variables related to medical applications.

Two principal components factor analyses[2] (one for food and one for medical applications) were run on a 116 (subjects) × 16 (dimensions) matrix. The factor analyses were run on the whole sample including the experts and the public, and the average factor scores of the subsamples were then compared. Tables 15.1 and 15.2 present the factor loadings resulting after the Varimax rotation for food and medical applications, respectively. The aim of the two factor analyses was to reduce the 16 dimensions to fewer factors, test the differences between experts

Table 15.1 *Rotated factor matrix of the 16 dimensions for biotech food applications*

	Factor 1 Harmful and dread application (31.4% var.)	Factor 2 Useful application (21.2% var.)	Factor 3 Science knowledge (10.2% var.)	Factor 4 New application (9.1% var.)
Personal exposure	**0.865**	−0.074	−0.161	−0.007
Harmful to environment	**0.800**	−0.385	−0.104	0.137
Collective exposure	**0.793**	−0.128	−0.039	−0.105
Harmful to humans	**0.780**	−0.327	−0.145	0.262
Risky for future generations	**0.775**	−0.205	−0.039	0.320
Severe negative consequences	**0.682**	−0.362	−0.255	0.175
Dread	**0.670**	−0.376	−0.143	0.327
Voluntary exposure	**−0.540**	0.221	0.321	−0.150
Acceptable risk	−0.221	**0.839**	0.101	−0.008
Benefits for humans	−0.309	**0.790**	0.153	−0.170
Personal benefits	−0.252	**0.774**	0.203	−0.250
Benefits for the environment	−0.424	**0.704**	0.086	0.031
Precise personal knowledge	0.059	**0.470**	0.199	−0.462
Observable damage	−0.098	0.108	**0.838**	−0.296
Precise scientific knowledge	−0.306	0.290	**0.740**	0.168
New risk	0.320	−0.090	−0.053	**0.824**

Table 15.2 *Rotated factor matrix of the dimensions for biotech medical applications*

	Factor 1 Useful and harmless application (21.8% var.)	Factor 2 Risk exposure (18.1% var.)	Factor 3 New and unknown risk (12.4% var.)	Factor 4 Potential damage to environment (8.9% var.)	Factor 5 Observable and voluntary (8.6% var.)
Benefits for humans	**0.852**	−0.227	−0.143	0.042	0.209
Acceptable risk	**0.798**	−0.107	−0.025	0.026	−0.074
Personal benefits	**0.761**	0.082	−0.118	0.377	0.138
Dread	**−0.631**	0.380	0.427	−0.046	−0.057
Harmful to environment	**−0.596**	0.518	0.181	0.306	−0.046
Harmful to humans	**−0.566**	0.547	0.342	−0.074	−0.116
Personal exposure	−0.073	**0.857**	0.051	0.113	−0.170
Collective exposure	−0.130	**0.842**	−0.135	−0.073	−0.082
Risk for future generations	−0.513	**0.626**	−0.318	−0.013	−0.118
New risk	−0.161	−0.117	**0.750**	0.036	−0.078
Personal knowledge	0.079	−0.086	**−0.679**	0.095	−0.086
Precise scientific knowledge	0.224	−0.178	**−0.501**	0.036	0.442
Benefits for environment	0.040	0.130	0.020	**0.872**	0.028
Severe consequences	−0.248	0.321	0.387	**−0.583**	0.181
Observable damage	0.008	−0.090	−0.082	−0.117	**0.868**
Voluntary exposure	0.207	−0.308	0.271	0.220	**0.487**

and the public on these factors, and examine the factor's explanatory power on the risk estimates.

The analysis relative to food applications revealed a four-factor solution accounting for 71.88 per cent of the total variance. We did not constrain the number of factors to be extracted. The first factor was labelled 'harmful and dreaded application' because the dimensions weighing heavily on this component relate to personal and collective exposure, harm to man and to environment, negative consequences, risk for future generations, dread and involuntary risk. The second factor was labelled 'useful application' since the dimensions included in this factor are related to benefits, acceptability of risk and knowledge of the application. The third factor was called 'science knowledge' and the components loading on this factor were related to science knowledge and observability of the damage. The fourth factor was defined by the only dimension of 'new'; therefore, it was labelled 'new application.'

Analysis of the medical applications revealed a five-factor solution accounting for 69.9 per cent of the total variance. We did not constrain the number of factors to be extracted. The first factor was labelled 'useful and harmless application' because the dimensions loading on this component related to benefits for man, personal benefits, acceptable risk, low harm to man and the environment, and lack of dread risk. The second factor was named 'risk exposure' and included the dimensions personal exposure, collective exposure and future generations. The third factor was called 'new and unknown' because the relevant dimensions related to personal and scientific knowledge and new risk. The fourth factor was related to the potential negative consequences that might damage the environment and it was labelled 'potential damage to environment.' The last factor included whether the risk was observable and voluntary and it was called 'observable and voluntary risk.'

The factor scores from both analyses were used as dependent variables in a multivariate analysis of variance (ANOVA) with *expertise* (experts vs. public) as the independent factor. The expertise factor was significant, $F(9,104) = 8.31; p = 0.00001$. Experts scored lower than the public on the 'harmful and dreaded application' factor for food ($M = -0.19$ vs. $M = 0.18$), $F(1,112) = 4.23; p = 0.042$. Experts also scored significantly higher than the public on the 'useful application' factor for food ($M = 0.46$ vs. $M = -0.44$), $F(1,112) = 28.95; p = 0.00001$. These differences are consistent with our expectation that experts perceive food applications as less harmful and more useful than the public. Analyses on medical applications showed that compared with the public, experts scored higher on the 'useful and harmless application' ($M = 0.29$ vs. $M = -0.28$), $F(1,112) = 10.52$; $p = 0.002$; and lower on the 'new and unknown' factor ($M = -0.42$ vs. $M = 0.41$), $F(1,112) = 23.37; p = 0.0001$. Compared with experts, the public perceive that both the food and medical applications have more harm and less benefit. The public judge the risks posed from medical biotech applications as newer and less acknowledged by the people and by science. No other differences were significant.

Regression analyses were performed separately for the expert and public samples, and for food and medical applications. The full linear regression model was tested (enter method) with the factor scores as the independent variables and the mean risk judgement as the predicted dependent variable.

The regression analysis for experts regarding food applications explained 44 per cent of the variance (adjusted R^2) and revealed a significant contribution of the first two factors: 'harmful and dread application' ($\beta = 0.57; p = 0.0001$) and 'useful application' ($\beta = -0.25; p = 0.02$). Experts judged the risk to be high when the food application was judged as harmful, dreaded and not useful. The same analysis carried out for the public explained 30 per cent of the variance (adjusted R^2), but revealed a significant contribution of all four factors: 'harmful and dreaded application' ($\beta = 0.54; p = 0.0001$), 'useful application' ($\beta = -0.57; p = 0.0001$), 'science knowledge' ($\beta = -0.41; p = 0.001$) and 'new risk' ($\beta = -0.27; p = 0.031$). The public judged the risk associated with biotech food to be high when the application was perceived as harmful, dreaded and not useful, as well as new

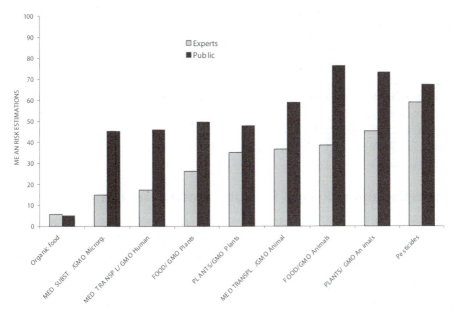

Figure 15.1 *Mean risk judgements of biotech applications by experts and the public*

or not well known by science. Compared with the experts, the public seems to have a broader perception (based on a greater number of factors) of the risk associated with food applications, and less variance in their perceptions is explained.

The regression analysis for experts regarding medical applications explained 37 per cent of the variance (adjusted R^2) and revealed a significant contribution of the first three factors: 'useful and harmless application' ($\beta = -0.36$; $p = 0.002$), 'risk exposure' ($\beta = 0.45$; $p = 0.0001$) and 'new and unknown risk' ($\beta = 0.37$; $p = 0.001$). Experts judged the risk from medical applications of biotechnology to be high when they thought the application was not useful and harmful, would expose themselves and many people (included future generations) to risk, and was new and unknown. The same analysis carried out for the public explained 45 per cent of the variance (adjusted R^2) and revealed a significant contribution only of the first factor: 'harmful and dread application' ($\beta = -0.70$; $p = 0.0001$). For the public, the risk was judged to be high only when the medical application was perceived to be not useful and harmful. Contrary to the food applications, public perception of medical applications is more defined (based on a fewer number of factors) and more variance in perceptions is explained. For experts, the perception of the risk of medical applications is broader and the variance is less well explained than it was for food applications.

Overall, the same factors had different predictive power for the two groups. Scientific knowledge and newness were more important in predicting the public's perception of risk from food applications. In other words, when judging the risk associated with an engineered food, the public is concerned not only with potential harm and potential benefits, but also with how much science knows and how familiar the product is. On the other hand, scientific knowledge and the number and type of individuals exposed to the risk were more important in predicting experts' perception of risk from medical applications. For example, when judging risk associated with a transplantation involving human GMOs, the general public is concerned with how useful and how harmful the application can be, whereas experts also consider factors such as the number of people potentially affected by a mass introduction of the application and how much science knows about the application.

Expertise and risk from food and medical applications

To test the difference in risk estimation of biotech applications between experts and the public, the risk judgements on a 0–100 scale of the nine applications (seven biotech applications and two filler items) were used as dependent variables in a multivariate ANOVA with *expertise* (experts vs. public) as the independent factor. The *expertise* factor was significant, $F(9,91) = 8.07$; $p = 0.0001$. Further analyses revealed that compared with the public, the experts significantly and systematically perceived lower risk for all seven biotech applications (all F-values were significant, ranging from 4.65 to 36.18). The only two items for which the experts and the public gave similar (not significantly different) estimates are the two filler items: pesticides and organic food (Figure 15.1).

To answer the question posed in previous literature about whether food applications are perceived as riskier than medical applications, we carried out a 2(*expertise*: expert vs. public) × 2(*nature* of the application: food vs. medical applications) ANOVA on the mean risk judgement, with the last factor within subjects. Results showed a main effect of the nature of the application, $F(1,112) = 27.70$; $p = 0.001$, and a main effect of expertise, $F(1,112) = 44.59$; $p = 0.001$, but no interaction effect, $F < 1$. In support of our hypotheses, the public judged both the risk from food-related applications ($M = 61.75$, $SD = 22.95$) and the risk from medical applications ($M = 50.03$, $SD = 27.79$) higher than did the experts ($M = 35.86$, $SD = 26.77$ and $M = 23.27$, $SD = 18.94$). Both groups judged the risk from food-related applications higher than the risk from medical applications.

To test whether the observed differences in mean risk judgements of food and medical applications among groups can be explained by variations in the quality of perceived risk, we analysed covariance with the risk factor scores as covariates and *expertise* as the independent variable. The analysis was carried out separately for food and for medical applications. All four risk factors had significant effects (Fs from 5.0 to 45.8) as covariates on the estimate of risk from food biotech applications. Nevertheless, the difference between experts and lay people still remained significant, $F(1,107) = 5.95$; $p = 0.016$. Only the first three risk factors had significant effects (Fs from 7.2 to 53.9) as covariates on the estimate of risk from medical biotech applications. Also in this case, the difference between experts and lay people remained significant, $F(1,107) = 7.47$; $p = 0.007$. These results indicate that the dimensions we used in the present study do not fully explain the difference between experts and the public, although they do make a difference.

We also conducted a 2(*expertise*: expert vs. public) × 2(*nature* of the application: food vs. medical applications) analysis of covariance, introducing 'benefits to man' (both those related to food applications and those related to medical applications) as covariates, on the mean risk judgement. The results showed a significant effect of the covariates, $F(1,110) = 5.39; p = 0.022; F(1,110) = 22.77; p = 0.001$, which eliminated the significance of the difference between food and medical applications, $F(1,110) = 3.04; p = 0.084$, but not the effect of expertise, $F(1,110) = 14.85; p = 0.001$. According to this result, the difference in risk perception between food and medical applications can be explained by their difference in benefits. However, expertise still had its main effect on risk ratings, apart from benefits.

Trust in information sources

Mean trust in each of the four information sources was computed separately for experts and the public. A 2(expertise) × 4(information source) ANOVA, with the second factor within subjects, was computed on the mean trust ratings. The main effect of expertise was not significant, $F(1,101) = 2.13; p = 0.147$, but there was a significant main effect of source, $F(3,303) = 53.49; p = 0.001$, and a significant interaction of source with expertise, $F(3,303) = 15.41; p = 0.001$. Information provided by research institutes and environmental groups was trusted the most ($M = 6.46$ and $M = 5.85$), followed by political organizations ($M = 4.24$), while information provided by industries was trusted the least ($M = 3.23$). Differences among sources were significant at $p < .05$ except for the comparison of research institutes with environmental groups. The expert and public samples were found to agree on the trustworthiness of all sources except for environmental groups, which were trusted significantly more by the public than by the experts ($M = 7.42$ and $M = 4.58$), $F(1,101) = 26.20; p = 0.001$.

Correlation coefficients were computed across individuals between trust in information source and risk judgements for the expert and the public samples. We predicted that if people perceived as reliable the information provided by a source (e.g. national and European Community political organ) about the risks associated with a biotech application, then they would perceive the application as low in risk. Therefore, we expected a negative correlation. The relationship, although weak, was generally negative and in line with the prediction and the existing literature. The judgement of risk from FOOD/GMO plants correlated negatively with trust in research institutes in the expert sample ($r = -0.41; p < .01$) and public sample ($r = -0.30; p < .05$) and with trust in product producer industries in the expert sample ($r = -0.37; p < .01$). The judgement of risk from PLANTS/GMO plants correlated negatively with trust in product producer industries in the expert sample ($r = -0.29; p < .05$). The only positive relationships with risk judgement were found for trust in information provided by environmental groups and risk from FOOD/GMO plants ($r = 0.29; p < .05$) and FOOD/GMO animal ($r = 0.26; p < .05$), but only for the expert sample.

Table 15.3 *Mean benefits and harm judgements for the expert and the public samples*

	Experts				Public			
	Benefits to humans	Harm to humans	Benefits to environ.	Harm to environ.	Benefits to humans	Harm to humans	Benefits to environ.	Harm to environ.
FOOD/GMO plants	6.86	5.48	4.30	5.79	5.41	6.40	3.79	7.14
FOOD/GMO animals	6.02	6.20	3.73	6.71	3.74	8.19	2.66	8.17
PLANTS/GMO plants	6.96	5.29	5.14	6.30	5.26	6.67	4.00	7.46
PLANTS/GMO animals	6.29	6.45	4.09	7.11	3.33	6.19	2.60	8.43
MED SUBST/GMO μ-org	8.61	4.39	4.13	4.18	6.43	5.64	3.89	5.41
MED TRANSPL/ GMO human	8.50	3.82	3.51	3.30	7.55	5.57	4.22	4.81
MED TRANSPL/ GMO animal	7.86	5.11	3.51	3.72	6.05	6.21	3.77	5.28
Pesticides	4.53	8.71	2.26	9.18	3.61	8.72	2.26	9.24
Organic food	8.05	3.00	8.80	2.66	9.47	2.49	9.80	2.69

Expert–public differences in benefit–harm correlations

Tables 15.3 and 15.4 show the mean and correlation coefficients between the dimensions related to harm and benefits to humans and the environment for each application and for the two samples. Harm and benefits were negatively correlated both in the expert and in the public sample. However, the experts think biotech applications have many benefits and cause low harm to humans, whereas the public sees biotech applications as having low benefits and causing high harm to humans. One exception is the benefits and harm to the environment posed by the medical applications, for which both experts and public gave low ratings, resulting in positive correlations (experts) or low correlations (public). Using the Fisher r-to-z transformation and then calculating the value of z, we assessed the significance of the difference between pairs of correlation coefficients in the two independent samples. Eight pairs of correlation coefficients were found to be significantly different from each other.

Table 15.4 *Correlations between benefits and harm for the expert and the public samples*

	Benefits/harm to humans			Benefits/harm to environment		
	Expert	Public	Difference (z-value)	Expert	Public	Difference (z-value)
FOOD/GMO plants	-0.639^{**}	-0.166	-03.06^{***}	-0.354^{**}	-0.375^{**}	n.s
FOOD/GMO animals	-0.743^{**}	-0.251	-03.62^{***}	-0.547^{**}	-0.506^{**}	n.s.
PLANTS/GMO plants	-0.294^{*}	-0.427^{**}	n.s.	-0.639^{**}	-0.498^{**}	n.s.
PLANTS/GMO animals	-0.604^{**}	-0.320^{**}	-1.89^{*}	-0.695^{**}	-0.484^{**}	-1.70
MED SUBST/GMO µ-org	-0.693^{**}	-0.360^{**}	-2.48^{**}	0.193	0.258	n.s.
MED TRANSPL/ GMO human	-0.556^{**}	-0.544^{**}	n.s	0.372^{**}	-0.011	-2.11^{*}
MED TRANSPL/ GMO animal	-0.328^{*}	-0.497^{**}	n.s.	0.442^{**}	-0.204	3.54^{**}
Pesticides	-0.415^{**}	-0.661^{**}	-1.72^{*}	-0.512^{**}	-0.587^{**}	n.s.
Organic Food	-0.628^{**}	-0.582^{**}	n.s	-0.654^{**}	-0.642^{**}	n.s.

Note: $* = p < .05; ** = p < .01; *** = p < .001.$

Discussion

When we investigated judgements on 16 dimensions of biotechnology and its applications, four (food domain) and five (medical domain) factors explained most of the variance. The factors that emerged for both food and medical applications were similar and related to the notions of harm and benefits, the number of people exposed, the scientific knowledge, the fact that biotech is a new risk, the potential damage to environment and the degree to which the consequences were voluntary or observable. The diverse set of dimensions used in the present study affected the factor analytic results. The 'rejection factor' found by Frewer et al (1997) split into separate factors in our study. No ethical factor emerged since no ethical dimension was used.

We observed several similarities and differences between the expert and public perceptions. The differences in risk perception were both quantitative and qualitative. The relevant results can be summarized as follows:

- Compared with the public, the experts significantly and systematically perceived less risk for all of the seven biotech applications.
- Both groups judged the risk from food-related applications higher than the risk from medical applications, in line with previous literature (Frewer et al, 1997).
- Compared with the public, the experts perceived food applications as less harmful and more useful.
- Compared with the public, the experts perceived medical applications as less harmful, more useful, better known to science, and less new.

- When estimating the risk of biotechnology applied to food, the public was concerned not only with potential harm and potential benefits, but also with how much science knows about it and how new they perceived the product to be, while experts were only concerned with how harmful and useful it is.
- When estimating the risk of biotechnology applied to the medical domain, the public was concerned with how useful and how harmful the application could be, whereas experts also considered factors such as the number and type of people potentially affected by a mass introduction of the application and how much science knew about the technology.

As previously found for other hazards, experts and the public differ in their perception of risk (Slovic et al, 1980; Kraus et al, 1992; Flynn et al, 1993a; Slovic et al, 1995; Savadori et al, 1998). However, experts' and non-experts' differences may be affected by the nature of the hazard. New and technological hazards, such as biotechnology, might be especially sensitive to the *expertise* factor because of the specialized knowledge surrounding this type of risk. When we tested if the observed differences in perceived risk levels among groups could be explained by variations in the quality of perceived risk, the results indicated that the dimensions we used in the present study did not fully explain the difference between experts and the public, although they did make a difference. Other factors not covered in this study (e.g. ethical factors) might have significantly contributed as well.

With respect to the communication of information related to biotech applications, these results suggest that public perceptions of risk from biotech applications could be reduced by providing information about benefits. On the other hand, experts' perception of risk from biotech applications could be increased by providing information on harmful effects and negative consequences. In both cases, however, the perception of risk should be conveyed by the general affective meaning that the experts and the public attribute to biotechnology.

The mean ratings of trust in information source were as we expected. Information provided by research institutes and environmental groups was trusted the most (especially for the public), followed by political organizations, while information provided by industries was trusted the least. However, we were surprised to find a low correlation between trust in information source and risk perception. This low correlation might be explained by the way we measured trust (as information reliability provided by a source rather than trust in risk management, as has been used in previous studies).

The negative correlations between harm and benefit across most applications for both experts and the public support the idea that people make judgements according to general affective feelings. If their feelings are positive, they will judge an application as high in benefits and low in risk; if their feelings are negative, these judgements will be reversed. Reliance on the affect heuristic may be producing the negative correlations observed in judgements of biotechnologies. Interestingly, several of the negative correlation coefficients were significantly larger for experts than the public. One explanation for this result is that compared with the public, experts are relying more on affect when judging harm and benefit. However, we would not expect experts to rely more on affect because they have significant technical knowledge to rely on. A more likely explanation is that the nature of the benefits and risks of the applications considered in this study are negatively correlated: the benefit may be saving lives or improving health and the risk is losing lives or hurting health. Experts know this well and thus show stronger negative correlations. Furthermore, public judgements about benefits and harm from biotech applications may be less reliable, thus resulting in smaller inverse correlations.

A final comment relates to the dread dimension, which weighed heavily on the first factor in both samples. Dread measures the emotional reaction (negative) when thinking about a hazard. Several studies and theories are reconsidering the direct role (not mediated by cognition) of affect in judgement and decision making (Alhakami and Slovic, 1994; Finucane et al, 2000a; Loewenstein et al, 2001). Our data further support this consideration and show how risk from biotech applications can be linked to the dread, affective reaction, both in experts and the public.

Appendix: Risk dimensions

1 Dread: How much does this application frighten you? (1 = *not at all*; 11 = *very much*).
2 New: Is it a new risk or an old and familiar risk? (1 = *absolutely old*; 11 = *absolutely new*).
3 Voluntary extent of exposure to risk: To what extent people can decide to voluntarily expose himself/herself to the risk? (1 = *exposure is involuntary*; 11 = *exposure is voluntary*).
4 Personal exposure to the risk: How much you think you are personally exposed to the potential risk derived from this application? (1 = *not at all exposed*; 11 = *completely exposed*).
5 Collective exposure to the risk: How many people in the world are exposed to these risks? (1 = *very few people*; 11 = *many people*).
6 Observability of the damage: To what extent is the potential damage produced by the application observable? (1 = *absolutely not observable*; 11 = *definitely observable*).
7 Severity of negative consequences: How severe are the potential negative consequences of this application? (1 = *not at all severe*; 11 = *extremely severe*).
8 Risk for future generations: To what extent does it pose a risk to future generations? (1 = *risk is very low*; 11 = *risk is very high*).
9 Personal knowledge of the risk: How precise is your personal knowledge of the risk associated with this practice? (1 = *absolutely not precise*; 11 = *extremely precise*).
10 Scientific knowledge of the risk: How precise is scientific knowledge of the risk associated with this application? (1 = *definite low knowledge*; 11 = *very high knowledge*).

11 Benefits for humans: To what extent will humans benefit from this application? (1 = *no benefits at all*; 11 = *many benefits*).
12 Personal benefits: To what extent will you personally benefit from this application? (1 = *no benefits at all*; 11 = *many benefits*).
13 Benefits for the environment: To what extent will the environment benefit from this application? (1 = *no benefits at all*; 11 = *many benefits*).
14 Harm to humans: How much harm will derive from this application to humans? (1 = *no harm at all*; 11 = *very much harm*).
15 Harm to environment: How much harm will derive from this application to the environment? (1 = *no harm at all*; 11 = *very much harm*).
16 Risk acceptability: To what extent do you think the risks associated with this application are acceptable to obtain the benefits? (1 = *not acceptable at all*; 11 = *definitely acceptable*).

Notes

1 Food-related applications generally apply DNA manipulation to agricultural seeds with the purpose of increasing plant resistance against pests or producing special characteristics in their fruit. The medical/pharmaceutical-related applications apply DNA manipulation on microorganisms to produce therapeutic substances, such as insulin, and study the possibility of producing organs for transplantation through the cloning of human cells or the use of organs of other animals.
2 Principal components analysis was preferred over principal factors analysis because in the former all of the variability in each item is used in the analysis, whereas in the latter only the variability in each item that it has in common with the other items is used. We preferred PCA because our aim was data reduction, whereas PFA is used when the goal of the analysis is to detect structure.

Chapter 16

Risk Perception of Prescription Drugs: Results of a National Survey

*Paul Slovic, Ellen Peters, John Grana, Susan Berger
and Gretchen S. Dieck**

Introduction

Knowledge of risk perceptions has been demonstrated to be vitally important in understanding how individuals and societies manage the risks of daily life. In medicine, perceptions of the risks and benefits associated with drugs are likely to influence patients' treatment choices, their compliance with treatment regimens, their views on the acceptability of adverse reactions and the drugs that cause them, and their attitudes toward government regulation of drugs. Understanding perceptions is a prerequisite for designing better communication materials for patients and the public and, ultimately, for ensuring the safe and effective use of pharmaceutical products.

During the period 1987–1991, national surveys in Sweden and Canada examined public attitudes and perceptions regarding prescription drugs (Slovic et al, 1989, 1991b). The present survey of US residents replicates and extends the earlier surveys. These studies (past and current) aimed to meet the following objectives:

- Describe precisely and quantitatively the public's perceptions of risk and benefit from the use of various kinds of prescription drugs.
- Place perceptions of prescription drugs within a broader context of

*   Reprinted from Slovic, P., Peters, E., Grana, J., Berger, S. and Dieck, G. S. (2007)
    'Risk perception of prescription drugs: Results of a national survey', *Drug Information Journal*, vol 41, no 1, pp81–100. Copyright © 2007 Drug Information Association. Reprinted with permission.

perceptions regarding many other activities (e.g. driving, smoking) and technologies (e.g. air travel, pesticides), including other medical technologies (e.g. X-rays, surgery).
- Provide baseline data that will allow the impact of new drug problems and controversies to be monitored and allow trends in relevant attitudes and perceptions to be followed over time.
- Provide data that will enhance understanding of how to inform patients more effectively about the risks and benefits of medicines.

Over the past decade, much has changed in the sociopolitical realm as well as in the science and technology of drug manufacture and delivery. The present survey examined public views toward medicines in light of these changes. It is also important to note that the earlier studies were conducted outside the United States. The current survey provides American data comparable to the Swedish and Canadian studies.

Design and administration of the survey

The survey was diverse in both content and methodology. It began by eliciting associations to the term 'prescription drugs.' Next came general questions about attitudes and perceptions, followed by questions about personal use of pharmaceutical products. A rating task then elicited quantitative judgements of risk, benefits and other characteristics found to be important in previous studies of risk perception. Additional questions asked about trust, stigma, worldviews and demographic characteristics. The survey was conducted by Knowledge Networks with a nationally representative sample of respondents who were presented with the questions over a specially designed Internet system.

Survey design

Section 1: Word associations to 'prescription drugs'
The first task asked respondents to read the words 'prescription drugs,' which appeared six times on the screen. Each time they read these words, they were instructed to type the first thought or association that came to their minds. This technique, called the method of continued associations, has been shown by Szalay and Deese (1978) to be a sensitive indicator of the imagery and meaning associated with people's mental representations for a wide variety of concepts. After providing the six associations, respondents were then asked to rate each one as very negative, negative, neutral, positive or very positive.

Section 2: General attitudinal questions
The second part of the survey employed a traditional survey format in which respondents were asked to indicate their attitudes, perceptions and opinions in response to specific questions. The questions asked about the following:

- perceptions of risk today as compared to 20 years ago;
- perceived frequency of side effects;
- the adequacy of performance by government regulators, drug manufacturers, doctors, pharmacists, hospitals, patients and patient's health plan in ensuring drug safety and efficacy;
- the respondent's personal experiences with drug side effects;
- perceived causes of side effects;
- opinions in response to a series of vignettes describing drug controversies.

Section 3: Product use

Respondents were then asked about their personal use of pharmaceutical products. They were asked if they were currently using or had previously used 23 pharmaceutical products. The list included vaccines, laxatives, antibiotic drugs, cancer chemotherapy, drugs for depression and so on.

Section 4: Psychometric questionnaire

During the past two decades, standard questionnaires such as that used in other parts of this survey have been supplemented by more quantitative studies of risk perceptions in what has come to be known as the psychometric paradigm (Slovic et al, 1985; Slovic, 1987). Within this paradigm, people are asked to make quantitative judgements about the relative riskiness of various hazards. Perceptions of risk are then related statistically to quantitative judgements of other properties of the hazards being studied, such as the degree to which the risks are known to those exposed to them or the expected seriousness of harm in the event of an accident or mishap.

In the present survey, respondents were asked to make quantitative judgements about the riskiness of 53 items. These included 32 pharmaceutical items (31 products and one general term called 'prescription drugs'); eight medical procedures, tests or devices; and 13 non-medical items. The non-medical items were included to provide a broad context against which to compare the medical and pharmaceutical items. The pharmaceutical items were carefully selected according to several criteria, including importance, familiarity to the general public and diversity. Four of these pharmaceutical items are available over the counter (laxatives, aspirin, herbal medicines and vitamins). Table 16.1 lists the 53 items; the asterisks denote new items that were not included in the Swedish or Canadian studies.

Each of the 53 items was rated on five characteristics of risk, similar to those found to be important in prior studies of perceived risk (Slovic, 1987). Respondents rated the risk and benefit for each item; the seriousness of harmful effects in the event of an accident or unfortunate event; the extent to which the risks are known to those exposed to them; and the degree to which a serious problem associated with the item, if it occurred, would serve as a warning sign indicating that the risk from this item might be greater than was thought before the problem occurred. The full set of rating scales for the five characteristics is shown in Table 16.2. Because of the length of the survey, a random sample of 60

Table 16.1 *Hazard items studied in Section 4*

---

1. Pharmaceutical items

Drugs for depression	Drugs for Alzheimer's disease*
Drugs for erectile dysfunction (Viagra)*	Drugs for anxiety*
Drugs for epilepsy*	Nicotine replacement (patches)*
Smallpox vaccination*	Antibiotic drugs
Drugs for osteoporosis*	Birth control pills
Sleeping pills	Herbal medicines
Drugs for AIDS	Laxatives
Drugs for arthritis*	Acne medicines*
Drugs for asthma*	Cancer chemotherapy
Drugs for ulcers*	Biotechnology drugs
Oestrogen replacement (HRT)†	Botox injections*
Nonsteroidal anti-inflammatory drugs*	Aspirin
Insulin	Drugs for cholesterol*
Vitamin pills	Prescription drugs†
Diet drugs*	Blood pressure drugs
Vaccines	Allergy drugs*

2. Medical procedures, tests, and devices

IUD	Heart surgery	Medical X-rays
MRI scanning*	Mammogram*	Appendectomy
Prostate screening tests*	Acupuncture	

3. Non-medical hazards

Cell phones*	Nuclear power plants	Pesticides
Cigarette smoking	Household cleaners	Artificial sweeteners
High-fat foods*	Food additives	Genetically modified food*
Automobiles	Alcoholic beverages	Coffee*
Air travel		

Note: * Items not included in Swedish and Canadian surveys;
† Items included in Canadian survey but not Swedish survey.

per cent of the respondents rated the 53 items on both the risk and benefit scales. The remaining 40 per cent of the sample were randomly assigned to rating only one of the other three scales.

Note that the responses on the rating scales are anchored by descriptive phases only at the extreme values (1 and 7). Thus, the responses have meaning primarily in relation to the other responses on that particular scale. Note also that risk is left undefined to allow the respondent to interpret the term freely. As a result, risk does not necessarily refer to the probability of an adverse event associated with the hazard, and there is no way to gauge the accuracy of a person's risk ratings by comparing them with statistical probabilities.

Table 16.2 *Scales on which the 53 items were rated*

Risk to those exposed

To what extent would you say that people who are exposed to this item are at risk of experiencing personal harm from it?

(1 = *They are not at risk;* 7 = *They are very much at risk*)

Benefits

In general, how beneficial do you consider this item to be?

(1 = *Not at all beneficial;* 7 = *Very beneficial*)

Seriousness of harm

If an accident or unfortunate event involving this item occurred, to what extent are the harmful effects to a person likely to be mild or serious?

(1 = *Very mild harm;* 7 = *Very serious harm*)

Knowledge of those exposed

To what extent would you say that the risks associated with this item are known precisely to people who are exposed to those risks?

(1 = *Risk level not known;* 7 = *Risk level known precisely*)

Warning signs

If you hear or read about a problem associated with this item in which people were seriously harmed, to what degree would this mishap serve as a warning sign, indicating that the risk of this item might be greater than was thought before the problem occurred?

(1 = *Not a warning sign;* 7 = *Very strong warning sign*)

Section 5: Additional questions

The psychometric portion of the survey was followed by several sets of questions asking about the following:

- respondents' perceptions of scientists' understanding of risks and benefits of prescription drugs, over-the-counter drugs and vitamins and herbal supplements;
- the extent to which doctors, pharmacists, hospitals, drug manufacturers, the Food and Drug Administration (FDA) and patients could reduce the current risks of prescriptions drugs to the American public;
- the level of trust in doctors, pharmacists, hospitals, drug manufacturers, FDA and patients to manage the safety of prescription drugs.

Section 6: Demographic characteristics

The survey ended with a series of demographic questions pertaining to the respondent's age, sex, health status, cigarette smoking, occupation, education, income, health consciousness and medicine usage.

Administration of the survey

The Internet survey firm Knowledge Networks conducted the survey on behalf of Decision Research; it used its online research panel that is representative of the entire US population. A total of 2900 Knowledge Networks panel members were invited to participate in the survey between 21 May 2003 and 11 June 2003, with an oversample of 430 people aged 65 years and older, 160 African-Americans and 160 Hispanics. The sample was randomly split, based on a 3:2 ratio, between a longer version and a shorter version of the survey. Respondents to the longer version received a $15 incentive, and those to the shorter version received a $10 incentive. Median lengths of the longer and shorter versions were 41 and 36 minutes, respectively.

A total of 2071 panel members completed the survey, resulting in a response rate of 71 per cent. Subgroup response rates ranged from 58.2 per cent for Hispanics to 88.9 per cent for respondents aged 65 and over. Of the 2071 respondents, 15 were excluded because they had an item non-response rate higher than 33 per cent. Another 55 respondents were excluded from the final analyses because of lack of variance in their responses on the psychometric item set. Thus, 2001 respondents were used in the analyses.

To provide the appropriate context for viewing the study results, it is important to note that the current survey was conducted prior to high-profile media reports of potential safety concerns with the use of Vioxx™ and other anti-inflammatory medications, as well as with the use of antidepressant drugs in children. Had the survey been conducted after these events, the study results may have been different. For example, a study conducted after the negative media reports may have shown respondents had higher perceptions of risk and lower perceptions of benefits for anti-inflammatory and antidepressant drugs (and possibly other drug categories) than we observed in this study.

Results

Characteristics of the sample

52 per cent of respondents were female. Their ages ranged from 18 to 94 years, with a mean of 46 years. 73 per cent of the overall sample was white; African-American and Hispanic individuals each made up 11 per cent of the sample. Approximately half of the sample (52 per cent) had at least some college education. Nearly three-quarters (73 per cent) of the respondents were from metropolitan areas. To analyse the overall sample, four sets of weights were created by Knowledge Networks. The weights adjust for gender, age, ethnicity, educational level and region. Each set of weights was applied to its respective sample or subsample.

The majority of the respondents rated their health as excellent (10.9 per cent), very good (31.4 per cent) or good (40.2 per cent); 13.8 per cent rated their health as fair and 3.2 per cent as poor. When asked how many prescription medications they were currently taking regularly, 44.6 per cent reported they were not taking any medications; 14.9 per cent reported taking three or more medications regularly.

Respondents were asked about medical conditions they had. They were presented with a list of 11 medical conditions. Half of the respondents indicated that they had none of the conditions listed. High blood pressure was the most commonly reported condition, with 22.8 per cent of the respondents reporting they had that condition. This was followed by 17.9 per cent reporting they had high cholesterol and 14.6 per cent with arthritis. 24 per cent of the respondents reported having two or more of the diseases.

Product use

More than two-thirds of the respondents (68.8 per cent) reported they were either currently using prescription drugs or had used them in the past. Antibiotic drugs had also been used by 62.6 per cent of respondents. No other pharmaceutical products had been used by over half of the respondents. Vaccine use was reported by 44.3 per cent of the sample; 33.6 per cent had used allergy drugs. The least-used products were biotechnology drugs, drugs for acquired immunodeficiency syndrome (AIDS) and drugs for Alzheimer's disease; less than 1 per cent of the respondents reported using these drugs.

Images of prescription drugs

More than 8000 associations were produced in response to the stimulus concept 'prescription drugs.' The major types of associations are listed in Table 16.3 in order of their frequency. The average rating for each association category is also displayed; ratings were coded as -2 for very negative, -1 for negative, 0 for neutral, 1 for positive and 2 for very positive. Concerns about cost clearly headed the list of associations, followed by types of illness or states pertaining to illness (e.g. sickness, pain). Strong positive images (helpful/necessary/beneficial) accounted for 459 (5.2 per cent) of responses. Other positive images of recovery, healing and cure accounted for 236 (2.7 per cent) of responses. Strong negative images took several forms: one had to do with general negatives such as bad taste, annoying, anger and avoid (187 responses, or 2.1 per cent); the second had to do with safety concerns (152 responses, or 1.7 per cent); and another had to do with side effects (148 responses, or 1.7 per cent). These results were similar to those found in Sweden and Canada except that cost concerns were much more common in the present survey. Whereas cost was by far the most frequent association in our US sample, accounting for almost 20 per cent of the responses, it was mentioned in only about 10 per cent of the associations in Canada (3rd highest) and only in 1 per cent in Sweden (18th on the list).

The negative association with cost is indicated by its low image affect rating (-0.8), which was similar to other negative associations: abuse and addiction (-1.2 and -1.1, respectively), death (-1.0) and general negative (-0.8). The most negative image affect scores were for profit/big business (-1.3), followed by

Table 16.3 *Associations with 'prescription drugs?*

Rank	Association category	Count	Average affect
1	Cost, price, money, expense concerns	1446	−0.8
2	States/types of illness, sickness, pain	818	−0.4
3	Definition of prescription drugs	676	0.9
4	Doctor, doctor's office, etc.	649	0.5
5	Pills/drug/medicine – unspecified	609	0.5
6	Pharmacy/drugstore	575	0.5
7	Helpful/beneficial/necessary	459	1.1
8	Miscellaneous (general)	378	0.2
9	Names of drugs (i.e. Valium, Allegra, etc.)	333	0.7
10	Types of drugs (e.g. antibiotics, vitamins, over the counter)	241	0.7
11	Recovery, healing, cure	236	1.4
12	Medical coverage, health insurance, prescription plan	230	0.1
13	Prescriptions	191	0.3
14	General negative (bad taste, annoying, anger, avoid)	187	−0.8
15	Safety concerns, dangerous, some risk, trouble, handle with care	152	−0.1
16	Side effects	148	−0.7
17	Health	136	0.9
18	Profit, big business	125	−1.3
19	Generic drugs	117	0.6
20	Overdose, overconsumption, overuse, overprescribed	91	−0.8
21	Elderly	82	−0.3
22	Is drug really needed/will it help?	82	0.5
23	Addiction, dependency	72	−1.1
24	Reliable, guaranteed	71	0.9
25	Co-payments	64	−0.1
26	Unnecessary/unworthwhile	62	−0.6
27	Hospital	59	−0.2
28	Industry, research, company	52	0.4
29	Lack of medical insurance/coverage	49	−0.7
30	Waiting in line	46	−1.2
31	Politics	45	−0.6
32	Canada/Mexico/mail order	44	0.6
33	Family, children, friend	40	0.2
34	Allergy, reactions	40	−0.7
35	Bottles, jars, boxes	36	0.3
36	Abuse	31	−1.2
37	TV ads/commercials	27	−0.8
38	Death	24	−1.0
39	Remembering to take	23	0.0
40	Effective	19	0.8
41	Warning	17	0.8
42	'Medicine' (i.e. liquid forms, syrup)	14	0.6
43	Chemicals	12	−0.9
44	Natural, herbal medicine	11	0.6
45	Need for more research/information on drugs	7	−0.1

Note: Image affect coding: −2 = *Very negative*, 0 = *Neutral*, 2 = *Very positive*

waiting in line (−1.2) and abuse (−1.2). The associations with the highest positive affect scores were recovery/healing/cure (1.4), followed by helpful/beneficial/necessary (1.1). Across the 45 association categories, there was no predominance of either negative or positive affect; 24 categories had mean affect ratings greater than zero (neutral), and 21 had means below zero.

Present and past risk

Respondents were asked to indicate whether they believed that there is more risk, less risk or about the same risk today than there was 20 years ago for each of several types of items. The results indicated that risks from chemicals and cancer were perceived to be greater today by 67–68 per cent of the respondents. Other percentages for the 'more risk' response were heart disease (64 per cent), global warming (57 per cent), infectious diseases excluding AIDS or severe acute respiratory syndrome (SARS) (54 per cent), food (54 per cent), health problems we face (52 per cent), methods of travel (51 per cent), quality of drinking water (48 per cent) and energy sources (43 per cent). At the bottom of the list are errors in prescribing drugs (42 per cent) and prescription drugs (37 per cent). As was found in the Swedish study, the perceived increase in risk from prescription drugs was substantially lower than that for other chemicals. One notable change from the Swedish study was in the percentage of respondents perceiving more risk from infectious diseases. In 1988, 30 per cent of Swedish respondents thought there was more risk today than 20 years ago compared to 54 per cent of the US

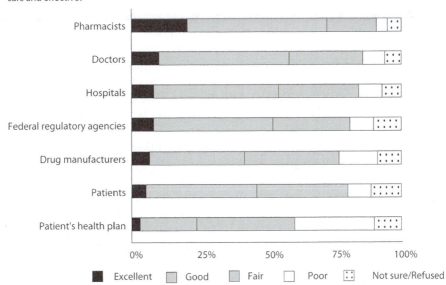

Figure 16.1 *Ensuring safety and efficacy: Confidence in selected health care groups*

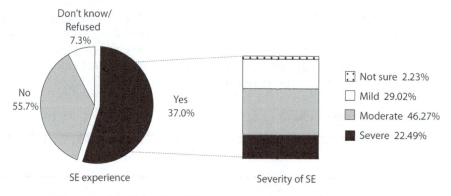

Figure 16.2 *Side effect (SE) experience within the past five years*

respondents in the present survey. This could well be the result of the emergence of AIDS as a major problem along with media attention to and awareness of highly publicized diseases in recent years (e.g. avian flu, swine flu, SARS, Ebola and anthrax).

Drug efficacy and side effects

Several questions asked about drug efficacy and the frequency, severity and causes of side effects. When asked to rate the job that various health care agents were doing to make sure that prescription drugs are safe and effective, pharmacists received the highest marks (73 per cent excellent or good), followed at quite a distance by doctors (58 per cent), hospitals (54 per cent), federal regulatory agencies (52 per cent), patients (46 per cent) and drug manufacturers (42 per cent). As shown in Figure 16.1, only 24 per cent of the respondents thought that the patient's health plan was doing an excellent or good job. The small percentage of excellent ratings for every group suggests that, in the public mind, there is room for improvement in this matter, especially regarding a patient's health plan. These results were similar to those found in the Swedish study, in which pharmacists received the highest marks (70 per cent excellent or good), followed by doctors (56 per cent), government regulatory agencies (50 per cent) and drug manufacturers (40 per cent).

When asked how often a drug works as intended for the patient, the majority of the respondents (83 per cent) said always, very often or often. However, when asked how often the patient experiences unwanted effects/side effects, 41 per cent said always, very often or often. When asked whether they personally had suffered a side effect from taking a prescription drug during the past five years, 37 per cent replied yes (see Figure 16.2). Of these, 22.5 per cent considered the side effect severe, 46.3 per cent moderate and 29.0 per cent mild.

Respondents were also asked to indicate how frequently each of 11 factors is the cause of a side effect. The results, shown in Figure 16.3, indicate that patient sensitivity was one of the most frequent perceived causes (39 per cent rated it

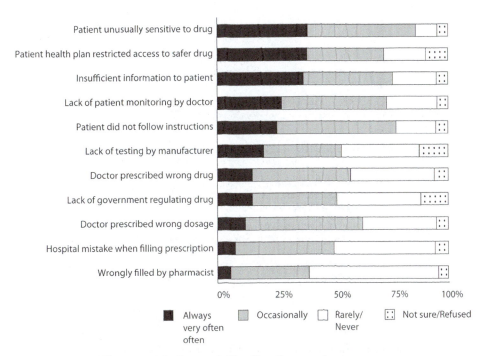

Figure 16.3 *Cause of side effect: Prompted responses*

always, very often or often a cause). This was closely followed by the patient's health plan restricting access to a safer drug (38 per cent always, very often or often) and insufficient information being given to the patient about the drug (37 per cent). Somewhat less frequent attributions of causality were assigned to improper monitoring of the patient by the doctor (27 per cent), lack of patient compliance with instructions (25 per cent) and lack of health and safety testing by the drug manufacturer (19 per cent). Pharmacists and hospital mistakes were seen as the least likely causes (5 per cent and 7 per cent, respectively).

A drug crisis scenario

The following hypothetical scenario was posed to each respondent, indicating a possible link between a drug and some fatalities among its users.

> Imagine that a new prescription drug becomes available in this country for treating a serious disease. Other drugs are also available for treating this disease. A study reveals that some people may have died from taking this new drug. What do you think the government should do in this case?
> - Leave the drug on the market.
> - Leave the drug on the market but warn doctors and patients.
> - Take the drug off the market.
> - Not sure.

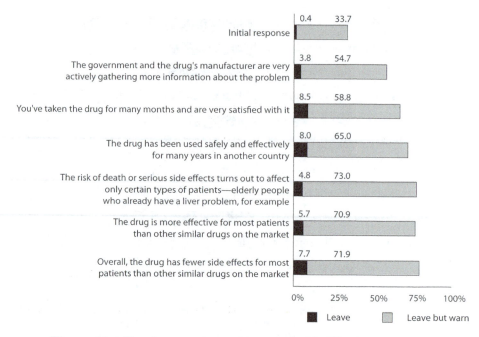

Figure 16.4 *Reactions to a drug crisis scenario: Modification of opinion in view of additional evidence*

The survey indicated that 54 per cent of respondents initially wanted the government to take the drug off the market, 34 per cent wanted it left on the market with a warning and 12 per cent were not sure. Fewer than 1 per cent wanted the drug left on the market. This is different from the 1988 Swedish survey, in which 75.0 per cent of respondents wanted the drug taken off the market, and 21.5 per cent wanted it left on the market with a warning. In Canada, 60.1 per cent wanted the drug taken off the market, 35.1 per cent wanted it left on the market with a warning and 3.3 per cent wanted it left on the market.

Respondents who wanted the drug taken off the market ($n = 1094$) were then asked to reconsider their views, taking into account each of six possible extenuating circumstances. The results, shown in Figure 16.4, indicate that there is no circumstance that, by itself, would convince more than 8.5 per cent of these respondents to leave the drug on the market. However, in combination with information warning doctors and patients about the possible problem, these circumstances led to considerable change in opinions, in some instances more than doubling the number of respondents willing to leave the drug on the market either with or without a warning. The knowledge that the drug has fewer side effects for most patients than other similar drugs was the most compelling of the scenarios studied in influencing respondents' decisions to leave the drug on the market. Conversely, knowledge that the government and the drug's manufacturer are actively gathering more information about the problem was least influential among the scenarios. These results were similar to those of the Swedish study.

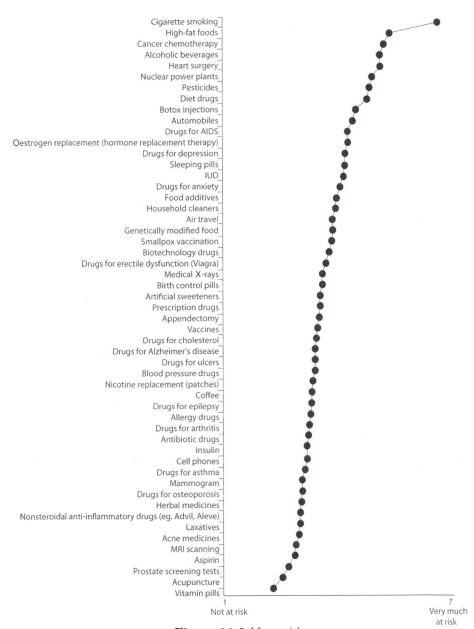

Cigarette smoking
High-fat foods
Cancer chemotherapy
Alcoholic beverages
Heart surgery
Nuclear power plants
Pesticides
Diet drugs
Botox injections
Automobiles
Drugs for AIDS
Oestrogen replacement (hormone replacement therapy)
Drugs for depression
Sleeping pills
IUD
Drugs for anxiety
Food additives
Household cleaners
Air travel
Genetically modified food
Smallpox vaccination
Biotechnology drugs
Drugs for erectile dysfunction (Viagra)
Medical X-rays
Birth control pills
Artificial sweeteners
Prescription drugs
Appendectomy
Vaccines
Drugs for cholesterol
Drugs for Alzheimer's disease
Drugs for ulcers
Blood pressure drugs
Nicotine replacement (patches)
Coffee
Drugs for epilepsy
Allergy drugs
Drugs for arthritis
Antibiotic drugs
Insulin
Cell phones
Drugs for asthma
Mammogram
Drugs for osteoporosis
Herbal medicines
Nonsteroidal anti-inflammatory drugs (eg, Advil, Aleve)
Laxatives
Acne medicines
MRI scanning
Aspirin
Prostate screening tests
Acupuncture
Vitamin pills

1
Not at risk

7
Very much
at risk

Figure 16.5 *Mean risk*

For those whose initial response to the scenario was to take the drug off the market (*n* = 1094), an index score was created according to the number of times they changed their response to leave the drug on the market or to leave it on the market with a warning when faced with each of the six extenuating circumstances. On average, changes were made 3.5 times of 6 (*SD* = 2.2). About 27 per cent changed six times; 16 per cent never changed. This change score was found to be

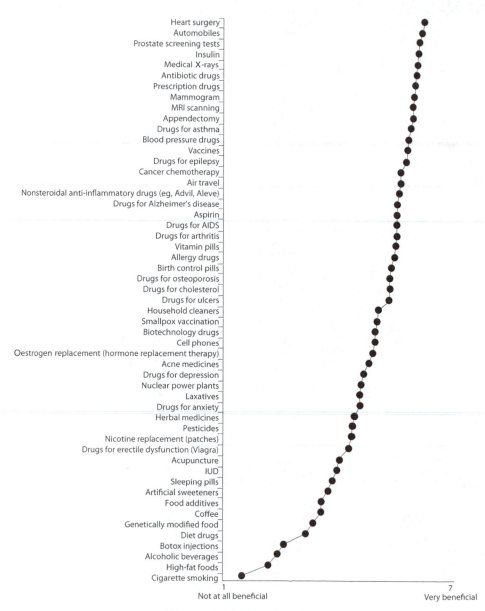

Figure 16.6 *Mean benefit*

significantly correlated with risk perception ($r = -0.14$; $p < .001$) and benefit perception ($r = 0.24$; $p < .001$). Individuals with lower perceptions of risk across the 32 pharmaceutical items and higher mean perceptions of benefits were more likely to change their responses to allow the drug to remain on the market. Education and the number of drugs the respondent had used also correlated positively with the change index ($r = 0.17$; $p < .001$; and $r = 0.09$; $p < .05$, respectively).

Psychometric questionnaire

Ratings of each hazard item were averaged across all respondents for each scale. The mean ratings for perceived risk, ordered from high to low, are shown in Figure 16.5. As with the Swedish study, cigarette smoking clearly stands out as the highest in perceived risk. This is followed by high-fat foods, cancer chemotherapy, alcoholic beverages and heart surgery. Next to cancer chemotherapy, the prescription drugs rated highest on risk are diet drugs; Botox injections; drugs for AIDS, depression, anxiety, oestrogen replacement; and sleeping pills – all with mean scores of 4.0 or higher on the risk scale that ranged from 1 to 7. Vitamin pills, acupuncture and prostate screening tests were judged lowest in risk. Vitamins were perceived as the lowest in risk in all three studies (United States, Sweden and Canada). The risk of prescription drugs fell in the middle range, with a mean score of 3.5.

Mean ratings of perceived benefit are shown in Figure 16.6. Heart surgery, automobiles, prostate screening tests, insulin, medical X-rays, antibiotic drugs and 'prescription drugs' were judged highest in perceived benefits, with mean scores of 6.0 or higher (on a scale from 1 to 7). Cigarette smoking was rated the lowest in perceived benefits. High-fat foods, alcoholic beverages and Botox injections were also perceived as having low benefit. The high ratings for prostate screening are notable in view of the controversial nature of this procedure (Wilt and Partin, 2003). Similar results were found by Farrell et al (2002).

A risk perception index and benefit perception index were created by averaging each respondent's risk and benefit judgements across the 32 pharmaceutical items. A person's score on this measure of perceived risk was predicted significantly by having experienced a side effect ($r = 0.13$; $p < .01$) and education ($r = -0.13$; $p < .01$). It was not predicted by the number of drugs used currently or in the past. Scores on the benefit perception index were predicted significantly by number of drugs used ($r = 0.19$; $p < .001$), experience with a side effect ($r = -0.11$; $p < .05$) and age ($r = -0.10$).

Analysis of means for specific subgroups of respondents showed that women perceived far higher risk from nuclear power than did men (mean rating, 5.1 for women and 4.5 for men; $p < .001$). Women had significantly higher risk perceptions for eight other items (diet drugs, air travel, smallpox vaccination, aspirin, alcoholic beverages, laxatives, intrauterine devices [IUDs] and food additives). Other studies have found that women typically have higher risk perceptions than men, especially regarding nuclear power and other technological hazards (see e.g. Flynn et al, 1994). In the present study, men had significantly higher risk perceptions for five drug items (drugs for depression, osteoporosis, blood pressure, AIDS and ulcers).

As found in other studies, nonwhite respondents tended to have higher perceptions of risk than white respondents. African-American respondents had significantly higher risk perceptions than whites for 23 items, of which 15 were drugs. Hispanics had significantly higher perceptions of risk than whites for seven items; four of the items were drugs. Whites had higher risk perceptions than Hispanics for herbal medicines.

As indicated, respondents who reported having experienced a side effect from a prescription drug generally showed slightly higher mean perceptions of risk than those without side effect experience for both drug and non-drug items. They were significantly higher on 19 items. The largest mean differences were 0.39 and 0.37 for pesticides and cancer chemotherapy, respectively. These respondents also showed a mean difference of 0.25 or greater for nuclear power plants, automobiles, air travel, drugs for cholesterol, diet drugs, prescription drugs, heart surgery, blood pressure drugs, drugs for arthritis and food additives.

Those who reported that they had experienced a side effect from a prescription drug still perceived high benefits from many drugs. Compared with those without such experience, they had significantly higher perceptions of benefits for five drugs or medical procedures (insulin, blood pressure drugs, acupuncture, appendectomy and drugs for osteoporosis) and one non-drug item (automobiles). Those who did not report experiencing side effects perceived significantly higher benefits from five items (laxatives, food additives, IUDs, alcoholic beverages and acne medications). All of these differences were statistically significant at $p < .05$ to $p < .001$.

African-Americans perceived higher benefits than whites for 11 items, including five drugs (biotechnology drugs, oestrogen replacement, laxatives, diet drugs and Botox injections). Whites perceived higher benefits than African-Americans for two items, insulin and appendectomy. Hispanics perceived significantly higher benefits than whites from five items (herbal medicines, genetically modified foods, Botox injections, alcoholic beverages and cigarette smoking). Whites had significantly higher perceptions of benefits than did Hispanics for nine items, including five drugs (insulin, antibiotic drugs, prescription drugs, blood pressure drugs and aspirin). African-Americans had significantly higher perceptions of benefits than Hispanics for two items (prescription drugs and blood pressure drugs).

The risk and benefit means are plotted in Figure 16.7. It is obvious that perceived risk and benefits are inversely related. The correlation of the mean responses across all items was −0.36. Across the subset of 32 pharmaceutical items, this correlation was −0.46. Some items are perceived as low risk and high benefit (e.g. prostate screening tests), and others are perceived as high risk and low benefit (e.g. cigarettes). Most prescription medications fall into the low-risk/high-benefit quadrant. Heart surgery, cancer chemotherapy, drugs for AIDS, hormone replacement therapy (HRT) and drugs for depression fall into the high-risk/high-benefit quadrant. Items seen as high risk and low benefit are cigarette smoking, high-fat foods and alcoholic beverages. Botox injections, diet drugs and sleeping pills also fall into this category. This result is consistent with previous findings, indicating that people base their risk and benefit judgements on how they feel about the activity or technology, a process called the affect heuristic. If their feelings are favourable, then they tend to judge the risks as low and the benefits as high. If their feelings are unfavourable, then they tend to judge the opposite – high risk and low benefit (Slovic et al, 2002).

Assuming that the seven-point scales are commensurate, the risk mean can be subtracted from the benefit mean for each item. According to this analysis,

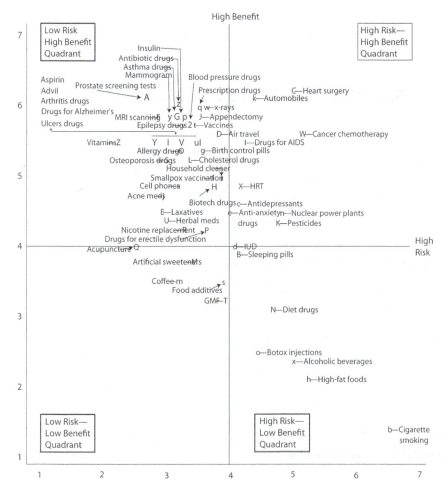

Figure 16.7 *Plot of benefit and risk means*

prostate screening tests, vitamins, magnetic resonance imaging (MRI) scanning, mammograms and insulin are judged highest in net benefits. Antibiotic drugs, drugs for asthma and prescription drugs are not far behind. Most drugs have positive net benefits, except for Botox injections, diet drugs and sleeping pills. Three non-drug or medical procedure items (cigarette smoking, high-fat foods and alcoholic beverages) show the most negative net benefits.

Turning to the other psychometric scales, seriousness of harm and warning signals were highly correlated with perceived risk ($r = 0.80$ and 0.83, respectively). Seriousness of harm ratings differed from perceived risk ratings in that nuclear power plants and heart surgery moved to the highest ranks along with cigarette smoking. This was similar to the findings in the Swedish study. Cigarette smoking ranked highest in rated knowledge of risk to those exposed. The risks of genetically modified food, cell phones and Botox injections were rated as least known. On the warning scale, most of the items took an intermediate position with very little variation among items. Perhaps this scale was not well understood by respondents.

Scientists' understanding of risks and benefits

Respondents were likely to report that scientists had a high understanding of the benefits of prescriptions drugs (69.3 per cent with ratings of 4 or 5 on the 1–5 scale where 5 was labelled *very high degree of understanding*). Perceptions of scientists' understanding of the benefits of over-the-counter drugs and vitamins and herbal supplements were lower, with 59.6 per cent and 45.9 per cent providing ratings of 4 and 5, respectively. For each of the three items, the benefits were perceived as better understood than the risks.

Reducing prescription drug risks

Drug manufacturers and the FDA were seen as the two groups that could do the most to reduce risks of prescriptions drugs, with 48–49 per cent giving ratings of 5 (for high degree of reduction). Patients were seen as least able to reduce the risks of prescription drugs, with only 15 per cent reporting that actions taken by the patient could reduce the current risk to a high degree. There was little variation in the responses for the other four groups (doctors, Congress, pharmacists and hospitals). About one-third (30–33 per cent) of the respondents thought the actions of these four groups could result in a high degree of risk reduction.

Trust in health care groups to manage safety of prescription drug risks

Pharmacists made up the group most trusted to manage the safety of prescription drugs, with 66 per cent of the respondents recording scores of 4 or 5 (where 5 means very great trust). They were followed by doctors, with 55 per cent ratings scores of 4 or 5; hospitals (47 per cent); FDA (44 per cent); drug manufacturers (33 per cent); patients (24 per cent); and Congress (19 per cent).

As each of the seven health care groups was rated on both trust and the extent to which they could reduce drug risks, we correlated these two responses for each group across the nearly 2000 respondents. We expected to find positive correlations for each group, indicating that higher ratings of trust were associated with greater ability to reduce risk. This was particularly evident for Congress ($r = 0.27$), patients ($r = 0.21$) and hospitals ($r = 0.20$). The FDA ($r = 0.15$), doctors ($r = 0.13$) and drug manufacturers ($r = 0.00$) exhibited less of a relationship between trust and perceived ability to reduce risks.

Medication avoidance

Finally, we examined responses to items across different parts of the survey to characterize participants who avoid taking medications appropriate to their medical condition. Our purpose here is to identify individuals who might benefit most from better communication about pharmaceuticals.

Participants in this survey were asked 'Do you have any of the following medical conditions' (e.g. diabetes, high blood pressure)? They also were asked to indicate 'which of the pharmaceutical products listed below you are using currently or have used in the past.' Ten medical conditions/medications were represented on both lists so that, for these items, we could identify participants with a medical condition who had completely avoided taking the matching medication for that condition. Two of the ten medical conditions, diabetes and cancer, were dropped from further analyses because it is not always recommended that an individual with cancer undergo chemotherapy or that a diabetic take insulin. The number of participants with Alzheimer's was quite low, and this medical condition also was dropped.

We constructed a summary variable based on the remaining seven conditions that reflected avoidance of drug therapy. For each condition a participant reported having, they were checked to see if they reported at least sometimes using the matching product either currently or in the past (high blood pressure/blood pressure drugs, arthritis/drugs for arthritis, high cholesterol/drugs for cholesterol, severe allergies/allergy drugs, ulcers/drugs for ulcers, osteoporosis/drugs for osteoporosis and asthma/drugs for asthma). Participants were then classified in the summary variable as not completely avoidant if they did not completely avoid medication for at least one medical condition or completely avoidant if they took no medications for any of the medical conditions (up to seven) they may have had (for all conditions; weighted n = 773.9 and 124.6, respectively).

We then attempted to characterize completely avoidant (CA) and not completely avoidant (NCA) patients (based on the summary measure) to look for clues about how to communicate with patients who completely avoid a medication appropriate to their condition. Who are these people, and how do their beliefs differ from those who do not completely avoid medicines?

Prescription drug use and experience of side effects
CA patients who were asked 'How many prescription medications are you currently taking regularly?' did take some prescription drugs, although they reported taking less than half as many prescription drugs as NCA patients (1.65 vs. 3.51, $p < .001$). CA patients were half as likely to have experienced a recent side effect (27 per cent and 55 per cent of CA and NCA patients, respectively, had experienced a side effect, $p < .001$). It may be that because CA patients take fewer medications regularly, the probability of experiencing a side effect from a single drug or drug–drug interaction is less.

What differentiates CA from NCA patients?
Negative information appears to influence the risk and benefit perceptions of CA patients more than those of NCA patients. Among complete avoiders, risk perceptions of prescription drugs were higher when a side effect was experienced

vs. not experienced (mean prescription drug risk perception index = 4.0 and 3.4, respectively), while among NCA patients this same index was 3.7 and 3.5, respectively, when a side effect was experienced versus not (interaction $F(3, 594) = 4.3$, $p < .05$). Benefit perceptions also were more reactive to the experience of a side effect, with complete avoiders perceiving less benefit if a side effect had been experienced (prescription drug benefit index = 4.7 and 5.2 with vs. without a side effect, respectively, for CA patients and 5.2 and 5.2, respectively, for NCA patients, interaction $F(3, 594) = 4.7$, $p < .05$).

Among those CA and NCA patients who had experienced a side effect in the past five years, CA patients perceived significantly less benefit from prescription drugs than did NCA patients ($p < .05$) and marginally more risk ($p < .10$). This finding is important and somewhat counter-intuitive. We might expect recent experience with side effects to influence perceived risk more than perceived benefit, but these data suggest that recent experience of a side effect (perhaps related, perhaps unrelated to the medical condition in the CA/NCA summary variable) may have an impact on avoidance of appropriate medications by decreasing the perceived benefits of prescription drugs in general as well as by increasing their perceived risks. This reciprocal impact on both risk and benefit may reflect the operation of the affect heuristic.

Reactivity results also are particularly interesting given that the data indicate that both CA and NCA patients who have experienced a side effect rated the severity of the most serious side effect about the same (mean scores = 1.96 and 1.98, respectively). This finding implies that perceptions regarding side effect severity are not driving the disparity in the risk and benefit perceptions.

In terms of what might make drugs safer, CA patients tended to believe that federal regulatory agencies, doctors, pharmacists and hospitals are not doing a good job of ensuring that drugs are safe and effective. They also tended to believe that side effects are more likely to be caused by the patient being unusually sensitive to the drug, the patient not following prescribed instructions and the doctor prescribing the wrong drug. It is possible that CA patients may be particularly receptive to information about how patients and others can increase patient safety by minimizing medical errors. However, CAs' beliefs that federal regulatory agencies, doctors, pharmacists and hospitals are not doing a good job might complicate efforts to identify appropriate messengers for the information.

Relative to NCA patients, those who completely avoid medications believed that scientists understand the benefits of prescription drugs less (mean = 3.73 and 3.96 for CA and NCA patients, respectively, $p < .01$). The CAs also seemed to react more to uncertainty about risks or about what we know about the risks. For example, CA versus NCA patients were more likely to want to take off the market a drug from which people might have died if the government and drug manufacturer were actively gathering more information about the problem (means = 2.40 and 2.29, respectively, $p < .05$). They were less likely than NCAs to want to take a drug from which people may have died off the market once they perceived greater certainty about the drug's effect (i.e. if the risks were only for certain types of patients, or the drug was more effective than similar drugs on the market). This result implies that CA patients may be more malleable to information that increases the perceived certainty of information about risks and benefits (just as they appeared more malleable or reactive to the experience of a side effect).

Perceptions of the specific drug appropriate to their condition
We have examined whether risk and benefit perceptions of drugs differed between CA and NCA patients (they did differ among those CA and NCA patients who had experienced a recent side effect). We now examine whether CA and NCA patients may differ in their beliefs about the specific drug appropriate to their condition.

Perceptions of medication benefits appeared to have an impact on use
Analyses revealed a trend that CA patients perceived less benefit from the medication for their specific conditions than NCA patients. For example, among patients with high blood pressure, those patients who had never taken medication for their condition perceived fewer benefits but similar risks from the medication (perceived drug benefits = 5.5 and 6.2, $p < .01$, for CA and NCA patients, respectively, while average perceived drug risks for both groups was 3.1). Results were similar for patients with high cholesterol and asthma. Thus, while patients on average perceived benefit from the drug that treats their condition, those who have taken the drug at least once (NCA patients) perceived greater benefit. This perception of fewer benefits among CA patients was as strong or stronger among the subset of CA patients who had not experienced a recent side effect. Thus, having a recent side effect does not explain these differences in perception of benefits.

The implication of the data is that the best communication strategy to lessen avoidance may revolve around educating CA patients about their drug's benefits. The findings also beg the question of which came first, the belief that the medication is beneficial or the act of taking it. It may be that initiating treatment is critical to belief in its benefit since those patients who had taken the drug at some point (NCA patients) were more likely to perceive its benefits. Overall findings suggest, however, that, if CA patients perceived more benefit from their drug by whatever means, then they might be less avoidant.

Those who were completely avoidant were younger and in better health and thus may perceive themselves as less vulnerable (more 'immortal') and may perceive their specific disease as less threatening, making the appropriate drug seem less beneficial. Alternatively, it may be, for at least some of them, that they can avoid taking medication without feeling the consequences immediately.

Discussion

The general pattern of results from this survey is quite consistent with the results from national surveys in Sweden and Canada more than a decade ago. In Sweden, Canada and now the United States, several results were clearly evident.

Prescription medicines were perceived to be high in benefit and low in risk. They appeared to be sharply differentiated from other chemicals (e.g. sweeteners, Botox injections, alcohol). The only exceptions to this favourable pattern of perceptions occurred with sleeping pills, antidepressants and diet drugs. Past or current use of prescription drugs was more strongly associated with perceived benefit than with perceived risk. When risk today was compared to risk 20 years ago (US and Sweden surveys only), prescription drugs had the highest percentage of less-risk responses and the smallest percentage of more-risk responses than any other source of hazard.

Despite the general acceptance of drug risks, a majority of respondents in all three surveys were quick to call for withdrawal from the market of a drug suspected of causing fatal reactions in some patients. This reaction was somewhat less frequent in the United States than in Sweden and Canada. However, evidence for safety and efficacy, in combination with warning information, led the majority of US respondents to want the drug left on the market. This tendency was strongest among persons whose overall risk perceptions of drugs were lower, whose benefit perceptions were higher and whose level of education was higher. Similar results had been found in Sweden and Canada. The fact that the government was gathering more information about the problem was least influential in creating tolerance; learning that the drug had fewer side effects than other similar drugs was the most influential information. It is unclear whether the diminished tendency among the less educated to leave a drug on the market despite mitigating information may be influenced by an inability to understand and process the information. It would be worthwhile to explore whether the use of communication materials tailored specifically for this population affects its tendency to leave drugs on the market.

Although we elicited ratings on characteristics such as seriousness of harm, knowledge of risk and strength of the warning signal triggered by a mishap, these three characteristics were highly correlated with perceived risk. Thus, the psychometric ratings led to only two basic dimensions, risk and benefit, and even these were strongly negatively correlated. This high negative correlation is suggestive of reliance on the affect heuristic. Such reliance suggests that information indicative of low risk or high benefit should greatly increase acceptability of a possibly risky drug, which is exactly what was found with the responses to the drug crisis scenario.

Unlike other studies of risk perception, women did not judge all items as riskier than did men. Sex differences were item specific, with women judging risks higher than men for diet drugs, smallpox vaccination, aspirin, laxatives and IUDs, and men perceiving higher risks with drugs for depression, osteoporosis, blood pressure, AIDS and ulcers. Hispanic respondents also exhibited different risk perceptions that were item specific, and African-American respondents had higher risk perceptions than whites for many items. Group differences in benefit perceptions were highly item specific. Recent findings by Voils et al (2006) pointed to the importance of understanding racial differences in risk-related affect as they may enhance understanding of racial differences in health behaviours and outcomes. These findings suggest that African-Americans and Hispanics may not believe that they are at greater risk for disease, despite observed differences in health outcomes. This diminished level of concern over disease may be one factor explaining our finding that African-Americans had lower perceptions of benefit than did whites for insulin and drugs for high blood pressure, despite the fact that African-Americans experience higher rates of diabetes and hypertension than do whites. Alternatively, this lower perception of benefit could reflect African-Americans' diminished access to health care, relative to whites, therefore limiting their ability to experience the benefits of these drugs.

The favourable perceptions of pharmaceutical products are somewhat marred, not by perceived risk but by concerns about cost, by far the dominant impression when people were asked for their images and associations to the term prescription drugs. Associations to profits, big business, lack of insurance and co-payments also surfaced.

Most respondents believed that prescription drugs tend to work as intended, but there is also awareness that side effects occur often (41 per cent of respondents) or occasionally (48 per cent). A significant proportion of respondents had personally experienced a drug side effect, although only about 8 per cent overall reported an effect that was severe. Side effects were most often attributed to patient sensitivity and least often attributed to mistakes by the manufacturer, hospital or pharmacist. Having experienced a side effect was associated not only with higher perceptions of risk but also with higher perception of benefit for many drugs and medical procedures. This is an interesting finding that seems to reflect the ability of respondents to separate their experiences with side effects from negatively influencing their perception of a drug's benefits. This bodes well for communication efforts aimed at educating the public that side effects are an inescapable, though unfortunate, risk of drugs, and that the presence of side effects does not necessarily eclipse the perceived benefits of a medicine.

Patients were viewed as the group that was least able to reduce the risks of prescription drugs, while drug manufacturers and the FDA were viewed as the groups that could do the most. Given that there are, in fact, many positive steps that patients themselves can take to improve drug safety, our results reveal a fertile area for educational outreach. Our results also indicated a low degree of trust afforded Congress in managing prescription drug safety, compared with the higher degrees of trust ascribed to pharmacists, doctors and the FDA. Our results may therefore indicate that the public would feel more confident in a drug safety initiative that involved pharmacists, doctors, the FDA and drug manufacturers rather than one that was driven solely by Congress.

Finally, extensive analysis was done to characterize persons who avoid taking medications prescribed for their medical condition and contrast CA individuals with those who are NCA. Risk and especially benefit perceptions appeared to have an impact on the use of medicines for these CA individuals. CA and NCA patients differed in important beliefs that may allow some leverage on decreasing CA patient avoidance. CA patients appeared to be more reactive to uncertain dangers or not knowing enough about a possible risk. Among CA patients, the experience of a side effect increased risk perceptions more than among NCA patients. CA patients appeared more malleable to information that clarified or made more certain the nature of the risk. They were less likely to want to take a drug off the market when people had died if the risks were known to be for certain types of patients.

CA patients also appeared more malleable with respect to their beliefs about benefits. Among CA patients, the experience of a side effect decreased benefit perceptions more than among NCA patients. However, CA patients were also less likely to want to take a drug off the market when people had died if the drug was more effective than others on the market. CA patients, however, also perceived less benefit than NCA patients from the specific drug appropriate to their condition. This important finding in combination with the other perceived benefit findings suggests that the best communication strategy with CA patients may be to provide more information about the benefits of prescription drugs.

There appear to be two groups of CA patients based on whether they have experienced a recent side effect. Different communication strategies may be appropriate for reducing each group's avoidance. Those with a recent side effect experience perceived fewer benefits from prescription drugs in general, and therefore communication concerning how prescription drugs have changed the lives of many for the better may be most effective. Those who had not experienced a recent side effect perceived similar benefits of pharmaceuticals as a class as the NCA patients. However, they tended to perceive less benefit from the drug appropriate for their condition. For these persons, communication targeted to the benefits of their specific drug may be best.

It would be interesting to explore further how risk and benefit perceptions are formed about specific drugs and prescription drugs in general and how these perceptions change over time and in response to events such as the emergence of new side effects. Of particular interest is how media coverage of potential drug safety concerns affects responses to the drug crisis scenarios discussed in our study. Additional research should examine how different communication strategies (e.g. providing benefit information to consumers) can encourage adherence to prescribed medicines. More generally, a great deal of research is needed to improve communication to consumers. Studying various formats for providing risk and benefit information is but one important direction. For example, recent research (Voils et al, 2006) suggesting that African-Americans and Hispanics do not acknowledge that they are at greater risk for disease than are whites points to the need to communicate their elevated risk of disease and to outline the steps they can take to mitigate this risk. It would also be important to focus a future study on medication adherence as opposed to medication avoidance.

Acknowledgement

This work was supported by a grant from Pfizer Inc.

Chapter 17

Predicting and Modelling Public Response to a Terrorist Strike

William J. Burns and Paul Slovic

Introduction

The goal of this chapter is to examine factors pivotal to understanding public reaction to a terrorist strike. To this end a survey addressing perceptions of different types of events is discussed. We also describe a system dynamics model that represents the important feedback mechanisms that probably drive a community's response. Following a terrorist attack, emergency response systems, information and communication channels, and social support organizations are likely to interact in a non-linear fashion to produce a wide range of physical, social and economic impacts (Kasperson et al, 1988; Maani and Cavana, 2000). This model simulates impacts (e.g. diffusion of fear) over a six-month period for different types of terrorist and accidental events.

This chapter is motivated by practical considerations as well. Public officials, business leaders and health care providers now feel the need to prepare for the impacts a major disaster might have on an urban community. Following the events of 11 September 2001, the anthrax attacks during the same period, and the London and Madrid bombings, individuals and organizations have become aware of their vulnerability with respect to explosions (bombing of tunnels and bridges), biological agents (smallpox, anthrax) and radiation releases ('dirty bombs,' attacks on nuclear reactors). Indeed, there is a clear need to provide researchers and practitioners with a better understanding of how a community is likely to prepare for and respond to an attack (Lasker, 2004).

Hazards examined in study

Hazards may be described from a number of vantage points and indeed have been examined along a variety of attributes. In this study we develop hypothetical threat scenarios that principally compare accidents to terrorism across two damage mechanisms: explosions and infectious diseases. Number of casualties, type of victim and whether negligence or suicide was involved were manipulated as well. The setting is a local theme park.

Conceptual and empirical underpinnings for study

The social amplification of risk

The conceptual basis for this study is guided by the social amplification of risk framework. It is also grounded in systems thinking and modelling to be discussed shortly. The core idea behind the social amplification framework is that an accident or act of terrorism, will interact with psychological, institutional and cultural processes in ways that may amplify (or attenuate) community response to the event (Kasperson et al, 1988). This theory contends the effects of an accident or act of terrorism can extend far beyond the direct damages to victims, property or environment, and may result in momentous indirect impacts. When such events occur, information flows through various channels to the public and its many cultural groups. This information is interpreted largely on the basis of its interaction with the above processes. This interaction, in turn, triggers risk-related behaviour. Such behaviour, together with the influence of the media and special interest groups, generates secondary social and economic consequences that eventually call for additional institutional responses and protective actions (Burns et al, 1993; Burns and Slovic, 2007).

Past studies

Many studies have investigated aspects of the social amplification framework. Investigations vary across particular disciplinary points of view and methodological approaches (Pidgeon et al, 2003) with applications from media and risk reporting (Freudenburg et al, 1996), organizational amplification and attenuation (Freudenburg, 1992; Kasperson, 1992; Pidgeon, 1997), institutional trust (Slovic, 1993, 2000a), nuclear power and stigma (Slovic et al, 1991c; Flynn et al, 2001), public policy (Renn, 1998b) and climate change (Leiserowitz, 2004, 2005). Much has been learned about the public perception of risk, but far less is known about the contexts under which amplification or attenuation occurs or how such amplification of risk perceptions are linked to secondary impacts (Kasperson et al, 2003). Only limited examination of its dynamic propositions (e.g. how amplification of risk plays out to create indirect impacts that far exceed the direct effects of the event) has been successfully attempted (Burns and Slovic, 2007).

Systems thinking

According to Maani and Cavana (2000), the modelling tools employed in systems thinking are useful for understanding dynamic complexity. Such complexity is likely to be present during times of crisis. According to Ackoff (1999), to understand community reaction to a terrorist act, attention must be placed on the interaction of the community's essential components and processes. From a policy standpoint, it is therefore highly useful to understand how change in one area affects the whole system and its parts over time. Indeed, one of the early applications of system dynamics modelling examined urban renewal policies and their counter-intuitive contribution to the acceleration of inner-city decay (Forrester, 1969).

Feedback loops

Sterman (2000, pp3–39, 845–891) maintains that the dynamics of such a systemic response can be understood in terms of the interaction of positive (self-reinforcing) and negative (self-correcting) feedback loops, along with time and information delays and non-linearities. The social amplification framework provides the conceptual guidance as to what processes should be modelled and how system feedback loops and delays may contribute to impacts far in excess of what one might expect based on the immediate and most tangible consequences of a terrorist act.

Positive loops are self-reinforcing and tend to amplify behaviours. Negative loops are balancing and tend to counter such change. For example, positive loops formed as the media began to follow the investigation of the anthrax attacks in Washington, DC and four other east-coast cities. Friends and co-workers across the country were warned about this new risk and information spread rapidly through conversation. Concern and fear began to rise in most cultural groups, according to news polls at the time. Ripple effects spread around the nation as people placed heavy demands on hotlines and health care providers, brought suspicious mail to local police and fire departments, and sought vaccines and antibiotics in case of exposure. Policy surrounding bioterrorism response and preparedness plans were reviewed. Shortly, negative loops also became evident. As conversation intensified, people had fewer new people to talk with or less fresh news to talk about and so declined. Likewise, as fear spread, communities intervened offering reassurance that the threat of anthrax was not as serious as imagined (e.g. not international terrorism), was limited to a small number of areas (e.g. cities on the east coast) and was being addressed (e.g. the postal service screening mail). Fear decreased and eventually so did the volume of telephone calls to health care facilities and demands for antibiotics. However, the call for bioterrorism preparedness persists (Stein et al, 2004).

Delays and non-linearities

Delays between actions and consequences are also important and make public response difficult to anticipate, much less manage (Senge, 1990). Despite an intensive federal investigation, it took law enforcement time to determine that international terrorism wasn't behind the anthrax attacks. It also took time for scientists to declare the Senate Office Building free of anthrax spores. Likewise, communities needed time to respond and offer help. Meanwhile the nation was on the alert and perceptions of risk were rising. Even after new information and reassurances became available, people needed time to adjust emotionally. Finally, the effects of terrorism are likely to be non-linear, that is, they will not be proportional to the direct damage they cause. For example, the anthrax attacks of 2001 were local events, unconnected to international terrorism, in which five people died. Yet, this event, in close proximity to 11 September, has led to massive efforts in bioterrorist research, disaster preparedness and the stockpiling of vaccines and antibiotics. Unexamined feedback mechanisms, delays and non-linearities increase the likelihood of policy decisions with unintended consequences.

Overview of study

This study intends to accomplish two goals. First we seek to examine differences in public response to non-terrorist vs. terrorist events. With this in mind, we systematically vary scenarios according to non-terrorism vs. terrorism, explosions vs. infectious diseases, terrorists' motives as demands to release prisoners vs. solely to instil fear, non-terrorists' motives as non-intentional vs. intentional (criminal), terrorist acts as non-suicidal vs. suicidal, non-terrorist incidents as involving no negligence vs. negligence, victims as government officials vs. tourists, and number of casualties (0, 15, 495). Second, we seek to illustrate how systems modelling may provide insight into how risk signals ripple through a community. Hence, we propose a preliminary systems model and provide simulation output depicting the diffusion of fear in a community.

Data collection

Methods

Participants
121 undergraduate business students from a university in San Diego County were recruited from four different classes during September of 2004. The median age was 23 (range 21–52) with 49 per cent being male.

Procedures
Participants were given a packet of survey materials and told they would be responding to 16 hypothetical scenarios or mishaps representing a mix of terrorist and non-terrorist events. They were then randomly assigned to one of six experimental conditions (described below) and asked to evaluate 16 scenarios on each of 12 survey questions shown in Table 17.3. To control for possible order effects, half the respondents began with scenario 1 and the other half began with scenario 16. Likewise, the sequence of scenarios was scrambled so as not to suggest that some events were of more concern than others. After finishing this task they answered questions pertaining to their use of media, their trust of various information sources (e.g. local officials, clergy, health care providers, experts), the size of their circle of friends, and demographic information. At the close of the exercise they also responded to ten questions taken verbatim from recent nationwide Gallup Polls relating to perceptions of terrorism. This was done to assess the generalizability of our findings beyond this student population. The entire task took between 60 and 90 minutes.

Experimental design

The setting for these hypothetical scenarios was a local theme park. We used a 2×3 factorial design with 16 repeated measures (scenarios). Participants were first randomly assigned to one of two conditions in which either all the scenarios involved park negligence (for the non-terrorist events) and suicide (for the terrorist events) or none of the scenarios involved negligence or acts of suicide. Within each of these two groups participants were randomly assigned to one of three conditions in which all scenarios involved either 0, 15 or 495 casualties. These factorial combinations created six between-subjects groups for later comparison. Within each of these six groups all participants evaluated 16 scenarios that varied in the following manner. Eight events focused on terrorism (four were bomb blasts and four were anthrax releases). Terrorist motives were either to obtain the release of prisoners or solely to instil fear. The remaining eight scenarios did not involve terrorism (four mishaps were propane tank explosions and four were infectious disease releases). The motives here were either intentional (criminal) or not intentional (accidental). In eight of the scenarios victims were government officials while in eight scenarios the victims were tourists.

To illustrate, Table 17.1 depicts the within-subjects design for the non-suicide/negligence group with 0 casualties. Within-subjects factor headings are in bold and between-subjects factor headings are italicized. For example, scenario 1 would be the first event evaluated by each participant. This event would have the following characteristics: Terrorist act, bomb blast, demands would be made for the release of political prisoners, government officials would be the target, no suicide would be involved, and no casualties would result. Whereas, scenario 2 in the non-suicide/negligence group with 0 casualties would have these attributes: Non-terrorist, release of an infectious disease by some park employee unintentionally, tourists would be the victims, no negligence by park authorities would be involved, and 0 casualties would result. The remaining five between-subjects groups had an identical design except with respect to the presence of suicide/negligence and level of casualties. For example, scenario 2 for a suicide/negligence group with 15 casualties would have the following characteristics: Non-terrorist, release of an infectious disease by some park employee unintentionally, tourists would be the victims, park authorities would be involved in some form of health code violation (negligence) and 15 casualties would result.

The sequence of scenarios depicted in Table 17.1 was purposefully chosen so as to mask our hypothesized order of perceived threat level. Our own ordering, which will be examined using multivariate procedures later in the chapter, was guided by the following propositions:

- Domain: Terrorist acts will be more threatening than non-terrorist acts because they are potentially more catastrophic and unpredictable and are driven by malevolence.
- Mechanism: Infectious diseases will provoke more concern than explosions because they are unseen and their effects are delayed.

Table 17.1 *Experimental design describing event characteristics for each of the 16 scenarios for the non-suicide/negligence and 0 casualties group*

Scenario	Domain	Mechanism	Motive	Target/ Victims	Suicide/ Negligence	Casualties
1	Terrorism	Bomb	Prisoners released	Officials	Non-suicide	0
2	Non-terrorism	Infectious disease released	Not Intentional	Tourists	Non-negligence	0
3	Non-terrorism	Propane tank	Not intentional	Officials	Non-negligence	0
4	Terrorism	Anthrax	Prisoners released	Tourists	Non-suicide	0
5	Non-terrorism	Propane tank	Intentional – criminal	Officials	Non-negligence	0
6	Terrorism	Anthrax	Solely to spread fear	Tourists	Non-suicide	0
7	Non-terrorism	Infectious disease released	Not intentional	Officials	Non-negligence	0
8	Terrorism	Bomb	Prisoners released	Tourists	Non-suicide	0
9	Non-terrorism	Infectious disease released	Intentional – criminal	Officials	Non-negligence	0
10	Terrorism	Bomb	Solely to spread fear	Tourists	Non-suicide	0
11	Non-terrorism	Infectious disease released	Intentional – criminal	Tourists	Non-negligence	0
12	Terrorism	Bomb	Solely to spread fear	Officials	Non-suicide	0
13	Non-terrorism	Propane tank	Intentional – criminal	Tourists	Non-negligence	0
14	Terrorism	Anthrax	Solely to spread fear	Officials	Non-suicide	0
15	Non-terrorism	Propane tank	Not intentional	Tourists	Non-negligence	0
16	Terrorism	Anthrax	Prisoners released	Officials	Non-suicide	0

- Motive for terrorist events: The stated goal to spread fear will be more worrisome than the demand to have prisoners released because the latter gives the impression there is an opportunity for negotiation and hence to reduce the risk.
- Motive for non-terrorist events: Mishaps that are perpetrated intentionally will be more worrisome than pure accidents because the former implies some

Table 17.2 *Examples of the scenarios used to examine the effect of domain, mechanism, motive, victim, suicide/negligence, and casualties on perceptions (e.g. risk perception) and behaviours (e.g. avoiding public places)*

Terrorism bomb blast (terrorism, explosion, fear as motive, suicide involved, tourists as victims, 495 casualties)
Reports are now coming out that a powerful bomb has gone off at a local theme park during unusually high attendance by tourists. An international terrorist group is claiming responsibility and promising to strike fear in the hearts of all Americans. It appears that a terrorist bent on suicide exploded the deadly bomb near a crowd of tourists. A large number of tourists have serious injuries and at least 495 have died.

Terrorism anthrax release (terrorism, infectious disease, release of prisoners as motive, no suicide, government officials as victims, no casualties)
Reports are now coming out that anthrax was released 16 days ago at a local theme park during a tour by over a thousand government officials from around the state. An international terrorist group is claiming responsibility and demanding the release of several of its members who are in prison. It appears that a terrorist released the deadly infectious disease near the group of officials. A number of officials may have been exposed but no one has died.

Non-terrorism *unintentional* propane tank explosion (non-terrorism, explosion, *not intentional*, negligence involved, government officials as victims, 495 casualties)
Reports are now coming out that a propane tank has exploded at a local theme park during a tour by over a thousand government officials from around the state. Authorities have ruled out foul play but are looking into the maintenance records of the tank. It appears that a faulty valve on the propane tank failed creating a massive explosion near the group of officials. Heavy fines may be issued pending an investigation. A large number of officials have serious injuries and at least 495 have died.

Non-terrorism *unintentional* infectious disease release (non-terrorism, infectious disease release, *not intentional*, no negligence involved, tourist as victims, 15 casualties)
Reports are now coming out that an infectious disease was released 16 days ago at a local theme park during unusually high attendance by tourists. Authorities have ruled out foul play and have determined it to be unintentional. It appears that a recently hired food server was unconcerned about present medical symptoms and reported no illness on the application. The server unknowingly exposed the deadly infectious disease to a crowd of tourists. No fines or criminal charges have been issued. A number of tourists have been exposed and at least 15 have died.

Non-terrorism *intentional* propane tank explosion (non-terrorism, explosion, *intentional*, negligence involved, tourists as victims, 495 casualties)
Reports are now coming out that a propane tank has exploded at a local theme park during unusually high attendance by tourists. Authorities have not ruled out foul play and are trying to determine if the explosion was intentional. Investigators are looking at the security precautions and maintenance records of the tank. It appears that a faulty valve on the propane tank may have actually been rigged to fail creating a massive explosion near a crowd of tourists. Heavy fines and possible criminal charges may be issued pending an investigation. A large number of tourists have serious injuries and at least 495 have died.

Non-terrorism *intentional* infectious disease release (non-terrorism, infectious disease release, *intentional*, negligence involved, tourist as victims, 0 casualties)
Reports are now coming out that an infectious disease was released 16 days ago at a local theme park during unusually high attendance by tourists. Authorities have not ruled out foul play and are trying to determine if the contamination was intentional. Investigators are looking at the security precautions and health screening procedures followed during hiring. It appears that a recently hired food server concealed present medical symptoms and reported having only the flu on the application. This illness was overlooked by management and the server may have knowingly exposed the deadly infectious disease to a crowd of tourists. Heavy fines and possible criminal charges may be issued pending an investigation. A number of tourists may have been exposed but no one has died.

Table 17.3 *Survey questions addressed for each scenario*

Risk perceptions and trust

1   To what degree do you trust *'first responders'* (police, firefighters and so forth) to quickly *reduce any danger* resulting from an event like this?

2   To what degree do you trust *'government officials'* (President, Governor, Mayor, and so forth) to quickly *reduce any danger* resulting from an event like this?

3   To what degree do you feel you could *protect yourself* from an event like this?

4   To what degree would you *feel at risk* after learning of this event?

Attention to media

5   How much time would you spend following news coverage of this event?

Your contact and conversations with friends and family

6   To what degree would you feel the need to *contact friends and family* to discuss this story after learning of this event?

Your behaviour during and following the event

7   To what degree would this event cause you to *worry about your safety throughout the day* until this event was resolved?

8   Assuming you were not at the theme park, which of these health care services would you *contact first for medical information* about any danger to you or your family?

9   How soon after learning of this event would you first contact the service you chose in the previous question to obtain information about any danger?

10   To what degree would not being able to reach a health care provider to obtain information about *information about* any danger cause you concern during such an event?

11   To what degree would you feel the need to *avoid public places* until this event was resolved?

12   To what degree would you feel the need to leave the area until this event was resolved?

Note: The scales are not shown but most have a format like that of 'Trust' (*Low trust* 1 2 3 4 5 6 7 8 9 *High trust*) or 'Risk' (*Low risk* 1 2 3 4 5 6 7 8 9 *High risk*). However, others list behaviours such as for 'Avoidance' (would not avoid any public places; would avoid 'theme parks' only; would avoid places like shopping malls, supermarkets, public transportation, as well as 'theme parks'; would avoid almost all public places but would continue to go to my job; would avoid almost all public places including going to my job).

degree of wanton disregard for others' safety.

•   Victim: Tourists as victims will be of more concern than government officials because the former have not volunteered to be put in harm's way and tourists may also appear more similar to the participants.

•   Suicide for terrorist events: Terrorist acts involving suicide will be more threatening than those not involving suicide because the former appear more difficult to stop and imply a much higher level of commitment on the part of an adversary.

•   Negligence for non-terrorist events: Mishaps involving negligence will be more threatening than those not involving negligence because the former imply a violation of public trust and portend a level of risk higher than previously thought.

- Casualties: The effect of casualties will be negligible because in the presence of other strong risk signals that predict potential exposure to harm this number may add little additional information.

Scenarios

There were 96 different scenarios (6 between-subjects groups and 16 scenarios within each group). Examples of six of these scenarios are shown in Table 17.2.

Questionnaire

Results

Regression analysis of event means

To better understand and predict mean perceptions of risk and trust for each of the 96 scenarios we developed linear regression models using the six variables depicted in Table 17.1 as predictors. Domain, mechanism, motive, victim, suicide or negligence were coded as 1 if terrorism, infectious disease, fear, tourist, and suicide or negligence were involved respectively (0 otherwise). Casualties was coded as 0, 15 or 495. The linear regression model for perceptions of risk is as follows: y (perceived risk) $= 3.03 + 1.39(\text{domain}) + 0.77(\text{mechanism}) + 0.32(\text{motive}) + 0.24(\text{victim}) + 0.74(\text{suicide or negligence}) + 0.00004(\text{casualties})$ with an $R^2 = 0.82$. These are unstandardized regression coefficients. Hence, the regression coefficient for domain implies that holding all other model variables at their current level, the mean perceived risk for terrorism is 1.39 scale points greater than for non-terrorism. In turn, the coefficient for mechanism reflects the mean risk perceptions differences for infectious disease versus explosions holding other model variables constant. Casualties was measured on a 0 to 495 scale thus in part explaining its comparatively small regression coefficient. Even so, its effect size is very small. All regression predictors were significant ($p < .001$) except casualties ($p = 0.85$) and terrorism appeared to have the largest effect on participants' perception of risk followed by the mechanism involved (infectious disease or anthrax), suicide or negligence, motive (fear) and victim (tourist). Interestingly, once these five factors were accounted for, the number of deaths did not appear to contribute to perceptions of risk. Note that these findings support our hypotheses (in 'Experimental design', above) that contend events involving terrorism, infectious disease, the spread of fear as a sole motive, tourists as victims, and suicide or negligence will have the highest perceived risk. The importance of these factors can clearly be seen by contrasting the three scenarios that had the highest mean risk perception ratings with the three scenarios that had the lowest risk perception ratings, as shown in Table 17.4.

Likewise, the regression model for perceptions of trust in first responders is as follows: y (perceived trust – first responders) $= 7.05 - 0.36(\text{domain}) - 0.90(\text{mechanism}) + 0.03(\text{motive}) - 0.07(\text{victim}) - 0.06(\text{suicide or negligence}) - 0.00132(\text{casualties})$ with $R^2 = 0.75$. Domain, mechanism and casualties were signif-

Table 17.4 *Ranking of mean risk perception based on event characteristics*

Rank in risk	Domain	Mechanism	Motive	Target/ Victims	Suicide/ Negligence	Casualties	Mean (1–9)
1	Terrorism	Anthrax	Solely to spread fear	Tourists	Suicide	0	6.48
2	Terrorism	Anthrax	Solely to spread fear	Tourists	Suicide	495	6.42
3	Terrorism	Anthrax	Solely to spread fear	Officials	Suicide	495	6.32
94	Non-terrorism	Propane tank	Not intentional	Tourists	Non-negligence	0	2.71
95	Non-terrorism	Propane tank	Not intentional	Tourists	Non-negligence	15	2.68
96	Non-terrorism	Propane tank	Not intentional	Tourists	Non-negligence	495	2.62

icant predictors of trust ($p < .001$). However, here the effect size for casualties is not trivial as it was for risk perception. It appears that trust in first responders is greatest for handling explosions rather than infectious disease, non-terrorism rather than terrorism and smaller numbers of casualties (negative regression coefficients). The regression model for trust in government officials is as follows: y (perceived trust – government officials)= $5.66 + 0.76$(domain) $- 0.05$(mechanism) $+ 0.22$(motive) $- 0.45$(victim) $- 0.0012$(suicide or negligence) $+ 0.00012$(casualties) with $R^2 = 0.50$. Domain and victim were significant ($p < .001$) as was motive ($p = 0.03$). Trust in government officials is highest for events involving terrorism directed at other government officials with the stated intent to spread fear. Interestingly, the presence of suicide or negligence does not appear to predict trust for either first responders or government officials. To understand better the differences in trust expressed for first responders versus government officials we debriefed a number of participants following the exercise. They explained they felt terrorism was essentially a political event requiring local and federal intervention whereas accidents are best handled by specifically trained professionals.

We also investigated the relationship of risk perception to other participant responses. Our regression analysis indicated that perceptions of risk predicted the degree to which participants reported they would pay attention to a news story ($R^2 = 0.72$), alert friends ($R^2 = 0.73$), contact health care providers ($R^2 = 0.53$), and avoid public places ($R^2 = 0.74$) or leave the area ($R^2 = 0.57$).

Analysing event differences at the participant level

To better understand how participants differed in their response to these 16 scenarios we began by examining the distribution of scores for a variety of our measures. As an example, we compare the distributions of risk perception responses for different levels of domain and damage mechanism, the within-subjects factors with the largest effects in the previous section. Figure 17.1 compares a terrorist bombing with a non-terrorist propane tank explosion and Figure 17.2 compares a terrorist release of anthrax with a non-terrorist release of an infectious disease. Notice that in both figures, there is clear upward shift in perceived risk for acts involving terrorism. However, this shift is more pronounced for explosions than for infectious disease. Figure 17.3 compares two non-terrorist events differing with regards to the damage mechanism involved while Figure 17.4 compares two terrorist events differing similarly. Observe that the release of an infectious disease is clearly perceived to pose greater risk than a propane tank explosion; however, the release of anthrax is only slightly more worrisome than a bomb blast. Figure 17.5 compares the relative contribution of each hazard event to various levels of risk perception. Notice that about 70 per cent of the highest risk ratings come from either bomb blasts or anthrax whereas about 40 per cent of the lowest risk ratings come from a propane tank explosion.

Consistent with our aggregate level analysis in the previous section the presence of terrorism or infectious disease greatly heightens risk perception with the largest effect coming from terrorism. However, these figures also reveal that the most of this difference comes in the realm of explosions. The comparatively low perceived risk for propane tank explosions may have a number of explanations. First, compared to infectious diseases, bomb blasts and anthrax, the public is very familiar and comfortable with this type of risk. Second, propane tank explosions, tragic though they be, have a clear end point in terms of risk exposure. Infectious diseases may continue to spread and the threat of future terrorist acts does not end with one incident of terrorism.

Multivariate analysis

In this section we further explore our hypotheses regarding the nature of the differences among the 16 scenarios. Recall (in 'Regression analysis of event means', above) that we found support for our hypotheses that predicted events involving terrorism, infectious disease, the spread of fear as a sole motive, tourists

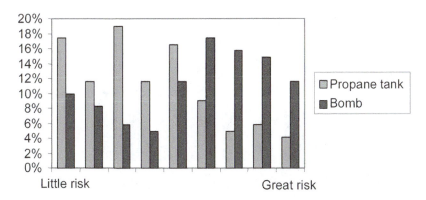

Figure 17.1 *Comparison of risk perceptions for a propane tank explosion (non-terrorist) versus bomb blast (terrorist)*

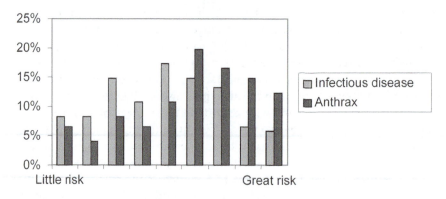

Figure 17.2 *Comparison of risk perceptions for an anthrax release (terrorist) versus an infectious disease (non-terrorist)*

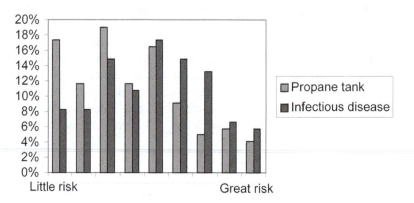

Figure 17.3 *Comparison of risk perceptions for an infectious disease release (non-terrorist) versus a propane tank explosion (non-terrorist)*

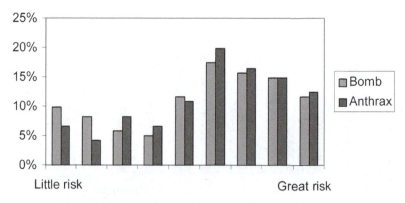

Figure 17.4 *Comparison of risk perceptions for an anthrax release (terrorist) versus a bomb blast (terrorist)*

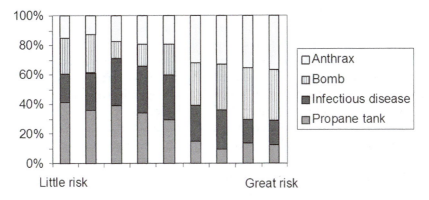

Figure 17.5 *Comparison of the relative contribution (100% scale) of four events to perceptions of risk*

as victims, and suicide or negligence would have the highest perceived risk, whereas casualties would have a negligible effect on perceived risk. These findings were based, however, on applying regression analysis to event means that were averaged across participants. Willis et al (2005) refer to this approach as an aggregate-level hazard-focused analysis. This approach had the important advantage of allowing us to examine the separate effects of each of the above six factors in a single regression model. Such modelling was not, however, conducive to investigating the many potential interactions and non-linearities among our six factors.

To address these interactions and non-linearities, as well as look more thoroughly at trends across our 16 scenarios, we decided to examine these hypotheses without averaging across participants by conducting a multivariate analysis of variance (MANOVA) using a general linear model capable of examining repeated measures in a factorial design. We felt it was important to corroborate our findings at a level closer to the participants. This approach also allowed us to examine three different effects on participant responses (e.g. risk perception): the overall within-subjects effects of domain, mechanism, motive and victim across the 16 scenarios (e.g. linear, quadratic), the between-subjects effects across the six groups described previously, and the effect of gender. However, this procedure too had its limitations. In a MANOVA, repeated measures are regarded as separate within-subjects treatments. Because our scenarios were analysed as 16 different treatments (which they were), we could not easily assess the separate contribution of domain, mechanism, motive and victim in the manner of our more aggregate level analysis described above. Hence, both approaches proved necessary and helpful. We limit our discussion here to participants' perception of risk and intention to avoid public places.

Concerning risk perceptions, we first examined the within-subjects effects. Multivariate tests of significance (e.g. Wilks' Lamda) indicated that there were significant differences among the 16 scenarios ($p < .001$). Using multivariate contrasts we were able to further determine that these (within-subjects) scenario effects were both linear and quadratic in nature ($p < .001$) with the former effect being large and positive while the latter being small and negative. The presence of a strong positive linear effect supported our hypothesis that events such as a non-terrorist propane tank explosion that was unintentional and whose victims were government officials would be the least worrisome, a terrorist anthrax release whose stated motive was solely to spread fear and whose target was tourists would be the most worrisome, and events such as a non-terrorist release of an infectious disease that was unintentional and whose victims were tourists would fall in between in a predicted order. The small negative quadratic effect did not contradict our hypothesis and will be discussed shortly. The interaction effects with the between-subjects factors of negligence or suicide and casualties were not significant hence these effects were consistent across the six between-subjects groups. Next we looked at the between-subjects effects of suicide/negligence and casualties on risk perception. Groups evaluating scenarios involving negligence (non-terrorist) or suicide (terrorist) had significantly higher perceived risk than those involving no negligence or suicide ($p = 0.045$), whereas groups evaluating scenarios with a larger number of casualties had no significant increase in risk perceptions was ($p = 0.851$). Both these findings were consistent with our hypothesis. There was no interaction effect between the two factors ($p = 0.918$). Gender was significantly related to risk perceptions ($p = 0.029$) with females having higher perceived risk.

Concerning the intention to avoid public places we found very similar results to that of risk perception. Multivariate tests indicated that there were significant differences among the 16 scenarios ($p < .001$). These effects were linear ($p < .001$) as well as quadratic ($p = 0.033$). Looking at the between-subjects factors, negligence or suicide was significant ($p = 0.022$) but casualties was not ($p = 0.155$). These results were also consistent with our hypothesis. Gender now was not significantly related to the intention to avoid public places ($p = 0.449$).

To examine the nature of these within-subjects linear and quadratic effects more closely we looked at how individual participants responded to each of the 16 scenarios in terms of risk perception and intention to avoid public places. Willis et al (2005) refer to this approach as a participant-level hazard-focused analysis. We selected 24 participants from our sample (four subjects from each of the six between-subjects groups) for closer evaluation. As a start, we attempted to overcome the limitation of our MANOVA by estimating the separate effects of domain, mechanism, motive and victim on individual participant risk perceptions. To do this, risk perception scores for the 16 scenarios were regressed on domain, mechanism, motive and victim for each participant resulting in 24 multiple regression equations. However, because of the small number of events relative to the number of parameters being estimated, our results proved unreliable (e.g. unusually large R^2s suggesting data fitting and many insignificant regression coefficients). We have guarded confidence that domain and to some extent mechanism appeared to predict risk perceptions.

We decided to reduce the number of parameters to be estimated by coding each scenario 1 through to 16 with a 1 corresponding to the hypothesized least worrisome event, a 2 relating to the next worrisome event and so forth. Regarding risk perception, for each participant we regressed their response (i.e. risk perception) for each event on the coded scenarios. We investigated a number of regression functions (e.g. linear, quadratic, power) for best fit. Consistent with the multivariate analysis we found that a quadratic function of the form $y = a + b_1x - b_2x^2$ worked well (about 75 per cent of cases) with a median R2 = .45 and 70 per cent of the R^2s greater than 0.30. We also found a similar quadratic function worked well (about 67 per cent of cases) for modelling the intention to avoid public places with a median $R^2 = 0.58$ and 69 per cent of the R^2s greater than 0.30. Regarding risk perception for these scenarios, we estimated this regression equation to be $y = 2.30 + 0.36x - 0.010x^2$ for events involving no negligence or suicide and $y = 3.13 + 0.38x - 0.012x^2$ for events involving negligence or suicide. Other types and numbers of hazards need to be examined to determine whether this quadratic function is idiosyncratic to our scenario development and data or has a more general application. What this function suggests is that first, it may be possible to use the factors domain, mechanism, motive and victim as a guide to ranking (value of x) a set of hazardous events in terms of threat level as we did here. For example, consider a set of events ranging from an accidental explosion involving firefighters to a terrorist anthrax release involving tourists. The former would be ranked lowest and the latter would be ranked highest. All other mix of events would be ranked in between according to their scores on domain, mechanism, motive and victim with the largest weight given to domain and the smallest to victim. Second, risk perception may increase linearly with our ordering (b_1x), but will taper off slightly at the upper range of our rankings $(-b_2x^2)$, that is change in risk perceptions between ranks is not equal. Understanding the nature of participants' response to our scenarios (i.e. $y = a + b_1x - b_2x^2$) was important because it would provide the input to a very influential component of our systems model to be discussed next.

Systems modelling

System dynamics modelling

Modelling procedures

As a brief explanation of our systems modelling procedures, consider the system dynamics model shown in Figure 17.6. For a more complete model description see Burns and Slovic (2007). This model is a stock and flow diagram designed to track how the system changes over time. Stocks (depicted as rectangles) are accumulations and represent the state of the system at any given moment. Flows (depicted as in-flowing and out-flowing pipes) increase or decrease the size of the stocks over time, respectively. Rates of flow are regulated by valves, which in turn are influenced by causal factors (depicted as circles and their corresponding causal arrows). The clouds at the beginning and end of the pipes are stocks (sources and sinks respectively) representing variables outside the boundary of the model. A number of causal factors and arrows have been omitted to make the

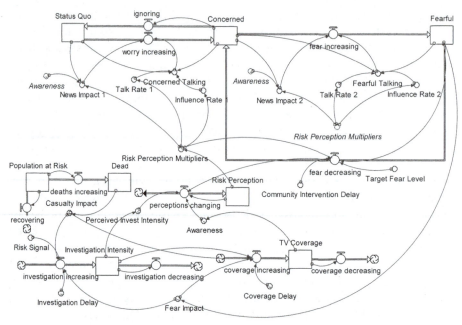

Figure 17.6 *System dynamics model of public response to a terrorist strike (abridged)*

figure more readable, but this figure provides the general idea.

The dynamic hypothesis underlying our model is based in part on the social amplification of risk framework, which predicts that events with higher risk signal will receive greater investigative attention and broader media coverage. It also suggests that the media may amplify this risk signal still further through sheer volume of coverage and selective content and imagery. Concerned citizens may also serve as amplifying stations through word-of-mouth and thus contribute to the rapid diffusion of fear in a community. High levels of fear may subsequently lead to costly secondary impacts as increasing demands are placed on community resources.

Concretely, the story behind the model begins with the stock 'Population at Risk' in which people are in the proximity of a terrorist act and some die ('Dead'). An investigation ensues based on these deaths, the risk characteristics (e.g. anthrax or bomb blast) of the event and subsequent fear. As the investigation intensifies ('Investigative Intensity'), media coverage ('TV Coverage') increases and alerts citizens about the event. Increased awareness of the terrorist strike causes perceived risk to increase which in turn causes people to become concerned ('Concerned') and alert others. Some people will also become fearful ('Fearful'). However, as the population becomes fearful the community begins to intervene and offer support and reassurance, which in turn begins to reduce the level of fear. As fear declines so does perceived risk. Eventually the community regains its equilibrium but the public remains at a higher state of concern (not shown here but was examined) than before the event.

Results

Systems model output

Now that our modelling and survey data have been discussed, consider the following example output (Figure 17.7) in which the diffusion of fear (the stock 'Fearful' from Figure 17.6) in a community is compared for a propane tank explosion, bomb blast, and anthrax release over a six-month period. We have construed 'fearful' to be not only an expression of fear but a propensity to take protective actions such as avoiding public places. This is a simple representation of a large urban community's response to terrorism or serious accident. It assumes a population of about one million adults of which 1000 people have been put in harm's way at a local theme park, half of whom die. It also postulates it takes much longer to investigate an anthrax attack than a bomb blast or a propane tank explosion.

The output is based in part on our survey data as well as personal assessments of the functional relationships among a number of model variables. For example, the risk characteristics input for different types of hazardous events in Figure 17.6 were derived from our prediction of risk perceptions based on the event's domain, mechanism, motive, victim, suicide/negligence and casualties profile discussed earlier. Likewise, the spread of news about a possible threat via word-of-mouth is depicted by 'Concerned Talking' and 'Fearful Talking'. These are in part a function of the average contact rate per person (talk rate) and the persuasiveness of each communication (influence rate). We were able to assign values for contact and persuasion rates based on our survey reports of an event's perceived risk, and ability to generate communication among friends, as well as the average number of friends per participant. We also assessed the relationship between a number of key model variables. For a detailed description see www.decisionresearch.org/pdf/TheDiffusionofFearFigureEquationsGraphs_000.pdf

Observe, in Figure 17.7, that about 45 per cent of citizens are predicted to be fearful even two months after an anthrax attack. While this percentage may appear high, Snyder and Park (2002) found in a nationwide survey two months after 11 September 2001 that 21 per cent of people described themselves as very afraid and 23 per cent were somewhat afraid. It's not unreasonable to think that, in terms of fear, the release of anthrax may have a larger and more lasting impact on local residents than 11 September had on people nationwide.

Notice the marked difference in the percentage of fearful people and the length of time they remain fearful for each event. This contrast is driven initially by differences in the risk characteristics of each event as shown in Table 17.1 and the duration of investigation. As inputs to the model, casualties are the same for all three events (500) but risk perception is greater for anthrax than for bomb blast or accidental propane tank explosion. However, the area under the curves representing number of fearful people by number of days they remain fearful is about 70 per cent greater for anthrax than for the propane tank explosion. The pronounced differences in the number of fearful people and the length of time they remain afraid has sobering implications for the physical and economic health

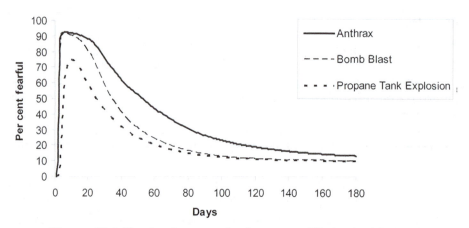

Figure 17.7 *Simulated response for three events differing in risk signal and investigation duration*

of a community, not to mention its quality of life. This kind of amplification results from the many reinforcing feedback loops, delays and non-linearities predicted by the social amplification of risk framework.

Discussion

Major findings

This study has examined threat scenarios across a number of variables pertaining to perceptions and likely behaviours during and following a mishap. These threat scenarios were investigated both at the aggregate level (averaging across participants) and at the disaggregate level (at the level of participants). The study has also involved different methodological approaches (e.g. univariate regression and MANOVA). The primary findings suggest that the threat of terrorism looms large in the public's mind relative to a comparable accident. Infectious diseases provoke considerably more concern than explosions especially for non-terrorist events. The use of suicide with the expressed motive to spread fear heightens perceptions of risk. Likewise, non-terrorist incidents that involve negligence and that are motivated by criminal intent also augment concern. Who the victims are appears to matter but to a lesser extent. Once these mentioned factors are taken into account the effect of casualties on perceived risk appears negligible. These effects are primarily linear but concern appears to taper off slightly at the upper range of worrisome events (e.g. bomb blast). Similar findings were found with regards to the intention to avoid public places during or following a mishap. Females reported a greater perceived risk for the scenarios presented in this study but not a greater intention to avoid public places during such events.

Trust in first responders appears greatest for non-terrorist events involving explosions rather than infectious diseases and resulting in smaller number of casualties. Conversely, trust in government officials is greatest for terrorist events regardless of whether they involve explosions or infectious diseases. This difference appears to be motivated by the perception that terrorism is to some extent political and hence naturally falls within the realm of government officials but accidents require the special professional skills of first responders. However, it is important to note that, since this data was collected, the nation has witnessed a largely ineffective response to Hurricane Katrina on the part of public officials and some first responders (i.e. some police officers). We suspect public trust would be somewhat more guarded if measured now.

We also found that perceived risk is a good predictor of the degree to which the public will report they will alert their friends or pay attention to the media during a threatening event. It also predicts the reported propensity to avoid public places or to leave the area until the event is resolved.

Survey findings were also incorporated into a systems model to examine how fear might diffuse within a community immediately following a terrorist attack or an accident. Scenarios differing in perceptions of risk and length of investigation were simulated to determine their impact on media coverage, word-of-mouth and fear over time. Small increases of either the level of perceived risk or length of the investigation had an amplifying effect on the number of fearful people, and rate of diffusion and duration of fear. Though not the focus of this study, we also varied the level of intervention by social support institutions (not treated separately) to determine its impact on the rate at which people become less fearful. We found that high levels of intervention, especially early on, produced a noticeable decline in fear. Predicted public response was dramatically different for accidents versus terrorist events, a finding consistent with the social amplification of risk framework. This study begins to demonstrate how responses to carefully designed scenarios can provide data and parameters for input into our system dynamics model.

Study limitations

121 students were recruited at a university in the San Diego area during September of 2004. Surveying only students raises questions about the generalizability of our findings beyond a college setting. To address this issue we had participants also respond to recent Gallup Poll questions pertaining to terrorism (e.g. 'How worried are you that you or someone in your family will become a victim of terrorism?') to compare their attitudes and perceptions to responses in a representative national sample. Student answers to these questions were very similar to the Gallup Poll results published in August 2004 suggesting that our participants' responses may be typical of the general population. This study also took place very near to the anniversary of 11 September 2001 and also during the last few months of a presidential campaign in which terrorism was a major issue. As a result, participants' awareness and level of concern about terrorism may have been higher than is typical for them. While our findings may somewhat overestimate public reaction to certain types of hazards, the timing of the study also tended to encourage participants to treat the exercise more seriously as evidenced

by the amount of time they devoted to the task and quality of their responses. In terms of our design, we decided to treat casualties as a between-subjects factor which may in part have accounted for its negligible effect size. However, we also treated suicide/negligence as a between-subjects factor and its effect size was quite large. This was a moderately small sample as well, which posed certain estimation challenges. Most notably our ability to detect higher order factor interactions was not very high (none appeared to be statistically significant but this may be due to low power as well). However, because of the statistical efficiency of our experimental design the main effects we report have very high precision (power calculations above 0.95).

Our model attempts to represent some of the dynamics likely to drive public response to a variety of hazardous events. Model construction was guided by the social amplification of risk framework. However, many of the functional relationships between model variables were based on reasonable but subjective assessments. For example, we know that social support groups and institutions engage the public during a crisis, but we had to subjectively predict the extent, timing and effectiveness of their response? Hence, it would be helpful to corroborative these findings with behavioural data from other terrorist attacks or major disasters. We did compare the level of fear predicted by our model 60 days after an anthrax attack with national surveys that tracked public perceptions following 11 September and found our projections reasonably close. Likewise, we have incorporated a number of important variables but some were not included. For example, we did not model the impact of government response. However, this response most probably would influence not only the behaviour of the media, public and various institutions but impact the magnitude of the event itself. Finally, several of the variables in our systems model are really an aggregate of a number of related variables. This was done for simplicity but these components may not always behave as an aggregate. For example, 'Investigative Intensity' represents the efforts of first responders, and local and federal authorities. However, a propane tank explosion might require intense efforts by first responders and local authorities whereas a terrorist threat may involve nationwide attention from a number of groups.

Policy implications

Policy makers need to prepare for a wide range of threatening events to their communities and the nation. Terrorist acts are likely to spark rapid and prolonged concern as the public learns to cope with the crisis. Conversely, non-terrorist explosions (non-nuclear at least) and natural disasters also have the potential to kill or injure large numbers of people, but events of this kind have a natural closure – it's reasonable to say the area is now safe or the storm is over. Here, it is possible to communicate what happened and why. It is also feasible to tabulate who has been injured and to what extent. In short, it's possible to begin resuming normal activities. Terrorist events are different. Is it reasonable to say the event is over? Is it possible to adequately explain why the attack took place? In the case of a biological, chemical or radiological attack, can we say in the short term, who has been effected and to what extent? The crisis subsides to be sure, but it is unlikely to be fully resolved. We in time make an uneasy truce with the situation and get back to our lives – not entirely unchanged, however. For these reasons terrorism presents a unique challenge to officials wishing to mitigate the effects of a terrorist strike in a community.

Our survey findings suggest that the public may have moderate trust in government officials' ability to reduce the danger during a terrorist event but only limited confidence in first responders' capability to effectively handle such a crisis, especially if it involves infectious diseases. Clearly government officials should play a more visible role in communicating with the public about precautions being taken and coordinating the response during a terrorist incident. Additionally, first responders should consider more actively engaging the community in a variety of terrorism simulations to help engender trust and foster communication with the public. Results from our simulation suggest that the longer the crisis goes unresolved in terms of investigative closure the more opportunity there is for the risk signal to amplify and for fear to spread throughout the community. Likewise, the greater the level of fear in the community the greater the effort required to restore normality among the public. Conversely, intervention by social support groups and institutions can help restore normality. These findings speak to the need for a careful, coordinated and rapid response on the part of government officials, first responders, and community leaders and support groups. An active effort should be made in advance to search for any and all delays in the community's delivery of health care, financial assistance and social support.

Suggestions for future research

Data collection
In this chapter we have focused on hazards that have involved either explosions or infectious diseases. However, it would be very helpful to extend this study to other types of damage mechanisms such as chemical and radiological explosions as well as natural disasters. Natural disasters are especially important because a great deal of behavioural data has been collected following hurricanes, tornados and floods. Comparing survey responses to natural disaster scenarios with reports of actual behaviours gathered in the field would serve as a useful benchmark to other types of disasters in which behavioural data is rare. Additionally, the setting here was a theme park, but of more general interest would be to couch these scenarios in terms of damage to our transportation, communication, energy, water or cyber-systems. These systems are important because damage here is likely to propagate throughout an entire community. We also know very little about how the public might react to multiple terrorist strikes similar to the London bombings. Do these events accelerate public fear or do people adapt depending on how effectively the attacks are handled? To what degree do threats of terrorist attacks provoke the same response as an actual strike? Finally, it would be helpful to know to what

extent people's level of fear during a disaster is influenced from observing the effectiveness of the government's response and the behaviours of others.

Modelling

Many variables likely to influence public reaction (risk signal, media coverage, community intervention) have been modelled. However, other variables such as trust and government response may be needed as well. It would also be helpful to know how these factors change and interact over time contributing to system feedbacks and delays. Hurricane Katrina and most recently the financial crisis have illustrated with devastating clarity how the effects of a calamity can be made much worse by systems delays. Additionally, understanding the influence of demographic characteristics and worldviews on risk perception may help forecast public reaction within a community. Finally, we have modelled the diffusion of fear, but we need to better understand how fear ripples through different sectors of our society potentially causing widespread impacts on the economy.

Acknowledgements

The authors would like to thank Dr Michael Osterholm, director of the Center for Infectious Disease Research and Policy (CIDRAP) at the University of Minnesota for his comments regarding our infectious disease scenarios. This research was supported by the National Science Foundation under grant number SES-0728934. However, any opinions, findings, and conclusions or recommendations in this chapter are those of the authors and do not necessarily reflect views of the National Science Foundation.

Chapter 18

Cultural Cognition of the Risks and Benefits of Nanotechnology

*Dan M. Kahan, Donald Braman, Paul Slovic, John Gastil and Geoffrey Cohen**

How is public opinion towards nanotechnology likely to evolve? The 'familiarity hypothesis' holds that support for nanotechnology will probably grow as awareness of it expands. The basis of this conjecture is opinion polling, which finds that few members of the public claim to know much about nanotechnology, but that those who say they do are substantially more likely to believe its benefits outweigh its risks (Cobb and Macoubrie, 2004; Macoubrie, 2006; Hart Research Associates, 2006, 2007). Some researchers, however, have avoided endorsing the familiarity hypothesis, stressing that cognitive heuristics and biases could create anxiety as the public learns more about this novel science (Scheufele and Lewenstein, 2005; Scheufele, 2006). We conducted an experimental study aimed at determining how members of the public would react to balanced information about nanotechnology risks and benefits. Finding no support for the familiarity hypothesis, the study instead yielded strong evidence that public attitudes are likely to be shaped by psychological dynamics associated with cultural cognition.

Cultural cognition refers to the tendency of people to base their factual beliefs about the risks and benefits of a putatively dangerous activity on their cultural appraisals of these activities (Wildavsky and Dake, 1990; DiMaggio, 1997). From a psychological point of view it is easier to believe that behaviour one finds noble is socially beneficial, and that behaviour one finds debased is dangerous, than vice versa (Douglas, 1966; Gutierrez and Giner-Sorolla, 2007). Those who are 'individualistic' and 'hierarchical' in their cultural worldviews tend to dismiss

---

* Reprinted from Kahan, D. M., Braman, D., Slovic, P., Gastil, J. and Cohen, G. (2008) 'Cultural cognition of the risks and benefits of nanotechnology', *Drug Information Journal*, vol 41, no 1, pp81–100. Supplementary Information accompanies this paper at www.nature.com/nnano/journal/v4/n2/suppinfo/nnano.2008.341_S1.html

claims of environmental risk, for example, because acknowledging such hazards would threaten the autonomy of markets and the authority of social elites. Persons who hold 'egalitarian' and 'communitarian' worldviews, on the other hand, take environmental risks seriously because they believe unregulated markets are a source of inequality and, therefore, harmful to society (Douglas and Wildavsky, 1982; Dake, 1991). Consistent with this dynamic, researchers have found evidence that people of opposing cultural outlooks polarize on various environmental and technological risks – from nuclear power (Peters and Slovic, 1996) and global warming (Leiserowitz, 2005) to genetically modified foods and 'mad cow' disease (Finucane, 2002).

The 'cultural cognition' hypothesis holds that these same patterns are likely to emerge as members of the public come to learn more about nanotechnology. That is, rather than adopt uniformly positive attitudes, as the familiarity hypothesis suggests, members of the public who hold relatively egalitarian and communitarian worldviews will perceive its risks to be greater and its benefits smaller than will those who hold relatively hierarchical and individualistic worldviews.

We designed a public opinion study to test the familiarity and cultural cognition hypotheses. The study reflected an experimental design aimed at detecting causal links, if any, between information exposure and attitude formation. We divided a diverse, national online sample of 1862 Americans into two groups. Those in the 'no-information condition' were told nothing about nanotechnology other than it is a scientific process for producing and manipulating very small particles. Those in the 'information-exposed condition,' in contrast, were furnished with two paragraphs of equal length and comparable information content, one identifying possible benefits of nanotechnology, the other possible risks. We then compared the two groups' perceptions of nanotechnology risks and benefits to see what effect information exposure had.

Like most members of the American public (Hart Research Associates, 2006, 2007), our study subjects reported being relatively unfamiliar with nanotechnology. The vast majority – over 80 per cent – reported having heard either 'just a little' (28 per cent) or 'nothing at all' (54 per cent) about it. Only 4 per cent reported having heard 'a lot' about nanotechnology before the study, and 14 per cent reported having heard 'some,' an amount in between 'just a little' and 'a lot.' Among subjects in the no-information condition, familiarity with nanotechnology was positively correlated with the perception that nanotechnology's benefits outweigh its risks ($r_s = 0.38$, $p < .001$), a finding also consistent with previous public opinion studies (Cobb and Macoubrie, 2004; Macoubrie, 2006; Hart Research Associates, 2006, 2007).

Information exposure had no discernable main effect on subjects' perceptions of nanotechnology risks and benefits. The mean assessment on a four-point risk–benefit measure (NANORISK) for subjects in the information-exposed condition ($M = 2.37$, $SD = 1.03$) was virtually identical to the mean assessment for subjects in the no-information condition ($M = 2.34$, $SD = 0.99$).

To assess whether the impact of information exposure varied based on either familiarity with nanotechnology or cultural worldviews, we performed a multivariate regression analysis. The dependent variable for the analysis was whether subjects perceived the benefits of nanotechnology to be greater than its risks or vice versa. Independent variables included cultural worldview measures, the interaction of those worldviews, the degree of self-reported knowledge, and appropriate interactions of these variables with the experimental condition to which subjects were assigned. This analysis (see Supplementary Information, Figure S1) can be used to determine how information exposure influences individuals either conditional on their cultural worldviews holding their level of familiarity constant, or conditional on their level of familiarity holding their cultural worldviews constant.

The results are illustrated in Figure 18.1. Holding cultural worldviews constant (at the sample mean), information exposure does not have a significant effect on the likelihood that either a subject who is relatively unfamiliar with nanotechnology or one who is relatively familiar with it will perceive the benefits of nanotechnology to be greater than its risks (Figure 18.1a).

In contrast, information on exposure has a relatively large and statistically significant impact on subjects defined with reference to their cultural worldviews (Figure 18.1b). In the no-information condition, subjects whose cultural worldviews are moderately hierarchical and individualistic, on the one hand, and subjects whose worldviews are moderately egalitarian and communitarian, on the other, are equally likely (61 per cent) to see the benefits of nanotechnology as outweighing its risks if we hold their level of self-reported knowledge constant (at the sample mean). In the information-exposed condition, however, the likelihood that

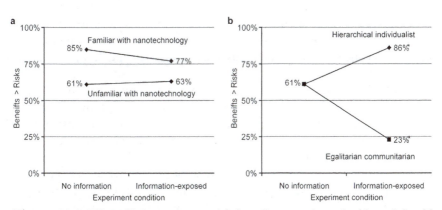

Figure 18.1 *Effect of information on risk–benefit perceptions of subjects defined by self-reported familiarity with nanotechnology and cultural worldviews*

Note: Likelihoods of response are derived by statistical simulation (Gelman and Hill, 2007) from the logistic regression analysis (see Supplementary Information, Table S1):
a Likelihoods of response for the benefits of nanotechnology exceeding the risks in the no-information and information-exposed conditions when cultural worldviews are controlled (set to their means) for respondents who are unfamiliar (bottom line) and familiar (top line) with nanotechnology
b Likelihoods of response across conditions when familiarity is controlled for (set to its mean) and the culture variables are set at values that reflect the worldviews of modestly hierarchical and individualistic subjects (top line), and modestly egalitarian and communitarian ones (bottom line). N = 1672
*Change in likelihood across conditions significant at p < .05.

hierarchical individualists will perceive benefits as greater than risks grows by 25 per cent, while the likelihood that egalitarian communitarians will do so shrinks by 18 per cent – opening up a 63 per cent gap (86 per cent to 23 per cent) between them.

These results support the cultural cognition hypothesis but not the familiarity hypothesis. Our subjects did not react uniformly, much less in a uniformly positive manner, when exposed to information. Instead, they reacted divergently, in a manner consistent with their opposing cultural predispositions toward technological risk generally. This finding displays the signature of 'biased assimilation and polarization' – the tendency of persons to conform information to their predispositions and thus to become more, not less, divided when exposed to balanced information (Lord et al, 1979).

This result also raises the question why those who report greater familiarity with nanotechnology – in the no-information condition of our study and in previous opinion surveys – tend to see the benefits of nanotechnology as great and the risks as small. One possibility is selection bias. The relatively small portion of the population who say they have heard either a modest amount or a great deal about nanotechnology are obviously different from the vast majority who have heard little or nothing. The same set of forces that creates their unique motivation to learn about nanotechnology might also be uniquely disposing these persons to form positive views about it.

The study also yielded two other findings that reinforce this conclusion. First, we found that the subjects (in both conditions) who reported being relatively familiar with nanotechnology – the 18 per cent who claimed to have heard either 'a lot' or 'some' about it – were not only less likely to perceive the risks of nanotechnology as greater than its benefits. They were also less likely than nanotechnology-unfamiliar subjects to be concerned with all manner of risk – whether from genetically modified foods, mad cow disease, nuclear power generation or the Internet (Figure 18.2). Obviously, it is not plausible to think that their familiarity with nanotechnology is the reason these persons are relatively unworried about these other risks. Instead, it is more sensible to think that there is something else that is causing people who are generally sceptical of environmental and technological risks to learn more about (or at least claim they have learned more about) nanotechnology.

The second finding sheds some light on what that influence – or set of influences – might be. Regressing self-reported familiarity with nanotechnology on various individual characteristics revealed that being simultaneously hierarchical and individualistic predicted greater familiarity with nanotechnology (see Supplementary Information, Table S2 and Figure S1). Because these worldviews generally dispose individuals to be sceptical about technological risks (Peters and Slovic, 1996; Finucane, 2002; Leiserowitz, 2005; Kahan et al, 2007), it is no surprise that experimental subjects of this sort reacted positively when exposed to balanced information on nanotechnology. By the same token, it is no surprise that egalitarians and communitarians, who are less likely in the normal course to learn about nanotechnology, react less favourably when such information is brought to their attention.

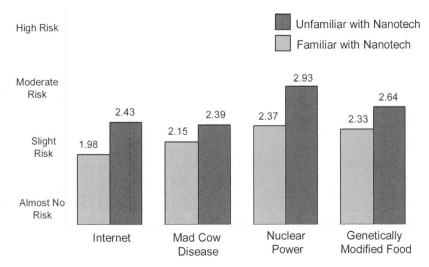

Figure 18.2 *How people familiar and unfamiliar with nanotechnology view the risks and benefits of other technologies*

Note: Risk variables are four-point measures of 'risk to people in American Society' posed by the Internet, mad cow disease, nuclear power and genetically modified food. Canonical correlation between familiarity and the risk measures significant at $p < .01$. Differences between group means all significant at $p < .01$.

In total, the study findings suggest a particular model of how cultural predispositions and exposure to information about nanotechnology work (Figure 18.3). In the model, such predispositions both affect the likelihood of information exposure and moderate how information affects risk–benefit perceptions. People who have a pro-technology cultural orientation are thus more likely to become exposed to information about nanotechnology and to draw positive inferences from what they discover. Individuals who lack that predisposition, in contrast, are less likely to become exposed to information, and when they do become exposed to it they are significantly more likely to react negatively.

Our study reinforces the conclusions of other researchers who have cautioned against assuming that enlightened public opinion will spontaneously emerge from accumulating scientific information on the risks and benefits of nanotechnology (Scheufele and Lewenstein, 2005; Currall et al, 2006). Indeed, because individuals in the real world are likely to select information in a biased fashion that matches their cultural and political dispositions (Mutz and Martin, 2001), one might anticipate even more extreme polarization outside the psychology laboratory than we observed in it when we exposed our subjects to a small bit of balanced information.

At the same time, nothing in our study suggests that cultural polarization over nanotechnology is inevitable. Social psychology is making important advances in identifying techniques for framing information on controversial policy issues in a manner that makes it possible for people of diverse values to derive the same factual information from it (Cohen et al, 2007). With further study, it is likely that

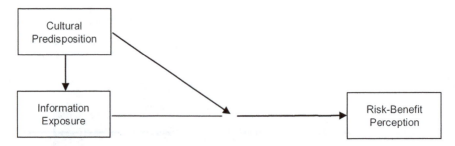

Figure 18.3 *Relationships between cultural worldviews, information*
exposure and risk–benefit perceptions

Note: The study results suggest that cultural worldviews influence perceptions of the risks and benefits of
nanotechnology both by influencing how likely subjects were to be exposed to information (or report being
exposed to information) about nanotechnology, and by determining what effect – positive or negative – they
gave to that information.

these techniques can be used to guide risk communication and thus enhance
democratic deliberations on risk-regulation policy – on nanotechnology
(Scheufele, 2006) and other issues (Kahan et al, 2006).

The practical lesson of our study, then, is that those who favour informed
public deliberations on nanotechnology should be neither sanguine nor bleak.
Instead they should be psychologically realistic. If they are, they will see the urgent
need for additional efforts to develop risk communication strategies that make it
possible for culturally diverse citizens to converge on policies that promote their
common interests.

Methods

The sample consisted of 1862 adults recruited by Knowledge Networks to be
members of a probability-based online panel representative of the United States
population. There has been considerable study of how probability-based online
sampling, which is becoming increasingly common in scholarly public opinion
research, performs relative to random-digit-dial telephone and other survey
methods (Chang and Krosnick, 2003; Miller et al, 2006; Heeren et al, 2008).
More information on the sampling methods of Knowledge Networks can be
found at www.knowledgenetworks.com/ganp/index.html. Subjects participated in
the study using Knowledge Networks' online facilities in December 2006.

In addition to standard demographic data, the study collected data on
subjects' cultural values. Measures, adapted from previous studies of cultural
cognition and the cultural theory of risk (Peters and Slovic, 1996; Peters et al,
2004; Kahan et al, 2007), assessed subjects' values with two scales,
'Individualism–Communitarianism' (α = 0.83) and 'Hierarchy–Egalitarianism'
(α = 0.81). Each scale was designed to measure a separate dimension of the
'group grid' worldview typology proposed by Mary Douglas (1970). In the

regression-based simulation (Figure 18.1), the culture variables for 'hierarchical individualists' were set at values one standard deviation from the mean towards the egalitarian and communitarian ends of those scales.

Subjects' perceptions of nanotechnology were also solicited. All subjects responded to a self-reported knowledge item (NANOKNOW) used in previous studies (Cobb and Macoubrie, 2004; Macoubrie, 2006; Hart Research Associates, 2006, 2007) that stated, 'How much have you heard about nanotechnology before today?' and permitted the responses, 'nothing at all,' 'just a little,' 'some' or 'a lot.' For certain analysis (see Supplementary Information, Table S2 and Figures S1, S2), subjects who answered 'some' or 'a lot' were deemed 'familiar' with nanotechnology, and those who answered 'nothing at all' or 'just a little' were deemed 'unfamiliar.' All subjects also responded to a four-point item (NANOBENEFIT), which required them to indicate whether they believed (1) 'the risks of nanotechnology will greatly outweigh its benefits,' (2) 'the risks of nanotechnology will slightly outweigh its benefits,' (3) 'the benefits of nanotechnology will slightly outweigh its risks,' or (4) 'the benefits of nanotechnology will greatly outweigh its risks.' A reverse-coded item (NANORISK) was used to compute the mean scores for subjects in both conditions. In the multivariate logistic regression analysis (see Supplementary Information, Table S1), responses to this item were collapsed into a dichotomous 'Benefit > Risk' (0) and 'Risk > Benefit' (1) measure.

Before responding to NANOBENEFIT, all subjects read this introductory statement:

> Now we would like to know what you think about nanotechnology. Nanotechnology is the ability to measure, see, predict and make things on the extremely small scale of atoms and molecules. Materials created with nanotechnology can often be made to exhibit very different physical, chemical and biological properties than their normal size counterparts.

Subjects assigned to the information-exposed condition were also asked to read the following two paragraphs (the order of which was rotated) before responding to NANOBENEFIT:

> The potential benefits of nanotechnology include the use of nanomaterials in products to make them stronger, lighter and more effective. Some examples are food containers that kill bacteria, stain-resistant clothing, high performance sporting goods, faster, smaller computers, and more effective skincare products and sunscreens. Nanotechnology also has the potential to provide new and better ways to treat disease, clean up the environment, enhance national security and provide cheaper energy.
>
> While there has not been conclusive research on the potential risks of nanotechnology, there are concerns that some of the same properties that make nanomaterials useful might make them harmful. It is thought that some nanomaterials may be harmful to humans if they are breathed in and might

cause harm to the environment. There are also concerns that invisible, nanotechnology-based monitoring devices could pose a threat to national security and personal privacy.

All subjects, before responding to the items relating to nanotechnology, also indicated their perceptions of a variety of other risks on a four-point scale that permitted them to characterize a set of activities or states of affairs as presenting almost no risk, slight risk, moderate risk or high risk. This item, too, was patterned after one used in previous risk-perception studies (Flynn et al, 1994; Satterfield et al, 2004). Because few subjects ever report seeing 'no risk,' 'almost no risk' has been shown more accurately to separate out the subjects who are the most risk-sceptical from those who are the next most risk-sceptical.

The complete study instrument is available on request from Dan M. Kahan.

Acknowledgements

This research was supported by the National Science Foundation (SES-0621840), the Project on Emerging Nanotechnologies at the Woodrow Wilson International Centre for Scholars, and the Oscar Ruebhausen Fund at Yale Law School. We thank E. Peters for advice on the study design, and R. MacCoun for valuable comments on earlier drafts.

Author contributions

All authors participated in the design of the study, in analysis of the results, and in drafting and revision of the chapter.

Part IV

Risk Knowledge and Risk Communication

Chapter 19

The Social Amplification of Risk: Assessing Fifteen Years of Research and Theory

*Jeanne X. Kasperson, Roger E. Kasperson, Nick Pidgeon and Paul Slovic**

The social amplification of risk framework in brief

More than a decade has elapsed since the introduction in 1988 of the social amplification of risk framework (SARF) by researchers from Clark University (Kasperson, Kasperson, Renn and colleagues) and Decision Research (Slovic and colleagues). During that time various researchers have enlisted the framework to complete a substantial number of empirical studies. All the while, the emergence of a much larger body of relevant knowledge has spawned a lively debate on aspects of the framework. In this chapter we consider these developments, enquiring into refinements, critiques, and extensions of the approach, the emergence of new issues, and the findings and hypotheses growing out of 15 years of empirical research.

The theoretical foundations of SARF are developed in five principal publications (Kasperson et al, 1988; Renn, 1991; Kasperson, 1992; Burns et al, 1993; Kasperson and Kasperson, 1996). The idea arose out of an attempt to overcome the fragmented nature of risk perception and risk communication research by developing an integrative theoretical framework capable of accounting for

---

*   Reprinted from Kasperson, J. X., Kasperson, R. E., Pidgeon, N. and Slovic, P. (2003) 'The social amplification of risk: Assessing fifteen years of research and theory', in N. Pidgeon, R. E. Kasperson and P. Slovic (eds) *The Social Amplification of Risk*, Cambridge University Press, UK. Copyright © 2003 Cambridge University Press. Reprinted with permission.

findings from a wide range of studies, including: from media research; from the psychometric and cultural schools of risk perception research; and from studies of organizational responses to risk. The framework also serves, more narrowly, to describe the various dynamic social processes underlying risk perception and response. In particular, those processes by which certain hazards and events that experts assess as relatively low in risk can become a particular focus of concern and sociopolitical activity within a society (risk amplification), while other hazards that experts judge more serious receive comparatively less attention from society (risk attenuation). Examples of significant hazards subject to social attenuation of risk perceptions might include naturally occurring radon gas, automobile accidents or smoking. On the other hand, social amplification of risk perceptions appears to have been one result of events such as the King's Cross and Lockerbie tragedies in the United Kingdom, the Bhopal (Wilkins, 1987), Chernobyl (Otway et al, 1988) and Three Mile Island accidents, as well as the recent concerns precipitated by 'mad cow' disease (Phillips et al, 2000) and by the future of genetically modified food in Europe (Anand, 1997; Marris et al, 2001).

The theoretical starting-point is the assumption that 'risk events,' which might include actual or hypothesized accidents and incidents (or even new reports on existing risks), will be largely irrelevant or localized in their impact unless human beings observe and communicate them to others (Luhmann, 1979). SARF holds that, as a key part of that communication process, risk, risk events and the characteristics of both become portrayed through various risk signals (images, signs and symbols), which in turn interact with a wide range of psychological, social, institutional or cultural processes in ways that intensify or attenuate perceptions of risk and its manageability (see Figure 19.1). The experience of risk therefore is not only an experience of physical harm but the result of processes by which groups and individuals learn to acquire or create interpretations of risk. These interpretations provide rules of how to select, order and explain signals emanating from the physical world (Renn et al, 1992, p40). With this framework, risk experience can be properly assessed only through the interaction among the physical harms attached to a risk event and the social and cultural processes that shape interpretations of that event, secondary and tertiary consequences that emerge, and the actions taken by managers and publics.

The authors adopt the metaphor of amplification from classical communications theory and use it to analyse the ways in which various social agents generate, receive, interpret and pass on risk signals. Kasperson et al (1988) argue that such signals are subject to predictable transformations as they filter through various social and individual amplification stations. Such transformations can increase or decrease the volume of information about an event, heighten the salience of certain aspects of a message or reinterpret and elaborate the available symbols and images, thereby leading to particular interpretations and responses by other participants in the social system. Amplification stations can include individuals, social groups and institutions, for example, scientists or scientific institutions, reporters and the mass media, politicians and government agencies, or other social groups and their members.

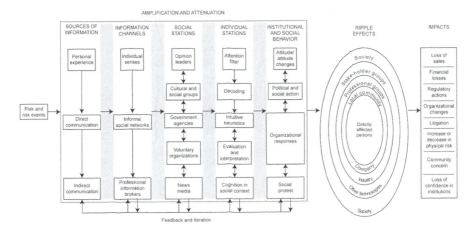

Figure 19.1 *The social amplification of risk framework*

For social stations of amplification, the likes of institutional structure, functions and culture influence the amplification or attenuation of risk signals. Even the individuals in institutions do not simply pursue their personal values and social interpretations; they also perceive the risks, those who manage the risks, and the risk 'problem' according to cultural biases and the values of their organization or group (Johnson and Covello, 1987; Dake, 1991; Rayner, 1992; Peters and Slovic, 1996; Marris et al, 1998).

Individual stations of amplification are affected by such considerations, well documented in the psychometric tradition, as risk heuristics, qualitative aspects of the risks, prior attitudes, blame and trust. These same individuals are also members of cultural groups (e.g. Vaughan, 1995; Palmer et al, 2001) and other social units that co-determine the dynamics and social processing of risk.

In a second stage of the framework, directed primarily at risk-intensification processes, Kasperson et al (1988) argue that social amplification can also account for the observation that some events will produce 'ripples' of secondary and tertiary consequences that may spread far beyond the initial impact of the event and may even eventually impinge upon previously unrelated technologies or institutions. Such secondary impacts include market impacts (perhaps through consumer avoidance of a product or related products), demands for regulatory constraints, litigation, community opposition, loss of credibility and trust, stigmatization of a product, facility, or community, and investor flight. The terrorist attacks of 11 September 2001 in the United States and their ensuing consequences (spanning a range of behavioural, economic and social impacts) provide perhaps the most dramatic recent example of such secondary social amplification effects (Slovic, 2002).

The analogy of dropping a stone into a pond (see Figure 19.1) is apt here as it illustrates the spread of these higher-order impacts associated with the social amplification of risk. The ripples spread outward, first encompassing the directly affected victims or the first group to be notified, then touching the next higher

Table 19.1 *Risk events with potentially high signal value*

Events	Messages
Report that chlorofluorocarbon releases are depleting the ozone layer	A new and possibly catastrophic risk has emerged
Resignation of regulators or corporate officials in 'conscience'	The managers are concealing the risks: they cannot be trusted
News report of off-site migration at a hazardous waste site	The risk managers are not in control of the hazard
Scientific dispute over the validity of an epidemiological study	The experts do not understand the risks
Statement by regulators that the levels of a particular contaminant in the water supply involve only very low risks as compared with other risks	The managers do not care about the people who will be harmed; they do not understand long-term cumulative effects of chemicals

Source: Kasperson et al (1998, p186)
Copyright © 1991 John Wiley & Sons. Reprinted with permission.

institutional level (a company or an agency), and, in more extreme cases, reaching other parts of the industry or other social arenas with similar problems. This rippling of impacts is an important element of risk amplification since it suggests that the processes can extend (in risk amplification) or constrain (in risk attenuation) the temporal, sectoral and geographical scales of impacts. It also points up that each order of impact, or ripple, may not only allocate social and political effects but also trigger (in risk amplification) or hinder (in risk attenuation) managerial interventions for risk reduction.

The record of empirical research

Since SARF is by design inclusive and integrative, the literature of relevant empirical work accomplished over the past 15 years is potentially very large indeed. We begin by addressing the studies that apply the general framework or core ideas and then proceed to more specialized applications and extensions of the framework.

The concept of 'signal'

Slovic et al (1984; also Slovic 1987, 1992) first proposed that hazardous events might hold a 'signal value.' They reported that risks in the upper right-hand sector of the classic dread/knowledge psychometric factor space have high signal value in terms of serving as a warning signal for society, providing new information about the probability that similar or even more destructive mishaps might occur with this type of activity. They also suggest that high signal value might be linked to the potential for second-order effects, and hence may provide a rationale in specific cases for stricter regulation of such risks. The 1988 article suggested risk events that could have high signal value (Table 19.1).

Building upon Slovic's work on risk signals, the research group at Clark University has developed a detailed methodology for identifying, classifying and assessing risk signals in the print media pertaining to the proposed nuclear waste repository at Yucca Mountain in the United States (Kasperson et al, 1992). Risk signals were defined as 'messages about a hazard or hazard event that affect people's perceptions about the seriousness or manageability of the risk.' They analysed the 'signal stream' as it appeared in the *Las Vegas Review Journal* between 1985 and 1989, including the symbols, metaphors and images in news headlines, editorials, letters to the editor and cartoons. The results reveal a dramatic shift in the discourse, symbols and imagery, in which risk-related matters recede in importance in the face of a growing depiction of victimization, distrust, unfairness and villainy.

In an individual difference analysis based upon the psychometric work of Slovic and colleagues, Trumbo (1996) uses people's judgements along the dread/knowledge dimensions to categorize individuals into risk 'amplifiers' and 'attenuators.' He concludes that perceived individual risk (for amplifiers) and satisfaction in institutional response (for attenuators) are the important differences between the two groups in their interpretation of risk signals (cf. also Vlek and Stallen, 1981). Interestingly, he also finds that, among amplifiers, concern over risk is driven more by interpersonal communication than by mediated communication (as in the mass media).

The 128-hazard-events study

This collaborative study between Clark University and Decision Research involved a large comparative statistical analysis of 128 hazard events, including biocidal hazards, persistent/delayed hazards, rare catastrophes, deaths from common causes, global diffuse hazards and natural-hazard events that had occurred in the United States. Researchers used the News file of the Nexis database to collect data on the actual volume of media coverage that each event received and then related the data to judgements made by experts and student panels of the physical consequences, risk perceptions, public response, potential for social group mobilization and the potential for second-order societal impacts of each event. Findings indicated particularly that social amplification processes are as important as direct physical consequences in determining the full array of potential risk consequences. Hence, a risk assessment that is based solely upon direct physical consequences might seriously underestimate the full range of consequences of an event. Among the conclusions from this work (Kasperson et al, 1992; Renn et al, 1992) are the following:

- A high degree of 'rationality' is evident in how society responds to hazards (e.g. volume of press coverage is roughly proportional to first-order physical consequences; risk perceptions incorporate aspects of human exposure and management performance).

- Extent of exposure to the direct consequences of a hazard has more effect on risk perceptions and potential social group mobilization than do injuries and fatalities.
- The contention that public perception mirrors media coverage needs further careful empirical study (no perceptual variable – except the ubiquitous dread – correlated with the extent of media coverage once the extent of damage was controlled for).
- The role of risk signals and blame attributable to incompetent risk management seemed particularly important to public concerns (see also Burns et al, 1993). Situations involving blame of corporations or government agencies after the event appear particularly worthy of further study.

Two limitations of this quantitative study bear noting. The outcome variable for the magnitude of secondary consequences was a judgement by experts rather than a direct measure of actual societal impact. Hence, the analysis neither demonstrates, nor concludes, that heightened perceptions as a result of media coverage will necessarily lead to secondary impacts and rippling, a point to which we return below. Secondly, the indices of media coverage used were primarily quantitative (volume) rather than qualitative (the content of what is presented in media reports), so did not allow a test of whether the media significantly alter risk representations (a question taken up by Freudenburg et al, 1996).

Qualitative field studies

The qualitative study by Kasperson and colleagues (reported in Kasperson, 1992) yielded complementary findings to the quantitative cross-risk work. Six risk events (four in the United States, one in Brazil and one in Germany) – all but one involving some form of nuclear hazard – were studied in depth. The cases were: a transportation accident involving low-level radioactive material in Queens, New York; a serious 1982 nuclear plant accident in Ginna, New York; a brine seepage controversy at a planned nuclear waste facility in Carlsbad, New Mexico; the closure of a hazardous waste site on Long Island (Glen Cove, New York); a construction accident at a planned nuclear waste disposal facility in Gorleben, Germany; and a radioactive accident in Goiania, Brazil (Petterson, 1988). Components of the amplification framework explored included physical impacts, information flow, social-group mobilization and rippling effects. Interviews with key participants were conducted in each case. This set of in-depth case studies yielded the following conclusions:

- Even heavy and sustained media coverage does not by itself ensure risk amplification or significant secondary effects. In some cases the secondary effects expected by the researchers failed to materialize. Trust (see also Kasperson et al, 1992; Slovic, 1993) appears to be a relevant critical issue, as are perceptions of the managerial handling of the accident and emergency response.

- The cases pointed to layering of attenuation/intensification effects across different groups and at different scales. Specifically, amplification at the national or regional scale accompanied by attenuation at the local scale may not be uncommon.
- Following on from the first point, it may be that several factors need to be present in combination (e.g. media coverage plus the focused attention of a local interest group, or an accident plus suspicions of incompetence) to generate what Kasperson (1992) terms 'take-off' (see also Gerlach, 1987; Cvetkovich and Earle, 1991) of an issue. Other examples of this can be found. Referring to the 1911 Triangle Shirtwaist Company fire in New York, Behrens (1983, p373) concluded that 'a disaster only prepares the groundwork for change ... the potential for reform created by a disaster can be fulfilled only if the appropriate interest groups recognize and successfully use the opportunities available to them.' With respect to nuclear power, Slovic et al (2000a) found much higher levels of trust in experts, government and science to manage the risks in France (where until quite recently this technology has not been a source of significant social conflict) as compared with the United States.
- The economic benefits associated with risks appear to be a significant source of attenuation at the local level (see also Metz, 1996).

As a result of both these quantitative and qualitative studies, further research might usefully focus upon the following: case studies giving insight into full social context; cultural studies (particularly those exploring the cultural prototypes drawn upon to interpret risk communications); and investigations of how different communities experience similar risks.

Desired risk

Arguing that studies of hazards and risks have virtually overlooked a range of human activity (e.g. hang-gliding, rock climbing, dirt biking, etc.) involving the deliberate seeking of risk, Machlis and Rosa (1990) have explored whether SARF can be extended to this domain of risk (also Rosa, 1998, 2003). Evaluating key propositions and current knowledge about desired risks, the authors reach several conclusions. First, they find the social amplification concept quite suitable for incorporating desired risk, although some terminology (e.g. 'victims') may need to be recast. Second, the key variables defined in the framework are appropriate but may need to be broadened to treat such issues as benefits as part of consequences and mass culture (as subsequently incorporated in the framework). Third, individual processing of risk can lead to increased risk-taking, an outcome not addressed in the early conceptual statements or empirical studies. Generally, their application of the social amplification conception led the authors to conclude that 'the framework has promise, since it generally performed well against the evidence examined' (Machlis and Rosa, 1990, p67).

Communications and the mass media

In one of the earliest studies of mass-media coverage of risks and public perceptions, Combs and Slovic (1979) analysed two United States newspapers for their reporting of various causes of death. They found that homicides, accidents and some natural disasters systematically received heavy coverage, whereas death from diseases received only light treatment. Whereas the authors noted that these patterns of coverage correlated with lay public judgements of the frequency of these causes of death, they also pointed out that substantial further research would be needed to define the relationships between mass-media coverage and the formation of opinion concerning risk.

Subsequent research suggests how complicated these relations are. Allan Mazur (1984) has examined media coverage of Love Canal and the Three Mile Island accident and argues that the massive quantity of media coverage, independent of the specific content, influenced public perceptions of the seriousness of the events and the political agenda of social groups and institutions. In a subsequent examination of mass-media coverage of nuclear power and chemical hazards, Mazur (1990, p295) found evidence that '... extensive reporting of a controversial technological or environmental project not only arouses public attention, but also pushes it toward opposition.' This may occur, Mazur argues, even when the treatment in the news is balanced. He proposes a theory with four interrelated propositions:

1   A few national news organizations are very influential in selecting which hazards receive most attention each year.
2   Public actions to alleviate a hazard or oppose a particular technology rise and fall with the amount of media reporting.
3   Public concerns over a risk or technology rise as press and television coverage increases.
4   It is important to distinguish between the substantive content of a news story about risk and the simple image that the story conveys.

Not all agree. Renn (1991) argues that the pure volume effect is only one of many influences of the media on public perceptions of risk. Filtering effects, deleting and adding information, mixing effects (changing the order of information in messages), equalizing effects (changing the context) and what he calls 'stereo effects' (multi-channel effects) can all be important. Some analyses (e.g. Singer and Endreny, 1993, p163) argue that the media report on risk events and not risk issues, and on harms rather than risks. Others see the media, whether providing warning or reassuring messages, as extensively framing discourse and perceptions in which the social processing of risk occurs (Wilkins, 1987; Wilkins and Patterson, 1991; Bohölm, 1998). Lichtenberg and MacLean (1991) have pointed out that cross-cultural media research is difficult to conduct because the news media are so diverse and are influenced by the political cultures in which they operate.

Using the 128 hazard events from the Clark University–Decision Research study, Freudenburg et al (1996) examined the amount of media coverage, public demand for further information, estimates of damage, dread, 'outrage' and anger and recreancy (the misuse of authority or failure to merit public trust; Freudenburg, 2003). As part of their analysis, the researchers read not only the Nexis abstracts but the entire original articles, complete with headlines and accompanying photography and artwork. The authors conclude, despite common beliefs to the contrary, that media coverage overall did not exaggerate risks or display an 'anti-technology' bias. Indeed, among the factors examined, only those involving the 'objective' severity of the event showed any significant predictive power for the amount of coverage devoted to risk events (Freudenburg et al, 1996, p40). Indeed, if anything, the general pattern was for full news articles to de-emphasize the severity of the risks and to provide reassurance. On the other hand, an analysis of television coverage of environmental biotechnology revealed a tendency to focus on extremes, and unknown risks, and to be superficial and incomplete (McCabe and Fitzgerald, 1991).

Although the dramatization of risks and risk events in the media has received much attention, the circularity and tight interrelations between the media and other components of social amplification processes (e.g. contextual effects, historical settings, interest-group activity, public beliefs) render it difficult to determine the specific effects of the volume and content of media coverage. There can be no doubt that the mass media are an important element in communication systems, the processing of risk in amplification stations, and, as Vaughan and Seifert (1992) have persuasively argued, how risk problems are framed and socially constructed. And Renn's (1991) recommended attention to coding, decoding, filtering and stereo processes remains a highly promising avenue of research. From a social amplification perspective, other interesting questions centre upon how the mass media interact with other elements of social amplification processes to construct, intensify, dampen and modify signals concerning risk and its manageability. In addition to analyses aimed at discerning of media-specific influence components of amplification, the search for patterns, syndromes or dynamics of interrelationship and the conditions under which they take particular forms is a promising avenue of amplification research.

Hidden hazards

Risk events, when they undergo substantial amplification and result in unexpected public alarms or what some would call 'social shocks' (Lawless, 1977), often surprise managers and others. No less remarkable is the extreme attenuation of certain risk events so that, despite serious consequences for the risk bearers and society more generally, they pass virtually unnoticed and untended, often continuing to grow in effects until reaching disaster proportions. Kasperson and Kasperson (1991) describe such highly attenuated risks as 'hidden hazards' and offer a theoretical explanation for their existence. Hidden hazards, in their view, have to do with both the nature of the hazards themselves and the nature of the societies and cultures in which they occur. The 'hiding' of hazards is at once purposeful and unintentional, life threatening and institution sustaining, systematic and incidental.

The Kaspersons describe five aspects of such hazards that drive attenuation, each associated with differing causal agents and processes. Global elusive hazards involve a series of complex problems (regional interactions, slow accumulation, lengthy time lags, diffuse effects). Their incidence in a politically fragmented and unequal world tends to mute their signal power in many societies. Ideological hazards remain hidden principally because they lie embedded in a societal web of values and assumptions that attenuates consequences, elevates associated benefits, or idealizes certain beliefs. Marginal hazards befall people who occupy the edges of cultures, societies or economies where they are exposed to hazards that are remote from or concealed by those at the centre or in the mainstream. Many in such marginal situations are already weakened or highly vulnerable while they enjoy limited access to entitlements and few alternative means of coping. Amplification-driven hazards have effects that elude conventional types of risk assessment and environmental impact analysis and are often, therefore, allowed to grow in their secondary consequences before societal intervention occurs. And, finally, value-threatening hazards alter human institutions, lifestyles and basic values, but because the pace of technological change so outstrips the capacity of social institutions to respond and adapt, disharmony in purpose, political will and directed effort impede effective responses and the hazards grow. The presence of some of these 'hidden hazards' has been documented in subsequent analyses of environmental degradation and delayed societal responses in nine regions around the world (Kasperson et al, 1995, 1999).

Organizational amplification and attenuation

As yet, limited attention has addressed the role of organizations and institutions in the social processing of risk. Pidgeon (1997) has suggested that linking risk amplification to the considerable empirical base of knowledge concerning organizational processes intended to prevent large-scale failures and disasters would be an important extension of the framework. Most contemporary risks originate in sociotechnical systems (see Turner, 1978; Perrow, 1984; Short and Clarke, 1992) rather than natural phenomena so that risk management and internal regulatory processes governing the behaviour of institutions in identifying, diagnosing, prioritizing and responding to risks are key parts of the broader amplification process. As Short (1992) points out, large organizations increasingly set the context and terms of debate for society's consideration of risk. Understanding amplification dynamics, then, requires insight into how risk-related decisions relate to organizational self-interest, messy inter- and intra-organizational relationships, economically related rationalizations and 'rule of thumb' considerations that often conflict with the view of risk analysis as a scientific enterprise (Short, 1992, p8). Since major accidents are often preceded by smaller incidents and risk warnings, how signals of incubating hazards are processed within institutions and communicated to others outside the institution do much to structure society's experience with technological and industrial risks.

Noting the relative void of work on organizational risk processing, Freudenburg (1992) has examined characteristics of organizations that serve to attenuate risk signals and ultimately to increase the risks posed by technological systems. These include such attributes as the lack of organizational commitment to the risk management function, the bureaucratic attenuation of information flow within the organization (and particularly on a 'bad news' context), specialized divisions of labour that create 'corporate gaps' in responsibility, amplified risk-taking by workers, the atrophy of organizational vigilance to risk as a result of a myriad of factors (e.g. boredom, routinization) and imbalances and mismatches in institutional resources. Freudenburg concludes that these factors often work in concert to lead even well-meaning and honest scientists and managers to under-estimate risks. In turn, such organizational attenuation of risk serves systematically and repeatedly to amplify the health and environmental risks that the organization is entrusted to anticipate and to control.

Other studies of organizational handling of risk confirm Freudenburg's analy-sis and provide further considerations. In an analysis of safety management at Volvo, Svenson (1988a) found that patterns of access to various parties to reliable information about hazards, understanding of the relation between changes in the product and changes in safety levels, attributes of the information network that informs various interested parties about changes in safety (either positive or negative) and the presence of organizational structures for negotiating about risk between the producer and other social institutions were all important. In her analysis of the Challenger accident in the United States, Diane Vaughan (1992, 1996) also found communication and information issues to be critical but argued that structural factors, such as pressures from a competitive environment, resource scarcity in the organization, vulnerability of important subunits and characteristics of the internal safety regulation system were equally important. In counterpoint to these assessments, the well-known DuPont safety culture has sought to identify characteristics that amplify even minor risks at the corporation so as to achieve high attentiveness to risk reduction throughout the organization (Kasperson and Kasperson, 1993). La Porte and colleagues have examined similar amplification mechanisms in high-reliability organizations that drive performance to error minimization (Weick, 1987; Roberts, 1989; La Porte, 1996), as have Pidgeon and O'Leary (1994, 2000) in their analysis of safety cultures and the use of incident reporting in aviation contexts.

Several theoretical perspectives on organizational processing of risk can be drawn upon within the amplification/attenuation framework. When considering individual responses to hazards within organizations, the idea of psychological denial of threatening information has had a particularly long history (see, for example, Leventhal, 1970). Perhaps surprisingly, however, this topic has only rarely been investigated in contemporary psychological risk research, where the current 'cold' cognitive paradigm for understanding responses to hazard and environmental threat, based upon the two traditions of cognitive psychology and decision-making research, has long undervalued the role of 'hot' motivational variables upon behaviour and choice. Notable exceptions are the studies by Janis and Mann (1977) on decision making under stress, the related threat-coping model of Stallen and Tomas (1988) and the treatment of worry by MacGregor (1991). More recent work has now begun to explore the relationship between affective variables and risk perceptions (Finucane et al, 2000a; Langford, 2002; Slovic et al, 2002).

Evidence of a range of broad social and organizational preconditions to large-scale accidents is available in the work of Turner (1978; see also Turner and Pidgeon, 1997). As a result of a detailed analysis of 84 major accidents in the United Kingdom, Turner concluded that such events rarely come about for any single reason. Rather, it is typical to find that a number of undesirable events accumulate, unnoticed or not fully understood, often over a considerable number of years, which he defines as the disaster incubation period. Preventive action to remove one or more of the dangerous conditions or a trigger event, which might be a final critical error or a slightly abnormal operating condition, brings this period to an end. Turner focuses in particular upon the information difficulties, which are typically associated with the attempts of individuals and organizations to deal with uncertain and ill-structured safety problems, during the hazard-incubation period.

Finally, in a series of persuasive case studies of foreign and domestic policy decisions, Janis (1982) describes the small group syndrome of groupthink, marked primarily by a strong concurrence-seeking tendency in highly cohesive policy-making groups. Particular symptoms of groupthink include an over-estimation by members of the group's inherent morality as well as of its power to influence events, a collective closed-mindedness (or mindset) to new information, and pressures within the group towards conformity to the majority view. Janis argues that the groupthink syndrome is responsible for a range of observable decision-making defects, including incomplete searches for new information, biased appraisal of available information and a failure to work out contingency plans to cope with uncertainties.

Despite these valuable explorations, our knowledge of risk amplification and attenuation in different types of institutions remains thin and eclectic. Systematic application of the amplification framework in a comparative study of organizations, issues and institutions (see e.g. the work comparing regulation of radon, chemicals and BSE by Rothstein, 2003) might well yield highly useful results, particularly demonstrating how signals are denied, de-emphasized or misinterpreted.

Imagery and stigma

The 1988 article that set forth SARF identified stigmatization as one of four major response mechanisms of amplification processes. Research on risk stigmatization was only beginning at that time, both in the path-breaking work of Edelstein (1987) and as part of the Decision Research studies on public perceptions of the proposed Yucca Mountain nuclear waste repository (Slovic et al, 1991a, c, 1994; Flynn et al, 1998). Subsequent work has underscored the importance of stigmatization as a principal route by which risk amplification can generate ripples and secondary consequences (Flynn et al, 2001).

It is clear from this work that stigma-induced effects associated with risky technologies, products or places may be substantial. Nuclear energy, for example, once so highly regarded for its promise for cheap, safe power, is today subject to severe stigmatization, reflecting public perceptions of abnormally great risk, distrust of management and the disappointment of failed promises. Certain products of biotechnology also have been rejected in part because of perceptions of risk. Milk produced with the aid of bovine growth hormone (BGH, or bovine somatotrophin, BST) is one example, with many supermarket chains refusing to buy milk products from BGH-treated cows. Startling evidence of stigmatization of one of the modern world's most important classes of technology comes from studies by Slovic and others. Asking people to indicate what comes to mind when they hear or read the word 'chemicals,' researchers find that the most frequent response tends to be 'dangerous' or some closely related term such as 'toxic,' 'hazardous,' 'poison' or 'deadly.' A study of public images of a proposed nuclear waste storage facility provides telling evidence of the potential stigmatization of such a facility (Table 19.2).

The ancient Greeks used the word 'stigma' to refer to a mark placed on an individual to signify infamy or disgrace. A person thus marked was perceived to pose a risk to society. An extensive literature, much stimulated by the seminal work of Goffman (1963), exists on the topic of stigma as it applies to people. By means of its association with risk, the concept of stigma recently has been generalized to technologies, places and products that are perceived to be unduly dangerous.

Stigmatized places, products and technologies tend to share several features (Gregory et al, 1995, p221). The source of the stigma is a hazard with characteristics, such as dread consequences and involuntary exposure, that typically contributes to high public perceptions of risk. Its impacts are often perceived to be distributed inequitably across groups (for example, children and pregnant women are affected disproportionately) or geographical areas (one city bears the risks of hazardous waste storage for an entire state). Often the impacts are unbounded, in the sense that their magnitude or persistence over time is not well known. A critical aspect of stigma is that a standard of what is right and natural has been violated or overturned because of the abnormal nature of the precipitating event (crude oil on pristine beaches and the destruction of valued wildlife) or the discrediting nature of the consequences (innocent people are injured or killed). As a result, management of the hazard is brought into question as concerns surface regarding competence, conflicts of interest or a failure to apply needed safeguards and controls.

Stigmatization of places has resulted from the extensive media coverage of contamination at sites such as Times Beach, Missouri, and Love Canal, New York. Other well-known examples of environmental stigmatization include Seveso, Italy, where dioxin contamination following an industrial accident at a chemical plant resulted in local economic disruptions estimated to be in excess of $100 million, and portions of the French Riviera and Alaskan coastline in the aftermath of the Amoco Cadiz and Exxon Valdez oil spills.

Table 19.2 *Images associated with an 'underground nuclear waste storage facility'*

Category	Frequency	Images included in category
1. Dangerous	179	Dangerous, danger, hazardous, toxic, unsafe, harmful, disaster
2. Death/sickness	107	Death, dying, sickness, cancer
3. Negative	99	Negative, wrong, bad, unpleasant, terrible, gross, undesirable, awful, dislike, ugly, horrible
4. Pollution	97	Pollution, contamination, leakage, spills, Love Canal
5. War	62	War, bombs, nuclear war, holocaust
6. Radiation	59	Radiation, nuclear, radioactive, glowing
7. Scary	55	Scary, frightening, concern, worried, fear, horror
8. Somewhere else	49	Wouldn't want to live near one, not where I live, far away as possible
9. Unnecessary	44	Unnecessary, bad idea, waste of land
10. Problems	39	Problems, trouble
11. Desert	37	Desert, barren, desolate
12. Non-Nevada locations	35	Utah, Arizona, Denver
13. Nevada/Las Vegas	34	Nevada (25), Las Vegas (9)
14. Storage location	32	Caverns, underground salt mine
15. Government/industry	23	Government, politics, big business

Note: Basis: $N = 402$ respondents in Phoenix, Arizona.

Source: Slovic et al (1991c, p693)

Copyright © 1991 John Wiley & Sons. Reprinted with permission

Stigmatization of products can also occur and result in severe losses. A dramatic example is that of the pain reliever Tylenol, where, despite quick action on the part of the manufacturer, Johnson and Johnson, seven tampering-induced poisonings that occurred in 1982 cost the company more than $1.4 billion. Another well-known case of product stigmatization occurred in the spring of 1989, when millions of United States consumers stopped buying apples and apple products because of their fears that the chemical Alar (used then as a growth regulator by apple growers) could cause cancer. Apple farmers saw wholesale prices drop by about one-third and annual revenues decline by more than $100 million. More recently, the BSE (bovine spongiform encephalopathy) affair stigmatized the European beef industry resulting in billions of dollars in losses and a crisis in trust and confidence in risk management in the United Kingdom (Phillips et al, 2000), while the perceptions of the spring 2001 foot-and-mouth epidemic in the United Kingdom (Poortinga et al, 2004) led to large losses to the rural economy as people cancelled trips to the United Kingdom countryside and Britain (see Harvey, 2001).

Kasperson et al (2001) have extended the social amplification model, as shown in Figure 19.2, to enhance its applicability to analysing stigmatization processes. In this adaptation, the early part of the amplification framework

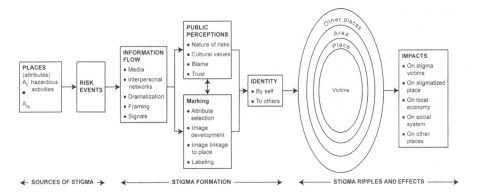

Figure 19.2 *Risk amplification and stigmatization*

remains the same, with risk events generating information flow and social communication treating the risk. Not only do public perceptions and imagery emerge or become modified, but the associated technologies, products or places become marked. Marking involves the selection of a particular attribute of a place or technology and focuses on some symbol or physical representation of the place. In Hawthorne's *The Scarlet Letter*, it was the letter A; in Nazi Germany, it was the yellow star. At Richland, the host community of the Hanford Reservation in the United States, it is the mushroom cloud insignia worn on school sport uniforms. Research by Mitchell et al (1988) has provided extensive evidence of such marking, imagery and stigmatization. Labelling, such as the use of the term 'dump site,' is an essential part of such marking. Eventually, amplification dynamics and imagery formation can fundamentally alter the identity of the place or technology, so that it is viewed as tainted and discredited by residents of the place, workers in the technology, and by outsiders. And, as a result, stigma-induced ripple effects and secondary consequences follow.

Extending the current knowledge base of risk-induced stigma and their effects is, in our opinion, a high-priority area for research on social amplification. Such stigma effects currently raise the spectre of gridlock for important avenues of technology development and for public policy initiatives. Can we anticipate which new technologies may become stigmatized through amplification processes? Can, and should, stigma effects be counteracted? How can responsible authorities act to ameliorate stigma-induced gridlock and the associated fallout on trust and confidence? What are the broad implications for risk management and risk communication?

Trust and confidence

The original framework article (Kasperson et al, 1988) hypothesized four major pathways or mechanisms – heuristics and values, social group relationships, signal value and stigmatization – in the second stage of amplification. High or growing social distrust of responsible institutions and their managers is certainly a fifth. A broad literature now indicates that recurrent failures in risk management stem in no small part from a failure to recognize the more general requirements of democratic society, and especially the need for social trust (see e.g. contributions to Cvetkovich and Löfstedt, 1999). Accordingly, risk control efforts have frequently gone awry due to a lack of openness and 'transparency,' a failure to consult or involve so-called 'interested' and 'affected' persons, a loss of social trust in managers, inadequacies in due process, a lack of responsiveness to public concerns or an insensitivity to questions of environmental justice. Such interpretations abound across a wide spectrum of environmental and risk debates: global warming, biodiversity, genetic engineering, clean-up of defence and other hazardous wastes, the siting of hazardous waste facilities and the protection of wetlands. As Ruckelshaus warned:

> *Mistrust engenders a vicious descending spiral. The more mistrust by the public, the less effective government becomes at delivering what people want and need; the more government bureaucrats in turn respond with enmity towards the citizens they serve, the more ineffective government becomes, the more people mistrust it, and so on, down and down.*
> (Ruckelshaus, 1996, p2)

Ruckelshaus's dread spiral is reminiscent of United States Supreme Court Justice Stephen Breyer's tripartite 'vicious circle – public perception, Congressional reaction and the uncertainties of the regulatory process' (Breyer, 1993, p50) – that thwarts effective risk management. Slovic (1993, 2000a) has argued that trust emerges slowly, is fragile and easily destroyed. And once lost, it may prove to be extremely difficult to recover. He posits an 'asymmetry principle' to explain why it is easier to destroy than to create trust: negative (trust-destroying) events are more visible or noticeable than positive (trust-building) events. Negative events often take the form of specific, well-defined incidents such as accidents, lies, discoveries of errors or other mismanagement. Positive events, although sometimes visible, are often fuzzy or indistinct. Events that are invisible or poorly defined carry little weight in shaping our attitudes and opinions. And even when events do come to our attention, negative (trust-destroying) events carry much greater weight than positive events (see Slovic, 1993; also Cvetkovich et al, 2002).

Trust is typically discussed in terms of an implicit relationship between two or more parties. It has long been discussed as a facet of political culture that facilitates the working of the political system (Almond and Verba, 1980; Inglehart, 1988), and more recently as an important dimension of social capital (Coleman, 1990, pp300–321; Putnam, 1993, 1995). It also functions to reduce complexity in our social environment (Barber, 1984), hence making life more predictable. Renn and Levine (1991) list five attributes of trust:

- competence (do you have the appropriate technical expertise?);
- objectivity (are your messages free from bias?);

- fairness (are all points of view acknowledged?);
- consistency (of your statements and behaviour over time?);
- faith (a perception of your good will?).

They argue that trust underlies confidence, and where this is shared across a community one has credibility. A somewhat different view of social trust is provided by Earle and Cvetkovich (1995; also Siegrist and Cvetkovich, 2000; Siegrist et al, 2000), who argue that it is similarity in our basic values, rather than attributes of technical competence, that underlies whom we trust or distrust. Hunt et al (1999) have recently shown that both perceived 'truthfulness' and 'expertise' are important but perhaps superficial factors as well. One public policy implication of the trust research is that we need to frame the principal goals of risk communication around building trust through participation (Royal Society, 1992; NRC, 1996; United Kingdom Interdepartmental Liaison Group on Risk Assessment, 1998b). The candid communication by an agency of risk uncertainties to people, however, can signal honesty for some while invoking greater distrust in others. Moreover, given that conflict is endemic to many risk controversies, effective risk communication may follow only if a resolution of conflict is obtained first, perhaps by searching for decision options that address all of the stakeholder's principal values and concerns (Edwards and von Winterfeldt, 1987; Renn et al, 1995; Arvai et al, 2001) or by identifying superordinate goals to which all parties can agree. Despite these difficulties, broad 'stakeholder' participation is also increasingly seen, often alas uncritically, as essential to the wider processes of risk assessment and management and a route to success (see, in particular, NRC, 1996).

Issues of social trust are clearly important components of the dynamics of social amplification. We know that distrust acts to heighten risk perceptions, to intensify public reactions to risk signals, to contribute to the perceived unacceptability of risk and to stimulate political activism to reduce risk (Flynn et al, 1993b; English, 1992; Jenkins-Smith, 1991; Kasperson et al, 1992; Löfstedt and Horlick-Jones, 1999). But a host of questions surrounds the interpretation of trust and its effects: there are many types of trust, the processes that create and destroy trust are not well understood, trust (or distrust) exists at multiple levels of the political system, complex attribution issues prevail, and policy responses and their effectiveness are opaque (see Cvetkovich and Löfstedt, 1999). From a social amplification perspective, trust is highly interrelated with other components and mechanisms in what we think of as 'amplification dynamics.' Understanding how trust is shaped, altered, lost or rebuilt in the processing of risk by social and individual stations of risk is a priority need in social amplification research.

Ripple effects

Since the 1988 framework article, the systematic, cross-hazard study of ripple effects and secondary/tertiary consequences has also been a priority research need. It has yet to occur. The 128-hazard-event study did elicit expert estimates, informed by documentary evidence, of event consequences. The results were highly suggestive. The societal processing of risk by media, social groups, institutions and individuals played a critical role in the overall magnitude and scope of societal impacts. For risk events that were highly amplified, the amplification-driven impacts frequently exceeded the primary (i.e. health, environmental and direct economic) effects. We also know that ripple effects can be charted and measured along temporal, geographical and sectoral dimensions. Such a broad-based and systematic empirical study could provide invaluable new information for understanding how social amplification processes affect the rippling of effects, the durability of such effects, possible contagion effects on other risks and overall impacts of rippling upon social capital, such as trust.

What we now have is some suggestive cases. In Goiania in Brazil, a strongly amplified radiological accident produced dramatic rippling of secondary risk consequences. As reported elsewhere (Petterson, 1988), within the first weeks of the media coverage, more than 100,000 persons, of their own volition, stood in line to be monitored with Geiger counters for indication of external radiation. Within two weeks of the event, the wholesale value of agricultural production within Goias, the Brazilian state in which Goiania is located, had fallen by 50 per cent, owing to consumer concerns over possible contamination, even though no contamination was ever found in the products. Even eight months after the event, when prices had rebounded by about 90 per cent, a significant adverse impact was still apparent. During the three months following the accident, the number and prices of homes sold or rented within the immediate vicinity of the accident plummeted. Hotel occupancy in Goiania, normally near capacity at this time of year, had vacancy levels averaging about 40 per cent in the six weeks following the São Paulo television broadcast, while the Hotel Castros, one of the largest in Goiania, lost an estimated 1000 reservations as a direct consequence of risk perceptions and stigma. Meanwhile, Caldas Novas, a hot-springs tourist attraction located a full one-hour drive from Goiania, experienced a 30–40 per cent drop in occupancy rates immediately following the São Paulo television broadcast. Hotels in other parts of Brazil refused to allow Goiania residents to register. Some airline pilots refused to fly airplanes that had Goiania residents aboard. Cars with Goias licence plates were stoned in other parts of Brazil. Even nuclear energy as a whole in Brazil was affected, as several political parties used the accident to mobilize against 'nuclear weapons, power, or waste' and to introduce legislation designed to split the National Nuclear Energy Commission into separate divisions. Increased public opposition to nuclear energy was apparent throughout Brazil. Even international ripples of the accident became apparent as Goiania became a frequent benchmark and rallying cry in anti-nuclear publications throughout the world.

Arvind Susarla (2003) at Clark University compared two risk events in India, one of which was highly amplified and the other attenuated. The amplified event was the discovery of bacterium *Yersinia pestis* in the city of Surat, which led to a plague scare in India. With media reports of increasing evidence of pneumonic plague, rumours about a large number of deaths due to the disease spread in the city. Despite assurances of safety and mitigative measures from local authorities, the rumours triggered widespread public concern and an extreme public response within hours of the initial reports of the plague. At its peak, over 200,000 persons are believed to have deserted the city of Surat, and hundreds of others reported to the public and private hospitals. Authorities in several nearby cities, meanwhile, were alerted to the possible arrivals of plague patients from Surat. Administrative officials responded by ordering a series of precautionary steps, including the medical screening of persons from Surat at the bus and train stations and the closure of schools, colleges, public gatherings and meetings, and theatres. These initiatives amplified concerns and alarm that the disease might spread to other parts of the country. Media coverage of the episode is complex as highly exaggerated death tolls were reported in the English-language dailies whereas Hindi-language newspapers insisted there was no plague and accused neighbouring Pakistan of a smear campaign aimed at bringing India's economy to its knees. The combination of public concern, media reporting and the actions of authorities also resulted in higher-order impacts due to the hazard event. Many countries imposed travel restrictions on people travelling to and from India. Iran's foreign minister postponed his visit to India. Trade embargoes, withdrawal of personnel by multinational firms and cancellations of many airline international flights reflect the extent of risk ripples produced by the hazard event.

Barnett et al (1992) report a clear decline (albeit temporary) of one-third, in the use of the DC-10 for domestic United States flights following a serious and heavily publicized crash at Sioux City, Iowa in 1989. Such secondary consequences may emerge only on a case-by-case basis and may require the presence of several factors in order to emerge fully (in this case, the DC-10 had a historically untrustworthy image following a spate of crashes in the 1970s). However, the effects were very temporary (less than two months). In a very different social 'risk' domain, that of the impacts of media violence, Hill (2001) argues that it is the politics of social group mobilization (around campaigns against particularly violent videos or movies) which is the key driver of secondary amplification effects such as increased censorship and regulation.

Metz (1996) has conducted a historical impact analysis of stigma (stage 2) effects around United States weapons sites. His claim is that, although anticipated stigma or other second-order amplification consequences might be a common response when individuals are asked to imagine the future, few of the anticipated negative consequences of siting a hazard in a community (loss of business, decline in land values etc.) were actually manifest in his research over the longer term. This is a controversial conclusion, given the central place that stigma and secondary consequences hold in discussions of risk perceptions, and his general argument has drawn vigorous critique (Slovic et al, 1994).

The one theoretical contribution that we know of linking stage 1 processes causally with stage 2 ripple effects is work by Slovic et al (1991c) on stigma effects at the Yucca Mountain nuclear repository site. They designed a series of empirical studies to (1) demonstrate the concept of environmental imagery and show how it can be measured, (2) assess the relationship between imagery and choice behaviour, and (3) describe economic impacts that might occur as a result of altered images and choices. The research tested three specific propositions:

1   Images associated with environments have diverse positive and negative affective meanings that influence preferences (e.g. preference for sites in which to vacation, retire, find a job or start a new business).
2   A nuclear-waste repository evokes a wide variety of strongly negative images, consistent with extreme perceptions of risk and stigmatization.
3   The repository at Yucca Mountain and the negative images it evokes will, over time, become increasingly salient in the images of Nevada and of Las Vegas.

Substantial empirical support was found for these propositions, demonstrating a set of causal mechanisms by which social amplification processes could adversely affect the attractiveness of the area to tourists, job seekers, retirees, convention planners and business developers, and produce adverse social and economic effects.

Despite these cases and the Decision Research theoretical work, it is clear that stage 1 relationships in the SARF have been more studied and are better understood than are those of stage 2. Stage 1 posits that signals from risk events become transformed to influence perceptions of risk and first-order behavioural responses. A relatively extensive set of findings from the risk perceptions literature now exists to suggest this is the case, although much remains to be done to pinpoint the specific contexts under which amplification or attenuation occurs. Stage 2 involves a direct link between amplification of risk perceptions and secondary consequences, such as calls for stricter regulation, market impacts and a generalization of responses to other similar risk events and hazards. In many respects it is stage 2 that is the most important for policy, given the potential here for large economic and social impacts. Despite prima facie evidence, stage 2 processes remain rather opaque, based largely upon current case-specific and anecdotal evidence rather than on systematic empirical evidence. It is also less clear what the direct secondary consequences of attenuation might be compared to the more visible impacts of amplification. Consequences of attenuation might include, however, the otherwise avoidable direct impacts of the hazard, and the impacts upon trust and credibility if degraded risk management is subsequently revealed in a serious unanticipated accident.

Having surveyed the empirical work that has tested, elaborated and extended the original conceptual paper, we next turn to a review of critiques and points of debate that have emerged over the past 15 years.

Critiques and contentions

The framework has prompted general critiques, principally in the set of peer review commentaries that accompanied the original 1988 article in *Risk Analysis*. Although most of these authors welcomed social amplification as a genuine attempt to provide more theoretical coherence to the field, they also highlighted points of issue, as well as avenues for further research. In a subsequent paper Kasperson (1992) sought to respond to many of these critiques. Here we review the various critiques and issues that have been raised, clarifying where we can and identifying unresolved questions where appropriate.

The amplification metaphor

Rayner (1988) has criticized the amplification metaphor itself, concerned that it might be taken to imply that a baseline or 'true' risk exists that is readily attached to risk events, which is then 'distorted' in some way by the social processes of amplification. He argues that the emphasis on signal and electronic imagery may be too passive to capture the complexity of risk behaviour. Rip (1988) worries that the focus of amplification work may be directed to what are regarded as 'exaggerated' risks.

It is quite clear, however, that the framework is not intended to imply that any single true baseline always and/or unproblematically exists, particularly in many of the heavily politicized, transcientific settings (Funtowicz and Ravetz, 1992) where amplification is most likely to occur. The conceptualization of the amplification process in terms of construction and transformation of signs, symbols and images by an array of social and individual 'stations' and actors is compatible with the view that all knowledge about risk entails some elements of judgement and social construction (Johnson and Covello, 1987; Holzheu and Wiedemann, 1993). The observation that experts and public sometimes disagree about risks is compatible with the claim that different groups may filter and attach salience to different aspects of a risk or a risk event. Amplification and attenuation, then, refer to the processes of signal interpretation, transformation, intensification and dampening as the dynamics of risk consideration proceed iteratively in society. At the same time, it is clear that risks do have real consequences (Rosa, 1998; Renn, 1998a), and these may be direct (as are usually treated in technical risk analyses) or indirect results from the social processing of risk (stigmatization, group mobilization, conflict, loss of trust).

The metaphor of amplification does come with some baggage, to be sure. Since the very term amplification, in its more general and common usage, refers to the intensification of signals, the framework nomenclature can be taken to have implicit semantic bias (Rip, 1988). The architects of SARF have repeatedly emphasized in their writings that this approach is intended to describe both the social processes that attenuate signals about hazards, as well as those involved in intensification. Alleged 'overreactions' of people and organizations should receive the same attention as alleged 'downplaying' of the risk. In his extensive review of the topic Renn (1991) discusses the processes and contexts that might be expected to lead to each.

What is amplified or attenuated are both the signals to society about the seriousness and manageability and, ultimately, the consequences of the risk through the generation, or constraining, of ripple effects. Indeed, the secondary risk consequences will often be connected causally with the various interactions involved in society's processing of risk signals. It is exactly this potential for signal transformation and amplification-driven social dynamics and consequences that has been so confounding to risk managers in various societies.

Is it a theory?

As emphasized in the 1988 article, SARF is not a theory, properly speaking, but '... a fledgling conceptual framework that may serve to guide ongoing efforts to develop, test, and apply such a theory to a broad array of pressing risk problems' (Kasperson et al, 1988, p180). A theory, as Machlis and Rosa (1990, p164) have emphasized, would require specification and explication of linked concepts, including the application of correspondence rules for converting abstract or inexact concepts into exact, testable ones. We are now beginning to see the first forays into such theorizing, as in the stigma work of Slovic and colleagues referred to above. Progress is also apparent in the empirical work linking events, trust, perceptions and imagery, also discussed above. Meanwhile, a continuing principal contribution of the framework is its 'net' function for catching a broad range of accumulated empirical research, for organizing and bringing into direct analytic interaction relevant phenomena, for theories concerning risk perception and its communication, and for deriving new hypotheses about the societal processing of risk signals (the latter could then, in principle at least, be tested directly).

One limitation of the risk amplification framework, despite its apparent face validity, is that it may be too general (rather as subjective expected-utility theory is) to test empirically and particularly to seek outright falsification. This has led some observers (e.g. Rayner, 1988; Wåhlberg, 2001) to doubt whether any genuinely new insights can be achieved beyond those already offered by existing approaches. Clearly, the usefulness of this social amplification approach will ultimately stand or fall upon its ability to achieve insights that can be subject to empirical test. Certainly the framework does, at minimum, help to clarify phenomena, such as the key role of the mass media in risk communication and the influence of culture on risk processing, providing a template for integrating partial theories and research, and to encourage more interactive and holistic interpretations. Kasperson (1992) has previously cited three potential contributions of such an integrative framework: to bring competing theories and hypotheses out of their 'terrain' and into direct conjunction (or confrontation) with each other; to provide an overall framework in which to locate a large array of fragmented empirical findings; and to generate new hypotheses, particularly hypotheses geared to the interconnections and interdependencies among particular concepts or components. These still seem highly relevant.

Communications and the mass media

The concern has been raised (Handmer and Penning-Rowsell, 1990) that the communications model on which the social amplification approach is founded unduly emphasizes too simple a conceptualization of risk communication, as a one-way transfer of information (i.e. from risk events and sources, through transmitters, and then onto receivers). So let us remove any existing doubt that this framework, as we conceive it, recognizes that the development of social risk perceptions is always likely to be the product of diverse interactive processes among the parties to any risk communication. Various reviews (NRC, 1989, 1996; Pidgeon et al, 1992) discuss the importance of viewing risk communication as a two-way process of dialogue. We would take this even further to note that any risk event generates coverage and signals that proceed through a broad array or fabric of ongoing communication networks. Purposeful risk communication programmes nearly always enter a terrain extensively occupied by existing communication systems. Thus, with the United States National Research Council, we see risk communication as

> *an interactive process of exchange of information and opinion among individuals, groups and institutions. It involves multiple messages about the nature of risk and other messages, not strictly about risk, that express concerns, opinions or reactions to risk messages or to legal and institutional arrangements for risk management.* (NRC, 1989, p21)

Certainly, applications of the framework should not lose sight of this important qualification, and although it is relatively easy to finger the public and media as the originators of risk communication problems, the communicators are also key parts of the process (Kasperson and Stallen, 1991).

In this context, a comment on the role of the mass media is also in order. Some have interpreted the framework to assume that we see high mass-media coverage as the principal driver of risk amplification. For example Sjöberg (1999) concludes that the framework predicts that enhanced media coverage should increase perceived risk. This is not the case. Although we find incidents where this has occurred, and some (e.g. Mazur, 1990) have advanced this argument, the conceptual work of Renn (1991) and Pidgeon et al (1999) and our empirical research as well reveal that the relationships among media coverage, public perceptions and stage 2 amplification processes are complex and highly interactive with other components of the amplification process. Indeed, we have speculated that no single amplification component may be sufficient to ensure 'take-off' of the amplification process. We also believe that layering of amplification and attenuation around scale-specific patterns of media coverage may not be uncommon (also Breakwell and Barnett, 2003). Indeed, we see the strength of amplification research as oriented to patterns of interacting amplification mechanisms, the nature of the risks and risk events, and social contextual effects. We have also concluded, surveying empirical work over the past 15 years, that the nature of discourse about risk that characterizes the social processing of the risk is important, including the political competition that occurs to control language, symbols, imagery and definition or framing of the risk problem.

Individual versus social processes

Two commentaries on the 1988 article expressed the concern that too much attention was given to the individual level of amplification and too little to social alignments, the mass media and social networks (Rip, 1988, p195). Svenson (1988b, p200) noted that future development of the framework might well benefit from a more articulated system and a broader social psychological approach that would put amplification processes 'even more firmly in the societal context.' As the foregoing discussion of organizational amplification and attenuation illustrates, the empirical work over the past 15 years has accorded the social 'stations' and processes of amplification as much, and perhaps even more, attention as individual processes have received. Indeed, even the extensions of the psychometric model to notions such as stigma, blame and social trust have emphasized heavily the interactions between social context and individual perceptions and behaviour. And, of course, it is precisely these interactions that are highlighted in the amplification framework.

With this review of empirical studies and extensions of the social amplification framework, as well as areas of critique and debate, in hand, we next turn to consider implications for public policy and future research directions.

Policy and research priorities

As yet, there has been no systematic exploration of how SARF and the empirical results of the past 15 years can be applied to various public policy matters. Yet there is an urgent need for social analysts of risk to suggest approaches and processes that have the potential to improve society's ability to anticipate, diagnose, prioritize and respond to the continuing flow of risk issues that confront, and often confound, society's risk processing and management functions. The recommendations calling for substantial overhauls in existing risk assessment and decision making, whether for an 'enlarged concept of risk' and trust-building (United Kingdom Interdepartmental Liaison Group on Risk Assessment, 1998a) or 'analytic and deliberative process' (NRC, 1996), potentially open the door for more socially informed approaches to risk decision making (e.g. see some of the contributions to Okrent and Pidgeon, 1998). The scope and structuring of the social amplification framework allows it to generate policy suggestions (with the usual caveats as to what is possible). And from the last 15 years of work, we do have several examples of substantial policy analysis that draw upon the amplification framework as well as a considerable body of empirical work to inform risk policy questions and ideas for further departures that may enhance management initiatives.

At the outset, it is important to recognize that any policy suggestions proceed from an underlying normative question: Is it possible to develop normative criteria for judging the outcomes of social risk amplification as 'good' or 'bad,' rather than merely addressing the pathologies of the most visible manifestations of 'over' and 'under' reaction? There is no research to date, as far as we are aware, on this critical issue. The question of when social amplification or attenuation becomes sufficiently pronounced, or more destructive than positive to the social construction and handling of the risk, is a complex one. Consider, for example, the case of social controversy over the siting of waste disposal facilities in the United States, an issue that generated widespread disapproval in the form of such acronyms as NIMBY (Not in my back yard), LULU (Locally unwanted land use), NIMTOF (Not in my term of office) and others, and has often been cited as a classic example of public overreaction. In fact, the resistance to land disposal of wastes has driven extensive waste reduction and recycling at source and, arguably, improved overall waste management.

In practical terms, agencies will still attempt to use the best available scientific knowledge and risk assessments in an attempt to produce estimates of 'risk,' although as Rappaport (1988) points out whereas scientific risk assessment is evaluated by its accuracy, one criterion for evaluating people's attention to risk signals is the adaptiveness of the information gained, and the two may not always correspond. Also, as Svenson (1988b) notes, we do not know when risk amplification has involved changes to people's basic mental models of a hazard (which may then, in principle, be judged as correct or incorrect with respect to some standard; see Morgan et al, 2001), or whether the modification of relevant values or thresholds of tolerability to the risk has occurred. Clearly a complete set of judgements oriented to the amplification process will probably be involved in any such evaluation process. And we should not lose sight of the desire of many responsible authorities to suppress the flow of signals in society so that control over the risk consideration process can be kept in the domain of the managers.

As noted earlier, two areas of policy analysis have drawn extensively on SARF. The first involves the future of radioactive waste management in the United States. The social amplification concept had its genesis in an ambitious programme of social and economic research funded by the state of Nevada and conducted between 1985 and 1995. Included was a broad array of research aimed at assessing the future potential impacts of the proposed nuclear waste repository at Yucca Mountain, including studies on perceptions and imagery, risk signals, patterns of media coverage, possible stigma-related and other ripple effects, and social distrust. Drawing upon this extensive body of empirical work, which covered much of the scope of SARF, a team of researchers, assisted by a well-known science writer, set forth a broad policy analysis entitled *One Hundred Centuries of Solitude: Redirecting America's High-Level Nuclear Waste Policy* (Flynn et al, 1995). The analysis argued that given the dismal failure of existing policy, a new approach was sorely needed, one that would be based on such elements as acceptance of the legitimacy of public concerns, an enhanced role for interim storage, a voluntary site selection process, negotiation with risk bearers and actions aimed at restoring credibility (Flynn et al, 1995, pp16–18).

A second policy area, one related to the Yucca Mountain case, is the impasse or gridlock over the siting of hazardous facilities more generically in a number of countries. Here the numerous empirical studies conducted as part of the social amplification approach have been an important part of the foundation for several policy prescriptions. Kunreuther and colleagues wedded the amplification concepts to the prescription and compensation research at the University of Pennsylvania's Wharton School and Lawrence Susskind's extensive experience with conflict resolution to develop a new Facility Siting Credo (Table 19.3), subsequently tested for its prescriptive power (Kunreuther et al, 1993). Similarly, Kasperson and colleagues have drawn heavily upon social amplification research in arguing for new approaches and procedures in facility siting, including such policy elements as clear demonstration of societal need, steps to narrow the risk debate, approaches that would remain resilient under conditions of high social distrust, building constituencies of support, and use of adaptive institutional processes (Kasperson et al, 1992; Kasperson, forthcoming). The scope of issues covered in these policy prescriptions, the attention to interactive effects and their links to rippling effects are suggestive of the types of policy analyses that might flow from amplification-based research.

One clear policy contribution could be to draw upon social amplification to improve society's capability to anticipate which new or emerging risks are likely to be highly amplified or attenuated. Given the inherent complexity of risk communication and social processes, it is clear that the framework cannot be expected to yield simple or direct predictions regarding which issues are likely to experience amplification/attenuation effects in advance. A parallel problem – which has in part epistemological and in part practical roots – occurs when researchers attempt to use knowledge of the human and organizational causes of past technological accidents and disasters to predict the likelihood of future failures (see Pidgeon, 1988; Turner and Pidgeon, 1997, esp. chapter 11). Here some practitioners have adopted more holistic methods, seeking to diagnose vulnerability in large organizational systems through screening against broad classes of risk management factors (see e.g. Groeneweg et al, 1994). In a similar way, knowledge of the factors likely to lead to amplification effects, and the sociopolitical contexts in which they might operate, could conceivably serve as a screening device for evaluating the potential for such consequences, particularly with respect to synergistic effects found among factors. Developing such a screening procedure and testing it retrospectively to explain past experience or against samples of new risks could be a particularly useful line of investigation.

Turning to the empirical foundations of social science research on risk, the extent to which existing empirical work reflects North American experience is striking. Clearly, we urgently need to conduct basic investigations on the transferability of the existing findings (for example, whether trust, blame and responsibility for risk management play as strong a role in Europe or Asia as is reported in the United States), as well as the ways in which different cultural contexts uniquely shape risk communication and risk amplification effects. However, as Renn and Rohrmann (2000) make clear, conducting well-founded cross-cultural risk perceptions research is a formidable task, particularly if we consider the multiple parties present in the amplification/attenuation construct. However, if we start from the standpoint of the key mediators of much risk

Table 19.3 *The facility siting credo*

When planning and building locally unwanted land uses (LULUs), every effort ought to be made to meet the following objectives
Institute a broad-based participatory process
Seek consensus
Work to develop trust
Seek acceptable sites through a volunteer process
Consider a competitive siting process
Set realistic timetables
Keep multiple options open at all times
Achieve agreement that the status quo is unacceptable
Choose the solution that best addresses the problem
Guarantee that stringent safety standards will be met
Fully address (compensate) all negative impacts of a facility
Make the host community better off
Use contingent agreements
Work for geographic fairness

Source: Kunreuther et al (1993)
Copyright © 1993 John Wiley & Sons. Reprinted with permission

communication – the mass media – then the framework should be capable of describing and organizing the amplification rules used by media institutions in their role between government and sections of society. How the media interface with the other different institutional players in what Slovic (1998b) terms the 'risk game' is a key issue ripe for investigation. There is also the question of whether different institutional arrangements can be characterized as operating with predictable sets of amplification or attenuation rules (see Renn 1991, p300), and whether evidence exists of causal links between such institutional behaviour and subsequent societal impacts. The influence of regional (e.g. EC) and national legal and cultural frameworks in setting overarching contexts for amplification processes should be part of this research direction.

Social amplification has provided a useful analytic structure for studying stigma-related policy questions (Flynn et al, 2001), although the existing policy options for addressing such amplification-driven processes appear quite limited, as Gregory et al (1995) have demonstrated. Litigating stigma claims under the aegis of tort law in the United States does not seem to offer an efficient or satisfactory solution. Project developers can, of course, simply pay whatever is asked for as compensation, but such a pay-and-move-on option fails to distinguish between valid claims for compensation and strategic demands based on greed or politically motivated attempts to oppose a policy or programme. In addition, claims are often made for economic losses predicted to take place years or even decades into the future, despite the many difficulties inherent in forecasting future economic activities or social responses. Stigma effects might be ameliorated if public fears could be addressed effectively through risk communication efforts, but such a simple solution also seems unlikely. All too often, risk communication efforts have been unsuccessful because they failed to address the complex interplay of psychological, social and political factors that is at the heart of social amplification and that drives profound mistrust of government and industry, and results in high levels of perceived risk and thus opposition. Accordingly, policy responses geared to the interacting factors contributing to stigma at multiple stages of amplification processes are also required.

More open and participatory decision processes could provide valuable early information about potential sources of stigmatization and amplification drivers (see Renn, 2003) and invest the larger community in understanding and managing technological hazards. This approach might even help to remove the basis for the blame and distrust that often occurs in the event of an accident or major risk policy failure, and improvements over time in our ability to identify and access the factors contributing to stigmatization may make it possible to predict the magnitude or timing of expected economic losses. This, in turn, could open the door to the creation of new insurance markets and to efforts for mitigating potentially harmful stigma effects. Finally, the societal institutions responsible for risk management must meet public concerns and conflicts with new norms and methods for addressing stigma issues, and improved arenas for resolving conflicts based on values of equity and fairness.

As a concluding comment, we reiterate that a particular policy strength of the framework is its capacity to mesh emerging findings from different avenues of risk research, to bring various insights and analytic leverage into conjunction, and (particularly) to analyse connections, interrelations and interactions within particular social and cultural contexts. Such strengths suggest that the search for patterns and broader-based interpretations may yield new insights and hypotheses, as research on stigma, social trust and 'take-off' of the amplification process suggests. Elsewhere, assessing risk amplification and attenuation in the particular context of transboundary risks, Kasperson and Kasperson (2001) have pointed to potential 'mirror' structures in the social processing of such risks, with social attenuation in the risk-source region and linked social amplification in the risk-consequence area. In global change research, German social scientists have provided new insights into vulnerability to environmental degradation by analysing 'syndromes' of change (Schnellnhuber et al, 1997). Throughout this chapter, and also in our more theoretical writings on social amplification, we have emphasized the potential research and policy value that a broadly based and integrative framework of risk affords. Such meso-level of theoretical analyses within the amplification framework could potentially open up new research questions and potential policy initiatives.

Chapter 20

Numeracy Skill and the Communication, Comprehension and Use of Risk–Benefit Information

Ellen Peters, Judith Hibbard, Paul Slovic
*and Nathan Dieckmann**

Increasingly, the emphasis of health care policy is to tap the potential power of informed consumers to improve health outcomes and the efficacy of health care. Employers and payers, recognizing the essential role that consumers can play in containing costs and improving care, have undertaken initiatives to influence consumers' behaviour. They have urged consumers to change the way they select and use health care and how they manage their day-to-day health. Attempts have been made to encourage consumers to select high-performing providers, health plans and facilities; choose evidenced-based, cost-effective treatments; collaborate with their providers; initiate and maintain healthy behaviour; and manage their own symptoms and conditions. At the same time, consumers are being asked to assume a greater share of their health care costs than ever before. As a result, choices have become more consequential for patients, in terms of both financial and health outcomes (Herzlinger, 2002; Iglehart, 2002).

However, not all consumers have the skills needed to use health information. A key concern is whether the policy approach of giving greater responsibility to patients will further disadvantage those with limited skills. Health literacy has been linked with higher health care costs and could be a driver of health disparities. In a recent study, health reading literacy and numeracy were found to independently influence the comprehension and use of information about hospital choices

* Reprinted from Peters, E., Hibbard, J., Slovic, P. and Dieckmann, N. F. (2007) 'Numeracy skill and the communication, comprehension, and use of risk–benefit information', *Health Affairs*, vol 26, pp741–748.

(Hibbard et al, 2007). Inadequate numeracy might be an important barrier to patients' understanding of their health situations and to their obtaining high-quality care.

Health care information can be complex, and different sources can yield contradictory advice. Chronic disease patients, for example, must make many choices daily that have major implications for their health and need for care. They often must follow complex treatment regimens with uncertain risks and benefits, monitor their own conditions, make lifestyle changes, and decide when to seek professional care. We tend to assume that simply providing information will result in a level playing field for all. However, many consumers lack the skills, knowledge and motivation to access credible sources, process information and make informed choices. Consequently, they have more health crises and functional declines than those who do have the skills, knowledge and motivation (Estrada et al, 2004; Marcus, 2006).

The purpose of this chapter is to examine the concept of numeracy, why numeric skill is important to health care decisions, and what the best practices are for the presentation of numeric health information. We limit our review to (1) what is known about the influence of numeracy on comprehension and use of risk–benefit information and (2) what strategies exist for supporting the use of numeric information in patient choice.

Definition of 'numeracy' and extent of innumeracy

Numeracy is an element of health literacy that refers to the ability to understand numbers. Researchers have measured it through both objective maths tests and self-reported perceptions of maths ability (Schwartz et al, 1997; Lipkus et al, 2001; Fagerlin et al, 2007). Based on the National Adult Literacy Survey, almost half of the general population has difficulty with relatively simple numeric tasks such as calculating (using a calculator) the difference between a regular price and a sales price or estimating the cost per ounce of a grocery item (Kirsch et al, 2002). These people do not necessarily perceive themselves as 'at risk' in their lives because of limited skills.

Having fewer numeric skills, however, is associated with lower comprehension and less use of health information. Many patients cannot perform the basic numeric tasks required to function in the current health care environment. For example, 26 per cent in one study were unable to understand information about when an appointment was scheduled (Williams et al, 1995). Another study found that 16 per cent of highly educated people incorrectly answered straightforward questions about risk magnitudes (for example, Which represents the larger risk: 1 per cent, 5 per cent or 10 per cent?; Lipkus et al, 2001). Understanding numeric information in real health situations is often much more difficult than in hypothetical situations.

Understanding numbers:
Essential for health decisions

Uncertainty abounds in health care settings, and successful communication of uncertain information to all patients becomes critical. The human mind, however, has difficulty coping with complicated information, and people tend to reduce the burden of processing such information by using simplifying strategies. At least four kinds of uncertainty exist in health care settings and result in the use of simplifying strategies.

Uncertainty in health care settings

To begin with, uncertainty exists about the magnitude or severity of possible benefits and risks (for example, the extent of pain reduction). Patients' testimonials may provide such information, but they can also overwhelm statistical information in health decisions (Fagerlin et al, 2005). Second, uncertainty may exist about the strength of current evidence – for example, concerning a treatment or the quality of care offered by a hospital. In processing information of uncertain accuracy or reliability, people tend to accept information fully or reject it completely, without adjusting for data quality. This 'best-guess' strategy simplifies information integration but ignores uncertainty (Gettys et al, 1973; Schum and DuCharme, 1971). Thus, showing confidence intervals, for example, might reduce use of information. Because the less numerate tend to trust numerical information less than their more numerate peers do, a reasonable expectation is that they will be more likely than others to reject information that they perceive to be inaccurate or unreliable (Gurmankin et al, 2004).

Third, patients and consumers are often uncertain about how to weigh risks and benefits in choices. Each of these topics is important, but no research appears to examine interactions of these topics with numeracy skill. Finally, uncertainty exists about the likelihood of different outcomes. Side effects or complications, for example, occur with almost all treatments. They do not necessarily happen to everyone, but physicians cannot predict exactly who will experience them. Instead, evidence-based medicine might provide a population-based likelihood (for example, the Gail model indicates that a woman has a 6 per cent lifetime chance of breast cancer). Similarly, the likelihood of receiving high-quality care in a hospital might vary across local hospitals, but exactly who will receive that care is unknown. Patients, however, can choose a hospital where high-quality care is more likely. Comprehension and use of likelihood information varies depending both on a person's numeracy skill and the format of the information (Schwartz et al, 1997; Peters et al, 2006b).

Skills needed to understand risk–benefit information

A hierarchy of skills is needed to comprehend and use information about the likelihood of risks and benefits. First, information must be available, accurate and timely, and the patient must be able to acquire it from tables, charts and text.[1]

Then, patients often must make calculations and inferences. For example, given survival rates for chemotherapy versus hormone therapy, a cancer patient must calculate the difference between therapies and infer the meaning of that difference. Next, patients must remember information either for a short period (if the decision is made quickly) or after an extended delay, and memory ability differs across patient populations. The patient must be able to weight factors to match his or her needs and values and, finally, must make trade-offs, either mundane or emotionally devastating, to ultimately arrive at a health decision. This process can be quite difficult.

Numeric skills associated with the quality of health decisions

Evaluating risks and benefits of health options

Those with inadequate numeracy have more difficulty using numeric information to inform their choices than do those with good numeric skills. For example, the National Institutes of Health (NIH) recommends that women aged 40–49 assess the need for mammography screening with their doctors. Patients, in this case, have to evaluate the risks and benefits of health options themselves, or else physicians must substitute their judgements for their patients' preferences (Elstein et al, 2005). Lisa Schwartz and colleagues concluded that quantitative descriptors of risk were necessary in such cases because qualitative descriptions were too ambiguous (Schwartz et al, 1997). However, less-numerate women in their study could not accurately determine the benefits of screening from the numbers provided.

Following complex health regimens

Numeracy skill also appears to influence the ability to follow complex health regimens. Low numeracy was common in a group of patients who took warfarin to reduce stroke risk and was associated with poorer anticoagulation control (Estrada et al, 2004). In addition, limited numeracy might be an important barrier to the meaningful assessment of patients' values. For example, less numerate women who were asked to assess the value of imaginary health states (such as heart disease and osteoporosis) using standard techniques had more difficulty and provided less valid assessments than those who were highly numerate (Woloshin et al, 2001; Zikmund-Fisher et al, 2007). A substantial minority of physicians also have difficulty understanding and interpreting numeric medical data, which suggests that physicians might not always be reliable translators of health information for patients (Sheridan and Pignone, 2002).

Weighing short-term against long-term benefits

Intertemporal choices represent an important, neglected area of health research, as patients are often asked to incur concrete costs now (take medication, feel anxious about getting a test) to reap long-term, but abstract and probabilistic, rewards later. Research in non-health-related domains suggests that (compared with more numerate patients) less numerate patients will be more likely to weigh short-term costs and benefits than those occurring in the distant future (Frederick, 2005; Benjamin et al, 2006).

Best practices in presenting numeric health information

People who differ in numeracy appear to have different needs for decision aids. Some preliminary research has focused on how comprehension and quality of decisions (for example, choosing the best insurance plans) vary as a function of the interaction between numeracy and the format of provided information.

Less is often more

People tend to comprehend more and make better-informed decisions when the presentation format makes the most important information easier to evaluate and when less cognitive effort is required (Peters et al, 2007a). Results from three experiments were particularly strong for those with lower numeracy skills and support the idea that 'less is more' when one is presenting consumers with comparative performance information to make hospital care choices. In one study, respondents who were given only the most relevant information about hospital quality (for example, percentage of patients receiving recommended care) were better able to comprehend that information and were more likely to choose a higher-quality hospital compared with respondents who received the same quality information plus less-relevant information (for example, the number of general care beds). In a second study, making only a more important quality measure easier to evaluate rather than making all indicators easier to evaluate led to more choices of higher-quality hospitals. In a third study, less cognitive effort was more; presenting quality information in a format in which a higher number means better (the number of registered nurses per 100 patients) compared to one where a lower number means better (the number of patients per registered nurse) facilitated comprehension and helped respondents make better choices.

If hospital decisions are to be aided by information about quality as well as cost, then reports need to show only important quality measures (or at least highlight them), make them easier to evaluate (for example, by using well-tested symbols), and present data in accordance with cognitive expectations (that is, higher numbers mean better performance). For those with poor numeracy skills, the effect of information presentation on comprehension and choice is even more marked.

Reduce required inferences and calculations

Other options for reducing cognitive effort have not been tested with numeracy but are likely to be effective. For example, information providers should reduce required inferences and calculations. In one study, a sizeable minority could not infer a monthly premium when told that the previous year's premium was $100 a month and the premium increase was 2 per cent (instead of being told that this year's premium would be $102; Finucane et al, 2002). Small probabilities should not be presented as one chance out of a larger number (1 of 50; 1 of 1000); instead, information providers should keep the denominator constant to reduce effort and increase comprehension and use of the information (20 of 1000; 1 of 1000). Risks should also be compared using the same time span. The use of visual cues such as stars to highlight the meaning of information is also likely to help, as is ordering and summarizing information (Hibbard et al, 2002). As mentioned earlier, presenting higher-level statistical concepts (for example, confidence intervals) to consumers should be avoided, because people tend to accept or reject information fully without adjusting for data quality (Gettys et al, 1973).

Test formats carefully to reduce numeracy effects

It is well known that people often respond more strongly to options that are described as losses rather than (equivalent) gains (Kahneman and Tversky, 1979). For example, patients are more likely to obtain a screening test if the costs associated with not getting screened are emphasized rather than the benefits of getting screened (Edwards et al, 2001). Although not yet tested in a health context, one of the authors (Peters) and other colleagues found that less numerate decision makers were influenced more by different (but equivalent) frames of numeric information than were those with high numeracy skills (Peters et al, 2006b). Carefully tested formats might reduce these effects.

Other aids

Research on presenting numeric information about risks and benefits is still relatively new, but some general themes have emerged. Visual displays, for example, can increase both comprehension and risk perceptions (Lipkus and Hollands, 1999; Stone et al, 2003). Hannah Faye Chua and colleagues demonstrated that visual displays of gum disease influenced cognitive and affective representations of risky options and increased willingness to pay to decrease risk (Chua et al, 2006). The affective influence, in particular, might be critical to risk perceptions and behaviour (Slovic et al, 2005; Peters et al, 2007b). Presenting absolute risks (for example, 3 out of 1000 will have a stroke) increases comprehension over the use of relative risks (50 per cent higher chance of stroke; Gigerenzer and Edwards, 2003). Results are mixed as to whether percentage (13 per cent) or frequency (13 out of 100) formats promote the greatest understanding (Gigerenzer and Edwards, 2003; Waters et al, 2006; Peters et al, 2006b). There is general agreement that decimals (its likelihood is 0.03) should not be used. Finally, individualized risk estimates rather than general population figures increase uptake of screening tests but might not be evidence of more-informed decisions (Edwards et al, 2003).

Highly numerate people are likely to pay more attention to numbers, comprehend them better, translate them into meaningful information, and ultimately use them in decisions, compared with their less numerate peers (Peters et al, 2006b). The decisions of the less numerate are likely to be informed less by numbers and more by other non-numeric sources of information such as their emotions, mood states and trust or distrust in physicians and the health system. Careful attention to information presentation should allow everyone – particularly the less numerate – to attend more to important numbers and use them more effectively in decisions. Approaches to presenting numeric information should be tested with target audiences whenever possible, and refinements should be made to increase the comprehensibility and usability of the information.

A new definition of 'health literacy'

To be a competent health care consumer in the current environment, one must be able to understand health care information and use it in making choices. Comprehension is based in large part on the difficulty of the material and on the individual's skills. It might also be a matter of motivation, or how much 'effort' a person is willing to exert to understand and make good choices (Hibbard et al, 2007). A traditional definition of health literacy concerns individual patients' abilities. We believe that this definition should also include the format of the provided information and what it requires from patients.

Of course, any deliberate framing of information raises ethical questions about manipulating patients' preferences. A strong case for such manipulation is presented by Cass Sunstein and Richard Thaler, who argue for a programme of 'libertarian paternalism' that acknowledges the fact that neutral framing of information does not exist and suggests that communications should employ formats that are likely to promote patients' welfare (Sunstein and Thaler, 2003). But the ultimate choice is left to the individual, following the libertarian perspective.

Ideally, we should strive to present important health information to patients and their families so as to encourage the best decisions for all, without hurting those who might already be disadvantaged. A further goal is to satisfy patients and other decision makers that they are adequately informed given the present state of knowledge. Meeting these goals requires careful thought devoted not only to the content of health information but also to the format in which it is presented. What format is chosen will influence how well the information is understood and used by people who vary in ability, time and motivation. Failing to meet these objectives will lead to dissatisfaction, system inefficiencies, and serious health and financial consequences for those struggling to make good choices within our complex health care environment.

Acknowledgements

This material is based on work supported by the National Science Foundation, under Grant No. SES-0517770, and the Agency for Healthcare Research and Quality (AHRQ) via the John M. Eisenberg Clinical Decisions and Communications Science Center, under Contract No. HHSA29020050013C.

Note

1   Information can also be acquired orally; it is not a focus of this chapter, however, as we are interested in how to maximize the comprehension and use of numeric information presented in print form.

Chapter 21

Public Understanding of the Illnesses Caused by Cigarette Smoking

*Neil D. Weinstein, Paul Slovic, Erika Waters
and Ginger Gibson*[*]

Introduction

Attempts to measure public understanding of the risks from cigarette smoking have focused mainly on the accuracy of beliefs about the likelihood of adverse health outcomes. Dozens of studies have been conducted in which respondents were asked to estimate the probability that death, 'serious illness' or specific health outcomes will result from smoking (Weinstein, 1999a). Often such studies also asked smokers whether they are more or less likely to experience harm than other smokers (Weinstein, 1999a). Similarly, the argument that the public overestimates the risks of smoking put forth by Viscusi (1990) has been based mainly on answers to probability questions, for example, 'Among 100 cigarette smokers, how many of them do you think will get lung cancer because they smoke?'

Beliefs about probability, however, are only one aspect of risk knowledge (Weinstein, 1999b). In formal decision-making models (Baron, 2000), choice depends on both the perceived probability and the perceived utility of the consequences of an action. Here, utility refers to the magnitude of costs or benefits that would accompany a particular outcome. Using the same concept, but different terminology, many of the most widely used theories of health behaviour (Conner and Norman, 1996) assert that actions depend on the expectancy (i.e. perceived probability) of particular outcomes and their value (i.e. the perceived magnitude of their costs or benefits). Other names for these same two hazard attributes are likelihood and severity.

[*]   Reprinted from Weinstein, N. D., Slovic, P., Waters, E. and Gibson, G. (2004) 'Public understanding of the illnesses caused by cigarette smoking', *Nicotine & Tobacco Research*, vol 6, pp349–355.

In contrast to the numerous studies of beliefs about smoking risk likelihood, very little has been published concerning public knowledge of the identity and nature of the illnesses caused by smoking. An accurate judgement of the severity of the threat posed by smoking requires more than a vague awareness that an activity is 'bad for you' or that it 'causes cancer.' When lung cancer, emphysema and heart disease are mentioned to survey respondents, most now agree that cigarettes can cause those illnesses (Gallup Organization, 1987; US Department of Health and Human Services [USDHHS], 1989). Yet, such prompted recall – in which the name of the specific illness is part of the question – is a much more lenient way to measure knowledge of smoking-caused illnesses than is unprompted recall. Whether people can identify these illnesses without being prompted is unclear.

Only a few investigators have asked laypeople to tell them what illnesses are caused by smoking. An early Gallup Poll (Gallup Organization, 1954) asked respondents who thought smoking was harmful, 'In what way do you think cigaret [sic] smoking is harmful?' A wide range of answers was received; 8 per cent of respondents mentioned 'cancer' or some form of cancer, 31 per cent said it was 'bad for the lungs,' and 7 per cent of responses were coded as 'interferes with circulation' or 'harmful to heart, causes heartburn, increases pulse rate.' For almost the next 50 years, no published study we are aware of asked an open-ended question about smoking effects. Wewers and colleagues (2000) reported the results of a survey of 249 adult smokers in two rural Ohio Appalachian counties. They found that cancer was identified as an adverse consequence of smoking by about 89 per cent of respondents; pulmonary disorders were reported second most frequently, and cardiovascular disorders were reported less often, by less than half of the sample (and by fewer young adults than older adults). A recent survey conducted by University of Pennsylvania Annenberg School of Communication (Annenberg 2) obtained similar results (Jamieson and Romer, 2001, p46). If individuals cannot identify the best-known, most severe health effects of smoking without prompting, they are certainly unable to apply that information in deciding whether to smoke. Thus, the first goal of this chapter was to find out whether laypeople can state the illnesses caused by smoking. We report data on this topic from our own study and also from the Annenberg 2 survey, the results of which have previously been presented only in graphical form, with smokers and nonsmokers combined.

Even less research has examined whether people understand the nature of the illnesses caused by smoking. We have not been able to locate any publications describing public knowledge about the nature of lung cancer and emphysema. Thus, the second goal of this chapter was to present data about the public's knowledge of these illnesses. Because any illness has many characteristics, we focused on the most serious aspects and selected questions for which there are correct answers. For lung cancer, we asked about the curability of the disease and about life expectancy after diagnosis. For emphysema, we asked about awareness of the illness, recognition that it is life threatening, and curability. It is difficult to determine with fixed-choice questions whether people have an accurate notion of what it would be like to experience an illness. Consequently, for both lung cancer and emphysema we asked respondents whether they felt they knew what the pain and suffering would be like if they contracted the illness.

Method

Subjects

Data in the present survey were collected over the telephone from two separate samples. The adult sample was obtained by random-digit dialling of exchanges within the 50 United States. Interviewers spoke with the person aged 20 years or older who had the most recent birthday. For reasons of cost, the adolescent sample was obtained by calling at random to those households in a national sample of listed telephone numbers that had been identified as containing a person aged 15–19 years. Interviewers spoke with the person in this age range or, if there was more than one person in this range, with the first one who could be reached by telephone. For individuals aged 15–17 years, parental permission was obtained before interviewing began. For both adults and adolescents, the interview was described as a survey about health issues.

For adults, a smoker was defined as someone who smoked any cigarettes in the past 30 days and smoked at least 100 cigarettes in his or her lifetime. An adult nonsmoker was someone who had never smoked or someone who had not smoked in the past 30 days and had not smoked 100 cigarettes in his or her lifetime. Former smokers were excluded from the interview. For adolescents, a smoker was defined as someone who had smoked any cigarettes in the past 30 days. An adolescent nonsmoker was someone who had never smoked or had not smoked in the past 30 days and had not smoked more than two cigarettes in his or her lifetime. Again, former smokers were not interviewed.

The survey was conducted between December 2000 and February 2001. Calling continued until approximately 200 interviews were completed in each of four categories: Adult smokers ($n = 173$), adult nonsmokers ($n = 205$), adolescent smokers ($n = 193$) and adolescent nonsmokers ($n = 205$). It proved difficult to reach adolescents, especially adolescent smokers, despite as many as 30 attempts. The Council of American Survey Research Organizations completion rate among eligible respondents was 43 per cent, and the refusal rate was 10 per cent.

Survey instrument

The telephone interview addressed the following main topics: Nature of the illnesses caused by smoking, probabilities of these illnesses, factors that affect these probabilities, nature and probability of addiction, support for tobacco control policies, and basic demographic characteristics. This chapter is limited to the first topic, with knowledge assessed by the following questions:

- Illnesses caused by smoking. 'To the best of your knowledge, what illnesses if any, are caused by smoking cigarettes? [Record verbatim] Anything else? [Probe until no more illnesses are generated. Probe unspecified 'cancer' with] What kind of cancer?' Answers were coded later, with 92 per cent inter-rater agreement. The same open-ended question with probing was asked in Annenberg 2, although the answers were not recorded verbatim but were immediately coded into the categories listed in the results section of this chapter.
- Lung cancer curability. 'Once someone gets an illness, there are three possible outcomes: They might get cured; or they might die from the illness; or they might not get cured but die of something else. Out of 100 people who get lung cancer, how many do you think get cured? Your best estimate is fine. How many people out of 100 who get lung cancer do you think die from it? Your best estimate is fine.' [The 'cured' and 'die' questions also were asked in the opposite order.]
- Lung cancer life expectancy. 'Once a person is diagnosed with lung cancer, how many years do you think he or she typically lives: 1 or 2 years, 3 to 5 years, 6 to 10, 11 to 20 or more than 20 years?'
- Lung cancer pain and suffering. 'Please tell me how much you know about the pain and suffering you would feel if you had lung cancer. Would you say you know a lot (4), a moderate amount (3), a little (2) or not much at all (1)?'
- Emphysema recognition. 'Have you ever heard of an illness called emphysema?'
- Emphysema seriousness. 'Do you think emphysema is more a nagging problem or a life-threatening illness?'
- Emphysema curability. 'If emphysema is detected early, is it always curable (4), usually curable (3), sometimes curable (2) or not curable (1)?'
- Emphysema pain and suffering. 'Please tell me how much you know about the pain and suffering you would feel if you had emphysema. Would you say you know a lot (4), a moderate amount (3), a little (2), or not much at all (1)?'

Annenberg 2

The Annenberg 2 survey was a random-digit-dialled telephone survey in the continental United States conducted between November 1999 and February 2000 (Jamieson and Romer, 2001). Interviews were conducted with smokers and nonsmokers aged 14 years or older. People aged 14–22 years were oversampled so that youth and adult smokers could be analysed separately. A smoker was defined as a person who reported smoking at least one cigarette in the past 30 days. Former smokers were grouped with nonsmokers. Altogether, the survey successfully interviewed 2002 people aged 14–22 years (including 487 current smokers) and 1504 people aged 23 years or older (including 310 current smokers). The response rate for the youth sample was 51 per cent, and the response rate for the adult sample was 38 per cent.

In the question relevant to this chapter, respondents were asked, 'To the best of your knowledge, what, if any, are the illnesses caused by smoking cigarettes?'

Table 21.1 *Characteristics of survey respondents*

	Adolescents (n = 398)	*Adults (n = 378)*
Gender (percentage male)	52	37
Race (percentage white)	91	85
Age (median; years)	17	46
Education (percentage with at least some college)	18	55
Smokers' cigarettes per day (percentage)		
≤ 5	58	19
6–9	27	36
≥20	15	45

Interviewers were instructed to 'probe until no further ideas come to mind.' Responses were coded by interviewers into the categories lung cancer, emphysema, heart disease, stroke, throat cancer, mouth cancer, diabetes, bronchitis and other.

Results

Sample

Characteristics of the adolescent and adult samples are presented in Table 21.1. Compared with the US population, our samples contained significantly fewer nonwhite respondents and more respondents who had college degrees. The adults in our sample were slightly older than the US population. However, because weighting our samples to resemble the US population affected response frequencies by 2 per cent or less, only the unweighted results are reported here.

Analyses

Tests for effects of age, smoking status, or their interaction on survey responses were based on analysis of variance (ANOVA) calculations for both numerical responses (e.g. number of lung cancer victims who are cured) and categorical responses (e.g. mentioning or not mentioning lung cancer). Although ANOVA is not designed for categorical data, with large samples, the results from this procedure become the same as those from categorical procedures, such as chi-square.

Identity of the illnesses caused by smoking

Respondents' ability to tell us what illnesses are caused by cigarette smoking was quite limited (Table 21.2). A large percentage mentioned lung cancer, though adult smokers were significantly less likely to mention this illness. However, only 18–34 per cent of the groups in this survey mentioned any kind of mouth, throat or gum cancer. Very few (3–7 per cent) named any other of the cancers related to

Table 21.2 *Illnesses believed to be caused by cigarettes*
(open-ended responses, percentage)

	Adolescents		Adults		Smoking (S)	Age (A)	S x A
	Smokers	Non-smokers	Smokers	Non-smokers			
Any cancer	88	91	73	87	**	***	*
Lung cancer	87	86	67	81	*	****	*
Mouth or throat cancer	24	34	18	20		**	
Other specified cancer	3	5	3	7	*		
Any non-cancer lung problem	71	54	61	62	*		**
Emphysema or chronic obstructive pulmonary disease	62	40	49	51	**		***
Bronchitis	8	4	7	2	**		
Asthma	4	7	8	4			*
Any cardiovascular problem	17	15	39	32		****	
Heart disease or heart problem	16	14	34	28		****	
Hypertension	1	2	5	4		**	
Stroke	0	0	4	2		**	

Note: Respondents were probed until they could generate no more illnesses. Answers were coded for specific illnesses and for broad categories.
$*p < .05, **p < .01, ***p < .001, ****p < .0001$.

smoking, such as those of the pancreas, cervix, bladder or kidney. (See Centers for Disease Control and Prevention, 2002, for a detailed list of the causes of death attributable to smoking.) Altogether, 73–91 per cent mentioned cancer in some way. About half of our sample mentioned emphysema or chronic obstructive pulmonary disease, but few mentioned bronchitis or asthma. Pneumonia and influenza, other illnesses for which smokers are at elevated risk, were rarely mentioned. Altogether, 54–71 per cent mentioned some kind of lung problem other than lung cancer.

Most striking was the limited recall of cardiovascular problems related to smoking, especially among adolescents. The fraction of adolescents who mentioned heart disease or heart problems was about 15 per cent, and the corresponding fraction of adults was about 31 per cent. Very few people mentioned hypertension, atherosclerosis, aneurisms or stroke. Only 15–17 per cent of adolescents and only 32–39 per cent of adults mentioned any kind of cardiovascular problem. Less than 1 per cent mentioned any perinatal conditions.

Table 21.3 *Illnesses believed to be caused by cigarettes (open-ended responses, percentage), Annenberg survey*

	Youth		Adults		Smoking	Age	
	Smokers (n = 478)	Nonsmokers (n = 1524)	Smokers (n = 310)	Nonsmokers (n = 1194)	(S)	(A)	S x A
Lung cancer	87	90	76	86	****	****	*
Mouth, throat or gum cancer	22	23	20	25			
Emphysema or chronic obstructive pulmonary disease	61	40	54	55	****	*	****
Bronchitis	9	7	6	8			*
Heart disease or heart problems	25	15	24	25	*	**	**
Stroke	3	1	2	2			
Diabetes	< 1	< 1	1	< 1			

Note: Respondents were probed until they could generate no more illnesses. Answers were precoded for the illnesses listed, except that mouth and throat cancer categories have been combined to facilitate comparison with Table 21.2.
*$p < .05$, **$p < .01$, ***$p < .001$, ****$p < .0001$.

Comparable data from Annenberg 2 are presented in Table 21.3. Because the Annenberg 2 youth and adult respondents were not from a single, random sample, the Annenberg 2 age categories (14–22 years and 23 years or older) were retained even though they differ from those in our study. A comparison of Tables 21.2 and 21.3 reveals both similarities and differences with respect to the subgroup contrasts that proved significant. In both surveys, smokers were somewhat less likely than nonsmokers to mention lung cancer, and young smokers were more likely than young nonsmokers to mention emphysema.

Despite occasional differences at the subgroup level, the relative frequencies with which different illnesses were mentioned were highly consistent across the two studies. Starting with the illness mentioned most often (percentages for the present study and Annenberg, respectively, combined across subgroups, are given in parentheses), they were lung cancer (81 per cent vs. 87 per cent), emphysema (50 per cent vs. 49 per cent), mouth or throat cancer (24 per cent vs. 23 per cent), heart disease (23 per cent vs. 21 per cent), bronchitis (5 per cent vs. 8 per cent, and asthma (5 per cent for the present study; this category was not covered in the Annenberg study). No other illness was mentioned by more than 5 per cent of the sample in either survey.

Severity of lung cancer and emphysema

Because the order in which people were asked about the likelihood of dying from lung cancer or being cured of lung cancer had no significant effect on the answers

Table 21.4 *Beliefs about severity of lung cancer*

	Adolescents		Adults		Smoking	Age	
	Smokers	Non-smokers	Smokers	Non-smokers	(S)	(A)	S x A
Mortality							
Die (mean n in 100)	67	67	69	70			
Cured (mean n in 100)	22	21	19	21			
Underestimate death rate (percentage)	82	82	71	71		****	
Estimated life expectancy (percentage)						****	
≤ 2 years	19	20	35	34			
3–5 years	50	50	45	43			
≥ 6 years	31	30	20	23			
Know little about the pain and suffering (percentage responding 'a little' or 'not much at all')	53	73	49	46		****	*

Note: * $p < .05$, ** $p < .01$, *** $p < .001$, **** $p < .0001$.

given ($p > 0.2$), the answers from the two different question orders were combined. The actual ten-year death rate is estimated to be 90 per cent (Ries et al, 2001). As seen in Table 21.4, all groups underestimated the percentage of people diagnosed with lung cancer who would die from it and overestimated the number who would be cured. (The third category, not explicitly assessed, would be people who are not cured but die from something else.) Adolescents, in particular, underestimated mortality from lung cancer; 82 per cent of young people and 71 per cent of adults gave estimates of deaths that were low. Adolescents also were more likely to underestimate how quickly lung cancer victims succumb. The median survival time from diagnosis is only ten months (Surveillance, Epidemiology, and End Results Program, 2001), but only about 20 per cent of adolescents and 35 per cent of adults selected the shortest option available, 'two years or less.' In addition, a large proportion of our sample said they knew only 'a little' or 'not much at all' about the pain and suffering associated with lung cancer; more adolescents said they were relatively uninformed.

Nearly all respondents said they had heard of emphysema, but this does not mean that they had an accurate understanding of this disease. Between 11 per cent and 17 per cent of adolescents and adults saw emphysema as a 'nagging problem' rather than as a life-threatening illness (Table 21.5). Furthermore, only

Table 21.5 *Beliefs about severity of emphysema*

	Adolescents		Adults		Smoking (S)	Age (A)	S x A
	Smokers	Non-smokers	Smokers	Non-smokers			
Have heard of emphysema (percentage responding 'yes')	99	91	99	94		****	
Nature of emphysema (percentage responding 'nagging problem')	17	17	15	11			
Curability (percentage responding 'not curable')	27	19	56	40	**	****	
Know little about the pain and suffering (percentage responding 'a little' or 'not much at all')	68	81	50	45		****	*

Note: $*p < .05, **p < .01, ***p < .001, ****p < .0001$.

about a quarter of adolescents and half of adults realized that emphysema, once diagnosed, is not curable. Smokers were better informed than nonsmokers. Finally, a large majority of adolescents and about half of adults said that they knew only 'a little' or 'not much at all' about the pain and suffering they would experience if they had emphysema.

Discussion

As the preceding results demonstrate, one cannot answer the question 'Do people understand the risks of cigarette smoking?' with a simple yes or no answer. Smoking is too complex to reduce understanding to a dichotomy. In the present study and Annenberg 2, the great majority of smokers and nonsmokers realized that smoking can cause life-threatening illnesses, but, except for lung cancer, no specific smoking-linked illness could be named by more than half of our respondents. About half mentioned emphysema, about a quarter mentioned any kind of cancer other than lung, and only about a quarter mentioned any kind of cardiovascular risk. About 10 per cent did not mention cancer at all. The preceding summary applies nearly equally to adolescents and adults. Adolescents mentioned lung cancer slightly but, significantly, more often than did adults, and adolescents mentioned cardiovascular problems less often in our study than did adults.

We used a probed, open-ended question to assess knowledge of the identity of smoking-related diseases rather than the more common approach in which respondents are asked whether they think a particular disease is related to smoking. The latter approach reminds people of the illness as the question is asked. We believe our approach is a more appropriate way to assess the extent to which this information would be available to smokers and potential smokers when they make decisions about smoking initiation or cessation.

Regarding the nature of lung cancer, respondents knew that victims are likely to die of that disease, but 71 per cent of adults and 82 per cent of adolescents underestimated the fatality rate. The longevity of people who are diagnosed with lung cancer also was greatly overestimated. Underestimating the severity of lung cancer was greater among adolescents than adults.

Nearly everyone said they had heard of emphysema. Most recognized it as a life-threatening illness, though a troubling minority viewed it as merely a 'nagging problem.' Still, people substantially overestimated the tractability of this illness; only a minority recognized that it is incurable. Finally, about half of our adult respondents and more than two-thirds of our adolescent respondents said they knew little about the suffering experienced by those who develop these illnesses.

In general, differences in knowledge between smokers and nonsmokers were small; however, smokers were more likely to cite emphysema as an illness related to smoking and said they were more familiar with the pain and suffering of these illnesses. Interestingly, in both surveys smokers were less likely than nonsmokers to cite cancer as an outcome related to cigarettes. Viscusi (1990) has argued that smokers choose this behaviour in part because they view the risks as smaller. Compared with nonsmokers, smokers rated negative consequences as less probable (Weinstein, 1999a), though this finding may simply be a justification for their behaviour rather than a cause of that behaviour. However, the present data showed that they do not, in general, view the consequences as less severe.

A limitation of the present study is that the adolescent respondents were drawn from a list of households identified as likely to contain teenagers, not from random-digit dialling or from some other sampling frame that is not preselected. Thus, the results from our adolescent sample may differ in unknown ways from a true random sample of youngsters in the same age range, and conclusions about differences between adults and adolescents must be tentative because of the different sampling approaches. Also, despite a low refusal rate, our completion rate was relatively low and may lead to differences between our data and the broader US population. However, because the completion rate was mainly a result of difficulty speaking to respondents, not refusals (in fact, nearly all refusals occurred before smoking was ever mentioned), a reluctance to talk about smoking issues was not a significant reason for failing to participate. It is difficult to think of reasons why people who are easier to reach at home should be less informed about smoking than people who are hard to reach.

The present results showed that investigating a multifaceted topic, such as understanding of smoking risks, is itself complex. A variety of questions is needed, to explore not only the different smoking consequences but also the depth of understanding of these concepts. For example, nearly everyone in our survey said they had heard of emphysema and a large majority believed it to be a life-threatening illness. If we had stopped at this point, we might have concluded that people have a good understanding of the severity of this disease. However, further questioning revealed a much different picture because many respondents thought that emphysema is curable and admitted to knowing little about what it would be like to experience this disabling illness.

Together with data demonstrating that smokers are unrealistically optimistic about their ability to quit (Slovic, 2001) and data demonstrating that smokers see themselves as having a less risky smoking pattern and lower risk than other smokers (Weinstein, 1999a), the present data reinforce a picture of smokers, especially adolescent smokers, as having a very superficial knowledge of the risks they face. The public does not yet have the minimal information needed to make a decision about cigarette use, and we have not come close to conveying a full appreciation of the harms in store for many who begin to smoke. Scare tactics are not the way to achieve this end and may even backfire. Providing a real sense of what it would mean to suffer prematurely from disabling or fatal illness and a more realistic appreciation of the cravings of nicotine addiction could be much more effective than the tobacco warnings typically offered. Yet, ways to achieve these goals have received little attention – not just in smoking research but in health promotion research in general – and certainly deserve further study.

The finding that both smokers and nonsmokers lack basic knowledge about the nature and severity of illnesses associated with smoking has important implications. We believe that society has a moral obligation to make all citizens knowledgeable about serious threats to health, and the present data point out major deficiencies in smoking knowledge. Such knowledge could influence the debate about smoking policies, such as taxation, minimum purchase age, government regulation of nicotine, and the permissibility of smoking in public places. Whether theories of decision making and health behaviour are correct that effective education about the seriousness of lung cancer and other smoking-related disease will deter people from smoking or increase smokers' efforts to quit remains an open question. The fact that smokers in the present study had almost as much, or sometimes even more, knowledge than nonsmokers does not demonstrate that such knowledge is irrelevant to smoking decisions. Correlational data cannot be used to demonstrate either causality or lack of causality. If nonsmokers had been much better informed than smokers, this might suggest an intervention to determine whether increasing the knowledge of smokers or potential smokers would decrease smoking. However, even nonsmokers were poorly informed, decreasing the possibility of finding such a relationship, and, furthermore, smokers are likely to have gained some of their knowledge after they began to smoke. Whatever factors motivated the smokers in the present study to initiate and continue this behaviour might have failed to do so had these individuals been more adequately informed.

Acknowledgements

The authors gratefully acknowledge support from the Robert Wood Johnson Substance Abuse Policy Research Program. They also thank Daniel Romer, Patrick Jamieson and Kathleen Jamieson of the Annenberg School of Communication, University of Pennsylvania, for providing access to the Annenberg smoking survey data.

Chapter 22

The Impact and Acceptability of Canadian-style Cigarette Warning Labels Among US Smokers and Nonsmokers

Ellen Peters, Daniel Romer, Paul Slovic, Kathleen Hall Jamieson, Leisha Wharfield, C. K. Mertz and Stephanie M. Carpenter[*]

Introduction

Smoking remains the largest preventable source of mortality in the United States (USDHHS, 2000). A review of successful programmes for prevention and cessation of tobacco use indicated that, apart from raising the price of tobacco products through taxation, several effective strategies involve dissemination of advice and information (Hopkins et al, 2001). In particular, media campaigns have reduced the uptake of smoking among adolescents and encouraged cessation among adults. In addition, reminders from health providers to their patients about the hazards of smoking and the benefits of quitting have been found to reduce smoking. However, increasing the quit rates among those who either use or are beginning to use cigarettes will require a range of strategies (USDHHS, 2000).

One particularly effective way of reaching cigarette users is through warning labels on cigarette packaging. The United States pioneered the use of such warnings when Congress mandated, in 1965, that the statement 'Cigarette smoking may be hazardous to your health' be placed on the side of all cigarette packs. A few years later the statement was changed to 'The Surgeon General has

[*] Reprinted from Peters, E., Romer, D., Slovic, P., Jamieson, K. H., Wharfield, L., Mertz, C. K. and Carpenter, S. M. (2007b) 'The impact and acceptability of Canadian-style cigarette warning labels among U.S. smokers and nonsmokers', *Nicotine & Tobacco Research*, vol 9, no 4, pp473–481

determined that cigarette smoking is dangerous to your health.' The only major change made since then was in 1984 when the labels were diversified to include four statements warning of health hazards in somewhat more specific terms (e.g. 'Surgeon General's Warning: Quitting smoking now greatly reduces serious risks to your health').

Research on the effects of these labels suggests that they have little influence on tobacco sales. They lack salience and persuasive power compared with the more colourful packaging and other forms of tobacco promotion (Fischer et al, 1989, 1993). Indeed, one study with adolescents found that users were virtually unaffected by the presence of these labels (Robinson and Killen, 1997). An expert panel commissioned by the National Academy of Sciences described the warnings as 'woefully deficient when evaluated in terms of proper public health criteria' (Lynch and Bonnie, 1994).

The new international Framework Convention on Tobacco Control sponsored by the World Health Organization (2005) encourages the use of larger warnings on cigarette packs that contain colour pictures to illustrate health hazards. Canada has had such a system in place since late 2000, with warning labels covering over 50 per cent of cigarette packs, front and back, with additional information on the inside about resources for quitting (see Figure 22.1 for an example of one such warning). The European Union has plans for similar labelling requirements, and Australia as well as countries in Asia (e.g. Thailand and Singapore) and South America (e.g. Brazil, Venezuela and Uruguay) have already implemented them. However, the United States has not ratified the treaty, and efforts to regulate cigarette labelling have stalled in Congress.

Any efforts to implement graphic warning labels in the US market will probably be met with stern resistance from the tobacco industry. One argument that may be deployed is that larger warnings violate the industry's commercial speech rights (Framework Convention Alliance for Tobacco Control, 2005). Unless it can be shown that larger and more graphic warnings provide an effective mechanism to inform cigarette users of the hazards of the product, the industry can claim that

Figure 22.1 *One of 16 warning labels used on cigarette packages in Canada*

the public health benefit of the warnings does not outweigh the burden imposed on the industry. To respond to this concern, it is important to demonstrate that larger graphic labels are appreciated by cigarette users while also communicating more effective information about the hazards for both users and non-users than current labels provide.

One of the ways that more graphic warning labels can help consumers appreciate the risks of smoking is to create unfavourable emotional associations with the behaviour. Bland descriptions of the health hazards of smoking, such as currently displayed on cigarette packs in the United States, are unlikely to create such associations, because they fail to attract attention (Argo and Main, 2004) or to make the health danger sufficiently compelling (Wogalter and Laughery, 1996). Affective associations, whether achieved through learning or simple primes, are important determinants of judgements and choice behaviour (Murphy and Zajonc, 1993; Damasio, 1994; Slovic et al, 2004) and are highly related to perceptions of risk and to the initiation and quitting of smoking (Brandon et al, 1999; Romer and Jamieson, 2001; Slovic, 2001). These affective associations are easily accessed and need not require deliberation to be effective (Epstein, 1994; Zajonc, 1980, 2001). More graphic warning labels may attach negative affect to the many smoking cues that elicit craving in smokers (Marlatt and Gordon, 1985; Niaura et al, 1988), thereby supporting their efforts to quit. The labels also could work to undermine the attractiveness of the smoker image, the favourableness of which has been a key goal of cigarette advertising and promotion (Pollay, 1995, 2000).

Survey research in Canada suggests that the larger labels with colour pictures and 16 separate messages about specific risks of smoking create more negative emotional associations with cigarettes and increase smokers' attempts to quit (Hammond et al, 2003, 2004a). However, this research relies on smokers' reports of exposure and attention to the labels. As noted by one critic, 'Smokers will often say they quit because of their health. Without an experimental design, there is no evidence that warning labels are responsible for these outcomes ...' (Ruiter, 2005). Furthermore, even though sales of cigarettes have declined since the introduction of the labels (Health Canada, 2007), taxes on cigarettes also increased, and new laws were passed restricting smoking in public places, making causal inferences regarding the role of the labels difficult (Mahood, 2004).

An important concern about the use of graphic warnings is the potential that such labels will prove to be too fear-arousing to be effective (Witte and Allen, 2000; Ruiter et al, 2001). As a critic of such labels put it, 'The evidence in this area suggests that especially those who are most at risk (i.e. smokers) react defensively to these messages ... Defensive reactions serve to get rid of the fear, not necessarily the threat. Policy makers should thus be reluctant to introduce cigarette warning labels ...' (Ruiter, 2005). Based on this reasoning, there is a risk that overly graphic warnings will cause users to avoid exposure to the labels, to derogate the messages, and potentially to reinforce favourable reactions to smoking. Although a study of the effects of Canadian labels (Hammond et al, 2004a) found little evidence for such defensive avoidance, the lack of research with controlled exposure to the labels leaves open the possibility that only those who were predisposed to find the labels helpful reacted favourably to them. It is important therefore to evaluate the potential for adverse effects of introducing Canadian-style labels in the US market with a design that compares exposure to the Canadian labels with exposure to current labels.

The present study randomly assigned a community sample of US smokers and nonsmokers to receive exposure in a controlled laboratory setting to either Canadian or US labels. To determine the breadth of effects of such exposure, we assessed the emotional impact of each set of labels as well as the effects of exposure on smoking-related cues and the smoker image. We assessed defensive reactions to the Canadian-style labels by unobtrusively measuring time spent examining them and by asking both smokers and nonsmokers to evaluate the credibility of the labels and whether they should be used in the US market.

Method

Participants

Participants ($N = 169$) were recruited through advertisements in local papers and flyers distributed in the local community (Eugene, Oregon). We used a two-way factorial design in which smokers and nonsmokers were randomly assigned to either a Canadian warning label condition ($n = 84$, with 43 smokers and 41 nonsmokers) or a US warning label condition ($n = 85$, with 45 smokers and 40 nonsmokers). Each participant received US$10 for completing the experiment individually in a one-hour session.

Procedure

Participants were asked, 'Do you ever smoke cigarettes?' so that they could be randomly assigned to either the Canadian or US label condition. Participants were seated at a computer and responded to an overall measure of attitude toward smoking: 'What is your attitude or opinion about cigarette smoking?' on a nine-point scale ranging from -4 (*extremely negative*) to $+4$ (*extremely positive*), and then commenced on Phase I of the task. In Phase I, those in the Canadian label condition viewed 16 different Canadian labels that appeared in a random order, whereas those in the US condition viewed the four current labels, each randomly appearing four times. The sizes of the two sets of labels as they appeared on the computer screen were roughly comparable. Participants controlled the exposure duration of each label, which was measured in milliseconds (ms) by the computer.

In Phase II, participants were asked to quickly but accurately give their impressions of a series of four smoking images (i.e. a close-up picture of a burning cigarette in an ashtray, a distant picture of a cigarette in an ashtray, an extreme close-up of a lit cigarette showing smoke and burning-red tobacco, and a picture of a lit cigarette in a smoker's hand) and four smoking-related words (i.e. nicotine, tobacco, cigarette and smoking). They provided similar reactions to eight food-related images (e.g. meat and vegetables on a plate) and words (e.g. nutrition). For each word and image, participants responded to the question 'What is your attitude or opinion?' by pressing one of two buttons for each of four adjective pairs (e.g. good–bad, positive–negative, favourable–unfavourable, and like–dislike). For example, if the word nicotine appeared on the screen with the good–bad adjective pair underneath it, and the participant felt good about it, she would press the button under the word good. The adjective pairs were presented in random order for each image with a randomized right–left orientation at the bottom of the screen. Response times (RTs) were recorded from the moment the adjectives appeared on the screen to the moment participants pushed one of the two response buttons. The resolution of the RTs was 16.7ms. Mean RTs were calculated from three target items for each image and word (RTs for the first target item for each image and word were deleted). Mean RTs were subjected to a 1/RT transformation to correct for skewness in all subsequent analyses (e.g. Fazio and Hilden, 2001). Untransformed mean RTs are reported in milliseconds in the text.

Participants then answered a series of questions on the computer. They were shown a US and a Canadian cigarette label and were asked whether Canadian labels should be used in the United States. They also were asked whether the minimum age for buying cigarettes should be raised. To assess vulnerability to becoming a smoker, we asked a question set developed by Pierce et al (1995). Based on their responses, current nonsmokers were classified as either not vulnerable or possibly vulnerable to becoming a smoker. Participants were considered possibly vulnerable if they had ever smoked a cigarette; if they had ever tried or experimented with cigarette smoking, even a few puffs; or if they answered yes to the question 'Do you think that you will try a cigarette soon?' Participants who went through the series of questions with a 'no' or 'definitely not' response to all questions were considered not vulnerable. Current smokers were simply asked how much they smoked using an eight-point scale ranging from less than one cigarette/day (1) to *11–14 cigarettes/day* (4) to *two packs/day or more* (8).

Participants next completed a task designed to measure affective images of smokers. Using a method inspired by Haire's (1950) 'Shopping List Survey,' we showed participants a shopping list of groceries bought by a student and asked them to 'project yourself into the situation as far as possible until you can more or less characterize the University of Oregon undergraduate who bought the groceries. Then write a brief description of his personality and character.' The shopping list contained six food items and a pack of cigarettes.

Participants then viewed all 16 Canadian labels or all four US labels again (depending on their condition) and were asked their affective reaction to each label, 'How does this warning label make you think and feel about cigarette smoking?' on a nine-point scale ranging from −4 (*extremely negative*) to +4 (*extremely positive*). In addition, they were asked to rate the credibility of the labels, 'How much do you believe the information in the warning label is true or false?' on a nine-point scale ranging from −4 (*completely false*) to +4 (*completely true*). Finally, participants provided demographics such as age, gender and education (1 = *8th grade or less* to 7 = *more than a four-year college degree*).

Table 22.1 *Characteristics of respondents in preent survey*

Characteristic	Status	Canadian	US	Average
Age (years)	Smoker	37	38	37
	Nonsmoker	37	32	34
	Mean	37	35	36
Education (1 = 8th grade or less to	Smoker	4.3	4.3	4.3
4 = vocational or trade school to	Nonsmoker	5.3	5.0	5.1
7 = more than a four-year college degree)	Mean	4.8	4.6	4.7
Gender (% female)	Smoker	30%	29%	30%
	Nonsmoker	46%	63%	54%
	Mean	38%	45%	41%
Amount smoked (1 = less than one cigarette to 4 = 11–14 cigarettes/day to 8 = two packs/day or more)	Smoker	3.5	4.1	3.8

Note: No significant differences existed between conditions or smoking status except that smokers were significantly less educated than nonsmokers.

Results

Approximately one-third of the sample was aged 18–24 years. Age, education, gender and amount smoked were not significantly different between participants exposed to Canadian and US warning labels (Table 22.1). Smokers were less educated than nonsmokers ($p < .001$). No other differences reached significance.

Looking time at warning labels

In Phase I, participants in the Canadian label condition looked at the warning labels for longer than did participants in the US label condition: Means (medians) = 8.4 (8.3) and 4.5 (4.4) seconds (s); $F(1, 165) = 115.7$, $p < .0001$. Neither smoker status nor its interaction with the label condition was a significant predictor of looking time (smokers' and nonsmokers' mean looking times were both 8.2s in the Canadian condition and were 4.1 and 4.3s, respectively, in the US condition).

Initial attitudes toward cigarette smoking

Not surprisingly, nonsmokers had significantly more negative initial attitudes toward cigarette smoking than did smokers (mean attitudes = −3.0 and 0.5, respectively, $p < .0001$). The initial attitudes of participants in the Canadian condition were marginally more negative than those in the US condition ($p = .10$); the interaction of smoker status and condition was not significant (initial-attitude means = −1.0 and −3.1 for smokers and nonsmokers, respectively, in the Canadian condition, and 0.0 and −3.0 for smokers and nonsmokers, respectively, in the US condition). A large proportion of nonsmokers gave the most extreme negative rating for their initial smoking attitude (49 per cent and 60 per cent of nonsmokers in the Canadian and US conditions, respectively, rated their attitude toward smoking as −4, compared with 16 per cent and 2 per cent of smokers in the same two conditions). In view of these initial attitude differences, it was important to control for them in all analyses.

Affective reactions to warning labels

We asked participants how the warning labels made them think and feel about smoking. In this direct measure of affect associated with the labels, participants in the Canadian label condition reported that their warning labels made them feel more negative toward smoking than those in the US label condition (Table 22.2; mean = −2.9 and −1.5, respectively, $p < .0001$). This finding remained significant after controlling for initial attitude toward smoking. The mean ratings of the 16 Canadian labels were uniformly more negative than any of the four US labels. Smoking status was not a significant predictor of affective reactions to the labels after controlling for initial attitude (mean affect for the Canadian labels was −2.4 and −3.5 for smokers and nonsmokers, respectively, whereas mean affect for the US labels was −0.9 and −2.1 for smokers and nonsmokers, respectively).

We asked participants how much they believed the information in the labels to be true or false using a scale from completely false (−4) to completely true (+4; see Table 22.2). Overall, participants in each of the four groups believed their labels to be truthful (mean belief in truth = 2.6 and 3.1 for smokers in the Canadian and US conditions, $p = .06$; mean belief in truth = 3.4 and 3.3 for nonsmokers in the Canadian and US conditions, *ns*).

Affect toward smoking words and images after exposure to warning labels

We assessed reactions to smoking-related words and images that might elicit craving in smokers and possible interest in nonsmokers. An index of affect toward smoking cues was created in response to four smoking-related words and four smoking-related images. This index was calculated from the mean response to each stimulus after deleting the first adjective pair encountered for each stimulus. As hypothesized, affect toward smoking cues was more negative for participants in the Canadian than in the US condition (mean affect ≈ ~0.8 and −0.5, respectively, RMANOVA, $p < .01$; eta-square = .05). Smokers and nonsmokers reported more negative affect toward smoking cues after exposure to the Canadian labels than after exposure to US labels. After controlling for initial smoking attitude, amount of smoking, age and gender, we found that a significant difference remained between the Canadian and US conditions (Figure 22.2). To examine the effect of the labels on individuals most likely to initiate smoking, we conducted this analysis again with young nonsmokers, aged 18–24 years, who were possibly vulnerable to smoking based on responses to the Pierce et al (1995) scale. Exposure to Canadian labels was still associated with significantly more negative

Table 22.2 *Mean rated affect toward and truthfulness of warning labels*

Label message	Affect	Truthfulness
US labels		
Smoking by pregnant women	−2.1	3.2
Smoking causes lung cancer, etc.	−2.0	3.4
Cigarette smoke contains carbon monoxide	−1.1	3.4
Quitting reduces serious risks	−0.8	2.9
Mean	−1.5	3.2
Canadian labels[*]		
Smoke hurts babies (baby in ICU)	−3.4	3.3
Mouth diseases	−3.2	3.1
Cigarettes hurt babies (pregnant)	−3.1	3.3
Equivalent of small city dies	−3.1	2.9
Lung cancer (person in hospital)	−3.1	3.3
Cigarettes cause strokes (brain)	−3.1	3.0
Lung cancer (lung)	−3.0	3.2
Children see children do	−2.9	2.9
Don't poison us (children)	−2.9	3.1
Leaves you breathless (cough)	−2.9	3.3
Heartbreaker (clogged arteries)	−2.9	2.9
Idle but deadly	−2.8	3.0
Highly addictive (heroin or cocaine)	−2.7	3.0
Hydrogen cyanide	−2.7	2.8
You're not the only one smoking	−2.6	2.7
Tobacco can make you impotent	−2.6	2.2
Mean	−2.9	3.0

Notes: Affect was rated in response to the question, 'How does this warning label make you think and feel about cigarette smoking?' (−4 = *extremely negative* to +4 = *extremely positive*). Truthfulness was rated in response to the question: 'How much do you believe the information in the warning label is true or false?' (−4 = *completely false* to +4 = *completely true*).
[*] Brief descriptions of graphics are given in parentheses.

affect toward smoking cues than was exposure to US labels (mean affect = −0.9 and −0.76, respectively, $p = .04$, one-tailed). We found no significant differences between participants in the Canadian and US label conditions in affect toward the food stimuli. Because the novelty of the Canadian warning labels could explain this effect, we conducted a final analysis controlling for the average time participants had spent looking at the labels. Condition remained significant after controlling for looking time.

The stronger negative associations with smoking cues for participants in the Canadian condition, compared with the US condition, could be the result of responding to perceived experimenter demand to evaluate cigarettes more unfavourably in the Canadian condition. This socially desirable response,

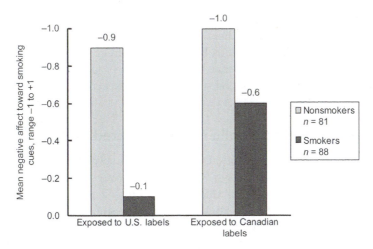

Figure 22.2 *Mean negative affect toward smoking cues among smokers and nonsmokers in the Canadian and US conditions*

however, should take longer because the subject has to first suppress the initial unconsidered response (Fazio and Olson, 2003), suggesting that responses in the Canadian condition should be slower. On the other hand, we hypothesized that the Canadian labels produce greater automatic negative affect, predicting that responses will be accessed faster in the Canadian than the US condition. A MANOVA of response times with condition, initial attitude, age and gender as independent variables revealed that responses in the Canadian condition were made faster than those in the US condition (mean response times = 970 and 1101ms, respectively, $p = .04$, one-tailed).

Affect toward the smoker image

In the final task, participants described the person who purchased groceries that included a pack of cigarettes. Two independent coders blind to condition rated the attitude or affective tone each participant conveyed about the person buying groceries on a three-point scale (-1 = *negative*, 0 = *neutral*, +1 = *positive*). The last author, also blind to condition, compared all responses and calculated the coders' overall reliability as a simple percentage by counting the number of times the coders agreed on the affect rating and dividing by the total number of affect ratings. With this analysis, coders averaged 82 per cent agreement. The last author resolved any differences prior to analysis.

In a two-way ANOVA (analysis of covariance) controlling for initial attitude toward smoking, participants exposed to Canadian labels were more negative in their descriptions of the shopper's personality and character (mean affect = -0.3 and -0.1, for the Canadian and US conditions, respectively, $p = .03$). This main effect was qualified by a significant interaction such that nonsmokers did not differ from smokers in their reaction to the US labels, but the two groups did differ in their reaction to the Canadian label. Means in the US condition were -0.1 for both smokers and nonsmokers and were −0.2 and −0.4 for smokers and nonsmokers, respectively, in the Canadian condition, $p = .04$. Smoking status was not significant as a main effect. In addition, controlling for the average amount of time spent looking at the labels did not influence the significance of the main effect of condition nor its interaction with smoking status. The results were similar among young nonsmokers, aged 18–24 years, who were possibly vulnerable to smoking.

Beliefs about cigarette policies in the United States

Those in the Canadian label condition were marginally more likely to favour raising the minimum purchase age for buying cigarettes to 21 compared with those in the US label condition (60 per cent and 42 per cent, respectively, favoured raising the age; $p = .06$ after controlling for smoking status, its interaction with condition, and initial attitude).

A strong majority of nonsmokers (81 per cent) thought the United States should use warning labels similar to the Canadian labels; a majority of smokers (60 per cent) thought the same. This finding did not differ by condition.

Discussion

The use of graphic colour warning labels, covering over 50 per cent of the cigarette package, was initiated in Canada in December 2000. Surveys beginning in October/November 2001 indicated that the extent to which smokers reported reading, thinking about and discussing the new labels was associated with greater intentions to quit smoking and with actual quit attempts (Hammond et al, 2003). Smokers who quit before and after the introduction of the new labels were asked whether warning labels were a factor in their decision (Hammond et al, 2004b). Those who quit after the introduction of new graphic labels were 2.8 times more likely to cite warning labels as a quitting influence than those who quit prior to their introduction (and would have seen only the old warning labels).

Despite these promising results, the causal influence of the new warning labels remained unclear. Smokers who already intended to quit may have been more likely to read the larger labels and discuss them. Also, as noted earlier, cigarette taxes were increased and laws requiring all indoor public places in the study region to be smoke-free were implemented prior to the study (Hammond et al, 2004b). Furthermore, reactions to the warnings may not generalize from Canada to the United States. These limitations motivated the present study, conducted in a laboratory setting in the United States, where exposure to Canadian and US warning labels could be randomly assigned and closely monitored among both smokers and nonsmokers.

The results showed that the Canadian labels were examined voluntarily for longer durations than were the US labels among both smokers and nonsmokers and also led to consistently more negative affect toward smoking cues and smokers themselves. A subset of young nonsmokers, aged 18–24 years, who were more vulnerable to smoking also demonstrated these effects. Nonsmokers appeared to be influenced more by the Canadian labels than were smokers. Smokers, nonetheless, showed evidence of significant transfer of negative associations and feelings after exposure to the Canadian warning labels, to smoking cues, and to a shopper who purchased cigarettes. Also noteworthy was greater support by both smokers and nonsmokers for raising the minimum purchasing age for cigarettes and for introducing Canadian-style labels in the United States.

We found little evidence to suggest that the Canadian labels elicited defensive avoidance of the warnings among smokers. Smokers spent as much time viewing the labels as nonsmokers, rated them as equally credible to existing US labels, and supported their use in the US market to nearly the same level as nonsmokers. At the same time, they reported that the Canadian labels were more emotionally powerful than the US labels and their reactions to smoking words and cues in the Canadian condition were both more negative and accessed more rapidly than in the US condition. This pattern of reactions was not unexpected given the careful research conducted by the Canadians in developing the warning labels (Health Canada, 2003; Mahood, 2004). This research also suggested that a majority of smokers are supportive of such labels and appreciate the information they provide. These results, in combination with the less favourable images of smokers created by the Canadian labels, support the contention that large, graphic warning labels, such as those used in Canada and proposed for use in the United States and many other countries, are more likely to serve as effective warnings against cigarette smoking than current warning labels and also may facilitate more attempts and greater success at smoking cessation (Hammond et al, 2004b).

The use of Canadian-style labels may be an important component of a national tobacco-control strategy for several reasons. First, current smokers and potential smokers can be easily and efficiently reached with these warnings whenever they purchase or use cigarettes. Indeed, there is no more efficient method of reaching smokers than through the use of graphic and highly visible warning labels. Current warnings in the United States are easily ignored and do not transmit the same level of emotional impact as the colourful and graphic Canadian warnings. Indeed, a major moderator of the effectiveness of product warnings is the salience and vividness of the label (Argo and Main, 2004). Second, considerable psychological research suggests that the mere presentation of hazard information is not sufficient to motivate perceptions of risk (Slovic, 2000a). Risk is most readily communicated by information that arouses emotional associations with the activity (Hibbard and Peters, 2003). The present results indicate that brief exposure to the Canadian-style labels produces emotional connotations that transfer to smoking cues and have the potential to convey the appropriate degree of risk associated with the use of the product. Third, emotional associations can be readily accessed from memory by the mere presentation of the relevant stimulus (Zajonc, 2000, 2001). These associations can then work to reduce attraction to the stimulus and motivate cessation. Indeed, emotional associations to smoking appear to be powerful predictors of smoking behaviour and may well be causally implicated in efforts to either start or stop smoking

376 Risk Knowledge and Risk Communication

(Romer and Jamieson, 2001; Slovic, 2001; Hammond et al, 2003, 2004a).

One limitation of the present study is the brief level of exposure to the labels. This is possibly more detrimental to the impact of the Canadian labels, which are new, than to the impact of the more familiar US labels. At the same time, it is possible that the novelty of the Canadian labels increased their salience, giving them more impact. This might explain the longer time spent looking at them and provides the alternative hypothesis that the effects we see are related to an experimenter demand effect that was different for Canadian labels than for US labels. Controlling for looking time, however, did not change the significance of condition, suggesting that this factor did not account for the greater impact of the Canadian labels. Furthermore, although US labels are smaller and less salient than the Canadian labels, both labels were presented as nearly equal in size on the computer screen and thus may have benefited the US labels. Nevertheless, the Canadian labels had more impact. In addition, all measures were taken very near in time to the exposure to the labels. Effects of long-term exposure (that could result in habituation to the labels) and effects at a time distant from exposure (when demand effects would lessen) were not studied. Of course, as mentioned previously, many of the people in Canada who stopped smoking attributed their quitting to the graphic warning labels; this non-laboratory finding is suggestive of a long-term causal effect. A final limitation is that our design did not allow us to separate the influence of the graphic pictures from the textual risk information provided by the Canadian labels. However, a long line of research on the fear-arousing capacity of health messages suggests that graphic pictures illustrating health risks adds considerably to the emotional reaction to the warning (Witte and Allen, 2000; Ruiter et al, 2001).

Despite these limitations, the present study, combined with similar results from non-laboratory surveys in Canada, lends support to recommendations to use Canadian-style warnings on all cigarette packages in the United States. Warning labels for tobacco products are controlled by Congress and cannot be mandated by federal regulatory agencies. One step toward achieving this objective would be for the president to submit and for the US Senate to ratify the international Framework Convention on Tobacco Control that encourages signatories to use Canadian-style warnings.

Acknowledgements

This work was undertaken with funding from the Annenberg Foundation to the Annenberg Public Policy Center. The Annenberg Foundation played no role in any stage of this study. Additional support was provided by the National Science Foundation under grants SES-0241313 and SES-0339204 to Decision Research. The first author has had full access to all of the data in the study and takes responsibility for the integrity of the data and the accuracy of the data analysis.

References

Ackerman, B. A. (1980) *Social Justice in the Liberal State*, Yale University Press, New Haven, CT, chapter 12

Ackerman, B. A and Fishkin, J. S. (2004) *Deliberation Day*, Yale University Press, New Haven, CT, chapter 12

Ackerman, B. A. and Stewart, R. B. (1988) 'Reforming environmental law: The democratic case for market incentives', *Columbus Journal of Environmental Law*, vol 13, pp171–199, chapter 12

Ackerman, F. and Heinzerling, L. (2004) *Priceless: On Knowing the Cost of Everything and the Value of Nothing*, The New Press, New York, chapter 12

Ackoff, R. L. (1999) *Re-creating the Corporation: A Design of Organizations for the 21st Century*, Oxford University Press, New York, chapter 17

Adler, R. and Pittle, D. (1984) 'Cajolery or command: Are education campaigns an adequate substitute for regulation?', *Yale Journal on Regulation*, vol 1, pp159–194, chapter 9

Albers, W. (2001) 'Prominence theory as a tool to model boundedly rational decisions', in G. Gigerenzer and R. Selten (eds) *Bounded Rationality: The Adaptive Toolbox*, MIT Press, Cambridge, MA, chapter 1

Alhakami, A. S. and Slovic, P. (1994) 'A psychological study of the inverse relationship between perceived risk and perceived benefit', *Risk Analysis*, vol 14, pp1085–1096, intro, chapter 2, chapter 7, chapter 15

Allen, K. A., Moss, A., Giovino, G. A., Shopland, D. R. and Pierce, J. P. (1993) 'Teenage tobacco use: Data estimates from the Teenage Attitudes and Practices Survey, United States, 1989', *Advance Data*, vol 224, no 1, chapter 7

Allen, M. W. and Ng, S. H. (2003) 'Human values, utilitarian benefits and identification: The case of meat', *European Journal of Social Psychology*, vol 33, pp37–56, chapter 12

Almond, G. A. and Verba, S. (1980) *The Civic Culture Revisited*, Little, Brown, Boston, chapter 19

Anand, P. (ed) (1997) 'Symposium: Economic and social consequences of BSE/CJD', *Risk Decision and Policy*, vol 2, no 1, pp3–52, chapter 19

Andrade, E. B. (2005) 'Behavioral consequences of affect: Combining evaluative and regulatory mechanisms', *Journal of Consumer Research*, vol 32, pp355–362, chapter 8

Andreoni, J. (1990) 'Impure altruism and donations to public goods: A theory of warm-glow giving', *The Economic Journal*, vol 100, pp464–477, intro

Argo, J. J. and Main, K. J. (2004) 'Meta-analysis of the effectiveness of warning labels', *Journal of Public Policy and Marketing*, vol 23, pp193–208, chapter 22

Ariely, D. (2001) 'Seeing sets: Representation by statistical properties', *Psychological Science*, vol 12, pp157–162, chapter 3

Arvai, J. L., Gregory, R. and McDaniels, T. L. (2001) 'Testing a structured decision approach: Value focused thinking for deliberative risk communication', *Risk Analysis*, vol 21, no 6, pp1065–1076, chapter 19

Associated Press (2001) 'Massive jackpot powers lottery mania', *The Register-Guard* [Eugene, OR], 25 August, p6A, chapter 1

ATSDR (Agency for Toxic Substances and Disease Registry) (1990) 'Case studies in environmental medicine: Arsenic toxicity', US Department of Health and Human Services, Washington, DC, chapter 13

ATSDR (1996), 'Exposure investigation CR #40W1', US Department of Health and Human Services, Public Health Service, Division of Health Assessment and Consultation, Atlanta, GA, chapter 13

ATSDR (2007) 'Case studies in environmental medicine: Lead toxicity', www.atsdr.cdc.gov/csem/lead/pbcover_page2.html, accessed 22 December 2009, chapter 10

Baird, B. N. R. (1986) 'Tolerance for environmental health risks: The influence of knowledge, benefits, voluntariness, and environmental attitudes', *Risk Analysis*, vol 6, pp425–435, chapter 9

Balkin, J. M. (1998) *Cultural Software*, Yale, New Haven, CT, chapter 11

Barber, B. R. (1984) *Strong Democracy: Participatory Politics for a New Age*, University of California Press, Berkeley, chapter 19

Barke, R. P., Jenkins-Smith, H. and Slovic, P. (1997) 'Risk perceptions of men and women scientists', *Social Science Quarterly*, vol 78, pp167–176, chapter 9, chapter 11, chapter 12

Barnett, A., Menighetti, J. and Prete, M. (1992) 'The market response to the Sioux City DC-10 crash', *Risk Analysis*, vol 14, pp45–52, chapter 19

Barrett, L. F. and Salovey, P. (eds) (2002) *The Wisdom in Feeling*, Guilford Press, New York, chapter 2

Baron, J. (1997) 'Confusion of relative and absolute risk in valuation', *Journal of Risk and Uncertainty*, vol 14, no 3, pp301–309, chapter 2, chapter 4

Baron, J. (2000) *Thinking and Deciding*, 3rd edn, Cambridge University Press, Cambridge, UK, chapter 21

Baron, R. M. and Kenny, D. A. (1986) 'The moderator-mediator variable distinction in social-psychological research: Conceptual, strategic, and statistical considerations', *Journal of Personality and Social Psychology*, vol 51, pp1173–1182, chapter 8

Bass, R. (1996) *The Book of Yaak*, Houghton Mifflin, New York, chapter 6

Basso, K. H. (1996) *Wisdom Sits in Places: Landscape and Language among the Western Apache*, University of New Mexico, Albuquerque, NM, chapter 13

Bateman, I. J., Munro, A. A. and Poe, G. L. (2005) *Asymmetric Dominance Effects in Choice Experiments and Contingent Valuation*, CSERGE Working Paper EDM 05-06, chapter 1

Bateman, I. J., Dent, S., Slovic, P. and Starmer, L. (2006a) *Exploring the Determinants of Affect: Examining Rating Scale Assessments of Gambles*, CSERGE Working Paper, University of East Anglia, Centre for Social and Economic Research on the Global Environment, Norwich, chapter 1

Bateman, I. J., Slovic, P. and Starmer, C. (2006b) *Incentivised Experimental Investigations of the Affect Heuristic*, CSERGE Working Paper, University of East Anglia, Centre for Social and Economic Research on the Global Environment, Norwich, chapter 1

Bates, M. N., Smith, A. H. and Cantor, K. P. (1995) 'Case-control study of bladder cancer and arsenic in drinking water', *American Journal of Epidemiology*, vol 141, no 6, pp523–530, chapter 12

Batson, C. D. (1990) 'How social an animal'? The human capacity for caring', *American Psychologist*, vol 45, pp336–346, chapter 3, chapter 5

Batson, C. D., Eklund, J. H., Chermok, V. L., Hoyt, J. L. and Ortiz, B. G. (2007) 'An additional antecedent of empathic concern: Valuing the welfare of the person in need', *Journal of Personality and Social Psychology*, vol 93, pp65–74, chapter 3

Baumeister, R. F. and Leary, M. R. (1995) 'The need to belong: Desire for interpersonal attachments as a fundamental human motivation,' *Psychological Bulletin*, vol 117, no 3, pp497–529, chapter 11

Beck, U. (1992) *Risk Society: Towards a New Modernity*, Sage, London, chapter 10

Beck, U. (1999) *World Risk Society*, Polity Press, Malden, MA, chapter 10

Behrens, E. G. (1983) 'The Triangle Shirtwaist Company fire of 1911: A lesson in legislative manipulation', *Texas Law Review*, vol 62, pp361–387, chapter 19

Bellinger, D., Leviton, A., Waternaux, C., Needleman, H. and Rabinowitz, M. (1987) 'Longitudinal analyses of prenatal and postnatal lead exposure and early cognitive development', *New England Journal of Medicine*, vol 316, no 17, pp1037–1043, chapter 10

Benjamin, D. J., Brown, S. A. and Shapiro, J. M. (2006) 'Who is "behavioral"? Cognitive ability and anomalous preferences', papers.ssrn.com/sol3/papers.cfm?abstract_id=675264 (accessed 31 December 2009), chapter 20

Bentham, J. (1823) *An Introduction to the Principle of Morals and Legislation* (Original work published 1789), www.constitution.org/jb/pml.htm, accessed 18 December 2009, intro

Benthin, A., Slovic, P. and Severson, H. (1993) 'A psychometric study of adolescent risk perception', *Journal of Adolescence*, vol 16, pp153–168, intro

Benthin, A., Slovic, P., Moran, P., Severson, H., Mertz, C. K. and Gerrard, M. (1995) 'Adolescent health-threatening and health-enhancing behaviors: A study of word association and imagery', *Journal of Adolescent Health*, vol 17, pp143–152, chapter 7

Berger, C. R., Lee, E.-J. and Johnson, J. T. (2003) 'Gender, rationality, and base-rate explanations for increasing trends,' *Communication Research*, vol 30, no 6, pp737–765, chapter 12

Bettman, J. R., Payne, J. W. and Staelin, R. (1987) 'Cognitive considerations in designing effective labels for presenting risk information', in K. Viscusi and W. Magat (eds) *Learning about Risk: Evidence on the Economic Responses to Risk Information*, Harvard University Press, Cambridge, MA, chapter 9

Berkowitz, L. (2000) *Causes and Consequences of Feelings*, Cambridge University Press, New York, intro

Birnbaum, M. H. (1999) 'How to show that 9 > 221: Collect judgments in a between-subjects design', *Psychological Methods*, vol 4, no 3, pp243–249, chapter 1

Bohölm, Å. (1998) 'Visual images and risk messages: Commemorating Chernobyl', *Risk Decision and Policy*, vol 3, no 2, pp125–143, chapter 19

Bord, R. J. and O'Connor, R. E. (1997) 'The gender gap in environmental attitudes: The case of perceived vulnerability to risk', *Social Science Quarterly*, vol 78, pp830–840, chapter 9, chapter 10, chapter 11

Bornstein, R. F. (1989) 'Exposure and affect: Overview and meta-analysis of research, 1968–1987', *Psychological Bulletin*, vol 106, pp265–289, chapter 7

Boudon, R. (1998) 'Social mechanisms without black boxes,' in P. Hedström and R. Swedberg (eds) *Social Mechanisms: An Analytical Approach to Social Theory*, Cambridge University Press, Cambridge, UK, chapter 11

Brandon, T. H., Juliano, L. M. and Copeland, A. L. (1999) 'Expectancies for tobacco smoking', in I. Kirsch (ed) *How Expectancies Shape Behavior*, American Psychological Association, Washington, DC, chapter 22

Brandstätter, E., Gigerenzer, G. and Hertwig, R. (2006) 'The priority heuristic: Making choices without trade-offs', *Psychological Review*, vol 113, pp409–432, chapter 1

Breakwell, G. M. and Barnett, J. (2003) 'Social amplification of risk and the layering method', in N. Pidgeon, R. E. Kasperson and P. Slovic (eds) *The Social Amplification of Risk*, Cambridge University Press, Cambridge, UK, chapter 19

Breyer, S. G. (1993) *Breaking the Vicious Circle: Toward Effective Risk Regulation*, Harvard University Press, Cambridge, MA, chapter 11, chapter 12

Brickman, P., Coates, D. and Janoff-Bulman, R. J. (1978) 'Lottery winners and accident victims: Is happiness relative?', *Journal of Personality and Social Psychology*, vol 36, pp917–927, chapter 7

Brody, C. J. (1984) 'Differences by sex in support for nuclear power', *Social Forces*, vol 63, pp209–228, chapter 9, chapter 11

Buckner, H. T. (1994) 'Sex and guns: Is gun control male control?', www.tbuckner.com/SEXGUN.HTM#Sex%20and%20Guns, accessed 23 December 2009, chapter 11

Bullard, R. D. (1990) *Dumping in Dixie: Race, Class and Environmental Quality*, Westview Press, Boulder, CO, chapter 10, chapter 13

Burkhalter, A., Gastil, J. and Kelshaw, T. (2002) 'A conceptual definition and theoretic model of public deliberation in small face-to-face groups', *Communications Theory*, vol 12, pp398–422, chapter 12

Burns, W. J. and Slovic, P. (2007) 'The diffusion of fear: Modeling community response to a terrorist strike', *Journal of Defense Modeling and Simulation*, vol 4, no 4, pp426–445, chapter 17

Burns, W. J., Slovic, P., Kasperson, R., Kasperson, J. X., Renn, O. and Scrinvas, E. (1993) 'Incorporating structural models into research on the social application of risk: Implications for theory construction and decision making', *Risk Analysis*, vol 13, pp611–623, chapter 17

Bush, G., Luu, P. and Posner, M. I. (2000) 'Cognitive and emotional influences in the anterior cingulate cortex', *Trends in Cognitive Science*, vol 4, pp215–222, chapter 3

Capek, S. M. (1993) 'The "environmental justice" frame: A conceptual discussion and an application', *Social Problems*, vol 40, pp5–24, chapter 10

Carstensen, L. L. (2006) 'The influence of sense of time on development', *Science*, vol 312, pp1913–1915, chapter 8

Centers for Disease Control and Prevention (1994) *Preventing Tobacco Use Among Young People: A Report of the Surgeon General* (No. S/N 017-001-00491-0), US Department of Health and Human Services, Washington, DC, chapter 7

Centers for Disease Control and Prevention (2002) 'Annual smoking-attributable mortality, years of potential life lost, and economic costs: United States, 1995–1999', *Morbidity and Mortality Weekly Report*, vol 51, pp300–303, chapter 21

Chaiken, S. (1980) 'Heuristic versus systematic information processing and the use of source versus message cues in persuasion', *Journal of Personality and Social Psychology*, vol 39, no 5, pp752–766, chapter 12

Chaiken, S. and Maheswaran, D. (1994) 'Heuristic processing can bias systematic processing: Effects of source credibility, argument ambiguity, and task importance on attitude judgment', *Journal of Personality and Social Psychology*, vol 66, no 3, pp460–473, chapter 12

Chaiken, S. and Trope, Y. (1999) *Dual-Process Theories in Social Psychology*, Guilford Press, New York, chapter 2, chapter 4

Chang, L. and Krosnick, J. (2003) 'Comparing oral interviewing with self-administered

computerized questionnaires: An experiment', www.comm.stanford.edu/faculty/
krosnick/Tel%20Int%20Mode%20Experiment.pdf, accessed 1 January 2010, chapter
18

Chen, S., Duckworth, K. and Chaiken, S. (1999) 'Motivated heuristic and systematic
processing', *Psychological Inquiry*, vol 10, no 1, pp44–49, chapter 11, chapter 12

Chua, H. F., Yates, J. F. and Shah, P. (2006) 'Risk avoidance: Graphs versus numbers',
Memory and Cognition, vol 34, no 2, pp399–410, chapter 20

Citizen's Assembly on Electoral Reform (2006) www.citizensassembly.bc.ca, accessed
26 December 2009, chapter 12

Clark, E. (1988) *The Want Makers: Inside the World of Advertising*, Penguin Books, New
York, chapter 1

Clark, M. S. and Fiske, S. T. (eds) (1982) *Affect and Cognition*, Erlbaum, Hillsdale, NJ,
chapter 2

Clark, R. D. and Maass, A. (1988) 'The role of social categorization and perceived source
credibility in minority influence,' *European Journal of Social Psychology*, vol 18, no 5,
pp381–394, chapter 11, chapter 12

Clore, G. L. and Huntsinger, J. R. (2007) 'How emotions inform judgment and regulate
thought', *Trends in Cognitive Science*, vol 11, pp393–399, chapter 8

Cobb, M. D. and Macoubrie, J. (2004) 'Public perceptions about nanotechnology: Risks,
benefits and trust', *Journal of Nanoparticle Research*, vol 6, pp395–404, chapter 18

Cohen, B. L. (1983) *Before It's Too Late: A Scientist's Case for Nuclear Energy*, Plenum
Press, New York, chapter 9

Cohen, G. L. (2003) 'Party over policy: The dominating impact of group influence on
political beliefs', *Journal of Personality and Social Psychology*, vol 85, no 5, pp808–822,
chapter 11, chapter 12

Cohen, G. L., Aronson, J. and Steele, C. M. (2000) 'When beliefs yield to evidence:
Reducing biased evaluation by affirming the self', *Personality & Social Psychology
Bulletin*, vol 26, no 9, pp1151–1164, chapter 11, chapter 12

Cohen, G. L., Sherman, D. K., Bastardi, A., Hsu, L., McGoey, M. and Ross, L. (2007)
'Bridging the partisan divide: Self-affirmation reduces ideological closed-mindedness
and inflexibility in negotiation', *Journal of Personality and Social Psychology*, vol 93,
no 3, pp415–430, chapter 11, chapter 12, chapter 18

Cohen, J. and Solomon, N. (30 January 1994) 'Media ignore world's dying kids', *The
Register-Guard*, p48, chapter 6

Cohen, J. T., Duggar, K., Gray, G. M., Kreindel, S., Abdelrahman, H., HabteMariam, T.,
Oryang, D. and Tameru, B. (2001) 'Evaluation of the potential for bovine spongiform
encephalopathy in the United States', www.aphis.usda.gov/newsroom/hot_issues/bse/
background/documents/mainreporttext.pdf, accessed 24 December 2009, chapter 12

Coleman, J. S. (1990) *Foundations of Social Theory*, Bellknap Press, Cambridge, MA,
chapter 19

Combs, B. and Slovic, P. (1979) 'Newspaper coverage of causes of death', *Journalism
Quarterly*, vol 56, no 4, pp837–843, 849, chapter 19

Compas, Inc, Multi-Audience Research (1995) 'Perceived blood safety and transfusion
acceptance: A report to the Canadian Red Cross Society on perceived safety of blood
and willingness to accept a blood transfusion', Ottawa, Canada, chapter 14

Conner, M. and Norman, P. (1996) *Predicting Health Behavior: Theory and Practice with
Social Cognition Models*, Open University Press, Philadelphia, PA, chapter 21

Cook, P. J. and Ludwig, J. (2000) *Gun Violence: The Real Costs*, Oxford University Press,
Oxford, chapter 11

Coombs, C. H. and Pruitt, D. G. (1960) 'Components of risk in decision making: Probability and variance preferences', *Journal of Experimental Psychology*, vol 60, pp265–277, intro

Cooper, R. S. (1994) 'A case study in the use of race and ethnicity in public health surveillance', *Public Health Reports*, vol 109, pp46–52, chapter 9

Crosby, N. and Nethercut, D. (2005) 'Citizens juries: Creating a trustworthy voice of the people', in J. Gastil and P. Levine (eds) *The Deliberative Democracy Handbook*, Jossey-Bass, New York, chapter 12

Cross, F. B. (1998) 'Facts and values in risk assessment', *Reliability Engineering and System Safety*, vol 59, pp27–40, chapter 9

The Cultural Cognition Project at Yale Law School (undated-a) 'Gun risk perceptions', www.culturalcognition.net/projects/gun-risk-perceptions.html, accessed 23 December 2009, chapter 12

The Cultural Cognition Project at Yale Law School (undated-b) 'First national risk & culture study', www.culturalcognition.net/projects/first-national-risk-culture-study.html, accessed 23 December 2009, chapter 12

The Cultural Cognition Project at Yale Law School (2006a) 'Culture and political attitudes', www.research.yale.edu/culturalcognition/content/view/91/100, accessed 15 January 2006, chapter 12

The Cultural Cognition Project at Yale Law School (2006b) 'Health risk perceptions', www.research.yale.edu/culturalcognition/content/view/102/100, accessed 15 January 2006, chapter 12

The Cultural Cognition Project at Yale Law School (2006c) 'What matters more: Consequences or meanings?', www.research.yale.edu/culturalcognition/index.php?option=content&task=view&id=104, accessed 15 January 2006, chapter 12

Currall, S. C., King, E. B., Lane, N., Madera, J. and Turner, S. (2006) 'What drives public acceptance of nanotechnology?', *Nature Nanotechnology*, vol 1, pp153–155, chapter 18

Cvetkovich, G. and Earle, T. (1991) 'Risk and culture', *Special issue of Journal of Cross-Cultural Psychology*, vol 22, no 1, pp11–149, chapter 19

Cvetkovich, G. and Löfstedt, R. E. (eds) (1999) *Social Trust and the Management of Risk*, Earthscan, London, chapter 19

Cvetkovich, G., Siegrist, M., Murray, R. and Tragesser, S. (2002) 'New information and social trust: Asymmetry and perseverance of attributions about hazard managers', *Risk Analysis*, vol 22, pp359–369, chapter 19

Dake, K. (1991) 'Orienting dispositions in the perception of risk: An analysis of contemporary worldviews and cultural biases,' *Journal of Cross-Cultural Psychology*, vol 22, no 1, pp61–82, chapter 11, chapter 18, chapter 19

Dale, N. (1999) 'Cross-cultural community-based planning: Negotiating the future of Haida Gwaii', in L. Susskind, S. McKearnan and J. Thomas-Larmer (eds) *The Consensus Building Handbook*, Sage, Thousand Oaks, CA, chapter 12

Damasio, A. R. (1994) *Descartes' Error: Emotion, Reason, and the Human Brain*, Avon, New York, intro, chapter 1, chapter 2, chapter 3, chapter 6, chapter 7, chapter 22

Damasio, A. R., Tranel, D. and Damasio, H. (1990) 'Individuals with sociopathic behavior caused by frontal damage fail to respond autonomically to social stimuli', *Behavioural Brain Research*, vol 41, pp81–94, chapter 7

Davidson, D. J. and Freudenburg, W. R. (1996) 'Gender and environmental risk concerns: A review and analysis of available research', *Environment and Behavior*, vol 28, pp302–339, chapter 10, chapter 11

Davis, M. H. (1994) *Empathy: A Social Psychological Approach*, Brown and Benchmark, Madison, WI, chapter 3

de Groot, A. D. (1978) *Thought and Choice in Chess*, Monton, New York, chapter 2

de Vries, M., Holland, R. W. and Witteman, C. L. M. (2008) 'In the winning mood: Affect in the Iowa gambling task', *Judgment and Decision Making*, vol 3, no 1, pp42–50, chapter 8

Denman, S., Pearson, J., Davis, P. and Moody, D. (1996) 'A survey of HIV- and AIDS-related knowledge, beliefs and attitudes among 14 year olds in Nottinghamshire', *Educational Research*, vol 38, pp93–99, chapter 14

Denes-Raj, V. and Epstein, S. (1994) 'Conflict between intuitive and rational processing: When people behave against their better judgment', *Journal of Personality and Social Psychology*, vol 66, pp819–829, chapter 2

DeVeillis, R. F. (1991) *Scale Development: Theory and Applications*, Sage, Newbury Park, CA, chapter 10

Dickert, S. (2008) 'Two routes to the perception of need: The role of affective and deliberative information processing in pro-social behavior', Doctoral Dissertation, University of Oregon at Eugene, OR, chapter 3

Diener, E. (1984) 'Subjective well-being', *Psychological Bulletin*, vol 95, pp542–575, chapter 8

DiFranza, J. R., Rigotti, N. A., McNeill, A. D., Ockene, J. K., Savageau, J. A., St Cyr, D. and Coleman, M. (2000) 'Initial symptoms of nicotine dependence in adolescents', *Tobacco Control*, vol 9, pp313–319, chapter 7

Dillard, A. (1999) *For the Time Being*, Knopf, New York, chapter 5, chapter 6

DiMaggio, P. (1997) 'Culture and cognition', *Annual Review of Sociology*, vol 23, pp263–287, chapter 18

Douglas, M. (1966) *Purity and Danger: An Analysis of Concepts of Pollution and Taboo*, Routledge & Kegan Paul, London, chapter 12, chapter 18

Douglas, M. (1970) *Natural Symbols: Explorations in Cosmology*, Barrie & Rockliff, London, chapter 11, chapter 12, chapter 18

Douglas, M. (1982) 'Cultural bias', in *In the Active Voice*, Routledge & Paul, London, chapter 11

Douglas, M. (1986) *How Institutions Think*, Syracuse University Press, New York, chapter 11, chapter 12

Douglas, M. and Wildavsky, A. B. (1982) *Risk and Culture: An Essay on the Selection of Technical and Environmental Dangers*, University of California Press, Berkeley, CA, chapter 11, chapter 18

Downing, P., Chan, A., Peelen, M., Dodds, C. and Kanwisher, N. (2006) 'Domain specificity in visual cortex', *Cerebral Cortex*, vol 16, pp1453–1461, chapter 3

Doyle, J. R., O'Connor, D. J., Reynolds, G. M. and Bottomley, P. A. (1999) 'The robustness of the asymmetrically dominated effect: Buying frames, phantom alternatives, and in-store purchases', *Psychology & Marketing*, vol 16, no 3, pp225–243, chapter 1

Drolet, A. and Luce, M. F. (2004) 'The rationalizing effects of cognitive load on emotion-based trade-off avoidance', *Journal of Consumer Research*, vol 31, no 1, pp63–77, chapter 4

Durant, J., Gaskell, G. and Buer, M. (1998) *Biotechnology in the Public Sphere: A European Sourcebook*, National Museum of Science and Industry, London, chapter 15

Earle, T. C. and Cvetkovich, G. T. (1995) *Social Trust: Toward a Cosmopolitan Society*, Praeger, Westport, CT, chapter 19

Eastwood, J. D., Smilek, D. and Merikle, P. M. (2001) 'Differential attentional guidance by unattended faces expressing positive and negative emotion', *Perception and Psychophysics*, vol 63, pp1004–1013, chapter 3

Edelstein, M. R. (1987) 'Toward a theory of environmental stigma', in J. Harvey and D. Henning (eds) *Public Environments*, Environmental Design Research Association, Ottawa, Canada, chapter 13, chapter 19

Edelstein, M. R. (1988) *Contaminated Communities: The Social and Psychological Impacts of Residential Toxic Exposure*, Westview, Boulder, CO, chapter 13

Edwards, A., Elwyn, G., Covey, J., Matthews, E. and Pill, R. (2001) 'Presenting risk information: A review of the effects of "framing" and other manipulations on patient outcomes', *Journal of Health Communication*, vol 6, no 1, pp61–82, chapter 20

Edwards, A., Unigwe, S., Elwyn, G. and Hood, K. (2003) 'Personalised risk communication for informed decision making about entering screening programs', *Cochrane Database of Systematic Reviews*, no 1: CD001865, chapter 20

Edwards, W. (1954) 'The theory of decision making', *Psychological Bulletin*, vol 51, pp380–417, intro

Edwards, W. and von Winterfeldt, D. (1987) 'Public values in risk debates', *Risk Analysis*, vol 7, no 2, pp141–158, chapter 19

Ellis, R. and Thompson, M. (1997) 'Seeing green: Cultural biases and environmental preferences,' in Wildavsky, A. B., Ellis, R. and Thompson, M. (eds) *Culture Matters: Essays in Honor of Aaron Wildavsky*, Westview Press, Boulder, CO, chapter 11

Elstein, A. S., Chapman, G. B. and Knight, S. J. (2005) 'Patients' values and clinical substituted judgments: The case of localized prostate cancer', *Health Psychology*, vol 24, no 4, ppS85–S92, chapter 20

English, M. R. (1992) *Siting Low-Level Radioactive Waste Disposal Facilities: The Public Policy Dilemma*, Quorum, New York, chapter 19

Epstein, S. (1994) 'Integration of the cognitive and the psychodynamic unconscious', *American Psychologist*, vol 49, pp709–724, chapter 2, chapter 4, chapter 6, chapter 7, chapter 22

Erikson, K. (1990) 'Toxic reckoning: Business faces a new kind of fear', *Harvard Business Review*, vol 68, no 1, pp118–126, chapter 13

Erikson, K. (1994) *A New Species of Trouble: The Human Experience of Modern Disasters*, Norton, New York, chapter 13

Eskridge, W. N. (2005) 'Pluralism and distrust: How courts can support democracy by lowering the stakes of politics', *Yale Law Journal*, vol 114, pp1279–1328, chapter 12

Estrada, C. A., Martin-Hryniewicz, M., Peek, B. T., Collins, C. and Byrd, J. C. (2004) 'Literacy and numeracy skills and anticoagulation control', *American Journal of the Medical Sciences*, vol 328, no 2, pp88–93, chapter 20

Fagerlin, A., Wang, C. and Ubel, P. A. (2005) 'Reducing the influence of anecdotal reasoning on people's health care decisions: Is a picture worth a thousand statistics?', *Medical Decision Making*, vol 25, no 4, pp398–405, chapter 20

Fagerlin, A., Zikmund-Fisher, B. J., Ubel, P. A., Jankovic, A., Derry, H. A. and Smith, D. M. (2007) 'Measuring numeracy without a math test: Development of the Subjective Numeracy Scale (SNS)', *Medical Decision Making*, vol 27, no 5, pp672–680, chapter 20

Farrell, M. H., Murphy, M. A. and Schneider, C. E. (2002) 'How underlying patient beliefs can affect physician–patient communication about prostate-specific antigen testing', *Effective Clinical Practice*, vol 5, pp120–129, chapter 16

Fazio, R. H. and Hilden, L. E. (2001) 'Emotional reactions to a seemingly prejudiced response: The role of automatically activated racial attitudes and motivation to control prejudiced reactions', *Personality and Social Psychology Bulletin*, vol 27, no 5, pp538–549, chapter 22

Fazio, R. H. and Olson, M. A. (2003) 'Implicit measures in social cognition research: Their meaning and uses', *Annual Review of Psychology*, vol 54, pp297–327, chapter 22

Fenske, M. J. and Raymond, J. E. (2006) 'Affective influences of selective attention', *Current Directions in Psychological Science*, vol 15, pp312–316, chapter 3

Fenske, M. J., Raymond, J. E. and Kunar, M. A. (2004) 'The affective consequences of visual attention in preview search', *Psychonomic Bulletin and Review*, vol 11, pp1055–1061, chapter 3

Fenske, M. J., Raymond, J. E., Kessler, K., Westoby, N. and Tipper, S. P. (2005) 'Attentional inhibition has social-emotional consequences for unfamiliar faces', *Psychological Science*, vol 16, pp753–758, chapter 3

Fetherstonhaugh, D., Slovic, P., Johnson, S. M. and Friedrich, J. (1997) 'Insensitivity to the value of human life: A study of psychophysical numbing', *Journal of Risk and Uncertainty*, vol 14, pp283–300, intro, chapter 1, chapter 2, chapter 4, chapter 5, chapter 6

Fife-Schaw, C. and Rowe, G. (1996) 'Public perceptions of everyday food hazard: A psychometric study', *Risk Analysis*, vol 16, pp487–500, chapter 15

Finucane, M. L. (2002) 'Mad cows, mad corn and mad communities: The role of socio-cultural factors in the perceived risk of genetically-modified food', *Proceedings of the Nutrition Society*, vol 61, pp31–37, chapter 18

Finucane, M. L., Alhakami, A., Slovic, P. and Johnson, S. M. (2000a) 'The affect heuristic in judgments of risks and benefits', *Journal of Behavioral Decision Making*, vol 13, pp1–17, intro, chapter 2, chapter 7, chapter 8, chapter 12, chapter 14, chapter 15, chapter 19

Finucane, M. L., Peters, E. and Slovic, P. (2003) 'Judgment and decision making: The dance of affect and reason', in S. L. Schneider and J. Shanteau (eds) *Emerging Perspectives on Judgment and Decision Research*, Cambridge University Press, Cambridge, UK, chapter 2

Finucane, M. L., Slovic, P., Hibbard, J. H., Peters, E., Mertz, C. K. and MacGregor, D. G. (2002) 'Aging and decision-making competence: An analysis of comprehension and consistency skills in older versus younger adults considering health-plan options', *Journal of Behavioral Decision Making*, vol 15, no 2, pp141–164, chapter 20

Finucane, M. L., Slovic, P., Mertz, C. K., Flynn, J. and Satterfield, T. A. (2000b) 'Gender, race, and perceived risk: The "white male" effect', *Health, Risk, & Society*, vol 2, no 2, pp159–172, chapter 10, chapter 11

Fischer, P. M., Richards, J. W., Berman, E. F. and Krugman, D. M. (1989) 'Recall and eye tracking study of adolescents viewing tobacco advertisements', *Journal of the American Medical Association*, vol 261, pp84–89, chapter 22

Fischer, P. M., Krugman, D. M., Fletcher, J. E., Fox, R. J. and Rojas, T. H. (1993) 'An evaluation of health warnings in cigarette advertisements using standard market research methods: What does it mean to warn?', *Tobacco Control*, vol 2, pp279–285, chapter 22

Fischhoff, B., Slovic, P., Lichtenstein, S., Read, S. and Combs, B. (1978) 'How safe is safe enough'? A psychometric study of attitudes toward technological risks and benefits', *Policy Sciences*, vol 9, pp127–152, intro, chapter 2, chapter 7, chapter 15

Fishkin, J. S. (1991) *Democracy and Deliberation*, Yale University Press, New Haven, CT, chapter 12

Fishkin, J. and Farrar, C. (2005) 'Deliberative polling: From experiment to community resource', in J. Gastil and P. Levine (eds) *The Deliberative Democracy Handbook*, Jossey-Bass, New York, chapter 12

Fitchen, J. M. (1989) 'When toxic chemicals pollute residential environments: The cultural meanings of home and home ownership', *Human Organization*, vol 48, no 4, pp313–324, chapter 13

Flynn, J., Slovic, P. and Mertz, C. K. (1993a) 'Decidedly different: Expert and public views of risks from a radioactive waste repository', *Risk Analysis*, vol 13, pp643–648, chapter 15

Flynn, J., Slovic, P. and Mertz, C. K. (1993b) 'The Nevada initiative: A risk communication fiasco', *Risk Analysis*, vol 13, no 5, pp497–502, chapter 19

Flynn, J., Slovic, P. and Mertz, C. K. (1994) 'Gender, race, and perception of environmental health risks', *Risk Analysis*, vol 14, no 6, pp1101–1108, intro, chapter 9, chapter 10, chapter 11, chapter 14, chapter 16, chapter 18

Flynn, J., Chalmers, J., Easterling, D., Kasperson, R., Kunreuther, H., Mertz, C. K., Mushkatel, A., Pijawka, K. D. and Slovic, P. with Dotto, L. (1995) *One Hundred Centuries of Solitude: Redirecting America's High-Level Nuclear Waste Policy*, Westview Press, Boulder, CO, chapter 19

Flynn, J., Kasperson, R., Kunreuther, H. and Slovic, P. (1997) 'Overcoming tunnel vision: Redirecting the U.S. high-level nuclear waste program', *Environment*, vol 39, no 3, pp6–11, 25–30, chapter 13

Flynn, J., Peters, E., Mertz, C. K. and Slovic, P. (1998) 'Risk, media, and stigma at Rocky Flats', *Risk Analysis*, vol 18, no 6, pp715–727, chapter 13, chapter 19

Flynn, J., Slovic, P. and Kunreuther, H. (eds) (2001) *Risk, Media, and Stigma: Understanding Public Challenges to Modern Science and Technology*, Earthscan, London, chapter 17, chapter 19

Forester, J. (1999) 'Dealing with deep value differences', in L. Susskind, S. McKearnan and J. Thomas-Larmer (eds) *The Consensus Building Handbook*, Sage, Thousand Oaks, CA, chapter 12

Forgas, J. P. (ed) (2000) *Feeling and Thinking: The Role of Affect in Social Cognition*, Cambridge University Press, Cambridge, UK, chapter 2

Forrester, J. W. (1969) *Urban Dynamics*, MIT Press, Cambridge, MA, chapter 17

Fox, E. (2002) 'Processing of emotional facial expressions: The role of anxiety and awareness', *Cognitive, Affective and Behavioral Neuroscience*, vol 2, pp52–63, chapter 3

Framework Convention Alliance for Tobacco Control (2005) *Tobacco Warning Labels: Factsheet No. 7*, World Health Organization, Geneva, Switzerland, chapter 22

Frederick, S. (2005) 'Cognitive reflection and decision making', *Journal of Economic Perspectives*, vol 19, no 4, pp24–42, chapter 20

Freudenburg, W. R. (1992) 'Nothing recedes like success? Risk analysis and the organizational amplification of risks', *Risk: Issues in Health and Safety*, no 3, pp1–35, chapter 17, chapter 19

Freudenburg, W. R. (2003) 'Institutional failure and the organizational amplification of risks: The need for a closer look', in N. Pidgeon, R. G. Kasperson and P. Slovic (eds) *The Social Amplification of Risk*, Cambridge University Press, Cambridge, UK, chapter 19

Freudenburg, W. R., Coleman, C. L., Gonzales, J. and Hegelund, C. (1996) 'Media coverage of hazard events – Analyzing the assumption', *Risk Analysis*, vol 16, pp31–42, chapter 17, chapter 19

Friedrich, J., Barnes, P., Chapin, K., Dawson, I., Garst, V. and Kerr, D. (1999) 'Psychophysical numbing: When lives are valued less as the lives at risk increase',

Journal of Consumer Psychology, vol 8, pp277–299, chapter 2, chapter 4

Frewer, L. J., Howard, C., Hedderley, D. and Shepherd, R. (1996) 'What determines trust in information about food-related risk? Underlying psychological constructs', *Risk Analysis*, vol 16, pp473–486, chapter 15

Frewer, L. J., Howard, C. and Shepherd, R. (1997) 'Public concerns in the United Kingdom about general and specific applications of genetic engineering: Risk benefit and ethics', *Science, Technology and Human Values*, vol 22, pp98–124, chapter 15

Fung, H. H. and Carstensen, L. L. (2006) 'Goals change when life's fragility is primed: Lessons learned from older adults, the September 11th attacks and SARS', *Social Cognition*, vol 24, pp248–278, chapter 8

Funtowicz, S. O. and Ravetz, J. R. (1992) 'Three types of risk assessment and the emergence of post-normal science', in S. Krimsky and D. Golding (eds) *Social Theories of Risk*, Praeger, Westport, CT, chapter 19

Gallup Organization (1954, January 9–14) *The Gallup Poll*, Princeton, NJ, chapter 21

Gallup Organization (1987) 'Survey of attitudes toward smoking', American Lung Association survey, Princeton, NJ, chapter 21

Ganzach, Y. (2001) 'Judging risk and return of financial assets', *Organizational Behavior and Human Decision Processes*, vol 83, pp353–370, chapter 2

Gardner, G. T. and Gould, L. C. (1989) 'Public perceptions of the risks and benefits of technology', *Risk Analysis*, vol 9, pp225–242, chapter 9

Gaskell, G. and Allum, N. (2001) 'Sound science, problematic publics? Contrasting representations of risk and uncertainty', *Notizie di Politea*, vol 63, pp13–25, chapter 15

Gaskell, G., Allum, N., Bauer, M. et al (2000) 'Biotechnology and the European public', *Nature Biotechnology*, vol 18, pp935–938, chapter 15

Gaskell, G. and Bauer, M. (2001) *Biotechnology 1996–2000: The Years of Controversy*, National Museum of Science and Industry, London, chapter 15

Gaskell, G., Bauer, M. W., Durant, J. and Allum, N. C. (1999) 'Worlds apart? The perception of genetically modified foods in Europe and the U.S.', *Science*, vol 258, pp385–387, chapter 15

Gasper, K. and Clore, G. L. (1998) 'The persistent use of negative affect by anxious individuals to estimate risk', *Journal of Personality and Social Psychology*, vol 74, no 5, pp1350–1363, chapter 2, chapter 8

Gastil, D. (1975) *Cultural Regions of the United States*, University of Washington Press, Seattle, chapter 12

Gastil, J. (2000) *By Popular Demand*, University of California Press, Berkeley, chapter 12

Gastil, J. and Dillard, J. P. (1999) 'Increasing political sophistication through public deliberation', *Political Commentary*, vol 16, no 1, pp3–23, chapter 12

Gastil, J., Black, L. and Moscovitz, K. (2008) 'Ideology, attitude change, and deliberation in small face-to-face groups', *Political Communication*, vol 25, no 1, pp23–46, chapter 12

Gelman, A. and Hill, J. (2007) *Data Analysis Using Regression and Multilevel/Hierarchical Models*, Cambridge University Press, New York, chapter 18

Gerber, A. and Green, D. (1999) 'Misperceptions about perceptual bias', *Annual Review of Political Science*, vol 2, pp189–210, chapter 12

Gerbert B., Maguire B. T. and Sumser, J. (1991) 'Public perception of risk of AIDS in health care settings', *AIDS Education and Prevention*, vol 3, pp322–327, chapter 14

Gerlach, L. P. (1987) 'Protest movements and the construction of risk', in B. B. Johnson and V. T. Covello (eds) *The Social and Cultural Construction of Risk*, Reidel, Dordrecht, The Netherlands, chapter 19

Gettys, C. F., Kelly, C. and Peterson, C. R. (1973) 'The best guess hypothesis in multi-stage inference', *Organizational Behavior and Human Performance*, vol 10, no 3, pp364–373, chapter 20

Gigerenzer, G. and Edwards, A. (2003) 'Simple tools for understanding risks: From innumeracy to insight', *British Medical Journal*, vol 327, no 7417, pp741–744, chapter 20

Gilbert, C. (2001) 'Cheney argues case for nuclear power', *Milwaukee Journal Sentinel*, 14 June, chapter 12

Gilligan, C. (1982) *In a Different Voice: Psychological Theory and Women's Development*, Harvard University Press, Cambridge, MA, chapter 12

Giner-Sorolla, R. and Chaiken, S. (1997) 'Selective use of heuristic and systematic processing under defense motivation,' *Personality & Social Psychology Bulletin*, vol 23, no 1, pp84–97, chapter 11, chapter 12

Glendon, M. A. (1987) *Abortion and Divorce in Western Law*, Harvard University Press, Cambridge, MA, chapter 12

Glöckner, A. and Betsch, T. (2008) 'Modeling option and strategy choices with connectionist networks: Towards an integrative model of automatic and deliberate decision making', *Judgment and Decision Making*, vol 3, pp215–228, chapter 3

Goffman, E. (1963) *Stigma*, Prentice-Hall, Englewood Cliffs, NJ, chapter 13, chapter 19

Goldstein, W. M. and Einhorn, H. J. (1987) 'Expression theory and the preference reversal phenomena', *Psychological Review*, vol 94, pp236–254, chapter 1, chapter 2

Graham, J., Beaulieu, N. D., Sussman, D., Sadowitz, M. and Li, Y. (1999) 'Who lives near coke plants and oil refineries? An exploration of the environmental inequity hypothesis', *Risk Analysis*, vol 19, pp171–186, chapter 10

Grandien, C., Nord, L. and Strömbäck, J. (2005) *'Efter flodvågskatastrofen (after the Tsunami disaster)'*, Krisberedningsmyndighetens temasserie, Stockholm, chapter 8

Greenberg, M. (1993) 'Proving environmental equity in siting locally unwanted land uses', *Risk: Issues in Health and Safety*, vol 235, pp235–252, chapter 10

Greenberg, M. and Schneider, D. (1995) 'Gender differences in risk perception: Effects differ in stressed versus non-stressed environments', *Risk Analysis*, no 15, pp503–511, chapter 10

Gregory, R. (2002) 'Incorporating value trade-offs into community-based environmental risk decisions', *Environmental Values*, vol 11, pp461–488, chapter 12

Gregory, R. and Failing, L. (2002) 'Using decision analysis to encourage sound deliberation: Water use planning in British Columbia, Canada', *Journal of Policy Analysis and Management*, vol 21, pp492–499, chapter 12

Gregory, R. and McDaniels, T. (2005) 'Improving environmental decision processes', in National Research Council (NRC), Committee on the Human Dimensions of Global Change, G. D. Brewer and P. C. Stern (eds) *Decision Making for the Environment: Social and Behavioral Science Research Priorities*, National Academies Press, Washington, DC, chapter 12

Gregory, R. and Wellman, K. (2001) 'Bringing stakeholder values into environmental policy choices: A community-based estuary case study', *Ecological Economics*, vol 39, no 1, pp37–52, chapter 12

Gregory, R., Flynn, J. and Slovic, P. (1995) 'Technological stigma', *American Scientist*, vol 83, pp220–223, intro, chapter 9, chapter 13, chapter 14, chapter 19

Gregory, R., Arvai, J. and McDaniels, T. (2001a) 'Value-focused thinking for environmental risk consultation', in G. Böhm, J. Nerb, T. McDaniels and H. Spada (eds) *Environmental Risks: Perception, Evaluation and Management*, Elsevier Science, Oxford, chapter 12

Gregory, R., McDaniels, T. and Fields, D. (2001b) 'Decision aiding, not dispute resolution: Creating insights through structured environmental decisions', *Journal of Policy Analysis and Management*, vol 20, no 3, pp415–432, chapter 12

Groeneweg, J., Wagenaar, W. A. and Reason, J. T. (1994) 'Promoting safety in the oil industry', *Ergonomics*, vol 37, pp1999–2013, chapter 19

Gross, J. (2002) 'Emotion regulation: Affective, cognitive, and social consequences', *Psychophysiology*, vol 39, pp281–291, chapter 3

Gross, J. L. and Rayner, S. (1985) *Measuring Culture: A Paradigm for the Analysis of Social Organization*, Columbia University Press, New York, chapter 11

Gurmankin, A. D., Baron, J. and Armstrong, K. (2004) 'The effect of numerical statements of risk on trust and comfort with hypothetical physician risk communication', *Medical Decision Making*, vol 24, no 3, pp265–271, chapter 20

Gustafson, P. E. (1998) 'Gender differences in risk perception: Theoretical and methodological perspectives', *Risk Analysis*, vol 18, no 6, pp805–811, chapter 10

Gusfield, J. R. (1968) 'On legislating morals: The symbolic process of designating deviance', *California Law Review*, vol 56, no 1, pp54–73, chapter 12

Gusfield, J. R. (1986) *Symbolic Crusade: Status Politics and the American Temperance Movement*, 2nd edn, University of Illinois Press, Champaign, chapter 12

Gutierrez, R. and Giner-Sorolla, R. (2007) 'Anger, disgust and presumption of harm as reactions to taboo-breaking behaviors', *Emotion*, vol 7, pp853–868, chapter 18

Gutteling, J. M. and Wiegman, O. (1993) 'Gender-specific reactions to environmental hazards in The Netherlands', *Sex Roles*, vol 28, pp433–447, chapter 9, chapter 10, chapter 11

Gwartney-Gibbs, P. A. and Lach, D. H. (1991) 'Sex differences in attitudes toward nuclear war', *Journal of Peace Research*, vol 28, pp161–176, chapter 9

Gyawali, D. (1999) 'Institutional forces behind water conflict in the Ganga plains', *GeoJournal*, vol 47, no 3, pp443–452, chapter 11

Hagstrom, J. (2004) 'U.S. should follow Japanese on mad cow testing', *Congress Daily*, 17 March 2004, chapter 12

Hahn, R. W., Lutter, R. W. and Viscusi, W. K. (2000) *Do Federal Regulations Reduce Mortality?*, AEI Press, La Vergne, TN, chapter 12

Hahn, R. W. and Stavins, R. N. (1991) 'Incentive-based environmental regulation: A new era from an old idea?', *Ecology Law Quarterly*, vol 18, pp1–42, chapter 12

Haidt, J. (2001) 'The emotional dog and its rational tail: A social intuitionist approach to moral judgment', *Psychological Review*, vol 108, no 4, pp814–834, chapter 5

Haidt, J. (2007) 'The new synthesis in moral psychology', *Science*, vol 316, pp998–1002, chapter 5

Haire, M. (1950) 'Projective techniques in marketing research', *The Journal of Marketing*, vol 14, pp649–656, chapter 22

Hamilton, D. L. and Sherman, S. J. (1996) 'Perceiving persons and groups', *Psychological Review*, vol 103, pp336–355, chapter 3

Hammond, D., Fong, G., McDonald, P., Cameron, R. and Brown, K. (2003) 'Impact of the graphic Canadian warning labels on adult smoking behavior', *Tobacco Control*, vol 12, pp391–395, chapter 22

Hammond, D., Fong, G., McDonald, P., Brown, K. and Cameron, R. (2004a) 'Graphic cigarette package warning labels do not lead to adverse outcomes: Evidence from Canadian smokers', *American Journal of Public Health*, vol 94, pp1442–1445, chapter 22

Hammond, D., McDonald, P., Fong, G., Brown, K. and Cameron, R. (2004b) 'The impact of cigarette warning labels and smoke-free bylaws on smoking cessation', *Canadian Journal of Public Health*, vol 95, pp201–204, chapter 22

Handmer, J. and Penning-Rowsell, E. (1990) *Hazards and the Communication of Risk*, Gower, Aldershot, chapter 19

Hart Research Associates (2006) 'Report findings: Based on a national survey of adults', www.nanotechproject.org/file_download/files/HartReport.pdf, accessed 1 January 2010, chapter 18

Hart Research Associates (2007) 'Awareness of and attitudes toward nanotechnology and federal regulatory agencies', www.nanotechproject.org/process/files/5888/hart_nanopoll_2007.pdf, accessed 1 January 2010, chapter 18

Harvey, D. R. (2001) 'What lessons from foot and mouth? A preliminary economic assessment of the 2001 epidemic', Working Paper No. 63, University of Newcastle upon Tyne, Centre for Rural Economy, chapter 19

Hastie, R. and Park, B. (1986) 'The relationship between memory and judgment depends on whether the judgment task is memory-based or on-line', *Psychological Review*, vol 93, pp258–268, chapter 3

Health Canada (2003) 'Canada's health warning messages for tobacco products: Labelling a legally available, inherently harmful product', www.wto.org/english/tratop_e/tbt_e/event_oct03_e/case7_e.ppt, accessed 2 January 2010, chapter 22

Health Canada (2007) 'Smoking prevalence in Canada', www.hc-sc.gc.ca/hc-ps/pubs/tobac-tabac/prtc-relct-2006/part2-eng.php#a1, accessed 6 January 2010, chapter 22

Heeren, T., Edwards, E. M., Dennis, J. M., Rodkin, S., Hingson, R. W. and Rosenbloom, D. L. (2008) 'A comparison of results from an alcohol survey of a prerecruited Internet panel and the national epidemiologic survey on alcohol and related conditions', *Alcoholism: Clinical and Experimental Research*, vol 32, pp222–229, chapter 18

Hendrickx, L., Vlek, C. and Oppewal, H. (1989) 'Relative importance of scenario information and frequency information in the judgment of risk', *Acta Psychologica*, vol 72, pp41–63, chapter 2

Hendriks, C. M. (2005) 'Consensus conferences and planning cells: Lay citizen deliberations', in J. Gastil and P. Levine (eds) *The Deliberative Democracy Handbook*, Jossey-Bass, New York, chapter 12

Henrich, J., Albers, W., Boyd, R., Gigerenzer, G., McCabe, K. A., Ockenfels, A. and Young, H. P. (2001) 'Group report: What is the role of culture in bounded rationality?', in G. Gigerenzer and R. Selten (eds) *Bounded Rationality: The Adaptive Toolbox*, MIT Press, Cambridge, MA, chapter 12

Herman, J. (1997) *Trauma and Recovery: The Aftermath of Violence from Domestic Abuse to Political Terror*, rev edn, Basic Books, New York, chapter 13

Hertwig, R., Barron, G., Weber, E. U. and Erev, I. (2004) 'Decisions from experience and the effect of rare events in risky choices', *Psychological Science*, vol 15, pp534–539, chapter 8

Herzlinger, R. E. (2002) 'Let's put consumers in charge of health care', *Harvard Business Review*, vol 80, no 7, pp44–55, chapter 20

Hibbard, J. H. and Peters, E. (2003) 'Supporting informed consumer health care decisions: Data presentation approaches that facilitate the use of information in choice', *Annual Review of Public Health*, vol 24, pp413–433, chapter 22

Hibbard, J. H., Slovic, P., Peters, E. and Finucane M. L. (2002) 'Strategies for reporting health plan performance information to consumers: Evidence from controlled studies', *Health Services Research*, vol 37, no 2, pp291–313, chapter 20

Hibbard, J. H., Peters, E., Dixon, A. and Tusler, M. (2007) 'Consumer competencies and the use of comparative quality information: It isn't just about literacy', *Medical Care Research and Review*, vol 64, no 4, pp379–394, chapter 20

Hill, A. (2001) 'Media risks: The social amplification of risk and the media debate', *Journal of Risk Research*, vol 4, pp209–226, chapter 19

Hillsman, Rev. M. and Krafter, M. (1996) Interview by author at the Shiloh Baptist Church, Marshall, Georgia, 29 July, chapter 13

Hirsch, J. M. (1999) 'Emissions allowance trading under the Clean Air Act: A model for future environmental regulations?', *New York University Environmental Law Journal*, vol 7, pp352–397, chapter 12

Hirschleifer, D. and Shumway, T. (2003) 'Good day sunshine: Stock returns and the weather', *The Journal of Finance*, vol 58, pp1009–1032, chapter 8

Hofstadter, R. (1970) 'America as a gun culture', *American Heritage*, vol 21, October, pp4–10, 82–85, chapter 11

Holmes, A., Vuilleumier, P. and Eimer, M. (2003) 'The processing of emotional facial expression is gated by spatial attention: Evidence from event-related brain potentials', *Cognitive Brain Research*, vol 16, pp174–184, chapter 3

Holzheu, F. and Wiedemann, P. (1993) 'Introduction: Perspectives on risk perception', in B. Rück (ed) *Risk Is a Construct*, Knesebeck, Munich, chapter 19

Hopkins, D. P., Briss, P. A., Ricard, C. J., Husten, C. G., Carande-Kulis, V. G., Fielding, J. E., Alao, M. O., McKenna, J. W., Sharp, D. J., Harris, J. R., Woollery, T. A. and Harris, K. W. (2001) 'Reviews of evidence regarding interventions to reduce tobacco use and exposure to environmental tobacco smoke', *American Journal of Preventive Medicine*, vol 20, pp16–66, chapter 22

Hsee, C. K. (1996a) 'Elastic justification: How unjustifiable factors influence judgments', *Organizational Behavior and Human Decision Processes*, vol 66, pp122–129, chapter 1

Hsee, C. K. (1996b) 'The evaluability hypothesis: An explanation for preference reversals between joint and separate evaluations of alternatives', *Organizational Behavior and Human Decision Processes*, vol 67, pp247–257, intro, chapter 1

Hsee, C. K. (1998) 'Less is better: When low-value options are valued more highly than high-value options', *Journal of Behavioral Decision Making*, vol 11, pp107–121, chapter 1

Hsee, C. K. and Kunreuther, H. (2000) 'The affection effect in insurance decisions', *Journal of Risk and Uncertainty*, vol 20, pp141–159, chapter 1, chapter 2, chapter 8

Hsee, C. K. and Menon, S. (1999) 'Affection effect in consumer choices', unpublished study, University of Chicago, chapter 2

Hsee, C. K. and Rottenstreich, Y. (2004) 'Music, pandas, and muggers: On the affective psychology of value', *Journal of Experimental Psychology: General*, vol 133, pp23–30, chapter 1, chapter 4

Hsee, C. K., Loewenstein, G., Blount, S. and Bazerman, M. H. (1999) 'Preference reversals between joint and separate evaluations of options: A review and theoretical analysis', *Psychological Bulletin*, vol 125, pp576–590, chapter 1

Huber, J., Payne, J. W. and Puto, C. (1982) 'Adding asymmetrically dominated alternatives: Violations of regularity and the similarity hypothesis', *Journal of Consumer Research*, vol 9, no 1, pp90–98, chapter 1

Hunt, S., Frewer, L. J. and Shepherd, R. (1999) 'Public trust in sources of information about radiation risks in the UK', *Journal of Risk Research*, vol 2, no 2, pp167–180, chapter 19

Hyde, D. and Spelke, E. (2009) 'All numbers are not equal: An electrophysiological investigation of small and large number representations', *Journal of Cognitive Neuroscience*, vol 21, pp1039–1053, chapter 3

Iglehart, J. K. (2002) 'Changing health insurance trends', *New England Journal of Medicine*, vol 347, no 12, pp956–962, chapter 20

Industrial Relations and Social Affairs (IRSA) (1995) 'Eurobarometer 41.0: Europeans and blood', ec.europa.eu/public_opinion/archives/ebs/ebs_083_en.pdf, accessed 28 December 2009, chapter 14

Inglehart, R. (1988) 'The renaissance of political culture', *American Political Science Review*, vol 82, pp1203–1230, chapter 19

Isen, A. M. (1993) 'Positive affect and decision making', in M. Lewis and J. M. Haviland (eds) *Handbook of Emotions*, Guilford Press, New York, chapter 2

Isen, A. M. (1997) 'Positive affect and decision making', in W. M. Goldstein and R. M. Hogarth (eds) *Research on Judgment and Decision Making: Currents, Connections, and Controversies*, Cambridge University Press, New York, chapter 8

Jamieson, P. and Romer, D. (2001) 'A profile of smokers and smoking', in P. Slovic (ed) *Smoking: Risk, Decision, and Policy*, Sage, Thousand Oaks, CA, chapter 21

Janis, I. L. (1982) *Victims of Groupthink*, 2nd edn, Houghton-Mifflin, Boston, chapter 19

Janis, I. L. and Mann, L. (1977) *Decision Making*, Free Press, New York, chapter 2, chapter 19

Jenkins-Smith, H. (1991) 'Alternative theories of the policy process: Reflections on research strategy for the study of nuclear waste policy', *PS: Political Science & Politics*, vol 24, no 2, pp157–166, chapter 19

Jenkins-Smith, H. (2001) 'Modeling stigma: An empirical analysis of nuclear waste images of Nevada', in P. Slovic, J. Flynn and H. Kunreuther (eds) *Risk, Media, and Stigma: Understanding Public Challenges to Modern Science and Technology*, Earthscan, London, chapter 11

Jenkins-Smith, H. and Smith, W. (1994) 'Ideology, culture, and risk perception', in D. J. Coyle and R. Ellis (eds) *Politics, Policy, and Culture*, Westview Press, Boulder, CO, chapter 11

Jenni, K. E. and Loewenstein, G. (1997) 'Explaining the "identifiable victim effect"', *Journal of Risk and Uncertainty*, vol 14, no 3, pp235–258, chapter 2, chapter 3, chapter 4

Johnson, B. B. (2002) 'Gender and race in beliefs about outdoor air pollution', *Risk Analysis*, vol 22, no 4, pp725–738, chapter 10

Johnson, B. B. and Covello, V. (1987) *Social and Cultural Construction of Risk*, Reidel, Dordrecht, The Netherlands, chapter 19

Johnson, E. J. and Tversky, A. (1983) 'Affect, generalization, and the perception of risk', *Journal of Personality and Social Psychology*, vol 45, pp20–31, chapter 2, chapter 8

Johnston, B. R. (ed) (1994) *Who Pays the Price? The Sociocultural Context of Environmental Crisis*, Island Press, Washington, DC, chapter 13

Johnston, B. R. (ed) (1997) *Life and Death Matters: Human Rights and the Environment at the End of the Millennium*, AltaMira Press, Walnut Creek, CA, chapter 13

Johnston, L. D., O'Malley, P. M. and Bachman, J. G. (1993) *National Survey Results on Drug Use from the Monitoring the Future Study* (No. 93-3598), National Institute on Drug Abuse, Rockville, MD, chapter 7

Jones, E. E., Farina, A., Hastorf, A. H., Marcus, H., Miller, D. T., Scott, R. A. and French, R. D. (1984) *Social Stigma: The Psychology of Marked Relationships*, W. H. Freeman, New York, chapter 10, chapter 13

Jones, R. E. (1998) 'Black concern for the environment: Myth versus reality', *Society and Natural Resources*, vol 11, pp209–228, chapter 10, chapter 11

Jungermann, H., Pfister, H. R. and Fischer, K. (1996) 'Credibility, information preferences, and information interests', *Risk Analysis*, vol 16, pp251–261, chapter 15

Just, R. (2008) 'The truth will not set you free: Everything we know about Darfur, and everything we're not doing about it', *The New Republic*, 27 August, pp36–47, chapter 4

Kahan, D. M. (1999) 'The secret ambition of deterrence', *Harvard Law Review*, vol 113, no 2, pp413–500, chapter 12

Kahan, D. M. (2007) 'The cognitively illiberal state', *Stanford Law Review*, vol 60, no 1, pp115–154, chapter 11

Kahan, D. M. and Braman, D. (2003) 'More statistics, less persuasion: A cultural theory of gun-risk perceptions', *University of Pennsylvania Law Review*, vol 151, no 4, pp1291–1327, chapter 11

Kahan, D. M. and Braman, D. (2006a) 'Cultural cognition and public policy', *Yale Journal of Law & Public Policy*, vol 24, p147, chapter 11

Kahan, D. M. and Braman, D. (2006b) 'Overcoming the fear of guns, the fear of gun control, and the fear of cultural politics: Constructing a better gun debate', *Emory Law Journal*, vol 55, no 4, pp569–607, chapter 12

Kahan, D. M. and Nussbaum, M. C. (1996) 'Two conceptions of emotion in criminal law', *Columbia Law Review*, vol 96, pp269–374, chapter 12

Kahan, D. M., Braman, D., Gastil, J., Slovic, P. and Mertz, C. K. (2005) 'Gender, race, and risk perception: The influence of cultural status anxiety', http://ssrn.com/abstract=723762, accessed 23 December 2009, chapter 12

Kahan, D. M., Slovic, P., Braman, D. and Gastil, J. (2006) 'Fear of democracy: A cultural critique of Sunstein on risk', *Harvard Law Review*, vol 119, pp1071–1109, chapter 11, chapter 18

Kahan, D. M., Braman, D., Gastil, J., Slovic, P. and Mertz, C. K. (2007) 'Culture and identity-protective cognition: Explaining the white-male effect in risk perception', *Journal of Empirical Legal Studies*, vol 4, pp465–505, chapter 18

Kahneman, D. (1994) 'New challenges to the rationality assumption', *Journal of Institutional and Theoretical Economics*, vol 150, pp18–36, chapter 2

Kahneman, D. (1997) 'New challenges to the rationality assumption', *Legal Theory*, vol 3, pp105–124, chapter 7

Kahneman, D. (2003) 'A perspective on judgment and choice: Mapping bounded rationality', *American Psychologist*, vol 58, pp697–720, chapter 1, chapter 3, chapter 4

Kahneman, D. and Frederick, S. (2002) 'Representativeness revisited: Attribute substitution in intuitive judgment', in T. Gilovich, D. Griffin and D. Kahneman (eds) *Heuristics and Biases: The Psychology of Intuitive Judgment*, Cambridge University Press, New York, chapter 2, chapter 4

Kahneman, D. and Snell, J. (1990) 'Predicting utility', in R. M. Hogarth (ed) *Insights in Decision Making*, pp295–310, University of Chicago, Chicago, IL, chapter 2, chapter 7

Kahneman, D. and Snell, J. (1992) 'Predicting a changing taste', *Journal of Behavioral Decision Making*, vol 5, pp187–200, chapter 2

Kahneman, D. and Tversky, A. (1979) 'Prospect theory: An analysis of decision under risk', *Econometrica*, vol 47, no 2, pp263–291, chapter 1, chapter 12, chapter 20

Kahneman, D., Slovic, P. and Tversky, A. (eds) (1982) *Judgment Under Uncertainty: Heuristics and Biases*, Cambridge University Press, New York, intro, chapter 2

Kahneman, D., Knetsch, J. L. and Thaler, R. H. (1991) 'Anomalies: The endowment effect, loss aversion, and status quo bias', *Journal of Economic Perspectives*, vol 5, no 1, pp193–206, chapter 12

Kahneman, D., Schkade, D. and Sunstein, C. R. (1998) 'Shared outrage and erratic awards: The psychology of punitive damages', *Journal of Risk and Uncertainty*, vol 16, pp49–86, chapter 1, chapter 2

Kaku, M. and Trainer, J. (eds) (1982) *Nuclear Power: Both Sides*, Norton, New York, chapter 12

Kalof, L., Dietz, T., Guagnano, G. and Stern, P. C. (2002) 'Race, gender and environmentalism: The atypical values and beliefs of white men', *Race, Gender & Class*, vol 9, no 2, pp1–19, chapter 10, chapter 11

Kasperson, J. X. and Kasperson, R. E. (1993) 'Corporate culture and technology transfer', in H. S. Brown, P. Derr, O. Renn and A. White (eds) *Corporate Environmentalism in a Global Economy*, Quorum Books, Westport, CT, chapter 19

Kasperson, J. X. and Kasperson, R. E. (2001) 'Transboundary risks and social amplification', in J. Linnerooth-Bayer and R. E. Löfstedt (eds) *Cross-National Studies of Transboundary Risk Problems*, Earthscan, London, chapter 19

Kasperson, J. X., Kasperson, R. E., Perkins, B. J., Renn, O. and White, A. L. (1992) *Information Content, Signals, and Sources Concerning the Proposed Repository at Yucca Mountain: An Analysis of Newspaper Coverage and Social-Group Activities in Lincoln County, Nevada*, Clark University, Center for Technology, Environment, and Development, Worcester, MA, chapter 19

Kasperson, J. X., Kasperson, R. E. and Turner, B. L. (eds) (1995) *Regions at Risk: Comparisons of Threatened Environments*, United Nations University, Tokyo, Japan, chapter 19

Kasperson, J. X., Kasperson, R. E., Pidgeon, N. and Slovic P. (2003). 'The social amplification of risk: Assessing fifteen years of research and theory', in N. Pidgeon, R. E. Kasperson and P. Slovic (eds) *The Social Amplification of Risk*, Cambridge University Press, Cambridge, UK, chapter 17

Kasperson, R. E. (1992) 'The social amplification of risk: Progress in developing an integrative framework of risk', in S. Krimsky and D. Golding (eds) *Social Theories of Risk*, Praeger, New York, chapter 13, chapter 17, chapter 19

Kasperson, R. E. (forthcoming) 'Process and institutional issues in siting hazardous facilities', chapter 19

Kasperson, R. E. and Kasperson, J. X. (1991) 'Hidden hazards', in D. G. Mayo and R. D. Hollander (eds) *Acceptable Evidence: Science and Values in Risk Management*, Oxford University Press, New York, chapter 19

Kasperson, R. E. and Kasperson, J. X. (1996) 'The social amplification and attenuation of risk', *The Annals of the American Academy of Political and Social Science*, vol 545, pp95–105, chapter 19

Kasperson, R. E. and Stallen, P. J. M. (eds) (1991) *Communicating Risks to the Public: International Perspectives*, Kluwer Academic, Dordrecht, The Netherlands, chapter 19

Kasperson, R. E., Renn, O., Slovic, P., Brown, H. S., Emel, J., Goble, R., Kasperson, J. X. and Ratick, S. (1988) 'The social amplification of risk: A conceptual framework', *Risk Analysis*, vol 8, pp177–187, chapter 12, chapter 13, chapter 17, chapter 19

Kasperson, R. E., Golding, D. and Tuler, S. (1992) 'Social distrust as a factor in siting hazardous facilities and communicating risks: Individual and collective responses to risk', *Journal of Social Issues*, vol 48, no 4, pp161–188, chapter 19

Kasperson, R. E., Kasperson, J. X. and Turner, B. L. (1999) 'Risk and criticality: Trajectories of regional environmental degradation', *Ambio*, vol 28, no 6, pp562–568, chapter 19

Kasperson, R. E., Jhaveri, N. and Kasperson, J. X. (2001) 'Stigma, places, and the social amplification of risk: Toward a framework of analysis', in J. Flynn, P. Slovic and H. Kunreuther (eds) *Risk, Media and Stigma: Understanding Public Challenges to Modern Science and Technology*, Earthscan, London, chapter 19

Keeney, R. L. (1990) 'Mortality risks induced by economic expenditures', *Risk Analysis*, vol 10, no 1, pp147–159, chapter 12

Kennedy, P. (1998) *A Guide to Econometrics*, 4th edn, MIT Press, Cambridge, MA, chapter 4

Kerr, N. L., MacCoun, R. J. and Kramer, G. P. (1996) 'Bias in judgment: Comparison individuals and groups', *Psychological Review*, vol 103, no 4, pp687–719, chapter 12

Kirsch, I. S., Jungeblut, A., Jenkins, L. and Kolstad, A. (2002) 'Adult literacy in America: A first look at the findings of the National Adult Literacy Survey', 3rd edn, National Center for Education Statistics, http://nces.ed.gov/pubs93/93275.pdf, accessed 31 December 2009, chapter 20

Kleck, G. (1996) 'Crime, culture conflict and the sources of support for gun control: A multilevel application of the general social surveys', *American Behavioral Scientist*, vol 39, no 4, pp387–404, chapter 12

Kletz, T. A. (1996) 'Risk – Two views: The public's and the experts", *Disaster Prevention and Management*, vol 15, pp41–46, chapter 15

Kogut, T. and Ritov, I. (2005a) 'The "Identified Victim" effect: An identified group, or just a single individual?', *Journal of Behavioral Decision Making*, vol 18, pp157–167, chapter 3, chapter 4

Kogut, T. and Ritov, I. (2005b) 'The singularity of identified victims in separate and joint evaluations', *Organizational Behavior and Human Decision Processes*, vol 97, pp106–116, chapter 3, chapter 4

Kraus, N., Malmfors, T. and Slovic, P. (1992) 'Intuitive toxicology: Expert and lay judgments of chemical risks', *Risk Analysis*, vol 12, pp 215–232, chapter 9, chapter 10, chapter 11, chapter 15

Kristof, N. D. (2005) 'Nukes are green', *New York Times*, 9 April 2005, chapter 12

Kroll-Smith, J. S. and Floyd, H. H. (1997) *Bodies in Protest: Environmental Illness and the Struggle over Medical Knowledge*, New York University Press, New York, chapter 13

Kunreuther, H. and Slovic, P. (1996) 'Science, values, and risk', *The Annals of the American Academy of Political and Social Science*, vol 545, pp116–125, chapter 9

Kunreuther, H., Fitzgerald, K. and Aarts, T. D. (1993) 'Siting noxious facilities: A test of the facility siting credo', *Risk Analysis*, vol 13, pp301–318, chapter 19

Kuyper, H. and Vlek, C. (1984) 'Contrasting risk judgments among interest groups', *Acta Psychologica*, vol 56, pp205–218, chapter 9

Kysar, D. A. (2003) 'The expectations of consumers', *Columbia Law Review*, vol 103, no 7, pp1700–1790, chapter 12

Kysar, D. and Salzman, J. (2003) 'Environmental tribalism', *Minnesota Law Review*, vol 87, pp1099–1137, chapter 12

La Porte, T. R. (1996) 'High reliability organizations: Unlikely, demanding and at risk', *Journal of Contingencies and Crisis Management*, vol 4, pp60–70, chapter 19

Lackritz, E. M., Satten, G. A., Aberle-Grasse, J. et al (1995) 'Estimated risk of transmission of the human immunodeficiency virus by screened blood in the United States', *New England Journal of Medicine*, vol 333, pp1721–1725, chapter 14

Lang, F. R. and Carstensen, L. L. (2002) 'Time counts: Future time perspective, goals and social relationships', *Psychology and Aging*, vol 17, pp125–139, chapter 8

Langford, I. L. (2002) 'An existential approach to risk perception', *Risk Analysis*, vol 22, pp101–120, chapter 19

Lasker, R. D. (2004) 'Redefining readiness: Terrorism planning through the eyes of the public', www.redefiningreadiness.net/pdf/RedefiningReadinessStudy.pdf, accessed 31 December 2009, chapter 17

Lau, J., Lau, M., Kim, J. H. and Tsui, H. I. (2006) 'Impacts of media coverage on the community stress level in Hong Kong after the tsunami on 26 December 2004', *Journal of Epidemiology and Community Health*, vol 60, pp675–682, chapter 8

Lavie, N., Ro, T. and Russell, C. (2003) 'The role of perceptual load in processing distractor faces', *Psychological Science*, vol 14, pp510–515, chapter 3

Lawless, E. W. (1977) *Technology and Social Shock*, Rutgers University Press, New Brunswick, NJ, chapter 19

Le Doux, J. (1996) *The Emotional Brain*, Simon and Schuster, New York, chapter 2

Lee, S. J., Liljas, B., Churchill, W. H. et al (1998) 'Perceptions and preferences of autologous blood donors', *Transfusion*, vol 38, pp757–763, chapter 14

Leiserowitz, A. (2004) 'Before and after *The Day After Tomorrow*: A U.S. study of climate change risk perception, *Environment*, vol 46, no 9, pp22–37, chapter 17

Leiserowitz, A. (2005) 'American risk perceptions: Is climate change dangerous?', *Risk Analysis*, vol 25, no 6, pp1433–1442, chapter 17, chapter 18

Lerner, J. S. and Gonzalez, R. M. (2005) 'Forecasting one's future based on fleeting subjective experiences', *Personality and Social Psychology Bulletin*, vol 31, pp454–466, chapter 8

Lerner, J. S., Gonzalez, R. M., Small, D. A. and Fischhoff, B. (2003) 'Effects of fear and anger on perceived risks of terrorism: A national field experiment', *Psychological Science*, vol 14, pp144–150, chapter 8

Lester, J., Allen, H. and Hill, K. (2001) *Environmental Justice in the United States: Myths and Realities*, Westview Press, Boulder, CO, chapter 10

Leventhal, H. (1970) 'Findings and theory in the study of fear communication', in L. Berkowitz (ed) *Advances in Experimental Social Psychology*, vol 5, Academic Press, New York, chapter 19

Lewin, K. (1946) 'Behavior and development as a function of the total situation', in L. Carmichael (ed) *Manual of Child Psychology*, Wiley, New York, intro

Lichtenberg, J. and Maclean, D. (1991) 'The role of the media in risk communication', in R. E. Kasperson and P. J. M. Stallen (eds) *Communicating Risks to the Public*, Kluwer Academic Press, London, chapter 19

Lichtenberg, J. and MacLean, D. (1992) 'Is good news no news?', *Geneva Papers on Risk and Insurance*, vol 17, pp362–365, chapter 15

Lichtenstein, S. and Slovic, P. (1971) 'Reversals of preference between bids and choices in gambling decisions', *Journal of Experimental Psychology*, vol 89, pp46–55, chapter 1

Lichtenstein, S. and Slovic P. (eds) (2006) *The Construction of Preference*, Cambridge University Press, New York, chapter 1, chapter 8

Lichtenstein, S., Slovic, P., Fischhoff, B., Layman, M. and Combs, B. (1978) 'Judged frequency of lethal events', *Journal of Experimental Psychology: Human Learning and Memory*, vol 4, pp551–578, chapter 2

Lifton, R. J. (1967) *Death in Life: Survivors of Hiroshima*, Random House, New York, chapter 6, chapter 13

Lifton, R. J. and Mitchell, G. (1995) 'The age of numbing', *Technology Review*, August/September, pp58–59, chapter 6

Lipkus, I. M. and Hollands, J. G. (1999) 'The visual communication of risk', *Journal of the National Cancer Institute: Monographs*, no 25, pp149–163, chapter 20

Lipkus, I. M., Samsa, G. and Rimer, B. K. (2001) 'General performance on a numeracy scale among highly educated samples', *Medical Decision Making*, vol 21, no 1, pp37–44, chapter 20

Loewenstein, G. F. (1996) 'Out of control: Visceral influences on behavior', *Organizational Behavior and Human Decision Processes*, vol 65, pp272–292, chapter 2

Loewenstein, G. F. (1999) 'A visceral account of addiction', in J. Elster and O-J. Skog (eds) *Getting Hooked: Rationality and Addiction*, Cambridge University Press, Cambridge, UK, chapter 2, chapter 7

Loewenstein, G. F. and Schkade, D. (1999) 'Wouldn't it be nice? Predicting future feelings', in E. Diener, N. Schwartz and D. Kahneman (eds) *Well-Being: The Foundations of Hedonic Psychology*, Russell Sage Foundation, New York, chapter 2, chapter 7

Loewenstein, G. and Small, D. (2007) 'The scarecrow and the tin man: The vicissitudes of human sympathy and caring', *Review of General Psychology*, vol 11, pp112–126, chapter 3

Loewenstein, G., Weber, E. U., Hsee, C. K. and Welch, E. S. (2001) 'Risk as feelings', *Psychological Bulletin*, vol 127, 267–286 intro, chapter 1, chapter 2, chapter 3, chapter 6, chapter 12, chapter 15

Loewenstein, G., Small, D. A. and Strand, J. (2006) 'Statistical, identifiable, and iconic victims', in E. J. McCaffery and J. Slemrod (eds) *Behavioral Public Finance*, pp32–46, Russell Sage Foundation Press, New York, chapter 4

Löfstedt, R. E. and Horlick-Jones, T. (1999) 'Environmental regulation in the UK: Politics, institutional change and public trust', in G. Cvetkovich and R. E. Löfstedt (eds) *Social Trust and the Management of Risk*, Earthscan, London, chapter 19

Lord, C. G., Ross, L. and Lepper, M. R. (1979) 'Biased assimilation and attitude polarization: The effects of prior theories on subsequently considered evidence', *Journal of Personality and Social Psychology*, vol 37, no 11, pp2098–2109, chapter 12, chapter 18

Lott, J. R. (2000) *More Guns, Less Crime: Understanding Crime and Gun-Control Laws*, 2nd edn, University of Chicago Press, Chicago, IL, chapter 11

Luhmann, N. (1979) *Trust and Power: Two Works by Niklas Luhmann*, Wiley, Chichester, chapter 19

Lukensmeyer, C. J., Goldman, J. and Brigham, S. (2005) 'A town meeting for the twenty-first century', in J. Gastil and P. Levine (eds) *The Deliberative Democracy Handbook*, Jossey-Bass, New York, chapter 12

Luker, K. (1984) *Abortion and the Politics of Motherhood*, University of California Press, Berkeley, CA, chapter 11

Lynch, B. S. and Bonnie, R. J. (1994) *Growing Up Tobacco Free: Preventing Nicotine Addiction in Children and Youths*, National Academies Press, Washington, DC, chapter 22

Maani, K. E. and Cavana, R. Y. (2000) *Systems Thinking and Modelling: Understanding Change and Complexity*, Prentice Hall, Auckland, New Zealand, chapter 17

MacGregor, D. G. (1991) 'Worry over technological activities and life concerns', *Risk Analysis*, vol 11, pp315–324, chapter 19

MacGregor, D., Slovic, P. and Morgan, M. G. (1994) 'Perception of risks from electromagnetic fields: A psychometric evaluation of a risk-communication approach', *Risk*

Analysis, vol 14, no 5, pp815–828, chapter 13

MacGregor, D. G., Slovic, P., Dreman, D. and Berry, M. (2000) 'Imagery, affect, and financial judgment', *Journal of Psychology and Financial Markets*, vol 1, pp104–110, chapter 7

Machlis, G. E. and Rosa, E. A. (1990) 'Desired risk: Broadening the social amplifications of risk framework', *Risk Analysis*, vol 10, no 1, pp161–168, chapter 19

MacKie, D. M. and Quellar, S. (2000) 'The impact of group membership on persuasion: Revisiting "who says what to whom with what effect?"', in D. J. Terry and M. A. Hogg (eds) *Attitudes, Behavior, and Social Context: The Role of Norms and Group Membership*, Erlbaum, Mahwah, NJ, chapter 11

MacKie, D. M., Gastardoconaco, M. C. and Skelly, J. J. (1992) 'Knowledge of the advocated position and the processing of in-group and out-group persuasive messages', *Personality and Social Psychology Bulletin*, vol 18, no 2, pp145–151, chapter 11

Mackie, D. M., Worth, L. T. and Asuncion, A. G. (1990) 'Processing of persuasive in-group messages', *Journal of Personality and Social Psychology*, vol 58, no 5, pp812–822, chapter 12

Macoubrie, J. (2006) 'Nanotechnology: Public concerns, reasoning and trust in government', *Public Understanding of Science*, vol 15, pp221–241, chapter 18

Madison, J. (1787) 'The Federalist No. 10: The utility of the union as a safeguard against domestic faction and insurrection (continued)', www.constitution.org/fed/federa10.htm, accessed 23 December 2009, chapter 12

Mahood, G. (2004) *Canada's Tobacco Package Label or Warning System: 'Telling the Truth' About Tobacco Product Risks*, World Health Organization, Geneva, Switzerland, chapter 22

Mandel, G. N. and Gathii, J. T. (2006) 'Cost–benefit analysis versus the precautionary principle: Beyond Cass Sunstein's "Laws of Fear"', *University of Illinois Law Review*, 2006, no 5, pp1037–1079, chapter 12

Mann, H. (2007) '*Upplevd nyhetsrapportering och associerade känslor i samband med katastrofer: En explorativ studie [News coverage and experienced feelings in connection to disasters: An explorative study]*', Reports from Stockholm University, http://urn.kb.se/resolve?urn=urn:nbn:se:su:diva6777, accessed 19 January 2007, chapter 8

Marcus, E. N. (2006) 'The silent epidemic: The health effects of illiteracy', *New England Journal of Medicine*, vol 355, no 4, pp339–341, chapter 20

Margolis, H. (1996) *Dealing with Risk: When the Public and Experts Disagree on Environmental Issues*, University of Chicago Press, Chicago, IL, chapter 11, chapter 12, chapter 14

Marlatt, G. A. and Gordon, J. R. (1985) *Relapse Prevention: Maintenance Strategies in the Treatment of Addictive Behaviors*, Guilford Press, New York, chapter 22

Marris, C., Langford, I. H. and O'Riordan, T. (1998) 'A quantitative test of the cultural theory of risk perceptions: Comparison with the psychometric paradigm', *Risk Analysis*, vol 18, no 5, pp635–647, chapter 11, chapter 19

Marris, C., Wynne, B., Simmons, P. and Weldon, S. (2001) *Public Perceptions of Agricultural Biotechnologies in Europe*, Final Report FAIR CT98-3844, DG12-SSMI, Commission of the European Communities, Brussels, Belgium, chapter 19

Matza, D. (1964) *Delinquency and Drift*, Transaction, Edison, NJ, chapter 12

Mazur, A. (1984) 'The journalist and technology: Reporting about Love Canal and Three Mile Island', *Minerva*, vol 22, pp45–66, chapter 19

Mazur, A. (1990) Nuclear power, chemical hazards, and the quantity of reporting', *Minerva*, vol 28, pp294–323, chapter 19

McCabe, A. S. and Fitzgerald, M. R. (1991) 'Media images of environmental biotechnology: What does the public see?', in G. S. Sayler, R. Fox and J. W. Blackburn (eds) *Environmental Biotechnology for Waste Treatment*, Plenum, New York, chapter 19

McGarity, T. O. (2002) 'Professor Sunstein's fuzzy math', *Georgetown Law Journal*, vol 90, p2341, chapter 12

McIntosh, P. L. (1996) 'When the surgeon has HIV: What to tell patients about the risk of exposure and the risk of transmission', *University of Kansas Law Review*, vol 44, no 2, pp315–364, chapter 12

McKelvie, S. J. (1997) 'The availability heuristic: Effects of fame and gender on the estimated frequency of male and female names', *Journal of Social Psychology*, vol 137, no 1, pp63–78, chapter 12

McKibben, B. (1989) *The End of Nature*, Doubleday, New York, chapter 6

McKibben, B. (1992) *The Age of Missing Information*, Random House, New York, chapter 6

McKibben, B. (1998) *Maybe One: A Personal and Environmental Argument for Single-Child Families*, Simon & Schuster, New York, chapter 6

McKibben, B. (2003) *Enough: Staying Human in an Engineered Age*, Times Books, New York, chapter 6

McNeil, B. J., Pauker, S. G., Sox, H. C. and Tversky, A. (1982) 'On the elicitation of preferences for alternative therapies', *The New England Journal of Medicine*, vol 306, pp1259–1262, chapter 9

Mellers, B. A. (2000) 'Choice and the relative pleasure of consequences', *Psychological Bulletin*, vol 126, no 6, pp910–924, chapter 2

Mellers, B. A., Ordóñez, L. and Birnbaum, M. H. (1992) 'A change-of-process theory for contextual effects and preference reversals in risky decision making', *Organizational Behavior and Human Decision Processes*, vol 52, pp331–369, chapter 1

Mellers, B. A., Schwartz, A., Ho, K. and Ritov, I. (1997) 'Decision affect theory: Emotional reactions to the outcomes of risky options', *Psychological Science*, vol 8, pp423–429, chapter 2

Melville, K., Willingham, T. L. and Dedrick, J. R. (2005) 'National issues forums: A network of communities promoting public deliberation', in J. Gastil and P. Levine (eds) *The Deliberative Democracy Handbook*, Jossey-Bass, New York, chapter 12

Merleau-Ponty, M. (1962) *The Phenomenology of Perception*, Routledge and Kegan Paul, London, chapter 13

Metz, W. C. (1996) 'Historical application of a social amplification of risk model: Economic impact of risk events at a nuclear weapons facility', *Risk Analysis*, vol 16, no 2, pp185–193, chapter 19

Miller, J. D., Scott, E. C. and Okamoto, S. (2006) 'Science communication: Public acceptance of evolution', *Science*, vol 313, pp765–766, chapter 18

Mitchell, M. L. (1989) 'The impact of external parties on brand-name capital: The 1982 Tylenol poisonings and subsequent cases', *Economic Inquiry*, vol 27, pp601–618, chapter 1, chapter 13

Mitchell, R. C., Payne, B. and Dunlap, R. E. (1988) 'Stigma and radioactive waste: Theory, assessment, and some empirical findings from Hanford, WA', in R. G. Post (ed) *Waste Management '88: Waste Processing, Transportation, Storage and Disposal, Technical Programs and Public Education*, vol 2, *High-Level Waste and General Interest*, University of Arizona, Tucson, AZ, chapter 19

Mohai, P. and Bryant, B. (1998) 'Is there a "race" effect on concern for environmental quality?', *Public Opinion Quarterly*, vol 62, pp475–505, chapter 10, chapter 11

Morgan, M. G., Fischhoff, B., Bostrom, A. and Atman, C. J. (2001) *Risk Communication: A Mental Models Approach*, Cambridge University Press, New York, chapter 19

Morris, W. N. (1999) 'The mood system', in D. Kahneman, E. Diener and N. Schwarz (eds) *Well-being: The Foundations of Hedonic Psychology*, Russell-Sage, New York, chapter 8

Mowrer, O. H. (1960a) *Learning Theory and Behavior*, Wiley, New York, intro, chapter 2, chapter 7

Mowrer, O. H. (1960b) *Learning Theory and the Symbolic Processes*, Wiley, New York, intro, chapter 7

Murphy, S. T. and Zajonc, R. B. (1993) 'Affect, cognition, and awareness: Affective priming with optimal and suboptimal stimulus exposures', *Journal of Personality and Social Psychology*, vol 64, pp723–739, chapter 3, chapter 22

Mutz, D. C. and Martin, P. S. (2001) 'Facilitating communication across lines of political difference: The role of mass media', *American Political Science Review*, vol 95, pp97–114, chapter 18

Needleman, H. L., Schell, A., Bellinger, D., Leviton, A. and Allred, E. N. (1990) 'The long-term effects of exposure to low doses of lead in childhood: 11-year follow-up report', *New England Journal of Medicine*, vol 322, no 2, pp83–88, chapter 10

New York Times (2001) 'Philip Morris issues apology for Czech study on smoking', 27 July, pC12

Niaura, R. S., Rohsenour, D. J., Blinkoff, J. A., Monti, P. M., Pedraza, M. and Abrams, D. B. (1988) 'Relevance of cue reactivity to understanding alcohol and smoking relapse', *Journal of Abnormal Psychology*, vol 97, pp133–152, chapter 22

Nisbett, R. E. and Cohen, D. (1996) *Culture of Honor: The Psychology of Violence in the South*, Westview Press, Boulder, CO, chapter 12

Noll, R. G. and Krier, J. E. (1990) 'Some implications of cognitive psychology for risk', *Journal of Legal Studies*, vol 19, no 2, pp747–779, chapter 12

Novemsky, N., Dhar, R., Schwarz, N. and Simonson, I. (2007) 'Preference fluency in choice', *Journal of Marketing Research*, vol 44, pp347–356, chapter 8

NRC (National Research Council) Committee on Risk Characterization (1989) *Improving Risk Communication*, National Academy Press, Washington, DC, chapter 19

NRC Committee on Risk Characterization (1996) *Understanding Risk: Informing Decisions in a Democratic Society*, National Academy Press, Washington, DC, intro, chapter 2, chapter 19

NRC Committee on Toxicology (2001) *Arsenic in Drinking Water: 2001 Update*, National Academy Press, Washington, DC, chapter 12

NRC Committee to Improve Research on Information and Data on Firearms (2004) *Firearms and Violence: A Critical Review*, National Academy Press, Washington, DC, chapter 12

Nussbaum, M. C. (2001) *Upheavals of Thought: The Intelligence of Emotions*, Cambridge University Press, New York, chapter 12

Ochsner, K. and Phelps, E. (2007) 'Emerging perspectives on emotion-cognition interactions', *Trends in Cognitive Sciences*, vol 11, pp317–318, chapter 3

Okrent, D. and Pidgeon, N. E. (1998) 'Risk perception versus risk analysis', *Reliability Engineering and System Safety*, vol 59, no 1, pp1–159, chapter 19

Oliver-Smith, A. (1996) 'Anthropological research on hazards and disasters', *Annual Review of Anthropology*, vol 25, p303, chapter 13

Ordóñez, L. and Benson, L., III (1997) 'Decisions under time pressure: How time constraint affects risky decision making', *Organizational Behavior and Human Decision Processes*, vol 71, no 2, pp121–140, chapter 2

Osgood, C. E., Suci, G. J. and Tannenbaum, P. H. (1957) *The Measurement of Meaning*, University of Illinois, Urbana, IL, intro, chapter 1

Otway, H., Haastrup, P., Connell, W., Gianitsopoulas, G. and Paruccini, M. (1988) 'Risk communication in Europe after Chernobyl: A media analysis of seven countries', *Industrial Crisis Quarterly*, vol 2, pp31–35, chapter 19

Packard, V. (1957) *The Hidden Persuaders*, David McKay, New York, chapter 1

Palmer, C. G. S. (2003) 'Risk perception: Another look at the "white male" effect', *Health, Risk & Society*, vol 5, no 1, pp71–83, chapter 11

Palmer, C. G. S., Carlstrom, L. K. and Woodward, J. A. (2001) 'Risk perception and ethnicity', *Risk Decision and Policy*, vol 6, pp187–206, chapter 19

Parducci, A. (1995) *Happiness, Pleasure, and Judgment*, Erlbaum, Mahwah, NJ, chapter 1

Pavot, W. and Diener, E. (1993) 'Review of the satisfaction with life scale', *Personality Assessment*, vol 5, pp164–172, chapter 8

Pearce, W. B. and Littlejohn, S. W. (1997) *Moral Conflict: When Social Worlds Collide*, Sage, Thousand Oaks, CA, chapter 12

Pennington, N. and Hastie, R. (1993) 'A theory of explanation-based decision making', in G. Klein, J. Orasano, R. Calderwood and C. E. Zsambok (eds) *Decision Making in Action: Models and Methods*, Ablex, Norwood, NJ, chapter 2

Perrow, C. (1984) *Normal Accidents: Living with High-Risk Technologies*, Basic Books, New York, chapter 19

Peters, E. (2006) 'The functions of affect in the construction of preferences', in S. Lichtenstein and P. Slovic (eds) *The Construction of Preference*, Cambridge University Press, New York, chapter 8

Peters, E. and Slovic, P. (1996) 'The role of affect and worldviews as orienting dispositions in the perception and acceptance of nuclear power', *Journal of Applied Social Psychology*, vol 26, pp1427–1453, chapter 7, chapter 11, chapter 19

Peters, E. and Slovic, P. (2000) 'The springs of action: Affective and analytical information processing in choice', *Personality and Social Psychology Bulletin*, vol 26, pp1465–1475, chapter 2, chapter 3, chapter 18

Peters, E., Burraston, B. and Mertz, C. K. (2004) 'An emotion-based model of risk perception and stigma susceptibility: Cognitive appraisals of emotion, affective reactivity, worldviews, and risk perceptions in the generation of technological stigma', *Risk Analysis*, vol 24, pp1349–1367, chapter 12, chapter 18

Peters, E., Västfjäll, D., Gärling, T. and Slovic, P. (2006a) 'Affect and decision making: A "hot" topic. The role of affect in decision making', *Journal of Behavioral Decision Making*, vol 19, no 2, pp79–85, chapter 1

Peters, E., Västfjäll, D., Slovic, P., Mertz, C. K., Mazzocco, K. and Dickert, S. (2006b) 'Numeracy and decision making', *Psychological Science*, vol 17, pp407–413, chapter 1, chapter 20

Peters, E., Dieckmann, N., Dixon, A., Hibbard, J. H. and Mertz, C. K. (2007a) 'Less is more in presenting quality information to consumers', *Medical Care Research and Review*, vol 64, no 2, pp169–190, chapter 20

Peters, E., Romer, D., Slovic, P., Jamieson, K. H., Wharfield, L., Mertz, C. K. and Carpenter, S. M. (2007b) 'The impact and acceptability of Canadian-style cigarette warning labels among U.S. smokers and nonsmokers', *Nicotine & Tobacco Research*, vol 9, no 4, pp473–481, chapter 20

Petterson, J. S. (1988) 'Perception vs. reality of radiological impact: The Goiania model', *Nuclear News*, vol 31, no 14, pp84–90, chapter 19

Pfister, H.-R. and Böhm, G. (2008) 'The multiplicity of emotions: A framework of emotional functions in decision making', *Judgment and Decision Making*, vol 3, no 1, pp5–17, chapter 8

Pham, M. T. (1998) 'Representativeness, relevance, and the use of feelings in decision making', *Journal of Consumer Research*, vol 25, pp144–159, chapter 8

Pham, M. T. (2007) 'Emotion and rationality: A critical review and interpretation of empirical evidence', *Review of General Psychology*, vol 11, pp155–178, chapter 3

Philipson, T. J. and Posner, R. A. (1993) *Private Choices and Public Health: The AIDS Epidemic an in Economic Perspective*, Harvard University Press, Cambridge, MA, chapter 12

Phillips, L. D. (1984) 'A theory of requisite decision models', *Acta Psychologica*, vol 56, pp29–48, chapter 2

Phillips, L., Bridgeman, J. and Ferguson-Smith, M. (2000) *The Report of the Inquiry into BSE and Variant CJD in the UK*, The Stationery Office, London, chapter 19

Picard, A. (1995) *The Gift of Death: Confronting Canada's Tainted-Blood Tragedy*, HarperCollins, Toronto, Canada, chapter 14

Pidgeon, N. F. (1988) 'Risk perception and accident analysis', *Acta Psychologica*, vol 68, pp355–368, chapter 19

Pidgeon, N. F. (1997) *Risk Communication and the Social Amplification of Risk – Phase 1 Scoping Study*, Report to the UK Health and Safety Executive (Risk Assessment and Policy Unit), RSU Ref 3625/R62.076, HSE Books, London, chapter 17, chapter 19

Pidgeon, N. F. and O'Leary, M. (1994) 'Organizational safety culture: Implications for aviation practice', in N. Johnston, N. McDonald and R. Fuller (eds) *Aviation Psychology in Practice*, Avebury Technical, Aldershot, chapter 19

Pidgeon, N. F. and O'Leary, M. (2000) 'Man-made disasters: Why technology and organizations (sometimes) fail', *Safety Science*, vol 34, pp15–30, chapter 19

Pidgeon, N. F., Henwood, K. and Maguire, B. (1999) 'Public health communication and the social amplification of risks: Present knowledge and future prospects', in P. Bennett and K. Calman (eds) *Risk Communication and Public Health*, Oxford University Press, UK, chapter 19

Pidgeon, N. F., Hood, C., Jones, D., Turner, B. and Gibson, R. (1992) 'Risk perception', in The Royal Society Study Group (ed) *Risk: Analysis, Perception and Management*, The Royal Society, London, chapter 19

Pidgeon, N. F., Kasperson, R. E. and Slovic, P. (eds) (2003) *The Social Amplification of Risk*, Cambridge University Press, Cambridge, UK, chapter 17

Pierce, J. P., Farkas, A. J., Evans, N. and Gilpin, E. (1995) 'An improved surveillance measure for adolescent smoking?', *Tobacco Control*, vol 4, no 1, pp47–56, chapter 22

Pollay, R. W. (1995) 'Targeting tactics in selling smoke: Youthful aspects of 20th century cigarette advertising', *Journal of Marketing Theory and Practice*, vol 3, pp1–22, chapter 22

Pollay, R. W. (2000) 'Targeting youth and concerned smokers: Evidence from Canadian tobacco industry documents', *Tobacco Control*, vol 9, pp136–147, chapter 22

Poortinga, W., Steg, L. and Vlek, C. (2002) 'Environmental risk concern and preferences for energy-saving measures', *Environment & Behavior*, vol 34, no 4, pp455–478, chapter 11

Poortinga, W., Bickerstaff, K., Langford, I., Niewöhner, J. and Pidgeon, N. (2004) 'The British 2001 foot and mouth crisis: A comparative study of public risk perceptions, trust and beliefs about government policy in two communities', *Journal of Risk Research*, vol 7, pp73–90, chapter 19

Posner, M. I. and Raichle, M. E. (1994) *Images of Mind*, Scientific American Books, New York, chapter 3

Posner, M. I. and Rothbart, M. K. (2007) 'Research on attention networks as a model for the integration of psychological sciences', *Annual Review of Psychology*, vol 58, pp1–23, chapter 3

Powell, D. (2001) 'Mad cow disease and the stigmatization of British beef', in J. Flynn, P. Slovic and H. Kunreuther (eds) *Risk, Media, and Stigma: Understanding Public Challenges to Modern Science and Technology*, Earthscan, London, chapter 1

Power, S. (2003) *A Problem from Hell: America and the Age of Genocide*, Harper Perennial, New York, chapter 5

Prentice, D. A. and Miller, D. T. (1993) 'Pluralistic ignorance and alcohol use on campus: Some consequences of misperceiving the social norm', *Journal of Personality and Social Psychology*, vol 64, no 2, pp243–256, chapter 12

Project 88 (1988) 'Harnessing market forces to protect our environment: Initiatives for the new president', www.hks.harvard.edu/fs/rstavins/Monographs_&_Reports/Project_88-1.pdf, accessed 26 December 2009, chapter 13

Putnam, R. D. (1993) *Making Democracy Work: Civic Traditions in Modern Italy*, Princeton University Press, Princeton, NJ, chapter 19

Putnam, R. D. (1995) 'Tuning in, tuning out: The strange disappearance of social capital in America', *PS Political Science and Politics*, vol 28, pp664–683, chapter 19

Quattrone, G. A. and Jones, E. E. (1980) 'The perception of variability within in-groups and out-groups: Implications for the laws of small numbers', *Journal of Personality and Social Psychology*, vol 38, no 1, pp141–152, chapter 12

Rappaport, R. A. (1988) 'Toward postmodern risk analysis', *Risk Analysis*, vol 8, pp189–191, chapter 19

Rawls, J. (1993) *Political Liberalism*, Columbia University Press, New York, chapter 12

Raymond, J. E., Fenske, M. J. and Tavassoli, N. T. (2003) 'Selective attention determines emotional responses to novel visual stimuli', *Psychological Science*, vol 14, pp537–542, chapter 3

Raymond, J. E., Fenske, M. J. and Westoby, N. (2005) 'Emotional devaluation of distracting patterns and faces: A consequence of attentional inhibition during visual search?', *Journal of Experimental Psychology: Human Perception and Performance*, vol 31, pp1404–1415, chapter 3

Rayner, S. (1988) 'Muddling through metaphors to maturity: A commentary on Kasperson et al, "The Social Amplification of Risk"', *Risk Analysis*, vol 8, pp201–204, chapter 19

Rayner, S. (1992) 'Cultural theory and risk analysis', in S. Krimsky and D. Golding (eds) *Social Theories of Risk*, Praeger, Westport, CT, chapter 11, chapter 19

Reber, R. and Schwarz, N. (1999) 'Effects of perceptual fluency on judgments of truth', *Consciousness and Cognition*, vol 8, pp338–342, chapter 8

Reber, R., Schwarz, N. and Winkielman, P. (2004) 'Processing fluency and aesthetic pleasure: Is beauty in the perceiver's processing experience?', *Personality and Social Psychology Review*, vol 8, pp364–382, chapter 8

Renn, O. (1991) 'Risk communication and the social amplification of risk', in R. E. Kasperson and P. J. M. Stallen (eds) *Communicating Risks to the Public: International Perspectives*, Kluwer Academic, Dordrecht, The Netherlands, chapter 19

Renn, O. (1998a) 'Three decades of risk research: Accomplishments and new challenges', *Journal of Risk Research*, vol 1, pp49–71, chapter 19

Renn, O. (1998b) 'The role of risk communication and public dialog for improving risk management', *Risk Decision and Policy*, no 3, pp5–30, chapter 17

Renn, O. (2003) 'Social amplification of risk in participation: Two case studies', in N. Pidgeon, R. G. Kasperson and P. Slovic (eds) *The Social Amplification of Risk*, Cambridge University Press, Cambridge, UK, chapter 19

Renn, O. and Levine, D. (1991) 'Credibility and trust in risk communication', in R. E. Kasperson and P. J. M. Stallen (eds) *Communicating Risks to the Public: International Perspectives*, Kluwer Academic, Dordrecht, The Netherlands, chapter 19

Renn, O. and Rohrmann, B. (2000) *Cross-Cultural Risk Perception: A Survey of Empirical Studies*, Kluwer Academic Press, Amsterdam, The Netherlands, chapter 19

Renn, O., Burns, W., Kasperson, J. X., Kasperson, R. E. and Slovic, P. (1992) 'The social amplification of risk: Theoretical foundations and empirical applications', *Journal of Social Issues*, vol 48, no 4, pp137–160, chapter 19

Renn, O., Webler, T. and Wiedemann, P. (1995) *Fairness and Competence in Citizen Participation: Evaluating Models for Environmental Discourse*, Kluwer Academic, Dordrecht, The Netherlands, chapter 19

Revesz, R. L. (1999) 'Environmental regulation, cost–benefit analysis, and the discounting of human lives', *Columbia Law Review*, vol 99, no 4, pp941–1017, chapter 11, chapter 12

Reyna, V. F. and Brainerd, C. J. (1995) 'Fuzzy-trace theory: An interim synthesis', *Learning and Individual Differences*, vol 7, pp1–75, chapter 3

Ries, L. A. G., Eisner, M. P., Kosary, C. L., Hankey, B. F., Miller, B. A., Clegg, L. and Edwards, B. K. (eds) (2001) 'Table XV-10. Lung and bronchus cancer (invasive): Incidence, mortality, and survival rates', in *SEER Cancer Statistics Review 1973–1998*, National Cancer Institute, Bethesda, MD, chapter 21

Rip, A. (1988) 'Should social amplification of risk be counteracted?', *Risk Analysis*, vol 8, pp193–197, chapter 19

Ro, T., Russell, C. and Lavie, N. (2001) 'Changing faces: A detection advantage in the flicker paradigm', *Psychological Science*, vol 12, pp94–99, chapter 3

Roberts, K. H. (1989) 'New challenges in organizational research: High reliability organizations', *Industrial Crisis Quarterly*, vol 3, pp111–125, chapter 19

Robinson, R. J. and Killen, J. D. (1997) 'Do cigarette warning labels reduce smoking? Paradoxical effects among adolescents', *Archives of Pediatrics and Adolescent Medicine*, vol 151, pp267–272, chapter 22

Romer, D. and Jamieson, P. (2001) 'The role of perceived risk in starting and stopping smoking', in P. Slovic (ed) *Smoking: Risk, Perception, and Policy*, Sage, Thousand Oaks, CA, chapter 22

Roosevelt, F. D. (1933) 'First inaugural address: Saturday, March 4, 1933', www.bartleby.com/124/pres49.html, accessed 23 December 2009, chapter 12

Rosa, E. A. (1998) 'Metatheoretical foundations for post-normal risk', *Journal of Risk Research*, vol 1, pp15–44, chapter 19

Rosa, E. A. (2003) 'The logical structure of the social amplification of risk framework (SARF): *Meta*theoretical foundations and policy implications', in N. Pidgeon, R. G. Kasperson and P. Slovic (eds) *The Social Amplification of Risk*, Cambridge University Press, Cambridge, UK, chapter 19

Rothman, A. J. and Schwarz, N. (1998) 'Constructing perceptions of vulnerability: Personal relevance and the use of experiential information in health judgments',

Personality and Social Psychology Bulletin, vol 24, pp1053–1064, chapter 8

Rothstein, H. (2003) 'Neglected risk regulation: The institutional attentuation phenomenon', *Health, Risk and Society*, vol 5, pp85–103, chapter 19

Rottenstreich, Y. and Hsee, C. K. (2001) 'Money, kisses, and electric shocks: On the affective psychology of risk', *Psychological Science*, vol 12, pp185–190, chapter 1, chapter 2, chapter 12

Rowe, G. and Wright, G. (2001) 'Differences in expert and lay judgments of risk: Myth or reality?', *Risk Analysis*, vol 21, pp341–356, chapter 15

The Royal Society (1992) *Risk: Analysis, Perception and Management*, The Royal Society, London, chapter 19

Rozin, P., Haidt, J. and McCauley, C. R. (1993) 'Disgust', in M. Lewis and J. M. Haviland (eds) *Handbook of Emotions*, Guilford Press, New York, chapter 2

Ruckelshaus, W. (1996, November) 'Trust in government: A prescription for restoration', www.napawash.org/resources/lectures/lecture_transcripts_web_1996.html, accessed 3 January 2010, chapter 19

Rueda, M. R., Posner, M. I. and Rothbart, M. K. (2005) 'The development of executive attention: Contributions to the emergence of self-regulation', *Developmental Neuropsychology*, vol 28, pp573–594, chapter 3

Ruiter, R. A. C. (2005) 'Saying is not (always) doing: Cigarette warning labels are useless', *European Journal of Public Health*, vol 15, pp329–330, chapter 22

Ruiter, R. A. C., Abraham, C. and Kok, G. (2001) 'Scaring warnings and rational precautions: A review of the psychology of fear appeals', *Psychology and Health*, vol 16, pp613–630, chapter 22

Russell, J. A. (2003) 'Core affect and the psychological construction of emotion', *Psychological Review*, vol 110, pp145–172, chapter 8

Sandman, P. (1989) 'Hazard versus outrage in the public perception of risk', in V. T. Covello, D. B. McCallum and M. T. Pavlova (eds) *Effective Risk Communication: The Role and Responsibility of Government and Nongovernment Organizations*, Plenum Press, New York, chapter 2

Sanfey, A. and Hastie, R. (1998) 'Does evidence presentation format affect judgment? An experimental evaluation of displays of data for judgments', *Psychological Science*, vol 9, no 2, pp99–103, chapter 2

Satterfield, T. A., Slovic, P., Gregory, R., Flynn, J. and Mertz, C. K. (2001) 'Risk lived, stigma experienced', in J. Flynn, P. Slovic and H. Kunreuther (eds) *Risk, Media, and Stigma: Understanding Public Challenges to Modern Science and Technology*, Earthscan, London, chapter 10

Satterfield, T. A., Mertz, C. K. and Slovic, P. (2004) 'Discrimination, vulnerability, and justice in the face of risk,' *Risk Analysis*, vol 24, no 1, pp115–129, chapter 11, chapter 18

Savadori, L., Rumiati, R. and Bonini, N. (1998) 'Expertise and regional differences in risk perception: The case of Italy', *Swiss Journal of Psychology*, vol 57, pp101–113, chapter 15

Scheufele, D. A. (2006) 'Five lessons in nano outreach', *Materials Today*, vol 9, p64, chapter 18

Scheufele, D. A. and Lewenstein, B. V. (2005) 'The public and nanotechnology: How citizens make sense of emerging technologies', *Journal of Nanoparticle Research*, vol 7, pp659–667, chapter 18

Schkade, D. A. and Johnson, E. J. (1989) 'Cognitive processes in preference reversals', *Organizational Behavior and Human Performance*, vol 44, pp203–231, chapter 1

Schnellnhuber, H.-J., Block, A., Cassel-Gintz, M., Kropp, J., Lammel, G., Lass, W., Lienenkamp, R., Loose, C., Lüdeke, M. K. B., Moldenhauer, O., Petschel-Held, G., Plöchl, M. and Reusswig, F. (1997) 'Syndromes of global change', *GAIA*, vol 6, pp19–34, chapter 19

Schum, D. A. and DuCharme, W. M. (1971) 'Comments on the relationship between the impact and the reliability of evidence', *Organizational Behavior and Human Performance*, vol 6, no 2, pp111–131, chapter 20

Schwab, J. (1994) *Deeper Shades of Green: The Rise of Blue Collar and Minority Environmentalism in America*, Sierra Club Books, San Francisco, CA, chapter 13

Schwartz, A. (1988) 'Proposals for products liability reform: A theoretical synthesis', *Yale Law Journal*, vol 97, no 3, pp353–419, chapter 12

Schwartz, L. M., Woloshin, S., Black, W. C. and Welch, H. G. (1997) 'The role of numeracy in understanding the benefit of screening mammography', *Annals of Internal Medicine*, vol 127, no 11, pp966–972, chapter 20

Schwarz, N. (2004) 'Meta-cognitive experiences in consumer judgment and decision making', *Journal of Consumer Psychology*, vol 14, pp332–348, chapter 8

Schwarz, N. and Clore, G. L. (1983a) 'Feelings and phenomenal experiences', in E. T. Higgins and A. W. Kruglanski (eds) *Social Psychology: Handbook of Basic Principles*, pp433–465, Guilford Press, New York, chapter 4

Schwarz, N. and Clore, G. L. (1983b) 'Mood, misattribution, and judgments of well-being: Informative and directive functions of affective states', *Journal of Personality and Social Psychology*, vol 45, pp513–523, chapter 8

Schwarz, N. and Clore, G. L. (1988) 'How do I feel about it? Informative functions of affective states', in K. Fiedler and J. Forgas (eds) *Affect, Cognition, and Social Behavior*, Hogrefe International, Toronto, Canada, chapter 2

Schwarz, N. and Clore, G. L. (2007) 'Feelings and phenomenal experiences', in A. Kruglanski and E. T. Higgins (eds) *Social Psychology: Handbook of Basic Principles*, 2nd edn, Guilford Press, New York, chapter 8

Schwarz, N. and Strack, F. (1999) 'Reports of subjective well-being: Judgmental processes and their methodological implications', in D. Kahneman, E. Diener and N. Schwarz (eds) *Well-being: The Foundations of Hedonic Psychology*, Russell-Sage, New York, chapter 8

Schwarz, N., Sanna, L., Skurnik, I. and Yoon, C. (2007) 'Metacognitive experiences and the intricacies of setting people straight: Implications for debiasing and public information campaigns', *Advances in Experimental Social Psychology*, vol 39, pp127–161, chapter 8

Scott, J. C. (1990) *Domination and the Arts of Resistance*, Yale University, New York, chapter 13

Sen, A. K. (1977) 'Rational fools: A critique of the behavioral foundations of economic theory', *Philosophy and Public Affairs*, vol 6, pp317–344, chapter 7

Senge, P. M. (1990) *The Fifth Discipline: The Art and Practice of the Learning Organization*, Doubleday, New York, chapter 17

Sexton, K. and Anderson, Y. B. (1993) 'Equity in environmental health: Research issues and needs', *Toxicology and Industrial Health*, vol 9, no 5, pp679–977, chapter 10

Sheridan, S. L. and Pignone, M. (2002) 'Numeracy and the medical student's ability to interpret data', *Effective Clinical Practice*, vol 5, no 1, pp35–40, chapter 20

Sherman, D. A., Kim, H. and Zajonc, R. B. (1998) 'Affective perseverance: Cognitions change but preferences stay the same', Paper presented at the annual meeting of the American Psychological Society, San Francisco, August, chapter 7

Sherman, D. K. and Cohen, G. L. (2002) 'Accepting threatening information: Self-Affirmation and the reduction of defensive biases?', *Current Directions in Psychological Science*, vol 11, no 4, pp119–123, chapter 11, chapter 12

Sherman, S. J., Beike, D. R. and Ryalls, K. R. (1999) 'Dual-processing accounts of inconsistencies in responses to general versus specific cases', in S. Chaiken and Y. Trope (eds) *Dual-process Theories in Social Psychology*, Guilford Press, New York, chapter 4

Shiv, B. and Fedorikhin, A. (1999) 'Heart and mind in conflict: The interplay of affect and cognition in consumer decision making', *Journal of Consumer Research*, vol 26, pp278–292, chapter 4

Shiv, B., Loewenstein, G., Bechara, A., Damasio, H. and Damasio, A. (2005) 'Investment behavior and the dark side of emotion', *Psychological Science*, vol 16, pp435–439, chapter 8

Short, J. F., Jr. (1992) 'Defining, explaining, and managing risks', in J. F. Short, Jr. and L. Clarke (eds) *Organizations, Uncertainties, and Risk*, Westview Press, Boulder, CO, chapter 19

Short, J. F., Jr. and Clarke, L. (1992) *Organizations, Uncertainties and Risk*, Westview Press, Boulder, CO, chapter 19

Sia, C.-L., Tan, B. C. Y. and Wei, K.-K. (2002) 'Group polarization and computer-mediated communication: Effects of communication cues, social presence, and anonymity', *Information Systems Resarch*, vol 13, no 1, pp70–90, chapter 12

Siegel, R. (2007) 'The new politics of abortion', *Illinois Law Review*, vol 2007, no 3, pp991–1053, chapter 11

Siemer, M. and Reisenzein, R. (1998) 'Effects of mood on evaluative judgments: Influence of reduced processing capacity and mood salience', *Cognition and Emotion*, vol 12, pp783–806, chapter 8

Siegrist, M. (1999) 'A causal model explaining the perception and acceptance of gene technology', *Journal of Applied Social Psychology*, vol 29, pp2093–2106, chapter 15

Siegrist, M. (2000) 'The influence of trust and perception of risk and benefits on the acceptance of gene technology', *Risk Analysis*, vol 20, pp195–203, chapter 15

Siegrist, M. and Cvetkovich, G. (2000) 'Perception of hazards: The role of social trust and knowledge', *Risk Analysis*, vol 20, pp713–719, chapter 15, chapter 19

Siegrist, M., Cvetkovich, G. and Roth, C. (2000) 'Salient value similarity, social trust and risk/benefit perception', *Risk Analysis*, vol 20, pp353–362, chapter 19

Singer, E. and Endreny, P. M. (1993) *Reporting on Risk: How the Mass Media Portray Accidents, Diseases, Disasters, and Other Hazards*, Russell Sage Foundation, New York, chapter 19

Sjöberg, L. (1999) 'Risk perception in western Europe', *Ambio*, vol 28, pp555–568, chapter 19

Sjöberg, L. (2001) 'Limits of knowledge and the limited importance of trust', *Risk Analysis*, vol 21, pp189–198, chapter 15

Sjöberg, L. (2002) 'The allegedly simple structure of experts' risk perceptions: An urban legend in risk research', *Science Technology and Human Values*, vol 27, pp443–459, chapter 15

Skitka, L. J., Mullen, E., Griffen, T., Hutchinson, S. and Chamberlin, B. (2002) 'Dispositions, scripts, or motivated correction? Understanding ideological differences in explanations for social problems', *Journal of Personality and Social Psychology*, vol 83, no 2, pp470–487, chapter 4

Sklansky, D. (1999) *The Theory of Poker*, 4th edn, Two Plus Two, Henderson, NV, chapter 12

Sloman, S. A. (1996) 'The empirical case for two systems of reasoning', *Psychological Bulletin*, vol 119, no 1, pp3–22, chapter 2

Slovic, P. (1987) 'Perception of risk', *Science*, vol 236, pp280–285, chapter 2, chapter 7, chapter 10, chapter 13, chapter 14, chapter 15, chapter 16, chapter 19, chapter 22

Slovic, P. (1992) 'Perception of risk: Reflections on the psychometric paradigm', in S. Krimsky and D. Golding (eds) *Social Theories of Risk*, Praeger, New York, chapter 10, chapter 13, chapter 19

Slovic, P. (1993) 'Perceived risk, trust, and democracy', *Risk Analysis*, vol 13, pp675–682, chapter 15, chapter 17, chapter 19

Slovic, P. (1995) 'The construction of preference', *American Psychologist*, vol 50, pp364–371, chapter 1, chapter 8

Slovic, P. (1997) 'Trust, emotion, sex, politics, and science: Surveying the risk assessment battlefield', in M. H. Bazerman, D. M. Messick, A. E. Tenbrunsel and K. A. Wade-Benzoni (eds) *Environment, Ethics, and Behavior*, New Lexington, San Francisco, CA, chapter 9, chapter 11, chapter 14

Slovic, P. (1998a) 'Do adolescent smokers know the risks?', *Duke Law Journal*, vol 47, pp1133–1141, chapter 7

Slovic, P. (1998b) 'The risk game', *Reliability Engineering and Systems Safety*, vol 59, no 1, pp73–77, chapter 19

Slovic, P. (1999) 'Trust, emotion, sex, politics, and science: Surveying the risk-assessment battlefield', *Risk Analysis*, vol 19, no 4, pp689–701, chapter 2, chapter 10

Slovic, P. (ed) (2000a) *The Perception of Risk*, Earthscan, London, intro, chapter 12, chapter 17, chapter 19

Slovic, P. (2000b) 'Rejoinder: The perils of Viscusi's analyses of smoking risk perceptions', *Journal of Behavioral Decision Making*, vol 13, pp273–276, chapter 7

Slovic, P. (2000c) 'What does it mean to know a cumulative risk? Adolescents' perceptions of short-term and long-term consequences of smoking', *Journal of Behavioral Decision Making*, vol 13, pp259–266, chapter 7

Slovic, P. (2001) 'Cigarette smokers: Rational actors or rational fools?', in P. Slovic (ed) *Smoking: Risk, Perception and Policy*, Sage, Thousand Oaks, CA, chapter 1, chapter 2, chapter 21, chapter 22

Slovic, P. (2002) 'Terrorism as hazard: A new species of trouble', *Risk Analysis*, vol 22, no 3, pp425–426, chapter 19

Slovic, P. (2007) '"If I look at the mass I will never act": Psychic numbing and genocide', *Judgment and Decision Making*, vol 2, pp79–95, chapter 1, chapter 3, chapter 5

Slovic, P. (2009) 'Can international law stop genocide when our moral intuitions fail us?', Report No. 09-06, Decision Research, Eugene, OR, chapter 5

Slovic, P. and Lichtenstein, S. (1968a) 'The importance of variance preferences in gambling decisions', *Journal of Experimental Psychology*, vol 78, pp646–654, chapter 1

Slovic, P. and Lichtenstein, S. (1968b) 'Relative importance of probabilities and payoffs in risk taking', *Journal of Experimental Psychology Monograph*, vol 78, no 3, pt 2, pp1–18, chapter 2

Slovic, P., Fischhoff, B. and Lichtenstein, S. (1979) 'Rating the risks', *Environment*, vol 21, no 3, pp14–20, 36–39, chapter 10, chapter 11, chapter 15

Slovic, P., Fischhoff, B. and Lichtenstein, S. (1980) 'Facts and fears: Understanding perceived risk', in R. Schwing and W. A. Albers (eds) *Societal Risk Assessment: How Safe Is Safe Enough?*, Plenum, New York, chapter 15

Slovic, P., Lichtenstein, S. and Fischhoff, B. (1984) 'Modeling the societal impact of fatal accidents', *Management Science*, vol 30, pp464–474, chapter 19

Slovic, P., Fischhoff, B. and Lichtenstein, S. (1985) 'Characterizing perceived risk', in R. W. Kates, C. Hohenemser and J. X. Kasperson (eds) *Perilous Progress: Technology as Hazard*, Westview, Boulder, CO, chapter 16

Slovic, P., Kraus, N. N., Lappe, H., Letzel, H. and Malmfors, T. (1989) 'Risk perception of prescription drugs: Report on a survey in Sweden', *Pharmaceutical Medicine*, vol 4, pp43–65, chapter 16

Slovic, P., Griffin, D. and Tversky, A. (1990a) 'Compatibility effects in judgment and choice', in R. M. Hogarth (ed) *Insights in Decision Making: A Tribute to Hillel J. Einhorn*, University of Chicago Press, Chicago, IL, chapter 1

Slovic, P., Layman, M. and Flynn, J. (1990b) 'What comes to mind when you hear the words "Nuclear waste repository"? A study of 10,000 images', Report No. NWPO-SE-028-90, Nevada Agency for Nuclear Projects, Carson City, NV, chapter 13

Slovic, P., Flynn, J. H. and Layman, M. (1991a) 'Perceived risk, trust, and the politics of nuclear waste', *Science*, vol 254, pp1603–1607, chapter 14, chapter 15, chapter 19

Slovic, P., Kraus, N., Lappe, H. and Major, M. (1991b) 'Risk perception of prescription drugs: Report on a survey in Canada', *Canadian Journal of Public Health*, vol 82, ppS15–S20, chapter 16

Slovic, P., Layman, M., Kraus, N., Flynn, J., Chalmers, J. and Gesell, G. (1991c) 'Perceived risk, stigma, and potential economic impacts of a high-level nuclear waste repository in Nevada', *Risk Analysis*, vol 11, no 4, pp683–696, chapter 1, chapter 7, chapter 17, chapter 19

Slovic, P., Flynn, J. and Gregory, R. (1994) 'Stigma happens: Social problems in the siting of nuclear waste facilities', *Risk Analysis*, vol 14, no 5, pp773–777, chapter 19

Slovic, P., Malmfors, T., Krewski, D., Mertz, C. K., Neil, N. and Bartlett, S. (1995) 'Intuitive toxicology II: Expert and lay judgments of chemical risks in Canada', *Risk Analysis*, vol 15, pp661–675, chapter 9, chapter 15

Slovic, P., Malmfors, T., Mertz, C. K., Neil, N. and Purchase, I. F. H. (1997a) 'Evaluating chemical risks: Results of a survey of the British Toxicology Society', *Human & Experimental Toxicology*, vol 16, pp289–304, chapter 9

Slovic, P., MacGregor, D. G., Malmfors, T. and Purchase, I. F. H. (1997b) *Influence of Affective Processes on Toxicologists' Judgments of Risk*, unpublished study, Decision Research, Eugene, OR, chapter 2

Slovic, P., Flynn, J., Mertz, C. K., Poumadére, M. and Mays, C. (2000a) 'Nuclear power and the public: A comparative study of risk perception in France and the United States', in O. Renn and B. Rohrmann (eds) *Cross-Cultural Risk Perception: A Survey of Empirical Studies*, vol 13, Springer, New York, chapter 12, chapter 19

Slovic, P., Monahan, J. and MacGregor, D. G. (2000b) 'Violence risk assessment and risk communication: The effects of using actual cases, providing instructions, and employing probability vs. frequency formats', *Law and Human Behavior*, vol 24, pp271–296, intro, chapter 2, chapter 7

Slovic, P., Finucane, M. L., Peters, E. and MacGregor, D. G. (2002) 'The affect heuristic', in T. Gilovich, D. Griffin and D. Kahneman (eds) *Heuristics and Biases: The Psychology of Intuitive Judgment*, Cambridge University Press, New York, intro, chapter 1, chapter 2, chapter 3, chapter 4, chapter 6, chapter 7, chapter 8, chapter 16, chapter 19

Slovic, P., Finucane, M. L., Peters, E. and MacGregor, D. G. (2004) 'Risk as analysis and risk as feelings: Some thoughts about affect, reason, risk, and rationality', *Risk Analysis*, vol 24, pp1–12, chapter 1, chapter 4, chapter 12, chapter 22

Slovic, P., Peters, E., Finucane, M. L. and MacGregor, D. G. (2005) 'Affect, risk, and decision making', *Health Psychology*, vol 24, no 4, ppS35–S40, chapter 20

Slovic, S. and Slovic, P. (2004/2005) 'Numbers and nerves: Toward an affective apprehension of environmental risk', *Whole Terrain*, vol 13, pp14–18, chapter 1

Small, D. A. and Loewenstein, G. (2003) 'Helping the victim or helping a victim: Altruism
and identifiability', *Journal of Risk and Uncertainty*, vol 26, no 1, pp5–16, chapter 4

Small, D. A. and Loewenstein, G. (2005) 'The devil you know: The effect of identifiability
on punitiveness', *Journal of Behavioral Decision Making*, vol 18, no 5, pp311–318,
chapter 4

Small, D. A., Loewenstein, G. and Slovic, P. (2007) 'Sympathy and callousness: Affect and
deliberations in donation decisions', *Organizational Behavior and Human Decision
Processes*, vol 102, pp143–153, chapter 3, chapter 5

Smith, T. W. (2000) *1999 National Gun Policy Survey of the National Opinion Research
Center: Research Findings*, National Opinion Research Center, Chicago, IL, chapter 11

Snyder, L. B. and Park, C. L. (2002) 'National studies of stress reactions and media
exposure to the attacks', in B. S. Greenberg (ed) *Communication and Terrorism: Public
and Media Responses to 911*, Hampton Press, Cresskill, NJ, chapter 17

Sokoloff, H., Steinberg, H. M. and Pyser, S. N. (2005) 'Deliberative city planning on the
Philadelphia waterfront', in J. Gastil and P. Levine (eds) *The Deliberative Democracy
Handbook*, Jossey-Bass, New York, chapter 12

Song, J. (2002) 'Every dog has its day – but at what price?', *The Register Guard*, 26 April,
p15A, chapter 4

Sparks, P. and Shepherd, R. (1994) 'Public perceptions of the potential hazards associated
with food production and food consumption: An empirical study', *Risk Analysis*,
vol 14, pp799–806, chapter 15

Sparks, P., Shepherd, R. and Frewer, L. (1995) 'Assessing and structuring attitudes
toward the use of gene technology in food production: The role of perceived ethical
obligation', *Basic and Applied Social Psychology*, vol 16, pp267–285, chapter 15

Spence, R. (1995) 'IOM Blood Forum explores alternative decision-making and risk
communications', *CCBC Newsletter*, 27 January, pp4–5, chapter 14

Srole, L. (1965) 'Social integration and certain corollaries', *American Sociological Review*,
vol 21, no 6, p709ff, chapter 10, chapter 13

Stallen, P. J. M. and Tomas, A. (1988) 'Public concern about industrial hazards', *Risk
Analysis*, vol 8, pp237–245, chapter 19

Stavins, R. N. (1998) 'What can we learn from the grand policy experiment? Lessons
from SO$_2$ allowance trading', *Journal of Economic Perspectives*, vol 12, no 3, pp69–88,
chapter 12

Steg, L. and Sievers, I. (2000) 'Cultural theory and individual perceptions of environmental risks,' *Environment & Behavior*, vol 32, no 2, pp250–285, chapter 11

Steger, M. A. and Witt, S. L. (1989) 'Gender differences in environmental orientations:
A comparison of publics and activists in Canada and the U.S.', *The Western Political
Quarterly*, vol 42, pp627–649, chapter 9, chapter 11

Stein, B. D., Tanielian, T. L., Eisenman, D. P., Keyser, D. J., Burnam, A. and Pincus, H. A.
(2004) 'Emotional and behavioral consequences of bioterrorism: Planning a public
health response', *The Milbank Quarterly: A Multidisciplinary Journal of Population
Health Policy*, vol 82, no 3, pp1–32, chapter 17

Steingraber, S. (1997) *Living Downstream*, Addison-Wesley, New York, chapter 13

Stephenson, M. T., Hoyle, R. H., Palmgreen, P. and Slater, M. D. (2003) 'Brief measures
of sensation seeking for screening and large-scale surveys,' *Drug and Alcohol
Dependence*, vol 72, no 3, pp279–286, chapter 11

Sterman, J. D. (2000) *Business Dynamics: Systems Thinking and Modeling for a Complex World*, McGraw-Hill, Boston, chapter 17

Stern, P. C., Dietz, T. and Kalof, L. (1993) 'Value orientations, gender, and environmental concerns', *Environment and Behavior*, vol 24, pp322–348, chapter 9, chapter 10, chapter 11

Stolz, B. A. (1983) 'Congress and capital punishment: An exercise in symbolic politics', *Law and Policy Quarterly*, vol 5, pp157–180, chapter 12

Stone, E. R., Sieck, W. R., Bulla, B. E., Yates, F., Parks, S. C. and Rusha, C. J. (2003) 'Foreground: Background salience: Explaining the effects of graphical displays on risk avoidance', *Organizational Behavior and Human Decision Processes*, vol 90, no 1, pp19–36, chapter 20

Strack, F. and Deutsch, R. (2004) 'Reflective and impulsive determinants of social behavior', *Personality and Social Psychology Review*, vol 8, no 3, pp220–247, chapter 4

Sunstein, C. R. (1996) *Legal Reasoning and Political Conflict*, Oxford University Press, New York, chapter 12

Sunstein, C. R. (2002) 'The laws of fear', *Harvard Law Review*, vol 115, no 4, pp1119–1168, chapter 12

Sunstein, C. R. (2003) 'Terrorism and probability neglect', *The Journal of Risk and Uncertainty*, vol 26, pp121–136, chapter 1, chapter 11

Sunstein, C. R. (2005) *Laws of Fear: Beyond the Precautionary Principle*, Cambridge University Press, New York, intro, chapter 12

Sunstein C. R. and Thaler, R. H. (2003) 'Libertarian paternalism is not an oxymoron', *University of Chicago Law Review*, vol 70, no 4, pp1159–1202, chapter 20

Surveillance, Epidemiology, and End Results Program (2001) 'Surveillance, Epidemiology, and End Results (SEER) program public-use data (1973–1998)', (Survival Matrix I), National Cancer Institute, DCCPS, Surveillance Research Program, Cancer Statistics Branch, Bethesda, MD, chapter 21

Susarla, A. (2003) 'Plague and arsenic: Assignment of blame in the mass media and the social amplification of attenuation risk', in N. Pidgeon, R. E. Kasperson and P. Slovic (eds) *The Social Amplification of Risk*, Cambridge University Press, Cambridge, UK, chapter 19

Svenson, O. (1988a) 'Managing product hazards at Volvo Car Corporation', in R. E. Kasperson, J. X. Kasperson, C. Hohenemser and R. W. Kates (eds) *Corporate Management of Health and Safety Hazards: A Comparison of Current Practice*, Westview, Boulder, CO, chapter 19

Svenson, O. (1988b) 'Mental models of risk communication and action: Reflections on social amplification of risk', *Risk Analysis*, vol 8, pp199–200, chapter 19

Svenson, O., Fischhoff, B. and MacGregor, D. (1985) 'Perceived driving safety and seatbelt usage', *Accident Analysis & Prevention*, vol 17, pp119–133, chapter 9

Szalay, L. B. and Deese, J. (1978) *Subjective Meaning and Culture: An Assessment through Word Associations*, Erlbaum, Hillsdale, NJ, intro, chapter 13, chapter 14, chapter 16

Szasz, A. (1994) *Ecopopulism: Toxic Waste and the Movement for Environmental Justice*, vol 1, University of Minnesota Press, Minneapolis, MN, chapter 10, chapter 13

Taylor, D. (2000) 'The risk of the environmental justice paradigm', *American Behavioral Scientist*, vol 43, pp508–580, chapter 10

Theeuwes, J. and Van der Stigchel, S. (2006) 'Faces capture attention: Evidence from inhibition of return', *Visual Cognition*, vol 13, pp657–665, chapter 3

Thomashow, M. (2002) *Bringing the Biosphere Home: Learning to Perceive Global Environmental Change*, MIT Press, Cambridge, MA, chapter 6

Thompson, M., Ellis, R. and Wildavsky, A. B. (1990) *Cultural Theory*, Westview Press, Boulder, CO, chapter 11

Tomkins, S. S. (1962) *Affect, Imagery, and Consciousness: Vol 1. The Positive Affects*, Springer, New York, chapter 2

Tomkins, S. S. (1963) *Affect, Imagery, and Consciousness: Vol. 2. The Negative Affects*, Springer, New York, chapter 2

Trumbo, C. W. (1996) 'Examining psychometrics and polarization in a single-risk case study', *Risk Analysis*, vol 16, no 3, pp429–438, chapter 19

Trumbo, C. W. (2002) 'Information processing and risk perception: An adaptation of the heuristic-systematic model', *Journal of Communication*, vol 52, no 2, p367–382, chapter 12

Turner, B. A. (1978) *Man-Made Disasters: The Failure of Foresight*, Wykeham, London, chapter 19

Turner, B. A. and Pidgeon, N. F. (1997) *Man-Made Disasters*, 2nd edn, Butterworth-Heineman, Oxford, chapter 19

Tversky, A. and Kahneman, D. (1973) 'Availability: A heuristic for judging frequency and probability', *Cognitive Psychology*, vol 5, pp207–232, chapter 2, chapter 7

Tversky, A. and Kahneman, D. (1974) 'Judgment under uncertainty: Heuristics and biases', *Science*, vol 185, pp1124–1131, chapter 7

Tversky, A. and Koehler, D. J. (1994) 'Support theory: A nonextensional representation of subjective probability', *Psychological Review*, vol 101, pp547–567, chapter 7

United Church of Christ (1987) *Toxic Waste and Race in the United States*, Commission for Racial Justice, New York, chapter 13

United Kingdom International Liaison Group on Risk Assessment (1998a) *Risk Assessment and Risk Management: Improving Policy and Practice Within Government Departments*, Health and Safety Executive, London, chapter 19

United Kingdom International Liaison Group on Risk Assessment (1998b) *Risk Communication: A Guide to Regulatory Practice*, Health and Safety Executive, London, chapter 19

US General Accounting Office (1988) 'Blood safety: Recalls and withdrawals of plasma products', Publication No. GAO/T-HEHS-98-166, www.gao.gov/archive/1998/he98166t.pdf, accessed 28 December 2009, chapter 14

USDHHS (US Department of Health and Human Services) (1989) 'Reducing the health consequences of smoking: 25 years of progress: A report of the surgeon general', DHHS Publication No. CDC89-84 11, US Government Printing Office, Washington, DC, chapter 21

USDHHS (2000) *Healthy People, 2010*, US Department of Health and Human Services, Washington, DC, chapter 22

US Senate, Subcommittee on Labor, Health and Human Services, and Education, and Related Agencies, Committee on Appropriations (2002) 'Cloning, 2002: Hearings before a subcommittee of the Committee on Appropriations, United States Senate, 107th Congress, second session', http://purl.access.gpo.gov/GPO/LPS24045, accessed 23 December 2009, chapter 12

Västfjäll, D., Friman, M., Gärling, T and Kleiner, M. (2002) 'The measurement of core affect: A Swedish self-report measure', *Scandinavian Journal of Psychology*, vol 43, pp19–31, chapter 8

Västfjäll, D., Peters, E. and Slovic, P. (2007) 'Affect and risk–benefit judgments in the aftermath of tsunami disaster', manuscript submitted for publication, chapter 8

Västfjäll, D., Peters, E. and Slovic, P. (2009) 'Compassion fatigue: Donations and affect are greatest for a single child in need', DR Report No. 09-05, Decision Research, Eugene, OR, chapter 3, chapter 5

Vaughan, D. (1992) 'Regulating risk: Implications of the Challenger accident', in J. F. Short, Jr. and L. Clarke (eds) *Organizations, Uncertainties, and Risk*, Westview Press, Boulder, CO, chapter 19

Vaughan, D. (1996) *The Challenger Launch Decision: Risky Technology, Culture, and Deviance at NASA*, University of Chicago Press, Chicago, IL, chapter 19

Vaughan, E. (1995) 'The significance of socioeconomic and ethnic diversity for the risk communication process', *Risk Analysis*, vol 15, pp169–180, chapter 10, chapter 19

Vaughan, E. and Seifert, M. (1992) 'Variability in the framing of risk issues', *Journal of Social Issues*, vol 48, no 4, pp119–135, chapter 19

Vercillo, A. P. and Duprey, S. V. (1988) 'Jehovah's Witnesses and the transfusion of blood products', *New York State Journal of Medicine*, vol 88, pp493–494, chapter 14

Viscusi, W. K. (1983) *Risk by Choice: Regulating Health and Safety in the Workplace*, Harvard University Press, Cambridge, MA, chapter 11, chapter 12

Viscusi, W. K. (1990) 'Do smokers underestimate risks?', *Journal of Political Economy*, vol 98, pp1253–1269, chapter 7, chapter 21

Viscusi, W. K. (1991) 'Age variations in risk perceptions and smoking decisions', *The Review of Economics and Statistics*, vol 73, pp577–588, chapter 7

Viscusi, W. K. (1992) *Smoking: Making the Risky Decision*, Oxford University Press, New York, chapter 2, chapter 7, chapter 12

Viscusi, W. K. (1998a) 'Perception of smoking risks', Paper presented at the International Conference on the Social Costs of Tobacco, Lausanne, Switzerland, 21–22 August 1998, chapter 7

Viscusi, W. K. (1998b) *Rational Risk Policy*, Oxford University Press, New York, chapter 12

Vlek, C. A. J. and Stallen, P. J. M. (1981) 'Judging risk and benefits in the small and in the large', *Organizational Behavior and Human Performance*, vol 28, pp235–271, chapter 19

Voils, C. I., Oddone, E. Z., Weinfurt, K. P. et al (2006) 'Racial differences in health concerns', *Journal of the National Medical Association*, vol 98, pp36–42, chapter 16

Vuilleumier, P. (2005) 'How brains beware: Neural mechanisms of emotional attention', *Trends in Cognitive Sciences*, vol 9, pp586–594, chapter 3

Vuilleumier, P. and Driver, J. (2007) 'Modulation of visual processing by attention and emotion: Windows on causal interactions between human brain regions', *Philosophical Transactions of The Royal Society*, vol 362, pp837–855, chapter 3

Vuilleumier, P., Armony, J. L., Driver, J. and Dolan, R. J. (2003) 'Distinct spatial frequency sensitivities for processing faces and emotional expressions', *Nature Neuroscience*, vol 6, pp624–631, chapter 3

Wåhlberg, A. (2001) 'The theoretical features of some current approaches to risk perception', *Journal of Risk Research*, vol 4, pp237–250, chapter 19

Wandersman, A. H. and Hallman, W. K. (1993) 'Are people acting irrationally? Understanding public concerns about environmental threats', *American Psychologist*, vol 48, pp681–686, chapter 9

Waters, E. A., Weinstein, N. D., Colditz, G. A. and Emmons, K. (2006) 'Formats for improving risk communication in medical tradeoff decisions', *Journal of Health Communication*, vol 11, no 2, pp167–182, chapter 20

Watts, M. and Bohle, H. (1993) 'The space of vulnerability: The causal structure of hunger and famine', *Progress in Human Geography*, vol 17, no 1, pp43–67, chapter 10

Weick, K. E. (1987) 'Organizational culture as a source of high reliability', *California Management Review*, vol 29, pp112–127, chapter 19

Weinstein, N. D. (1998) 'Accuracy of smokers' risk perceptions', *Annals of Behavioral Medicine*, vol 20, pp135–140, chapter 7

Weinstein, N. D. (1999a) 'Accuracy of smokers' risk perceptions', *Nicotine & Tobacco Research*, vol 1, ppS123–S130, chapter 21

Weinstein, N. D. (1999b) 'What does it mean to understand a risk? Evaluating risk comprehension', *Journal of the National Cancer Institute Monograph*, vol 25, pp15–20, chapter 21

West Virginia State Board of Education v. Barnette (1943) www.oyez.org/cases/1940-1949/1942/1942_591, accessed 27 December 2009, chapter 12

Wewers, M. E., Ahijevych, K. L., Chen, M. S., Dresbach, S., Kihm, K. E. and Kuun, P. A. (2000) 'Tobacco use characteristics among rural Ohio Appalachians', *Journal of Community Health*, vol 25, pp377–388, chapter 21

Wiener, J. B. (2002) 'Precaution in a multirisk world', in D. J. Paustenbach (ed) *Human and Ecological Risk Assessment: Theory and Practice*, Wiley, New York, chapter 2

Wildavsky, A. and Dake, K. (1990) 'Theories of risk perception: Who fears what and why?', *Daedalus*, vol 119, no 4, pp41–59, chapter 11, chapter 18

Wilkins, L. (1987) *Shared Vulnerability: The Media and the American Perspective on the Bhopal Disaster*, Greenwood Press, Westport, CT, chapter 19

Wilkins, L. and Patterson, P. (1991) *Risky Business: Communication Issues of Science, Risk and Public Policy*, Greenwood Press, Westport, CT, chapter 19

Williams, M. V., Parker, R. M., Baker, D. W., Parikh, N. S., Pitkin, K., Coates, W. C. and Nurss, J. R. (1995) 'Inadequate functional health literacy among patients at two public hospitals', *Journal of the American Medical Association*, vol 274, no 21, pp1677–1682, chapter 20

Willis, H. H., DeKay, M. L., Fischhoff, B. and Morgan, M. G. (2005) 'Aggregate, disaggregate, and hybrid analyses of ecological risk perceptions', *Risk Analysis*, vol 25, pp405–428, chapter 17

Wilson, T. D. and Brekke, N. C. (1994) 'Mental contamination and mental correction: Unwanted influences on judgments and evaluations', *Psychological Bulletin*, vol 116, pp117–142, chapter 4

Wilson, T. D., Lisle, D. J., Schooler, J. W., Hodges, S. D., Klaaren, K. J. and LaFleur, S. J. (1993) 'Introspecting about reasons can reduce post-choice satisfaction', *Personality and Social Psychology Bulletin*, vol 19, no 3, pp331–339, chapter 2

Wilson, T. D., Gilbert, D. T. and Wheatley, T. P. (1998) 'Protecting our minds: The role of lay beliefs', in V. Y. Yzerbyt, G. Lories and B. Dardenne (eds) *Metacognition: Cognitive and Social Dimensions*, pp171–201, Sage Publications, New York, chapter 4

Wilson, T. D., Lindsey, S. and Schooler, T. Y. (2000) 'A model of dual attitudes', *Psychological Review*, vol 107, no 1, pp101–126, chapter 4

Wilt, T. J. and Partin, M. R. (2003) 'Prostate cancer intervention', *Postgraduate Medicine*, vol 114, pp 43–49, chapter 16

Winkielman, P., Zajonc, R. B. and Schwarz, N. (1997) 'Subliminal affective priming resists attributional interventions', *Cognition and Emotion*, vol 11, pp433–465, chapter 7

Winkielman, P., Schwarz, N., Fazendeiro, T. and Reber, R. (2003) 'Hedonic marking of processing fluency: Implications for evaluative judgment', in J. Musch and K.C. Klauer (eds) *Psychology of evaluation: Affective processes in cognition and emotion*, Erlbaum, Mahwah, NJ, chapter 3

Winship, C. (2006) 'Policy analysis as puzzle solving', in M. Moran, M. Rein and R. E. Goodin (eds) *The Oxford Handbook of Public Policy*, Oxford University Press, New York, chapter 12

Witte, K. and Allen, M. (2000) 'A meta-analysis of fear appeals: Implications for effective public health campaigns', *Health Education and Behavior*, vol 27, pp591–615, chapter 22

Wogalter, M. S. and Laughery, K. R. (1996) 'Warning sign and label effectiveness', *Current Directions in Psychological Science*, vol 5, pp33–37, chapter 22

Woloshin, S., Schwartz, L. M., Moncur, M., Gabriel, S. and Tosteson, A. N. (2001) 'Assessing values for health: Numeracy matters', *Medical Decision Making*, vol 21, no 5, pp382–390, chapter 20

World Health Organization (2005) 'Global tobacco treaty enters into force with 57 countries already committed: Parties represent 2.3 billion people', www.who.int/mediacentre/news/releases/2005/pr09/en/index.html, accessed 2 January 2010, chapter 22

Wright, G., Pearman, A. and Yardley, K. (2000) 'Risk perception in the U.K. oil and gas production industry: Are expert loss-prevention managers' perceptions different from those of members of the public?', *Risk Analysis*, vol 20, pp681–690, chapter 15

Wright, W. F. and Bower, G. H. (1992) 'Mood effect on subjective probability assessment', *Organizational Behavior and Human Decision Processes*, vol 22, pp276–291, chapter 8

Yamagishi, K. (1997) 'When a 12.86% mortality is more dangerous than 24.14%: Implications for risk communication', *Applied Cognitive Psychology*, vol 11, pp495–506, chapter 2

Zajonc, R. B. (1968) 'Attitudinal effects of mere exposure', *Journal of Personality and Social Psychology*, vol 9, pp1–27, chapter 3, chapter 7

Zajonc, R. B. (1980) 'Feeling and thinking: Preferences need no inferences', *American Psychologist*, vol 35, pp151–175, chapter 2, chapter 4, chapter 7, chapter 22

Zajonc, R. B. (2000) 'Feeling and thinking: Closing the debate over the independence of affect', in J. P. Forgas (ed) *Feeling and Thinking: The Role of Affect in Social Cognition*, Cambridge University Press, Cambridge, UK, chapter 22

Zajonc, R. B. (2001) 'Mere exposure: A gateway to the subliminal', *Current Directions in Psychological Science*, vol 10, pp224–228, chapter 22

Zechendorf, B. (1994) 'What the public thinks about biotechnology', *Biotechnology*, vol 12, pp870–875, chapter 15

Zikmund-Fisher, B. J., Smith, D. M., Ubel, P. A. and Fagerlin, A. (2007) 'Validation of the Subjective Numeracy Scale (SNS): Effects of low numeracy on comprehension of risk communications and utility elicitations', *Medical Decision Making*, vol 27, no 5, pp663–671, chapter 20

Zimmerman, R. (1993) 'Social equity and environmental risk', *Risk Analysis*, vol 13, pp649–666, chapter 10, chapter 13

Index

race
  arsenic contamination event 226, 227
  cultural-identity protective risk percep-
    tion 168, 176, 179
  environmental health-risks 141, 142,
    147–149, 159
  prescription drugs 282–283
  see also white male effect
radioactive waste management *see* nuclear
  waste repository
Rappaport, R. A. 341
rationality 18, 23, 36, 105–107
rational system *see* analytic thinking
rational-weigher model 186
Rayner, S. 337
registration bounties, guns 203
relative frequency 29
remediation contexts, environmental
  health 160
Renn, O 324, 325, 332, 337, 339, 342
representations of risk 29
representativeness heuristic xx, 14, 25, 89
reproduction 83
Rip, A. 337
ripple effects 320, 333–336
risk
  as analysis 21
  as politics 21
  see also affect heuristic
risk amplification *see* social amplification
  of risk
risk analysis, experiential thinking 34–35
risk attenuation 318, 325, 327, 337
risk-benefit information, health care
  345–351
risk and benefit judgements 26–28, 91–94
risk communication
  biotechnology 258
  cultural cognition 185
  environmental health 159–160
  social amplification of risk 338–339
  trust 333
  worldviews 177
risk management 34–36, 70
risk panics 184, 191, 199
risk perception
  affect 81, 110–111, 118, 189
  cultural-identity-protective 167–168
  cultural theory 165–166

  measuring 116
  risk regulation 184
  see also white male effect
risk ratings, environmental health
  145–147
risk regulation 177–178
  cultural-evaluator model 201, 210
  and democracy 185, 208–209, 210
  effective 183–184
  fear 190
  irrational-weigher model 187
  liberal dilemma 208–209
  politics 200–201
  rational-weigher model 186
  Sunstein 201
Ritov, I. 53
Rohrmann, B. 342
Rosa, E. A. 323, 338
Ro, T. 48
Rothman, A. J. 120
Ruckelshaus, W. 332

Sandman, P. 26
Sanfey, A. 29
Satterfield, T. A. 160
Schwartz, L. M. 348
Schwarz, N. 110, 114, 117, 120
scientists, prescription drugs 278
secondary amplification effects 319–320
Seifert, M. 325
self-affirmation 202
sex *see* gender; white male effect
Sherman, D. A. 90
Short, J. F., Jr. 326
side effects, prescription drugs 270–271,
  283
signal, concept of 320–321
single victims *see* identifiable victims
Sjöberg, L. 339
Skitka, L. J. 66
Sloman, S. A. 28
Slovic, P.
  imagery 242
  probability judgements 29
  proportion dominance 30
  risk and benefit judgements 26, 27, 92
  sympathy 37, 38
  system dynamics modelling 299
  white male effect 126